SMYTH & HELWYS BIBLE COMMENTARY

MARK

R. ALAN CULPEPPER

SMYTH&HELWYS
PUBLISHING, INCORPORATED • MACON, GEORGIA

Smyth & Helwys Bible Commentary: Mark
Publication Staff

President & CEO
Cecil P. Staton

Publisher & Executive Vice President
Lex Horton

Vice President, Production
Keith Gammons

Senior Editor
Mark K. McElroy

Book Editor
Leslie Andres

Graphic Designer
Dave Jones

Assistant Editors
Betsy Butler
Kelley F. Land

Smyth & Helwys Publishing, Inc.
6316 Peake Road
Macon, Georgia 31210-3960
1-800-747-3016
© 2007 by Smyth & Helwys Publishing

Library of Congress Cataloging-in-Publication Data

Culpepper, R. Alan.
Mark / R. Alan Culpepper.
p. cm. — (The Smyth & Helwys Bible commentary ; v. 20)
Includes bibliographical references and indexes.
ISBN 978-1-57312-077-7 (hardcover : alk. paper)
1. Bible. N.T. Mark—Commentaries. I. Title.

BS2585.53.C85 2007
226.3'07—dc22
2007006198

DEDICATION

To teachers who loved the New Testament,
called forth the best in their students,
and lived what they taught.

William E. Hull
Harold S. Songer
Frank Stagg
W. D. Davies
D. Moody Smith, Jr.

Project Editor
R. Scott Nash
Mercer University
Macon, Georgia

Old Testament
General Editor
Samuel E. Balentine
Union Theological Seminary and
Presbyterian School of Christian
Education
Richmond, Virginia

New Testament
General Editor
R. Alan Culpepper
McAfee School of Theology
Mercer University
Atlanta, Georgia

Area
Old Testament Editors
Mark E. Biddle
Baptist Theological Seminary
at Richmond, Virginia

Kandy Queen-Sutherland
Stetson University
Deland, Florida

Paul Redditt
Georgetown College
Georgetown, Kentucky

Area
New Testament Editors
R. Scott Nash
Mercer University
Macon, Georgia

Richard B. Vinson
Baptist Theological Seminary
at Richmond, Virginia

ADVANCE PRAISE

This is a large book in many respects. It is large in conception — it includes a large fund of relevant material drawn from ancient primary sources as well as more modern secondary sources. It is large in scope — it covers the message of Mark from its meaning in its own time to the way modern interpreters can go about making that message their own. It is large in execution — it begins with an introduction that is an excellent survey of Markan scholarship, and contains a multitude of side-bars that provide helpful cultural, geographic, and theological information. It is, in sum, an excellent commentary on the first Gospel that will richly reward the careful reader: preacher, scholar, and student alike.

— *Paul J. Achtemeier*
Union Theological Seminary and
Presbyterian School of Christian Education

Alan Culpepper brings to the task of reading Mark his considerable skills, honed in his pioneering work on John, a Gospel of dramatic qualities second only to Mark. The skills and insights he developed in his literary-critical work are fully utilised in this sophisticated and sensitive reading of the narrative of Mark. Culpepper focuses on the text of Mark, its meaning, literary patterns and themes, and probes the text to reveal what Mark is saying and why it is expressed as it is. In this way he illuminates the meaning of Mark as a whole while providing a detailed and convincing treatment of all the details. In doing this he draws on a deep appreciation of the tradition underlying Mark and the tradition of interpretation down to our time. The commentary builds on Culpepper's incisive analysis of the text and the insights arising from imaginative illumination critically assessed. All of this is harnessed to nurture the life of discipleship in our world today.

— *John Painter*
St. Mark's National Theological Centre
Charles Sturt University

When it comes to literary or narratological analysis of the Gospels, Alan Culpepper has few peers and no masters. Here in his Gospel of Mark commentary we find the ripe fruit of that sort of literary reading of a Gospel. Eloquently written, fully in touch with the latest scholarship on Mark, and unfailingly fair to various points of view, Professor Culpepper is a sure guide through the complexities of our earliest Gospel.

The usual helpful sidebars and supplementary resources on the CD-ROM also help make this a very helpful tool for pastors and teachers who want accessible and useable material for their teaching and sermonic preparation. Highly recommended.

— *Ben Witherington, III*
Asbury Theological Seminary

Alan Culpepper's commentary on Mark is creative, innovative, and user-friendly. In short, it is outstanding. It belongs in the library of every pastor, student, and scholar. I recommend it highly.

— *Craig A. Evans*
Acadia Divinity College

Alan Culpepper reads Mark with an eye for the literary sophistication and for the theological meaning of the text. This volume, with its helpful "connections" comments will be welcome in the library of every preacher and teacher of the Bible.

— *Sharyn Dowd*
Baylor Univeristy

Alan Culpepper's offering on Mark is a major contribution to the estimable *Smyth & Helwys Bible Commentary*. Here we benefit from the author's recognized gifts as biblical exegete: literary creativity and theological insight, appreciation of Scripture's historical grounding and history of interpretation, admirable clarity and level-headedness. The book's abundant maps, photographs, charts, and illustrations add elegance while fulfilling this series' promise of an intelligent user-friendliness. Upon publication Culpepper's *Mark* should rise to the highest rank of serious biblical commentaries for the widest audience imaginable. I applaud its achievement.

— *C. Clifton Black*
Princeton Theological Seminary

CONTENTS

ABBREVIATIONS USED IN THIS COMMENTARY

Books of the Old Testament, Apocrypha, and New Testament are generally abbreviated in the Sidebars, parenthetical references, and notes according to the following system.

The Old Testament

Genesis	Gen
Exodus	Exod
Leviticus	Lev
Numbers	Num
Deuteronomy	Deut
Joshua	Josh
Judges	Judg
Ruth	Ruth
1–2 Samuel	1–2 Sam
1–2 Kings	1–2 Kgs
1–2 Chronicles	1–2 Chr
Ezra	Ezra
Nehemiah	Neh
Esther	Esth
Job	Job
Psalm (Psalms)	Ps (Pss)
Proverbs	Prov
Ecclesiastes	Eccl
or Qoheleth	Qoh
Song of Solomon	Song
or Song of Songs	Song
or Canticles	Cant
Isaiah	Isa
Jeremiah	Jer
Lamentations	Lam
Ezekiel	Ezek
Daniel	Dan
Hosea	Hos
Joel	Joel
Amos	Amos
Obadiah	Obad
Jonah	Jonah
Micah	Mic
Nahum	Nah
Habakkuk	Hab
Zephaniah	Zeph
Haggai	Hag

| Zechariah | Zech |
| Malachi | Mal |

The Apocrypha

1–2 Esdras	1–2 Esdr
Tobit	Tob
Judith	Jdt
Additions to Esther	Add Esth
Wisdom of Solomon	Wis
Ecclesiasticus or the Wisdom of Jesus Son of Sirach	Sir
Baruch	Bar
Epistle (or Letter) of Jeremiah	Ep Jer
Prayer of Azariah and the Song of the Three	Pr Azar
Daniel and Susanna	Sus
Daniel, Bel, and the Dragon	Bel
Prayer of Manasseh	Pr Man
1–4 Maccabees	1–4 Macc

The New Testament

Matthew	Matt
Mark	Mark
Luke	Luke
John	John
Acts	Acts
Romans	Rom
1–2 Corinthians	1–2 Cor
Galatians	Gal
Ephesians	Eph
Philippians	Phil
Colossians	Col
1–2 Thessalonians	1–2 Thess
1–2 Timothy	1–2 Tim
Titus	Titus
Philemon	Phlm
Hebrews	Heb
James	Jas
1–2 Peter	1–2 Pet
1–2–3 John	1–2–3 John
Jude	Jude
Revelation	Rev

Other commonly used abbreviations include:

BCE	Before the Common Era
CE	Common Era
C.	century
c.	*circa* (around "that time")
cf.	*confer* (compare)
ch.	chapter
chs.	chapters
ed.	edition or edited by or editor
eds.	editors
e.g.	*exempli gratia* (for example)
et al.	*et alia* (and others)
f./ff.	and the following one(s)
gen. ed.	general editor
ibid.	*ibidem* (in the same place)
i.e.	*id est* (that is)
lit.	literally
n.d.	no date
sg.	singular
trans.	translated by or translator(s)
vol(s).	volume(s)
v.	verse
vv.	verses

Selected additional written works cited by abbreviations include the following. A complete listing of abbreviations can be referenced in *The SBL Handbook of Style* (Peabody MA: Hendrickson, 1999):

AB	Anchor Bible
ABD	*Anchor Bible Dictionary*
ANET	Ancient Near Eastern Texts Relating to the Old Testament
BibInt	*Biblical Interpretation*
BR	*Bible Review*
BZAW	Beihefte zur Zeitschrift für die alttestamentliche Wissenschaft
CBQ	*Catholic Biblical Quatrerly*
CBQMS	Catholic Biblical Quarterly, Monograph Series
ChrLit	*Christianity and Literature*
DCH	*Dictionary of Classical Hebrew*
ER	*The Encyclopedia of Religion*
FRLANT	Forschungen zur Religion und Literatur des Alten und Neuen Testaments
HBT	*Horizons in Biblical Theology*
HTR	*Harvard Theological Review*

HUCA	*Hebrew Union College Annual*
IB	*Interpreter's Bible*
Int	*Interpretation*
JB	Jerusalem Bible
JBL	*Journal of Biblical Literature*
JNES	*Journal for Near Eastern Studies*
JQR	*Jewish Quarterly Review*
JSOT	*Journal for the Study of the Old Testament*
JSOTSup	Journal for the Study of the Old Testament, Supplement Series
JSS	*Journal of Semitic Studies*
JTS	*Journal of Theological Studies*
KAT	Kommentar zum Alten Testament
KJV	King James Version
LXX	Septuagint
MDOG	Mitteilungen der Deutschen Orient-Gesellschaft
MT	Masoretic Text
NAB	New American Bible
NIB	The New Interpreter's Bible
NICOT	New International Commentary on the Old Testament
NIV	New International Version
NJB	New Jerusalem Bible
NJPS	New JPS Translation (Tanakh)
NRSV	New Revised Standard Version
OTL	Old Testament Library
PRSt	*Perspectives in Religious Studies*
RB	*Revue Biblique*
REB	Revised English Bible
ResQ	*Restoration Quarterly*
RevExp	*Review & Expositor*
SBLDS	Society of Biblical Literature, Dissertation Series
TEV	Today's English Version
TLOT	Theological Lexicon of the Old Testament
TOTC	Tyndale Old Testament Commentaries
VT	*Vetus Testamentum*
VTSup	Supplements to Vetus Testamentum
WBC	Word Biblical Commentary
WMANT	Wissenschaftliche Monographien zum Alten and Neuen Testament
ZAW	*Zeitschrift für alttestamentliche Wissenschaft*

SERIES PREFACE

The *Smyth & Helwys Bible Commentary* is a visually stimulating and user-friendly series that is as close to multimedia in print as possible. Written by accomplished scholars with all students of Scripture in mind, the primary goal of the *Smyth & Helwys Bible Commentary* is to make available serious, credible biblical scholarship in an accessible and less intimidating format.

Far too many Bible commentaries fall short of bridging the gap between the insights of biblical scholars and the needs of students of God's written word. In an unprecedented way, the *Smyth & Helwys Bible Commentary* brings insightful commentary to bear on the lives of contemporary Christians. Using a multimedia format, the volumes employ a stunning array of art, photographs, maps, and drawings to illustrate the truths of the Bible for a visual generation of believers.

The *Smyth & Helwys Bible Commentary* is built upon the idea that meaningful Bible study can occur when the insights of contemporary biblical scholars blend with sensitivity to the needs of lifelong students of Scripture. Some persons within local faith communities, however, struggle with potentially informative biblical scholarship for several reasons. Oftentimes, such scholarship is cast in technical language easily grasped by other scholars, but not by the general reader. For example, lengthy, technical discussions on every detail of a particular scriptural text can hinder the quest for a clear grasp of the whole. Also, the format for presenting scholarly insights has often been confusing to the general reader, rendering the work less than helpful. Unfortunately, responses to the hurdles of reading extensive commentaries have led some publishers to produce works for a general readership that merely skim the surface of the rich resources of biblical scholarship. This commentary series incorporates works of fine art in an accurate and scholarly manner, yet the format remains "user-friendly." An important facet is the presentation and explanation of images of art, which interpret the biblical material or illustrate how the biblical material has been understood and interpreted in the past. A visual generation of believers deserves a commentary series that contains not only the all-important textual commentary on Scripture, but images, photographs, maps, works of fine art, and drawings that bring the text to life.

The *Smyth & Helwys Bible Commentary* makes serious, credible biblical scholarship more accessible to a wider audience. Writers and editors alike present information in ways that encourage readers to gain a better understanding of the Bible. The editorial board has worked to develop a format that is useful and usable, informative and pleasing to the eye. Our writers are reputable scholars who participate in the community of faith and sense a calling to communicate the results of their scholarship to their faith community.

The *Smyth & Helwys Bible Commentary* addresses Christians and the larger church. While both respect for and sensitivity to the needs and contributions of other faith communities are reflected in the work of the series authors, the authors speak primarily to Christians. Thus the reader can note a confessional tone throughout the volumes. No particular "confession of faith" guides the authors, and diverse perspectives are observed in the various volumes. Each writer, though, brings to the biblical text the best scholarly tools available and expresses the results of their studies in commentary and visuals that assist readers seeking a word from the Lord for the church.

To accomplish this goal, writers in this series have drawn from numerous streams in the rich tradition of biblical interpretation. The basic focus is the biblical text itself, and considerable attention is given to the wording and structure of texts. Each particular text, however, is also considered in the light of the entire canon of Christian Scriptures. Beyond this, attention is given to the cultural context of the biblical writings. Information from archaeology, ancient history, geography, comparative literature, history of religions, politics, sociology, and even economics is used to illuminate the culture of the people who produced the Bible. In addition, the writers have drawn from the history of interpretation, not only as it is found in traditional commentary on the Bible but also in literature, theater, church history, and the visual arts. Finally, the *Commentary* on Scripture is joined with *Connections* to the world of the contemporary church. Here again, the writers draw on scholarship in many fields as well as relevant issues in the popular culture.

This wealth of information might easily overwhelm a reader if not presented in a "user-friendly" format. Thus the heavier discussions of detail and the treatments of other helpful topics are presented in special-interest boxes, or *Sidebars,* clearly connected to the passages under discussion so as not to interrupt the flow of the basic interpretation. The result is a commentary on Scripture that focuses on the theological significance of a text while also offering the reader a rich array of additional information related to the text and its interpretation.

An accompanying CD-ROM offers powerful searching and research tools. The commentary text, sidebars, and visuals are all reproduced on a CD that is fully indexed and searchable. Pairing a text version with a digital resource is a distinctive feature of the *Smyth & Helwys Bible Commentary.*

Combining credible biblical scholarship, user-friendly study features, and sensitivity to the needs of a visually oriented generation of believers creates a unique and unprecedented type of commentary series. With insight from many of today's finest biblical scholars and a stunning visual format, it is our hope that the *Smyth & Helwys Bible Commentary* will be a welcome addition to the personal libraries of all students of Scripture.

The Editors

HOW TO USE
THIS COMMENTARY

The *Smyth & Helwys Bible Commentary* is written by accomplished biblical scholars with a wide array of readers in mind. Whether engaged in the study of Scripture in a church setting or in a college or seminary classroom, all students of the Bible will find a number of useful features throughout the commentary that are helpful for interpreting the Bible.

Basic Design of the Volumes

Each volume features an Introduction to a particular book of the Bible, providing a brief guide to information that is necessary for reading and interpreting the text: the historical setting, literary design, and theological significance. Each Introduction also includes a comprehensive outline of the particular book under study.

Each chapter of the commentary investigates the text according to logical divisions in a particular book of the Bible. Sometimes these divisions follow the traditional chapter segmentation, while at other times the textual units consist of sections of chapters or portions of more than one chapter. The divisions reflect the literary structure of a book and offer a guide for selecting passages that are useful in preaching and teaching.

An accompanying CD-ROM offers powerful searching and research tools. The commentary text, Sidebars, and visuals are all reproduced on a CD that is fully indexed and searchable. Pairing a text version with a digital resource also allows unprecedented flexibility and freedom for the reader. Carry the text version to locations you most enjoy doing research while knowing that the CD offers a portable alternative for travel from the office, church, classroom, and your home.

Commentary and Connections

As each chapter explores a textual unit, the discussion centers around two basic sections: *Commentary* and *Connections*. The analysis of a passage, including the details of its language, the history reflected in the text, and the literary forms found in the text, are the main focus of the *Commentary* section. The primary concern of the *Commentary* section is to explore the theological issues presented by the Scripture passage. *Connections* presents potential applications of the insights provided in the *Commentary* section. The *Connections* portion of each chapter considers what issues are relevant for teaching and suggests useful methods and resources. *Connections* also identifies themes suitable for sermon planning and suggests helpful approaches for preaching on the Scripture text.

Sidebars

The *Smyth & Helwys Bible Commentary* provides a unique hyperlink format that quickly guides the reader to additional insights. Since other more technical or supplementary information is vital for understanding a text and its implications, the volumes feature distinctive Sidebars that provide a wealth of information on such matters as:

• Historical information (such as chronological charts, lists of kings or rulers, maps, descriptions of monetary systems, descriptions of special groups, descriptions of archaeological sites or geographical settings).

• Graphic outlines of literary structure (including such items as poetry, chiasmus, repetition, epistolary form).

• Definition or brief discussions of technical or theological terms and issues.

• Insightful quotations that are not integrated into the running text but are relevant to the passage under discussion.

• Notes on the history of interpretation (Augustine on the Good Samaritan, Luther on James, Stendahl on Romans, etc.).

• Line drawings, photographs, and other illustrations relevant for understanding the historical context or interpretive significance of the text.

• Presentation and discussion of works of fine art that have interpreted a Scripture passage.

Each Sidebar is printed in color and is referenced at the appropriate place in the *Commentary* or *Connections* section with a color-coded title that directs the reader to the relevant sidebar. Select Sidebars may be located on the CD-ROM only. These are noted as [CD:] and can be found in a separate collection on the CD-ROM. In addition, helpful icons appear in the Sidebars, which provide the reader with visual cues to the type of material that is explained in each Sidebar. Throughout the commentary, these four distinct hyperlinks provide useful links in an easily recognizable design.

AΩ

Alpha & Omega Language

This icon identifies the information as a language-based tool that offers further exploration of the Scripture selection. This could include syntactical information, word studies, popular or additional uses of the word(s) in question, additional contexts in which the term appears, and the history of the term's translation. All non-English terms are transliterated into the appropriate English characters.

Culture/Context

This icon introduces further comment on contextual or cultural details that shed light on the Scripture selection. Describing the place and time to which a Scripture passage refers is often vital to the task of biblical interpretation. Sidebar items introduced with this icon could include geographical, historical, political, social, topographical, or economic information. Here, the reader may find an excerpt of an ancient text or inscription that sheds light on the text. Or one may find a description of some element of ancient religion such as Baalism in Canaan or the Hero cult in the Mystery Religions of the Greco-Roman world.

Interpretation

Sidebars that appear under this icon serve a general interpretive function in terms of both historical and contemporary renderings. Under this heading, the reader might find a selection from classic or contemporary literature that illuminates the Scripture text or a significant quotation from a famous sermon that addresses the passage. Insights are drawn from various sources, including literature, worship, theater, church history, and sociology.

Additional Resources Study

Here, the reader finds a convenient list of useful resources for further investigation of the selected Scripture text, including books, journals, websites, special collections, organizations, and societies. Specialized discussions of works not often associated with biblical studies may also appear here.

Additional Features

Each volume also includes a basic Bibliography on the biblical book under study. Other bibliographies on selected issues are often included that point the reader to other helpful resources.

Notes at the end of each chapter provide full documentation of sources used and contain additional discussions of related matters.

Abbreviations used in each volume are explained in a list of abbreviations found after the Table of Contents.

Readers of the *Smyth & Helwys Bible Commentary* can regularly visit the Internet support site for news, information, updates, and enhancements to the series at <**www.helwys.com/commentary**>.

Several thorough indexes enable the reader to locate information quickly. These indexes include:

• An *Index of Sidebars* groups content from the special-interest boxes by category (maps, fine art, photographs, drawings, etc.).

• An *Index of Scriptures* lists citations to particular biblical texts.

• An *Index of Topics* lists alphabetically the major subjects, names, topics, and locations referenced or discussed in the volume.

• An *Index of Authors* organizes contemporary authors whose works are cited in the volume.

INTRODUCTION

Commentaries are not like other books. They are books about other books, so they are woven into a fabric of other texts and the readings of texts. Most readers of this commentary probably will not read it through from start to finish. Instead, it will be a resource, probably one among several, that will be used in studying particular passages in the Gospel of Mark in preparation for teaching or preaching. At other times, the reader may consult the commentary looking for an answer to a specific question. Still others may read through the commentary over a period of time as part of their systematic study of the Bible for their own personal enrichment. Because commentaries are used for different specific purposes, they must be written so that they do not presuppose or require linear reading. In other words, the writer cannot assume that the reader has read the material presented earlier in the volume. Where such knowledge is needed, cross-references are supplied.

Writing requires the writer to make countless decisions about what needs to be said, emphasized, clarified, referenced, and documented. Inevitably these decisions in turn require that the writer make assumptions about his or her readers and how they will use the commentary. The process is also based on assumptions about the purpose and role of a commentary. The following paragraphs, therefore, are an introduction, not to the Gospel of Mark—for that see the following sections—but to the commentary.

THE FUNCTION OF A COMMENTARY

First and foremost, a commentary should prepare the reader to read the text, in this case the Gospel of Mark. It therefore serves a mediating role. The commentator is a guide, consultant, and advisor concerning this enigmatic text. If the commentary does its job well, it will not substitute for reading and studying Mark but will prompt and motivate the reader to study Mark itself with greater interest and insight.

Reading Beside Other Readers Whispering the Text

In this process, the commentary can explain the foreign and ancient terms, customs, and references in Mark that a modern reader may not understand. For example, Mark uses terms like "the Son of Man" (e.g., 2:10), "the sons of the bridal-chamber" (2:19), and "Corban" (7:11) that are not only foreign to us but remind us that the Gospel of Mark comes to us from another time and culture. It was not written for modern readers, except in God's greater purpose for it, and we are outsiders to its thought world.

A commentary can also collect other texts that provide a context for our reading of the Gospel. Mark draws from the historical, social, religious, and conceptual context in which it was written. The reader will therefore find numerous references to the books of the Old Testament but also to contemporary writers and historians (Philo, Josephus, the Dead Sea Scrolls), the Apocrypha and Pseudepigrapha, later Jewish writings (the Mishnah and Talmud), early Christian writings (New Testament Apocrypha, Church Fathers, and gnostic texts), and Greco-Roman writers. These ancient writings provide illuminating insights into the Gospel and its world and times.

Mosaic of St. Mark with the Gospel

Large arch over cantoria. Mosaic. S. Marco, Venice, Italy. (Credit: Cameraphoto / Art Resource, NY)

Still, we cannot assume that we can simply come to Mark with fresh eyes and read it for the first time in the light of sources contemporary with it. Mark, like the other books of Scripture, has been read and interpreted continuously through the centuries. We are part of a culture and churches that have been shaped by the reading of these texts, and in this instance by interpretations of Mark. One aspect of studying Mark's Gospel, therefore, is becoming aware of this rich tradition of Bible reading and interpretation and the ways in which it has focused the issues, passages, problems, and interpretations that guide our understanding of Mark today. For this reason, the reader will find in the pages of this volume a sample of quotations from church fathers and medieval scholars, and images of artwork related to the text that provide interpretation in a visual medium. Finally, the introduction to the commentary, occasional references within it, the bibliography, and the endnotes acknowledge the contributions to our understanding of Mark from a vigorous community of modern scholars. No one can come to the text alone, and no one can read it without the echoes of other readings conditioning what we see and hear, nor should one want to. The generations of readers who have gone before us have greatly enriched and illuminated what we can see in the text, and the community of informed readers today can guard us from idiosyncratic interpretations.

"Narrative Texts Create Their Own Worlds"

By virtue of being a narrative rather than an epistle, homily, or some other form of writing, Mark has a narrator who tells the story to an implied reader, a cast of characters who interact with one another, and events or scenes that cover a span of time and form a more or less coherent plot. Mark is also based on the history of Jesus' life and set in a particular historical context. Some readers may wish to explore questions of historicity and theories regarding Mark's sources. For such questions they should consult other commentaries and sources. The focus of this commentary (especially in the Commentary sections) is on the text of Mark itself, its meanings, literary patterns, and themes. We ask, what was Mark saying, and why was it written in this way? The reader will therefore find that many passages, motifs, and terms are part of larger patterns in the Gospel. This commentary takes pains to point out those patterns, connect references, and trace themes so that the reader is continually reading each passage in the context of its setting and function within the Gospel as a whole.

In addition, the commentary (especially in the Connections sections) suggests ways in which the Gospel speaks to contemporary issues and concerns and provides reflections that may offer ways in which the reader can find the Gospel to be personally meaningful. The Gospel of Mark is not just a classic, ancient text; it is inspired Scripture, a part of the church's canon of Scripture that sustains and guides worship, spiritual formation, and personal discipleship. It is our hope that this commentary will foster biblical preaching, devotional reading, and moral decision-making for those who draw inspiration from Mark. The more one studies the Gospel, the more one will see in it, and the more one will be challenged by its vision of Jesus' ministry, death, and resurrection.

FIVE ERAS IN MARKAN SCHOLARSHIP

Mark has been at the center of debate about the nature of the Gospels and their relationships to one another. The history of Markan scholarship therefore offers a good overview of basic issues in the study of the Gospels. It also provides an orientation to different perspectives on the basic introductory questions: who wrote the Gospel, when, where, and why? The history of Markan studies up until the current period can be sketched in five eras: (1) the clumsy Mark (the church fathers until the rise of modern critical scholarship), (2) the chronicler Mark (the source critics), (3) the compiler Mark (the form critics), (4) the clever Mark (the redaction critics), and (5) the creative Mark (the narrative critics). The recent spate of publications on Mark has taken various directions, so it is best to leave the naming of a common theme among them (if there is one) to future surveys.

The Clumsy Mark

The rubric "the clumsy Mark" reflects not only the general view that Mark was the abbreviator or epitomizer of Matthew but specifically the testimony of Papias that Mark wrote everything accurately but not in order and the Anti-Marcionite Prologue's comment that Mark was "stump-fingered."

Papias

Papias (c. 120–140), according to Eusebius (c. 325): "And the Presbyter used to say this, "Mark became Peter's interpreter and wrote accurately all that he remembered, not, indeed, in order, of the things said or done by the Lord. For he had not heard the Lord, nor had he followed Him, but later on, as I said, followed Peter, who used to give teaching as necessity demanded but not making, as it were, an arrangement of the Lord's oracles, so that Mark did nothing wrong in thus writing down single points as he remembered them. For to one thing he gave attention, to leave out nothing of what he had heard and to make no false statements in them."

Eusebius, *Ecclesiastical History* 3.39.15; LCL 1:297

The earliest external evidence about the Gospel of Mark is preserved in fragments of the writings of Papias (c. AD 120–140). [Papias] Matthew was already becoming the church's favorite Gospel. Marcion chose the Gospel of Luke, which he edited to excise references to the Old Testament. About the same time, Papias wrote to defend the authority of Mark, claiming that John the elder had said that Mark was the interpreter of Peter. As an associate of the principal apostle, Mark collected Peter's words. Papias claimed that Mark wrote down what he remembered. His writings say nothing about Peter checking his work, so the implication is that Peter was not around when Mark wrote— presumably he was already dead. Then Papias acknowledges that Mark's account is not in order. We can contrast here Luke's claim that he would write everything in order. Alternatively, Papias may have known of John's different chronology. Still, Papias defends Mark against omission or error while acknowledging also that Mark adapted his material to the needs of the hearers.

The Papias tradition is tremendously important, although many scholars now doubt there was any real connection between Mark and Peter. How accurate is the tradition Papias claims to have received from

John the Elder? Papias may have had no more than 1 Peter 5:13 on which to base this tradition: "Your sister church in Babylon, chosen together with you, sends you greetings; and so does my son Mark."

The Anti-Marcionite Prologue adds that Mark was called "stump-fingered" and that he wrote after Peter's death. [The Anti-Marcionite Prologue] This prologue (traditionally dated c. 160–180 but now thought to be later) appears to be dependent upon the Papias tradition. The note that Mark was composed after Peter's death may be an attempt to explain why Mark did not consult Peter about the order of events.

Irenaeus (c. 180) concurs that Mark was the interpreter of Peter and that he wrote his Gospel (i.e., "the things preached by Peter") after Peter's death. [Irenaeus] The problem is that there is no evidence that Irenaeus knew anything about Mark other than the Papias tradition. On the other hand, he agrees with the Anti-Marcionite Prologue (or the Anti-Marcionite Prologue later drew from Irenaeus) in saying that the writing occurred after Peter's death. Clement of Alexandria adds that Peter ratified the Gospel, and Jerome adds that Mark was the first bishop of Alexandria.

The most important evidence from the patristic period is the statement by Papias, but its value is debated. Most conservative scholars accept it at face value,[1] while acknowledging that Mark had other sources beside Peter. The fact that its order is criticized at this early date should caution against taking Mark to be an accurate chronology of the ministry of Jesus. Because of the possibility that Papias may have been motivated by an interest in countering the Marcionites and linking Mark more closely with apostolic authority—and may have adapted 1 Peter 5:13 to this end—many scholars regard the Papias tradition with some skepticism. This skepticism is heightened by those who hold 1 Peter to be a pseudonymous writing dating from the reign of Domitian. While Mark stands solidly within the mainstream of the apostolic tradition about Jesus, and doubtlessly contains material derived from eyewitnesses, there is little in the Gospel to support Papias's claim that it preserves Peter's preaching. If Mark was Peter's interpreter, it is certainly odd that he placed Peter and the Twelve in a more negative light than any of the other Gospels.

Very early, Mark suffered from neglect, chiefly because it was viewed as merely an abridgment of Matthew. This opinion, however, is clearly irreconcilable with the Papias tradition. Nevertheless, Augustine held

The Anti-Marcionite Prologue

". . . Mark related, who was called 'stumpy-fingered' [*colobodactylus*], because for the size of the rest of his body he had fingers that were too short. He was Peter's interpreter [*interpres*]. After the departure [or 'death,' *post excessionem*] of Peter himself, the same man wrote this Gospel in the regions of Italy."

C. Clifton Black, *Mark: Images of an Apostolic Interpreter* (Columbia: University of South Carolina Press, 1994), 119.

Irenaeus

"And after the death of these Mark, the disciple and interpreter of Peter, also transmitted to us in writing the things preached by Peter."

Irenaeus, *Haer.* 3.1.2, qtd. by William L. Lane, *The Gospel of Mark* (NICNT; Grand Rapids: Wm. B. Eerdmans, 1974), 9.

Augustine

"Mark follows him [Matthew] closely, and looks like his attendant and epitomizer. . . . Luke, on the other hand, had no one connected with him to act as his summarist in the way that Mark was attached to Matthew."

Augustine, *De con. evang.* 1.2.3-4; 3.6, qtd. by C. Clifton Black, *Mark: Images of an Apostolic Interpreter* (Columbia: University of South Carolina Press, 1994), 128.

that Mark was an abridgment of Matthew. [Augustine] Ironically, where Matthew and Mark report the same events, Matthew's account is usually briefer than Mark's. Victor of Antioch in the fifth century says he could not find an earlier commentary on Mark,[2] and Mark was virtually ignored until the dawn of modern critical scholarship nearly two centuries ago.[3]

The Chronicler Mark

Comparative study of the Gospel accounts gradually led to a reversal in perspectives on Mark, from Matthew's epitomizer to "the saint who first found grace to pen the life which was the Life of men."[4] Mark became the first evangelist and the one who gave us the most reliable outline of Jesus' ministry: "the chronicler Mark." The crucial developments leading up to the theory of Markan priority are presented here merely in outline form.[5]

In 1774–1775 J. J. Griesbach published the first true "synopsis," from which the first three Gospels were called "synoptic." Griesbach recognized that no real harmonization of the Gospel accounts was possible, and John was left out. In 1783, Griesbach proposed his theory: Matthew was written first, then Luke, who used Matthew, then Mark, who followed both Matthew and Luke but omitted some passages where they both agreed. Both D. F. Strauss and F. C. Baur, key figures in Gospel studies in the mid-nineteenth century, accepted the Griesbach hypothesis.

In 1782 J. B. Koppe observed that Mark cannot be explained as Matthew's epitomizer. Koppe showed that Mark does not slavishly follow Matthew, thereby challenging the dominant view that dated back to Augustine. Karl Lachmann (1835) discovered that the order of events in all three Synoptics is based on the Gospel of Mark. When Matthew and Luke agree with each other, they agree with Mark; when they depart from Mark (and where Mark is silent), they depart from one another. From this it was inferred that Mark was the earliest Gospel. This inference was later called the "Lachmann fallacy," but it is one of the foundations of the two-source hypothesis.[6] A further step was taken when C. H. Weisse (1838) theorized that Matthew and Luke were based on a "proto-Gospel" that lay behind Mark, which Matthew and Luke combined with a "sayings source." That same year C. G. Wilke concluded that Matthew and Luke were based on Mark itself, not an Ur-Mark. He also said that Matthew and Luke used the sayings source, but Matthew also used Luke.

The "two-source" hypothesis reached its definitive form in 1863 in the work of H. J. Holtzmann. Drawing on Weisse, Holtzmann postulated that Matthew and Luke drew from some form of Mark and the sayings source, which by the 1890s was called Q. Mark therefore provides the earliest form of the Gospel tradition. With this development Mark was thrust into the limelight. The era of its neglect was over. The priority of Mark meant that Mark could be used as the chronology for the life of Jesus. In 1924 B. H. Streeter published *The Four Gospels*, the classic statement of the two-source theory in English. He proposed that Matthew and Luke used Mark as we have it, and each drew on Q and their own special sources as well ("M" and "L").[7]

Chart of Synoptic Relationships

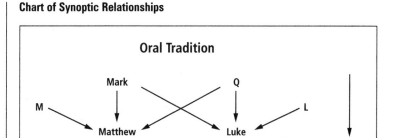

The Compiler Mark

The form critics reduced the work of the evangelist to collecting the fragments, units, and brief collections of oral tradition and compiling them in a connected narrative account, hence "the compiler Mark."

In 1896 Martin Kähler published a small book that revolutionized the study of the Gospels.[8] Kähler reacted against the subjective portraits and psychologizing efforts of current lives of Jesus. He reacted against the implications that the Christian faith stood or fell on the results of historical investigation so that the basis for one's faith hung on the latest study of the historical Jesus. The living Lord, he said, is the Christ proclaimed by the apostles. To this end, he asserted that the Gospels do not provide us with historical data with which one can write a life of Jesus. Rather, they portray the Christ of faith. The Gospels have a religious purpose—to nurture faith. They are not concerned about historical detail, psychological understanding of Jesus, or biographical information. Moreover, he claimed that the Gospels should be understood as "passion narratives with extended introductions."[9] Only when their purpose and content is understood in this way—as the presentation of the Christ of faith, the Christ preached by the apostles—can the Christian faith find a *sturmfrei Gebiet*, an invulnerable area. The result of Kähler's work is that he raised serious questions about whether Mark can be taken as uninterpreted history.

At the beginning of the twentieth century, the prevailing view was that Mark provides an accurate historical reflection of the life of Jesus. In particular, scholars believed that Mark accurately portrays the gradual awakening of the recognition of Jesus' identity among his disciples and their cooperation in keeping his identity secret from the general populace. William Wrede, who more than any other influenced the course of Markan scholarship in the last century, asked, "Did Jesus consider himself to be the Messiah?" and "Was Jesus regarded as the Messiah by others?" And if so, when?[10] Wrede called attention to four lines of evidence that Jesus deliberately suppressed the messianic character of his ministry: (1) Jesus forbids the demons to make him known (1:25, 34); (2) he commands secrecy to those who might reveal the messianic character of his ministry—those whom he healed and his disciples (1:43-45; 5:43; 7:36; 8:30; 9:9); (3) Jesus withdraws from the crowds in order to give special or esoteric teachings (4:34; 7:17); and (4) according to Mark, Jesus taught in parables in order to conceal the mystery of the kingdom of God from outsiders (4:10-12).

Saint Peter dictating the Gospels of Saint Mark

Fra Angelico (1387–1455). *Saint Peter dictating the Gospels of Saint Mark*, from the predella of the Linaiuoli altarpiece, 1433–1435. Museo di S. Marco, Florence, Italy. (Credit: Nicolo Orsi Battaglini / Art Resource, NY)

From this evidence, Wrede concluded the following: (1) The description Mark gives is historically impossible. The commands to remain silent when people were cured miraculously, and often in view of others, would have been pointless; and if the secret was revealed to the disciples, and they were taught about Jesus' death and resurrection, why were they discouraged when his prediction about his death came true? (2) Since the secrecy motif cannot be historically accurate, it must be a theological construct imposed on the account of Jesus' ministry. This conclusion was important because for the first time it raised the possibility that Mark was more theologian than historian and that he wrote the Gospel with theological and apologetic interests: ". . . as a whole the Gospel no longer offers a historical view of the real life of Jesus. Only pale residues of such a view have passed over into what is a suprahistorical view for faith. In this sense the Gospel of Mark belongs to the history of dogma."[11] (3) Mark 9:9 is an indication that, according to

Mark, the messiahship of Jesus was a closely guarded secret during his earthly ministry; it was made known only after the resurrection. (4) The early church originally believed that Jesus became the Messiah through the resurrection (Acts 2:36; Rom 1:4). Gradually the belief that Jesus was the Messiah was thrust back into the period of the earthly ministry of Jesus. Mark lived in the period in which the two views were in tension. Mark resolved this tension by saying that Jesus was the Messiah during his earthly life, but that he did not want others to know. Thus, his messiahship was kept secret until after the resurrection. Mark therefore developed the secrecy motif to explain how it was that Jesus was not recognized as the Messiah during his lifetime but was proclaimed to be the Messiah after his death and resurrection. (5) Finally, Wrede concludes that Mark did not originate this conception but took it from his community and heightened it in his Gospel.

Most conservative New Testament scholars now argue that Wrede forced a false dichotomy between the mind of Jesus and the mind of Mark. The emphasis on secrecy probably originated with Jesus rather than with Mark. Jesus may well have commanded secrecy to avoid the misunderstanding that he was merely a wonder worker and to discourage further suspicion from the religious and political authorities. After all, secrecy was inherent in the nature of his mission—God in the form of a servant.

About 1920 three German scholars (Karl L. Schmidt, Martin Dibelius, and Rudolf Bultmann) working independently developed a new method for the study of the Gospels: form criticism. The German name was more accurate: *Formgeschichte*, or form history. This breakthrough revolutionized Gospel studies. As we have seen, there was a keen interest in pushing behind the Gospels to their sources for more reliable material with which to write a life of Jesus. This interest led to discussion of the sources of the Gospels. The purpose of form criticism was to enable the interpreter to move behind the written sources into the period of the oral transmission of the sayings of Jesus and accounts of his deeds. Form critics isolated independent units of oral tradition (each parable, aphorism, pronouncement story, or miracle story) and studied their form. They postulated a life situation (*Sitz im Leben*) in which such tradition might be used and looked for evidences of embellishment or development beyond the basic form of the material.

Karl Ludwig Schmidt focused on the framework of the history of Jesus in the Gospel of Mark.[12] He concluded that the most primitive form of the Jesus tradition is the pericope, i.e., an individual saying or narrative. The framework (*Rahmen*) or outline in which these units are set represents the work of the evangelist. The pericopae are generally arranged on the basis of topical or theological considerations, with the exception of the Passion Narrative. Thus, even though Mark is the earliest Gospel there is no reason to assume that it provides a historically accurate sketch of the ministry of Jesus. He also noted that Mark occasionally supplied summary sections (*Sammelberichte*) as transitions. Schmidt found pre-Markan collections of material, however, and occasionally pre-Markan geographical and chronological references. For the most part, however, the pericopae were preserved within the community without details of time or place. Much of what appears to be chronology or geography is only the (Markan) framework that has been imposed on individual units.[13]

Dibelius took the life of the early church as the guide for interpreting the forms of the Gospels.[14] Bultmann, on the other hand, began with the text and moved from it to the setting of the forms in the life of the church. Dibelius's method has consequently been labeled "constructive" and Bultmann's "analytical." Dibelius focused on the preaching of the early church. In his interpretation of Mark, Dibelius basically followed Wrede and observed that Mark is "a book of secret epiphanies." [Martin Dibelius]

After analyzing each pericope in the synoptics, Bultmann concludes *The History of the Synoptic Tradition* with a section on each Gospel.[15] He notes that Mark "has nowhere used a source which itself already portrayed a thoroughly coherent life of Jesus which could have been described as a Gospel."[16] In other words, Mark was the first to write a Gospel and his framework of the life of Jesus cannot be traced to an earlier source. "The only instance of close linking together over a larger portion of narrative is to be found in the story of the Passion."[17] He also noted Mark's use of stock scenes: lake and lakeside, house and road, synagogue, and mountain and concluded, "It is a misconception to infer from Mark's ordering of his material any conclusions about the chronology and development of the life of Jesus."[18]

Bultmann felt that names generally represented secondary additions to the tradition, but allowed that the passages in Mark that use the names of individual disciples may come from an early period when the idea of the Twelve had not yet influenced the synoptic tradition.[19] He agreed with Dibelius's characterization of Mark as a book of "secret epiphanies," saying it was "just right."[20] The veil of secrecy drawn over these revelations is apologetic—as "a veiling of the fact that faith in Jesus' Messiahship begins from belief in his resurrection."[21] In fact, Mark could have been the Gospel of Pauline, Hellenistic Christianity.[22]

Martin Dibelius

Mark's purpose was "... to represent Jesus as the Messiah, but without placing his work in a supernatural sphere which had no room for tradition—although this was done in the Fourth Gospel. It is also to emphasize those characteristics in the tradition which disclose Jesus as the Messiah, but at the same time to show why He was not recognized as Messiah by the people and why He was opposed, despised, and finally sent to the cross. In this way the Gospel of Mark was written as a book of secret epiphanies."

Martin Dibelius, *From Tradition to Gospel* (Cambridge: James Clarke, 1971), 230.

Mark's purpose was to unite the Hellenistic kerygma about Christ with the tradition of the story of Jesus.[23]

As we have seen, one of the primary conclusions of Schmidt and the other form critics was that the earliest form of the synoptic materials was the individual pericope. The framework that links these pericopae into a continuous, coherent narrative was added later by the evangelist when for the first time the attempt was made to gather and organize the Gospel materials. This means, if they are correct, that the outline or framework of Mark is of questionable value for any attempt to describe the chronology or geography of Jesus' life.

In 1932, C. H. Dodd took up this question.[24] Dodd affirms that the pericope was the earliest form of the tradition and concedes that Schmidt has shown that the framework was superimposed on these units. Dodd argues, however, that the framework is not "indeed quite arbitrary" and "nothing more than an artificial construction of the Evangelist." He begins by pointing out that Schmidt agreed that the evangelist also received blocks or complexes of material. These complexes (like 3:7–6:13 and 8:27–10:45) include material that does not fit the theory of topical arrangement, and the complexes reflect the emphases in Jesus' teaching at particular times, e.g., sayings on the hardening of the people at the time of the collapse of his Galilean ministry, and a collection of teachings on the passion after he had made his decision to go to Jerusalem. Finally, Dodd observes that if one collects the statements and summaries from the first part of the Gospel that Schmidt identifies as the work of the evangelist, one has a neat summary of the ministry of Jesus. Moreover, if one reads these one after another, they fit together very smoothly. [The Framework of Mark] He asks, therefore, whether such would be the result of "casual links supplied here and there where the narrative seemed to demand it." Then, if the pericopae do not always seem to fit the frame it is because the evangelist had a frame he respected. If he had constructed the frame to fit the units, he could have fit them in better. Moreover, if we compare this outline in Mark with the primitive preaching in Acts (10:37-41 and 13:23-31), we find that the summaries of the early Christian preaching in Acts contain a similar outline of the ministry of Jesus. Therefore, Dodd concludes that Mark had three kinds of material: isolated pericopae, larger complexes of various kinds (continuous narratives and topical collections), and an outline of the ministry of Jesus. But the outline was too meager to indicate where all of the material fit in the ministry, and some of the complexes were already topically organized. So the evangelist did the best job he could of fitting pericopae and complexes into the outline using whatever clues the pericopae contained.

The Framework of Mark

Transitions in the early chapters in Mark identified by C. H. Dodd as elements of a traditional outline of Jesus' life:

(1:14-15) Now after John was arrested, Jesus came into Galilee, preaching the gospel of God, and saying, "The time is fulfilled, and the kingdom of God is at hand; repent, and believe in the gospel."

(1:21-22) And they went into Capernaum; and immediately on the Sabbath he entered the synagogue and taught. And they were astonished at his teaching, for he taught them as one who had authority, and not as the scribes.

(1:39) And he went throughout all Galilee, preaching in their synagogues and casting out demons.

(2:13) He went out again beside the sea; and all the crowd gathered about him, and he taught them.

(3:7b-19) . . . and from Judea and Jerusalem and Idumea and from beyond the Jordan and from about Tyre and Sidon a great multitude, hearing all that he did, came to him. And he told his disciples to have a boat ready for him because of the crowd, lest they should crush him; for he had healed many, so that all who had diseases pressed upon him to touch him. And whenever the unclean spirits beheld him, they fell down before him and cried out, "You are the Son of God." And he strictly ordered them not to make him known. And he went up into the hills, and called to him those whom he desired; and they came to him. And he appointed twelve, to be with him, and to be sent out to preach and have authority to cast out demons. Simon whom he surnamed Peter; James the son of Zebedee and John the brother of James, whom he surnamed Boanerges, that is, sons of thunder; Andrew, and Philip, and Bartholomew, and Matthew, and Thomas, and James the son of Alphaeus, and Thaddaeus, and Simon the Cananaean, and Judas Iscariot, who betrayed him.

(4:33-34 omitted because it pertains to his manner of teaching; 6:7) And he called to him the twelve, and began to send them out two by two, and gave them authority over the unclean spirits.

(6:12-13) So they went out and preached that men should repent. And they cast out many demons, and anointed with oil many that were sick and healed them.

(6:30) The apostles returned to Jesus, and told him all that they had done and taught.

See C. H. Dodd, "The Framework of the Gospel Narrative," *ExpT* 43 (1931-32): 396-400; reprinted in his *New Testament Studies*, 1-11.

In 1955, D. E. Nineham set out to reexamine Dodd's arguments.[25] He observes that Dodd's conclusions are more tentative, modest, and restrained than subsequent claims. The outline was brief, and the evangelist could place only a few pericopae in it with confidence that he knew where they belonged. Moreover, about half of Mark's account of the ministry consists of material that was already topically organized. In response to Dodd's argument that the complexes reflect actual periodic emphases in Jesus' ministry, Nineham observes that "it is one thing to claim that an account of the past is historically plausible and quite another to know it to be historically accurate."[26]

The upshot of this debate is that the Gospels show attention both to chronological and geographical data and to topical organization. We cannot take Mark as a simple, historically accurate account. On the other hand, we cannot say that early Christians had no interest in the life of Jesus or that they preserved no information about the course of his ministry. Here it is wise to be cautioned by the fact that Paul shows little or no interest in such matters and John's Gospel gives a completely different framework. Still, it is probable that some outline existed in the kerygma. Nevertheless, it must have been brief and of limited value for organizing the independent pericopae, and it does not account for the way in which much of the material in Mark is organized. This leads us to the question, Why did Mark organize his material and write his Gospel as he did?

The Clever Mark

About 1954, Günther Bornkamm, Willi Marxsen, and Hans Conzelmann developed the method of study known as redaction criticism. In reaction against the excesses of form criticism in breaking the Gospels into hundreds of units and reducing the evangelists to scissors-and-paste editors, the redaction critics contended that the Gospels must be studied as whole literary units, the creations of intelligent writers who wrote with specific purposes and theological views: "the clever Mark." Redaction criticism also focused attention on the setting of the evangelist. What was the situation that called forth the writing of the Gospels? What was the theology of the evangelist? Why did he write? What did he want to communicate to his community? In an effort to answer these questions, the redaction critics contended that the evangelist's theology and purposes may be inferred from what he did with the tradition he received. How did he arrange it? What do the editorial comments, summaries, transitions indicate? Why has he omitted some material and expanded other verses? In this way, the redaction critics focused attention on the work of the evangelist in an effort to infer why he worked as he did.

Marxsen coined the term "redaction criticism" in 1954 and published his book, *Mark the Evangelist*, in 1956.[27] After a preface setting forth the basic principles of redaction criticism, Marxsen develops the method in four separate studies on Mark.

1. John the Baptist. In Mark, John the Baptist is a bridge between Old Testament prophecy and Jesus. Therefore Mark uses "the wilderness" theologically and separates the ministry of Jesus chronologically from that of John (1:14). Galilee appears in 1:14 as the place where Jesus preached. Later the reference is historicized by Matthew and Luke.

2. The Geographical Outline. Following Ernst Lohmeyer, Marxsen contends that "the second Gospel scarcely notes one biographical detail which does not have theological significance."[28] The geographical references serve Mark's theological purpose. He organized the ministry of Jesus around his preaching in Galilee, his trip to Jerusalem, and his death there. Galilee has special significance for Mark, so it becomes the place of Jesus' activity. Mark gives scant attention to the names of cities but always notes that the decisive preaching occurred in Galilee. Places around Galilee were doubtlessly mentioned in the tradition Mark received, but it was Mark who first gave Galilee special prominence.

Mark 1:14-15 summarizes the whole Gospel. Galilee is again mentioned in 14:28 and 16:7. Why then doesn't Mark tell us of resurrection appearances in Galilee? The answer, Marxsen argues, is that Mark is writing after the resurrection, in anticipation of the Parousia. Mark, writing from Galilee, is calling Christians out of war-torn Judea to Galilee, the place of Jesus' preaching and the place of his Parousia. Mark therefore presupposes the existence of a Christian community in Galilee.

3. Euangelion. Mark calls his work a Gospel (1:1). Furthermore, where *euangelion* appears in Mark (1:1, 14; 8:35; 10:29; 13:10; 14:9) it is always used absolutely, without qualification, and Marxsen argues it is always inserted by Mark. Thus, his Gospel is to be read as a proclamation, not as a report about Jesus. Mark introduced the term "gospel" into the traditions about Jesus, but behind Mark stands the Pauline use of the term. The proclamation Mark offers to Christians from Galilee is "I am coming soon." Thus Mark writes a sermon that is "gospel." He incorporated the Jesus tradition into "gospel" for the first time in writing.

4. Mark 13. In reaction against past analyses of this chapter, Marxsen argues that it must be approached as a unity. As such it helps us locate the setting of Mark. For example, 13:1-4 looks forward to the imminent destruction of the temple. The emphasis in vv. 5-23 is on not being misled by messianic pretenders who appeared at the time of the war. Other references point to the same time: "rumors of war," "the beginning of the woes," "pray that it will not be in winter," "flee to the mountains"—to Galilee.

Like many Markan scholars before him, Marxsen asked some insightful questions, but his work raises other questions. (1) It is important to ask what Mark did with the tradition he received, but since we can only venture some tentative theories about Mark's sources from the Gospel itself, can observations about how Mark handled his sources yield information reliable enough to help us identify Mark's setting, theology, and purposes? (2) It appears that Mark gives special emphasis to "Galilee" in his Gospel, but if Mark uses "Galilee" symbolically and theologically for the place(s) where Jesus preached, why does its use in Mark compel us to think that the Gospel was written in Galilee? Would not someone writing elsewhere (Rome perhaps) be more likely to use "Galilee" symbolically? (3) Is it really credible that Mark would have written a Gospel, particularly one with such a veiled ending, if he had been intent on urging Christians to flee from Judea to Galilee in the middle of a war?

The Creative Mark

Redaction criticism shifted attention from the history and sources behind the Gospels to the work of the evangelists. Marxsen notwithstanding, Mark posed a particular challenge for redaction critics because its sources must be reconstructed from Mark itself. Interpreters also realized that the decision to reproduce a source unchanged could potentially reflect the evangelist's situation and thought just as clearly as a decision to alter the source. Gradually interpreters became concerned more generally with the composition of the Gospel and its literary patterns: "the creative Mark."

The work of Norman Perrin and his student Werner Kelber foreshadowed the development of narrative criticism of Mark shortly later. Both viewed Mark as a response to the Jewish War after 70. Perrin characterized Mark as apocalyptic drama,[29] stressing that Mark was writing for Christians in his own time and that he taught them by telling a story about Jesus and the disciples. He taught about discipleship by telling about Peter. Perrin agrees with Marxsen that 14:28 and 16:7 look forward to the Parousia. The resurrection came after three days, and the transfiguration, which he claims anticipates the Parousia, came "after 6 days." Mark lived in the interim (9:9). He was writing after the destruction of the temple. The false Christs about whom he warns in 13:5b-6, 21-22 were "Parousia pretenders," men claiming to be the risen Jesus (at this point Perrin follows Kelber): "The readers of Mark are, therefore, the men and women of the church caught up in a resurgence of apocalyptic expectation occasioned by the circumstances of the Jewish war, especially the destruction of the Jerusalem temple, but led astray by false teaching."[30]

Mark uses "Galilee" as a symbol for the Gentile mission. He was concerned about the Gentile mission (7:26; 12:8-11; 13:10, 27; 14:9, and references to Gentiles in chs. 5–7; 15:39). Galilee in Mark, therefore, comes to "symbolize the Christian mission to the world, especially to the Gentile world."[31]

In his analysis of Mark 13, Perrin argues for a post-70 date by pointing out that the destruction of the temple is

Saint Peter Dictating the Gospel to Saint Mark

Saint Peter Dictating the Gospel to Saint Mark. 11th c. South Italian (?) ivory, Romanesque, Victoria and Albert Museum, London, Great Britain. (Credit: Victoria & Albert Museum, London / Art Resource, NY)

the last dateable event in Mark, and it is common to date apocalyptic material by its latest dateable references (as with Daniel and Revelation). The end would come shortly. In preparation for the Parousia, Mark sought to instruct his readers in the correct understanding of Christology and Christian discipleship. In doing this he wrote not letters, or discourses or visions, but a Gospel. Perrin then points out the similarity between Mark and Revelation—both were written to instruct the church in a troubled time and during a resurgence of apocalyptic. Both have essentially the same purpose: to prepare their readers for the Parousia and tell them how Christians ought to live in the interim. The basic difference is that "Mark's narratives are deliberately realistic; John's deliberately symbolic."[32]

Werner Kelber begins by describing the impact the destruction of Jerusalem must have had on Palestinian Christians.[33] Kelber focuses on Mark 1:14-15 as giving the gospel program for a new existence. He interprets these verses as proclaiming a realized eschatology (like C. H. Dodd): "The kingdom has come." The kingdom of God has attained its earthly destination in Galilee: "Not the risen Christ, but the presence of the Kingdom in Galilee constitutes the gist of the gospel program."[34] Mark therefore writes in the aftermath of the war to summon his people to undergo a change of heart and a renewal of courage in view of the presence of the kingdom. Chapter 4 in Mark is devoted to revealing the mystery of the kingdom: "the Kingdom in miniature will phase into the Kingdom which covers the length and breadth of the land."[35] By their present sufferings, the people are participating in this mystery.

In chapters 5–8 the spread of the kingdom is described first in terms of its power—miracles—then in reference to the role of the disciples in carrying on the work of Jesus, and finally through the motif of crossing the sea to spread the kingdom among the Gentiles. Kelber claims the east side of the Sea of Galilee, because it was primarily Gentile, represents the Christian mission to the Gentiles. Thus there is first a Jewish feeding miracle, then a Gentile one. The polemic in this section is against the family of Jesus and against the disciples. These were associated with the church in Jerusalem. Therefore, it is not unreasonable to see Mark as a representative of northern (Galilean) Christianity. In the next section—chapters 8 through 10—we find the story centering on teaching about discipleship and this cast in terms of a journey from Galilee to Jerusalem. In terms of their understanding at least some of the disciples figuratively fall by the wayside on the journey. Through the travel narrative Mark has Jesus correct false notions of discipleship commonly held by Petrine Christians. Peter's false understanding of Christ is corrected by Jesus' teaching on the suffering Son of Man.

Chapter 11 drives a wedge between the kingdom of God and the kingdom of David. There is a break with Jerusalem, and the kingdom is oriented around a new center. The temple is displaced. In chapter 13, Mark looks upon the destruction of the temple as an event recently accomplished. This chapter deals with the dangers facing the Christians in the aftermath of the destruction of Jerusalem. The danger of being misled by messianic pretenders—those who have miscalculated the time and the place of the Parousia—is real. At the same time, watchfulness is imperative because the Parousia is at hand—but not yet. Mark therefore wrote his Gospel about the beginning of the gospel of Jesus in order to provide a new beginning for Christians at the end of the war. For this reason, he retells the past (the beginning) in order to open the way for the future (the Parousia).

Kelber synthesizes many trends in Markan studies and gives adept analyses of the Gospel. His study of the relationship of Jesus to the temple, Jerusalem, and the disciples also furnishes strong arguments for a post-70 date. Nevertheless, we may be reticent about Kelber's concentration on Galilee. We know precious little about "Northern Christianity," and Mark's interest in the Gentile mission means "Galilee" may represent the Christian mission to the world in Mark, as Perrin contended.

Norman Petersen led the Literary Aspects of the Gospels Group of the Society of Biblical Literature in reading literary theory. Robert Tannehill traced the narrative development of Mark's theology in an article on the disciples in Mark.[36] David Rhoads and Donald Michie introduced narrative criticism of Mark to non-specialists in *Mark as Story*, in which they analyzed the role of the narrator in Mark, its narrative patterns, settings, plot, and the functions of characters.[37] [David Rhoads]

David Rhoads

"In the story dying for the good news—trusting God enough to lose one's life in service for others—is the basic expression of following God's way. The narrative leads the reader to be a faithful follower of Jesus by preparing the reader to face death. In the Jerusalem scenes, the reader sees all the characters dealing with death. By identifying with these different characters, the reader experiences the desire to save one's self, the avoidance of death, and the unwillingness to deal with the weakness of the flesh. But the narrator leads the reader to reject these, to identify and align with the hero Jesus, to want to be courageous as he is, and to want to have such faith in God's salvation as to relinquish one's own life in spite of fears and desires. Then through the powerful depiction of Jesus' death, the reader experiences vicariously the isolation, the pain, the rejection, and the despair of death. By facing death vicariously through the story, the implied reader is purged of some of the fear of death and is therefore better prepared to be faithful as Jesus was."

David Rhoads and Donald Michie, *Mark as Story: An Introduction to the Narrative of a Gospel* (Philadelphia: Fortress, 1982), 139–40.

With the monograph by Mary Ann Tolbert, narrative criticism of Mark reached a new level of maturity. In regard to its genre, she interprets Mark as an example of Hellenistic popular literature accessible to a wide spectrum of society, an ancient novel.[38] Internally, Mark's narrative has two parts. The first is primarily concerned with Jesus' mission, the second with the issue of Jesus' true identity. The parable of the sower and its interpretation (4:1-20) serves as a "parabolic plot

Mary Ann Tolbert

"The characters, groups, and events of Division One are all portrayed as the concrete illustrations of these four fundamental kinds of responses to Jesus' word [in the parable of the Sower]. Every episode and every character or group can be understood by the audience as an example of one of these four alternatives: the instant rejection of Jesus by the scribes and the Pharisees illustrates the first response; the immediate joy but ultimate failure of the disciples, the second; the wealth, too great to give up, of the rich man (10:17-22), the third; but what of the fourth type? The task of the material following the parable of the Sower, Mark 4:21–5:43, is to clarify the nature of the good earth that produces fruit."

Mary Ann Tolbert, *Sowing the Gospel: Mark's World in Literary-Historical Perspective* (Minneapolis: Fortress, 1989), 124.

synopsis" through which the reader can see in miniature the various figures who surround Jesus and the meaning of their responses to his message. [Mary Ann Tolbert] Similarly, the parable of the wicked tenants functions as a plot synopsis for the coming Passion Narrative, interpreting the meaning of Jesus' identity, rejection by the authorities, and death on the cross.[39]

The literature on Mark is extensive. The articles and monographs mentioned here are at best a selective sample of the available literature, chosen to provide a sense of the direction of Markan studies over the past two centuries. With this background, the reader will have a richer context for interacting with the text of the Gospel itself.

MARK'S LEADING THEMES

The commentary that follows highlights Markan themes and makes numerous cross-references between related passages. Nevertheless, the following overview of five of these themes will help the reader be alert to them when they appear in the Gospel.

Jesus' Identity as the Son of God

The Gospel begins by announcing that it is the "gospel" of Jesus Christ, and most of the manuscripts add "the Son of God." See the discussion of this verse and the textual variants in the commentary on Mark 1:1. Normally textual criticism favors the shorter text, a principle that rules against accepting "the Son of God" as part of the earliest text of Mark 1:1, but in this case there are offsetting considerations: (1) the reference to Jesus as "my son" by the voice from heaven in Mark 1:11 and 9:7; (2) the occurrence of the title in the centurion's confession following Jesus' death (15:39); (3) the sequence of the two christological titles in Mark 1:1 that foreshadows the strategic placement of the confessions of Jesus by Peter and the centurion in the Gospel's narrative Christology; and (4) the fact that the title might have been dropped by accident if it was abbreviated (see the commentary on Mark 1:1).

Regardless of one's decision about the occurrence of "the Son of God" in Mark 1:1, the Gospel builds to the disclosure of Jesus' identity not merely as the Messiah ("Christ") but specifically as the Son of God. The secrecy motif, noted so influentially by Wrede, focuses the reader's attention on the question of how Jesus' true identity was revealed. Mark's theological achievement was that he integrated the traditions of the life and ministry of Jesus with the proclamation of the gospel of the cross.[40] The teachings of Jesus were being used in preaching and instruction. Collections of Jesus' miracles may have been used to justify the activities of some apostles (for example, the "super apostles" to whom Paul refers in 2 Cor 11:5; 12:11). Perhaps following Paul's lead, Mark placed priority neither on Jesus' words nor on his works but on his death and resurrection. In Mark, therefore, the reader finds that no one confesses that Jesus is the Son of God as a result of hearing his parables or witnessing his mighty works. It is only in the context of his death that his identity can be understood (14:62), so it is only when he is hanging dead on the cross that the Roman centurion can confess his true identity. ["Son of God" in Mark]

> **"Son of God" in Mark**
>
> AΩ 1:1 "The beginning of the good news of Jesus Christ, the Son of God."
>
> 1:11 The voice from heaven: "You are my Son, the Beloved; with you I am well pleased."
>
> 3:11 "[the unclean spirits] fell down before him and shouted, 'You are the Son of God!'"
>
> 5:7 "[The Gerasene demoniac] shouted at the top of his voice, 'What have you to do with me, Jesus, Son of the Most High God?'"
>
> 9:7 The voice from heaven: "This is my Son, the Beloved; listen to him!"
>
> 14:61 "Again the high priest asked him, 'Are you the Messiah, the Son of the Blessed One?'"
>
> 15:39 "Now when the centurion, who stood facing him, saw that in this way he breathed his last, he said, 'Truly this man was God's Son!'"

The centurion's confession, "Truly, this man was the Son of God" (15:39), is strikingly emphatic, as though to deny that any other could be confessed with this title. Craig Evans surveyed the use of the title "Son of God" in divine epithets of the Roman emperors from Julius Caesar to Vespasian.[41] Based on this evidence and other parallels with the veneration of the emperors, Evans concluded that "the Markan evangelist presents Jesus as the true son of God and in doing so deliberately presents Jesus in opposition to Rome's candidates for a suitable emperor, savior, and lord."[42] If the effect of Mark's presentation of the "good news" of Jesus was to present Jesus as the true "Son of God" in contrast to the emperor—and *euangelion* was often used in reference to the accession and activities of the emperor—Mark's Gospel would have set in dramatic relief the choice the early believers faced: choose between Jesus and Caesar! Jesus is Lord, not Caesar.

The Testing of God's Son

Conflict pervades the Gospel of Mark. Jesus is tested in turn by Satan, unclean spirits, forces of nature, religious authorities, his hometown, his family, and even his disciples. The effect is that Jesus is progressively isolated as the nature of his mission and its eventual cost become clearer with each new trial.

The Gospel begins in the place of Israel's testing: the wilderness. As soon as Jesus is baptized by the wilderness prophet, the Spirit drives him into the wilderness, where he is "tested" (1:12-13). The Greek verb *peirazein* means primarily to "try, make trial of, put to the test" and by extension to "tempt."[43] This scene sets the theme that is developed through the rest of the Gospel. In the synagogue in Capernaum Jesus is confronted by the first of a series of unclean spirits and demons who challenge his authority (1:24, 34, 39; 3:15 passim). The crowds press around Jesus and threaten to hinder his work (1:37-39; 3:7-10; 6:30-31, 54-55; 8:1). In Mark 2:1–3:6 Jesus is repeatedly challenged by the religious authorities, and the section ends with the first reference to their intent to kill him. Scribes from Jerusalem come to investigate his activities (3:22), and his own family comes to take him home (3:31). In the first of his parables, Jesus likens his ministry to plundering Satan's house after having bound "the strong man" (3:27). Jesus is like a farmer who sows, but Satan "immediately" takes the seed (4:15). Storms at sea seem to be a metaphor for the life-threatening opposition Jesus and his disciples will face in proclaiming the coming kingdom among the Gentiles (4:35-41; 6:45-52). Again the Pharisees and the scribes challenge Jesus for not teaching "the tradition of the elders" (7:5-13). In the region of Tyre a Syrophoenician woman tests Jesus (7:24-30). The Pharisees test him, demanding a sign (8:11) and asking about divorce (10:2; cf. 12:15). Peter, his own disciple, becomes "Satan" when he objects to Jesus' announcement that he must suffer and die (8:32-33). A crowd, some scribes, and an unclean spirit confront Jesus after his transfiguration (9:14, 17, 29). The disciples' lack of understanding and hardness of heart and finally their abandonment and denials test Jesus (6:52; 8:14-21, 32-33; 9:33-34; 10:35-45). The corruption of the temple tests Jesus (11:15-17), and his prophetic action there leads the chief priests and scribes to renew their determination to kill him (11:18). Repeatedly, the religious and political authorities challenge Jesus' authority (11:27–12:44).

The night before Jesus' death is also a time of testing, first through the failure of the disciples (14:29-31, 32-42, 51, 66-72), then through the trials before the Jewish authorities (14:53-65) and Pilate (15:1-20). Jesus is interrogated, challenged to prophesy, confronted with false witnesses, mocked, flogged, and then crucified. The mockers taunt Jesus for not saving himself and for claiming he would destroy the temple and build another (15:29-32). Even God's failure to intervene tests Jesus (15:34).

Through it all Jesus remains steadfast in his mission to proclaim the kingdom and confront the forces that oppose it. Peter, like a man who could see but not clearly (8:22-26), sees that Jesus is the Christ (8:27-30) but cannot fully grasp who he is or what his work will require of him. The centrality of the cross in revealing Jesus' true identity as the Son of God is underscored by the fact that it is only after his death that anyone—the Roman centurion—is able to offer this confession (15:39).

The testing of Jesus reveals not only his identity but also the means by which God will defeat Satan and the demons and establish the kingdom. It also sets the example for all who take up the cross and follow him (8:34).

The Testing of Jesus' Disciples

Jesus' life is set in the context of persecution. John the Baptist comes preaching. He is arrested and subsequently killed. Jesus preaches the kingdom, is arrested, tried, and crucified. His disciples too—not surprisingly—will face similar hostility.

Jesus calls the Twelve and appoints them to "be with him" and to be sent out to preach and to cast out demons (3:14-15). [*Peirazein*, To "Tempt" or "Test," in Mark] As insiders, they have the secret of the kingdom; but still they do not understand Jesus' parables (4:10-13). The disciples will face "trouble or persecution on account of the word" (4:17). When the storm arises on the sea, they are terrified, and Jesus rebukes them for their lack of faith: "Why are you afraid? Have you still no faith?" (4:40). When Jesus sends them out by twos with strict instructions, "They cast out many demons, and anointed with oil many who were sick and cured them" (6:13), but their success is fleeting. The disciples are at a loss to know how to feed the crowd (6:35-36). When they see Jesus walking on the sea, they are terrified and "they did not understand about the loaves, but their hearts were hardened" (6:52). Their lack of understanding is underscored by Jesus' questioning. They are no more understanding than outsiders (8:14-21). They are like the man who could see but not clearly (8:22-26), and in stark contrast to Matthew's account of Peter's confession at Caesarea Philippi (Matt 16:17-19), in Mark Jesus rebukes Peter (8:30, 32-33).

From this point on, the disciples move from lack of understanding to renewed self-seeking as they seek personal greatness, advantage over

---

Peirazein, To "Tempt" or "Test," in Mark

AΩ 1:13 "He was in the wilderness forty days, tempted by Satan."

8:11 "The Pharisees came and began to argue with him, asking him for a sign from heaven, to test him."

10:2 "Some Pharisees came, and to test him they asked, 'Is it lawful for a man to divorce his wife?'"

12:15 "But knowing their hypocrisy, he said to them, 'Why are you putting me to the test?'"

others, and places of honor (9:32-34; 10:35-45). By contrast, when the blind Bartimaeus receives his sight he follows Jesus "on the way" (a phrase Mark uses for discipleship and the way to the cross, 10:52; cf. 1:2-3; 8:27; 9:33-34; 10:32; 12:14). In the course of prophesying the destruction of Jerusalem and the coming of false prophets and false messiahs who would mislead the people, Jesus warns the disciples that "they will hand you over to councils; and you will be beaten in synagogues; and you will stand before governors and kings because of me" (13:9). They "will be hated by all because of my name" (13:13). They will have to be on guard against those who will mislead the elect (13:5-6, 21-22). Like a trusted doorkeeper, they should keep alert and watch (13:33-37). The events of the night Jesus was betrayed by Judas prove that they are incapable of watching with Jesus for even one hour. Judas betrays Jesus to the authorities (14:10-11, 43-45), Peter is unaware of his own vulnerability (14:29-31), and the three closest to Jesus sleep while he prays (14:32-42). Finally, the disciples all abandon Jesus (14:50-52), and Peter denies Jesus three times (14:66-72).

Others too are tested: the leper (1:40-45), the four who bring the paralytic to Jesus (2:1-12), Jesus' family (3:31-35), the Gerasene demoniac (5:1-20), Jairus and the woman with a hemorrhage (5:21-43), Jesus' hometown (6:1-6a), John the Baptist (6:14-27), the Syrophoenician woman (7:24-30), the blind man (8:22-26), the father of the epileptic boy (9:17-27), Bartimaeus (10:46-52), and the authorities, Jewish and Roman.

The effect of this constant testing is to underscore Jesus' warnings to the disciples about the necessity for self-denial, cross bearing, faithfulness, and vigilance. The failure of the disciples not only dramatizes the consequences of failure to meet the tests of persecution, but also heightens Jesus' faithfulness in continually returning to bring sight to the blind and a second chance for those who stumble: "Go to Galilee, there you will see him" (16:7). Eduard Schweizer's comment aptly interprets the other side of Mark's oppressive emphasis on the disciples' failure: "So man's continued inability to understand is contrasted with Jesus' promise to go before them and accomplish what human hearts cannot do; despite every failure he would call the disciples again to discipleship and would encounter them in a way that would enable them to see him."[44]

The Temple Not Made with Hands

Early in the Gospel Jesus begins to call together a new community, one that crosses all geographical, social, and ethnic boundaries. He casts out demons and touches a leper (1:40-45). He eats with tax collectors and sinners (2:15-17). He travels to "Judea, Jerusalem, Idumea, beyond the Jordan, and the region around Tyre and Sidon" (3:8). He visits a cemetery in a Gentile region (5:1-20). He is touched by a woman in a state of impurity and accepts her faith (5:24-34). Then he takes the hand of a dead girl and raises her to life (5:35-43). He shows that it is not what enters a person that defiles but the thoughts of the heart and the "evil things [that] come from within" (7:23). A Syrophoenician woman (7:24-30), a deaf and mute man from the region of the Decapolis (7:31-37), a blind man who requires a second touch (8:22-26), a persistent father (9:14-29), blind Bartimaeus (10:46-52), and a widow who gave all she had are among those who represent the new community of the kingdom. In this new community prevailing conventions are overturned: one who would be great must be the servant of all (9:35; 10:42-45), children are valued and accepted (9:36-37; 10:13-16), women and marriage are protected (10:2-12), and those who have much should sell all they have and give to the poor (10:17-22).

In Jerusalem Jesus condemns the corruption of the temple, recalling the words of Isaiah and Jeremiah (11:17). The temple has become like a fig tree that gives every appearance of health but bears no fruit (11:12-14, 20-21). After Jesus' death the temple will be destroyed (13:14-20). False witnesses say they heard Jesus say he would destroy the temple and build another not made with hands (14:58), and mockers at the cross repeat the charge (15:29). Although false witnesses introduce the charge, its repetition in a context in which the other things are said in mockery is ironically a true call for further reflection. Jesus' death will lead to the establishment of a new community of faith in which those like the centurion who confess Jesus find a new Lord, a renewed faith, and the presence of God among them (16:7). They will continue the work of the kingdom that Jesus began, preaching the gospel to all nations (11:17; 13:10). To these Jesus promises,

> Truly I tell you, there is no one who has left house or brothers or sisters or mother or father or children or fields, for my sake and for the sake of the good news, who will not receive a hundredfold now in this age—houses, brothers and sisters, mothers and children, and fields, with persecutions—and in the age to come eternal life. (10:29-30)

The Hope of the Kingdom

Because the Gospel of Mark was written for a persecuted community, it is first and foremost a gospel of hope. Nothing else compares to the announcement that God's eschatological sovereignty has torn the heavens, crossed the boundaries, and been proclaimed by God's Son.

The long-expected Messiah had come, accompanied by wonders and mighty works associated with Moses (testing in the wilderness, crossing the sea, and feeding the multitude), Elijah and Elisha (giving sight to the blind, hearing to the deaf), and the words of Isaiah (hardness of heart). He had condemned the corruption of the temple (like Jeremiah) and announced its destruction—a cataclysmic event that was either imminent and clear when Mark was written or else had already occurred.

Jesus prophesied that his followers would be persecuted, just as he was and just as John the Baptist had been. Indeed, discipleship is defined by taking up the cross and following him (8:34). But the kingdom will not be defeated. Although Jesus had been crucified, God raised him from the grave. The angel at the tomb had commissioned the women to tell his disciples and Peter to go to Galilee. The fact that they failed to deliver this good news either implies that it was delivered in other ways or that it is now the reader's duty to do what the women failed to do.

In Mark, Galilee is the place of the kingdom, where the kingdom was announced and where its power was seen in Jesus' words and works, in the exorcism of demons, and in the response of the people. Mark therefore challenges the followers of Jesus to carry on the work of the kingdom and preach the gospel among the Gentiles, in fact to "all nations" (13:10).

All of these events are a sign, like a fig tree in leaf (13:28-29). The signs of the kingdom confirm to those who have eyes to see and ears to hear that the Son of Man is coming (9:1; 13:26-27) to vindicate and gather the faithful (8:38; 13:27; 14:62). Therefore the faithful should "take heart" (6:50) and watch, like a doorkeeper watching for the return of his master (13:34-37). Do not be misled by the false claims of other messiahs and prophets or by the claims of governors and kings (13:5-6, 9, 21-22). Even the Roman emperor who is worshiped as divine, a savior, and God's son, pales by comparison. Jesus alone is truly the Son of God

Map of Galilee

(15:39), and those who follow him will be vindicated and gathered with the elect when the Son of Man "comes in the glory of his Father with the holy angels" (8:39).

MARK'S SETTING

Locating the setting of the Gospel is important not because it would confirm the authenticity or historical accuracy of Mark or the tradition about it but because identifying the setting of the Gospel creates a context for reading it that may illuminate or bring new significance to otherwise obscure features. The problem is that the early testimonies about the Gospel are of questionable value and reconstructing the Gospel's setting depends heavily on data derived from the Gospel itself. Some circularity is inevitable and the issues remain unsettled, so at best our conclusions must be tentative and serve as theories to be tested by further close reading of the Gospel.

We have already noted that Mark makes specific references to the persecution of Jesus' disciples "because of Jesus and the gospel" (4:17; 8:35; 10:29; 13:9). Moreover, Mark gives evidence of having been written for a particular community or a group of house churches in a specific locality. In support of this contention and reasons for rejecting the notion that Mark was written for the church at large, as proposed by Richard Bauckham,[45] H. N. Roskam adduces evidence that there was a close relationship between Mark and his readers: the readers are familiar with certain persons (Alexander and Rufus, 15:21; James the Younger and Joses, 15:40) and various Galilean sites (Magdala, 15:40, 47; 16:1, and Dalmanutha, 8:10).[46] Roskam also concludes that Mark's readers were associated with each other and that they were Christians; they are familiar with titles such as "Son of Man" and accept Christian interpretations of Old Testament passages.[47]

The Case for Galilee

Building on the work of earlier scholars, especially, R. H. Lightfoot, Willi Marxsen, and Werner H. Kelber, the argument in favor of Galilee or Syria as the provenance for the Markan community is based on observations regarding Mark's handling of geographical references, especially "Galilee" and the Syrophoenician woman, the accuracy of its description of the rural context of Jesus' ministry,[48] and Josephus's account of Galilee during the Jewish War (AD 66–70).

H. N. Roskam argues that Mark's knowledge of the geography of Galilee is more accurate than his description of the sites in Judea, the

Galilee

(Credit: Jim Pitts)

Decapolis, or the Transjordan.[49] The confused reference in Mark 7:31, that Jesus "returned from the region of Tyre, and went by way of Sidon towards the Sea of Galilee, in the region of the Decapolis," he argues, reflects ignorance not of Galilee but of the location of Sidon.[50] Joel Marcus (drawing on the work of Gerd Theissen) concludes that while the reference to the "Syrophoenician" woman would make no sense in Syria if it designated a particular kind of Phoenician, it may have denoted a particular kind of Syrian and the entire pericope reflects an interesting knowledge of the local social setting (see the commentary on 7:24-30).[51]

Mark seems to presume a rather detailed knowledge of the course of the war in 13:14-20, especially in the aside, "let the reader understand." The appearance of the desolating sacrilege was the signal that they should "flee to the mountains" (13:14). Joel Marcus reasonably suggests that "The sort of detailed knowledge of the course of the Jewish War that seems to be reflected in Mark 13 is most easily explained by the theory that the Gospel was composed in geographical and temporal proximity to it."[52] Galilee was a war zone between AD 66 and 70, however, making it difficult to think that anyone found the time to write a Gospel there at this time, and there is no evidence that Christians were persecuted in Galilee during the war. Marcus favors Syria rather than Galilee.[53] Roskam, on the other hand, argues that Galilee was more pro-Roman than has often been alleged and that Mark reflects the persecution of Christians in Galilee by Jewish and Roman authorities after the war.[54]

The Case for Rome

The argument that Mark originated from Rome can be traced to (and some argue that it derives from) Papias. Clifton Black notes that the connection between Mark and Rome in early Christian literature is always through Mark's association with Peter and never appears in the absence of this association.[55] Early in the twentieth century, B. W. Bacon's *Is Mark a Roman Gospel?* focused attention on Mark's affinities with Pauline teaching (or at least interpretations of Pauline teaching) and argued for the Roman origin of Mark.[56]

Bacon's arguments summarized the data for a debate that continues to the present. First, Bacon examined the tradition from Papias and concluded that Papias had nothing more to work from than the statement in 1 Peter 5:13. Nevertheless, 1 Peter shows special respect for Mark and holds that past association with Peter was the basis for this respect. Since it is likely that 1 Peter was written from Rome, this tells us that Mark was held in special regard in Rome near the end of the first century.

Bacon then turned to the internal evidence, maintaining that whatever Aramaisms there may be in Mark prove no threat to Rome as its place of origin. Although Aramaic oral or written sources probably lie behind Mark, the Gospel itself was not composed in Aramaic and is not merely a translation.

Rome
(Credit: Jim Pitts)

Mark uses more Latin terms than any other Gospel, but many of these are terms that would have been known widely, and his preference for them over Greek terms does not necessarily indicate he was writing from Rome (cf. 15:39, 44, 45; 6:27; 7:4, 8). More persuasive are 12:42 and 15:16 in which Mark explains Greek terms with Latin terms.

Mark's editorial glosses and explanations (e.g., 7.3-4) habitually explain to the readers things and customs peculiar to a Jewish setting—even *abba* (14:36). Mark finds it necessary to explain Palestinian climate and seasons (11:13). Such explanations would have been superfluous in Palestine. Mark also appears to have only a fuzzy knowledge of Palestinian geography (e.g., Gerasa in 5:1-20 and Sidon, the Sea of Galilee, and the Decapolis in 7:31). Mark shows a lack of understanding about local history (e.g., 6:17 using "king" for the tetrarch Antipas). He also seems ignorant of the complicated family relationships of the Herods.

Bacon found in Mark an affinity with the sentiments of "the strong" in Romans 14. In particular Bacon argued that Mark reflects a hardening of the attitude of "the strong" in Romans 14, that is, the anti-judaic attitude of the Paulinists against the Petrine conciliatory attitude of "the weak." Bacon did not claim that Mark knew the Pauline epistles, but was positive that Mark shows a direct dependence upon the teachings of Paul: "Our contention is that the paulinism of Mark is precisely of the type Paul seeks to hold in check. It has little to do with the literary Paul, but is characterized by exactly this overbearing, inconsiderate, intolerant attitude of the 'strong' toward the Jewish 'distinctions.'"[57] These observations led Bacon to conclude that Mark originated in Rome.

More recently Brian J. Incigneri revisited the issue in a volume tellingly titled *The Gospel to the Romans*.[58] He responds to Marxsen's argument that Mark's emphasis on Galilee indicates that the Gospel was written there by pointing out that Christians continued to identify with Galilee because it was the place of Jesus' ministry and the origin of the movement, and Mark reads like a text written at a distance: "In Rome, adherents of foreign cults were used to stories and images of their religion's origins in another land."[59] His response to the contention that Mark reflects the local color and rural setting of Galilee or Syria is similar: these elements of the Gospel derive from traditional material rather than from the setting of the Gospel's composition.

The significance of the Latinisms in Mark has been debated. The sheer number of Latinisms is significant in itself. Kelber responded that Mark's Latinisms are mainly military, administrative, and commercial terms that could have been spread by the Roman army and known anywhere in the Roman Empire,[60] but Incigneri and Gundry point out that some of the Latinisms in Mark do include domestic, social, and religious terms, some of which are listed above. Twice Mark uses Latin terms to explain Greek terms: Mark 12:42 explains that two *lepta* are a *kodrantēs* and Mark 15:16 explains that the courtyard, *aulēs*, was a *praitōrion*. [Latin Tems in Mark] The most likely setting for such frequent use of Latin in a Greek document is Rome,

---

Latin Terms in Mark

ΑΩ

dēnarion	a denarius (coin)	6:37; 12:15; 14:5
kenturion	a centurion	15:39, 44, 45
kēnsos	[census] tax	12:14
kodrantēs	copper coin, a quadrans	12:42
legiōn	a Roman legion	5:9, 15
modios	a measure of grain	4:21
phragello«	flog	15:15
praitōrion	quarters of a Roman governor	15:16
pykmē	"with a handful of water" (Hengel)	7:3
spekoulatōr	executioner	6:27
symboulion	a council	15:1
to hikanon poiēsai (satisfacere)	to satisfy	15:15
xestēs	a liquid measure, a sextarius	7:4

Martin Hengel, "Mk 7.3 *pugmē*: Der Geschichte einer exegetischen Aporie und der Versuch ihrer Lösung," *ZNW* 60 (1969): 182-98; Brian J. Incigneri, *The Gospel to the Romans: The Setting and Rhetoric of Mark's Gospel* (BIS 65; Leiden: E. J. Brill, 2003), 101; Vincent Taylor, *The Gospel according to St. Mark* (London: Macmillan, 1952), 45, 657. See also the commentary on 15:18.

"where the Latin and Greek languages were closely intermingled as nowhere else at that time."[61]

Other factors support a Roman provenance: the tradition from the church fathers (Papias, the Anti-Marcionite Prologue, Irenaeus, Clement of Alexandria), the fact that the persecution of Christians in Rome is more strongly attested than anywhere else in the first century, and the evidence assembled by Craig Evans that Mark makes use of terms and motifs from the emperor cult.[62] The latter would again have been significant in other provincial centers (though presumably not in rural Syria), but Rome was its epicenter.

One other consideration, though inconclusive, fits Rome better than Galilee or Syria. One might have assumed that Mark would be forgotten after it was incorporated into Matthew and Luke. The survival of Mark may be due in part to the belief that it was thought to contain Peter's preaching, but also to the probability that an important Christian center stood behind it—Rome.

After examining what is known of the ethnicity and social background, economic and social standing, religious organization, and political turbulence of the sixties in Rome and what may be inferred from Mark, Clifton Black concludes, rightly I think, that "our relevant evidence is strong enough to lend support to a location of Mark's Gospel in Rome; at the same time it remains too equivocal to nail that theory down."[63]

THE DATE OF THE COMPOSITION OF MARK

Considerations regarding the date of Mark are again rather evenly divided between those that favor a date in the late 60s and those that favor a date in the early 70s. The difference is significant because the year 70 marks the destruction of the temple in Jerusalem and the end of the Jewish War (although a group of Zealots held out on Masada until 74). The fact that scholarship is virtually unanimous in dating the Gospel in the decade from 65 to 75 should not be missed in the arguments for and against the earlier or latter part of this decade. No other Gospel can be dated with such precision.

Earlier critical scholarship assigned the Gospel to the mid-60s, following the persecution of Christians in Rome under Nero. More recently Mark 13 and Mark's relationship to the course of the Jewish War have overshadowed the Neronian persecution. As Joel Marcus notes, "If Mark 13 really came out of the Neronian persecution, would we not expect it to focus more, as Daniel and Revelation do, on a bestial, anti-God figure?"[64] For some interpreters Mark 13 supports a pre-70 date because the prophecy it contains does not match the course

Pre-70 Date

"So I believe that in contrast to the other Gospels, we can determine the time of the composition of the second Gospel relatively accurately, as also its author and the tradition which shaped him. It presumably came into being in the politically turbulent time after the murder of Nero and Galba and before the renewal of the Jewish War under Titus, i.e. say between the winter of 68/69 and the winter of 69/70."

Martin Hengel, *Studies in the Gospel of Mark* (trans. John Bowden; Philadelphia: Fortress, 1985), 28.

of events exactly: the temple was not completely destroyed ("not one stone will be left here," 13:2), and there is no mention of the great fire that accompanied the destruction. See the discussion of Mark 13:14-20 in the commentary and the outline of the chronology of the war (see [Chronology of the Jewish War, AD 66–70]). Martin Hengel has been one of the recent advocates for a pre-70 date for Mark. [Pre-70 Date]

Proponents of a post-70 date argue that the Gospel should be dated after the latest specifically identifiable events in it, which would include the flight of believers in Jerusalem to Pella (in 68) and the destruction of the temple (13:2; 15:38) and the removal of Jewish authorities and insurgents in Judea. Roskam proposes that the transfer of authority in AD 70 is reflected in Mark 12:9.[65] Before 70 Judea was administered by Roman governors who were subordinate to the legate of the province of Syria. After 70, Judea became a separate province, and the Jewish Sanhedrin no longer exercised the authority over internal affairs that it had earlier. Mark writes to reassure the community and challenge it to remain faithful amid the agitation of false prophets and the speculation that the fall of Jerusalem meant that the end was near.[66]

S. G. F. Brandon proposed that the Gospel of Mark was written in Rome in the year following Titus's march of triumph through the streets of Rome, as an apology for the Christians who worshiped a Jewish teacher who was crucified by the Romans. Mark shows special interest in the veil of the temple (15:38), and according to Josephus (*J.W.* 7.162) the veil of the temple was among the items displayed during the march of triumph in Rome. So Mark did not find it necessary to explain its significance, as he does other Jewish words and customs. There is also late tradition in the rabbinic materials that Titus had split the veil with his sword. Brandon argues that Mark includes this detail to say that the temple had been made obsolete long before the death of Jesus.

Brandon relates the "abomination of desolation" (13:14) to Titus, pointing out that in Mark the term is masculine.[67] Gaius in AD 39 had attempted to erect Roman standards in the temple, and that is often thought to be the reference here. Brandon says Mark points out that what was threatened by Gaius in 39 was accomplished by Titus. So Mark uses a well-known reference to make a potentially inflammatory claim. The Roman Christians would have understood.

The argument over the date of the Gospel will continue, although most scholars date it between AD 68 and AD 73, which is already a narrow range.

AUTHORSHIP

Papias claims that the Gospel was written by Mark, Peter's interpreter. The relationship between the Gospel and Peter is probably more indirect than Papias claimed, though it may still be related to the Petrine tradition.[68] On the basis of this tradition, Papias's Mark has been identified as John Mark, who appears in Acts (12:12, 25; 15:37, 39). By tradition, the Mark referred to in Colossians 4:10; 2 Timothy 4:11; Philemon 24; and 1 Peter 5:13 is also John Mark. Clifton Black distinguishes the "minimalist reconstruction" that questions these identifications from the "maximalist reconstruction" that accepts the traditional identifications.[69] Mark was one of the five most common Latin names in all periods of Roman history,[70] so the New Testament writings may refer to more than one Mark, who may or may not have been the Mark to whom Papias refers.

In favor of accepting the Papias tradition is the consideration that Papias links the Gospel only indirectly to an apostle, when the church was moving toward claiming apostolic authority for the canonical writings. There is no reason to doubt that the Gospel was written by Mark, who in all probability was John Mark. Nevertheless, this traditional identification is only of limited value for reading the Gospel. A popular view has suggested that the young man in the garden who fled naked was the evangelist himself, John Mark, but this is nothing more than interesting speculation. We know so little about John Mark that the contention that he is the evangelist makes little practical difference for the interpretation of the Gospel. Whoever wrote the Gospel drew on early tradition of the miracles, teachings, and passion of Jesus, and interpretation must begin with the Gospel itself rather than tradition about its authorship. The Gospel tells us more about the evangelist and his setting than the tradition of Papias does. The Gospel, moreover, remains one of the pillars of the Christian faith and tradition, one that is endlessly fascinating, inspiring, and pivotal for our understanding of Jesus.

NOTES

[1] See, for example, Robert H. Gundry, *Mark: A Commentary on His Apology for the Cross* (Grand Rapids: Wm. B. Eerdmans, 1993), 1026-41, who contends that Papias wrote between AD 101–108 and that the elder John was the apostle John.

[2] C. Clifton Black, *Mark: Images of an Apostolic Interpreter* (Columbia: University of South Carolina Press, 1994), 131, 213.

[3] Ibid., 135 n. 34.

[4] Laurence Housman, *Songs of Praise*, no. 228, quoted by A. M. Hunter, *Saint Mark* (London: SCM Press, 1948), 15.

[5] For full accounts of this history see Seán P. Kealy, *Mark's Gospel: A History of Its Interpretation from the Beginning until 1979* (New York: Paulist, 1982).

[6] William R. Farmer, *The Synoptic Problem* (Dillsboro: Western North Carolina Press, 1976), 66.

[7] For a history of the study of synoptic relationships, see Werner Georg Kümmel, *Introduction to the New Testament* (trans. Howard Clark Kee; Nashville: Abingdon, 1975), 38-80; Farmer, *Synoptic Problem*.

[8] Martin Kähler, *The So-called Historical Jesus and the Historic Biblical Christ* (trans. Carl E. Braaten; Philadelphia: Fortress, 1964).

[9] Ibid., 80.

[10] William Wrede, *Das Messiasgeheimnis in den Evangelien* (1901) (trans. J. C. G. Grieg as *The Messianic Secret*; Edinburgh: T. & T. Clark, 1971).

[11] Wrede, *The Messianic Secret*, 131.

[12] Karl Ludwig Schmidt, *Der Rahmen der Geschichte Jesu* (Berlin: Trowitzsch & Sohn, 1919).

[13] Schmidt, *Rahmen*, v.

[14] Martin Dibelius, *From Tradition to Gospel* (Cambridge: James Clarke, 1971).

[15] Rudolf Bultmann, *The History of the Synoptic Tradition* (2d ed.; trans. John Marsh; Oxford: Blackwell, 1968).

[16] Ibid., 338.

[17] Ibid., 340.

[18] Ibid., 349.

[19] Ibid., 345.

[20] Ibid., 346.

[21] Ibid., 347.

[22] Ibid.

[23] Ibid., 347-48.

[24] C. H. Dodd, "The Framework of the Gospel Narrative," *ExpT* 43 (1931–1932): 396-400; reprinted in his NTS, 1-11.

[25] D. E. Nineham, "The Order of Events in St. Mark's Gospel—An Examination of Dr. Dodd's Hypothesis," in *Studies in the Gospels: Essays in Memory of R. H. Lightfoot* (ed. D. E. Nineham; Oxford: Oxford University Press, 1955), 223-39.

[26] Ibid., 228.

[27] Willi Marxsen, *Mark the Evangelist* (Nashville: Abingdon, 1969).

[28] Ibid., 55.

[29] Norman Perrin, *The New Testament: An Introduction* (2d ed.; New York: Harcourt Brace Jovanovich, 1974), 143-45, 149.

[30] Ibid., 149.

[31] Ibid., 151.

[32] Ibid., 165.

[33] Werner H. Kelber, *The Kingdom in Mark* (Philadelphia: Fortress, 1974), 1-2.

[34] Ibid., 11.

[35] Ibid., 41.

[36] Robert Tannehill, "The Disciples in Mark: The Function of a Narrative Role," *JR* 57 (1977): 386-405.

[37] David Rhoads and Donald Michie, *Mark as Story: An Introduction to the Narrative of a Gospel* (Philadelphia: Fortress, 1982; rev. ed. with Joanne Dewey, Minneapolis: Fortress, 1999).

[38] Mary Ann Tolbert, *Sowing the Gospel: Mark's World in Literary-Historical Perspective* (Minneapolis: Fortress, 1989), esp. 70-79.

[39] Ibid., 122-23, 232.

[40] Eduard Schweizer, *The Good News according to Mark* (trans. Donald H. Madvig; Atlanta: John Knox, 1970), 380-86.

[41] Craig A. Evans, *Mark 8:27–16:20* (WBC 34B; Nashville: Thomas Nelson, 2001), lxxxii-lxxxiii.

[42] Ibid., lxxxix.

[43] BDAG, 792-93.

[44] See Schweizer, *The Good News according to Mark*, 373.

[45] Richard Bauckham, ed., "For Whom Were Gospels Written?" in *The Gospels for All Christians: Rethinking the Gospel Audiences* (Grand Rapids: Wm. B. Eerdmans, 1998), 9-48.

[46] H. N. Roskam, *The Purpose of the Gospel of Mark in Its Historical and Social Context* (NovTSup 114; Leiden: E. J. Brill, 2004), 15.

[47] Ibid., 16.

[48] Howard Clark Kee, *Community of the New Age: Studies in Mark's Gospel* (Philadelphia: Westminster, 1977), 102-103.

[49] Roskam, *The Purpose of the Gospel of Mark*, 104-14.

[50] Ibid., 108.

[51] Joel Marcus, *Mark 1–8* (AB 27; New York: Doubleday, 1999), 32; Gerd Theissen, *The Gospels in Context: Social and Political History in the Synoptic Tradition* (trans. Linda M. Maloney; Minneapolis: Fortress, 1991), 245-49.

[52] Marcus, *Mark 1–8, 35*.

[53] Ibid., 36.

[54] Roskam, *The Purpose of the Gospel of Mark*, 139.

[55] Black, *Mark: Images*, 224-25.

[56] Benjamin W. Bacon, *Is Mark a Roman Gospel?* (Harvard Theological Studies 7; Cambridge: Harvard University Press, 1919).

[57] Ibid., 69.

[58] Brian J. Incigneri, *The Gospel to the Romans: The Setting and Rhetoric of Mark's Gospel* (BIS 65; Leiden: E. J. Brill, 2003).

[59] Ibid., 65.

[60] Kelber, *The Kingdom in Mark*, 129 n. 1.

[61] Incigneri, *The Gospel to the Romans*, 102.

[62] Evans, *Mark 8:27–16:20*, lxxxi-xciii.

[63] Black, *Mark: Images*, 237.

[64] Marcus, *Mark 1–8*, 33.

[65] Roskam, *The Purpose of the Gospel of Mark*, 83-84.

[66] Kelber, *The Kingdom in Mark*, 117.

[67] Francis J. Moloney comes to the same conclusion in *The Gospel of Mark* (Peabody MA: Hendrickson, 2002), 259.

[68] Black, *Mark: Images*, 236.

[69] Ibid., 1-7.

[70] Roskam, *The Purpose of the Gospel of Mark*, 80 n. 17; citing H. Solin, "Names, Personal, Roman," in S. Hornblower, A. Spawforth, eds., *The Oxford Classical Dictionary* (Oxford: Oxford University Press, 1996), 1024-1026, esp. 1024.

AN OUTLINE OF
THE GOSPEL ACCORDING TO MARK

I. Introduction 1:1-13
  A. The Herald of Jesus 1:1-8
  B. The Baptism of Jesus 1:9-11
  C. The Temptation of Jesus 1:12-13
II. The Authority of Jesus Revealed 1:14–3:6
  A. Introduction 1:14-20
    1. The Proclamation of the Kingdom 1:14-15
    2. The Call to Discipleship 1:16-20
  B. Conflict with the Demons: Jesus' Authority over Sickness 1:21-45
    1. The Authority of Jesus in Teaching and Healing 1:21-28
    2. The Healing of Peter's Mother-in-law 1:29-31
    3. The Healings in the Evening 1:32-34
    4. The Departure from Capernaum 1:35-39
    5. The Cleansing of a Leper 1:40-45
  C. Conflict with the Religious Leaders: Jesus' Authority over Sin 2:1–3:6
    1. Authority to Forgive Sins 2:1-12
    2. Authority to Eat with Outcasts 2:13-17
    3. Authority to Dispense with Fasting 2:18-22
    4. Authority over the Sabbath 2:23-28
    5. Authority to do a Good Work 3:1-5
  D. Conclusion: The Plot to Kill Jesus 3:6
III. The Authority of Jesus Rejected 3:7–6:6a
  A. Introduction 3:7-19
    1. Summary Statement 3:7-12
    2. The Call to the Twelve 3:13-19
  B. The Rejection of Jesus by His Family 3:20-35
    1. Jesus and the Crowd 3:20-21
    2. Jesus and Beelzebul 3:22-30
    3. Jesus and His Family, the Crowd 3:31-35
  C. The Kingdom of God Proclaimed in Parables 4:1-34
    1. The Parable of the Sower 4:1-9
    2. The Purpose of the Parables 4:10-12
    3. The Interpretation of the Parable of the Sower 4:13-20
    4. A Collection of Exhortations 4:21-25
    5. The Parable of the Growing Seed 4:26-29
    6. The Parable of the Mustard Seed 4:30-32
    7. The Use of the Parables 4:33-34
  D. The Kingdom of God Manifest in Miracles 4:35–5:43
    1. The Power of Jesus over the Sea 4:35-41
    2. The Power of Jesus over Demons 5:1-20

JESUS AND THE COMING KINGDOM

Mark 1:1-45

As with the Gospel of Luke, the curtain rises in the Gospel of Mark in a specific location, but in contrast to Luke one finds oneself not in the temple but in the wilderness with John the Baptist (see John 1:19ff.). The wilderness setting—with its overtones of events from Israel's history, testing, wildness, and demonic forces—pervades the atmosphere of the opening scenes in Mark. John the Baptist, a wild, hairy man, announces the coming of one stronger than he. When Jesus comes to be baptized, the heavens are violently ripped open and a gentle dove descends on Jesus. When he is tempted in the wilderness, he overcomes Satan, and the peace of Eden is restored. The proclamation that the kingdom of God is at hand will be the theme of Jesus' ministry, both through what he says and what he does, so Jesus' work of vanquishing the demonic forces and restoring wholeness continues throughout the first chapter of Mark. [Outline of 1:1-13] Jesus calls disciples

Mark the Evangelist

The Ebbo Gospels. c. 816–835. Illumination, Bibliothèque Municipale, Epernay. (Credit: Art Resource, NY)

Before the prevalence of Ottonian Art, the Reims School created manuscript miniatures with fluid modeling and the classical effects of an ancient Roman statue. This was translated into a uniquely Carolingian style, filled with the vibrant energy of the pose and swirling garments.

Susan Wright, *The Bible in Art* (New York: Smithmark, 1996), 76–77.

to be "fishers of men," casts out a demon in the synagogue in Capernaum, and heals Peter's mother-in-law and many others before going on to other places to proclaim the kingdom. Finally, he heals a leper, who immediately goes out to become a proclaimer also.

COMMENTARY

Introduction, 1:1-13

Opening Mark's Gospel immediately confronts the reader with a series of knotty, interrelated problems. [Problems] Is the first verse Mark's title for the Gospel? What does the "beginning" include? Does "gospel" mean the oral proclamation of the "good news" or a written account of Jesus' life? How should one resolve the textual difficulties posed by the opening verse? How far does the introduction extend, what are its themes, and how do they relate to the rest of the Gospel?

The first question is whether v. 1 should be read as a superscription. There are three possibilities: the first verse may be (1) Mark's title for the Gospel, (2) part of the first sentence of the Gospel, or (3) a superscription or textual marker added by a scribe in the latter half of the second century. There is no verb in the first verse, and most modern translations treat it as a title, put a period after the verse (JB, NEB, NIV, RSV, NRSV), and begin the next sentence with "As" (NRSV). The connection between v. 1 and v. 2 is rough, however, and the other twenty-two occurrences of the phrase "as it is written" in the New Testament are all closely linked to the preceding main clause of the sentence. Only twice in the New Testament does this phrase stand at the beginning of a sentence (Rom 8:36 and 10:15), and in both of these instances it follows a question. Therefore, the phrase "as it is written" seems to presume a relationship to the preceding statement (see Mark 9:13; 14:21) that is not at all obvious in the first two verses of Mark.

Mark 1:1 has typically been read as Mark's introduction to his Gospel. Scholars have debated whether "beginning" refers to the first section of the book (1:1-8, 1:1-13, or 1:1-15) or to the whole story of Jesus' life. If "beginning" means the preaching and baptizing of John the Baptist, then Mark 1:1 is not the evangelist's title for the Gospel but merely an introduction to the first section (similar to Matt 1:1). Later

Problems

"The opening of Mark has long been as difficult a problem to commentators as its close, in some ways even more difficult. Verse 1 offers a subject with no predicate; vv. 2 and 3 a subordinate clause with no main clause; and v. 4 gives a statement of fact about John the Baptist, which seems to have some links in thought with what has gone before, but no obvious grammatical connexion."

T. W. Manson, "The Life of Jesus: A Survey of the Available Material: 2. The Foundation of the Synoptic Tradition," *John Rylands Library Bulletin* 28/1 (1944): 121–22; reprinted in *Studies in the Gospels and Epistles* (Manchester: Manchester University, 1962), 30–31.

sections, however, do not have comparable superscriptions or introductions. On the other hand, Mark may be calling for the reader to understand that the whole life of Jesus is the "beginning" of the gospel, by which he means the oral proclamation of the "good news" in the early church. If "gospel" means the written account of Jesus' life, then Mark has taken a striking step, coining a use of the term "gospel" that would not be repeated by any other early Christian writer for nearly a century. The first references to the written accounts of Jesus' life as "gospels" [Gospels] do not occur until the middle of the second century, after Marcion, who interpreted Paul's references to "my gospel" (Rom 2:16; 16:25) as references to the Gospel of Luke (Eusebius, *E.H.* III.4.7).[1] Matthew wrote of the "book of the genealogy" of Jesus in Matthew 1:1, and Luke called his writing a "narrative" (Luke 1:1). So, if Matthew and Luke knew Mark, as is generally held, they either did not have Mark 1:1 or did not understand "gospel" as a reference to the book that followed. In Paul's letters [Paul's Letters] and in the early church fathers up to the middle of the second century "gospel" is always used in the sense of the proclaimed message about Jesus.

The Gospel of Mark ends abruptly at Mark 16:8, and scholars have often speculated that the original ending may have been lost. The beginnings and endings of manuscripts were most susceptible to damage in antiquity, so it may be that both the beginning and the ending of Mark were lost before it was widely copied. If so, Mark 1:1 is a scribe's notation, added in the second century as a superscription or textual marker.[2] This theory, though bold, solves a number of difficulties. "Beginning" would signal that this was the beginning of the Gospel text, which began abruptly with v. 2, "as it is written," and "gospel" would mean the written text that follows rather than the oral proclamation of the "good news" (as it does in Mark 1:14-15).

The roots of the announcement of "good news" as the inauguration of a new era of peace and prosperity can be traced in the Old Testament, especially in

Gospels

AΩ The earliest uses of "gospel" to refer to a book are found in Justin Martyr (d. c. 165):

"The apostles in the memoirs which have come from them, which are also called gospels [*euangelia*], have transmitted that the Lord had commanded." (*1 Apol* 66.3)

"(Trypho said:) . . . I know that your commandments which are written in the so-called gospel [*euangeliō*] are so wonderful and so great that no human being can possibly fulfill them." (*Dial.* 10.2)

"And in the gospel [*euangeliō*] it is recorded that he (Jesus) said, 'Everything has been handed over to me by the Father. . . .'" (*Dial.* 100.1)

Helmut Koester, *Ancient Christian Gospels: Their History and Development* (Philadelphia: Trinity Press International, 1990), 40–41.

Paul's Letters

AΩ "Gospel" occurs sixty times in Paul's letters in passages such as the following:

"Paul, a servant of Jesus Christ, called to be an apostle, set apart for the gospel [*euangelion*] of God. . . ." (Rom 1:1)

". . . so that from Jerusalem and as far around as Illyricum I have fully proclaimed the good news [*euangelion*] of Christ." (Rom 15:19)

"Now I would remind you, brothers and sisters, of the good news [*euangelion*] that I proclaimed to you. . . ." (1 Cor 15:1)

". . . inflicting vengeance on those who do not know God and on those who do not obey the gospel [*euangeliō*] of our Lord Jesus." (2 Thess 1:8)

Isaiah's announcement of hope for the faithful exiles (Isa 40:9; 52:7; 61:1). The herald of good news pointed to a hope that lay in the future. In the more immediate, Greco-Roman background of Mark, "good news" is linked with the announcement of military victories:

> The messenger appears, raises his right hand in greeting and calls out with a loud voice: *chaire . . . nikōmen* ["Greetings . . . we are victors!"]. By his appearance it is known already that he brings good news. His face shines, his spear is decked with laurel, his head is crowned, he swings a branch of palms, joy fills the city, *euangelia* [sacrifices for good news] are offered, the temples are garlanded . . . , and the one to whom the message is owed is honoured with a wreath.[3]

By the time of Mark, the term was closely connected with the acclamations of Caesar Augustus as a divine man who by his victories had inaugurated a new era of peace for all the world. An inscription from Priene [The Priene Inscription (9 BC)] in Asia Minor links the term "good news" to Augustus, who is also called "savior." Against this background, Mark 1:1 would have been understood as both the fulfillment of the messianic hopes of Israel and a polemic against the cult of the emperor. Jesus Christ, not the emperor—the crucified, not the enthroned—should be worshiped for overcoming evil and ushering in a new kingdom of peace and deliverance.

The combination "Jesus Christ" appears frequently in Paul's letters (e.g., Rom 1:1, 4, 6, 7, 8) and in other books of the New Testament, but the familiar designation occurs only rarely in the Gospels (Matt 1:1, 16, 18; 16:21; 27:22; John 1:17; 17:3; 20:31), never in Luke but a dozen times in Acts, and only in the first verse of Mark. "Christ" was originally a messianic title, meaning

---

The Priene Inscription (9 BC)

"Since the Providence which has ordered all things and is deeply interested in our life has set in most perfect order by giving us Augustus, whom she filled with virtue that he might benefit mankind, sending him as a savior, both for us and for our descendants, that he might end war and arrange all things, and since he, Caesar, by his appearance [excelled even our anticipations], surpassing all previous benefactors, and not even leaving to posterity any hope of surpassing what he has done, and since the birthday of the god Augustus was the beginning for the world of the good tidings [*euangeliōn*] that came by reason of him [may it therefore be decided that. . . .]"

Eugene Boring et al., eds., *Hellenistic Commentary to the New Testament* (Nashville: Abingdon Press, 1995), 169

Record of Paulus Fabius Maximus
Record of Paulus Fabius Maximus, Roman governor of Asia, proposing to the Asian League of cities that they change their calendar so that Augustus' birthday would be henceforth New Year's Day. Uses the term "Gospel" (euaggelion) for Augustus. 29 BCE.

Antikensammlung, Staatliche Museen zu Berlin, Berlin, Germany. (Credit : Bildarchiv Preussischer Kulturbesitz / Art Resource, NY)

"anointed" or "the anointed," that was later used as an extension of Jesus' name. In the Gospel of Mark the term is used as a messianic title (9:41; 12:35; 13:21; 14:61; 15:32) and has a special significance because throughout his ministry Jesus conceals his identity. The unclean spirits know who Jesus is (1:34), but the disciples do not discover Jesus' messianic identity until it is revealed to Peter at Caesarea Philippi (8:29; see the commentary on this verse).

The addition of the title "Son of God" in Mark 1:1 is uncertain because it is absent from some ancient manuscripts, including the original reading of Codex Sinaiticus (4th C.). Nevertheless, important early manuscripts include the title, and it plays an important role at key points in the Gospel, including the centurion's climactic confession in Mark 15:39. It is unlikely that a scribe would have omitted it intentionally or because of fatigue or carelessness (in the first verse of the Gospel!). On the other hand, because ancient scribes usually abbreviated titles for Jesus, the latter part of Mark 1:1 would have appeared as IΥ ΧΥ ΥΥ ΘΥ, and the latter abbreviation might easily have been dropped from this series by accident.[4]

Like the term "gospel," the title "Son of God" can be traced to the Old Testament but was also current in the Greco-Roman world. In ancient Israel the king was acclaimed as "son of God" (see 2 Sam 7:14; Pss 2:7; 89:26-27). Greco-Roman readers would have associated the title generally with heroes, miracle workers, and figures such as Alexander the Great, of whom it was said that it had been revealed to him that he was a son of Zeus Ammon. More recently, following the murder of Julius Caesar, Augustus took the title *divi filius* (son of the divine one).[5]

Within the New Testament, the reference in Romans 1:3 is especially important because it preserves a very early Christian confession. Paul was called to be an apostle of "the gospel of God" that was promised through the prophets, "the gospel concerning His Son, who was descended from David according to the flesh and was declared to be Son of God . . . by resurrection from the dead, Jesus Christ our Lord" (Rom 1:3-4). The similarities with Mark are striking, where the Gospel begins with a quotation from Isaiah and extends through Jesus' resurrection from the dead. The voice from heaven claims Jesus as God's son (1:11; 9:7), and the unclean spirits know who Jesus is (3:11; 5:7), but only when Jesus has died on the cross does anyone confess that he is the Son of God. This confession, by the Roman centurion, is the climactic confession in Mark. As a result, Mark 1:1, by proclaiming Jesus to be the Christ and the Son of God, anticipates the confessions that stand at the midpoint and end of the Gospel. Whatever its origin, therefore, this verse is a fitting title for the Gospel. Only as the reader recognizes the

Composite Quotation

Note Mark's use of key words to stitch together the quotation in Mark 1:2-3.

"I am going to send an angel in front of you, to guard you on *the way* and bring you to the place I have prepared." (Exod; 23:20)

"See, I am sending my messenger to *prepare the way* before me, and the Lord whom you seek will suddenly appear in his temple. The messenger of the covenant in whom you delight—indeed, he is coming, says the Lord of hosts." (Mal 3:1)

"A voice cries out: '*In the wilderness prepare the way of the Lord, make straight in the desert a highway* for our God.'" (Isa 40:3)

"See, I am sending my messenger ahead of you, who will prepare your way; the voice of one crying in the wilderness: 'Prepare the way of the Lord, make his paths straight.'" (Mark 1:2-3)

Isaiah as a Subtext

Mark quotes Isaiah eight times:

Sharyn Dowd, *Reading Mark: A Literary and Theological Commentary on the Second Gospel* (Macon: Smyth & Helwys, 2000), 3.

truth of these claims can he or she understand the "good news" that Mark announces (see ["Son of God" in Mark]).

The origin of the Gospel, however, can be traced not just to the beginning of Jesus' ministry, or even to John the Baptist. Mark found an allusion in the prophet Isaiah that he took as a prophecy of the coming of John the Baptist, Jesus' herald. Actually, the words quoted in Mark 1:2-3 are a composite of Exodus 23:20, Malachi 3:1, and Isaiah 40:3. [Composite Quotation] The three passages share key words and each of the three can be seen as illuminating aspects of John's role as the forerunner. Exodus 23:20 promises the protection of Israel in the conquest of Canaan. The Greek word "angel" can also mean "messenger." Malachi 3:1 contains the announcement that the Lord will send a messenger of the covenant to the temple to purify the descendants of Levi. Malachi identifies this messenger as the prophet Elijah, so Mark understands that John the Baptist is the fulfillment of the expectation of the return of Elijah before "the great and terrible day of the Lord" (cf. Mal 4:5; Mark 9:11-13).

Isaiah 40:3 comforts the faithful exiles that their God will come to them. The highway in the wilderness may well have been an allusion to the roads built by the Babylonians. From the wilderness the faithful will return to Judah, and ultimately God's glory will be declared to all the nations (Isa 66:18-23). The opening verses of Mark, therefore, tie the story that is about to unfold to Israel's experience of testing in the wilderness, exile, the temple, and her expectations of a great future deliverance. Because these themes are so prominent in Isaiah, it is no surprise that Mark repeatedly uses Isaiah as a subtext for his Gospel [Isaiah as a Subtext], which may explain why the quotation in vv. 2 and 3 is attributed to Isaiah when it is actually a conflation of these several verses.

Isaiah 40:3 is also quoted in a section of the Manual of Discipline (1QS 8:13) found at Qumran that may have been the manifesto for the community. Following the reading contained in the Masoretic text, the Essenes read, "In the wilderness prepare the way of the Lord" (Isa 40:3) and went to found the community at Qumran not far from the northwest shore of the Dead

Sea. For Mark the story begins in the wilderness with John the Baptist preaching a baptism of repentance, but the community of the kingdom will not be founded there. Mark follows the Septuagint text, which makes it clear that the voice was "crying out in the wilderness" (Mark 1:3). The Essenes interpreted preparing the way to mean continuous study of Scripture and living in obedience and purity. In Mark "the way" is the path that Jesus himself follows, which ultimately leads to the cross in Jerusalem (see esp. Mark 8:27; 9:33, 34; 10:32, 52; 12:14), and in Acts the first Christians were called followers of "the Way" (Acts 9:2; 18:25; 19:9, 23; 22:4; 24:14, 22). What began there in the wilderness, therefore, was nothing less than the prelude to the coming of the Messiah and the inbreaking of the kingdom of God.

Following the title in v. 1 and the quotation of Scripture in vv. 2-3, the third stage of the introduction to the story of Jesus begins with the description of John the Baptist in vv. 4-8. Mark 1:4 begins with the same verb that is used at the beginning of the introduction of the Baptist in John 1:6, but whereas in John his function is to bear witness, in Mark John is introduced first as the one who was baptizing in the wilderness and preaching "a baptism of repentance for the forgiveness of sins" (1:4). John was a common Hebrew name (*Johanan*) meaning "God has been gracious" (1 Chr 26:3; Ezra 10:6). The phrase "in the wilderness" in v. 4 picks up the same phrase from the quotation in v. 3, providing a natural transition to the description of John and his work.

The Wilderness of Judea
The "wilderness" of Judea near Jericho.
(Credit: R. Alan Culpepper)

The "wilderness" or desert was significant in the history of Israel as a place of testing. Moses led the people of Israel in the wilderness for forty years before they crossed into the promised land. If the wilderness was a place of disobedience and testing, however, it was also the place where God did wonders and mighty acts for the people of Israel: providing manna, water, and the bronze serpent that delivered the people from death. The wilderness had therefore been romanticized by the first century, and the people looked to it as the place where they could await God's final act of deliverance. By beginning in the wilderness and moving to Jerusalem, the gospel story recapitulates the history

Baptism

AΩ The following lines from Josephus, the first-century Jewish historian, show that the contemporary secular meaning of "baptize" was to immerse, dip, or sink.

". . . in my opinion there could be no more arrant coward than the pilot who, for fear of a tempest, deliberately sinks (*ebaptisen*) his ship before a storm." (Josephus, *J.W.* 3.368; LCL 2:679)

". . . before they had time to do anything they instantly came to grief and were sent to the bottom (*ebaptizonto*) with their skiffs." (Josephus, *J.W.* 3.368; LCL 2:725)

"Seeing him in this condition, sunken (*bebaptismenon*) into unconsciousness and a drunken sleep. . . ." (Josephus, *Ant.* 10.169; LCL 6:253)

"I know of some who when they are half-seas-over and before they have completely gone under (*baptisthēnai*) arrange donations and subscriptions. . . ." (Philo, *Contempl.* 46; LCL 9:141)

of Israel, showing in yet another way that it is a fulfillment as well as a promise of hope.

The baptism of John did not have the same meaning as Christian baptism (see Acts 19:1-7)—no baptismal practice prior to the death and resurrection of Jesus could have the significance of dying to an old way of life and being raised to a new life (cf. Rom 6:3-4). [Baptism] Nevertheless, the Essenes at Qumran, perhaps not far from where John was baptizing, practiced repeated self-administered ritual washings, and it is possible that John was influenced by their practices. Like the Essenes, he called fellow Jews to repent and prepare for the coming eschatological events. According to Josephus and the Gospel descriptions of John's baptism, its distinguishing feature was that it was coupled with repentance. [Repentance] The call to repentance was also coupled with John's warning of eschatological urgency: the time of judgment of the wicked and deliverance of the righteous was at hand. For those who repented of their sins, the washing of baptism brought forgiveness. Injunctions from the Manual of Discipline illustrate how repentance was essential for the effectiveness of ritual purification: one who maintains the stubbornness of his heart "will not become clean by the acts of atonement, nor shall he be purified by the cleansing waters, nor shall he be made holy by the seas or rivers, nor shall he be purified by all the water of the ablutions. Defiled, defiled shall he be all the days he spurns the decrees of God" (1QS 3.4-6).[6] The Greek word for "repentance" signals a profound conversion: a transformation of mind, or a change in the way one appropriates reality (*metanoia*).

When Mark reports that all the people from Judea and Jerusalem were "going out" to John, he may be implying that this was the beginning of a new Exodus (Exod 13:4, 8; Deut 23:4 [LXX 23:5]; Josh 2:10).[7] John's dress and diet were those of a prophet. King Ahaziah recognized Elijah when his messengers reported that they had met "a hairy man, with a leather belt around his

Judea, Jerusalem, and the Jordan River

waist" (2 Kgs 1:8), and Zechariah says that on the day of the Lord the prophets will be ashamed; "they will not put on a hairy mantle in order to deceive" (13:4). Like his dress, John's diet of locusts (Lev 11:21-22) and wild honey (1 Kgs 14:33; 2 Kgs 18:32; Rev 10:9-10) identified him as a "wilderness man."

In contrast to Matthew and Luke, but similar to John, Mark's report of John's preaching is limited to his proclamation that one greater than he was coming. The two sayings in vv. 7-8 report the measure of the greater standing of the coming one (v. 7) and the greater work that he would do (v. 8). Various interpretations have been proposed in an effort to clarify John's expectations, but the two sayings that follow suggest a messianic or eschatological figure sent by God as an agent of the Spirit. Since the John the Baptist movement continued even after the rise of the early church, early Christians may have appealed to this saying as a way of arguing that Jesus was superior to John even though he came to John and was baptized by him. Removing sandals was such a menial task that students were not required to remove their rabbi's sandals: "a pupil does for his teacher all the tasks that a slave does for his master, except untying his shoe" (*b. Ketub.* 96a). So much greater would the Coming One be that John would not be worthy to serve even as his slave (see Matt 3:11; Luke 3:16; John 1:26-27; Acts 13:25).

The Greater One would baptize not with water but with the Holy Spirit. The Essenes at Qumran also looked forward to the time when God would cleanse them with "the spirit of holiness." [The Spirit of Holiness] Their own repeated self-washings may therefore have been practiced in anticipation of this washing with the Spirit, just as John's baptism was in anticipation of the purifying work of the Coming One. The irony is that when John baptizes Jesus, the Spirit descends on Jesus. The coming of the Spirit upon Jesus, however, confirms John's announcement about him.

Repentance

Josephus reports that John the Baptist "exhorted the Jews to lead righteous lives, to practise justice towards their fellows and piety towards God, and so doing to join in baptism. In his view this was a necessary preliminary if baptism was to be acceptable to God. They must not employ it to gain pardon for whatever sins they committed, but as a consecration of the body implying that the soul was already thoroughly cleansed by right behaviour." (*Ant.* 18.117; LCL 81–83)

A Hairy Man

Because of John's connection with Elijah, who is described as "a hairy man" in 2 Kgs 1:8, Byzantine icons typically depict John the Baptist with a full beard and long hair.

Byzantine, c. 395-1453. *St. John the Baptist.* c. 1300. British Museum, London, Great Britain. (Credit: HIP / Art Resource, NY)

The Spirit of Holiness

"Meanwhile, God will refine, with his truth, all man's deeds, and will purify for himself the configuration of man, ripping out all spirit of injustice from the innermost part of his flesh, and cleansing him with the spirit of holiness from every irreverent deed. He will sprinkle over him the spirit of truth like lustral water (in order to cleanse him) from all the abhorrences of deceit and from the defilement of the unclean spirit." (1QS 4.20–22)

Florentino García Martínez, *The Dead Sea Scrolls Translated: The Qumran Texts in English* (trans. Wilfred G. E. Watson; Leiden: E. J. Brill, 1994), 7.

Verses 9-11 shift the subject from John to Jesus. Neither Jesus nor John speaks (cf. Matt 3:13-13). The only words that are spoken are those of the voice from heaven, lending an even greater sense of mystery to this scene. Mark knows nothing of the birth of Jesus in Bethlehem; he introduces Jesus as "from Nazareth of Galilee" (see the commentary on Mark 6:1-6). The identification of Jesus with Galilee is important because Galilee will be the place of the inbreaking of the kingdom through Jesus' ministry, and at the end of the Gospel the disciples will be instructed to go to Galilee: "There you will see him" (16:7).

Mark apparently has no qualms about reporting that Jesus was baptized by John in the Jordan (v. 9). Matthew has John protest that he should be baptized by Jesus (Matt 3:14). Luke reports that John was thrown in prison before he says that Jesus was baptized, without saying explicitly that he was baptized by John (Luke 3:18-22), and John records John the Baptist's testimony concerning the Spirit descending on Jesus without actually saying that John baptized Jesus (John 1:32-34). In each of the other Gospels, therefore, the evangelist shows great sensitivity about the baptism of Jesus, either because John's baptism was "for the forgiveness of sins," which might imply that Jesus needed forgiveness, or because of arguments with followers of the Baptist about the superiority of Jesus over John. Apparently Mark was writing for a community that was not in debate with John's followers. In all likelihood, Jesus was one of the followers of the Baptist before beginning his own ministry, but significantly Mark says nothing about Jesus making any confession as the others did (cf. v. 5 and v. 9).

The Jordan River
(Credit: R. Alan Culpepper)

Verse 10 reports two features of Jesus' vision, and v. 11 the words that he heard. Mark records only that Jesus saw the heavens opened and the dove descending and heard the words spoken by the heavenly voice; there is no report that anyone else was privy to this experience. If that is so, it was a private or secret theophany that declared Jesus' identity. The reader is now allowed to share this private knowledge. As readers, we know who Jesus is because of the superscription in Mark 1:1, which is now confirmed by the events at Jesus' baptism, but none of the characters in the Gospel share in this secret. Indeed, much of the plot of Mark revolves around how the secret of Jesus' identity comes to be known. In short, if Jesus looked like any other man, how did anyone know that he was the Son of God? Most modern readers would say that Jesus' uniqueness lay in his power to do miracles, but that is not Mark's view. None of those who witness the miracles in Mark conclude that Jesus is God's son. Neither do any who hear his teachings respond with this confession. For Mark it is only Jesus' death that reveals his divinity (Mark 15:39).

The term "immediately" is a Markan favorite. Mark includes less teaching material than any other Gospel, so it moves along more rapidly. The frequent repetition of this adverb lends a sense of urgency to Mark's account. The kingdom is "at hand," and Jesus moves swiftly to complete his eschatological mission. Literally, as he was coming up out of the water, Jesus saw the heavens being torn apart. [Torn Apart] It is a strong, picturesque verb, and one that has apocalyptic overtones. Isaiah pleads, "O that you would tear open the heavens and come down so that the mountains would quake in your presence . . . to make your name known to your adversaries" (Isa 64:1-2). At the end of Mark, the rending of the heavens is answered by the rending of the veil in the temple, but both are acts of God's self-disclosure. The good news is that God has become known and accessible through the person and work of Jesus.

The dove visibly represents the Spirit of God that hovered over the waters at creation (Gen 1:2). [The Dove] The descent of the Spirit, literally "into" Jesus, and the declaration of his divine sonship are the two features that define his unique identity. He could pray "Abba, father," and he was the Spirit-endowed agent of the kingdom. The words of the voice from heaven appear to be a composite of Psalm 2:7 and Isaiah 42:1. The psalm text was used at the coronation of a king, as a litany for the divine sonship being conferred on the one who was ascending to the throne: "He said to me, '*You are my son*; today I have begotten you. Ask of me, and I will make the nations your heritage, and the ends of the earth your possession'" (Ps 2:7-8). The verse from Isaiah stands at the beginning of the first of the servant songs in Isaiah: "Here is my servant, whom I uphold, *my*

Torn Apart

"In Mark, then, God has ripped the heavens irrevocably apart at Jesus' baptism, never to shut them again. Through this gracious gash in the universe, he has poured forth his Spirit into the earthly realm."

Joel Marcus, *Mark 1–8* (AB 27; New York: Doubleday, 2000), 165.

The Dove

"But why in the form of a dove? The dove is a gentle and pure creature. Since then the Spirit too, is 'a Spirit of gentleness' [Gal 5:22], he appears in the form of a dove, reminding us of Noah, to whom, when once a common disaster had overtaken the whole world and humanity was in danger of perishing, the dove appeared as a sign of deliverance from the tempest, and bearing an olive branch, published the good tidings of a serene presence over the whole world [Gen 8:11]. All these things were given as a type of things to come. . . . In this case the dove also appeared, not bearing an olive branch, but pointing to our Deliverer from all evils, bringing hope filled with grace. For this dove does not simply lead one family out of an ark, but the whole world toward heaven at her appearing."

Chrysostom, *The Gospel of St. Matthew* 12.3; *Nicene and Post Nicene Fathers* 1 10:77.

chosen, in whom my soul delights, I have put my spirit upon him; he will bring forth justice to the nations" (Isa 42:1). For emphasis, Mark has quoted freely from these two verses, selecting phrases from each and changing the word order. The words from Psalm 2:7 follow the Septuagint, while the words from Isaiah are closer to the Hebrew, adding "beloved" (*agapētos*, cf. Mark 9:7; 12:6) and "well pleased" (*eudokēsa*) that are not in the Septuagint text of Isaiah 42:1. The term "beloved" may have been suggested by the reference to Isaac, the child of the covenant, in Genesis 22:1 (see [The Voice of God]).

The significance of the remainder of each of these verses suggests that Mark was using them as a commentary on the meaning of Jesus' baptism and the divine mission that was being conferred upon him. Jesus' sonship is affirmed by God, and God empowers Jesus with the Spirit so that he can overcome evil. Jesus was both unique son and suffering servant. The paradox of the gospel is that the mighty one is put to death, the chosen one rejected, and the servant exalted. Jesus will carry out this commission in the rest of the Gospel: the good news will spread to all the nations (Mark 13:10), to bring forth justice and to secure them for God from the Evil One.

The two references to "in(to) the wilderness" in vv. 12 and 13 balance the two references to "in the wilderness" in vv. 3 and 4. Again, the action takes place "immediately" (v. 12). This time, it is the Spirit that has just descended upon Jesus that acts, driving Jesus into the wilderness to confront Satan. Matthew and Luke record the tradition of three temptations, with Jesus responding to each with a quotation from Scripture. Mark notes only the location of the temptations, the length of the temptations, the identity of the tempter, the curious detail that Jesus was with wild beasts, and that angels ministered to him. For the significance of the wilderness, see above (1:3-4) (see [*Peirazein*, To "Tempt" or "Test," in Mark]).

The elements of Mark's brief report of the temptation of Jesus suggest that Mark is again interpreting Jesus' identity in light of scriptural, and especially Isaianic, expectations that the last days will be like the first. Adam was tempted in the garden, where he lived in harmony with the animals and the angels, at least according to legend. The apocryphal *Life of Adam and Eve*, which may also have been written in the first century, reports that Eve was tempted while the angels were away (*Vita* 33.3) and that Adam did penance, standing in the Jordan River for forty days (*Vita* 17.3) while the angels interceded for him (*Vita* 9.3), "and all the angels and all the creatures of God surrounded Adam as a wall around him, weeping and praying to God on behalf of Adam" (*Apocalypse of Moses* 29.14).[8] The similarity of the imagery shows that

Mark's account of the temptation conjures up images of Eden and Paradise, the unsoiled beginning and the eschatological restoration. Christ is a new Adam, a stronger one (see v. 7). Here Mark employs an Adam/Christ typology like that Paul develops in Romans: "Adam . . . is a type of the one who was to come. . . . Therefore just as one man's trespass led to condemnation for all, so one man's act of righteousness leads to justification and life for all" (Rom 5:14, 18). The hope of paradise is also shared by Isaiah, who looked forward to the coming of a shoot from the stump of Jesse on whom "the spirit of the Lord shall rest" (11:2) and who will bring about a return to paradise: "The wolf shall live with the lamb, the leopard shall lie down with the kid" (11:6; cf. Isa 65:25; *T. Naph.* 8:4, 6; *2 Bar.* 73:6; *b. Sanh.* 59b).

The meaning of Mark's imagery, therefore, is that when Jesus is driven into the wilderness by the Spirit he confronts Satan—for evil spirits were thought to dwell in desolate places (Mark 5:10; Matt 12:43; Luke 11:24). Satan tempts Jesus to abandon his messianic mission, but Jesus dwells in peace with the animals and is served by the angels, showing that he is the Strong One who will restore the creation and fulfill Isaiah's vision of Paradise.

The Announcement of the Kingdom, 1:14-15

The position and function of vv. 14 and 15 have led to a debate that many interpreters have called a draw. These two verses articulate some of Mark's leading themes and serve as a summary of Jesus' preaching. The question is whether they are the climax and conclusion of the introduction to the Gospel (1:1-15) or the introduction to the first main section of the Gospel (1:14-45, or 1:14–3:6, or 1:14–8:30). Those who favor 1:1-15 as the introduction can point to the repetition of "the gospel" (v. 1 and vv. 14-15), "preaching" (vv. 4 and 14), and "repentance/repent" (vv. 4 and 15). On the other hand, it is just as likely that vv. 14 and 15 introduce the next section by repeating key terms from the beginning of the introduction, and that "in(to) the desert" in vv. 12 and 13 echoes "in the desert" in vv. 3 and 4, drawing the introduction neatly to a close with v. 13. One may also detect a pattern of summary statements (1:14-15; 3:7-12; and 6:6b) followed by reports concerning the disciples (1:16-20; 3:13-19; 6:7-13, 30-34) in the first half of the Gospel. This latter pattern will be followed here.

The section that begins with v. 14 and extends through Mark 3:6 develops the theme of Jesus' authority. The coming of the kingdom is announced (1:14-15), and Jesus calls the first disciples (1:16-20). In his first public act Jesus teaches with authority and casts an unclean spirit out of a man in the synagogue in Capernaum (1:21-28). At the end of the Sabbath Jesus heals Peter's mother-in-law (1:29-31) and people brought from the surrounding area (1:32-34). After leaving Capernaum to carry his ministry of the kingdom through the region (1:35-39), he heals a leper (1:40-45). Mark 2 continues the same theme with a collection of acts and teachings that declare Jesus' authority over sin, tradition, and even the Sabbath.

Mark 1:14 opens with a clause marking the passage of time and a new beginning: "Now after John was arrested." Nothing more is said about John's arrest until chapter 6, but this notation cleanly separates Jesus' ministry from John's. The Gospel of John (3:22) provides evidence of a period of parallel ministries, but Mark treats John the Baptist chronologically as well as functionally as Jesus' forerunner. The sequence also sets up the parallel: John preaches, is arrested, and put to death; Jesus then comes preaching, and he too will be arrested and put to death; Jesus calls the disciples and then sends them to preach. What should these (and by implication later) disciples expect?

The place of Jesus' ministry throughout the first half of the Gospel (with only brief forays into nearby regions) is Galilee. For the reader, Galilee takes on the symbolic role "the land of the gospel" in Mark. It is the place where Jesus preached and his miracles gave evidence of the power of the kingdom.

In Galilee Jesus proclaimed "the good news of God." The genitive construction is usually taken as meaning "the good news about God," but here it should probably be read as "God's good news"—as in Isaiah 52:7 and 61:1. [Isaiah 52:7 and 61:1] Jesus proclaimed God's good news of the fulfillment of history and the coming of the kingdom. The "kingdom of God" has various nuances in the New Testament, but basically it means God's triumph or God's sovereign rule.

Isaiah 52:7 and 61:1

"How beautiful upon the mountains are the feet of the messenger who announces peace, who brings *good news*, who announces salvation, who says to Zion, 'Your God reigns.'" (Isa 52:7)

"The spirit of the Lord God is upon me, because the Lord has anointed me; He has sent me to bring *good news* to the oppressed, to bind up the brokenhearted, to proclaim liberty to the captives, and release to the prisoners. . . ." (Isa 61:1; cf. Luke 4:16-18)

Verse 15 consists of two statements and two imperatives. In each part the second statement or imperative seems to repeat and clarify, sharpen, or extend the first. The first statement is "The time is fulfilled"—"the *kairos*" (season, significant era, or moment in time) has been fulfilled or completed. The second statement moves on: "the kingdom of God has come near." The verb in this statement has been variously interpreted as "has come" (C. H. Dodd) or "is at hand" (J. Jeremias and W. G. Kümmel).[9] Dodd emphasized the in-breaking of the kingdom in the person of Jesus, while Jeremias and Kümmel took the view that the kingdom is "already" but "not yet"—already here but not yet fully established. The "kingdom of God" is the most common theme of Jesus' teachings, occurring some 118 times in the Synoptic Gospels. Two imperatives follow from these two declarations—the time is fulfilled: "repent"; the kingdom of God is at hand: "believe in the gospel." Here "the gospel" refers to the oral proclamation of the good news about Jesus (cf. the discussion of "gospel" in v. 1).

Calling the First Disciples, 1:16-20

The first public act of Jesus' ministry in the Gospel of Mark is to call the first disciples, the four fishermen, from their nets. The Sea of Galilee, an inland lake 8 miles across and about 13 miles from north to south, was the fishery that supplied the fish that was the most common meat item in the regional diet. [Fish] The two sets of brothers were not only called first, but they are also named first in all four lists of the Twelve in the New Testament (see Mark 3:17). Simon and Andrew were "casting" their nets into the lake, and James and John were cleaning, mending, and folding their nets. [Nets] The fact that Zebedee had boats and hired hands suggests that he operated a small fishing business. While it is unlikely that they were among the families of the upper class, neither did they share the desperate lot of hired servants and day laborers.

Fishermen
Fishermen working their nets on the Sea of Galilee.
(Credit: R. Alan Culpepper)

Jesus' call to the disciples was direct and simple: "follow me" and "I will make you fishers of men." Although in some respects unique, Jesus' call to the fishermen has parallels in both Elijah's call to Elisha (1 Kgs 19:19-21) and in Socrates's call to Strepsiades ("Don't chatter there, but come and follow me"; Aristophanes, *The Clouds* 497-517) and to Xenophon ("Then follow me and learn"; Diogenes Laertius, *Lives* 2.48).[10] Similarly, the metaphor "fishers of

Fish

"The eighteen species of fish in the Sea of Galilee fall into three main groups. The *Cichlidae*, called *Musht* by the Arabs, include the Tilapia or 'St. Peter's fish,' a mouth-breeding fish of Ethiopic origin that looks something like an American panfish (crappie or bluegill). Also found are the *Cyprinidae*, the carp family, which range from the large Barbels to the small fresh water 'sardines' (*Acanthrobrama terrae-sanctae*). This latter variety were probably the 'small fish' in the boy's lunch [Mark 6:38]. Finally, there are the *Siluridae* or catfish (*Clarias lazera*), called *Barbut* in Arabic, which were also common in the Nile River and in the lakes around Alexandria."

R. Alan Culpepper, *John the Son of Zebedee: The Life of a Legend* (Columbia: University of South Carolina Press, 1994), 11.

Nets

"There is almost certainly a close correlation between the kinds of nets used by Arab fishermen until recent decades and the various words for nets found in the Gospels. The casting net (Gk. *amphiblēstron* [Mark 1:16]; in Arabic, *shabaka*) is a circular net up to twenty feet across with weights along the circumference. The fisherman wades out, watches for signs of fish, casts the net in a circle and, drawing it in by means of a center cord, and entraps the fish. The trammel net, or *diktyon* (though this is a generic word for nets in Greek; in Arabic, the word is *mubattan*) is a compound net—three nets of equal length suspended from a rope. The outer two have a wide mesh, but the mesh of the center net is fine. The top of the net is held up by floats, while the bottom is anchored with weights. Fish can swim through the outer nets but become entangled in the center net and cannot retreat. The largest of the nets is the *sagēnē* (Gk. [Matt 13:47]; in Arabic, *jurf*). It may be 400 yards long. The net is set out by boat in a large semi-circle with the two ends near the shore. As with the *diktyon*, the top is held up with floats, and the bottom is anchored with weights. Men on the shore then draw the net in by means of ropes attached to its upper and lower corners. Care is taken to keep the net in uninterrupted motion while it is being retrieved."

R. Alan Culpepper, *John the Son of Zebedee: The Life of a Legend* (Columbia: University of South Carolina Press, 1994), 13.

---

men" evokes both overtones of judgment that metaphorical references to fishing carried in Jewish literature (Amos 4:2; Hab 1:14-15; Jer 16:16; 1QH 5.7-8) and the activity of teaching and learning that it has in Greek philosophical literature (Plato, *Sophist* 218d-222d). In the Gospels, where it becomes a call to gather men and women for the kingdom, it retains eschatological overtones from the biblical traditions, authorizes the disciples as representatives of their teacher and agents of the kingdom, and looks on to the church's evangelistic mission.[11]

A Day in Capernaum: Jesus' Authority over Demons and Sickness, 1:21-45

The next section reports a series of events that took place in and around Capernaum, so it has often been called "A Day in Capernaum." [A Day in Capernaum] Capernaum was a fishing village on the northwest shore of the Sea of Galilee that seems to have been the home base for Jesus (see 2:1). The name means "Village of Nahum," and the ruins (Tell Hum) extend for a mile along the shore. Because it was located near the border between Galilee and Gaulanitis, there was a toll station there. The site of the synagogue was not far from the site later Christians revered as Peter's house. The synagogue was a local gathering place, under lay leadership, for the study of Scripture, prayer, and social activities.

Because there was not yet a clear process of ordination or legitimation of rabbis, Jesus could be invited to read and expound the Scriptures, as he does in Luke 4:16-18. Jesus' first public act in each of the Gospels

A Day in Capernaum

Conflict with the Demons: Jesus' Authority over Sickness 1:21-45

1. The Authority of Jesus in Teaching and Healing 1:21-28
2. The Healing of Peter's Mother-in-law 1:29-31
3. The Healings in the Evening 1:32-34
4. The Departure from Capernaum 1:35-39
5. The Cleansing of a Leper 1:40-45

telegraphs the themes each of the evangelists will emphasize.[12] The Sermon on the Mount declares the fulfillment of Scripture in Jesus (Matthew), Jesus' teaching in the synagogue in Nazareth announces good news to the poor and the outcast (Luke), and the wedding at Cana is the first of the signs that announce the replacement of Jewish rites and point to Jesus' identity as the Logos (John). In the synagogue in Capernaum Jesus teaches with authority and then demonstrates his authority by exorcising an unclean spirit.

The Synagogue in Capernaum
Remains of the synagogue from the 4th–5th centuries that probably stand over the remains of an earlier synagogue.
(Credit: R. Alan Culpepper)

The word "immediately" in vv. 21 and 23 again lends a sense of urgency to Jesus' actions, even though it is grammatically out of place. The verb to teach (*didaskein*) occurs seventeen times in Mark, and the verb to preach (*kēryssein*) occurs fourteen times, but Mark appears to use the two with little distinction in meaning (cf. 1:21 and 1:39). The people who heard him were amazed. Mark explains that "he taught them as one having authority, and not as the scribes" (v. 22). Authority denotes "ability to perform an action to the extent that there are no hindrances in the way," and in the New Testament it denotes "the power of God in nature and the spiritual world."[13] The scribes derived their authority from the Law and cited the judgments of their predecessors. [Scribes] Jesus' teachings, in contrast, were direct, pithy, and illustrated by parables and metaphors so that the hearer was immediately challenged by them.

While Jesus was teaching, a man cried out, challenging him. The exorcism follows the general pattern of a miracle story, reporting (1) the setting (1:21-22), (2) the illness, problem, or challenge (1:23-24), (3) Jesus' word or act (1:25), (4) the miraculous act (1:26), and (5) the response of the witnesses, confirming the miracle (1:27-28). The distinctive feature about

Scribes

"The scribes presented in the Synoptic Gospels are best understood as bureaucrats and experts on Jewish life. They could have been low-level officials and judges both in Jerusalem and in the towns and villages of the country."

"In Mark the scribes are associated with Jerusalem and the chief priests as part of the government of Judaism. Though their roles are not specified, their close association with the chief priests means they functioned as high officials and advisors. Some scribes who appeared in Galilee were identified as coming from Jerusalem (3:22; 7:1). Their teachings are referred to in an offhand way, which suggests that they were recognized as authoritative teachers of Jewish law and custom (1:22; 9:11). Mark presents them as a unified political group because for him their salient unifying characteristic is opposition to Jesus. Actually, the scribes probably stand for a plethora of Jewish community officials, many of them actual scribes, who opposed Jesus' claim to authority and his growing popularity."

Anthony J. Saldarini, "Scribes," *ABD* (New York: Doubleday, 1992), 5:1015.

this miracle story is the way it is intertwined with the report of Jesus' teaching with authority.

Literally, Mark says he was "a man in an unclean spirit," that is a man enveloped and consumed by an unclean spirit. In the worldview of first-century Palestine, evil spirits, minions of Satan, could possess and take control of a person's actions and speech (Josephus, *J. W.* 7.185; *T. Benjamin* 5:2; 1QM 13:4-5) (see [Demon Exorcism]). [Evil Spirits] Unclean spirits and demoniacs rarely appear in the Old Testament (Job 4:15-17), the Gospel of John (where only Jesus is said to have a demon; cf. 7:20; 8:48-52; 10:20-21), Paul's letters, or Revelation (16:13; 18:2). In the biblical writings one finds demoniacs and exorcisms only in the Synoptic Gospels and Acts (5:16; 8:7; 16:16; 19:12-16). Having been tempted by Satan in the wilderness, Jesus is now confronted by an unclean spirit, lending further evidence that Mark characterizes Jesus' ministry as warfare with the power of evil.

The unclean spirit first asks what the basis for the relationship between Jesus and the spirit is, or what the issue is between them: "What have you to do with us?" (5:7; cf. Judg 11:12; 2 Sam 16:10; 19:22; 1 Kgs 17:18; 2 Kgs 3:13; 9:18; 2 Chr 35:21; John 2:4). Ironically, the spirit correctly surmises Jesus' intent: "Have you come to destroy us?" or "You have come to destroy us!" Then the spirit declares Jesus' identity, perhaps seeking to gain control over him by doing so. The disclosure is particularly significant in Mark, where Jesus' messianic identity remains a secret throughout his ministry and becomes the issue around which the plot of the Gospel revolves. The reader has been told who Jesus is (1:1, 7-8, 11), but the people in the synagogue, the disciples, and the scribes do not know who he is. Because it belongs to the spirit realm, however, the unclean spirit knows who Jesus is and seeks to make him known, declaring that he is "Jesus of Nazareth" and "the Holy One of God" (v. 24; cf. 2 Kgs 4:9; Ps 106:16; 1Q30; John 6:69), perhaps suggesting that like Samson Jesus is a Nazirite, or the Strong One (Judg 13:7 LXX; 16:17; Mark 1:7-8).[14] Jesus' response is to silence the unclean spirit. It cannot gain power over him in this way, and he will not have his identity revealed by the evil powers. Literally, he commands the spirit to "be muzzled," implying it is like a wild animal (cf. 4:39), and to come out of the man. After convulsing, tearing, or throwing the man to and fro (cf. 9:20, 26) and crying out in a loud voice (cf. 15:37)—which could be a final act of resistance or its death throes—the spirit comes out of the man.

Evil Spirits

"[Describing Baaras, a plant said to be fatally poisonous to the touch unless the entire root is dug up and the plant carried off in a prescribed manner]. . . . With all these attendant risks, it possesses one virtue for which it is prized; for the so-called demons—in other words, the spirits of wicked men which enter the living and kill them unless aid is forthcoming—are promptly expelled by this root, if merely applied to the patients."

Josephus, *J. W.* 7.185; LCL 3:559.

The response of the people is astonishment or amazement. The response will be repeated following Jesus' miracles throughout the Gospel (cf. 2:12; 5:42; 10:24, 32). It signals a lack of comprehension of the meaning of the event that they have witnessed, the demonstration of an incomprehensible power. Mark uses their question, "What is this?" as a device to focus attention on the issue of Jesus' identity and power (4:41; 6:2). The response of the people ties together the two parts of this story—Jesus' teaching and the exorcism. Both demonstrate his authority. Note the repetition and parallel of "astounded" and "authority" in reference to Jesus' teaching in v. 22 and "amazed," "a new teaching—with authority" in v. 27 in reference to the exorcism. By linking teaching and miracle in this way, Mark suggests that Jesus' miracle-working power continues to be present wherever Jesus' "new teaching" is repeated and heard. [Common Men on an Uncommon Mission]

The word "immediately" is repeated for the third time in this pericope in v. 28 (cf. vv. 21, 23). The casting out of demons was a sign that Satan's dominion had been broken and God's kingdom was breaking into history with its expected suddenness. With some irony, Mark says that the report of what Jesus had done spread throughout Galilee, even though Jesus had silenced the unclean spirit. Galilee was the locus of Jesus' kingdom work, and from his first public act the "gospel of God" (1:14) began to spread throughout the region.

Mark again reports that "immediately" after they left the synagogue they entered Peter and Andrew's house (see [Synagogues]). In fact, Peter's house seems to have been located only a matter of yards from the synagogue. The sites in question can now be located with a greater degree of confi-

Common Men on an Uncommon Mission

"Reflect on the nature and grandeur of the one Almighty God who could associate himself with the poor of the lowly fisherman's class. To use them to carry out God's mission baffles all rationality. For having conceived the intention, which no one ever before had done, of spreading his own commands and teachings to all nations, and of revealing himself as the teacher of the religion of the one Almighty God to all humanity, he thought good to use the most unsophisticated and common people as ministers of his own design. Maybe God just wanted to work in the most unlikely way. . . . When he had thus called them as his followers, he breathed into them his divine power, and filled them with strength and courage. As God himself spoke God's true word to them in his own way, enabling them to do great wonders, and made them pursuers of rational and thinking souls, by empowering them to come after him, saying: 'Come, follow me, and I will make you fish for people.'"

Eusebius, *The Proof of the Gospel* 3.7, in Thomas C. Oden and Christopher A. Hall, eds., *Ancient Christian Commentary on Scripture, New Testament II: Mark* (Downers Grove IL: InterVarsity Press, 1998), 18–19.

Peter's House

Remains of the 5th-century octagonal basilica built over a house revered as "St. Peter's House" from the early centuries.

(Credit: R. Alan Culpepper)

dence than nearly any other site in the Gospel. Remains of an earlier structure that may have been a synagogue have been excavated beneath the remains of the fifth-century synagogue in Capernaum. Not far away, in the fifth century, stood an octagonal Christian basilica that is built over an ordinary house whose walls had been plastered and inscribed with Christian graffiti, suggesting that it had been used as a site of Christian worship since the late first or second century. Mark 1:21-39 summarizes Jesus' "Day in Capernaum" and no doubt served as the foundational story for the church that grew there.[15] About AD 400 the pilgrim Egeria wrote, "At Capharnaum the house of the Prince of the Apostles has become a Church: The walls of the house are still preserved."[16]

According to Mark, Peter's mother-in-law was ill "with a fever." Knowing nothing about infections or the cause of fever, the ancients looked on the fever as the illness. In the parallel account in Luke 4:39, Jesus "rebuked the fever" as though it were a demon and it left her. Mark's account, although it follows the exorcism in the synagogue, is more nearly a foreshadowing of resurrection: Jesus took her by the hand and "raised her up" (v. 31; cf. 5:41; 9:27; 12:26; 14:28; 16:6).

Peter's Mother-in-Law
Although Mark says that Jesus "took her by the hand and lifted her up" (1:31), the artist focuses on the moment of Jesus' healing touch.

Jesus healing the mother-in-law of Saint Peter. Mosaic in the narthex. Byzantine, 14th c. Hora Church (Kariye Camii), Istanbul, Turkey. (Credit: Erich Lessing / Art Resource, NY)

The comment that she began to serve them probably means that she prepared a meal for them, but it resonates with other occurrences of the same verb in Mark: the angels had "served" Jesus in the wilderness (1:13), Jesus himself came to serve, not to be served (10:45), and at the end of the Gospel there are still the women who "served" him when he was in Galilee (15:41), so the Gospel is bracketed by references to women serving Jesus.[17]

Verses 32-34 contain generalizations ("he cured many who were sick with various diseases, and cast out many demons") and hyperbole ("all who were sick," "the whole city was gathered around the door") that are common to the Markan summaries, such as 3:7-17 and 6:53-56, but they also contain some specific data that suggests pre-Markan tradition. Double time references, such as "that evening, at sundown," are common in Mark. The specificity of "at sundown" is important because it marks the end of the Sabbath. Carrying burdens [Carrying Burdens as Violation of the Sabbath] and healing the chronically ill were both considered violations of Sabbath law. Having heard of the exorcism in the synagogue (1:21-28), the townspeople waited until the end of the Sabbath to bring the sick and possessed to Jesus. Jesus, on the other hand, had already cast out the demon and healed Peter's mother-in-law on the Sabbath, demonstrating the priority of human need over Sabbath observance, which will be an issue of contention in 2:23-28 and 3:1-6.

Because the houses in Capernaum were small, one- or two-room structures around a common courtyard, and the streets were narrow, it would not have taken a large crowd to block an entire area. Although Jesus was introduced as the one who proclaimed the kingdom of God in 1:14-15, Mark's description of his early activity centers on his healing and exorcism of demons, which establishes that all of his ministry, as it declares the coming of the kingdom, is also an attack on Satan's dominion. Jesus heals and restores to wholeness all who come to him, with no questions about their faith. Concluding the summary, Mark's comment that Jesus would not allow the demons to speak reminds the reader of his silencing the demon in the synagogue (v. 25) and continues the theme of secrecy in Mark.

Verses 35-39 report Jesus' withdrawal for prayer and his departure from Capernaum. Another double time reference opens the paragraph ("In the morning, while it was still very dark"). The dual references

> ### Carrying Burdens as Violation of the Sabbath
>
> "Thus says the LORD: For the sake of your lives, take care that you do not bear a burden on the sabbath days or bring it in by the gates of Jerusalem. And do not carry a burden out of your houses on the sabbath or do any work, but keep the sabbath day holy, as I commanded your ancestors." (Jer 17:21-22)
>
> "And they shall not bring in or take out from house to house on that day because it is more holy and it is more blessed than any day of the jubilee of jubilees." (*Jub.* 2:29-30; Charlesworth, *Old Testament Pseudepigrapha*, 2:58)
>
> "The main classes of work are forty save one: . . . and taking aught from one domain to another." (*m. Shab.* 7.2; Danby, *The Mishnah*, 106)

continue ("he got up and went out," "to a wilderness place"; cf. 6:31, 32, 35) but then give way to a singular activity ("and there he prayed"). Jesus prays only three times in Mark (1:35; 6:46; 14:32-39; and we may assume 9:2-8). Each time he withdraws to a "wilderness place," a mountain, or a garden. The narration of the story continues through Peter's point of view, lending weight to the theory that the "Petrine" material in Mark came to Mark from Peter's preaching.[18] The disciples who had been called to be "fishers of men" have to "hunt" (NRSV) for Jesus. The verb usually means to "pursue" in a hostile sense. Here the hostility is muted, but some frustration is evident in the first words the disciples speak in Mark: "Everyone is searching for you" (v. 37). Implicit is a profound difference of purpose between Jesus and the disciples. They assume that Jesus should be responding to and perhaps cultivating the adulation of the crowds. If Jesus preached the coming of the kingdom in the synagogue in Capernaum, then they may have expected him to set up an administrative center for the new kingdom there and that they would have been power brokers in the new kingdom. On the contrary, Jesus had no such kingdom in mind, did not regard healing and exorcism as a means of spreading his fame, and did not regard his work as healer and exorcist as either limited to a particular locality or as primary for his mission. While none of this is explicit at this point, the lack of understanding and the faithlessness of the disciples will dominate the interaction between Jesus and the disciples throughout the Gospel.

At the same time, as agent of the kingdom, Jesus is elusive and enigmatic. He will not allow his identity to be revealed by the demons, he withdraws from his followers so that they have to "seek" (v. 36) and "find" (v. 37), and his followers can predict neither his actions nor his priorities. The theme of seeking and finding is common in the Wisdom tradition, where Wisdom is sought and found (Deut 4:29; Job 28:12; Prov 1:28; Isa 55:6; Hos 5:6; Bar 3:14-15; Wis 6:12). In spite of their misunderstanding, Jesus extends a second call to the first disciples, "Let us go on" (v. 38). Jesus would not be a village healer, exorcist, or shaman; but his healing and exorcizing need not be interpreted as competing with his purpose of proclaiming the message of the kingdom. His claim, "for this I came out" (v. 38), is suggestively ambiguous. It may indicate the reason for his early morning departure from Capernaum, his reason for embarking on his public ministry, or it may extend the characterization of Jesus' ministry as a military campaign.[19]

Verse 39 draws to a close the summary of Jesus' "Day in Capernaum," recapping themes established to this point in the Gospel: Jesus' movements (vv. 9, 14, 16, 21, 35), the centrality of Galilee (vv. 9, 14, 28), Jesus' preaching (vv. 14-15), the synagogues (vv. 21-29), and demon exorcism (vv. 23-27, 32, 34). Just as John the Baptist had reached "the whole Judean countryside and all the people of Jerusalem" (1:5), so Jesus' fame spread "throughout the surrounding region of Galilee" (vv. 28, 39).

The story of Jesus healing a leper serves as a climax to the healings of the previous section (the "day at Capernaum," 1:21-39) and an introduction to the conflicts with the authorities in following section (2:1–3:6). It follows the familiar pattern of a healing narrative: (1) the malady (1:40), (2) the healing act (1:41), (3) the confirmation of the healing (1:42), and (4) the response to the healing (1:45). Drawing attention as distinctive elements are Jesus' stern instructions to the man to tell no one but to go and show himself to the priests (1:43-44) and the report of how the news of this healing spread (1:45). The most perplexing feature of this story, however, is its

Healing a Leper
Byzantine (476–1453). *Healing of the Leper*. From the manuscript "The Four Gospels" from Mount Athos Monastery, Iberon, Greece. (2nd half 12th c.) National Library, Athens, Greece. (Credit: Erich Lessing / Art Resource, NY)

strong, hostile, and confrontive language. Finding the language inappropriate, scribes and commentators have often found means to soften the language in order to yield a picture of Jesus moving compassionately to heal the man from his wretched condition. Doing so, however, obscures the force of the passage, which continues the theme of Jesus' attacks on the power of evil, as he here both drives out the leprosy (an exorcistic healing that caps off the previous section) and exposes the impotence of the ritual system while ostensibly complying with it (foreshadowing the conflicts with the authorities in 2:1–3:6).

In the Gospels, Jesus frequently encounters "lepers," but the term probably covers a variety of skin diseases, scales, and scabbing. The levitical law [Levitical Laws regarding Lepers] treats such diseases as a sign of ritual impurity and imposes strict restrictions on those who suffer from them. The rabbis [Rabbinic Regulations regarding Lepers] devoted an entire tractate of the *Mishnah* to regulations regarding the treatment of lepers.

Mark does not tell us where the healing occurred or anything about the leper except that he knelt before Jesus. His request for healing takes the form of an astounding assertion about Jesus' power: "If you choose, you can make me clean" (v. 40). It was commonly thought that

Levitical Laws regarding Lepers

"The person who has the leprous disease shall wear torn clothes and let the hair of his head be disheveled; and he shall cover his upper lip and cry out, 'Unclean, unclean.' He shall remain unclean as long as he has the disease; he is unclean. He shall live alone; his dwelling shall be outside the camp." (Lev 13:45-46)

Rabbinic Regulations regarding Lepers

"All can contract uncleanness from leprosy-signs excepting gentiles and resident aliens. All are qualified to inspect leprosy-signs, but only a priest may pronounce them unclean or clean." (*m. Negaim* 3.1)

"If a man unclean [from leprosy] stood beneath a tree and one that was clean passed by, he becomes unclean; if he that was clean stood beneath the tree and he that was unclean passed by, he remains clean; but if [he that was unclean] stood still the other becomes unclean." (*m. Negaim* 13.7)

"If a leper enters a house every vessel therein becomes unclean." (*m. Negaim* 13.11)

"How did they cleanse the leper? . . . he brought two birds that had lived in freedom. The priest slaughtered one of them over the earthenware vessel and over the living water, and dug a hole and buried it in his presence. . . . He then came to set free the living bird. . . . He then came to cut off the hair of the leper. . . . On the seventh day he cut off his hair a second time after the manner of the first cutting. He washed his garments and immersed himself; and thus he became clean so that he no more conveyed uncleanness. . . ." (*m. Negaim* 14.1-3; H. Danby, trans., *The Mishnah* [Oxford: Oxford University Press, 1933], 678, 694–95)

---

healing a leper was akin to raising the dead—something only God could do—and there are only two accounts of the healing of lepers in the Old Testament (Miriam: Num 12:10-15; Naaman: 2 Kgs 5:1-14). We may suppose that the leper had either witnessed or been told of Jesus' healings in Capernaum and that he had come to the conclusion that Jesus could heal even leprosy without the authority of the priests, the temple cult, or the prescribed process for the cleansing of lepers.

Jesus responds with the first of several indications of intense emotion and conflict. Most manuscripts read "moved with pity" (*splanchnistheis*), but a few "Western" manuscripts read "moved with anger" (*orgistheis*). Although the latter is a weaker reading, it is also the more difficult, meaning it may be the original reading: one can easily see why scribes would have changed it, but it is unlikely that any scribe would have changed "moved with pity" to "moved with anger." Jesus' anger was at the disease, or the demon that caused the disease, not the victim of the disease who had come to him with such a daring statement of trust in his power.

Although Jesus has already exorcised a demon by means of an authoritative command, here he touches the leper [Jesus Touches the Leper], demonstrating complete disregard for its infectious and defiling power. He deliberately crosses the boundary between clean and unclean, thereby accepting the leper's uncleanness. His statement, then, is a response to the leper's challenge regarding Jesus' will to heal: "I do choose. Be made clean" (v. 41).

Mark describes the healing in two stages, or better, with two metaphors (exorcism and purification). Perhaps with intentional overtones of an exorcism, Mark says the leprosy "left him" (cf. 1:25-26). As a result, he was made clean, just as he had requested (cf. vv. 41-42). Mark then uses a term for violent emotion that occurs only rarely in the New Testament or other Greek literature (Matt 9:30; Mark 14:5; John 11:33-38) to describe Jesus' instructions to the healed leper. In classical literature it means to "bellow" or "snort," but here it has the meaning "to insist on something sternly" or "warn sternly."[20] We must presume that the substance of Jesus' warning follows (out of sequence) in v. 44: to tell no one, but to go and show himself to the priest and to make the prescribed offerings (see Lev 14), as a testimony either "to them" (NRSV) or "against them." In this case the difference depends on interpretation, not a textual

> **Jesus Touches the Leper**
>
> 📖 "He did not simply say, 'I will, be cleansed,' but he also 'extended his hand, and touched him'—an act we do well to analyze. If he cleansed him merely by willing it and by speaking it, why did he also add the touch of his hand? For no other reason, it seems to me, than that he might signify by this that he is not under the hand of the law, but the law is in his hands. Hence to the pure in heart, from now on, nothing is impure. . . . He touched the leper to signify that he heals not as servant but as Lord. For the leprosy did not defile his hand, but his holy hand cleansed the leprous body." (Chrysostom, *The Gospel of St. Matthew, Homily* 25.2; NPNF 1, 10:173)
>
> In Thomas C. Oden and Christopher A. Hall, eds., *Ancient Christian Commentary on Scripture, New Testament II: Mark* (Downers Grove IL: InterVarsity Press, 1998), 26.

variant. Those who take the positive sense interpret the testimony as confirming that the leper was actually cleansed, that Jesus was being faithful to the Law, or that the miracle had in fact occurred. Nevertheless, the linguistic evidence, the strong language in this healing story, and the location of the story just before the coming section on Jesus' conflict with the authorities all support the negative sense—"as a testimony against them," meaning either an indictment of the power- lessness of the cultic system in contrast to the power of Jesus or a condemnation of their unbelief. Other occurrences of this phrase in the New Testament can signify a witness against the person in question (as in 6:11), but in Mark 13:9, which precedes the command to preach "the gospel" in 13:10, it should probably be read with the positive sense.[21]

Continuing the strong language of the passage, and perhaps the over- tones of exorcism, Mark reports that Jesus "cast out" or "drove away" the man he had just healed. Mark then adds another report of the spread of Jesus' fame (cf. vv. 28, 39). In spite of Jesus' stern warning, and perhaps demonstrating that it was impossible for the in-breaking power of the kingdom to be kept secret, the healed leper too became a proclaimer—note the use of this verb for both John the Baptist (1:4, 7) and Jesus (1:14, 38, 39). The result is that Jesus is forced to stay out of the cities and remain in the "wilderness places" (1:3, 4, 12, 13, 35). Just as the chapter opened with John the Baptist and the people coming out to him from all over Judea, so it closes with Jesus in wilderness places and the people coming out to him from everywhere.

CONNECTIONS

Mark 1:1-13

To make a beginning is to divide time, to place a marker that says that one era has ended and another has begun. The past is closed, but the future holds infinite possibilities. The blank sheet of paper before the writer has the potential to hold the words of a Shakespearian sonnet, the Declaration of Independence, or the Gettysburg Address. A newborn baby may become an artist, a musician, a scientist, or a great leader in a time of crisis. New beginnings are therefore rightly celebrated. They speak something of God's grace, that the future may be better than the past, and that the future is open to new disclosures of God's creative love. When we celebrate birthdays, weddings, New Year's, the beginning of a new school year, or the inauguration of a new president, we are setting hope over against despair and giving thanks for what may yet be. But only God could draw a line in time and announce the beginning of the gospel, the coming of the Messiah, and the arrival of the kingdom of God.

Such "good news" has the power to shape the future. The marathon is run at the Olympics every four years in honor of the legend that an Athenian named Pheidippides ran from Marathon to Athens, a distance of 26 miles, to bring the good news of the victory at Marathon (in the Greeks' defense of their homeland against the Persians in 490 BC). History hung in the balance, but now the way was open for democracy to flourish, for the Parthenon to be built, for Plato and Aristotle to teach and write, and for drama, rhetoric, and architecture to develop—the cradle of western civilization had survived.

Later in the Gospel of Mark, Jesus will send his disciples to proclaim the "good news" to all the nations. Satan had frustrated God's earlier attempts to redeem humanity, to vanquish the demonic, dehumanizing powers, to empower a redemptive community, to overcome the barriers that divide one people from another, and to restore the creation to its primal peace. Now Jesus has come, the heavens have been opened, the Spirit has descended, the demons are exorcised, the estranged are reconciled, and death has given way to life. No wonder such good news has to be shared. This good news is the gospel that Jesus Christ, the Son of God brought, so only by trusting him can we receive it. But he was no mere messenger. Jesus announced the coming of God's kingdom, but he also inaugurated that kingdom, broke the power of Satan, and triumphed over death. What might the future hold after such a beginning?

The kingdom comes to those who are ready to receive it. John the Baptist was sent to call people to repentance and to readiness for the coming Messiah. Jesus likewise called people to "repent and believe in the gospel" (1:15). "The way of the Lord" ["The Way of the Lord"] must therefore be prepared within us, but this is a lifelong task. As his followers, we give our lives to preparing ourselves to be able to know God more fully and live in deeper appreciation of God's fellowship. We cultivate "the way of the Lord" through study, as did the ancient Essenes, through prayer and mediation, as did the contemplative monks, and through lives of charity and service, as did many of the saints.

The wilderness is our time of testing. It can take many forms. The wilderness can be the despair that denies hope, the cynicism that goads us to believe that our doubts are truer than our insights, the grief that binds us to our losses, the hostility that will not let us enjoy friends or family, or the addictions that degrade us, forcing us to give away all we have. Our spirits often drive us to wildernesses of our own making: desolate, lonely, godforsaken places populated with all sorts of wild beasts. It is important, therefore, that Jesus first appears in the wilderness. He comes to the wilderness to confront the evil powers that dwell there, and he overcomes them and restores a garden-like quality to life. He is at peace with nature, surrounded by animals, and the angels serve him.

The mention of angels will communicate to many today that we are dealing with a mythic story with mythical creatures. For the ancients, however, angels evoked the mystery and wonder of God's presence in the world. The early church told its story and found the power to go on. The medieval church wrote, sang, and painted its stories. It built them into cathedrals, and they spoke stability and purpose amid the anarchy and violence of their age. But we children of the Enlightenment and modernism demand rational explanations. As soon as we begin to sense that the story defies our attempts to interpret it and make it fit our worldview, we challenge it with our incredulity, and its people slip away from us and leave us with hollow abstractions.

Naturally, since abstractions are all we have left, we reduce the scope of our believing to the most abstract concepts we can conceive. We don't believe in Yahweh; we believe in monotheism. We don't believe in Jesus; we believe in the Son of God. We don't believe in the virgin birth; we believe in the incarnation. We don't believe in the end of the world; we believe in eschatology, realized but not completed. We don't

"The Way of the Lord"

"The way of the Lord must be prepared within the heart; for great and spacious is the heart of man, as if it were a whole world. But see its greatness, not in bodily quantity, but in the power of the mind which enables it to encompass so great a knowledge of the truth. Prepare, therefore, in your hearts the way of the Lord, by worthy manner of life, so that the words of the Lord may enter in without hindrance." (Origen, *Homily 21*)

In Thomas C. Oden and Christopher A. Hall, eds., *Ancient Christian Commentary on Scripture, New Testament II: Mark* (Downers Grove IL: InterVarsity Press, 1998), 1–2.

believe in Jesus' death; we believe in the atonement. Like technological marvels poisoning the natural world, we have defoliated and depopulated our stories. They cannot live in our world, so we go through the motions, believing that the irrationality of our stories means that we can answer our ultimate questions ourselves. Instead of allowing the gospel story to give us life, we try to force it into our parameters of rationality. The result is an eerie silence. The music has stopped, and the stories are being forgotten. Soon there may be no more angels for us to hear. So remember the story and tell it to your children. Tell it to those who don't know the words, to those who have never heard it, and to those who have forgotten it. Tell it to those who have never heard an angel before. Jesus came into the wilderness and tamed it.

Mark 1:16-20

The fishermen were going about their routine tasks when Jesus passed by. We are not told whether they had heard or met Jesus before. Mark reports the encounter with no hint of any preparation for it (such as the account of the first disciples' association with John the Baptist in John 1). Their response is based only on Jesus' call, which was unlike any other. Rabbis did not call students; students were instructed to seek out a rabbi. Philosophers preached and taught in the marketplaces and called others to adopt their teachings. Zealot groups called the uncommitted to their militant cause. But Jesus gave no hint of his teachings or his cause. He offered no guarantees or promises of success. He posed no time frame or trial period for the commitment. His was an absolute, person-centered call: "You follow me!" ["You Follow Me"]

"You Follow Me"

"He comes to us as One unknown, without a name, as of old, by the lakeside, He came to those men who knew Him not. He speaks to us the same word: 'Follow thou me!' and sets us to the tasks which he has to fulfil in our time. He commands. And to those who obey Him, whether they be wise or simple, He will reveal Himself in the toils, the conflicts, the sufferings which they shall pass through in His fellowship, and, as an ineffable mystery, they shall learn in their own experience Who He is."

Albert Schweitzer, *The Quest of the Historical Jesus* (trans. W. Montgomery; New York: Macmillan, 1950), 403.

Many summers ago, a teenager who had grown up on a farm near Groesbeck, Texas, had a chance to go to college on a scholarship. He had worked all summer picking cotton and saving his cotton money. When the big day came, he put on his best clothes, hugged his mother, shook his father's hand, and walked to the end of the road. Everything he had was in an old suitcase, everyone he knew lived along that road, and all his family was back in the old house nestled under the trees. He stood there for a long minute and almost turned back, but he knew God was calling him to do something besides be a farmer, so he turned again and walked on. Following that inner prompting led him to become a pastor, and later a much-loved vice president of student affairs at a Baptist university who

Exorcists

"Rabbinic charismatic miracle-workers can be demonstrated for the period at the turn of the eras. [Geza] Vermes refers to Honi in the first century BCE, who was well known for his miracles with rain (performed by drawing a magic circle); the rabbinic tradition was somewhat critical of him (Taan III.8), but Josephus is more positive (*Ant.* 14, 22-24). Most interesting of all is Hanina ben Dosa in the first century CE, who like Jesus worked in Galilee. . . . Traditions about Hanina ben Dosa describe a miraculous immunity to snake bites (bBer 33a), two healings at a distance through prayer (bBer 34b), and power over demons (bPes 112b). . . . He could have come from the same milieu as Jesus. It is also striking that charismatic miracle-workers in the rabbinic tradition were given the status of sons of God: Hanina ben Dosa is designated 'my son' by God himself (bTaan 24b; cf. Mark 1.11; 9.7 par.). It is said of Honi that he was 'like a son of the house' before God (mTaan 3.8). . . . The parallels to Jesus, who particularly in the context of miracles is regarded as 'son of God' and is known for addressing God as 'Abba', is [sic] obvious. Differences to be mentioned are that the Jewish charismatic miracle-workers were active primarily through their prayer; it was not they but their God who performed miracles. There are no eschatological miracles whatsoever among the Jewish charismatic miracle workers."

Gerd Theissen and Annette Merz, *The Historical Jesus: A Comprehensive Guide* (trans. John Bowden; Minneapolis: Fortress, 1998), 307–308.

---

made a difference in the lives of hundreds of students over the years— all because he did not turn away from that inner leading when he stood at the bend in the road.

Mark 1:21-45

This section confronts modern interpreters with several difficult issues: Did Jesus perform miracles, and if so how do we interpret them for our skeptical age, and, related, how do we interpret demons in the twenty-first century? Both are difficult issues since they have clear implications for one's view of the nature of Scripture and one's understanding of Jesus.

The view taken here is that Jesus shared the worldview of his time, and one of the common data in the historical record is that he was regarded as an exorcist and a healer. [Exorcists] Similarly, the Gospels reflect the worldview of the first century, so the accounts of Jesus' exorcisms and healings did not raise questions of science and natural law for either the evangelists or their readers, as they do for modern readers.

The understanding of the world that was common in ancient Mediterranean culture was that natural processes and events that affect human life are subject to fate and controlled by spiritual forces. In place of a scientific understanding of cause and effect and intermediate causes, ancients looked for ultimate, direct, and divine or demonic causes. If one were sick, it was because a capricious divine being or a malicious demon had caused it. Therefore, one had to offer sacrifices to appease the gods, practice ritual and magic to ward off demons, and trust fate (Gk. *tychē*). They had no understanding of infections, diseases, or mental illnesses. Instead, they looked for causes in the external world of spirits and demons.

The modern worldview is grounded in science and assumes that all events must have a rational, scientific explanation (Gk. *technē*). To explain symptoms and behaviors, we appeal to pathology and psychology. In the process, the spiritual has often been discarded as simply superstition, a holdover from the prescientific era. Natural processes replace divine actions in our worldview. Because science can explain some phenomena, we assume it will ultimately allow us to understand all human experience. If God served as the explanation for all that we could not explain, then—because we are now confident that we will eventually be able to explain everything by natural process—God no longer has any place or function: God is unnecessary. [God Is Unnecessary]

Our mistake, therefore, is likely to be the opposite of that of ancient culture. While ancients assumed everything happened by direct, divine or demonic causes, everything was mystery, and natural causes were excluded or ignored, moderns assume we can understand everything and therefore exclude all mystery and fail to recognize the spiritual realities in human experience. The Truth (that which conforms to reality), however, excludes neither the material nor the spiritual, recognizes that God works both through and beyond natural processes, and leaves room for mystery we may never penetrate.

The question the interpreter should start with is not whether the miracles are historical but what they mean. How then do we discover their meaning? One important guide is to analyze the form of each miracle story. As indicated in the Commentary section, the miracle stories typically follow a common pattern: (1) a brief description of the situation—the need; (2) Jesus' word or action; (3) the effect of Jesus' word or action; (4) confirmation of the miracle by witnesses; and (5) a response of awe or praise. Where any of these elements is expanded, or other material is added, the evangelist is using the miracle story to make a particular point. In the case of the exorcism of the unclean

---

God Is Unnecessary

"This is also a book about God . . . or perhaps about the absence of God. The word of God fills these pages. Hawking embarks on a quest to answer Einstein's famous question about whether God had any choice in creating the universe. Hawking is attempting, as he explicitly states, to understand the mind of God. And this makes all the more unexpected the conclusion of the effort, at least so far: a universe with no edge in space, no beginning or end in time, and nothing for a Creator to do." (x)

"So long as the universe had a beginning, we could suppose it had a creator. But if the universe is really completely self-contained, having no boundary or edge, it would have neither beginning nor end: it would simply be. What place, then, for a creator?" (141)

"However, if we do discover a complete theory, it should in time be understandable in broad principle by everyone, not just a few scientists. Then we shall all, philosophers, scientists, and just ordinary people, be able to take part in the discussion of the question of why it is that we and the universe exist. If we find the answer to that, it would be the ultimate triumph of human reason—for then we would know the mind of God." (175)

Stephen W. Hawking, *A Brief History of Time* (Toronto: Bantam Books, 1988).

spirit in Mark 1:21-28, that point is Jesus' authority and the power of his teachings. In the case of the healing of the leper in Mark 1:40-45, the hostile language emphasizes Jesus' attack on the evil power responsible for the leprosy and his condemnation of the priests and the system of ritual purity (see the commentary on 1:40-45).

Miracle stories can serve various functions. First, the miracle stories serve a *theological function*: they are signs of God's power and glory. They affirm that God is sovereign over all other powers, sovereign over the world in which we live, and sovereign over the evil powers that degrade human beings and deprive them of life as God intended it. Second, the miracle stories serve a *christological function*: the miracles tell us who Jesus was. They affirm that Jesus was the Son of God and that God was acting through Jesus. When Jesus walks on the sea, he does what God alone does in the Old Testament, and he answers the cry of the disciples with a reassuring "I am he" (*egō eimi*) that echoes the divine name disclosed to Moses at the burning bush (Exod 3:14; see the commentary on Mark 6:45-52). The miracle story, therefore, affirms that God's fullest revelation came through Jesus and God is revealed in what Jesus did.

Third, the miracle stories may serve a *hermeneutical function*: they link Jesus to "the Law and the Prophets" and show that he was the fulfillment of the Hebrew Scriptures. Most of the miracles are related to events associated with Moses (commanding the forces of nature, crossing the sea, feeding the multitude, providing water) or Elijah and Elisha (healing the sick, the lepers, the blind, the deaf, and raising the dead; see also Isa 35:5 and 61:1). In order to grasp the significance of many of the miracle stories, therefore, it is necessary to read the related stories in the Old Testament (e.g., 1 Kgs 17:8-16, 17-24; 2 Kgs 4:42-44; 5:1-14).

Fourth, the miracle stories often serve a *kerygmatic function*: they demonstrate the power of Jesus' word. This function is clearly evident in Mark's account of the exorcism of the demon in Mark 1:21-28. The setting is the first account of Jesus' teaching. Mark comments that he taught as one with authority. Then Jesus silences the demon and exorcises it with a double command: "Be silent and come out of him!" (1:25). The response of the crowd links together Jesus' teaching and the exorcism, the authority of his teaching and the power of his word: "What is this? A new teaching—with authority? He commands even the unclean spirits and they obey him" (1:27). The repetition of the word "authority" in vv. 22 and 27, after his teaching and after the exorcism, establishes the theme of this section of the Gospel. Having received the Holy Spirit at his baptism, Jesus now acts and speaks with divine authority.

Finally, the miracle stories often have a *didactic function*: they offer a lesson on discipleship. In the wilderness, the angels served Jesus, and when Jesus healed (lit., "raised") Peter's mother-in-law, she served Jesus and the disciples. Serving is important because Jesus himself came to serve (10:45), but Mark never says that the disciples served Jesus—an observation that underscores the theme of the failure of the disciples in Mark. Believers, therefore, should imitate not the disciples, but the "angelic" role of Peter's mother-in-law and the women from Galilee (1:31; 15:41).

In short, the miracles invite us to live in a world over which God is sovereign and to have faith that God is indeed sovereign over the world in which we live. Our task as interpreters is to recognize the rhetorical function of the Gospel stories and be responsive to the truth they declare. The Gospels are grounded in the life and person of Jesus of Nazareth, so historical research is essential. On the other hand, the concern of the Gospels is primarily kerygmatic and didactic: they mean to preach Jesus and teach what it means to follow him. Among the competing worldviews of antiquity rooted in superstition, magic, and speculation, the Gospels offer a vision of a world in which God is sovereign but combating the destructive powers of evil. Jesus, God's beloved son, came to liberate humanity from the power of evil and establish a new power, God's kingly sovereignty. The rest of the Gospel teaches us how God's kingdom is different from that of earthly authorities, how we can recognize God's work in the world, and how God's faithful live.

The competing worldviews of our time are generally not based on superstition and magic but on science and technology. The human questions, however, are still ultimately religious: Is there a God, and if so who is God? Does life have purpose and meaning? Does God control the world and history, or are we on our own in a chaotic world with forces beyond our control? The temptations of our era are despair and resignation—the real antitheses of faith. The poet Matthew Arnold evokes the materialism of our age and the denial of any meaning or purpose to existence in his poem "Rugby Chapel." [Rugby Chapel]

In response to such nihilism, Mark offers timeless answers that are illustrated especially in the miracle stories: God cares about human suffering, God has the power to overcome demonic forces, and the end of history will be marked by the fulfillment of God's redemptive work on earth. Human life and history, therefore, have *eternal* meaning, and individually we find

Rugby Chapel

Most men eddy about
Here and there—eat and drink,
Chatter and love and hate,
Gather and squander, are raised
Aloft, are hurl'd in the dust,
Striving blindly, achieving
Nothing; and then they die—
Perish;—and no one asks
Who or what they have been,
More than he asks what waves,
In the moonlit solitudes mild
Of the midmost Ocean, have swell'd,
Foam'd for a moment, and gone.

Matthew Arnold, "Rugby Chapel," *The Poetical Works of Matthew Arnold* (New York: Oxford University Press, 1957), 288.

purpose and meaning through faithfulness to Jesus' revelation and teachings in the quest for experiential knowledge of God's fellowship. The choice that faces each of us, we might say, is whether we will live in the world evoked by Matthew Arnold or the world evoked by Mark the Evangelist.

NOTES

[1] Hans von Campenhausen, *The Formation of the Christian Bible* (trans. J. A. Baker; Philadelphia: Fortress Press, 1972), 155-56; Robert H. Gundry, "ΕΥΑΓΓΕΛΙΟΝ: How Soon a Book?" *JBL* 115/2 (1996): 321-25.

[2] N. C. Croy, "Where the Gospel Text Begins: A Non-Theological Interpretation of Mark 1:1," *NovT* 43 (2001): 105-27.

[3] Gerhard Friedrich, *"euangelizomai,"* *TDNT* (ed. Gerhard Kittel; trans. Geoffrey W. Bromiley; Grand Rapids: Wm. B. Eerdmans, 1964), 2:722.

[4] Robert A. Guelich, *Mark 1–8:26* (WBC 34a; Dallas: Word, 1989), 6, who cites C. H. Turner, "Marcan Usage: Notes, Critical and Exegetical, on the Second Gospel," *JTS* 26 (1925): 150.

[5] See Martin Hengel, *The Son of God* (trans. John Bowden; Philadelphia: Fortress, 1976), 30.

[6] Florentino García Martínez, *The Dead Sea Scrolls Translated: The Qumran Texts in English* (trans. Wilfred G. E. Watson; Leiden: E. J. Brill, 1994), 5.

[7] Joel Marcus, *Mark 1–8* (AB 27; New York: Doubleday, 2000), 151.

[8] James H. Charlesworth, *The Old Testament Pseudepigrapha* (Garden City NY: Doubleday, 1985), 2:261.

[9] For helpful surveys of this debate, see George Eldon Ladd, *A Theology of the New Testament* (Grand Rapids: Wm. B. Eerdmans, 1974), 58-60; Norman Perrin, *Jesus and the Language of the Kingdom* (Philadelphia: Fortress, 1976), esp. 32-40, 89-107.

[10] Vernon K. Robbins, "Mark 1.14-20: An Interpretation at the Intersection of Jewish and Graeco-Roman Traditions," *NTS* 28 (1982): 220-36.

[11] R. Alan Culpepper, *John the Son of Zebedee: The Life of a Legend* (Columbia: University of South Carolina Press, 1994), 21; cf. the full discussion of this passage on pp. 7-27.

[12] Marcus, *Mark 1–8*, 190.

[13] Werner Foerster, *"exousia,"* *TDNT* 2:562, 565.

[14] Marcus, *Mark 1–8*, 188.

[15] Ibid., 202-203.

[16] Eugene Hoade, o.f.m., *Guide to the Holy Land* (Jerusalem: Franciscan Printing House, n.d.), 759.

[17] Malbon, "Fallible Followers: Women and Men in the Gospel of Mark," *Semeia* 28 (1983): 41.

[18] See esp. Vincent Taylor, *The Gospel according to St. Mark* (London: Macmillan, 1952), 102.

[19] For the latter, see Marcus, *Mark 1–8*, 204.

[20] *"embrimaomai,"* BDAG, 322.

[21] Guelich, *Mark 1–8:26*, 77, who cites H. Strathmann, *"martys,"* *TDNT* 4:502-03, who cites similar usage of the phrase in Ignatius (*Trallians* 12.3; *Philadelphians* 6.3). George R. Beasley-Murray, *Jesus and the Last Days: The Interpretation of the Olivet Discourse* (Peabody MA: Hendrickson, 1993), 401, offers a critique of Strathmann's interpretation.

CONFLICT WITH THE RELIGIOUS LEADERS

Mark 2:1-28

Chapter 2 is actually part of Mark 2:1–3:6. The earliest manuscripts have no chapter or verse divisions. Indeed, the numbering of chapters in the New Testament can be traced to Stephen Langton (c. 1150–1228), Archbishop of Canterbury, who added the chapter divisions to the Latin Vulgate.[1] Stephanus added the verse divisions in 1551, while he was traveling from Paris to Lyons (some say while he was traveling on horseback!), and the Geneva Bible (1560)—the Bible of Shakespeare, John Bunyan, and the Mayflower pilgrims— was the first English translation to have chapter and verse divisions. Modern interpreters would choose to mark some chapters and verses differently, but Langton's chapter divisions have now become the standard.

As we have seen, Mark 1 characterizes Jesus' ministry as a conflict between spiritual powers: the reign of God is displacing the power of the devil; angels attend Jesus, and demons invade human personalities. In response, Jesus exercises the power of the Spirit to silence and banish the demons. In the second cycle of events, which begins in Capernaum, Jesus encounters the opposition of the religious authorities. The cycle contains five controversy stories in which the authorities question Jesus about his actions and Jesus responds with a definitive pronouncement. [Five Controversy Stories: The Structure of Mark 2:1–3:6] The narrative serves as a frame for Jesus' pronouncement. The controversies focus on Jesus' authority to forgive sin, table fellowship, and Sabbath violations. Throughout Mark 2:1–3:6 we can detect a rising level of hostility toward Jesus that culminates in plans to put him to death: "questioning in their hearts . . . 'It is blasphemy!'" (2:6-7), the authorities watch Jesus (2:15), they ask an accusing question (2:24), they watch him "so that they might accuse him" (3:2), Jesus is angry and grieved "at their hardness of heart" (3:5), and finally the Pharisees conspire with the Herodians "how to destroy him" (3:6).

Other patterns are evident also. Mark 2:1–3:6 balances the cycle of controversy stories set in Jerusalem in Mark 11–12. Mark 2:1–3:6 also begins and ends with a miracle story, but the similarities do not stop there.[2] Mark 2:1-12 and 3:1-6 both occur indoors, a controversy is embedded in the miracle story, and in each Jesus challenges a man

---

Five Controversy Stories: The Structure of Mark 2:1-3:6

1. Authority to Forgive Sins (2:1-12)
   Controversy: "Why does this fellow speak in this way? It is blasphemy! Who can forgive sins but God alone?"
   Pronouncement: (". . . the Son of Man has authority on earth to forgive sins")

2. Authority to Eat with Outcasts (2:13-17)
   Controversy: "Why does he eat with tax collectors and sinners?"
   Pronouncement: "Those who are well have no need of a physician, but those who are sick; I have come to call not the righteous but sinners."

3. Authority to Dispense with Fasting (2:18-22)
   Controversy: "Why do John's disciples and the disciples of the Pharisees fast, but your disciples do not fast?"

   Pronouncement: "The wedding guests cannot fast while the bridegroom is with them, can they?. . . ."

4. Authority over the Sabbath (2:23-28)
   Controversy: "Look, why are they doing what is not lawful on the Sabbath?"
   Pronouncement: "The Sabbath was made for humankind, and not humankind for the Sabbath; so the Son of Man is lord even of the Sabbath."

5. Authority to Do a Good Work (3:1-5)
   Controversy: ("They watched him to see whether he would cure him on the Sabbath")
   Pronouncement: "Is it lawful to do good or to do harm on the Sabbath, to save life or to kill?"
   Conclusion: The Plot to Kill Jesus (3:6)

---

to "rise" (2:9, 11; 3:3). Whereas the response to the healing of the paralytic is positive ("They were all amazed and glorified God"; 2:12), the response to the healing of the man with a withered hand is the plot to destroy Jesus.[3]

The sequence of these five controversy stories reflects the work of the church in clustering Jesus' teachings and stories about Jesus into topical collections for ease of teaching and transmission before the Gospels were written. We see evidence of such topical collections throughout Mark: parables on the kingdom (Mark 4), teachings on Jewish traditions (Mark 7:1-23), teachings on discipleship (Mark 8:31–9:1), controversies with the Jerusalem authorities (Mark 11–12), and teachings on the fall of Jerusalem and the coming of the Son of Man (Mark 13).

The five controversy stories are connected by brief editorial notices and occur in settings that are typical in Mark: "When he returned to Capernaum after some days, it was reported that he was at home" (2:1); "Jesus went out again beside the sea" (2:13); "and as they sat at table in Levi's house" (2:15); "one Sabbath he was going through the grainfields" (2:23); and "Again he entered the synagogue" (3:1). A pattern develops in which Jesus debates with the authorities in public and gives instruction to the disciples in private settings.

The conflict between Jesus and the religious authorities represents a clash between two kinds of authority. The scribes and Pharisees represent established religious tradition, sanctioned by Scripture, oral tradition, and scribal authorities. This authority established and controlled the local religious and legal status quo. Jesus represents a

Honor and Shame

"Honor can be understood as the status one claims in the community together with the all-important recognition of that claim by others. It thus serves as an indicator of social standing, enabling persons to interact with their social superiors, equals, and inferiors in certain ways prescribed by society.

"Honor can be *ascribed* or *acquired*. Ascribed honor derives from birth: being born into an honorable family makes one honorable in the eyes of the entire community. Consider the poignant scenario in Mark 3:21, where Jesus' family comes to seize him 'for the people were saying, "He has gone out of his mind."' Acquired honor, by contrast, is the result of skill in the never-ending game of challenge and response. Not only must one win to gain it; one must do so in public because the whole community must acknowledge the gain. To claim honor that the community does not recognize is to play the fool. Since honor is a limited good, if one person wins honor, someone else loses. . . .

"Since the honor of one's family determines potential marriage partners as well as with whom one can do business, what functions one can attend, where one can live, and even what religious role one can play, family honor must be defended at all costs. The smallest slight or injury must be avenged, or honor is permanently lost."

Bruce J. Malina and Richard L. Rohrbaugh, *Social-Science Commentary on the Synoptic Gospels* (Minneapolis: Fortress, 1992), 213.

---

charismatic authority, empowered by the Spirit and guided by God's direction for his life. Jesus' authority is that of the coming kingdom, which supersedes that of the religious authorities.

In any public exchange, challenge, or questioning, the ancient code of honor and shame controlled the way the participants and bystanders viewed the event. [Honor and Shame] Every person belonged to a family, a town, and a people, and it was imperative that the group maintain its honor in relationship with other groups. In any public exchange honor was at stake. It could be gained, maintained, or lost. When the authorities challenge Jesus, they can either gain honor by imposing their authority on him, or lose honor if he successfully answers them or fends off their effort to control him. If he is more clever than they, or asks a counter-question they cannot answer, he gains honor and they are shamed.

Throughout Mark 2:1–3:6 the theme of the new age of the kingdom is evident. The lame are restored, sins are forgiven, table fellowship with outcasts confirms the beginning of a new, inclusive community, and human needs take precedence over religious tradition. The coming of the kingdom brought a sharp division between the old and the new. Jesus' mission to announce the coming of the kingdom of God meant, therefore, that he also had to demonstrate the new order of the kingdom and confront all who opposed this new order, even when the authorities plotted to kill him.

COMMENTARY

Authority to Forgive Sins, 2:1-12

The healing of the paralytic sets the tone for the rest of this section. In contrast to the typical healing story, it contains an extended section of debate with the scribes over Jesus' authority to pronounce the man's sins forgiven. It also includes the Gospel's first reference to the Son of Man.

Capernaum seems to have been the center of Jesus' ministry in Galilee. He is actually reported to be in this fishing village only in Mark 1:21-39, 2:1-12, and 9:33-50, but most of the Galilean ministry takes place around the Sea of Galilee. Every time Jesus is in Capernaum, he is in a house. In 1:29 it is specifically identified as "the house of Simon and Andrew." In 2:1 the definite article is not used; some translate it as "in the house" (KJV) and others as an idiom, "at home" (NRSV, NASB), or "had come home" (NIV). In 9:33 the definite article is used, presuming that the reader will know which house: "in the house." The natural implication, therefore, is that Jesus passed through Capernaum often and that when he was there he stayed in the house of Simon and Andrew.

The phrase "after some days" is more naturally taken with the preceding phrase, meaning that Jesus had been gone from Capernaum for some days, than that he had been back for some days before his presence became known. Just as a crowd had gathered around the door following the exorcism in the synagogue (1:33), and he healed many, so once again a crowd gathers around the door, and they bring a paralyzed man to him. Jesus had been speaking "the word" (2:2). Mark uses this expression as a technical term for the gospel. His readers would have understood it as a reference to the early Christian preaching, but in context it must mean Jesus' announcement of the kingdom and call to repentance (1:14-15, 38-39; cf. 1:45; 4:14-20).

Four men carry the paralyzed man [Paralyzed Man] to Jesus on a pallet or stretcher. When they cannot get to Jesus because of the crowd, they carry the man up on the roof. Mark describes their actions on the roof in two phrases: "they removed the roof" and they "dug through it." Mark has in mind a typical Galilean peasant's home [Galilean Peasant's Home], whereas Luke is familiar with a Mediterranean-style home: the men "let him down with his bed

Paralyzed Man

"In the Synoptic Gospels much of Jesus' public reputation derives from healing the sick. Terms for healing appear 25 times in Luke, 17 times in Matthew, and 8 times in Mark. By contrast, there are only three healing stories in the entire Gospel of John. . . .

"In non-Western medicine, the main problem with sickness is the experience of the sick person being dislodged from his/her social moorings and social standing. Social interaction with family members, friends, neighbors, and village mates comes to a halt. To be healed is to be restored to one's social network."

Bruce J. Malina and Richard L. Rohrbaugh, *Social-Science Commentary on the Gospel of John* (Minneapolis: Fortress, 1998), 113–14.

Galilean Peasant's Home

"An appreciable portion of the ancient village [of Capernaum] has been excavated since 1968, providing an insight to the living quarters. The private houses so far excavated are rather unpretentious but by no means poor, at least according to the living standard of an ancient village. They also betray no sharp economic differentiation. Local volcanic basalt stones in their natural state were used to build walls and pavements. Walls were built without true foundations, and the one storey rooms could hardly reach more that [sic] 3 m in height, judging from several staircases leading to the roof. Fairly regular courses were levelled with small pebbles and soil, but with no help of strong mortar, at least in the Hellenistic and Roman periods; even in the Byzantine period mortar was employed only in some cases, and not as a rule. Light roofs made up of wooden beams and of beaten earth mixed with straw covered the squat rooms, and they were reached from open courtyards through a flight of stone steps."

Capharnaum: The Town of Jesus, "The Village," online: http://198.62.75.1/www1/ofm/sites/TScpvill.html.

through the tiles" (Luke 5:19). The homes in Capernaum typically had flat roofs (which doubled the space of the cramped quarters) and steps leading up to the roof. Beams were laid from one wall to the other, a matting of vines and briars covered the beams, and then mud thatch was placed over the matting. The four "dug up the roof" and let the man down between the beams.

Their actions demonstrate their faith (2:5). There is no indication whether the man had solicited his friends to carry him to Jesus or whether it was their initiative. Neither is there any indication of what they knew or believed about Jesus—simply the confidence that he could help the man and their determination to get the man to Jesus in spite of the obstacles in their way. Mark measures faith not by its orthodoxy but by its determination, courage, and persistence. It is not the "i's" dotted or the "t's" crossed but the obstacles overcome that count.

As we noted in the commentary on the miracles in Mark 1, the standard form of a miracle story includes (1) the setting (2:1-2), (2) the illness, problem, or challenge (2:3-4), (3) Jesus' word or act (2:5-11), (4) the miraculous act (2:12), and (5) the response of the witnesses, confirming the miracle (2:12). The distinctive feature of this miracle story is the debate with the scribes in 2:6-10. The exorcism of the unclean spirit from the man in the synagogue in Mark 1:21-28 is intertwined with the report of Jesus' teaching with authority. When Jesus healed the leper (1:40-45), he instructed him to show himself to the priest "as a testimony *against* them" (author's translation; see commentary above). Now, Jesus debates with the scribes over his authority to declare the man's sins forgiven before he heals him.

The story gives evidence of a complicated composition history: (1) the inclusion of a controversy dialogue (2:6-10) within a miracle story is unusual; (2) several phrases are repeated, possibly indicating seams formed by the insertion of new material into the original story; and (3) the story contains one of only two "Son of Man" sayings (2:10, 28) in the first part of Mark. It is difficult to distinguish the development of this story at the time Mark received it from editorial additions he may have made to it.

The repetition of the statement "he said to the paralytic" in 2:5 and 2:10, where the continuity is so rough that it is set off by dashes, has been taken by many interpreters as an indication that the dialogue in the intervening verses was added to the story of the healing of the paralyzed man and the statement was repeated at the end of the dialogue to serve as a transition back to the original story. The healing story reads well if one drops out the insertion and skips from v. 5, "he said to the paralytic," to v. 11, "I say to you, stand up, take your mat and go to your home." It is clear that the controversy dialogue represents an expansion of the original story, but it is difficult to know whether the addition was made by Mark or before Mark received it. In either case, the controversy dialogue is probably a secondary stage in the development of the tradition. It does not have enough context to have been transmitted as an independent unit.

The situation becomes more complicated when one notices other repetitions in these verses: "your sins are forgiven" (vv. 5, 9), "questioning in their hearts/among themselves/in your hearts" (vv. 6, 8), and "stand up (and) take up your mat and walk/go to your home" (vv. 9, 11). These repetitions, however, are a part of the flow of the narration and dialogue, and while they add emphasis they do not seem to mark places where material has been inserted.

Whether Mark expanded the healing story by inserting the challenge-riposte [Challenge-Riposte] in 2:6-10 or merely placed the already expanded story at the beginning of this new section of the Gospel, it builds on the conflict already introduced in Mark 1 and elevates Jesus' authority. The scribes question Jesus' actions, Jesus poses a counter-question, "which is easier" (2:9), Jesus not only heals but pronounces the man's sins forgiven, and Jesus uses the title "Son of Man" in reference to himself in the context of claiming "authority" (2:10). This key term is used earlier in the exorcism story in Mark 1:22 and 27 (see the commentary there). Mark clearly establishes that the miracles confirm Jesus' authority, the authority of his teaching, and his authority to forgive sins.

Sin and sickness were often linked together in Jewish theology, at least in its popular form. In

Challenge-Riposte

"Just as concern for money, paying the bills, or perhaps affording something is perpetual and pervasive in American society, so was the concern about honor in the world of the Gospels. In this competition for honor the game of challenge-riposte is a central phenomenon and one that must always be played out in public. It consists of a challenge (almost any word, gesture, or action) that seeks to undermine the honor of another person and a response that answers in equal measure or ups the ante (and thereby challenges in return). Both positive (gifts, compliments) and negative (insults, dares) challenges must be answered to avoid a serious loss of face.

"In the Synoptic Gospels Jesus demonstrates considerable skill at challenge and riposte and thereby reveals himself to be an honorable man, capable of defending God's honor, his group's honor, and his own honor. The exchange here in Mark 2:6-9 is a good example. In Mark we find these challenge-riposte scenarios presented, first, in an initial set of five: 2:1-12; 2:15-17; 2:18-22; 2:23-28; 3:1-6; and then interspersed throughout the work: 3:20-34; 7:1-8; 10:1-12; 11:27-33; 12:13-17; 12:18-27."

Bruce J. Malina and Richard L. Rohrbaugh, *Social-Science Commentary on the Synoptic Gospels* (Minneapolis: Fortress, 1992), 188.

Healing and Forgiveness

Healing and forgiveness are often closely associated in the Old Testament:

"O Lord, be gracious to me; heal me, for I have sinned against you"; Ps 41:4

[the Lord] "who forgives all your iniquity, who heals all your diseases"; Ps 103:3

"And no inhabitant will say, 'I am sick'; the people who live there will be forgiven their iniquity"; Isa 33:24

"so that they may not turn again and *be forgiven*"; Mark 4:12, quoting Isa 6:10

"and turn—and I would *heal* them"; Matt 13:15, quoting Isa 6:10

---

the Old Testament sin could lead to illness ("some were sick through their sinful ways, and because of their iniquities endured affliction"; Ps 107:17), so healing and forgiveness are often closely associated. [Healing and Forgiveness] In the Gospel of John, Jesus warns the man whom he healed at the Pool of Bethesda, "See, you have been made well! Do not sin any more, so that nothing worse happens to you" (John 5:14). When they pass a man born blind, his disciples echo popular assumptions when they ask Jesus, "Rabbi, who sinned, this man or his parents, that he was born blind?" (John 9:2), but Jesus healed the man, demonstrating that sin lay not in being born blind but in being willfully blind (John 9:39-41).

Jesus' declaration, "Son, your sins are forgiven" (2:5), can be taken either as a divine passive, meaning "God has forgiven your sins," or as a statement on his own authority, meaning "I forgive your sins." The divine passive was often used to avoid a direct reference to the divine name (see 2:20; 3:28; 4:12, 25; etc.).[4] Only God can forgive sins (Exod 34:6-7; Isa 43:25; 44:22), but God's prophets at times announced forgiveness: "Nathan said to David, 'Now the LORD has put away your sin; you shall not die'" (2 Sam 12:13). Even if Jesus used the divine passive, the scribes recognize the authority implied in his statement.

By the time of the New Testament, blasphemy was construed not only as cursing God but as any "violation of the power and majesty of God."[5] The scribes heard Jesus' use of the divine passive as either a claim to be able to pronounce the forgiveness of sins or to speak for God. Either way, for them, Jesus was usurping a divine prerogative. According to levitical law, anyone who blasphemes is to be stoned to death (Lev 24:15-16); rabbinic law specified that blasphemy required that one pronounced "the Name itself" and that the offense was confirmed by witnesses (*m. Sanhedrin* 7.5). The scribes' question, "Who?" advances one of the Gospel's main themes by focusing on the issue of Jesus' identity.

Jesus perceives that the scribes were questioning "in their hearts" (2:6). In doing so, ironically, he manifests a prerogative attributed to God in the Old Testament, "the knower of hearts" (1 Sam 16:7; 1 Kgs 8:39; Pss 7:9; 139:23; Prov 24:12; Jer 11:20).[6] His response is to ask,

The Son of Man

📖 The Son of Man sayings in the Gospels are typically divided into three categories. The fourteen occurrences of the term in Mark include all three categories:

(1) The Earthly Son of Man

Mark 2:10—"The Son of Man has authority on earth to forgive sins"

Mark 2:28—"The Son of Man is lord even of the sabbath"

(2) The Suffering Son of Man

Mark 8:31—"The Son of Man must undergo great suffering, and be rejected by the elders, the chief priests, and the scribes, and be killed, and after three days rise again."

Mark 9:9—"He ordered them to tell no one about what they had seen, until after the Son of Man had risen from the dead."

Mark 9:12—"How then is it written about the Son of Man, that he is to go through many sufferings and be treated with contempt?"

Mark 9:31—"The Son of Man is to be betrayed into human hands, and they will kill him, and three days after being killed, he will rise again."

Mark 10:33—"The Son of Man will be handed over to the chief priests and the scribes, and they will condemn him to death; then they will hand him over to the Gentiles; they will mock him, and spit upon him, and flog him, and kill him; and after three days he will rise again."

Mark 10:45—"The Son of Man came not to be served but to serve, and to give his life a ransom for many."

Mark 14:21—"The Son of Man goes as it is written of him, but woe to that one by whom the Son of Man is betrayed!"

Mark 14:41—"The Son of Man is betrayed into the hands of sinners."

(3) The Coming Son of Man

Mark 8:38—"Those who are ashamed of me and of my words in this adulterous and sinful generation, of them the Son of Man will also be ashamed when he comes in the glory of his Father."

Mark 13:26—"Then they will see 'the Son of Man coming in clouds' with great power and glory."

Mark 14:62—"I am; and 'you will see the Son of Man seated at the right hand of the Power,' and 'coming with the clouds of heaven.'" (Ps 110:1; Dan 7:13-14)

"which is easier, to say to the paralytic, 'Your sins are forgiven,' or to say, 'Stand up and take up your mat and walk'?" (2:9). From a theological perspective, since only God can forgive sins, it would be easier to tell the paralyzed man to stand up and walk. Forgiving sins requires divine authority, whereas healing does not. On the other hand, healing can be verified, whereas forgiveness cannot. It would be easier for a deceiver to claim to forgive than for him to claim to be able to heal. Jesus therefore heals the man (the empirically more difficult) as a demonstration that he has the authority to forgive (the theologically more exclusive act). Healing is also the outward demonstration of wholeness that reflects the internal, redemptive effect of forgiveness.

By healing and forgiving, Jesus both demonstrates his divine authority as the Son of God empowered by the Holy Spirit as the agent of the kingdom and carries out his mission to inaugurate the kingdom. With one exception (Acts 7:56, the only occurrence outside the Gospels), the term "Son of Man" [The Son of Man] occurs exclusively on the lips of Jesus in the New Testament. No one ever addresses him with this title, and Paul does not use it. Part of the explanation for this situation is linguistic: the term derives from Aramaic (*bar enasha*) and is awkward in Greek. In Daniel 7:13, the prophet says, "I saw one like a son of man coming with the clouds of heaven. And he came to the

Ancient One. To him was given dominion and glory and kingship, that all peoples, nations, and languages should serve him." The term is not

a messianic title here, but in the course of time it acquired messianic significance in some contexts. The phrase "on earth" in Mark 2:10, therefore, appears to be a deliberate extension of the assignment of authority "in heaven" to the Son of Man in Daniel 7:13-14.[7] The Similitudes of Enoch speak of a messianic Son of Man [The Messianic Son of Man], but this part of 1 Enoch was not among the fragments of the book discovered at Qumran, leading to suspicion that it was composed later. The history and meaning of term is a matter of great debate. In some contexts (Ezek 2:1, 3, 6, 8, etc.) it means no more than "human being." In later Aramaic texts it appears to be a circumlocution one might use in reference to oneself when referring to one's suffering or honor. Such usage fits the occurrence in Mark 2:10, but elsewhere in Mark it is clear that some of the Son of Man sayings echo Psalm 110:1, Daniel 7:13-14, and the suffering servant in Isaiah. The phrase "on earth" implies a counterpoint to "in heaven," the setting of Daniel's vision in 7:13.

The Messianic Son of Man

"This is the Son of Man, to whom belongs righteousness, and with whom righteousness dwells. And he will open all the hidden storerooms; for the Lord of the Spirits has chosen him, and he is destined to be victorious before the Lord of the Spirits in eternal uprightness. This Son of Man whom you have seen is the One who would remove the kings and the mighty ones from their comfortable seats and the strong ones from their thrones. He shall loose the reigns of the strong and crush the teeth of the sinners. He shall depose the kings from their thrones and kingdoms. For they do not extol and glorify him, and neither do they obey him, the source of their kingship." (*1 En.* 46:3-5)

"For the Son of Man was concealed from the beginning, and the Most High One preserved him in the presence of his power; then he revealed him to the holy and the elect ones. The congregation of the holy ones shall be planted, and all the elect ones shall stand before him. On that day, all the kings, the governors, the high officials, and those who rule the earth shall fall down before him on their faces, and worship and raise their hopes in that Son of Man; they shall beg and plead for mercy at his feet." (*1 En.* 62:7-9; cf. 62:14; 69:27–70:1; 71:17)

Again, some scholars contend that this is a later reflection of the messianic development of the term in the early church, while others believe that Jesus himself was influenced by and understood his role in the light of these biblical motifs. The Son of Man acts as God's agent on the earth: forgiving sins and healing the sick are both works that foreshadow the coming of the kingdom.

Verses 11-12 contain the healing and the response of the bystanders, both typical elements of a healing story. Jesus orders the man to do three things: stand up, take up his mat , and go home (v. 11). Mark's report underscores that his orders were carried out precisely: "And

"Take Up Your Mat"

Christ Healing the Paralytic in Bethesda. 6th c. Early Christian Mosaic. S. Apollinare Nuovo, Ravenna, Italy. (Credit: Scala / Art Resource, NY)

he stood up, and immediately took up the mat and went out before all of them." As a polished unit of oral tradition, the story ends with the result Mark desired from his readers: they all—presumably even the grumbling scribes—were amazed and glorified God. No one had ever seen anything like it before: "the new aeon, which no eye has previously see (Isa 64:4; 1 Cor 2:9), is here breaking in."[8]

Authority to Eat with Outcasts, 2:13-17

The double story of the calling of Levi and Jesus eating with "tax collectors and sinners" takes the modern reader deeper into the world of first-century Galilee. In these stories we meet the tax collectors, "scribes of the Pharisees," and learn about the social and religious practices that governed table fellowship. These brief verses contain four different scenes: (1) Jesus teaching by the Sea of Galilee (v. 13); (2) the call of Levi (v. 14); (3) a meal scene in Levi's house (v. 15); and (4) a controversy dialogue over Jesus' eating with outcasts (vv. 16-17).[9]

Verse 13 serves as a transition from the previous scene. The sea can evoke various associations from its role in the imagery of the Old Testament, as it will later in Mark, but there is no evidence in the present context that it is anything more than a typical setting during Jesus' ministry in Galilee. Although one might assume that the crowd followed Jesus from the house where he healed the paralyzed man, it is more likely that a new scene is being introduced and that the crowd "gathered" around him rather than that it "followed" him (see the role of the crowd in 3:7, 9, 32; 4:1; 6:31-34, 45). Teaching was Jesus' normal response when a crowd gathered around him (4:1-2; 6:2, 6, 34; 10:1).

The calling of Levi closely parallels the earlier calling of the four fishermen (1:16-20), except that Jesus does not commission him to be a "fisher of men." Levi is mentioned only here and in v. 15, and in the parallel account in Luke 5:27

Saint Matthew and the Angel

Michelangelo depicts the calling of St. Matthew, the tax collector, not by an earthly Jesus but by a heavenly being. Matthew is presumably at work recording entries in a tax ledger, but his writing also foreshadows his later work as an evangelist.

Michelangelo Merisi da Caravaggio (1573-1610). *Saint Matthew and the Angel*. S. Luigi dei Francesi, Rome, Italy. (Credit: Scala / Art Resource, NY)

Tax Collectors in Mishnah

"If tax-collectors entered a house (so, too, if thieves restored [stolen] vessels), they may be deemed trustworthy if they say, 'We have not touched.'" (*m. Hagigah* 3.6)

"Men may vow to murderers, robbers, or tax-gatherers that what they have is Heave-offering even though it is not Heave-offering; or that they belong to the king's household even though they do not belong to the king's household. The School of Shammai say: They may so vow in any form of words save in the form of an oath. And the School of Hillel say: Even in the form of an oath." (*m. Nedarim* 3.4)

"None may take change or money from the counter of excisemen or from the wallet of tax-gatherers, or take any alms from them [Since such money is deemed got by robbery]; but it may be taken from them at their house or in the market [When they are not practicing their calling]. If tax-gatherers took a man's ass and gave him another, or if robbers robbed a man of his coat and gave him another, they become his own, since the owner cherishes no hope of recovering them." (*m. Baba Kamma* 10.1-2)

"If tax gatherers entered a house [all that is within it] becomes unclean. . . . What do they render unclean? Foodstuffs and liquids and open earthenware vessels; but couches and seats and earthenware vessels having a tightly stopped-up cover remain clean. If a gentile or a woman was with them all becomes unclean." (*m. Tohoroth* 7.6)

In Herbert Danby, trans., *The Mishnah* (Oxford: Oxford University Press, 1933).

---

and 29. He is called "the son of Alphaeus" only in Mark 2:14 and is not named in the lists of the twelve disciples. James the son of Alphaeus, presumably his brother, was one of the Twelve (Matt 10:3; Mark 3:18; Luke 6:15; Acts 1:13). In an effort to include Levi among the Twelve, some have identified Levi with James ("the son of Alphaeus") or with Matthew, whose name appears in the parallel account in the Gospel that bears his name (Matt 9:9). For the meaning of Jesus' call, "Follow me," see the commentary on 1:16-20. Here again, "follow" is used as a technical term for discipleship: "And he got up and followed him."

Mark reports that Jesus called Levi while Levi was "sitting at the tax booth" (2:14). In actuality, Levi was probably a Jewish toll collector. Direct taxes were collected by tax collectors [Tax Collectors in Mishah] employed by the Romans, while tolls, tariffs, and custom fees were collected at toll booths by toll collectors. Toll collectors [Toll Collectors] paid in advance for the right to collect tolls, which led to widespread corruption, so the toll collectors were scorned because of their dishonesty.

We also meet the Pharisees for the first time in this passage. The Pharisees were pious laypersons who ordered their lives to live in obedience to the Law in every respect. Their sages built up an oral tradition (see Mark 7:3), "a fence around the law," [A Fence around the Law] that interpreted the meaning of each of the laws contained in the books of Moses so that they

Toll Collectors

"One of the chief functions of the prefect of Judea was his role of financial overseer. During the rule of the prefects and procurators the direct taxes, the poll tax and the land tax were not farmed out. The officials in charge of collecting these were in direct employ of the Romans. Though Roman citizenship was not required for the office of tax collector, it was often granted and many of the tax collectors *de facto* were Jews. The tolls and numerous other tariffs were probably at this time auctioned off to the highest bidder, so that *ho telōnēs* [the Greek term in Mark 2:15 and 16] is properly a toll collector and not a tax collector.

"In Galilee at the time of Jesus' ministry the collection of taxes and tolls would have been under the supervision of Antipas. The collection of customs at travel points such as Capernaum would have been the responsibility of the *telōnai*."

John R. Donahue, S.J., "Tax Collectors and Sinners," *Catholic Biblical Quarterly* 33 (1971): 45.

would not inadvertently violate one of them. In the early part of the first century the Pharisees appear to have been particularly concerned about tithing, table fellowship, and maintaining ritual purity. For this reason, Pharisees ate only in their own homes or with other Pharisees. Mark's reference to "the scribes of the Pharisees" is unusual (see Mark 7:1). Many of the Jerusalem scribes were probably priests, but these Galilean scribes were Pharisees.

The transition between vv. 14 and 15 is abrupt. One must assume that in his gratitude, to honor Jesus, or to introduce Jesus to his friends, Levi gave a banquet at his house and invited Jesus and his disciples.

Parenthetically, this is the first time the disciples as a group are mentioned in Mark; the Twelve will not be named until 3:13-19. Verse 15 is actually more ambiguous in Greek than it appears in the English translations, reading literally, "And as he sat [or reclined] in his house," leaving it unclear whether it was Levi's house or Jesus' house. Since we are never told that Jesus had a house (see Mark 2:1; 9:33), and since Luke, one of the first interpreters of the gospel, removes the ambiguity by saying explicitly, "Then Levi gave a great banquet for him in his house" (5:29), we may follow Luke in understanding that Jesus was a guest in Levi's house. The banquet evokes allusions to the great messianic or eschatological banquet at which the chosen will feast while the sinners and Gentiles are excluded. A banquet shall be provided for the righteous, "and from thenceforth they shall never see the faces of the sinners and the oppressors" (*1 Enoch* 62:13).[10] At the banquet at Levi's home, however, tax collectors are invited to the banquet [Tax Collectors at the Banquet] in a dramatic reversal of the popular theological scenario. A banquet in a Galilean village would have been a very public affair. Even those who had not been invited would have come to see the spectacle and watch those who had been invited.

The Pharisees held that the Law brought the possibility of holiness, or conformity with God's intentions and commandments. Only Jews, therefore, could be holy. Gentiles were by definition "sinners," as were all who lived without regard for the Law. That included the openly immoral and dishonest (murderers, robbers, adulterers, deceivers, etc.) and those who practiced one of the despised vocations that were associated with dishonesty (tax collecting, sheep herding, and money lending, but also tanners, camel drivers, and at times even physicians).[11] The Pharisees also regarded as sinners the *Am-haaretz*, the "people of the land," the common peasants and artisans who could not scrupulously maintain ritual purity as the Pharisees did. On the other hand, those who ordered their lives in accord with the Law were righteous (cf. Luke 18:11-12; Phil 3:5-6).

The pharisaic scribes were scandalized that Jesus was eating with "tax collectors and sinners" because by doing so he was crossing the boundary of clean/unclean, flaunting the religious customs of the day, and rendering himself unclean by doing so: "He that undertakes to be trustworthy . . . may not be the guest of an *Am-haaretz*" (*m. Demai* 2.2).[12] When Jesus heard the scribes' question, he responded with the proverb [The Proverb] "Those who are well have no need of a physician, but those who are sick" (2:17).

The rest of the verse applies the proverb to Jesus' eating with the "tax collectors and sinners" by way of metaphor: "I have come to call not the righteous but sinners" (2:17). The saying belongs to a group of sayings in the Synoptic Gospels that begin with "I have come" ["I Have Come"] and define Jesus' mission. The scandal of this good news is both that Jesus

The Proverb

William L. Lane cites two instances of the proverb:

"If they are not sick, why do they need a physician?" (Mekilta to Exod 15:26)

"The physicians, he said, are not to be found among the well but customarily spend their time among the sick." (Pausanias, according to Plutarch, *Apophthegmata Laconica* 230f.)

Healing was also a metaphor for God's redemptive work:

"I am Yahweh your healer." (Exod 15:26)

"May it be Thy will, O Lord my God, that this action may serve to heal me, and do Thou heal me, for Thou, O God, art the true Physician, and Thine healing is true." (*b. Berakoth* 60a).

God is "the only doctor for the sicknesses of the soul" (Philo, *Sacrifices of Abel and Cain* 70).

William L. Lane, *The Gospel according to Mark* (Grand Rapids: Wm. B. Eerdmans, 1974), 104 n. 43.

"I Have Come"

"Do not think that I have come to abolish the law or the prophets; I have come not to abolish but to fulfill." (Matt 5:17)

"Do not think that I have come to bring peace to the earth; I have not come to bring peace, but a sword." (Matt 10:34)

"For I have come to set a man against his father. . . ." (Matt 10:35)

"For the Son of Man came not to be served but to serve, and to give his life a ransom for many." (Mark 10:45; Matt 20:28)

"I came to bring fire to the earth, and how I wish it were already kindled!" (Luke 12:49)

"For the Son of Man came to seek out and to save the lost." (Luke 19:10)

"I have come in my Father's name, and you do not accept me." (John 5:43)

"The Righteous"

"For the life of the righteous (goes on) forever,
    but sinners shall be taken away to destruction,
  and no memory of them will ever be found." (*Pss. Sol.* 13:11)

"For God's mark is on the righteous for (their) salvation.
Famine and sword and death shall be far from the righteous;
    for they will retreat from the devout like those pursued by famine.
But they shall pursue sinners and overtake them,
    for those who act lawlessly shall not escape the Lord's judgment. . . .
And the inheritance of sinners is destruction and darkness,
    and their lawless actions shall pursue them below into Hades." (*Pss. Sol.* 15:6-10)

Domesticating the Tradition

Mark 2:17—"I have come to call not the righteous but sinners." (Matt 9:13b)

Luke 5:32—"I have come to call not the righteous but sinners to repentance."

Luke 19:10—"For the Son of Man came to seek out and to save the lost."

1 Timothy 1:15—"The saying is sure and worthy of full acceptance, that Christ Jesus came into the world to save sinners—of whom I am the foremost."

Barnabas 5:9—"But when he chose out his own Apostles who were to preach his Gospel, he chose those who were iniquitous above all sin to show that 'he came not to call the righteous but sinners.'"

justifies his eating with the outcasts and that he declares that he did not come to call the righteous. The Pharisees would have assumed that they were righteous. Indeed, "the righteous" ["The Righteous"] may have been a self-designation of the Pharisees.[13]

The tension and opposition in the saying in the latter part of v. 17—"not the righteous but sinners"—was typical of Jesus' sayings. Over time, however, the tension was removed. When the righteous were no longer associated with the Pharisees but with believers, the negation "not the righteous" was omitted. Alternatively, the righteous magnified the power of God's grace by pointing to their sinfulness. The history of the transmission of this saying, therefore, provides a fascinating study in how the tradition was domesticated [Domesticating the Tradition] so that it could serve the purposes of the church.

Authority to Dispense with Fasting 2:18-22

Having responded to challenges about his table fellowship, Jesus is now challenged because his disciples do not fast. On closer reading, however, this central unit of the five controversy stories in Mark 2:1–3:6 is concerned with much more than whether Jesus' disciples should fast or not. It unveils the complete incompatibility of the new era inaugurated by Jesus with the religious observances of the old era and intimates that the conflict between the two will result in his being "taken away" from them. In form these verses represent an expanded controversy over fasting (2:18-20) to which a related couplet of sayings has been appended (2:21-22).

Verse 18 introduces the setting and the issue: fasting. Jesus responds with a counter-question (v. 19) and the conclusion that follows from the question. Verse 20 is an appendix or digression that recognizes that for the church there will be a time for fasting later. Verses 21-22 contain related aphorisms or proverbs that deepen and extend the incompatibility of the new and the old, thereby putting the question of fasting in an entirely "new" perspective.

"The Bridegroom's Friends"

AΩ The phrase "bridegroom's friends" translates a phrase that means literally "sons of the bridal-chamber." In order to understand this obscure phrase, one must know how weddings were celebrated among the Jews in the 1st century:

In antiquity a wedding did not celebrate the marriage of two individuals, but of two families. Wedding celebrations were of immense significance as public demonstrations of family honor. Families often went deeply in debt trying to outdo each other in the honorific competition to provide the best wedding the village had ever seen. Because a wedding celebration would often include a whole village, arrangements were usually quite elaborate and could take many days to complete. . . .

In order to . . . ensure a wedding that brought a family public honor, associations (Hebrew *shushbinim*) were formed among village men for the purpose of mutual assistance (probably the ones referred to as the "sons of the bridal-chamber" in Mark 2:19). Those designated by this term usually included close relatives and friends, especially age-mates of the groom, who formed an in-group of celebrants at a wedding feast. The closest of them were sometimes involved in negotiations for a betrothal, and among all of them it was common to send gifts ahead of the wedding that could be used as provisions for the feast.

Each time another member of this in-group got married, reciprocal obligations came into play. . . . Obviously, then, a wedding celebration was not a private family affair. It culminated in festivities at the home of the groom, and everyone in the village participated. The wedding day began with the village women washing the bride in her own home. It was a joyful ritual of preparation that included perfuming, anointing, and dressing the bride. Elaborate clothing and adornment were provided. Then came the "home-taking," a torchlight procession in which the bride was accompanied to the groom's house. There was much singing and dancing as she walked, or even rode in a decorated carriage. If a virgin, she wore her hair loose and a wreath upon her head. Both men and women participated in the procession. The well-known Pharisaic scribes of Jesus' day (Hillel and Shammai) argued over whether it was permissible to exaggerate a bride's beauty during the singing. Roasted ears of grain, wine, and oil were strewn in the path of the procession.

After arriving at the groom's house, the bride was introduced into her husband's family and then the celebration began in the home of the groom. Such wedding celebrations traditionally began on a Wednesday and lasted seven days if the bride was a virgin and if the family and its village had enough resources; they would begin on a Thursday and last three days if the bride was a widow (Judg. 14:12; Tob. 11:19; *m. Ket. 1.1*).

Bruce J. Malina and Richard L. Rohrbaugh, *Social Science Commentary on the Gospel of John* (Minneapolis: Fortress Press, 1998), 70–71.

Fasting had various meanings in first-century Judaism. Generally it was associated with mourning: mourning for the dead (1 Sam 31:13), contrition and submission to God (Ps 35:13; 1 Kgs 21:27). Fasting was also practiced on the Day of Atonement (Lev 16:31; 23:27) and Purim (Esther 4:16). By the first century, the Pharisees also fasted twice a week (Luke 18:12; *Didache* 8.1), on Mondays and Thursdays. Ascetics, like the Essenes, the Therapeutae, Haninah ben Dosa, and John the Baptist (Matt 11:18), were also known for their fasting. Fasting had a different meaning for John's disciples than for the followers of the Pharisees, since John's disciples probably fasted as an expression of repentance and preparation for the coming judgment that John had announced.

Were Jesus' disciples less pious than these other groups? Why did they not fast? Jesus' counter-question employs a striking metaphor for his own messianic role and returns to the basic meaning of fasting. Jesus likens his disciples to the bridegroom's friends ["The Bridegroom's Friends"] at a wedding and thereby casts himself in the role of the

Wedding

"After these things it was reported to Jonathan and his brother Simon, 'The family of Jambri are celebrating a great wedding, and are conducting the bride, a daughter of one of the great nobles of Canaan, from Nadabath with a large escort. . . . They looked out and saw a tumultuous procession with a great amount of baggage; and the bridegroom came out with his friends and his brothers to meet them with tambourines and musicians." (1 Macc 9:37-39)

bridegroom. Wedding [Wedding] imagery was common in connection with the celebration of the end time, but the metaphor of the Messiah as the bridegroom does not appear until much later in Jewish literature. A wedding was a time of joy and celebration for a whole town, so it was unthinkable that anyone would fast during such a time.

Verse 20 can be read in two ways. In the context of Jesus' dispute with his critics—apparently still the scribes and Pharisees (see 2:16, 18)—Jesus knowingly alludes to his own death. In that time, there will be an appropriate occasion for his disciples to fast, when he is "taken from them." In the context of the church in Mark's time the verse may have served as a defense of fasting by Christians when Jesus' pronouncement in the previous verse had seemed to leave no place for it among those who belonged to the new era of the kingdom. Fasting was also practiced in time of war, following the holy war code of ancient Israel, to affirm that one's only hope was in God and to prepare for eschatological redemption (1 Macc 3:47; Josephus, *Life* 290). Therefore, Mark 2:20 may also be a prophetic allusion to the Jewish Revolt of AD 66–70, about the time when the Gospel was written.[14]

Verses 21 and 22 contain two proverbs that underscore the incompatibility of the old and the new. The two sayings also occur in the Gospel of Thomas (47), but in reverse order. They may have once circulated independently. In the present context, the two proverbs have the effect of underscoring the incompatibility of fasting with the celebration of the new era. It is not just that fasting would be inappropriate; it belongs to an old order that cannot even be grafted onto the new. The term for "patch" in Greek means literally "a thing put upon." The new cannot simply be added or put on the old. Galilee was known for its linen and Judea for its wool, and fullers served as a kind of ancient dry cleaning service (see [Fuller]). New material, particularly if it were not fine material, would shrink. Therefore, if one patched an old garment with new cloth, when it was washed, the new would shrink and tear away from the old. Ironically, the new will not repair the old; it will destroy it.

Similarly, one never put new wine into old (leather) wineskins. The old skins would have grown stiff and lost their elasticity. The new wine put off gas in the fermentation process, which could burst the old skins, so new wine had to be put into new wineskins. [Wineskins] Not only could the new not be put upon the old; the old is unusable in producing the new. Each of the three sayings that respond to the question about fasting, therefore, serve to drive the wedge deeper, separating Jesus and his mission from the established religious traditions and practices: (1) the times made the old no longer appropriate—like fasting at a wedding; (2) the new cannot simply be stitched onto the old—like a patch on an old garment; and (3) the old is of no use for the new—as useless as old wineskins. The depth of the conflict between Jesus and the authorities now lies fully exposed. For Mark it may also have meant that there could be no going back. Gentile Christianity could neither be grafted onto Judaism nor contained by Jewish structures. New wine required new wineskins.

Authority over the Sabbath, 2:23-28

A minor incident in a grain field gave Jesus the occasion to define religious priorities. This fourth of the controversy stories in Mark 2:1–3:6 continues the theme of eating (2:13-17—eating with outcasts; 2:18-22—fasting). Verse 23 defines the setting, and v. 24 poses the accusing question. In the remaining verses Jesus offers three responses: (1) an appeal to the example of David, (2) a pronouncement regarding the Sabbath and human need, and (3) a pronouncement on the authority of the Son of Man. The greatest challenge for the interpreter is how to understand the relationship among these three responses. Because the pronouncement story would have been complete without vv. 27 and 28, these latter two sayings, which may have circulated independently, are probably secondary additions added either by Mark or a pre-Markan compiler.

One Sabbath, as Jesus was walking through the grain fields, his disciples began to "make a way" picking (and presumably eating) the grain. The expression "make a way" is somewhat unusual and reminds the reader of the quotation of Isaiah 40:3 in Mark 1:3—"prepare *the way* of the Lord, *make* his paths straight"—because it echoes words from each line of this verse. Rather than following Jesus, therefore, the disciples may have been making a path for him.

Wineskins

"The first stage of fermentation, which began as soon as six hours after the pressing, took place in the lower vat itself. Then the wine was transferred to jars (Jer. 13:12; 48:11) or skins for further fermentation and storage. These skins were usually made from whole goat hides, the neck and the feet being tied. Naturally an opening was left to allow for the escape of gases formed by fermentation. Elihu, 'full of words,' says:

Behold, my heart is like wine that has no vent; like new wineskins, it is ready to burst. (Job 32:18-19)"

J. F. Ross, "Wine," *IDB* (Nashville: Abingdon Press, 1962), 4:850.

(Credit: Barclay Burns)

A Neighbor's Field

"If you go into your neighbor's vineyard, you may eat your fill of grapes, as many as you wish, but you shall not put any in a container. If you go into your neighbor's standing grain, you may pluck the ears with your hand, but you shall not put a sickle to your neighbor's standing grain." (Deut 23:24-25)

Picking grain from a neighbor's field [A Neighbor's Field] was not against the law, but picking grain was one of the thirty-nine varieties of work that was forbidden on the Sabbath (*m. Shabbath* 7.2; cf. Exod 34:21). Moses and Aaron allowed the congregation of Israel to stone a man to death for gathering sticks on the Sabbath (Num 15:32-36). Most of the references to the Sabbath occur early in Mark (1:21; 2:23-28; 3:1-6; 6:2; and 16:1-2). Other than healing, this is the only other offense for which Jesus is accused of Sabbath violation, and significantly both are responses to human needs. The Pharisees, whom we must presume were watching Jesus—even in a grain field—question Jesus about his disciples' actions because as their master or teacher he would have been responsible for their conduct. By making the issue the disciples' conduct (cf. 2:18), the pronouncement story may have been used to justify the early Christians' departures from Jewish Sabbath observances. The term "lawful" ["Lawful"] or "permitted" in v. 24 implies a transgression of the Mosaic Law. Jesus' answer, "have you not read?" implies an ironic rebuke (cf. 12:10, 26). If they raise an issue on the basis of the books of Moses, they should also have read what David did. God had made a covenant with the house of David (2 Sam 7:5-16), so identification with David always conferred monarchical authority. Here Jesus appeals to David's action in justification of his own, and later Jesus will be hailed as the "son of David" (see 10:47-48; 11:10; 12:35, 37).

"Lawful" in Mark

AΩ "Look, why are they doing what is not *lawful* on the Sabbath?" (Mark 2:24)

"He entered the house of God, when Abiathar was high priest, and ate the bread of the Presence, which is not *lawful* for any but the priests to eat." (Mark 2:26)

"Is it *lawful* to do good or to do harm on the Sabbath, to save life or to kill?" (Mark 3:4)

"It is not *lawful* for you to have your brother's wife." (Mark 6:18)

"Is it *lawful* for a man to divorce his wife?" (Mark 10:2)

"Is it *lawful* to pay taxes to the emperor or not?" (Mark 12:14)

In defense of the disciples, Jesus cites the account of David entering the temple at Nob and taking the "bread of the presence" [Bread of the Presence] for his men (1 Sam 21:1-6). This bread was sacred—it had been devoted to the service of God. Some interpreters have argued that David's taking of the bread occurred on the Sabbath because fresh bread was baked every Friday in preparation for the Sabbath, but the parallel between the two incidents lies in the supplying of sustenance even when ritual law is violated in the process. Jesus was providing for his disciples, just as David provided for his men.

One of the anomalies of this passage is that it names Abiathar as the high priest when David took the bread of the presence, but Abimelech is the priest named in 1 Samuel 21:1-2. Abiathar (1 Sam 22:20) was

Bread of the Presence

AΩ "According to the priestly regulations (which may not have been codified until after David's time), twelve cakes of pure wheat flour were to be baked every Friday. As part of the Sabbath observance on Friday evening, the warm loaves were placed in two rows (or perhaps, 'two piles'—the word means 'arrangement') before the Lord. The bread was accompanied by frankincense, all placed upon a rather small table covered with gold plate. On the following Sabbath, fresh bread was offered, and the old bread was removed (1 Sam 21:6) for distribution to the priests. The gift of the bread as provision for the priests is significant because it makes a direct statement that God was not expected to eat the bread (as other religions expected of food placed before their gods). Rather, the bread was symbolic of God's provision for Israel and the mutual covenant between them.

"Rules" governing the preparation and use of the bread of the Presence (called 'shewbread' in the KJV) are found in Exod 25:30 and Lev 24:5-9, which requires that each loaf should contain 1/5 of an ephah of choice flour. Since an ephah may have been about 7/10 of a bushel (dry measure equivalents are not certain), this represented about 3 quarts—or about 3 pounds—of flour for each loaf. The resulting loaves would have been huge, rendering their symbolic presence highly visible and providing a significant amount of food for the priests (see G. J. Wenham, *The Book of Leviticus* [NICOT; Grand Rapids: Eerdmans, 1979], 309-10). In later years, certain kindred of the Kohathites were responsible for preparing this bread (1 Chr 9:32)."

Tony W. Cartledge, *1 & 2 Samuel* (Smyth and Helwys Bible Commentary; Macon GA: Smyth & Helwys, 2001), 253.

the son of Abimelech and the better known of the two, which may account for the confusion. The manuscript variants in v. 26 represent scribal efforts to correct the mistaken identification.

Verse 27 contains the first of two pronouncements on the Sabbath that are appended to the story. As with Jesus' explanations of the practice of fasting (2:19-20) and the provisions for marriage and divorce (10:1-9), it returns to the original, divine purpose for the principle of Sabbath rest. Although the Sabbath was created after humankind (Gen 2:2-3), humanity was not made to honor the Sabbath. Rather, the Sabbath was a gift from God. The rabbis interpreted the Sabbath requirement as a gift to sanctify and bless Israel (see *Jub.* 2:17-33). A similar pronouncement on the Sabbath, attributed to Rabbi Simeon ben Menasya (c. AD 180), appears in the Mekilta, the rabbinic commentary on Exodus: "The Sabbath is delivered over for your sake, but you are not delivered over to the Sabbath."[15] The parallel may be superficial, however, since it applies to saving a life on the Sabbath. The Sabbath restrictions were suspended by the Maccabees, who agreed that they could fight on the Sabbath when threatened (1 Macc 2:34-41). Similarly, healing was permitted if a person were mortally ill ("whenever there is doubt whether life is in danger this overrides the Sabbath," *m. Yoma* 8.6), a woman giving birth could be attended on the Sabbath (*m. Shabbath* 18.3), rescue operations were permitted if a fire broke out on the Sabbath (*m. Shabbath* 16.1-7), and circumcision was to take place on the eighth day, even if it were the Sabbath (Gen 17:10-12; Lev 12:3; Phil 3:5; *m. Shabbath* 18.3; 19.1-3).[16]

Jesus' pronouncement was radically different from these exceptions to the Sabbath regulations because it allowed the Sabbath to be superseded by ordinary human need (hunger), not just by a critical need in a life-and-death situation. In so doing, he placed the religious priority on meeting the basic human needs of others rather than on ritual observance, even of the Sabbath. God is served above all when, out of love, religious persons serve the needs of others. The Sabbath is not to be taken lightly ("the Sabbath was made for humankind"), but Sabbath observance should not supersede meeting human needs ("and not humankind for the Sabbath").

The third pronouncement on the Sabbath (v. 28) builds on the other two in context, although it may once have circulated as an independent saying. The first pronouncement (vv. 25-26) justifies superseding the Sabbath in this particular instance on the basis of an appeal to the example of David. The second pronouncement extends the argument by universalizing it: the Sabbath was created to serve humankind, not vice versa. Therefore, by implication, Sabbath observance should always be secondary to meeting human needs, one's own or those of others. The third pronouncement is christological: the Son of Man has authority over the Sabbath. For the use of "Son of Man" in Mark, see the commentary on Mark 2:10. The force of the first word in v. 28 is important; it normally introduces a result clause or expresses a logical consequence. The question may be raised how v. 28 follows from v. 27, or how the claim of v. 28 is significant in light of the prior claim that the Sabbath is secondary to the needs of any and every human being. (In the first-century context, it would have been understood that Sabbath observance applied only to Jews, not Gentiles.) One can make sense of the argument by the following line of reasoning: Jesus had just shown that if David could supersede the Sabbath law in order to meet the needs of his men, then Jesus could too. The principle, Jesus declared, was that the Sabbath was created to serve human needs. By pronouncing when the Sabbath could be superseded, Jesus was in effect demonstrating that as the Son of Man he had authority over the Sabbath.

The christological focus of this conclusion is consistent with that of each of the preceding sections of Mark 2. As the Son of Man Jesus had authority to heal and to forgive sins on earth (2:10). By having table fellowship with "tax collectors and sinners," he acted appropriately and authoritatively as a physician among the sick, a savior among sinners (2:17). He was the messianic bridegroom, ushering in the eschatological celebration (2:19). His work could not be grafted onto the old or contained by it (2:21-22). His authority was even greater than that of David; it was the authority of the Son of Man.

CONNECTIONS

Mark 2:1-12

The story of the healing of the paralytic is a hopeful story. Friends have faith, Jesus heals and forgives, and it ends with everyone praising God. It also offers a great deal of food for thought. First, it illustrates faith in action. Given the context of the story, we can only assume that the people in Capernaum had seen or heard of Jesus healing others. The faith of the friends who carried the paralyzed man to Jesus was probably as simple as it was pure. They knew or cared nothing about the fine points of Christology that would define later creeds and theological debates. They just knew that Jesus could heal him, if they could only bring him to Jesus. In this respect they illustrate the faith community at its best, caring for the sick and for friends who need Jesus. Bringing persons in need to Jesus is also an act of prayer: it can be enacted through prayer or motivated by prayer, but that is what the church does when it prays for persons in need—it brings them to Jesus.

The friends also illustrate the nature of faith. When their initial intentions were blocked by the crowd around the house, they improvised.[17] Sometimes faith requires that we improvise. What do you do when the economy is bad and you lose your job? What do you do when Mother falls and breaks her hip and can't care for Dad anymore? What do you do when circumstances block your well-laid plans? You improvise. You find another way, you do something you would not have thought of otherwise. You keep on finding a way to make life work and take care of your loved ones and those who depend on you, and you don't give up the confidence that life matters, the hope that things will work out, or the conviction that Jesus' love is unfailing.

When Jesus became aware of the scribes' questions, he asked, "Which is easier?" As children of modernity (or post-modernity) we are so preoccupied with the question of miracles and the assumptions of natural law that like the scribes we may miss the wonder of the miracle of forgiveness. What does our experience of being forgiven, or being able truly to forgive one who has hurt or wronged us, say about the reality of God's love? Where does the capacity to forgive come from? If we know that God has forgiven us, even though there is no basis on which we might justify or merit God's forgiveness, then we have experienced something that puts the world in an entirely new perspective. So which is easier to believe, that Jesus healed a paralyzed man or that he forgives sins—even our sins?

Mark 2:13-17

The story of Jesus eating with tax collectors and sinners illustrates two paradoxes: the paradox of holiness and the paradox of righteousness. Being "a holy people" (1 Pet 2:5, 9-10; Hos 2:23) has often been interpreted, from the Pharisees to the Puritans and by many today, to mean that one must keep oneself separate from and "unstained by the world" (Jas 1:27). When that happens, piety turns inward and loses sight of its transforming mission. The paradox of holiness is that the more a person, or a community of believers, comes to appreciate the character of God and grows in Christlikeness, the more God's love will drive them outside the religious community to serve and mediate God's love to the wretched and the despised. All too often, those who cross ethnic, racial, economic, and social barriers following the mandate of love are criticized by other members of the religious community, and usually by persons in their own religious tradition.

The paradox of righteousness [The Paradox of Righteousness] is that it leads all too easily to pride and self-righteousness. The more one's life, values, and activities are shaped by obedience, discipline, and faithfulness, the more one may be tempted to feel superior to others less faithful. True righteousness, however, is not a result of one's faithfulness but of God's spirit working within the human person. Self-righteousness, on the other hand, prevents one from humbly depending on God's mercy and cuts off the lifeline of righteousness. No human achievement of righteousness can ensure one's salvation. As a result, the righteous stand in as great a need of mercy as sinners, yet they are less open to it and less grateful for it. The story of Jesus healing the man born blind in John 9 makes the same point. At the end of the story, Jesus says, "I came into this world for judgment so that those who do not see may see, and those who do see may become blind." The Pharisees ask, "Surely we are not blind, are we?" and Jesus answers, "If you were blind, you would not have sin. But now that you say, 'We see,' your sin remains" (John 9:39-41).

The Paradox of Righteousness

"Among those who need the new relationship to God Jesus also and especially numbers the righteous. In doing so He does not dispute their righteousness or call it sin. But He judges it in respect of its nature. . . . The reason for this is to be found in the egoistic nature of this righteousness, which is satisfied with the fulfillment of the divine commands and which thus becomes inwardly self-confident, and outwardly proud and pitiless. Such emphasis on oneself and one's achievements inevitably leads to an attitude in which one does not bow before God but treats with Him. . . . His ultimate accusation was that there is not here the serious opposition to sin which is meet and proper for the sake of God, so that a true righteousness is achieved, but it is a righteousness which measures up only to human standards and does not satisfy the divine judgment. This insight leads Jesus sharply to call the pious and righteous as well to repentance, not for their sin but for their righteousness, which prevents them from seeing clearly either the greatness of God or their own situation."

Karl Heinrich Rengstorf, "*hamartōlos*," *TDNT* 1:331–32.

Mark 2:18-22

This paragraph is the reveille that announces the arrival of a new day. There can be no delaying, no waiting until tomorrow to start living by one's new priorities. Neither can one go on living with the comfortable habits, values, and relationships that belong to the old order. A new day has come. Jesus marks the arrival of the kingdom in history and in one's individual life. The kingdom requires a radical break with the old and an opening of one's life completely to the new leadings of God's spirit.

The challenge for organized religion has always been that it has difficulty distinguishing the new wine from the wineskins. The forms and practices of religion that served so well in one generation can become impediments for the next. The new wine is always the prompting of God's spirit to love and worship God, to find the purpose of life in living in response to the grace of God revealed in Jesus Christ, and to share God's grace and love with others. All the rest is wineskins: the forms of worship, the organizations, and the influence of social patterns on religious practice are all wineskins that change from generation to generation. But the sad truth is that many religious communities spend most of their energy dealing with debates over wineskins rather than celebrating the gift of the new wine.

Mark 2:23-28

The issue of Sabbath observance has lost significance for most Christians. Sabbath observance was replaced early on by worship on Sunday, the day of Jesus' resurrection. Even in the memory of recent generations, there were restrictions in Christian families about forms of recreation (such as card playing or fishing) on Sunday. Sunday was a day for worship, rest, and family. With the pace of modern life, the extension of business hours on Sunday for many stores and service providers, and the general influence of secularism, Sunday has become no different from any other day except that church services are held on Sunday.

Perhaps it is time that the church rediscovered the gift of the Sabbath, the creation of a day of rest. Even in generations when the pace of life was much, much slower, the Sabbath was a gift that gave individuals and families the opportunity to be at home together, to rest from the week, to worship and pray, and to walk, talk, and eat together. Is it not ironic that in a time when more people take tranquilizers and antacids to relieve the stress of the pace of modern life, so many Christians neglect the gift of the Sabbath?

The fact that "the Son of Man is Lord even of the Sabbath" (v. 28) is no reason for believers not to observe a Sabbath every week. The emphasis of the message of this text should not be put on our freedom from Sabbath observance but on the good news that "the Sabbath was made for humankind." It is one of God's most gracious gifts and one not to be neglected.

NOTES

[1] F. L. Cross and E. A. Livingstone, eds., *The Oxford Dictionary of the Christian Church*, 2nd ed. (Oxford: Oxford University Press, 1974), 798-99; Alec Gilmore, *A Dictionary of the English Bible and Its Origins* (Sheffield: Sheffield Academic Press, 2000), 42, 101.

[2] The definitive work on Mark 2:1–3:6 is Joanna Dewey, *Markan Public Debate: Literary Technique, Concentric Structure, and Theology in Mark 2:1–3:6* (SBLDS 48; Chico: Scholars Press, 1980), who finds evidence of a concentric structure in this section.

[3] See Sharyn Dowd's summary of Joanna Dewey's analysis in *Reading Mark* (Macon: Smyth & Helwys, 2000), 22-23.

[4] See Joachim Jeremias, *New Testament Theology: The Proclamation of Jesus* (New York: Charles Scribner's Sons, 1971), 9-14.

[5] H. W. Beyer, "*blasphēmeō*," *TDNT* 1:622.

[6] Robert A. Guelich, *Mark 1–8:26* (WBC 34A; Dallas: Word, 1989), 88.

[7] Craig Evans, *Mark 8:27–16:20* (WBC 34B; Nashville: Thomas Nelson, 2001), 2002-03.

[8] Joel Marcus, *Mark 1–8* (AB 27; New York: Doubleday, 2000), 224, quoting W. Schmithals, *Das Evangelium nach Markus* (Ökumenischer Taschenbuchkommentar zum Neuen Testament; Gütersloh: Mohn, 1979), 1:163.

[9] Marcus, *Mark 1–8*, 229.

[10] James H. Charlesworth, ed., *The Old Testament Pseudepigrapha* (Garden City NY: Doubleday, 1983), 1:44.

[11] See Joachim Jeremias, *Jerusalem in the Time of Jesus* (trans. F. H. and C. H. Cave; Philadelphia: Fortress, 1969), 303-12.

[12] Herbert Danby, trans., *The Mishnah* (Oxford: Oxford University Press, 1933), 21.

[13] Jeremias, *New Testament Theology*, 116.

[14] Marcus, *Mark 1–8*, 236.

[15] Mekilta, *Shabbata* I to Exod 31:14, cited by William L. Lane, *The Gospel according to Mark* (NICNT; Grand Rapids: Wm. B. Eerdmans, 1974), 119.

[16] Eduard Lohse, "*sabbaton*," *TDNT* 7:14.

[17] Marcus, *Mark 1–8*, 220: "Jesus perceives this improvisation as an expression of faith."

THE COMING KINGDOM
BRINGS DIVISIONS

Mark 3:1-35

The effect of Jesus' revelation of the kingdom was to call some to discipleship while exposing the hardness of heart in others. In Luke, Jesus says that he has not come to bring peace but division (11:51) and that Satan would sift them all like wheat (22:31). In the Gospel of John, the light shines in the darkness, and some "loved darkness rather than light because their deeds were evil" (3:19). The same motif is evident in Mark, and especially in this chapter. The authorities watch Jesus to see whether he will heal on the Sabbath, then make plans to kill him (3:1-6). Nevertheless, Jesus extends his healing ministry (3:7-12) and calls the twelve disciples (3:13-19). When he goes home, the crowds press about him, but scribes from Jerusalem say, "He has Beelzebul" (3:22), and when his family comes, apparently wanting to take him away, Jesus says that his real family is those who do the will of his Father (3:31-35).

COMMENTARY

Doing Good and Doing Harm on the Sabbath, 3:1-6

At the end of the previous paragraph, Jesus declares, "the Son of Man is Lord even of the Sabbath" (2:28). The healing of the man with the withered hand on the Sabbath now illustrates Jesus' lordship while it exposes opposing views regarding the priority of Sabbath observance or healing. Mark 3:1-6 concludes the series of controversy stories that set Mark 2:1–3:6 off as a distinct unit. Parallels between the first and the last stories in this unit can also be detected. Both the healing of the paralytic (2:1-12) and the healing of the man with the withered hand (3:1-6) contain elements of a controversy dialogue embedded in the healing narrative. The controversies concern Jesus' authority vis-à-vis the law. Can he forgive sins? Can he heal on the Sabbath? In both, Jesus' opponents watch him and Jesus challenges them with a question, but they make no response. Jesus tells the man in need to rise (2:11; 3:3), and in both accounts Jesus heals with a command.

Withered Hand

"In the Gospel which the Nazarenes and the Ebionites use, which we have recently translated out of Hebrew into Greek, and which is called by most people the authentic (Gospel) of Matthew, the man who had the withered hand is described as a mason who pleaded for help in the following words: I was a mason and earned (my) living with (my) hands; I beseech thee, Jesus, to restore to me my health that I may not with ignominy have to beg for my bread." Jerome, *Commentary on Matthew*, on 12:13, in Wilhelm Schneemelcher, ed., *New Testament Apocrypha* (English trans. ed. R. McL. Wilson; rev. ed.; Louisville: Westminster/John Knox Press, 1991), 1:160.

Withered Hand, Withered Minds

Athanasius, bishop of Alexandria in the 4th century, commented, "In the synagogue of the Jews was a man who had a withered hand. If he was withered in his hand, the ones who stood by were withered in their minds."

Athanasius, *Homilies* 28, in Thomas C. Oden and Christopher A. Hall, eds., *Ancient Christian Commentary on Scripture: New Testament II, Mark* (Downers Grove IL: InterVarsity Press, 1998), 37.

The Penalty for Sabbath Violation

"You shall keep the Sabbath, because it is holy for you; everyone who profanes it shall be put to death; whoever does any work on it shall be cut off from among the people. Six days shall work be done, but the seventh day is a Sabbath of solemn rest, holy to the Lord; whoever does any work on the Sabbath day shall be put to death." (Exod 31:14-15)

"These are they that are to be stoned: . . . and he that profanes the Sabbath. . . ." (*m. Sanhedrin* 7.4)

Herbert Danby, trans., *The Mishnah* (Oxford: Oxford University Press, 1931), 391.

This time, however, instead of responding in amazement, Jesus' opponents plot to kill him.

Although the translations obscure this "defect" in an effort to improve Mark's style, every sentence in this story starts with the conjunction "and." Mark does not specify whether the healing took place in the synagogue in Capernaum, as the reader may naturally assume based on the references to the synagogue there in 1:21, 23, 29, or in some other town in Galilee (see 1:39). This time, Jesus takes the initiative toward a man with a withered hand. Although the legend that the man was a mason is apocryphal [Withered Hand], it is true that in a society where most men worked with their hands, having a withered hand would have meant that the man was prevented from working and was therefore reduced to begging.

Jesus' opponents, presumably the Pharisees (2:24; 3:6), watched Jesus for any violation they might use against him. [Withered Hand, Withered Minds] Healing on the Sabbath was permitted only in critical cases in which the person might not live until the Sabbath had passed. Legally, violation of the Sabbath was punishable by death [The Penalty for Sabbath Violation], but in practice stoning a person for Sabbath violation was probably rare. The Mishnah specifies that a warning must be given first (*m. Sanh.* 7.8).

Just as a prophet had withered Jeroboam's hand (1 Kgs 13:4) to demonstrate God's protection of the prophet, so Jesus restored a man's hand to demonstrate God's outrage against those who would use religious prescriptions to block the relief of suffering and the restoration of wholeness. Jesus first called the man to rise and stand "in the middle" (3:3), either so that there would be no question of his healing in secret or as an effort to soften the hearts of his critics. [Soften the Hearts]

The distinguishing feature of this healing miracle is Jesus' response to his opponents. He asks a double question about what is permitted on the Sabbath. Actually, the relationship to the Sabbath only intensifies the ethical question that might be applied universally: to do good or to do evil, to save life or to kill? The second half of the question intensifies the alternatives posed by the first half, just as the application of the alternatives is intensified by the fact that it is the Sabbath. The peculiar relevance of the question lies in the provision for doing work on the Sabbath if by doing so one might save a life. By implicitly appealing to this provision in the case of a man with a withered hand, Jesus was radically expanding what might be considered saving a life. Interpreters have debated whether there is also an implicit accusation or irony in Jesus' question. His intent was to heal and restore the man, while his opponents' intent was to catch him in a violation of the Sabbath so that they might kill him. So who was keeping the Sabbath and who was violating it? What is permitted on the Sabbath? [What Is Permitted?]

> **Soften the Hearts**
>
> "Note the tender compassion of the Lord when he deliberately brought the man with the withered hand right into their presence. He hoped that the mere sight of the misfortune might soften them, that they might become a little less spiteful by seeing the affliction, and perhaps out of sorrow mend their own ways. But they remained callous and unfeeling."
>
> Chrysostom, *Gospel of St. Matthew*, Homily 40.1, in Thomas C. Oden and Christopher A. Hall, eds., *Ancient Christian Commentary on Scripture: New Testament II, Mark* (Downers Grove IL: InterVarsity Press, 1998), 38.

> **What Is Permitted?**
>
> "Moreover R. Mattithiah b. Heresh said: If a man has a pain in his throat they may drop medicine into his mouth on the Sabbath, since there is doubt whether life is in danger, and whenever there is doubt whether life is in danger this overrides the Sabbath."
>
> *m. Yoma* 8.6, in Herbert Danby, trans., *The Mishnah* (Oxford: Oxford University Press, 1931), 172.

Faced with a question that unmasked their evil intentions while justifying Jesus' healing of the man with the withered hand, his opponents were silent. When Jesus perceives that his opponents are challenging him, he responds with a question (2:6-10, 16-17, 18-19, 24-26), but when Jesus puts a question to them, they are silent. The silencing of his opponents fits a pattern in Mark. Jesus silences unclean spirits (1:25, 34) and a storm at sea (4:39). When he asks the disciples what they had been talking about (when they had been discussing which of them was the greatest), they were silent (9:34), but when the people tell the blind Bartimaeus to be silent, Jesus invites him to speak (10:48). Ironically, though, Jesus remains silent before those who bear false witness against him (14:61).

> **Jesus Was Angry**
>
> Matthew and Luke omit Mark's reference to Jesus' anger:
>
> Mark 3:5—"He looked around at them with anger."
> See Matthew 12:9-14
> Luke 6:10—"After looking around at all of them. . . ."

Jesus' response to their silent malevolence is anger and grief. Mark is the only Gospel that explicitly says Jesus was angry. [Jesus Was Angry] Anger is implicit in such actions as Jesus' demonstration in the temple, but the Gospels are reticent to report Jesus' anger. The New Testament recognizes, however, that anger is not in and of itself evil but that anger can be used redemptively (see Eph 4:26).

Jesus is also grieved at his opponents' "hardness of heart." The phrase evokes memories of Pharaoh's hardness of heart in Exodus (7:3, 13, 22; 8:15, 19, 32) and Israel's hardness of heart in response to the prophets (Jer 7:24; 9:14; 13:10; 16:12). Hardness of heart is at times willful rejection of God's redemptive work and at other times the inability to grasp the significance of God's activity (see Isa 6:10). Jesus is therefore both angered and grieved by his opponents. Even the disciples were afflicted with hardness of heart (6:52; 8:17).

Moved by compassion, anger, and grief, Jesus commands the man to stretch out his hand. Because the healing is accomplished by this verbal command, rather than by touching or anointing, it would have been difficult to demonstrate that Jesus had violated the prohibition against doing work on the Sabbath.[1] When the man stretched out his hand, however, it was restored. ["Restored"]

"Restored"

AΩ The verb translated "restored" (*apokathistēmi*) is used in two other contexts in Mark: when the blind man's sight is fully restored (8:25) and in Jesus' eschatological prediction that Elijah will come first to restore all things (9:12). Similarly, in the book of Acts, the disciples ask Jesus if it was the time when he would restore the kingdom to Israel (Acts 1:6).

Bested both by being unable to answer Jesus' question about the Sabbath and by being unable to catch Jesus doing work on the Sabbath, the Pharisees and the Herodians immediately begin to plot how they might destroy Jesus. From this point on the shadow of the cross falls across the Gospel story. We know that Jesus' opponents are plotting his death. The escalating conflict in the series of controversy stories in Mark 2:1–3:6 has reached its conclusion, but with a twist. The followers of Herod—a political group—have been introduced for the first time. Their reasons for wanting to destroy Jesus are not explained, though later in the narrative we may draw some inferences about their motives when Mark reports the death of John the Baptist at Herod's hands (6:14-29). At this point it is simply ominous that a religious group and a political group have entered into collusion against Jesus (see later references to the Pharisees and Herod or the Herodians in Mark 8:15; 12:13). [Herodians]

Withdrawal to the Sea, 3:7-12

Like the summary section in Mark 1:14-15, these verses serve as a bridge, drawing together themes from the preceding section while introducing motifs that will be found in the next section of the Gospel. Commentators have debated how much of this summary section is drawn from tradition and how much comes from Mark. Mark 3:7, 9-10 bear marks of traditional material, while Mark's hand is more visible in vv. 8 and 11-12.[2] Five words in the traditional core appear nowhere else in Mark: the Greek terms for "departed," "[little] boat," "have ready," "crush," and "pressed upon."

In structure, this summary section has three sections, each of which has two parts:

Herodians

The only reference to the "Herodians" outside the New Testament is found in Josephus, *J.W.* 1.319: "Infuriated by his discomfiture, he [Machaeras, Herod's ally] killed all the Jews whom he met on his march, not even sparing the Herodians, but treating all alike as friends of Antigonus." Josephus also refers to "the partisans of Herod" in *Ant*. 14.450. The Herod to whom Mark refers was Herod Antipas, Tetrarch of Galilee and one of the sons of Herod the Great:

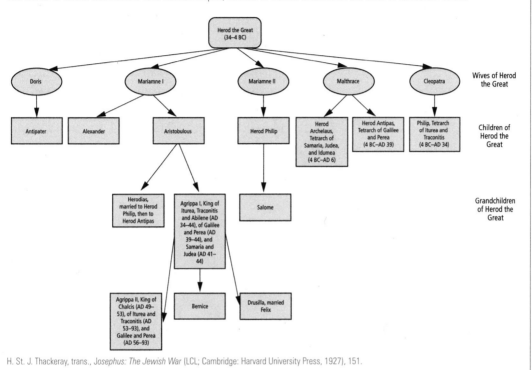

H. St. J. Thackeray, trans., *Josephus: The Jewish War* (LCL; Cambridge: Harvard University Press, 1927), 151.

I. Withdrawal to the sea (v. 7) and list of regions from which the crowds came (v. 8)

II. Instruction to secure a boat (v. 9) and report of healing activity (v. 10)

III. Confession of the unclean spirits (v. 11) and silencing of the spirits (v. 12)

Following the geographical notices of vv. 7 and 8, Mark summarizes first the human response to Jesus' ministry and then the demonic response.[3]

In Mark, as in the other Gospels, Jesus periodically attempts to withdraw from the crowds, sometimes unsuccessfully (1:35; possibly 2:13; 4:35-36; 6:31; 6:46; possibly 7:24; 8:13; possibly 8:27; 9:2; and 14:32). The sea (of Galilee) was the site of the calling of the first disciples (1:16-20; 2:13) in the preceding section, and it will be the place of teaching (4:1) and storm, miracle and boundary crossing in the coming chapters (4:35-41; 5:1, 13, 21; 6:45-52; 8:13). The disciples, who are

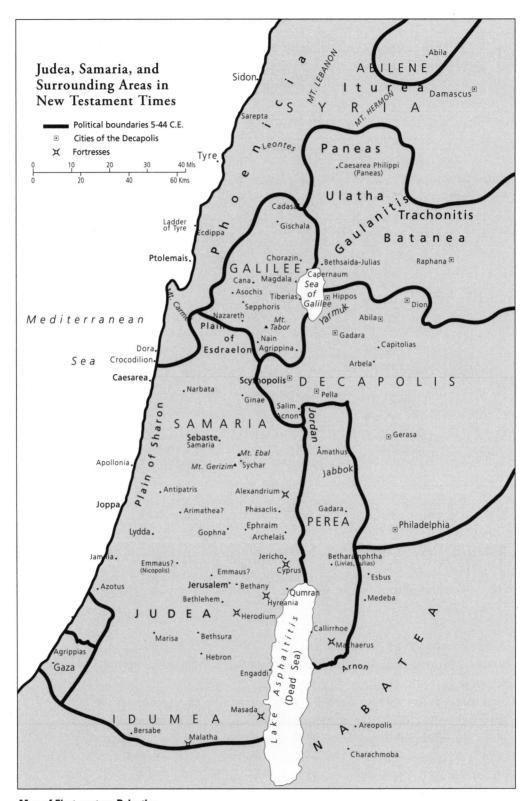

Map of First-century Palestine

not mentioned in Mark 3:1-6, are reintroduced at this point, perhaps anticipating Jesus' appointment of the Twelve in Mark 3:13-19.

The list of the areas from which the crowds came presents its own enigmas: Why are these areas included and not others? Do they bear some relationship to the areas of Jesus' ministry, the extent of Israel or Jewish communities, or the locales of early Christian churches? Seven locales are listed: Galilee, Judea, Jerusalem, Idumea, Transjordan, Tyre, and Sidon. From Galilee, the author looks first to the south, then to the southeast, and then to the north. Notably missing from the list are Samaria (neither Samaria nor Samaritans are ever mentioned in Mark), the Decapolis (5:20; 7:31), and Caesarea Philippi (8:27).

The position of Galilee and Judea at the head of the list is predictable because most of Jesus' ministry occurs in Galilee, prior to his journey to Jerusalem and his death there. *Galilee* is named in significant passages in Mark 1:14-15, 14:28, and 16:7. In all, Mark refers to Galilee ten times, not counting two references to the "Sea of Galilee." [Galilee] By contrast, the other references to *Judea* in Mark are fewer and less significant (1:5; 10:1; 13:14). *Jerusalem* is the home of the scribes (3:22) and Pharisees (7:1) who opposed Jesus, but Jesus' "way" (i.e., road) will lead him eventually to Jerusalem (10:32; 11:1; 15:41), where he will curse the fig tree, condemn the temple (11:11, 15), and debate with the chief priests, scribes, and elders (11:27). *Idumea*, the home of Herod the Great, is not mentioned anywhere else in the New Testament. Jesus travels once to the Transjordan (10:1), to the region of Tyre and Sidon (7:24, 31; see the textual variant in 7:24). [Idumea, the Transjordan, Tyre, and Sidon]

The crowds came to Jesus because they had heard reports of the things he was doing. Mark calls attention to the spread of Jesus' fame (1:28, 45) so that from this point on Jesus is followed by crowds wherever he goes. Jesus' instruction to the disciples to get a boat ready for him is interesting in view of the numerous references to Jesus getting into or traveling by boat in the coming chapters (4:1, 36, 37; 5:2, 18, 21; 6:32, 45-51, 54; 8:10, 14). The sick, who suffered from various afflictions, literally "whips" or "lashes" (as in Acts 22:24), pressed upon him. The same term is used to describe the condition

Galilee

🔍 Selected bibliography of recent works on Galilee:

Freyne, Seán. *Galilee, from Alexander the Great to Hadrian, 323 B.C.E. to 135 C.E.: A Study of Second Temple Judaism.* Wilmington DE: M. Glazier; Notre Dame IN: University of Notre Dame Press, 1980.

———. *Galilee, Jesus, and the Gospels.* Philadelphia: Fortress Press, 1988.

Horsley, Richard A. *Archaeology, History, and Society in Galilee: The Social Context of Jesus and the Rabbis.* Valley Forge PA: Trinity Press International, 1996.

———. *Galilee: History, Politics, People.* Valley Forge PA: Trinity Press International, 1995.

Lapin, Hayim. *Early Rabbinic Civil Law and the Social History of Roman Galilee: A Study of Mishnah Tractate Baba' Mesi'a'.* Atlanta: Scholars Press, 1995.

Levine, Lee I., ed. *The Galilee in Late Antiquity.* New York: Jewish Theological Seminary of America; Cambridge: Harvard University Press, 1992.

Meyers, Eric M., ed. *Galilee through the Centuries: Confluence of Cultures.* Winona Lake IN: Eisenbrauns, 1999.

Sawicki, Marianne. *Crossing Galilee: Architecture of Contact in the Occupied Land of Jesus.* Harrisburg PA: Trinity, 2000.

Idumea, the Transjordan, Tyre, and Sidon

Idumea is located on the southern border of Judea and extends from the Gaza strip to the Dead Sea and the Judean desert. The name may be derived from "Edom" or from the Hebrew word for "earth" (*'dmh*). John Hyrcanus I conquered Idumea in 129 BC, and it was later incorporated by the Hasmoneans. The father and grandfather of Herod the Great, both named Antipater, were governors of Idumea. Following Herod's death, Idumea and Judea were governed by his son Archelaus (4 BC–AD 6). When Archelaus was deposed, Idumea was placed under the jurisdiction of the Roman procurators (AD 6–41) and Agrippa I (AD 41–44). After AD 44 Idumea was again governed by procurators until it was merged with Judea following the Jewish revolt in AD 66–70.

The *Transjordan* usually designates the area east of the Jordan River—Gilead and Bashan. It was settled by the tribes of Reuben, Gad, and part of Manasseh. Later, the Ammonites, the Moabites, and the Edomites dwelt there. In New Testament times, it was governed by the Seleucids, the Hasmoneans, and then the Romans. When Herod the Great died, the northern part of the area (Paneas, Gaulanitis, and Batanea) passed to Philip (4 BC–AD 34) and then to Agrippa I (AD 34–44). Along with Galilee, the central region (Perea) was ruled by Herod Antipas from 4 BC until AD 39, when it passed to Agrippa I (AD 39–44), while the Nabateans continued to rule the southern part from their stronghold at Petra.

Tyre and *Sidon* were ancient Phoenician centers, and the latter is mentioned in the Homeric epics. Tyre was originally an island located off the Phoenician coast between Sidon and Acco. The city was completely destroyed by Alexander the Great in 322 BC following a seventh-month siege, and the rubble of the city was used to build a causeway between the island and mainland. A keen rivalry developed between Tyre and Sidon during the Seleucid period, with each claiming to be the "mother" of the other. Herod the Great visited Tyre often and financed various building projects for it. Both Jesus (see the commentary on Mark 7:24, 31) and Paul (Acts 21:3-7) visited Tyre, and Jesus contrasted Tyre and Sidon with Bethsaida and Chorazin (Matt 11:21-22/Luke 10:13-14).

---

of the woman with the hemorrhage (5:29, 34). They pressed upon him in the hope that they might touch him. Jesus often healed by touching (1:41; 7:33; 8:22; cf. 10:13), and the sick hoped to be healed by touching him or his garments (5:27-31; 6:56). This detail recalls the healing of the leper in Mark 1:40-45 and anticipates the healing that will follow.

For a discussion of exorcism and evil spirits see the commentary and connections on Mark 1:21-28. Mark typically describes evil spirits as "unclean" (1:23, 26-27; 3:30; 5:2, 8, 13; 6:7; 7:25; 9:25). According to the purity codes of ancient Israel, bodily secretions, blood, births, skin diseases, corpses, various liquids, prohibited foods, vessels used for unclean things, and contact with Gentiles all rendered a person "unclean." There were ten degrees of uncleanness in men (*m. Kelim* 1.5). Unclean persons were ritually defiled and were therefore excluded from the community or from worship (entering into the presence of God) for specified periods of time or until they bathed or underwent ritual purification. The sixth division of the Mishnah ("Tohoroth"), some 185 pages in translation, deals with cleanness and uncleanness. [Uncleanness] Just as the sick "pressed upon" (*epipiptein*) him, so the unclean spirits "fell down before" (*prospiptein*) him. The woman with the hemorrhage (5:33) and the Syrophoenician woman (7:25) fall at his feet in the coming chapters as a sign of contrition and supplication. The unclean spirits yell out or scream Jesus' true but hidden identity:

Uncleanness

The tractate on vessels (*m. Kelim*) begins: "These Fathers of Uncleanness [things that can convey uncleanness to persons and vessels], [namely] a [dead] creeping thing, male semen, he that has contracted uncleanness from a corpse, a leper in his days of reckoning, and Sin-offering water too little in quantity to be sprinkled, convey uncleanness to men and vessels by contact and to earthenware vessels by [presence within their] air-space; but they do not convey uncleanness by carrying." It goes on to list things that are even more potently unclean.

m. Kelim 1.1, in Herbert Danby, trans., *The Mishnah* (Oxford: Oxford University Press, 1933), 604.

"You are the Son of God," echoing Mark 1:1 and the voice from heaven at Jesus' baptism (1:11), and foreshadowing the transfiguration (9:7) and the centurion's confession at the cross (15:39). While the "confession" of the unclean spirits is true, Jesus' identity cannot be disclosed openly apart from his death and resurrection. Jesus therefore silences the unclean spirits, issuing an authoritative order that they not make him known. Mark's use of this term (*epitimaō*) fittingly summarizes the authority that Jesus demonstrates in Mark 2:1–3:6 and continues to exercise in the next section of the Gospel. Robert Guelich comments that Mark uses this verb "as a technical expression for an action by which God establishes control over evil powers" (cf. 1:25; 4:39; 8:30, 32, 33; 9:25; 10:13, 48).[4]

Calling the Twelve, 3:13-19

The calling of the twelve disciples introduces the second major section of the first half of the Gospel (3:13–6:6). The pattern is consistent: each section begins with a report on Jesus' disciples (1:16-20; 3:13-19; 6:7-13). The first two sections end with reports of the rejection of Jesus (3:1-6; 6:1-6a), while the third ends with Peter's confession of Jesus (8:27-30). Whereas the first disciples were mentioned in the first section at the home of Peter's mother-in-law (1:29), hunting for Jesus when he withdrew for prayer (1:36), at the dinner at Levi's house (2:16), in the Pharisees' question about fasting (2:18), plucking grain on the Sabbath (2:23), and withdrawing with Jesus (3:7, 9), they are constantly with Jesus from Mark 4 on (see ["Son of God" in Mark]).

In Mark 3:13–6:6 the hostility against Jesus is clarified, concentrated, and extended. Jesus is empowered by the Spirit, while his adversary is Satan (3:20-27; 4:15) and his legions (5:1-20). Identities are both clarified and blurred: Jesus' true family is those who do the will of his Father (3:31-35), while his flesh and blood family does not understand him (3:21, 31). Scribes from Jerusalem question him (3:22), and his hometown does not accept him (6:1-6). Still, Jesus finds faith in a demoniac from the Decapolis (5:1-20), a hemorrhaging woman (5:25-34), and one of the leaders of the synagogue (5:21-24, 35-43). The first indication of the dullness and eventual failure of the disciples also appears: although the disciples have been with Jesus, they apparently understand no more of Jesus' teachings than those who are outside the kingdom (4:10-13). The teachings of Jesus, which were reported in the previous section only in summary statements and aphorisms, are now expanded by parable and explanation in Mark 4. Miracles also continue to announce and interpret the inbreaking of the kingdom through Jesus' ministry: the sea, which functions as a symbolic barrier between Galilee and the Decapolis, is tamed and stilled (4:35-41); the dehumanizing power of Satan is cast out of the demoniac (5:1-20), health and dignity are restored to a woman who had been rendered unclean (5:25-34), and a twelve-year-old girl is restored to life (5:21-24, 35-43).

The calling of the Twelve is reported in sparse, almost stylized phrases. At the same time, the paragraph gives evidence of tradition, Markan redaction, and later attempts at harmonization with the other synoptic accounts. The appointment and the list of the Twelve (3:13-14, 16b-19) probably come from tradition, while Mark's hand may be detected in 3:15-16a, the nickname *Boanerges* (3:17c), and the comment about Judas (3:19b).[5] Scribal efforts to harmonize these verses with Matthew 10:1-4 and Luke 6:12-16 are evident in the textual variants in 3:14, 15.

Mark's statement that Jesus went up "the mountain" (3:13) is odd because this is the first reference to a mountain in the Gospel. Later, Jesus will go up "the mountain" to pray (6:46), but the mount of transfiguration is introduced as "a high mountain" (9:2; see 9:9). The mountain may be a stock setting evoking associations with Moses and Elijah in the Old Testament. Jesus' choosing of the Twelve resonates with the election of the twelve tribes of Israel, marking both continuity and fulfillment, reconstitution and a new beginning. As with Abraham and Moses, God chose a people through whom to bless all peoples (Gen 12:1-3). This time, the covenantal promise of a land and a nation was transformed into the promise of the kingdom of God and a people that would eventually be drawn from all nations, but the purpose of the covenant was still the same—to call out a people through whom God could bless all peoples.

The relationship between the groups in vv. 13 and 14 is unclear. "Those whom he wanted" in v. 13 are either the Twelve or a larger group from whom Jesus chose the Twelve. If the latter, then we have foreshadowed here all of those who would later be led by the Twelve. On the other hand, if the groups are synonymous, the Twelve may still be representative of all who would follow Jesus—the church. Commitment to Jesus necessarily means leaving behind other commitments and pursuits: "and they came (*apēlthon*; lit., "came away") to him" (3:13). The act of appointing the Twelve is described in oddly suggestive language, echoing God's creative work: literally, "and he made twelve." The phrase "whom he also named apostles" (v. 14) is omitted by Codex Alexandrinus (A), Codex Bezae (D), and the majority of manuscripts, and appears to be a harmonization with Luke 6:13. Mark uses the term "apostles" elsewhere only once (6:30).[6]

The most distinctive feature of this paragraph is Mark's inclusion of two purpose clauses that explain why Jesus appointed the Twelve: first that they might "be with him," and second that they might "be sent out to proclaim the message, and to have authority to cast out demons" (3:14-15). The two are not contradictory but follow in sequence. The disciples provided companionship for Jesus, modeled the inclusive nature of the kingdom he proclaimed, and learned from him. Jesus then sent them out to multiply his own kingdom-inaugurating work: proclaiming the kingdom and casting out demons (see 6:7-13). Luke has no purpose clauses at this point (cf. Luke 6:13), and Matthew adds healing but omits proclamation (cf. Matt 10:1). Later, when Jesus sends out the Twelve, he gives them authority over the unclean spirits, but they proclaim the call to repentance, cast out demons, and heal the sick (6:7-13).

Four lists of the twelve disciples appear in the New Testament [The Lists of the Twelve], and none of the four are the same, which probably reflects the reality that while some of the disciples had prominent roles, memory of the others faded quickly. Each evangelist filled out the list from the tradition he received. Interesting observations arise from the variations in the lists and Mark's comments about the key disciples. Three traditions are reflected in these lists: the call of the two sets of brothers (Matthew and Luke), the role of the "inner three" (Mark), and the importance of Peter and John in the early church (Acts). Simon

---

The Lists of the Twelve

Mark 3:16-19	*Matthew 10:2-4*	*Luke 6:14-16*	*Acts 1:13*
Simon	Simon	Simon	Peter
James	Andrew	Andrew	John
John	James	James	James
Andrew	John	John	Andrew
Philip	Philip	Philip	Philip
Bartholomew	Bartholomew	Bartholomew	Thomas
Matthew	Thomas	Matthew	Bartholomew
Thomas	Matthew	Thomas	Matthew
James son of Alphaeus	James son of Alphaeus	James son of Alphaeus	James son of Alphaeus
Thaddaeus	Thaddaeus	Simon the Zealot	Simon the Zealot
Simon the Cananaean	Simon the Cananaean	Judas son of James	Judas son of James
Judas Iscariot	Judas Iscariot	Judas Iscariot	

The Inner Three

Mark makes greater use of the group of three than any of the other Gospels. Matthew retains the group only at the transfiguration (which may be evidence that the group was firmly attached to this story), while elevating the role of Peter elsewhere. Luke omits references to the group at the Mount of Olives and Gethsemane, so all of the disciples function for the later church as models for those who seek to follow Jesus.

In Mark, the inner three serve as Jesus' closest companions. They witness the most secret, intimate events of Jesus' ministry. They see his power to raise the dead, the glory of his transfiguration, the prophecy of the destruction of the temple and the coming of the Son of Man, and the agony of his prayer in the garden. In the end, they along with the rest abandon him. In contrast to Matthew and Luke, Mark does not seem to exalt these disciples as the apostolic authorities of the later church. Instead, they enhance two of Mark's major themes: the secrecy surrounding Jesus' messiahship and the failure of the disciples.

The identification of the inner three as the group closest to Jesus can be traced to Mark with some confidence. This group appears in the other Gospels only in scenes derived from Mark, and only in Mark does the separation of these three fit the larger themes of the Gospel. Mark probably found this group in the early tradition, but we are unable to locate which scene or scenes featured this group in the pre-Markan traditions. Some have conjectured that the memory of the group of three leaders of the church in Jerusalem led Mark to insert the three disciples into pivotal scenes in his Gospel. The similarity of the list in Galatians 2:9 (James, Cephas, and John) is such that the possibility of confusion or the suggestion of a group of three leading disciples cannot be excluded, even though the James in question is different in the two groups. On the whole, however, it is dubious that the "pillars of the church" were the origin of the "inner three" in the synoptic tradition.

James, Peter, and John

Monaco, Lorenzo (1370–1423). *Agony in the garden.* Accademia, Florence, Italy.

(Credit: Finsiel/Alinari / Art Resource, NY)

R. Alan Culpepper, *John, the Son of Zebedee: The Life of a Legend* (Columbia: University of South Carolina Press, 1994), 37–38.

Peter is always named first. Rather than merely listing Peter, Mark begins the listing awkwardly by saying, literally, "and he gave the name Peter to Simon." Cephas is not attested as a proper name in Aramaic, where it means simply "rock" or "stone." John 1:42 translates the Aramaic into the Greek: *Petros.* Proper names are not ordinarily translated, but Mark may have regarded the nickname as a new name. Oscar Cullmann commented, therefore, that "in order to bring out the power of the nickname as the authors and early readers of the NT felt it, we ought perhaps to follow the NT practice and reproduce the name as 'Simon Rock.'"[7] Whether Jesus gave Simon this nickname when he met him (John 1:42), when he appointed the Twelve (Mark 3:16), or at Caesarea Philippi (Matt 16:18) is difficult to say. The nickname probably refers more to Simon's promise and the new role he would assume than to his strength of character. After Simon Peter, Mark lists James and John, thereby placing the "inner three" (Peter, James, and John) first in the list. [The Inner Three] Only these three are given special names, and only in Mark does the name *Boanerges* appear in the list of the

"*Boanerges*, the Sons of Thunder"

AΩ Only Mark 3:17 records that Jesus called James and John "Boanerges, that is, Sons of Thunder." Two issues must be distinguished: (1) the etymology and meaning of the Aramaic *Boanerges* and (2) the meaning of the interpretation "sons of thunder." Scholars have withheld neither energy nor imagination in attempts to explain the etymology of *Boanerges*. The word is clearly a transliteration of a Semitic expression which should be divided *Boane-rges*. The first part derives from the Hebrew (and Aramaic) word *b^{e}ne*, "sons of," but the transition from *b^{e}ne* to *boane-* has been explained in several ways. A consensus seems to be building, however, that *Boanerges* is derived from either *b^{e}ne* regem or *b^{e}ne r'sh* and that the explanation "sons of thunder" is therefore an accurate translation of the Semitic expression that lies behind the corrupt transliteration.

Interpretations of the Hebrew or Aramaic words that lie behind *Boanerges* do not explain why Jesus called the two by this name. Unfortunately, Mark gives no clues. Explanations have ranged from the suggestion that James and John spoke with loud voices to the conjecture that as followers of John the Baptist, they had witnessed the voice from heaven, spoken in thunder. Generally, however, interpreters such as Swete have concluded that the name was given to the brothers either because of "the impetuosity of their natural character" or to signal "their place in the new order." James and John were noted for their zeal, which is evident in the censure of the unauthorized exorcist (Mark 9:38-41) and their offer to call down fire on the Samaritan village (Luke 9:52-56). Alternatively, by the giving of the name *Boanerges*, Jesus may have announced that James and John would become "sons of thunder," mighty witnesses, voices as from heaven (see Bietenhard, 5:281). Only the inner three, Peter, James, and John, are given new names. In Jewish tradition, names were often given either as a promise or as an act of laying upon the recipient a specific task (Bietenhard, 5:254). Accordingly, the "sons of thunder" were probably recognized by Jesus for their potential as thundering witnesses, not because they were hot-tempered. [This paragraph is an abridgement of a more detailed discussion of *Boanerges* in R. Alan Culpepper, *John the Son of Zebedee: The Life of a Legend* (Columbia: University of South Carolina Press, 1994), 38-40.]

Henry Barclay Swete, *The Gospel according to St. Mark* (1898 rpt.: Grand Rapids: Wm. B. Eerdmans, 1956), 60.

Hans Bietenhard, "*onoma*," *TDNT* 5:281, 254.

Twelve. ["*Boanerges*, the Sons of Thunder"] Mark has evidently arranged the names in this order and supplied the Semitic nicknames. Andrew, who was called at the same time and who appears with the other three at the eschatological discourse on the Mount of Olives (Mark 13:1), is named in fourth place. Mark's list, therefore, sets up the first three as a significant group that will appear in important scenes later in the Gospel. Outside of the first four disciples, none of the others except for Judas Iscariot is mentioned elsewhere in the Gospel.

The second group of four (Philip, Bartholomew, Matthew, and Thomas) is the same in all four New Testament lists except for the sequence of the names. Philip and Andrew, who both have Greek names, appear together in the Gospel of John (6:5-8; 12:21-22), which also reports that, along with Peter and Andrew, Philip came from the town of Bethsaida (John 1:44). Bartholomew means "Son of Talmai" (cf. 2 Sam 3:3). Matthew has traditionally been identified with Levi, son of Alphaeus, the toll collector (2:14; see Matt 9:9; 10:3). Thomas is an Aramaic name that means "twin" (see John 11:16; 14:5; 20:24-29; 21:2).

Other variations in the four lists of the Twelve occur in the third group of four. Mark lists the third group as James the son of Alphaeus, Thaddaeus, Simon the Cananaean, and Judas Iscariot. Luke and Acts omit Thaddaeus and add Judas the son of James (cf. John 14:22). James the son of Alphaeus may also be James the Younger (15:40) and the brother of Levi, the son of Alphaeus (2:14). Luke and Acts also identify Simon the Cananaean as Simon the Zealot, correctly translating the Aramaic *qan'ānā'* in order to avoid confusion with the place name Canaan. The name Iscariot probably comes from the Hebrew *'îšqĕrîyōt*,

---

The Twelve Apostles

📖 **Simon Peter**

NT, outside the Gospels and Acts: Gal 2:7-8; 1 Pet 1:1; 2 Pet 1:1; Cephas: 1 Cor 1:13; 3:22; 9:5; 15:5; Gal 1:18; 2:9, 11, 14

Legend: According to early tradition, Peter preached to the Jews in Asia Minor, traveled to Rome, instituted the episcopal succession, and was martyred and buried there (*1 Clem.* 5.4; Irenaeus, *Against Heresies* 3.1.2; 3.3.1; Eusebius, *Ecclesiastical History* 2.25.5-8). Origen reported that Peter requested to be crucified head downward (*Ecclesiastical History* 3.1.2-3). Fragments from Papias maintain that the preaching of Peter lies behind the Gospel of Mark.

Apocryphal Writings: The Acts of Peter; The Acts of Peter and Paul; The Gospel of Peter; The Martyrdom of Peter; The Passion of Peter; The Passion of Peter and Paul; The Preaching of Peter; The Acts of Peter and the Twelve Apostles (Nag Hammadi Codex VI); *The Letter of Peter to Philip* (Nag Hammadi Codex VIII); *The Apocalypse of Peter* (Nag Hammadi Codex VII, 3). See Pheme Perkins, *Peter: Apostle for the Whole Church* (Columbia: University of South Carolina Press, 1993).

James, son of Zebedee

NT, outside the Gospels: Acts 12:2

Legend: James (James the Great), the only apostle whose death is recorded in the New Testament, was put to death by Herod Agrippa, probably in AD 44. The *Apostolic History* of Abdias records fictional deeds of James. Eusebius records that his guard became a believer and went with James to be beheaded with him (*Ecclesiastical History* 2.9.2-3). James became the patron saint of Spain. Tradition claims that his body was put on a ship and guided to Spain by angels, where his remains rest in the shrine at Santiago de Compostela. The evolution of the name James is interesting: *Iakob* (Greek), Iago, St. Iago, Santiago, San Diego. See Abdias, *Apostolic History*.

John, son of Zebedee

NT, outside the Gospels: Acts 3:1, 3, 4, 11; 4:13, 19; 8:14; 12:2; Gal 2:9; John the Seer: Rev 1:1, 4, 9; 22:8

Legend: According to early tradition, this John is the author of the Gospel, letters, and apocalypse that bear his name. Apocryphal acts of John record his travel to Ephesus, ministry there, drinking a poison cup unharmed, exile on Patmos, and confrontation there with the demon Kynops before his death at an advanced age. Augustine said that the earth rose and fell over his grave, over which the Basilica of St. John was built, near Ephesus, in the 6th century.

Apocryphal Writings: Acts of John; Acts of John at Rome; Acts of the Holy Apostle and Evangelist John the Theologian, Written by His Disciple Prochorus. See R. Alan Culpepper, *John the Son of Zebedee: The Life of a Legend* (Columbia: University of South Carolina Press, 1994; Minneapolis: Fortress, 2000).

Andrew

NT, outside the Gospels: none

Legend: Andrew left Jerusalem to evangelize Achaea, left Achaea to rescue Matthias from cannibals, traveled by sea (like Odysseus), and worked miracles. When he returned to Achaea, he converted the wife of the proconsul, Aegeates, who crucified Andrew near the sea because his wife would no longer have sex with him. Andrew was later (8th century) claimed as the founder of Byzantium. His relics lay in Constantinople until the crusaders brought them back to Amalfi, Italy, in 1204. The British Isles also claimed his influence.

Apocryphal Writings: The Acts of Andrew; The Acts of Andrew and Matthias. See P. M. Peterson, *Andrew: Brother of Simon Peter, His Story and His Legends* (Supplements to Novum Testamentum 1; Leiden: E. J. Brill, 1958).

Philip

NT, outside the Gospels: none

Legend: According to Clement of Alexandria, Philip was the one who asked to go and bury his father (*Stromata* 3.4; 4.9). He was often confused with Philip the Evangelist (from Acts 6:5; see Eusebius, *Ecclesiastical History* 3.31.2-5; 3.39.8-10). Polycrates of Ephesus connects him with

"Man from Kerioth," meaning a town near Hebron (Josh 15:25) or in Moab (Jer 48:24).[8] The name is ascribed to Judas's father, Simon, in John 6:71 and 13:26. Others, less convincingly, have interpreted the name as meaning "false one," from the Aramaic *'išqaryā'*, or "assassin," from the Latin *sicarius*.[9] Mark's comment, "who betrayed him," like

---

Asia Minor and says that he died at Hierapolis, apparently of natural causes.

Bartholomew
NT, outside the Gospels: none
Legend: Since the 9th century he has often been identified with Nathanael, but this identification is inconclusive. Eusebius (*Ecclesiastical History* 5.10.3) claimed that Bartholomew preached in India, where he left the Gospel of Matthew, written in Hebrew. After preaching in India and Greater Armenia, he was flayed alive and beheaded. According to the *Martyrdom of Bartholomew*, he was placed in a sack and cast into the sea.

Apocryphal Writings: Gospel of Bartholomew; Questions of Bartholomew; the Coptic *Book of the Resurrection of Christ by Bartholomew*.

Matthew
NT, outside the Gospels: none
Legend: Matthew "compiled the oracles [of the Lord] in the Hebrew language, and each interpreted them as best he could" (Papias, quoted by Eusebius, *Ecclesiastical History* 3.39.16; Loeb, 1:297). Eusebius records that Matthew preached to Hebrews and wrote his Gospel for them (3.24.6). Clement of Alexandria adds that Matthew was a vegetarian (*Instructor* 2.1). Heracleon records that he died a natural death (Clement, *Stromata* 4.9), but later legends describe his death by fire or the sword. See Edgar J. Goodspeed, *Matthew, Apostle and Evangelist* (Philadelphia: Winston, 1959).

Thomas
NT, outside the Gospels: none
Legend: According to the Gnostics, Thomas received secret revelations from the risen Lord. Eusebius (*Ecclesiastical History* 3.1) says Thomas evangelized the Parthians, while the *Acts of Thomas* record his preaching and martyrdom in India. The Syrian Christians of Malabar, who call themselves "Christians of St. Thomas," claim he was martyred and buried near Madras. His body was later transported to Edessa, and his relics are preserved at Ortóna. See James

H. Charlesworth, *The Beloved Disciple* (Valley Forge: Trinity Press International, 1995), esp. 360-89.

Apocryphal Writings: Acts of Thomas; Apocalypse of Thomas; The Book of Thomas the Contender; Gospel of Thomas; The Infancy Gospel of Thomas.

James, son of Alphaeus
NT, outside the Gospels: none
Legend: James the Less, according to tradition, worked in southern Palestine and Egypt before being crucified in lower Egypt or in Persia (Nicephorus 2.40; J. Migne, *Patrologia* 30.478).

Thaddaeus
NT, outside the Gospels: none
Legend: Eusebius identified Thaddeus as one of the seventy (*Ecclesiastical History* 1.13.4, 11; 2.1.6-8). He is also sometimes identified as Judas, not Iscariot. According to Greek and Syriac sources, Thaddeus healed and converted many in Edessa.

Apocryphal Writings: Acts of Thaddeus

Simon the Cananaean (or Zealot)
NT, outside the Gospels: none
Legend: Simon ("the Less") was identified by some as Simeon son of Clopas, who succeeded James as the head of the church in Jerusalem (Eusebius, *Ecclesiastical History* 3.11.1).
Apocryphal Writings: The Passion of Simon and Jude

Judas Iscariot
NT, outside the Gospels: Acts 1:16, 25
Legend: A fragment from Papias (early 2d century), preserved by Apollinaris of Laodicea (4th century), records a gruesome account of Judas's death.
Apocryphal Writings: A Gospel of Judas, no longer extant, according to Irenaeus (*Against Heresies* 1.31.1), Theodoret, and Epiphanius. See B. Gärtner, *Iscariot* (Philadelphia: Fortress, 1971); William Klassen, *Judas: Betrayer or Friend of Jesus* (Minneapolis: Fortress, 1996).

Mark 3:6, foreshadows the events that led to Jesus' death. Although the Greek verb *paradidonai* can mean simply to "hand over" or "hand on," it is connected with Judas early in the tradition (1 Cor 11:23b) and took on the meaning "betray" in the gospel tradition (13:9, 11-12; 14:21).[10] (See [The Twelve Apostles].)

Excursus: The Role of the Twelve in Mark

In the Gospel of Mark, the disciples are portrayed as moving from a lack of understanding to complete failure. They do not understand the parable of the sower (see Mark 4:10-13). Their greatest success comes when they follow Jesus' instructions after he sends them out by twos (6:7-13), but then they do not grasp the meaning of the feeding of the 5,000 or the feeding of the 4,000. Jesus challenges them: "Do you still not perceive or understand? Are your hearts hardened? Do you have eyes, and fail to see? Do you have ears, and fail to hear? And do you not remember?" (8:17-18; compare the plight of the outsiders in Mark 4:10-12). Mark indicates that indeed their hearts were hardened (6:52).

Even following Peter's confession at Caesarea Philippi, the disciples do not understand what Jesus is doing. Three times, Jesus tells the disciples that he is going up to Jerusalem, where he will be killed and rise on the third day. Each time, the disciples (Peter in Mark 8:32-33, all the disciples in 9:33-34, and then James and John in 10:35-37) show not only that they do not understand but that they are pursuing the self-centered objectives of glory and reward (10:28-29). Only those to whom sight is given can follow Jesus (10:52). In Jerusalem, Jesus instructs the disciples to watch so that they will be ready for the trauma of the destruction of Jerusalem and the coming of the Son of Man, but in the Garden of Gethsemane, they cannot watch with Jesus for even one hour (14:34-42). When Jesus is arrested, they flee into the night, abandoning him and their call to follow him (14:50). The failure of the disciples could hardly be more complete; only the promise of a meeting with the risen Lord holds out hope for their future usefulness (16:7; see also 13:9-13).[11]

Jesus' Opponents and Jesus' True Family, 3:20-35

The calling of the Twelve is followed by a scene in which Mark depicts the response of various groups to Jesus: the crowd that thronged around him; his family, who sought to protect him from himself; the scribes from Jerusalem; and his true family, those who do the will of God. Mark demonstrates his compositional skill by bringing together a series of discrete traditions into an example of his distinctive framing technique. [Markan Sandwiches] Varying the monotony of simple sequence and juxtaposing events or drawing parallels between them, Mark often introduces one event or scene, narrates a second, and then returns to the first. The technique creates dramatic tension and suspense and invites comparison between the two sandwiched events. In this case, the response of Jesus' family is placed in parallel with the charge of demonic possession that is leveled against him by the scribes. An outline of Mark 3:20-35 reveals the structure of the framing technique in these verses. [Outline of Mark 3:20-35] Jesus' pronouncement at the end of this unit dramatically declares his rejection of his family and the adoption of his followers as his true family.

The note that Jesus came to a house echoes 2:1 and 9:33 and prepares for the exchange in 3:31-35. Mark may intend that we understand that it was the same house referred to in 2:1, and possibly the home of Simon and Andrew (1:29). Translating the phrase "at home" (NRSV, 2:1 and 3:20) suggests either that Jesus had a home in Capernaum (for which there is no other evidence) or that he went home to Nazareth, which does not fit 9:33 (in Capernaum) and makes it strange that Jesus and his followers are inside while his family is outside in 3:31-35. Mark emphasizes the demands of the crowd by noting that Jesus could not even eat; literally, could not even eat bread (see also 6:31), which means they could not have a meal.

Markan Sandwiches

Mark 2:1-5/11-12—The healing of the paralytic and Jesus' authority to forgive sins

Mark 5:21-24/35-43—Raising Jairus's daughter and healing the woman with a hemorrhage

Mark 6:7-13/30-32—The mission of the Twelve and the death of John the Baptist

Mark 9:37/42—Receiving the children and the unauthorized exorcist

Mark 11:12-14/20-25—Cursing the fig tree and cleansing the temple

Mark 14:1-2/10-11—The betrayal of Jesus and the anointing of Jesus

Mark 14:54/66-72—Peter's denials and Jesus' testimony before the high priest

Outline of Mark 3:20-35

Key words introduce the setting, each group of characters, and their responses to Jesus:

A. House, crowd, and family 3:20-21
  "in a house" 3:20
  "the crowd" 3:20
  "his family: 'He has gone out of his mind'" 3:21
B. The scribes from Jerusalem
  "the scribes: 'He has Beelzebul'" 3:22
    Jesus' first response 3:23-29
  "they had said, 'He has an unclean spirit'" 3:30
A'. House, crowd, and family 3:31-35
  family: "his mother and his brothers" 3:31
  "standing outside [the house]" 3:31
  "a crowd" 3:32
    Jesus' second response 3:33-35

While probably correct, the NRSV translation of v. 21 ("When his family heard it") obscures an ambiguity. Literally the text says, "those around him." In other texts the phrase refers either to friends and associates (1 Macc 11:73; 12:27) or family and relatives (Josephus, *Ant.* 1.193), so an interpretation must be based on context. In this instance, if Mark had intended a reference to the disciples, he could have used "his disciples," "the twelve," or "the apostles," picking up language from the preceding paragraph. The reference to "hearing" implies that those who came to take him away had not been with him, as we assume the disciples were. Finally, the framing technique implies that "those around him" in v. 21 are the same as "his mother and his brothers" in v. 31. Implicitly, Mark is already showing that simply being with Jesus (see the first purpose clause in 3:14) was no guarantee that one would understand what Jesus was doing.

The verb "to seize" or "restrain" (NRSV) in v. 21 occurs frequently in Mark, where it can mean either to take someone's hands, hold fast to tradition, or arrest. The apparent sense is that Jesus' family heard that he was being thronged by crowds, and, possibly fearing for his safety since popular uprisings were inherently dangerous in an occupied territory, they came to take him home. They (or less likely others, NRSV) were saying, "He has gone out of his mind" (see John 10:20). Mark uses this verb elsewhere (2:12; 5:42; 6:51) to mean "be amazed" or "astonished." Here it has a stronger sense: whereas others were amazed, confused, or astounded (i.e., in a state in which things seemed to make little or no sense) as a result of seeing what Jesus had done, Jesus—guided by insight that others did not have—seemed to them to be "out of his mind."

A new group appears suddenly—scribes sent from Jerusalem—presumably to investigate Jesus' activities. The reference to sending implies concern at some official level, either among the chief priests (who assume a prominent role later in Mark; see also Acts 9:1) or the Sanhedrin (see Acts 5:27-40). Scribes were active in Jerusalem, but little is known about the role of scribes in Galilee or their relationship to Jerusalem scribes. Although Jerusalem lay to the south of Galilee, the scribes "came down" from Jerusalem because one came down from or went up to Jerusalem both literally and figuratively regardless of which direction one was traveling.

The scribes' charge is twofold: (1) Jesus has Beelzebul, and (2) he casts out demons by the power of the ruler of the demons. The Hebrews contemptuously referred to a Canaanite god as Baal-zebub or "Lord of the flies" (2 Kgs 1:2). While Beelzebul does not occur in Jewish literature, the name, or variations of it, are picked up in later Christian writings. The two most commonly proposed derivations are "Lord of dung" or "Lord of the dwelling" (see "the ruler of this world"; John 12:31; 14:30; 16:11).[12] The charge that Jesus was demon-possessed occurs in the Gospel of John (7:20; 8:48, 52; 10:20), in later rabbinic literature, and as a charge to which the apologists responded. [Jesus the Magician in Later Sources]

Jesus the Magician in Later Sources

"Yeshu of Nazareth was hanged on the day of preparation for the Passover because he practiced sorcery and led the people astray" (*b. Sanhedrin* 43a, Baraitha).

"And as a master has said, 'Yeshu the Nazarene practiced magic and led Israel astray'" (*b. Sanhedrin* 107b, Baraitha).

"and they dared to say that he was a magician and seducer of the people" (Justin Martyr, *Dialogue* 69).

[Jesus] "in the capacity of a man whom they took to be a magician with miraculous signs and a rival in teaching" (Tertullian, *Against Marcion* 3.6).

"Celsus says that Christians are strong through the names and enchantments of certain demons. . . . He further laid it to the Savior's charge that he had been enabled to perform the fancied miraculous feats by sorcery" (Origen, *Against Celsus* 1.6).

William L. Lane, *The Gospel according to Mark* (Grand Rapids: Wm. B. Eerdmans, 1974), 142 n. 88; cf. Morton Smith, *Jesus the Magician* (San Francisco: 1978).

Mark 3:22-27 follows the form of a pronouncement story. The accusations of the scribes from Jerusalem set up Jesus' response, which contains Jesus' first reference to the parables in the Gospel of Mark. Joachim Jeremias contended that Jesus often used parables in order to respond to his accusers.[13] Parables are ideally suited for this purpose because they leave it to the hearer to infer the meaning of the parable and to see how it relates to them. Mark uses the term *parabolē* here in its broad sense, which can include can include proverbs and riddles, like the Hebrew *mašal*.

Jesus' response confirms that *Beelzebul* and "the ruler of the demons" are references to Satan. His question traps his accusers: how can he be empowered by Satan if exorcisms are a casting out of Satan? Jesus' challenge understands the conflict between good and evil in personal and corporate terms. The powers are communities in conflict. Neither a kingdom (today we would say "a country") nor a family will be able to withstand an attack from the outside if inside it is divided against itself. Therefore, if he were indeed acting by the power of Satan to cast out Satan's minions, then his exorcisms show that the dominion of evil is divided and therefore that its end is near. Satan's end has come (3:26), but not because of division with Satan's domain. The unclean spirits themselves cry out that Jesus is "the Holy One of God" and ask, alternatively, "Have you come to destroy us?" (1:24) and "What have you to do with me?" (5:7). Satan's kingdom is falling not because Satan has risen up against himself but because of the inbreaking of the kingdom of God in the ministry of Jesus. Jesus is indeed spirit empowered, but it is the spirit of God that is at work in him, not that of the "ruler of the demons."

Jesus, therefore, changes images, extending the metaphor of an attack on a household. The mini-parable of the strong man is actually an allegorical metaphor. The strong man is Satan, his house is this world, his possessions ("property," NRSV) are those spirits or people under his control, the one entering the strong man's house is Jesus, and the plundering of the strong man's property is the casting out of the unclean spirits. The metaphor, therefore, confirms Jesus' response to the scribes: he is not acting under the power of Satan; his exorcising activity is actually an attack on the house of Satan. The logic of the metaphor, however, is not merely that Jesus would not be able to cast out demons unless he were stronger than Satan, but that because he is able to "plunder" Satan's house in this way he has already bound "the strong man."

The question then is what is meant by "binding the strong man." On this point, the Gospel is not clear. The decisive binding of Satan is undoubtedly related to the death and resurrection of Jesus, and eventually to the triumphal coming of Jesus as the Son of Man to judge the nations and raise the dead. In the immediate context, however, with reference to the exorcisms of Jesus during his ministry, the binding of Satan may be assumed to have occurred either in connection with the baptism of Jesus and his wrestling with Satan during the forty days of temptation in the wilderness (1:12-13),[14] or more generally in the inauguration of the kingdom through Jesus' ministry. John the Baptist's witness was true: Jesus' exorcisms demonstrate that he is indeed "the stronger one" (1:8).

Like others of Jesus' sayings (the good Samaritan or the unjust steward), the riddle of the strong man involves a scandalous association. Jesus casts himself in the role of a thief plundering another's house. On further reflection, the metaphor invites contemplation on God's role as liberator. At the exodus, God's paradigmatic redemptive act, God bound Pharaoh and liberated the children of Israel. The ministry of Jesus, therefore, marks a new exodus, the liberation of the people of God. [God, the Liberator]

God, the Liberator

"Can the prey be taken from the mighty,
　　or the captives of a tyrant be rescued?
But thus says the LORD:
　Even the captives of the mighty shall be taken,
　and the prey of the tyrant be rescued;
　for I will contend with those who contend with you,
　and I will save your children. . . .
Then all flesh shall know
　that I am the Lord your Savior,
　and your Redeemer, the Mighty One of Jacob."
(Isa 49:24-26)

"Therefore it is said,
　'When he ascended on high he made captivity itself a captive;
　he gave gifts to his people.'" (Eph 4:8, adapting Ps 68:18)

Having turned aside the charge that his exorcisms were the work of Satan and having clarified his own role as rescuer or liberator, Jesus takes the offensive. He charges that by accusing him of being in league with Satan his accusers are blaspheming against the Holy Spirit and therefore show that it is they who are doing the work of Satan. Both the language and the substance of the argument are thoroughly Semitic. The solemn formula, "Amen," normally occurred at the end of a prayer or priestly pronouncement as the response of the assembly, meaning, "let it be so." Only in rare instances is it found at the beginning of a statement (1 Kgs 1:36; Jer 11:5; 28:6; *m. Sotah* 2.5), and in none of these instances does the speaker dare to say, "Amen, I say to you. . . ." To begin a statement with this formula was tantamount to claiming divine authority. The formula never occurs in the Jewish literature, and is found only on the lips of Jesus in the New Testament. Because no Jewish rabbi would speak in such a way, Joachim Jeremias identified the "Amen" formula as one of the distinguishing characteristics of Jesus' speech.[15] The opposing absolute declarations of Jesus are also Semitic in style: literally, "all things will be forgiven the sons of men. . . , but whoever blasphemes the Holy Spirit never has forgiveness. . . ."

The scribes had earlier accused Jesus of blasphemy (2:7). Jesus now turns the charge back on the scribes who had come from Jerusalem. The seriousness of the offense is set off by Jesus' initial declaration that all sinful activity and all blasphemy could be forgiven. His declaration of forgiveness is again reminiscent of his pronouncing the sins of the paralytic forgiven (2:6-10), continuing Mark's emphasis on the authority of Jesus. (See the discussion of blasphemy in the commentary on 2:7.) But the affirmation that all sins could be forgiven for those who repent was common in Judaism. [Forgiveness for the Repentant]

Jesus' declaration introduces an unpardonable sin, different from other forms of blasphemy: blasphemy against the Holy Spirit. Blasphemy is the repudiation of the holiness or power of God, and the levitical law prescribed stoning as the punishment for blasphemers (Lev 24:13-16). In terms similar to Mark's, the Damascus Document declares, "And also they defile his holy spirit, for with blasphemous tongue they have opened their mouth against the statutes of God's covenant, saying: 'they are unfounded'" (CD 5.11-12).[16] While it is difficult to distinguish blasphemy against the Holy Spirit from other forms of blasphemy, it is clear in the present context that the scribes had charged Jesus, the agent of the kingdom of God, God's beloved son (1:11; 9:7), and they had said that he had an unclean spirit (3:30, see the commentary on 1:23), that he had Beelzebul, and that he exorcised demons by the power of Satan. They had therefore rejected the one through whom they might have found forgiveness.

The issues of spirit inspiration and blasphemy were particularly important in the Markan context (see the introduction to this commentary) in which believers were being betrayed by family members and dragged before magistrates because of their Christian faith. In such instances, they were instructed to rely on the Holy Spirit. Their accusers, who rejected their testimony, were by implication rejecting the gospel of Jesus Christ (Mark 1:1) and the utterances given to the Markan Christians by the Holy Spirit. Like the scribes sent from Jerusalem, they were in danger of the one unpardonable sin—rejecting the witness of the spirit of God.

The aside or parenthetical comment in v. 30 serves as a frame for the exchange between Jesus and the scribes by recalling their charges in v. 22. It also concludes the intercalated unit in vv. 22-30 with a charge against Jesus, just as the introductory frame ended with a charge in v. 21. The reader is prepared, therefore, to resume the story of Jesus and his family in vv. 31-35.

The sandwich construction (A. family, vv. 20-21; B. scribes, vv. 22-30; A'. family, vv. 31-35) invites reflection on the parallel between the scribes' accusations of Jesus and his family's judgment that he was "out

Forgiveness for the Repentant

"The *individuals* who were excluded from the world to come were, as we have repeatedly seen, those who effectively deny the claims of God. Those excluded from salvation, in other words, are those who exclude themselves from the covenant.

"That only the most unregenerate sinners were excluded from the covenant and the covenant promises becomes most apparent when we study the passages on atonement for transgression. The universally held view is this: God has appointed means of atonement for every transgression, except the intention to reject God and his covenant."

E. P. Sanders, *Paul and Palestinian Judaism* (Philadelphia: Fortress Press, 1977), 157.

of his mind" (3:21). Both were stumbling blocks to his ministry, and Jesus was rejected by the two groups who should have recognized that God was working through him: the Torah experts (the scribes and the Pharisees) and his family.

The scene is set in vv. 20-21. Jesus was in a house surrounded by a crowd. Jesus' family thought he was "standing outside himself," "beside himself," or "out of his mind" (NRSV). Returning to this scene, Mark reports that Jesus' mother and his brothers came and, standing outside, were calling him. Each element of Mark's narration is significant. For the debates over whether Jesus' brothers were also Mary's sons see the commentary on Mark 6:3. The observation that they were standing "outside" sets up the contrast between insiders and outsiders that will be developed further in Mark 4:11, "To you has been given the secret of the kingdom of God, but for those outside, everything comes in parables." Ironically, those who said Jesus was "outside himself" (3:21) now find themselves outside the circle of those who do God's will.[17] Their action in calling Jesus should be considered on both a literal and a thematic level. Literally, the reader gathers that Jesus' family, thinking that Jesus had perhaps been carried away by the fervor of the movement gathering around him, had come to take him home. Thematically, the call of Jesus' family is diametrically opposed to the call of God. Would he do the will of his earthly family or his heavenly Father? It was the same decision that confronted Jesus' disciples. Jesus himself had called the fishermen, who "left their father" (1:20) to follow him. Jesus also promised that those who left their families for his sake would receive houses, brothers, sisters, and children one hundredfold (see 10:28-30). Luke sharpens the radical demand of calling over family: "Whoever comes to me and does not hate father and mother, wife and children, brothers and sisters, yes, and even life itself, cannot be my disciple" (Luke 14:26; cf. Matt 10:35-37). In the face of persecution, no doubt a reflection of Mark's own time, unbelieving family members would betray believing brothers, children, and parents to the authorities (13:12). Therefore, Mark allows the call of the gospel and the call of one's family to stand in sharp opposition. Having called the disciples to leave their families and follow him, Jesus now turns aside his family's call for him to leave his disciples. [Fictive Kin Groups]

Commentators have noted that there is no mention of Jesus' father in v. 31. The omission is probably intentional, either because Joseph had

Fictive Kin Groups

"In antiquity, the extended family meant everything. It was not only the source of one's status in the community but also functioned as the primary economic, religious, educational, and social network. Loss of connection to the family meant the loss of these vital networks as well as loss of connection to the land. But a surrogate family, what anthropologists call a fictive kin group, could serve the same functions as the family of origin, and thus the Christian community acting as a surrogate family is for Mark the locus of the good news. It transcends the normal categories of birth, class, race, gender, education, wealth, and power."

Bruce J. Malina and Richard L. Rohrbaugh, *Social-Science Commentary on the Synoptic Gospels* (Minneapolis: Fortress Press, 1992), 201–202.

died or because Mark is setting up the substitution of doing "the will of God" for "the will of my father" in v. 35. The reference to Jesus' sisters in v. 32 is probably original even though the phrase is omitted by significant early manuscripts (note the reference to his sisters in v. 35 and their absence from vv. 31 and 33).

Because Jesus' family could not get to him through the crowd, they "sent" to him (cf. the sending in 3:14), meaning no doubt that they passed a message through the crowd to him. In Mark the verb "to seek" (*zētein*) is usually used with negative connotations (see 1:37; 8:11-12; 11:18; 12:12, etc.). Dramatically, Jesus first asks who his mother and brothers are. The question appears to confirm his family's fears: he has lost his senses; he is out of his mind; he does not even know his own family. But Jesus poses the question in order to answer it on a metaphorical level that exposes one's scale of priorities. Looking around at those sitting in a circle "around him" (v. 34; contrast those "with him" in v. 21), he pronounces them his true family: "Here are my mother and my brothers" (3:34). Jesus' declaration is performative language—it accomplishes the reality it declares. Jesus has displaced his earthly family and brought into being a new family.

The displacement of Jesus' family functions on several levels. First, by rejecting his family's summons, Jesus demonstrates his complete devotion to God's claim on his life. In effect, he places the first commandment ("You shall have no other gods before me"; Exod 20:3) above the fifth commandment ("Honor your father and your mother"; Exod 20:12). In the next verse, however, he shows that he is in fact honoring his "father." Second, he creates a new community. This scene should therefore be taken with the calling of the Twelve, which it extends, as the genesis for the church. Third, Mark may reflect the conflict in the early church between the Jerusalem church that was dominated by Jesus' family and the disciples (both of whom are portrayed in a negative light in Mark), and the Galilean communities or Gentile communities that grew up independent of the leadership of Peter, the Twelve, James (the brother of Jesus), and the elders (cf. 1 Cor 15:5-7; Gal 2:11-14; and note the omission of Galilee from Acts 1:8). Matthew and Luke both stand closer to the Jerusalem church, and both soften the polemic against Jesus' family. [Jesus' Family in the Other Gospels] And fourth, by rejecting the claims of his own family for the sake of his mission and his true family, Jesus sets an example for his persecuted followers in Mark's time.

Jesus' declaration in v. 35 assumes the structure and household code of the ancient family (cf. Eph 5:22–6:4; Col 3:18-21; 1 Pet 3:1-7) in which other members of the family were subject to the will of the pater familias. One notes first that Jesus pointedly does not say, "Whoever does the will of God is my father. . . ." The silence or omission makes it clear who Jesus' real father is. Second, whereas "sisters" were omitted earlier, at least in vv. 31 and 33, they are now expressly included in the new family that transcends social status and brings an end to all forms of oppression. And finally, membership in this new family is achieved by doing the will of the Father. Mark is not concerned here with the Pauline opposition of faith and works, but takes a position closer to that of James, who insists that faith is demonstrated by the works that grow from it: "Be doers of the word, and not merely hearers who deceive themselves" (Jas 1:22; cf. 1:23-25; and 2:14-26, which incidentally begins with an address to the community as "my brothers and sisters"). In Mark 3:35 the reference to doing God's will further clarifies the distinction between those on the "inside" and those "outside." By following Jesus, those around him were doing God's will, and by coming to Jesus they had entered into a new community, a new kin group that transcended the calls even of one's family.

The variety of responses to Jesus that are exposed in this section leads to the question, why did some receive Jesus' word while others rejected it? The question will be answered through the parables of the next chapter.

CONNECTIONS

Mark 3:1-6

One point at which the healing of the man with the withered hand on the Sabbath connects with our own experience is neither the healing nor the rules for Sabbath observance. Rather, like the story of the disciples plucking grain on the Sabbath, this story exposes the difference between Jesus and his opponents in regard to ultimate religious values. We miss the relevance of the story if we focus on the hypocrisy of the Pharisees. Instead, we should try to understand their values and their religious tradition. The Law of Moses commanded the observance of the Sabbath as a day of rest. Sabbath observance was one of the clearest issues that distinguished Jews from their pagan neighbors: every week they observed the Sabbath. All of one's life was to be lived in obedience to God's commands. Therefore, obedience even in trivial matters was an act of faith and devotion. It protected the Jews from being absorbed by their pagan neighbors, and it connected them with the covenants God made with Israel. Disregard for the Sabbath was a violation of God's commandments and a breach of the covenant. Sabbath observance, therefore, took precedence over the healing of chronic ailments.

The force of this issue is difficult to grasp today in large measure because we have become so cavalier about religious observances generally. The importance of setting aside a day for worship, study of Scripture, prayer, rest, and family is often casually discarded in favor not of meeting real human needs—as Jesus did when he healed the man—but in favor of other pursuits that have little to do with our professed convictions. Sabbath observance was easier in a society in which all work stopped on the Sabbath, but the issue is not Saturday or Sunday, it is the importance of making time for a Sabbath in our lives. Until one is seriously seeking an answer to the first part of Jesus' question, "Is it proper on the Sabbath . . . ?" one is hardly prepared to go on to the dilemma that Jesus posed to his opponents. The question presupposes that we are already ordering our lives around a regular Sabbath observance. How can we look in judgment on the Pharisees who sought to protect the Sabbath if we do not make the Sabbath a vital part of the rhythm of our lives? [Sabbath Resistance]

Mark 3:7-12

Not only did Jesus observe the Sabbath, but he also regularly took time to withdraw from the crowds and the pace of his ministry. At times he withdrew for prayer by himself (1:35) or with a few of his disciples (9:2). At other times, he led the disciples out to a desolate area (6:31). There is a rhythm of initiative and retreat, emptying and replenishing, prayer and ministry to Jesus' life. Sometimes a withdrawal follows a period of intense activity; at other times it anticipates a time of looming crisis. Making time regularly for rest, reflection, prayer, and time with family or close associates is one of the least imitated aspects of Jesus'

Sabbath Resistance

Barbara Brown Taylor described her growing sense of Sabbath in the following paragraphs in the *Christian Century*.

"In his book *Jewish Renewal*, Rabbi Michael Lerner says that anyone engaging the practice of Shabbat can expect a rough ride for a couple of years at least. This is because Sabbath involves pleasure, rest, freedom and slowness, none of which comes naturally to North Americans. Most of us are so sold on speed, so invested in productivity, so convinced that multitasking is the way of life that stopping for one whole day can feel at first like a kind of death.

As the adrenaline drains away, you can fear that your heart has stopped beating since you cannot hear your pulse pounding in your temples anymore. As you do no work, you can wonder if you are running a temperature since being sick is the only way that you ever get out of work. As time billows out in front of you, you can have a little panic attack at how much of it you are wasting since time is not only money but also the clock ticking on your life.

For reasons like these, plenty of us take an hour here or there and call it Sabbath, which is like driving five miles to town and calling it Europe. Two hours on a Friday afternoon is not enough, Lerner says. We need ten times longer than that to calm down enough to draw a deep breath. We need ten times ten to trust the saving rhythm of Sabbath without worrying that our own ambition will yank the rug of rest out from under us. 'You haven't had the experience,' he says, 'until you've tried doing it for the full 25 hours, and doing it for a year or two minimum.'

I have been doing it for seven years now, which is how I know the rabbi is right. For the first couple of years, I paced as much as I rested. Every few hours I caught my mind posing inventive questions. If I enjoyed yard work, was it really work? Was browsing a mail order catalog really shopping? By year three I had come to count on Sabbath the same way I count on food or breath. I could work like a demon the other six days of the week as long as I knew the seventh was coming. For the first time in my life, I could rest without leaving home.

With sundown on the Sabbath, I stopped seeing the dust balls, the bills and the laundry. They were still there, but they had lost their power over me. One day each week I lived as if all my work were done. I lived as if the kingdom had come and when I did the kingdom came, for 25 hours at least. Now, when I know Sabbath is near, I can feel the anticipation bubbling up inside of me. Sabbath is no longer a good idea or even a spiritual discipline for me. It is an experience of divine love that swamps both body and soul. It is the weekly practice of eternal life, marred only by the fact that I do it alone."

Barbara Brown Taylor, "Sabbath Resistance," *Christian Century* (May 31, 2005).

---

life, however. There is no record in the book of Acts or the letters of Paul that the disciples ever followed Jesus' example. How might the history of the early church have been different if they had continued the practice of regular individual and group retreats? Would they have been more sensitive to God's leading? Would there have been fewer rifts and tensions in the early church? Jesus came to save the world, but he made time to withdraw from his work for rest and renewal. Yet, our "messianic complex" leads us to think that we are so busy or so indispensable that we cannot leave our regular responsibilities even for a brief time. Self-care is the first step in giving effective care to others. How does the rhythm of your life differ from the rhythm of Jesus' life? When and how do you replenish your soul's emotional and spiritual reserves?

A second reflection arising from this summary section concerns the parallel actions of the sick, who pressed upon Jesus, and the unclean spirits that fell before him. Note the similarity of the Greek verbs discussed in the commentary section above. Although both groups came to Jesus, their reasons and Jesus' responses to them were different. The sick came in desperate faith, hoping and trusting that they would be healed if they even touched him. On the other hand, why did the unclean spirits cry out to Jesus, and why did he silence them? We can only surmise. The unclean spirits asked for nothing; they either confessed Jesus as the Son of God, or more likely they sought to reveal his identity and perhaps thereby to gain power over him. Jesus healed many (3:10), but he commanded the unclean spirits not to make him known. In other words, those who came in faith and desperate need found their needs met, while those who came seeking to promote themselves or diminish his power were rebuffed. The act of falling before Jesus, therefore, is not in and of itself effective; more important are the motive, need, and sincerity of the one who comes to Jesus.

The alternative explanation for why Jesus silenced the unclean spirits is that while their confession or declaration was true, it was a truth out of time, a truth that could not yet be disclosed because there was not yet a context in which it could be understood. To declare that Jesus was the Son of God apart from his death and resurrection would be to conjure up a false understanding of Jesus. The title "Son of God" was associated in Hebrew thought with David and with the kings of Israel. In Greco-Roman thought it was related to Julius Caesar. Octavian, or Caesar Augustus, then claimed the title. For Jesus, however, divine descent meant not royal power but a single-minded devotion to God's redemptive mission. Because Jesus was the Son of God, he could not turn aside from the death that awaited him, and because Jesus was the Son of God, the resurrection of Jesus had a significance that the resurrection of any other person would not have had. The resurrection of Jesus declared God's validation of Jesus' ministry and message and God's vindication of Jesus over his opponents and the power of evil. Truth is time-bound. All things must be understood in context, and there are some things that we are not now ready to grasp (see John 14:26; 16:12). According to at least one early Christian confession, it was the death and resurrection of Jesus that established his divine sonship: ". . . the gospel concerning his Son, who was descended from David according to the flesh and was declared to be the Son of God with power according to the spirit of holiness by resurrection from the dead, Jesus Christ out Lord" (Rom 1:3-4). This being the case, confessing Jesus to be the Son of God before his death and resurrection would only have brought misunderstanding of Jesus' true identity and mission.

Mark 3:13-19

We face a daunting challenge—how to be the church in the twenty-first century. Both the church and the society in which we live have undergone far-reaching changes during the lifespan of our older members. Some of us can remember training union, study courses, and a time when everyone used the King James Version and the same Sunday school material. The church occupied a central position in the life of a small town, denominational traditions were more important than they are now, and ministers held a more respected position in society at large. Now we face the challenge of being the church in a society in which there is growing polarization. Daily schedules are stretched by time spent commuting. The Bible belt in which Christians, Protestants, and especially Baptists predominated has given way to a multicultural society in which Asians, Afrian Americans, Hispanics, Jews, Arabs, and many other ethnic groups have their own foods, festivals, and religious practices. We know how to grow churches in affluent suburbs, but where are the instructions for how to be the church today?

Did Jesus intend to found the church? This is the question that Reformers and historians have asked at pivotal times in our history. Martin Luther looked at the church of his day and asked, is the church with its hierarchical structure, its ministry and sacraments, its sale of indulgences, its saints, angels, and relics the legitimate outgrowth of the life and teachings of Jesus? What would Jesus say about what the church has become? Is the modern alternative, covenant church or praise church the fulfillment of Jesus' design for the church? Is the televangelists' church of the airwaves or the Internet a legitimate extension of what it means to be the church? Where are the instructions, the map, the blueprint, the foundation for the future of the church?

The question is made all the more difficult because when we read through the Gospels we find that Jesus does not use the word *church* except in the Gospel of Matthew, and then only two times. Jesus says to Peter at Caesarea Philippi, "And I tell you, you are Peter, and on this Rock I will build my church" (16:18), and then in giving instructions on how to deal with conflict, he says to go to the person, then to take one or two others, then "tell it to the church; and if he refuses to listen even to the church, let him be to you as a Gentile and a tax collector" (18:17). Important as these passages are, we cannot limit our study of Jesus' plan for the church to the places where he uses the term "church." Much of the teaching of Jesus was intended to guide his followers in how they should continue to be the people of God on mission in the world after his death. The Gospels were written for exactly this purpose—to guide the church by reminding the early Christians of what Jesus had done and said that could serve as a blueprint for the church in their own time.

In a real sense, the church began on a hillside near the Sea of Galilee, when Jesus called his followers to him and singled out twelve individuals. None of the words spoken on that occasion have been preserved, but Mark records that "Jesus appointed twelve to be with him, and to be sent out to preach and have authority to cast out demons," and then he lists the names of the twelve disciples. Here we have the church in embryonic form and a digest of Jesus' purposes for it.

As soon as we read that Jesus went up on a mountain, we are reminded of Moses, who went up on Mount Sinai and brought down the Ten Commandments, or Elijah who went up on Mount Horeb, where he experienced the presence of God in silence, "a still, small voice." But instead, Jesus called a group of men up on a mountain to be with him and to join him the work of the kingdom. Instead of a new law, Jesus created a new people, a people bound to a divine purpose.

The text says that Jesus called Twelve, but they would be leaders of what the book of Revelation ultimately describes as "a great multitude which no man could number, from every nation, from all tribes and peoples and tongues, standing before the altar and before the lamb" (Rev 7:9). It is God's purpose to call all men and women into a new relationship with God.

In Mark 3:14 two purposes for the calling of the Twelve are stated that are foundational for God's plan for the church. The first is "in order that they might be with him." At the heart of God's redemptive activity is the purpose of restoring all people to fellowship with God. God created human beings to tend the earth and to live in fellowship with their Creator. The greatest of God's commandments is that "you shall love the Lord your God with all your heart, and with all your soul, and with all your mind, and with all your strength" (12:30), and in the majestic opening verses of Ephesians Paul repeats three times that we are to live "for the praise of the glory of God" (Eph 1:6, 12, 14). The church fulfills an essential part of its purpose through worship. Perhaps Mark has given us the simplest definition of worship: "being with our Lord." [William Temple's Definition of Worship]

William Temple's Definition of Worship

William Temple, a devout English theologian, gave us a much fuller definition of worship: *Worship is the submission of all our nature to God. It is the quickening of conscience by His holiness; the nourishment of mind with His truth; the purifying of imagination by His beauty; the opening of the heart to his love; the surrender of will to His purpose—and all of this gathered up in adoration.*

William Temple, *Readings in St. John's Gospel* (New York: St. Martin's Press, 1959), 68.

In worship we experience in more intense ways than in other activities the mystery of God's presence and immanence in life. Worship requires our active participation, our thought, our will, our imagination, and our sense of beauty. Worship that is devoid of aesthetic elements is impoverished. Worship that does not engage all of our nature and lead us to praise, confess, give thanks, celebrate, deepen awareness, make covenants, and recommit ourselves to our defining relationships and values scarcely fulfills our Lord's purpose that we "be with him."

"Being with him," however, also involves Christian nurture and education. During the years that the disciples spent with Jesus, they saw what he did, they listened to his teachings, and they learned by example. Being with Jesus led the disciples to become more mature in their faith so that they could carry on the work of the kingdom after Jesus' departure. The book of Acts records that one of the hallmarks of the Jerusalem church's practice was that they "devoted themselves to the apostles' teachings." The early church adapted the Jewish emphasis on nurture and the Greek ideal of *paideia* or education. Christian schools, monasteries, and later universities played important roles in perpetuating and undergirding the life of the church. In 1780 Robert Raikes started the first Sunday school program, and its good legacy continues to this day. Before the disciples would be prepared for anything else, they had to spend time with Jesus. Worship and education, therefore, are essential elements of Jesus' plan for the church.

The second purpose stated in Mark 3:14 is twofold: "in order that he might send them out to proclaim the message and to have authority to cast out demons." Here is a basic truth about the Christian life: God has called us both to be with him and to be sent out, both a "journey inward" and a "journey outward."[18] If we see discipleship merely as our private relationship with God, it becomes a sterile, self-centered experience with no outlet. If we see discipleship merely as going out, it becomes frenetic activism, and we soon exhaust our resources to keep going or to confront the demonic forces around us. Worship and education give us power for going out, and evangelism and ministry fulfill God's redemptive purpose for the church.

Unfortunately evangelism has gotten tied to certain outdated approaches to evangelism that no longer work well. Revivalism, knocking on strangers' doors, and confrontive, deductive religious sales pitches do not work well. Instinctively we have resisted such ways of sharing our faith with others. Sharing good news, establishing caring relationships in which we can tell others about Jesus and what he means to us, however, is a natural and essential part of responding to Jesus' call to follow him. The challenge to find appropriate and effective ways to proclaim the good news of Jesus' love is not a new one, but it is one of the most important challenges we face.

The second part of the mission purpose is that we have "authority to cast out demons." Here the language is couched in first-century terms, but terms that remind us of the powerful forces of evil that constantly claw at the fabric of human life and society. Poverty, oppression, and the lack of education or hope spawn drug abuse, violence, and hatred.

Daily, we see around us the work of these demonic forces, but Jesus has called the church to have authority to cast out the demons, to be God's instrument for breaking the cycle of poverty, hopelessness, and violence. [A Blueprint for the Church in Mark 3:14-15]

Responding to the call to follow Christ created a fellowship that transcended social differences. The group of twelve included fishermen who had left their livelihood, a tax collector who taxed the fishermen for Herod Antipas, Simon the zealot who had been ready to take up arms against the oppressive rulers, brothers who were ready to call down fire on a Samaritan village, and even Judas. With these men Jesus created a new kind of fellowship.

A Blueprint for the Church in Mark 3:14-15

"And [Jesus] appointed twelve, whom he also named apostles,

to be with him	WORSHIP and CHRISTIAN EDUCATION
and to be sent out to preach	EVANGELISM
and to have authority to cast our demons."	SOCIAL MINISTRIES

The church is to be a community that is marked by caring and discipline. We care for each other and for the church too much to let anyone take church membership too lightly. We care for those who need forgiveness, for those who need comfort, for those who need encouragement to go on under difficult circumstances, and for those who are lonely and friendless.

The circumstances of the church change from generation to generation. New forms and structures are called for, and each generation faces the challenge of finding the right wineskins for the new wine of the kingdom. Whatever its form or structures, though, when the church is fulfilling God's purposes for it, the life of the church is marked by meaningful worship, caring nurture and education, evangelistic sharing of the gospel, compassionate and courageous ministry in the name of Jesus, and a fellowship that transcends divisive social barriers. That was Jesus' blueprint for the church when he called those first twelve disciples.

Mark 3:20-35

This section poses difficult issues. Is it possible for persons to commit an "unpardonable sin," and if so what sins are unpardonable? And second, does Jesus' rejection of his own family offer biblical support for those who turn away from their families? Both issues require sensitivity to the full range of biblical teachings and the way in which the interpreter moves from what the sayings of Jesus meant in the context of his ministry, what they meant in the early church, what they meant in

Mark's context, what they have meant in various eras of Christian history, and what they may mean today. It is all too easy either to ignore and bypass a difficult passage, or to lift it out as the exclusive biblical word on a particular topic. It would be wrong, for example, to take Mark 3:28 to mean that if one ever says a blasphemous word against the Holy Spirit, that person can never be forgiven. Equally, it would be wrong to build one's understanding of the biblical teachings on the family exclusively on Mark 3:31-35.

Jesus' instruction about the unpardonable sin has troubled the conscience of many whose remorse over something they have done has led them to agonize over whether what they have done will separate them from God's mercy forever. Three observations should be made in response to this fear: (1) the Bible assures us that God's mercy and forgiveness are beyond our comprehension; (2) whenever the New Testament speaks of the impossibility of forgiveness it is always in the context of a warning, and it is never Jesus' response to a penitent sinner (see Heb 6:4-9; 1 John 5:14-17); and (3) as C. E. B. Cranfield reminds us, "It is a matter of great importance pastorally that we can say with absolute confidence to any one who is overwhelmed by the fear that he has committed this sin, that the fact that he is so troubled is in itself a sure proof that he has not committed it."[19]

Jesus' warning to the scribes about blasphemy against the Holy Spirit should be understood first in its particular historical context. The religious authorities of their day failed to perceive that God was acting in a new way in Jesus. Instead of assisting in his ministry, they were an obstacle to it. Through Jesus, God was breaking down the social barriers that religious tradition had established between Jews and Gentiles, the religious and the "people of the land," men and women (see elsewhere Acts 2:17-18; Gal 3:28; Eph 2:15-16). Jesus was forgiving sins and restoring persons to wholeness. The sin of the scribes was not merely uttering forbidden words. They were threatening to prevent Jesus from fulfilling his kingdom-bringing mission. If one is looking for analogous actions today, one might look to the pronouncements of religious, denominational, and church leaders who are so out of touch with the movement of God's spirit in our time that they champion sectarian causes by polarizing religious communities and stirring up fear, hatred, and divisiveness. Rather than fostering understanding and finding common ground between Christians, Jews, Muslims, and persons of other religious faiths, they accuse and slander. For example, in an era when the Christian witness has been severely compromised by anti-Semitism, it is irresponsible to say, "God does not hear the prayers of a Jew." In an era when Middle Eastern Muslims and American Christians perceive each other as enemies, for a Christian religious leader to say, "Mohammed was a demon-possessed pedophile," poses a serious hindrance to the reconciling, forgiving, and peace-making work of the Holy Spirit. In our time as in Jesus' time, it is misguided religious leaders who are most in danger of blaspheming against the Holy Spirit.

Jesus' words about his family should not be taken to justify breaking ties to one's family over family issues or strained relationships. Jesus was setting in sharp relief the ultimate call of God upon the life of an individual and making the family the model for the experience of the Christian community. Rather than devaluing the family, Jesus made it the paradigm for the church. The love and sustained commitment of siblings, parents, and children should characterize the relationships between disciples in the company of Jesus. In our mobile and fragmented society, in which many do not have family around them, the church can become an important "kin group," offering support, mutual accountability, and sustained, stable relationships.

The inclusiveness of Jesus' accepting word, "*whoever* does the will of God is my brother and sister and mother," should challenge every devout person to enter into community with others who are sincerely seeking God's will, regardless of the differences in their backgrounds or beliefs.

NOTES

[1] Joel Marcus, *Mark 1–8* (AB 27; New York: Doubleday, 2000), 253.

[2] Leander E. Keck, "Mark 3,7-12 and Mark's Christology," *JBL* 84 (1965): 341-58; Robert A. Guelich, *Mark 1–8:26* (WBC 34A; Dallas: Word, 1989), 142-43; and Marcus, *Mark 1–8*, 259.

[3] Marcus, *Mark 1–8*, 260.

[4] Guelich, *Mark 1–8:26*, 148.

[5] Ibid., 155.

[6] See Rengstorf, "*apostolos*," *TDNT*, esp. 1:407-20.

[7] Oscar Cullmann, "*Petros*," *TDNT* 6:101.

[8] Guelich, *Mark 1–8:26*, 163.

[9] See Raymond E. Brown, *The Death of the Messiah* (New York: Doubleday, 1994), 2:1410-16.

[10] See William Klassen, "Judas Iscariot," *ABD* (New York: Doubleday, 1992), esp. 1092.

[11] These paragraphs are reproduced from R. Alan Culpepper, *John, the Son of Zebedee: The Life of a Legend* (Columbia: University of South Carolina Press, 1994; Minneapolis: Fortress Press, 2000), 29-30.

[12] Werner Foerster, "*Beelzeboul*," *TDNT* 1:605-606.

[13] Joachim Jeremias, *The Parables of Jesus* (rev. ed.; trans. S. H. Hooke; New York: Scribner's Sons, 1963), 21, 38, 42.

[14] Ernest Best, *The Temptation and the Passion: The Markan Soteriology* (SNTSMS 2; Cambridge: Cambridge University Press, 1965), 15.

[15] Joachim Jeremias, *New Testament Theology: The Proclamation of Jesus* (trans. John Bowden; New York: Charles Scribner's Sons, 1971), 35-36.

[16] Florentino García Martínez, *The Dead Sea Scrolls Translated* (Leiden: E. J. Brill, 1994), 36.

[17] Marcus, *Mark 1–8*, 285.

[18] Elizabeth O'Connor, *Journey Inward, Journey Outward* (New York: Harper & Row, 1968).

[19] C. E. B. Cranfield, *The Gospel according to Saint Mark* (CGTC; Cambridge: Cambridge University Press, 1959), 142.

PARABLES OF THE KINGDOM

Mark 4:1-41

By the end of Mark 3, it has become clear that Jesus came as the Son of God, authorized to inaugurate a new era that will be characterized by God's sovereign rule. Jesus has authority to cast out demons, and he teaches "as one with authority" (1:22), but the scribes and the Pharisees, the religious authorities, resist his teaching and even plot to kill him (3:6). In response, Jesus calls twelve disciples. They are men from ordinary walks of life, and one of them will betray him (3:19). Ominously, the scribes sent from Jerusalem say he is in league with Satan, and even his own family thinks he is out of his mind. Still, there is hope—a new community of those who do the will of God (3:35).

At this point Mark inserts the largest block of teaching material in the Gospel except for the discourse on the Mount of Olives in Mark 13. Jesus teaches in parables so that his teaching will remain an enigma to those outside the kingdom (4:10-12). The parable of the sower and the seed explains why so many have resisted Jesus' announcement of the kingdom and affirms that, nevertheless, its coming will be glorious. When the disciples do not understand the parable, Jesus explains the rhetorical strategy of the parables (4:10-12) and interprets the parable for them.

Parables can generally be distinguished from allegories in that a parable typically has one point, while the characters and events in an allegory each stand for realities the hearer must identify. [A Synopsis of Parable Studies] In contrast to most interpretations of the parables, which treat the parables in isolation from their narrative contexts, recent narrative criticism interprets the parables as embedded narratives that interact with the larger Gospel narratives in fascinating ways. Because of its position as the first of Jesus' parables and because it is the only one he interprets, the parable of the sower and the seed functions as a lens, or an embedded commentary, that prepares the reader to understand the actions of the characters in Jesus' ministry, just as the parable of the wicked tenants in Mark 12:1-12 prepares the reader to understand the betrayal, trial, death, and resurrection of Jesus.[1]

The theme of hiddenness and revelation runs through Mark 4:1-34. Jesus teaches in parables because the kingdom is a mystery. The

Synopsis of Parable Studies

Cyril of Alexandria said, "Parables are word pictures not of visible things, but rather of things of the mind and the spirit" (Oden and Hall, 55). Since Adolf Jülicher parables have been divided into four groups: similitudes, parables, example stories, and allegories. C. H. Dodd, who regarded the parables as vehicles for Jesus' message of the kingdom of God, offered the following suggestive definition of a parable: "At its simplest the parable is a metaphor or simile drawn from nature or common life, arresting the hearer by its vividness or strangeness, and leaving the mind in sufficient doubt about its precise application to tease it into active thought" (Dodd, 16).

Joachim Jeremias recognized both how thoroughly Jesus' parables breathed the atmosphere of 1st-C. Palestine and how thoroughly they have been reinterpreted in the tradition of the early church. He therefore set about to reconstruct the original parables from the tradition, identify the actual words of Jesus, and set the parables in the context of Jesus' ministry (rather than in the literary context of the Gospels or the moralizing and allegorizing tradition of the early church). As Norman Perrin records, Amos Wilder regarded Jesus as "a poet who imparted to his hearers his own vision of reality in the metaphorical language of his parables" (Perrin, 131). In *Early Christian Rhetoric*, Wilder interpreted the parables as extended metaphors, writing that "a true metaphor or symbol is more than a sign, it is a bearer of the reality to which it refers" (Wilder, 84). Robert Funk took as his point of departure a reconsideration of Dodd's definition of a parable: "This definition provides four essential clues to the nature of the parable: (1) the parable is a metaphor or simile which may (*a*) remain simple, (*b*) be elaborated into a picture, or (*c*) be expanded into a story; (2) the metaphor or simile is drawn from nature or common life; (3) the metaphor arrests the hearer by its vividness or strangeness; and (4) the application is left imprecise in order to tease the hearer into making his own application" (Funk, 133).

Funk argued that a parable is a metaphor not a simile. A simile illustrates the nature of the kingdom or some aspect of it. With metaphor, "the kingdom confronts us through the power of the metaphor to produce an impact on the imagination, to be the bearer of reality, to induce vision" (Perrin, 135). Funk then took up the assertion that a parable has one point. In contrast to both Jülicher and Dodd, Funk contended that because the parable can be addressed to different audiences and situations, it is possible that "the parable, as metaphor, had not one but many 'points,' as many points as there are situations into which it is spoken" (151). Metaphors are open-ended and evoke a response from the hearer. Funk then turned to the second and third elements of Dodd's definition. The story is drawn from ordinary life, but it turns that everydayness on its head. The parables generally have an unexpected twist that points through the everydayness to a new reality: "They are language events in which the hearer has to choose between worlds" (Funk, 162).

The work continues. Building on Funk's treatment of parable as metaphor, Dan O. Via (*The Parables: Their Literary and Existential Dimension* [Philadelphia: Fortress Press, 1967]); John Dominic Crossan (*In Parables: The Challenge of the Historical Jesus* [New York: Harper & Row, 1973]); Bernard Brandon Scott (*Hear Then the Parable* [Minneapolis: Fortress Press, 1989]); and Charles W. Hedrick (*Parables as Poetic Fictions: The Creative Voice of Jesus* [Peabody MA: Hendrickson, 1994]) have made significant contributions to the field of parable studies. For a recent survey of parable research, see David B. Gowler, *What Are They Saying about the Parables?* (New York: Paulist Press, 2000). Also not to be missed is the fine treatment of the parables by Peter Rhea Jones, *Studying the Parables of Jesus* (Macon GA: Smyth & Helwys, 1999).

The sheer volume of the literature on the parables is proving Origen right: "Not even the whole world itself could contain the books that might be written to fully clarify and develop the parables" (Oden and Hall, 50).

Dodd, C. H., *The Parables of the Kingdom* (New York: Charles Scribner's Sons, 1935), 16.

Funk, Robert W., *Language, Hermeneutic, and Word of God* (New York: Harper and Row, 1966), 133.

Jeremias, Joachim, *The Parables of Jesus* (rev. ed.; trans. S. H. Hooke; New York: Charles Scribner's Sons, 1963).

Jülicher, Adolf, *Die Gleichnisreden Jesu* (2 vols.; Tübingen: J. C. B. Mohr, 1888, 1899).

Oden, Thomas C. and Christopher A. Hall, eds., *Ancient Christian Commentary on Scripture: New Testament II, Mark* (Downers Grove IL: InterVarsity Press, 1998), 55.

Perrin, Norman, *Jesus and the Language of the Kingdom: Symbol and Metaphor in New Testament Interpretation* (Philadelphia: Fortress Press, 1976), 131.

Wilder, Amos, *Early Christian Rhetoric: The Language of the Gospel* (rev. ed.; Cambridge MA: Harvard University Press, 1971), 84.

mystery has been given to the disciples, but they do not understand it (4:10-12). A lamp is for revelation and therefore is not put under a bushel basket (4:21). Everything that is hidden will be revealed (4:22). Seeds grow of themselves (4:26-29). The harvest, an eschatological image, is certain, and the kingdom, which had such obscure beginnings in a group of fishermen gathered around an itinerant teacher, will surely come. The seed grows secretly (4:26-29), and the mustard seed becomes the greatest of the shrubs (4:30-32). The section ends with a summary comment about Jesus' teaching in parables (4:33-34) and the first sea crossing, during which Jesus stills a storm (4:35-41). If the kingdom is dynamic and growing, it must reach beyond Galilee into the Gentile Decapolis also. [Outline of Mark 4]

Outline of Mark 4

4:1-2 Introduction: Jesus Teaching by the Sea
4:3-20 The Parable of the Sower and Its Interpretation
    4:3-9 The Parable of the Sower
    4:10-12 The Secret of the Kingdom
    4:13-20 The Interpretation of the Parable of the Sower
4:21-32 Teachings on Hiddenness and Revelation
    4:21-25 The Lamp and the Bushel Basket
    4:26-29 The Seed Growing Secretly
    4:30-32 The Mustard Seed
4:33-34 Summary

COMMENTARY

The Parable of the Sower and the Secret of the Kingdom, 4:1-20

The introduction to this section emphasizes Jesus' teaching and the size of the crowd that came to him. The setting is the seaside, the most frequently mentioned locale of Jesus' Galilean ministry (1:16; 2:13; 3:7; 5:1, 21; [6:34]; 7:31). Teaching, whether by the sea or in the synagogue, was also the most characteristic activity of Jesus' ministry—the verb "to teach" occurs seventeen times in Mark. The emphasis is evident in Mark 4:1-2, where the verb occurs twice and the noun "teaching" once. The size of the crowd is characterized by the superlative "greatest" or "largest." Joel Marcus translates the phrase "the biggest crowd yet," noting that the crowd around Jesus had been growing steadily (1:33; 2:2, 13; 3:7-10, 20).[2] The size of the crowd prompts Jesus to get into a boat in order to teach the crowd that gathered on the shore. Presumably, it is the boat first mentioned in 3:9, where it was also coupled with a reference to

The Sea of Galilee

(Credit: R. Alan Culpepper)

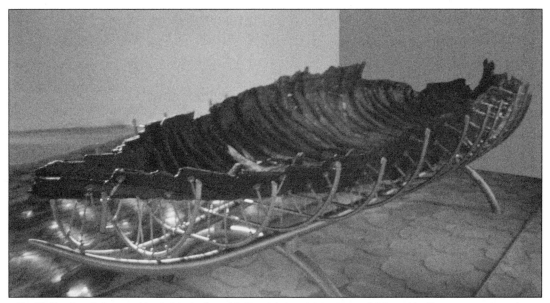

The "Galilee-Boat," discovered in 1986 in the Sea of Galilee. It is (now) 8.2m long and 2.3 m wide. Numerous repairs and many different types of timber show that the boat had a long working life.

Yigal Allon Center, Ginosar, Israel. (Credit: Erich Lessing / Art Resource, NY)

Galilean Fishing Boat

Late in January 1986, two brothers, Moshe and Yuval Lufan, discovered the outline of a boat in mud flats of the Sea of Galilee created by the drought of the previous summer. The shell of the boat, which is 26.5 feet long, 7.5 feet wide, and 4.5 feet high, was buried in the mud between Kibbutz Ginnosar and Migdal. Initially there was speculation that the boat may have been one of those used in the Battle of Migdal (AD 67), because Josephus reports that the Jews "were sent to the bottom with their skiffs" and "the beaches were strewn with wrecks" (*J.W.* 3.525, 530 [Loeb 2.725]). Detailed study, however, revealed that the boat had been stripped of reusable parts before it was pushed into the lake. The mast block, stempost, and sternpost had been removed.

The boat could have been either rowed or sailed. Just as the boat is depicted in a first-century mosaic from Migdal, it was designed for a crew of four rowers and a helmsman, who would have stood on a large stern platform. It could have carried about fifteen people. The converging evidence of the building techniques that were used in its construction, the pottery found around the boat, and carbon 14 testing of the wood itself indicates that boat was built about 40 BC plus or minus 80 years. By all accounts, it appears to have been a typical fishing vessel used during the period of Jesus' ministry.

R. Alan Culpepper, *John, the Son of Zebedee: The Life of a Legend* (Columbia: University of South Carolina Press, 1994), 13–14. See further Shelley Wachsmann, "The Galilee Boat—2,000-Year-Old Hull Recovered Intact," *Biblical Archaeology Review* 14/5 (1988): 18-33.

the size of the crowd. [Galilean Fishing Boat] Some find here a fulfillment of Psalm 29—"The voice of the LORD is over the waters" (29:3) and "The LORD sits enthroned over the flood" (29:10). Mark's comment that Jesus was teaching them "many things" shows that what follows is merely representative of Jesus' teaching. For the second time Mark notes that Jesus taught in parables (see 3:23). The imperfect tense can signal either the beginning of an action, "he began to teach them" (NRSV), or recurring action, "he was teaching . . . and he used to say. . . ."

The parable of the sower is introduced emphatically: "Listen! Behold. . . ." The command to hear, when taken with the concluding admonition, "Let anyone with ears to hear listen!" (4:9), serves as a frame for the story that commands attention, as if to say, "It is very important that you hear this!" (cf. 4:13, 24). After such an introduction, the opening line of the parable is mystifyingly commonplace: "A sower went out to sow." Because the introduction commands attention the first line does not seem to merit, the parable hooks the hearer's interest by creating suspicion that there must be more here than is apparent, as in a riddle, a paradox, or a mystery (cf. 4:11).

After the introductory line, the sower is not mentioned again, leading some interpreters to suggest that "the parable of the sower" is a misnomer. Interpretations place varying degrees of emphasis on the sower, the seeds, and the harvest. Placing emphasis on the sower leads to reflection on Jesus' role as the agent of the kingdom, whose ministry will lead to such a bountiful harvest in spite of the obstacles he confronts. In the parable, however, the sower does nothing unusual, sowing seemingly indiscriminately on the path, on the rocky soil, and among the thorns. Broadcasting seed is wasteful, as is sowing seed on the path. Jeremias made the case for the necessity of interpreting the parables in their historical context by arguing that sowing and then plowing was the normal sequence. [Sowing before Ploughing] The sower sowed on the path and on the rocky soil because he had not yet plowed the field: "What appears to the western mind as bad farming is simply customary usage under Palestinian conditions."[3]

Sowing before Ploughing

"The main classes of work are forty save one: sowing, ploughing, reaping, binding sheaves, threshing, winnowing, cleansing crops, grinding, sifting, kneading, baking. . . ." (*m. Shab.* 7.2)

"And Prince Mastema sent crows and birds so that they might eat the seed which was being sown in the earth in order to spoil the earth so that they might rob mankind of their labors. Before they plowed in the seed, the crows picked it off the surface of the earth." (*Jub.* 11:11)

Prompted by this threat, Abram invented a device that allowed the farmers to plant the seed as they plowed:

"Abram taught those who were making the implements for oxen, the skilled carpenters. And they made implements above the ground facing the handle of the plow so that they might place seed upon it. And the seed would go down from within it onto the point of the plow, and it would be hidden in the earth. And therefore they were not afraid of the crows." (*Jub.* 11:23)

The most detailed portion of the parable describes the fate of the seeds, which leads to the interpretation in vv. 13-20. Again, however, as every farmer knew, there is nothing remarkable about the loss of seed to the elements: birds, rocks, and thorns. Here the triadic structure of the parable becomes visible. The parable describes two sets of three groups of seeds: three that failed to produce (those sown on the path, the rocky soil, and among the thorns) and three that produced in varying degrees (thirty, sixty, and a hundredfold). The fate of each of the unproductive groups is described in three stages: the sowing, the threat, and the result.[4]

Alternatively, one may focus on the harvest. The harvest was measured in terms of the ratio of yield to seed. Jeremias concluded that a harvest of seven-and-a-half fold was normal, and a tenfold harvest was good.[5] Harvest of thirty, sixty, and a hundredfold would therefore be extraordinary. Here is the piece that does not fit—the hyperbole that signals there is more to the story than one first suspects. If the farmer did nothing unusual, and met the all-too-familiar problems of farming, how did he reap such a bountiful harvest? The harvest was a common image for eschatological bounty. [Bountiful Harvests] As a parable of the kingdom, the parable of the sower promises that even if the beginnings of the kingdom are altogether unremarkable, and even if the disciples' experience of persecution and suffering seemed to indicate that their hopes were in vain, the harvest would be spectacular. The parable is therefore a challenge to believe that the kingdom could be present even in such insignificant beginnings and that the fulfillment of the kingdom was indeed coming.

Bountiful Harvests

"Isaac sowed seed in that land, and in the same year reaped a hundredfold. The LORD blessed him, and the man became rich." (Gen 26:12)

"For these alone the fertile soil yields fruit from one- to a hundredfold, and the measures of God are produced." (*Syb. Or.* 3.261–64)

"Its corn is so abundant that it yields for the most part two hundred fold, and even three hundred fold when the harvest is best." (Herodotus 1.193; LCL 1:243–44)

"Around Sybaris in Italy the normal yield is said to be even a hundred to one, and a like yield is reported near Gadara in Syria, and for the district of Byzacium in Africa." (Varro, *On Agriculture* 1.44.2)

"The days will come, in which vines shall grow, each having ten thousand branches, and in each branch ten thousand twigs, and in each true twig ten thousand shoots, and in each one of the shoots ten thousand clusters, and on every one of the clusters ten thousand grapes, and every grape when pressed will give five and twenty metretes of wine." (Irenaeus, *Against Heresies* 5.33.3)

"The world to come is not like this world. In this world there is the trouble of harvesting and treading [of the grapes], but in the world to come a man will bring one grape on a wagon or a ship, put it in a corner of his house and use its contents as [if it had been] a large wine cask, while its timber [branches] would be used to make the firs for cooking. There will be no grape that will not contain thirty kegs of wine." (*b. Ketub.* 111b, Soncino 7:721–22)

Mark 4:10-12 is one of the most difficult passages in the Gospel. The difficulty is posed by its use of Isaiah 6:9-10 as an explanation for why Jesus taught about the kingdom of God in parables. The explanation presumes that there are two ways in which one may be related to the kingdom—one is either an "insider" or an "outsider." The kingdom is "given" to the insiders, but for those outside everything about Jesus and his ministry is a riddle or a mystery, "so that they may not turn again and be forgiven" (4:12). Therein lies the difficulty. Why would Jesus teach in such a way that many of his hearers would not be able to perceive, understand, and repent?

Mark's handling of these verses posed problems even for his earliest interpreters: Matthew and Luke, both of whom edit them to take away some of their offensiveness. [The Purpose of the Parables in the Synoptic Parallels]

Mark 4:10-12 poses other problems for the interpreter. It does not fit smoothly in its context. Verse 10 signals a change of time and place:

The Purpose of the Parables in the Synoptic Parallels

Matthew 13:10-16
10 *Then* the *disciples* came and asked him, "Why do you speak to them in parables?"
11 He answered, "To you it has been given *to know* the *secrets* of the kingdom of heaven, but *to* them it has not been given.
12 For to those who have, more will be given, and they will have an abundance; but from those who have nothing, even what they have will be taken away.
13 The reason *I speak* to them in parables is that 'seeing they do not perceive, and hearing *they* do not listen, nor do they understand.' 14 With them indeed is fulfilled the prophecy of Isaiah that says:
'You will indeed listen, but never understand, and you will indeed look, but never perceive.
15 For this people's heart has grown dull, and their ears are hard of hearing, and they have shut their eyes; so that they might not look with their eyes, and listen with their ears, and understand with their heart and turn—and I would heal them.'
16 But blessed are your eyes, for they see, and your ears, for they hear.

Mark 4:10-12
When he was alone, those who were around him along with the twelve asked him about the parables. 11 And he said to them, "To you has been given the secret of the kingdom of God, but for those outside,
everything comes in parables;
12 in order that 'they may indeed look, but not perceive, and may indeed listen, but not understand; so that they may not turn again and be forgiven.' "

Luke 8:9-10
9 *Then* his *disciples* asked him what this parable meant. 10 He said, "To you *it* has been given *to know* the *secrets* of the kingdom of God; but *to* others *I speak* in parables,
so that 'looking they may not perceive, and listening *they* may not understand.' "

"When he was alone." But vv. 35 and 36 return to the scene set in 4:1-2—later the same day they leave the crowd behind and cross the lake in the boat. Furthermore, Jesus says that the secret of the kingdom has been given to the disciples, while for those outside everything is in parables (i.e., riddles). Nevertheless, the disciples do not understand the parables, not even the parable of the sower (see v. 13).

Jesus' explanation of the parables introduces the pattern of public teaching and private explanation in Mark (see 4:33-34; 6:30-31; 7:14-17; 9:28, 33; 10:10). The group asking Jesus about the parables includes more than the Twelve (cf. 3:13). The reference to "those who were around him" recalls the crowd that was sitting around Jesus when his family came for him (3:32). The connection to this scene establishes an important context for interpreting the reference to "those outside." Accordingly, those who have responded to Jesus' teachings and follow him have been given the secret of the kingdom of God. Through Jesus they have access to the kingdom. For those who reject Jesus (the scribes and Pharisees, and Jesus' family), everything is in riddles. Paradoxically, however, having been given the secret of the kingdom does not automatically mean that the disciples would understand the parables. The disciples too can be blind and hard of heart.

Literally, Jesus says that the "mystery" of the kingdom has been given to his followers. The term had strong associations both for Jews and for Gentiles. The pagan mystery religions promised eternal life to their initiates, who were given secret knowledge and shown secret objects during elaborate initiation rituals. [Mystery Religions] In the prophetic and apocalyptic literature, God is "the revealer of mysteries" (Dan 2:18-19, 27-30, 47). At Qumran, the initiates believed that revelation occurred in two stages: God had inspired the prophets to write, but they did not understand the full meaning of what they wrote. The interpretation (Heb. *pesher*) of the mystery (Heb. *raz*) was given to their Teacher of Righteousness. By following his teachings they were able to discern the real meaning of the Scriptures. They therefore wrote the first commentaries (Heb. *pesharim*) on the Scriptures, quoting a verse and then introducing the commentary with the phrase "and its interpretation (*pesher*) is. . . ." The difference was that at Qumran the key to understanding the Scriptures was provided by the teachings of the Teacher of Righteousness; for Mark Jesus himself was the secret of the kingdom of God, and the text to be interpreted was the words of Jesus, not the Scriptures. [Pesher Interpretation] In both Mark and the Qumran scrolls, however, the fulfillment of the Scriptures is seen in the events surrounding the

Mystery Religions

Note how closely the following description of the mystery religions approximates the language of Mark 4:10-12: "A person (Gk. *mystēs*, pl. *mystai*) who had experienced the *mystērion* [mystery] was required to maintain closed lips in order not to divulge the secret revealed at the private ceremony. Pledges of silence were intended to ensure that the holy secret would not be disclosed to profane outsiders. . . . An initiate into the mysteries also participated in the closing (and subsequent opening) of the eyes. As people with closed eyes remain in darkness until they open their eyes to see the light, so the *mystai* whose eyes were opened moved from darkness to enlightenment, both literally and metaphorically."

Marvin W. Meyer, "Mystery Religions," *ABD* 4:942.

Pesher Interpretation

"But God remembered the covenant of the very first, and from Aaron raised men of knowledge and from Israel wise men, and forced them to listen. And they dug the well: *Num 21:18* 'A well which the princes dug, which the nobles of the people delved with the staff.' The well is the law. And those who dug it are the converts of Israel, who left the land of Judah and lived in the land of Damascus, all of whom God called princes, for they sought him, and their renown had not been repudiated in anyone's mouth. *Blank* And the staff is the interpreter of the law, of whom Isaiah said: *Isa 54:16* 'He produces a tool for his labours.' *Blank* And the nobles of the people are those who have arrived to dig the well with the staves that the scepter decreed, to walk in them throughout the whole age of wickedness, and without which they will not obtain it, until there arises he who teaches justice at the end of days."

Damascus Document 6.2-11, in Florentino García Martínez, *The Dead Sea Scrolls Translated* (trans. Wilfred G. E. Watson; Leiden: E. J. Brill, 1994), 36–37.

founder of their movement—Jesus and the Teacher of Righteousness. The New Testament writers, Paul in particular, used "mystery" to denote the revelation of divine knowledge that had been withheld from earlier generations but revealed in Christ. The effect was to underscore the role of Jesus as the revealer and to confirm that they were living in the last days. Paul, who used the term more than any other New Testament writer, also used "mystery" specifically to mean the revelation of God's plan to redeem Gentiles as well as Jews through the gospel (Rom 11:25; 16:25; Eph 3:1-9; Col 1:25-27).

For Mark the issue was why some rejected the gospel while others became disciples. The hardheartedness and hostility of some confirmed for the early Christians Isaiah's sharp judgment on Israel for its failure to understand and obey. Quotations of Isaiah 6:9-10 appear, therefore, at significant points in the New Testament: at the close of Jesus' public ministry in the Gospel of John (12:40), at the end of the book of Acts, where Paul says, "Let it be known to you then that this salvation of God has been sent to the Gentiles; they will listen" (Acts 2:26-28), and in paraphrase in Paul's explanation for why a hardening had come upon part of Israel (Rom 11:8).

Interpreters have sought to soften the offense of these verses by appealing to the Aramaic syntax or adopting alternative translations that weaken the force of the initial "in order that" (NRSV, NASB; 4:12, a purpose clause introduced by the Greek *hina*, which may also introduce a result clause, "so that," NIV) and the closing "so that they may not" (NRSV) or "lest" (NASB; Greek *mēpote*), which some translate as "otherwise" (NIV, NEB). The Contemporary English Version removes the offense by translating the last line of 4:12 as "If they did [understand], they would turn to God, and he would forgive them" (also GNB).

In the end, however, all of these efforts to remove the offense misrepresent the meaning of Mark 4:10-12. The contrast here is between those who followed Jesus and those who remained "outside" (who did not accept him), picking up the language of Mark 3:31-35. Mark 4:10-12 speaks only implicitly to the question of why Jesus spoke in parables, in contrast to Matthew and Luke, which introduce the phrase "I speak in parables" (Matt 13:13; Luke 8:10). When the disciples ask Jesus about the parables, Jesus responds that for those outside, he and his ministry ("all things") are "in parables," which can also mean "riddles," so that they might not turn and be forgiven. The Messiah who will not allow his identity to be broadcast openly offers a veiled kingdom. The offense here is the christological exclusiveness of the gospel: one cannot understand the kingdom of God apart from accepting Jesus, the agent of the kingdom.

The importance and function of the parable of the sower is under-scored by its position as the first of Jesus' parables in Mark, by the fact that it is the only parable for which an interpretation is attached, and by Jesus' sharp question to the disciples: "Do you not understand this parable? Then how will you understand all the parables?" (4:13). For the first time, Mark underscores the disciples' lack of understanding—a theme that will be developed repeatedly in the rest of the Gospel. Their inability to understand the parable is jarring because Jesus has just assured the disciples that they are "insiders." The kingdom is mys-terious, however, and even insiders may not understand it or the parables Jesus used to explain it.

The interpretation that follows allegorizes the parable, using it as a vehicle for reflecting on the effectiveness of preaching the gospel in spite of its rejection by various hearers. The interpretation, therefore, shows how the early church interpreted the parable in reference to the mission of the church. In its literary setting in the Gospel of Mark, the parable functions as a "plot synopsis" for the first part of the Gospel, interpreting for the reader Jesus' role as the proclaimer of the kingdom and the meaning of the various responses to Jesus represented by dif-ferent characters and groups in Mark.[6]

Just as the parable begins with the simple declaration that the sower went out to sow, so the interpretation begins with the five-word state-ment "The sower sows the word" (4:13). Elsewhere, Mark uses "the word" in an unqualified sense to mean Jesus' teachings or reports of Jesus' activities (1:45; 2:2; 4:33; 8:32). In the early church "the word" became a technical term for the preaching of the gospel (e.g., Mark 16:20; Luke 1:2; Acts 4:4; 6:4; 8:4; Gal 6:6; etc.). The interpretation of the parable can therefore be read on two levels: as it relates to responses to Jesus during his ministry and as it relates to responses to the preaching of the gospel in Mark's own time. Verse 15 must be read carefully, as it makes the transition from the word that is sown to the locations (or types of hearers) where the word is sown. In a similar way, *4 Ezra* (a Jewish apocalyptic writing from the latter part of the first century AD) uses the metaphor of seed for both the law and the responses of the people to it. [The Seed Metaphor in *4 Ezra*] Most of the interpretation of the parable concerns the three types of unproductive soils (i.e., hearers of the word). Similarly, the rabbis

The Seed Metaphor in *4 Ezra*

"For just as the farmer sows many seeds upon the ground and plants a multitude of seedlings, and yet not all that have been sown will come up in due season, and not all that were planted will take root; so all those who have been sown in the world will not be saved.

"I answered and said, 'If I have found favor before you, let me speak. For if the farmer's seed does not come up, because it has not received your rain in due season, or if it has been ruined by too much rain, it perishes. But man, who has been formed by your hands and is called your own image because he is made like you, and for whose sake you have formed all things—have you also made him like the farmer's seed?" (*4 Ezra* 8:41-44)

"For behold, I sow my Law in you, and you shall be glorified through it for ever." (*4 Ezra* 9:31)

James H. Charlesworth, ed., *The Old Testament Pseudepigrapha* (Garden City NY: Doubleday, 1983), 1:543, 545.

described four types of students. [Four Types of Students]

"The road" or "the way" is used in Mark as a metaphor for the path of discipleship or suffering servanthood, the way to the cross (1:2, 3; 8:27; 9:33, 34; 10:32, 52; 12:14). The depiction of Satan as a bird is found in other writings from the period also. [Satan as a Devouring Bird] In Mark the seed sown on the path characterizes the demoniacs, the scribes, the Pharisees, and the Herodians, who immediately (Gk. *euthys*) reject Jesus and his teaching. Just as there is immediacy to Jesus' actions, so also the demonic responds immediately:

- "Just then (*euthys*) there was in their synagogue a man with an unclean spirit" (1:23).
- "The Pharisees went out and immediately (*euthys*) conspired with the Herodians against him, how to destroy him" (3:6).
- "And when he had stepped out of the boat, immediately (*euthys*) a man out of the tombs with an unclean spirit met him" (5:2).
- "Immediately (*euthys*) the king sent a soldier of the guard with orders to bring John's head" (6:27).
- "When the spirit saw him, immediately (*euthys*) it convulsed the boy" (9:20).
- "Immediately (*euthys*), while he was still speaking, Judas, one of the twelve, arrived" (14:43).
- "As soon as (*euthys*) it was morning, the chief priests held a consultation with the elders and the scribes and the whole council." (15:1).

The verb to "take away" is also used in a hostile sense elsewhere in Mark (4:25; 11:23).

The rocky ground characterizes those who (1) "immediately" receive the word with joy, (2) hold to it only for a while because they have no

---

Four Types of Students

"There are four types among them that sit in the presence of the Sages: the sponge, the funnel, the strainer, and the sifter. 'The sponge'— which soaks up everything; 'the funnel'—which takes in at this end and lets out at the other; 'the strainer'—which lets out the wine and collects the lees; 'the sifter'—which extracts the coarsely-ground flour and collects the fine flour." (*m. Aboth* 5.15)

Herbert Danby, trans., *The Mishnah* (Oxford: Oxford University Press, 1931), 457.

Satan as a Devouring Bird

"And Prince Mastema [i.e., Satan] sent crows and birds so that they might eat the seed which was being sown in the earth in order to spoil the earth so that they might rob mankind of their labors. Before they plowed in the seed, the crows picked it off the surface of the earth." (*Jub.* 11:11)

"And an unclean bird flew down on the carcasses, and I drove it away. And the unclean bird spoke to me and said, 'What are you doing, Abraham. . . .' And it came to pass when I saw the bird speaking I said this to the angel: 'What is this, my lord?' And he said, 'This is disgrace, this is Azazel!' And he said to him, 'Therefore the Eternal Ruler, the Mighty One, has given you a dwelling on earth. Through you the all-evil spirit (is) a liar, and through you (are) wrath and trials on the generations of men who live impiously.'" (Apocalypse of Abraham 13:3-9)

James H. Charlesworth, ed., *The Old Testament Pseudepigrapha* (Garden City NY: Doubleday, 1983), 1:695; 2:78.

(Credit: Barclay Burns)

Rootlessness

"But the prolific brood of the ungodly will be of no use, and none of their illegitimate seedlings will strike a deep root." (Wis 4:3)

"Her children will not take root, and her branches will not bear fruit." (Sir 23:25)

"The children of the ungodly put out few branches; they are unhealthy roots on sheer rock." (Sir 40:15)

root, and then (3) stumble (Gk. *skandalizontai*) when they encounter persecution. In the Gospel of Mark this role is played by the disciples. When Jesus calls them, they immediately leave everything to follow him (1:18, 20; 2:14). Rootlessness described the condition of the wicked [Rootlessness], and like the world itself they pass quickly from the scene (2 Cor 4:18; Heb 11:25; 1 John 2:17). Likewise, the faithful response of the disciples is "for a time" only. They do not understand the nature of the kingdom or the demands of discipleship. Judas betrays him, Peter denies him, and when Jesus is arrested the disciples abandon Jesus and flee into the night (14:50). One may even suspect a play on words between the "rocky" soil and the nickname given to Simon: "Rock." The reference to "trouble or persecution on account of the word" is the clearest indication that the interpretation of the parable has in view the persecution of converts to the preaching of the gospel in Mark's time. The terms used here are used elsewhere to describe the persecution of the early church: "trouble" (Gk. *thlipsis*), which is sometimes used for tribulations preceding the coming of the Son of Man (Mark 13:19, 24; Rev 2:22; 7:14), can also mean "persecution" (Acts 11:19; 14:22), and the two terms (*thlipsis* and *diōgmos*) are found together in Romans 8:35 and 2 Thessalonians 1:4. John was on the island of Patmos and the faithful are persecuted "because of the word of God" (Rev 1:9; 6:9; 20:4). The verb "to fall away" (4:17, Gk. *skandalizein*) is a picturesque term that connotes falling into a trap, stumbling, or causing offense. Jesus' hometown takes offense at him (6:3), and later he warns his disciples that they will all fall away, fulfilling the plot synopsis provided by the interpretation of the parable of the sower (14:27-29; see also 9:42-47).

The interpretation of the fate of the seed sown among the thorns is again reported in patterns of threes: (1) "the ones who hear the word," (2) "[the thorns] choke the word," and (3) "and it yields nothing" (4:18-19). After warning against the sin of apostasy, the author of Hebrews uses the image of thorns in a similar way: "Ground that drinks up the rain falling on it repeatedly, and that produces a crop useful to those for whom it is cultivated, receives a blessing from God. But if it produces thorns and thistles, it is worthless and on the verge of being cursed; and its end is to be burned over" (Heb 6:7-8). The thorns that choke the word are also three: (1) "the cares of the world," (2) "the lure of wealth," and (3) "the desire for other things" (4:19). None of the key words in these phrases appears elsewhere in Mark, but they are common in the ethical teachings of the New Testament. In Luke, Jesus warns that "cares" or "worries" (Gk. *merimnai*) may keep some from being ready for the coming of the Son of Man (Luke 21:34-36), and 1 Peter admonishes, "Cast all your anxiety on him, because he cares for you" (1 Pet 5:7). The term "world" (Gk. *aiōn*) can also mean "age," and suggests the Jewish distinction between "this world" and "the world to come."

The ethical teachings of the early church often warn believers against the dangers of deception (Eph 4:22; Col 2:8; 2 Thess 2:10) and wealth (1 Tim 6:17; Jas 5:1-6; 1 John 2:15-17). Drawing on common imagery of the prophets (Isa 40:6-8) and the wisdom tradition (Job 15:29-30; Ps 103:15-16), James echoes the sentiments of this verse: ". . . the rich will disappear like a flower in the field. For the sun rises with its scorching heat and withers the field; its flower falls, and its beauty perishes. It is the same way with the rich; in the midst of a busy life, they will wither away" (Jas 1:11). [Cares and Riches] The list ends with "desires," a "catch-all" for various lusts, desires, and vices (Rom 1:24; 6:12; 7:8; 13:14, etc.). In the Gospel of Mark, the rich man and Herod illustrate this response to the gospel.[7] Jesus challenges the rich man to sell all his possessions and follow him. His response parallels the interpretation of the fate of the seed that fell among the thorns: "[1] When he heard this, [3] he was shocked and went away grieving, for [2] he had many possessions" (10:22). And Jesus laments that it is hard for those who have wealth to enter the kingdom of God (10:23). Herod too illustrates this pattern. Initially, he protected John the Baptist and "heard" him gladly (6:20), but after his thoughtless pledge, when Salome asked for John's head, "The king was deeply grieved; yet out of regard for his oaths and for his guests, he did not want to refuse her" (6:26). Both Herod and the rich man start well but are led astray by wealth and the cares that accompany their position in the world.

After such a discouraging list of failures, one might wonder whether there will be any harvest at all. If the scribes and Pharisees, the disciples—even Peter, James and John—and the rich and powerful like Herod and the rich man will not bear fruit, then who? Jesus assures the disciples that there will be those who (1) "hear the word," (2) "accept it," and (3) "bear fruit," and the harvest will be astounding: (1) "thirty," (2) "sixty," and (3) "a hundredfold" (4:20). In the gospel the examples of the seed falling upon good soil are few and paradoxical. John the Baptist responds to his call to prepare the way, proclaims "the one who is more powerful than I is coming after me" (1:7), and baptizes "people from the whole countryside and all the people of Jerusalem" (1:5). Then, still preparing the way, he is arrested (1:14). The fruitful soil may

---

Cares and Riches

"When the Word is choked, it is not merely due to the thorns as such, but to the negligence of those allowing them to spring up. There is a way, if there is a will, to hinder evil growth and use wealth appropriately. For this reason he warned not of 'the world' but of the 'care of the world,' not 'riches' as such but 'the deceitfulness of riches.'" (Chrysostom, "Homilies on The Gospel of St. Matthew," 44.6)

Thomas C. Oden and Christopher A. Hall, eds., *Ancient Christian Commentary on Scripture: New Testament II, Mark* (Downers Grove IL: InterVarsity Press, 1998), 57.

also be illustrated by "the little people" as David Rhoads called them:[8] the men who bring the paralytic to Jesus, the Gadarene demoniac who goes home to tell about Jesus, Jairus the synagogue ruler, the woman with a hemorrhage who presses through the crowd to touch Jesus, the Syrophoenician woman who matches wits with Jesus, the father of the epileptic boy, the children who come to Jesus, the blind Bartimaeus who refuses to be quiet, the poor widow who gives all she has, and Joseph of Arimathea who buries Jesus' body while his disciples are nowhere around. Typically these characters persist in their faith in Jesus in spite of obstacles that might have deterred them. Of such is the harvest. The good earth, as Jesus goes on to explain in the following parables, produces of itself and is capable of transforming even the smallest seed into a great plant. The kingdom will not be hidden forever.

Parables of Hiddenness and Fruition, Mark 4:21-34

Verses 21-25 are a collection of independent sayings found in other contexts in Matthew and Luke. Their distinctive meaning in Mark is shaped by his handling of these traditional sayings, their arrangement, and their location following the parable of the sower and its interpretation. The structure of this paragraph reveals the design of its arrangement. Mark supplies the introductory line, "And he said to them," in vv. 21 and 24 (cf. vv. 26, 30), which divides the paragraph into two parts. Each part contains two sayings and an exhortation:

I. Mark 4:21-23
  A. The lamp and the lampstand
  B. The secret disclosed
  C. "Let anyone with ears to hear listen!"
II. Mark 4:24-25
  A. "Pay attention to what you hear!"
  B. The measure you give and the measure you receive
  C. The haves and the have-nots

Although these sayings follow the interpretation of the parable, in theme they develop the paradox of hiddenness in Mark 4:10-12. Why is the kingdom hidden and secret?

The metaphor of the lamp appears in different forms in Matthew 5:15, Luke 8:16, and the *Gospel of Thomas* 33. The form of the saying in Mark is distinctive in several respects: Mark uses the verb "is brought in" (NRSV), which can also mean "comes" (Gk. *erchetai*), and Mark uses the definite article with "lamp" (lit., "the lamp") as with the other nouns (the bushel, the bed, the lampstand), which may signal that the riddle has a symbolic meaning. Whereas Matthew speaks of placing the lamp under a bushel basket, and Luke under a bed, Mark conflates the tradition and has both a bushel and a bed. In Mark the saying takes the form of two questions, one that expects a negative answer and one a positive. And finally, Mark alone among the four Gospels omits the concluding purpose statement, "so that everyone who enters may see the light."

The saying is drawn from everyday life. Of course, a lamp is not hidden but put where it can give light. [The Lamp] The suggestive verb "comes" may echo statements of the kingdom coming, which can be found both in Jewish literature and in the teachings of Jesus (cf. 9:1; 11:9). Although there is a series of sayings that begin, "I have (not) come . . ." (see ["I Have Come"]), the association here is probably with the hidden kingdom rather than with the hidden Messiah. God did not bring the kingdom (in Jesus' ministry) so that it would remain hidden but so that it might become manifest to all. The veil is therefore temporary. This is the time to hear and respond, because the kingdom will not remain hidden for long.

Parallels to the saying on that which is hidden, Mark 4:22, are found in Matthew 10:26; Luke 8:17; 12:2; and the *Gospel of Thomas* 5-6. [*Gospel of Thomas* 5-6] The thought of light revealing attracted the independent saying on the hidden becoming manifest. Luke

The Lamp

AΩ "'Lamp' serves as a metaphor in a number of ways in the OT and Judaism (for God—2 Sam 22:29; David—2 Sam 21:17; Messiah—Zech 4:2; Torah—Ps 119:105; Israel, Jerusalem, Temple—cf. Wisd 18:4). The different contexts for this saying in the Gospels (Matt 5:15—applied to disciples; Luke 11:33—with other sayings about light and darkness and the *Gos. Thom.* 33) indicate that it circulated in the early Church as an isolated saying, so we can only speculate about its setting and consequent meaning in Jesus' ministry."

Robert A. Guelich, *Mark 1–8:26* (WBC 34A; Dallas: Word, 1989), 229.

Lampstand

Lampstands were common, but only a wealthy person would have had an elegant metal lampstand such as this one.

(Credit: Kelsey Museum of Archaeology)

appends the further saying, "Therefore whatever you have said in the dark will be heard in the light, and what you have whispered behind closed doors will be proclaimed from the housetops" (Luke 12:3). Whatever its original context or meaning, in its present context it extends the theme of the now hidden kingdom becoming manifest (see 4:10-12). The connection with v. 21, though secondary, is conveyed by the logical inference, "for." The double saying contains a play on words that may be missed in translation: "there is nothing hidden (*krypton*), except to be disclosed (*phanerōthē*); nor is anything secret (*apokryphon*), except to become light (*phaneron*)" (4:22).

If the unusual use of the verb "come" in v. 21 is related to the coming kingdom, and v. 22 in its current context continues that theme, the reoccurrence of the verb at the end of v. 22, literally, "in order that it may come into the open," provides a subtle continuity. Mark's form of the saying is further distinctive in that it contains the fourth of the four purpose clauses in vv. 21-22. The words translated "except to be" or "except to become" might be translated more fully "except in order that it may be" and "but in order that it may become." Why would anyone hide something *in order that* it might become known? The paradox invites further reflection. Not only will the hidden kingdom become known, but its present hiddenness serves a divine purpose that will lead to its full disclosure.

If one misses the subtle clues, such as the repeated use of the definite article, the odd use of the verb "come," and the repeated purpose clauses, these sayings may seem commonplace and proverbial. Therefore, Mark again warns his readers, "Let anyone with ears to hear listen!" (4:23; see 4:3, 9).

Mark's editorial, "And he said to them" (4:24), introduces the second trilogy of sayings. The warning, literally, "See what you hear!" mixes seeing and hearing in an odd way. Translations convey the apparent sense of the admonition—"Pay attention to what you hear" (NRSV)—but blur the combination of verbs for seeing and hearing that resonates with the Isaianic warning quoted in Mark 4:12. The warning can mean that the hearer is responsible for what he or she understands or fails to understand. Alternatively, because "hear" can also mean "hear and heed" (as in "Hear, O Israel," Deut 6:4), the warning may mean "Take care to heed (or obey) what you hear!" Because "the sower sows the word" (4:14), "pay attention to what you hear" (4:24).

The saying on receiving by the measure in which one measures is again an independent saying with parallels elsewhere (Matt 7:2; 13:12; Luke 6:38). It is a proverbial saying drawn from the marketplace in a culture in which measures were inexact and weights were used as standards of quantity and value—as they still are: "a pound of ten-penny nails" or "a pound of ground round." Be careful, the proverb warns, for if you use false measures and cheat others, you will eventually get your due. The passive voice can also be used to speak of God's action—a "divine passive"—and the absence of a subject is appropriate for the theme of the hiddenness of the kingdom. When God acts, we see the action, but the agent of the action remains hidden.

Scales

Commodities were placed in the pan. Then their weight could be determined by sliding the weight along the arm of the balance scale.

Bronze balance with one pan and a weight shaped like a bust. Imperial Period, 1st–3rd century. Musee des Antiquites Nationales, Saint-Germain-en-Laye, France. (Credit: Erich Lessing / Art Resource, NY)

Following the admonition to watch what one hears, this proverb may take on the sense that in the measure that one sees and perceives, listens and understands (4:12), he or she will receive understanding, and Mark adds, "and still more will be given to you."[9] Or, as Cranfield observed, "According to the measure of your response to the Word, so will be the blessing which you will receive from God—or rather God in his generosity will give you a blessing disproportionately large."[10]

The saying on measures suggested the final saying in this paragraph, the haves and the have-nots. Parallels to this saying occur in Matthew 13:12; 25:29; Luke 8:18; 19:26; and *Thomas* 41 (cf. Prov 11:24-26; 2 Cor 9:6-12). The law of recompense works with ruthless consistency. The rich get richer and the poor get poorer. This principle was axiomatic for the "limited goods" society of the first century. If anyone received wealth or status, it necessarily meant that someone else suffered a commensurate loss of wealth or status. Three factors give this principle of privilege and deprivation a more specific interpretation in

Mark: (1) its context in this collection of sayings that interpret the "mystery of the kingdom," introduced in 4:10-12, (2) the repetition of the divine passive, and (3) the use of the future tense. The latter two signal that the giving and taking away will be God's action in the future, presumably at the Last Judgment. In the context of Mark 4:10-12, "those who have" are those to whom the secret of the kingdom of God "has been given," while "those who have nothing" are "those outside." Consequently, those who have been given the kingdom of God through their response to Jesus will find that even more than they have now perceived, understood, or experienced will be given to them (by God). On the other hand, those who remain "outside" will find that even what they have will be taken from them. The seed that falls along the path will therefore suffer two catastrophic losses: "Satan immediately comes and takes away the word that is sown in them" (4:15), and then "even what they have will be taken away" (4:25). This eschatological warning underscores the ultimate importance of Jesus' teachings on the kingdom and concludes this series of sayings. The four principal sayings in Mark 4:21-25, while they occur in other contexts and may have had other meanings, have therefore been woven into a commentary on the mystery of the kingdom, and in their present context they draw their significance from Mark 4:10-12.

If the collection of sayings in Mark 4:21-25 ends on a note of warning, the two seed parables that follow return to a positive note. They are parables of the good soil. The good soil has the power to germinate the seed and produce the harvest, and the seed, though tiny, can produce a great plant.

The parable of the seed growing secretly, or as Mary Ann Tolbert suggested, the parable of the earth producing of itself, appears only in Mark.[11] In fact, it is the only section of Mark that has no parallel in the other Gospels. Mark introduces this parable and the parable of the mustard seed (4:30-32) with the formula, "He also said" (cf. 4:21, 24). No change of audience is indicated. Both parables are introduced as kingdom parables, explicitly linking them to the mystery of the kingdom that has been given to the disciples but that they do not understand (4:10-13). Again the parable begins with a sower sowing. The brevity of this parable's description of the sower's action, "as if someone would scatter seed on the ground" (4:26), may be due to the fact that it follows the detailed account of sowing in the parable of the sower (4:3-8). The reader already knows about the sowing of the seed. The focus of the present parable is on the interaction of the seed and the good soil to produce the harvest. The shift from the sower to the soil is further underscored by the description of the sower's inactivity and ignorance in v. 27. The sower sleeps and rises "night and day." He does nothing, and time passes. The sequence of night and day follows

"automatē"

ΑΩ The Greek term *automatē* is used for "something that happens without visible cause, *by itself*." It appears in classical Greek literature, in Homer, in the Old Testament (LXX), Philo, Josephus, and the rabbinic literature. The only other occurrence in the New Testament is in Acts 12:10, where an iron gate opens "of its own accord." The usage of the term in the Greek Old Testament is consistent with its nuances in the New Testament. The Wisdom of Solomon describes the terror of the Egyptians on the night of the plague, when "nothing was shining through to them except a dreadful, self-kindled fire" (17:6). The Lord tells Joshua that when the people surround Jericho, "when they shout together, the walls of the city shall fall of themselves" (Josh 6:5 LXX). And Job 24:24 describes the fall of an evil man as an ear of grain that falls from the stalk by itself. Applying the term to the growth of plants, Leviticus legislates against gathering the uncultivated growth of the field after the harvest: "You shall not reap the aftergrowth of your harvest or gather grapes of your unpruned vine: It shall be a year of complete rest for the land" (Lev 25:5). The Brown-Driver-Briggs *Hebrew and English Lexicon of the Old Testament* defines the term here as "what springs up of itself in [the] second year, and serves as food when no grain could be sown" (p. 705). The land is the Lord's, and the grain is the Lord's. In 2 Kgs 19:29, the fruit that grows of itself is a sign of God's grace: "And this shall be the sign for you: This year you shall eat what grows of itself, and in the second year what springs from that; then in the third year sow, reap, plant vineyards, and eat their fruit." From this linguistic background, Bernard Brandon Scott concludes, "To the attuned hearer, the contrast between the ignorance of the man, his nonaction, and the mention of *automatos* indicates that the land is on sabbatical. The allusion is meant not literally but as a metaphorical reference to the graced character of the growth event."

Bernard Brandon Scott, *Hear Then the Parable* (Minneapolis: Fortress Press, 1989), 368-69. See also Robert A. Guelich, *Mark 1–8:26* (WBC 34A; Dallas: Word, 1989), 241–42.

from the Hebrew understanding that a new day begins at sunset: "And there was evening, and there was morning" (Gen 1:5). Nothing is said of the farmer's work (hoeing and weeding) or of the processes of nature (sun and rain). The point is the mystery of the process of germination and growth. Just as the disciples do not understand the parable (4:13), so the farmer does not understand how the seed grows. The earth produces "of itself" (Gk. *automatē*). ["automatē"] So we have a dramatic contrast between the sleeping farmer and sprouting seed.[12] This contrast prevents the interpreter from focusing exclusively on the sower or the harvest, or even the contrast between the sowing and the harvest. The seed and the good earth combine to bring forth the kingdom.[13]

The mystery is that "the earth produces of itself, first the stalk, then the ear, then the full grain in the ear" (4:28, RSV). Up to v. 28 all the verbs are in the subjunctive mood, expressing potential, but in v. 28 the verb is in the indicative mood, affirming the reality of the action. The mysterious growth leading to the harvest despite the farmer's inactivity invalidates every human effort to force the coming of the kingdom in power. As Schweizer observed so elegantly,

> The parable with its assurance that the harvest will come stands in opposition to any form of doubt or care which, instead of waiting for God to fulfill his promise, endeavors to force the coming of the Kingdom or to build it—by a revolution like the Zealots, by exact calculations or preparation like the Apocalyptists, or by complete obedience to the law like the Pharisees.[14]

Apocalyptic Timetable

"A divine necessity (*dei* = "it is necessary") demands that certain events occur before the eschaton can come: Elijah must come first (9:11-13); the Son of Man must suffer, die, and rise again (8:31; 9:31-32; 10:32-34); the disciples must face suffering and persecution themselves (13:9-13); many must be led astray (13:21-22); the 'abomination of desolation' must occur (13:14); judgment must come on the Temple and the Jewish leaders (12:1-12; 13:2); and the Gospel must be preached to all nations (13:10). Knowledge of one's position on this eschatological timeline is vital: 'Do not be disturbed; these things must occur, but the end is not yet' (13:7). But since 'these things' have, from the perspective of the Markan community *already* occurred, the end cannot be far away!"

Joel Marcus, *Mark 1–8* (AB 27; New York: Doubleday, 2000), 329.

The automatic growth of the seed, however, through the stages described in v. 28, echoes the deterministic view of history of apocalyptic theology. Because the course of history is foreordained, according to the Apocalyptists, the end will come suddenly after the events set by God have been fulfilled. For Mark's community, these events include the preaching of the word and the spread of the gospel. [Apocalyptic Timetable]

The growth of the seed in the good earth leads inexorably to the harvest. The scattering of the seed corresponds to Jesus' ministry (or the preaching of "the good news of Jesus Christ, the Son of God," 1:1), the growth of the seed to the period of the church, and the harvest to the eschaton. The sower may sleep while the seed is growing (see Prov 10:5; 20:5; Ps 126:5-6), but when the time for the harvest comes, "he goes in with his sickle, because the harvest has come" (4:29).[15] The language of v. 29 echoes Joel 3:13, where the harvest is a metaphor for the coming apocalyptic war, the beating of "plowshares into swords" (Joel 3:10; cf. Isa 2:4):

> Proclaim this among the nations:
> Prepare war, stir up the warriors. . . .
> Put in the sickle, for the harvest is ripe.
> Go in, tread, for the wine press is full.
> The vats overflow, for their wickedness is great. (Joel 3:9, 13)

The coming of the kingdom is mysterious because it comes in God's providence. Still, because this is so, the faithful live in hope of the great harvest—not war but the gathering of the "full grain in the ear."

The third of the seed parables is the parable of the mustard seed (4:30-32). The Markan form of the parable differs slightly from its form in Matthew 13:31-32 and Luke 13:18-19 and in *Thomas* 20. Interpretations have focused variously on the sowing of the mustard seed, the size of the mustard plant, the contrast between the two, the ordinariness of mustard, and the transforming power of the earth. Like the first two seed parables, it implicitly responds to the challenges to Jesus' authority raised in Mark 2 and 3. The beginnings, and even the present experience, of the kingdom may be small and seemingly powerless, but by the mystery of God's transforming power, the future manifestation of the kingdom will be great, and all will see it.

The parable of the mustard seed is introduced elaborately, with a doubled question. The doubled question (3:4; 7:18-19; 10:38; 11:28; 12:14-15) and other forms of duality are common in Mark. "Parable" (v. 30) may have originally had the broader meaning "riddle" and then taken on the more specific meaning "parable" when placed in the context of Mark's collection of parables. Similarly, the introductory questions set a context for understanding the parable, guiding the reader to see it as a simile for the kingdom of God.

The mustard seed was widely regarded as the smallest of the seeds (Matt 17:20/Luke 17:6; *m. Niddah* 5.2), and Jesus no doubt chose it because of the striking contrast between the mustard seed and the mustard plant, which could grow to a height of eight to ten feet,[16] and because it was a common plant. Mark twice repeats the phrase *epi tēs gēs*, "upon the ground" or "on earth" (cf. 4:20, 26), and again the good earth does its work. The point is not in the growth of the plant but in the contrast between the seed and the full-grown plant. Citing 1 Corinthians 15:35-38; John 12:24; *1 Clement* 24:4-5; and b. Sanhedrin 90b, Jeremias observes, "The Oriental mind sees two wholly different situations: on the one hand, the dead seed, on the other, the waving corn-field, here death, there, through the divine creative power, life."[17] Mark correctly says the mustard seed becomes "the greatest of all shrubs," while Matthew and Luke heighten the contrast by speaking of the mustard as a tree. Common to all forms of the parable, the reference to the coming of birds to nest in the shade of its branches already dramatizes the size of the full-grown mustard plant. The description serves a second function, however, as it resonates with descriptions of kingdoms as trees in the Old Testament. [The Great Tree] In the context of these familiar uses of the metaphor of the great tree, the birds depict the Gentiles who will come, fulfilling Isaiah's vision (66:18-21) of the revelation of God's glory among the nations and the gathering of the nations to Jerusalem. By appealing to this image, therefore, Jesus affirms that the future will belong neither to the Gentile kingdoms (e.g., Nebuchadnezzar, Darius, or Rome) nor to Israel but to the kingdom of God. For Mark, the parable offered hope to the persecuted community of the faithful. The good earth will do its work. The present condition of hiddenness and suffering will soon give way to the glory of the kingdom come in power, the downfall of the nations, and the gathering of all the faithful to the shelter of God's dominion.

The Great Tree

AΩ "On the mountain height of Israel I will plant it,
in order that it may produce boughs and bear fruit,
and become a noble cedar.
Under it every kind of bird will live;
in the shade of its branches will nest winged creatures of every kind." (Ezek 17:23; cf. 31:6)

"The tree grew great and strong . . .
the birds of the air nested in its branches. . . ."
(Dan 4:12; cf. 4:14, 21)

Verses 33 and 34 conclude the section of Jesus' teaching in parables. The contrast between the insiders and outsiders, the reference to "parables" and "everything," and the explanation in a private setting all bind the interpretation of vv. 33-34 to 4:10-12. "The word" Jesus spoke in the parables (v. 33) echoes the reference to "the word" the sower sows in 4:14. Several important elements emerge from the conclusion, especially when it is read in the context of the introduction in 4:1-2 and Jesus' explanation of the mystery of the kingdom in 4:10-12. First, Mark makes it clear that he has included only a sample of Jesus' teachings. The Q material in Matthew and Luke preserves a much larger sample, though it is not clear whether Mark knew this tradition or not. Second, the parables are vehicles for "the word," the gospel of the kingdom to which they point. The pronoun "them" in v. 33 is undefined. Presumably it means the crowd rather than the disciples because of the contrast between these two groups in v. 34. Third, and standing in some tension with 4:12, Jesus spoke the word "as they were able to hear it." In light of its explanation in the next verse, this phrase must mean that Jesus accommodated his teaching to the people's ability to grasp it. Because they could only understand it in riddles or parables, Jesus spoke to them only in this veiled manner. Nevertheless, his teaching was limited not by a desire to keep the crowds in the dark but by their own inability to hear more of his teaching. In the circumstances, he could not give them more. Verse 34 continues the Markan pattern of public teaching and private explanation (see 6:30-31; 7:14-17; 9:28, 33; 10:10). For "those outside, everything comes in parables" (or riddles, 4:11), but "he explained everything in private to his disciples" (4:34).

Stilling the Storm, Mark 4:35-41

The story of the stilling of the storm introduces a new section in Mark. Following the collection of parables in Mark 4:1-34, Mark 4:35–5:43 will contain four miracle stories. The Markan attachment formula, literally, "and he says to them," in v. 35 signals more than the simple attachment of one story to another. The motif of the boat that runs through Mark 3:7, 9-10; 4:1-2 and the stilling of the storm may have followed from these references in Mark's sources. The stilling of the storm may also have introduced a cycle of miracle stories that began with 4:35-41 and ended with the walking on the water in 6:45-52, in which Jesus' identity, the focus of the first sea crossing, is more fully revealed. Alternatively, Paul Achtemeier has proposed a pre-Markan cycle of miracle stories organized in two "catenae," or connected series.

[Pre-Markan Miracle Catenae]

Pre-Markan Miracle Catenae

Catenae I
Stilling of the Storm (4:35-41)
The Gerasene Demoniac (5:1-20)
The Woman with a Hemorrhage (5:25-34)
Jairus's Daughter (5:21-23, 35-43)
Feeding of the 5,000 (6:34-44, 53)

Catenae II
Jesus Walks on the Sea (6:45-51)
The Blind Man of Bethsaida (8:22-26)
The Syrophoenician Woman (7:24b-30)
The Deaf Mute (7:32-37)
Feeding of the 4,000 (8:1-10)

Paul J. Achtemeier, "Toward the Isolation of Pre-Markan Miracle Catenae," *JBL* 89 (1970): 265–91, esp. 291.

Our reading of the story is greatly enriched by uncovering its "intertextual" connections with the Old Testament and Jewish literature during the period of the early church. As with every part of Mark, locating the story within the development of the Gospel narrative opens new insights for the reader. The stilling of the storm is the first of the "nature miracles." To this point Jesus has healed various diseases and cast out demons, but the stilling of the storm shows Jesus exercising God-like authority over the creation and focuses the question of his identity ("Who then is this?" 4:41) even more sharply. The disciples serve as a foil for the issue of Jesus' identity as we simultaneously begin to see more clearly their lack of understanding.

The sea was typically a place of chaos and terror in Jewish literature, and the stilling of the storm picks up motifs rooted in the exodus, the story of Jonah, and reflections on these stories in other Jewish writings. [The Ship of Jacob] In particular one may suspect early Christian reflection on Psalm 107:23-25, 28-29:

The Ship of Jacob

"And behold a ship came sailing past full of dried fish, without sailor or pilot. Inscribed on it was 'The Ship of Jacob.' So our father said to us, 'Get into our boat.' As we boarded it, a violent tempest arose, a great windstorm (Gk. *lailaps*), and our father, who had been holding us on course, was snatched away from us. After being tossed by the sea, the boat was filled with water and carried along on the waves until it broke apart. Joseph escaped in a light boat while we were scattered about on ten planks; Levi and Judah were on the same one. Thus we were all dispersed, even to the outer limits. Levi, putting on sack cloth, prayed to the Lord in behalf of all of us. When the storm ceased, the ship reached the land, as though at peace. Then Jacob, our father, approached, and we all rejoiced with one accord." (*Testament of Naphtali* 6.2-10)

James H. Charlesworth, ed., *The Old Testament Pseudepigrapha* (Garden City NY: Doubleday, 1983), 1:813.

Some went down to the sea in ships,
    doing business on the mighty waters;
they saw the deeds of the LORD,
    his wondrous works on the deep.
For he commanded and raised the stormy wind,
    which lifted up the waves of the sea. . . .

Then they cried to the LORD in their trouble,
    and he brought them out from their distress;
he made the storm be still,
    and the waves of the sea were hushed.

The Storm at Sea and the Conflict of Light and Darkness

Giorgio de Chirico (1888–1978). *Christ and the Tempest*. Collezione d'Arte Religiosa Moderna, Vatican Museums, Vatican State. (Credit: Scala / Art Resource, NY)

Rembrandt van Rijn (1606–1669). *The Storm on the Sea of Galilee*. 1633. Oil on canvas. Isabella Stewart Gardner Museum, Boston, MA. (Credit: The Bridgeman Art Library)

By commanding the waves and the sea into submission, Jesus does what only God can do and reveals that he is greater than Jonah. The repetition of the word "great," which also occurs in Jonah (eleven times), structures the story in three movements:

I. The Crisis—"a great windstorm" (v. 37)
II. The Result of Jesus' Command—"a great calm" (v. 39)
III. The Response of Jesus' Disciples—"a great fear" (v. 41)[18]

Verses 35-36 introduce the story. The phrase "on that day" (v. 35) connects the story with the setting established by 4:1-2. After teaching the crowd from the boat, "when evening had come" (v. 35), Jesus proposes that they should cross "to the other side" (v. 35). The evening setting has been developed by artists who have portrayed the scene with striking contrasts between light and darkness. The phrase "to the other side" recurs at significant points in the next four chapters, in contexts that suggest that when Jesus is on the west side of the Sea of Galilee he is among Jewish crowds, and when he crosses to the east side he is among Gentiles. The Sea of Galilee functions as a symbolic barrier between the two. Breaking the social barrier, Jesus crosses the sea, but the sea crossing is rough and fraught with danger.[19] By crossing the sea and exercising the power of the coming kingdom among both Jews and Gentiles, Jesus revealed the power of the kingdom to transcend barriers and bring unity.

The crowd has not been mentioned since 4:1 (but see 4:33), and their reappearance in v. 36 stands in tension with the teaching of the disciples in private in 4:10ff. (see also 4:34). That they took Jesus "just as he was" (v. 36) probably means "without going back to shore." The reference to other boats is problematic because they play no role in the story. The detail may therefore be a vestige from an earlier tradition or narrative setting (see the plural "boats" in Ps 107:23).

The Sea of Galilee was famous for sudden storms. The storm is described as "a great windstorm" (see Jonah 1:4, 12). The terms for the storm are different in Jonah (*klydōn*) and Mark (*lailaps*; cf. 2 Pet 2:17; and *T. Naphtali* 6.4 [The Ship of Jacob]). Whereas *klydōn* means "a succession of waves, rough water," *lailaps* means a "whirlwind" or "hurricane" (cf. Job 27:20; 38:1).[20] A storm at sea was also an image connected with apocalyptic events in Jewish literature of the intertestamental period. [Apocalyptic Storm]

Meanwhile, in dramatic contrast to the fury of the storm and the disciples' terror, Jesus is asleep, apparently under the platform in the stern. Jesus' sleep also resonates with biblical motifs. As D. E. Nineham observed, "The ability to sleep peacefully and untroubled is a sign of perfect trust in the sustaining and protective power of God" (Pss 3:5; 4:8; Prov 3:24; Job 11:18-19; Lev 26:6; cf. Jonah 1:5-6).[21] With perhaps a knowing glance at the hearer, Mark reports that the disciples "raised" Jesus (4:38). Their cry is not a plea for help (cf. Matt 8:25) but a complaint in which we may hear overtones of the frustration of Mark's community: "Teacher, do you not care that we are perishing?"

Awakened (see Ps 44:23-24; Isa 51:9-10), Jesus "rebuked" the wind as though confronting a demon (see 1:25; 3:12, where the same verb is used, and Ps 104:7, "At your rebuke they flee"). Then he commanded the sea, "Peace, be still" (4:39), fulfilling the tribute of the psalmist, "You silence the roaring of the seas, the roaring of the waves,

Apocalyptic Storm

"I, Daniel, saw in my vision by night the four winds of heaven stirring up the great sea, and four great beasts came up out of the sea, different from one another." (Dan 7:2-3)

They have counted me, and have put the soul
like a boat in the depths [of the sea], . . .

The foundations of the wall shake
like a ship on the surface of the sea,
and the clouds echo with the uproar.
And both he who lives in the dust
and he who sails upon the sea
are terrified by the din of the water.
For them their wise men are like sailors on the deeps,
for all their wisdom is perplexed
by the roar of the sea,
by the welling up of the deeps
upon the springs of water;
[they churn] to form huge waves,
the gates of the water, with clamorous sound." (1QH 11.6, 13-16 = 3.6, 13-16)

"[I am] like a sailor in a ship
in the raging sea,
its waves and torrents roar over me,
a whirlwind [without a] lull for taking breath,
without tracks which direct the path over the surface of the sea.
The deep thunders at my sigh,
[my soul nears] the gates of death." (1QH 14.22-24 = 6.22-24)

". . . my entrails heave like a boat in the rage of the storm,
my heart pulsates to destruction,
a whirlwind overwhelms me,
due to the wickedness of their sin." (1QH 15.4-5 = 7.4-5)

Florentino García Martínez, *The Dead Sea Scrolls Translated* (Leiden: E. J. Brill, 1994), 331–32, 341, 343.

the tumult of the peoples" (Ps 65:7; cf. 89:9). The only other occurrence of the verb "be still" in Mark appears in the exorcism of the man with an unclean spirit in the synagogue at Capernaum (1:25). Cranfield suggests the translation "be silent and remain so."[22] The assumption that spirits controlled the elements of nature can also be traced in Jewish writings (*Jub.* 2:2; Rev 7:1-3). When Jesus commanded the waves to be still, therefore, he commanded the spirits that control the waves. In the Old Testament, "creation is described in terms of a struggle between God and the sea" (Eduard Schweizer).[23] By stilling the storm, Jesus demonstrates that he exercises the sovereign power over nature that is reserved for God alone (Gen 8:1; Josh 10:12-13; Job 9:5-10; Ps 74:13-14).

The wind ceased (cf. 6:51), and there was "a great calm" (4:39). Then Jesus turned to the disciples, to address the real problem: "Why are you afraid? Have you still no faith?" Fear is here juxtaposed to faith. Because the disciples do not yet recognize Jesus' role as Savior, they still fear the elements that threaten them. The implications for Mark's community are clear: the fearful have no faith, and the faithful have no fear. Now the disciples are filled with a great fear, but it is a different kind of fear (*deilos* in v. 40; *phobos* in v. 41). It is "the fear of the Lord," a reverential awe (see the references to "great fear" in Jonah 1:10, 16; cf. Jonah 4:1 "great grief," and 4:6, "great joy"). Awe still does not bring understanding, however. In place of a confession, the disciples can only raise the question that will concern Mark through the rest of the Gospel, preparing the way for Peter's confession at Caesarea Philippi (8:29) and the centurion's confession at the cross (15:39): "Who then is this, that even the wind and the sea obey him?" (4:41).

CONNECTIONS

Mark 4:1-20

The parable of the sower and its interpretation offer rich possibilities for reflection, meditation, and application to modern contexts. Primarily the parable is an assertion of the mystery of hope. For the Christian, of course, hope is not like Annie: "Tomorrow, tomorrow—I love you, tomorrow. You're only a day away." Hope is based on the goodness of God and the promise of God's redemptive purposes. The kingdom of God is already present in the world through the gospel of Jesus Christ, and its fulfillment is as mysterious as a bountiful harvest. What we see is the fruitlessness of the seed: prosperous secular communities dismissing the church as irrelevant; poverty, hunger, and disease running rampant over large portions of the globe; races, ethnic groups, and nations bent on doing violence to one another; families torn apart and children hurt by drug abuse, infidelity, and domestic violence; exploitation of the land, the poor, and the powerless—the evidence of fruitless soil can be overwhelming. Yet, still, the parable calls those who have ears to hear, assuring the gospel will be heard, God's will shall be done, and the great harvest will come.

The parable does not so much call for hearers to be good soil as it calls for Jesus' disciples to live in the faith and confidence that, appearances to the contrary, the seed will bear fruit, and the harvest will come.

Jesus' explanation of the mystery of the kingdom in Mark 4:10-12 is a notoriously difficult passage. It is difficult to imagine that Jesus spoke in parables in order that some would not understand what he was saying. While open to various interpretations, the parables are typically brief, picturesque, drawn from everyday life, and seemingly open to any willing hearer. They do not have a given meaning that is accessible only if one has information not conveyed by the parable itself or its context in the ministry of Jesus (or the gospel). Instead, they tease the mind into active discernment that can lead to further insight, and a parable like the parable of the sower is open to multiple fruitful interpretations.

The distinction between "insiders" and "outsiders" is inviting but dangerous. We all want to be insiders—part of the "in group," "in the know," accepted, and privileged. No doubt most Bible readers assume they are "insiders"—like the disciples, they are among those to whom Jesus said, "To you has been given the secret of the kingdom of God" (4:11). Mark immediately undermines the position of the insiders, however, by revealing that the disciples do not understand the parable either, and Jesus asks, "Then how will you understand all the parables?" For both insiders and outsiders, therefore, the kingdom remains veiled and mysterious. Everything about God is enigmatic and paradoxical. The movement of God's spirit is so elusive it is best seen in retrospect. Neither ritual nor emotion can assure God's presence in our worship. God's sovereign presence among us was dramatically revealed in the person of Jesus, but the cross is still more evident in our experience than the empty tomb.

On the one hand, the "mystery" of the kingdom of God is now clear and simple: Jesus, the Son of God, was God's agent in establishing the kingdom. Apart from Jesus one can neither enter nor understand the kingdom. The kingdom is also open to Gentiles as well as to Jews—Paul's great insight. The kingdom, while "already" present, is "not yet" fulfilled but awaits the final consummation of God's redemptive work in history. Therefore, we live in the "in-between" times—between the resurrection of Jesus and the end of history when Jesus will be revealed as the coming Son of Man, raise the dead, and judge the nations.

During the "in-between" time, however, the kingdom remains elusive and mysterious. In our world, wealth, power, and status still determine the circumstances in which we live and divide "haves" from "have nots." The life of the spirit must be cultivated by a mysterious process of experience, reflection, prayer, study, and sacrificial living. And yet, even the spiritually mature among us remain embarrassingly (and sometimes scandalously) human. As a result, we live in the paradox that the mystery of the kingdom has been given to us but we do not understand even its first lessons.

The parable of the sower is a metaphor of hope, but it tells us first that God acts on hope and sows the seed, knowing that only a fraction of it will be fruitful. Our hope does not lie in confidence in our own receptiveness but in the hope of the sower. Because God continues to prepare for the harvest, we too can live in hope that the kingdom, now elusive and veiled, will one day be triumphant, fulfilling all God's redemptive work among us. Living in the twilight, we look forward to the dawn.

Mark 4:21-34

The sayings that follow the interpretation of the parable of the sower develop further the theme of the hidden kingdom. Because ours is an age of paradox and searching, these sayings speak to the tenor of our time. All the proffered answers to life's ultimate questions are held in suspicion. If there are any answers, it is widely assumed they are relative at best. If there is a kingdom, it is certainly a hidden one. The metaphor of kingdom is itself archaic. We might better say, if there is a divine presence and purpose at work in the world, it is mysterious and veiled. Just as Mark's community—persecuted and possessing no wealth, power, organization, or influence in the larger setting of the Roman Empire—struggled to remain faithful to the gospel of the suffering Messiah and the veiled kingdom, the church today, though it possesses far more resources than the first-century church, struggles to continue to be faithful to its mission to be light in the darkness.

Mark reminds the church that the kingdom—the light—came in the person of Jesus. From this foundational Christian confession flows the Christian's basis for hope regardless of how oppressive the current darkness is. Just as the purpose of the lamp is to give light, so the coming of Jesus confirms that divine purpose of bringing light to the world. The essential function of light is to reveal or make visible. Therefore, that which is now hidden will be brought to light. The sovereign mercy of

God will be fully revealed. Both the secret purposes of God and the secret sins of the wicked and the faithless will be exposed. Therefore, Mark exhorts, hear the word of God. Even in the present darkness and confusion the principles of the God's sovereignty are already in force. The first is a warning—the law of just rewards. The merciful will be treated mercifully, the spiteful will be treated spitefully, the fair will be treated fairly, the narrow of spirit will be treated meanly. But even more so, with the result that those who strive to hold forth the light will be enlightened, while those who hide in the shadows will be consigned to the darkness: "even what they have will be taken away" (4:25).

While Jesus' words connect with the confusion, compromise, and cynicism of our age, they inject a warning of consequences that will threaten and offend the morally lax. Our tendency is to reason from the prevailing wisdom that there are no universal answers that there are therefore no moral consequences. Therefore, we can live as we want, only we should allow everyone else the same license. Jesus' words cut on two edges: God is surely and inexorably at work in the world through the gospel of Jesus Christ, and although the kingdom is still hidden, its principles already determine what the ultimate consequences of our choices will be.

For those who despair that humanity will never learn the lessons of justice, peace, and reconciliation—and even less those of spiritual maturity, love, mercy, and sacrifice—the parable of the seed growing secretly offers a word of encouragement. When the revelation of the kingdom through the ministry of Jesus meets a receptive human response, that seed will germinate and grow to produce a harvest of biblical proportions. The processes of the kingdom are as mysterious but as sure as the mystery of growth. The power of the kingdom does not depend on us. Just as light shines and seeds grow, so the kingdom is coming "of itself."

The sayings in vv. 21-25 already prevent us from reasoning that if the kingdom is coming of itself, it does not matter what we do. On the contrary, the parable calls for a response of resolute faith. Look at how seeds germinate, acorns become strong oaks, and children grow up before our eyes. We accept that growth is taking place imperceptibly all around us. Why then is it so difficult to "see" that the kingdom still hidden is moving toward its fruition?

The parable of the mustard seed makes a corollary point and has an appropriately veiled subtext. Look at the contrast between the size of the mustard seed and the size of the plant it produces. The subtext is the prophetic-apocalyptic image of a kingdom as a great tree with birds coming to nest in its branches. Like the birds of the air, people from all nations will find shelter in God's kingdom. The parables call for us to see the reality of the supernatural in natural processes.

Let us tell the stories of small beginnings. How could the poor and unschooled receive religious training, especially when there was no public education and many worked six days a week? In 1780 Robert Raikes started the first Sunday schools. What could God do with a shoemaker in England whose imagination was fired by Captain James Cook's discoveries in the Pacific? William Carey founded the Baptist Society for Propagating the Gospel among the Heathen in 1792, and then went to India as its first missionary. Who can calculate what great things have come from these small beginnings? So what is the kingdom of God like? Just plant a mustard seed, and see what God can do!

Offer God your best gifts, and watch the mustard seed grow. A personal story: My father was a sickly child. When he was nine he almost died of pneumonia, but the doctors cut a hole in his back between his ribs and inserted a tube to drain his lungs for several days. His father had only a grammar school education, but he got a senator from Arkansas to appoint my father to the Naval Academy. Still, he could not go because he failed to make the cut on the math exam. After a year studying at a prep school in Marion, Alabama, he made the highest grade on the exam the next year. During his first year at Annapolis, he felt a definite call to the ministry. He was the first in his family to go to college. He had spent a year studying math just to get there. A senator had gone to bat for him. It was the Depression, and he had the prospect of a comfortable career as a naval officer. His family was proud of him, and now he wanted to leave and come home to be a preacher. Still, he held to his convictions—the seed was growing "of itself." He enrolled at Ouachita College in Arkadelphia, Arkansas, and then went on to Baylor University. After finishing the basic degree at Southern Seminary, my father and mother, still in their twenties, volunteered to be missionaries, hoping to spend their lives in China, but it was not to be. They were prisoners of war under the Japanese for the entire Second World War. Still, they were committed to serving God as missionaries. After two terms in South America, the son of a women's shoe salesman with a grammar school education was asked to join the faculty at Southern Seminary to teach missions. Five years later, the head of the Home Mission Board invited him to come to Atlanta to be the director of the Missions Division and guide the work of more than 2,300 missionaries working in more than 30 states across the country.[24] See what God can do with a mustard seed!

[The Spreading Tree]

The Spreading Tree

"It is up to us to sow this mustard seed in our minds and let it grow within us into a great tree of understanding reaching up to heaven and elevating all our faculties; then it will spread out branches of knowledge, the pungent savor of its fruit will make our mouths burn, its fiery kernel will kindle a blaze within us inflaming our hearts, and the taste of it will dispel our unenlightened repugnance. Yes, it is true: a mustard seed is indeed an image of the kingdom of God." (Peter Chrysologus, "Sermons," 17)

Thomas C. Oden and Christopher A. Hall, eds., *Ancient Christian Commentary on Scripture: New Testament II, Mark* (Downers Grove IL: InterVarsity Press, 1998), 61–62.

Mark 4:35-41

The history of interpretation of the stilling of the storm suggests a number of ways in which interpreters have found this passage meaningful. The almost primal setting—a storm at sea—readily communicates danger and terror. At least as early as Tertullian (early third c.) this passage suggested the ship as a symbol for the church. [The Ship as the Church] Whatever hardships or persecutions the church might face, have faith: the Lord is present with the faithful and will bring the church safely through its trials. With Augustine, allegorical interpretation of the passage reached full flower: The wind represents the abuse the faithful suffer, the waves suggest the anger that swells within them, the danger to the boat mirrors the danger to their heart. Like the disciples, one should rouse Christ, whose presence they have forgotten. [Awakening the Christ Asleep in You] Ingenious as this allegorical interpretation is, it goes well beyond any symbolic interpretation suggested by the text itself.

If Mark uses the story symbolically, it is to rebuke the persecuted church of his time for its fear in the face of danger. The word of assurance that the power of the Lord is far greater than that of the forces that threaten the community carries the corollary that fear demonstrates a lack of faith. The believer should not be foolhardy, but disciples of Jesus can face hardship and uncertainty with a deep and abiding confidence in the sufficiency of God's power. In the end God will prevail, and that is all that matters. Therefore, if our lives are invested in God's mission in the world, ultimately we too shall be vindicated. The connection of the stilling of the storm to the mission of the church is rooted in the function of the sea crossings in Mark (see commentary above). The storms in view are not just the common hardships of life; they are the persecutions the church faces when it acts on Jesus' command to cross to the other side. On the other side one encounters the "other"—cultures and persons different from one's own "kith and kin." The boat is ready and the Lord commands. The Lord who commands even the wind and the waves and they obey him will go with us, but will we leave the familiar shore?

The Ship as the Church

"But that little ship did present a figure of the Church, in that she is disquieted 'in the sea,' that is, by persecutions and temptations; the Lord, through patience, sleeping as it were, until, roused in their last extremities by the prayers of the saints, He checks the world, and restores tranquility to His own." (Tertullian, "On Baptism," 12)

Alexander Roberts and James Donaldson, eds., *The Ante-Nicene Fathers, vol. 3: Latin Christianity: Its Founder, Tertullian* (rpt., Grand Rapids: Wm. B. Eerdmans, 1986), 675.

Awakening the Christ Asleep in You

"When you have to listen to abuse, that means you are being buffeted by the wind. When your anger is roused, you are being tossed by the waves. So when the winds blow and the waves mount high, the boat is in danger, your heart is imperiled, your heart is taking a battering. On hearing yourself insulted, you long to retaliate; but the joy of revenge brings with it another kind of misfortune—shipwreck. Why is this? Because Christ is asleep in you. What do I mean? I mean you have forgotten his presence. Rouse him, then; remember him, let him keep watch within you, pay heed to him. . . . A temptation arises: it is the wind. It disturbs you: it is the surging of the sea. This is the moment to awaken Christ and let him remind you of those words: 'Who can this be? Even the winds and the sea obey him.'" (Augustine, *Sermons* 63.1-3)

Thomas C. Oden and Christopher A. Hall, eds., *Ancient Christian Commentary on Scripture: New Testament II, Mark* (Downers Grove IL: InterVarsity Press, 1998), 65.

NOTES

[1] Mary Ann Tolbert, *Sowing the Gospel: Mark's World in Literary Historical Perspective* (Minneapolis: Fortress Press, 1989), esp. 121–24.

[2] Joel Marcus, *Mark 1–8* (AB 27; New York: Doubleday, 2000), 291.

[3] Joachim Jeremias, *The Parables of Jesus* (rev. ed.; trans. S. H. Hooke; New York: Charles Scribner's Sons, 1963), 12. See further K. D. White, "The Parable of the Sower," *JTS* 15 (1964): 301–302; P. Payne, "The Order of Sowing and Ploughing in the Parable of the Sower," *NTS* 25 (1978–1979): 123–29; Bernard Brandon Scott, *Hear Then the Parable* (Minneapolis: Fortress Press, 1989), 353.

[4] Robert A. Guelich, *Mark 1–8:26* (WBC 34a; Dallas: Word, 1989), 190.

[5] G. Dalman, *Arbeit und Sitte* (Gütersloh, 1933), 3:153–65, cited by Jeremias, *The Parables of Jesus*, 150. See further Scott, *Hear Then the Parable*, 355–58; Marcus, *Mark 1–8*, 292–93.

[6] See above note 1.

[7] Tolbert, *Sowing the Gospel*, 157–58.

[8] David Rhoads and Donald Michie, *Mark as Story: An Introduction to the Narrative of a Gospel* (Philadelphia: Fortress Press, 1982), 129–36.

[9] Marcus, *Mark 1–8*, 320.

[10] C. E. B. Cranfield, *The Gospel according to Saint Mark* (CGTC; Cambridge: Cambridge University Press, 1959), 166.

[11] Tolbert, *Sowing the Gospel*, 161.

[12] Peter Rhea Jones, *Studying the Parables of Jesus* (Macon: Smyth & Helwys, 1999), 110.

[13] Tolbert, *Sowing the Gospel*, 163.

[14] Eduard Schweizer, *The Good News according to Mark* (trans. Donald H. Madvig; Atlanta: John Knox Press, 1970), 103.

[15] Scott, *Hear Then the Parable*, 367.

[16] Jeremias, *The Parables of Jesus*, 148.

[17] Ibid., 148.

[18] The three occurrences of "great" have been observed by others. See Marcus, *Mark 1–8*, 336.

[19] Werner H. Kelber, *The Kingdom in Mark: A New Place and a New Time* (Philadelphia: Fortress Press, 1974), esp. 62–63.

[20] BDAG, 581.

[21] D. E. Nineham, *The Gospel of Saint Mark* (Baltimore: Penguin Books, 1963), 146.

[22] Cranfield, *The Gospel according to Saint Mark*, 174.

[23] Schweizer, *The Good News according to Mark*, 109.

[24] See further R. Alan Culpepper, *Eternity as a Sunrise: The Life of Hugo H. Culpepper* (Macon GA: Mercer University Press, 2002).

JESUS' POWER TO GIVE LIFE

Mark 5:1-43

Chapter 5 continues the collection of four miracle stories that begin with the stilling of the storm in Mark 4:35-41. When Jesus and the disciples reach "the other side" of the Sea of Galilee, Jesus is immediately confronted by a man with an unclean spirit. The exorcism of the Gerasene demoniac is related with great delight and detail. Underlying this dramatic tale is a stark depiction of the destructive, dehumanizing power of evil and the liberating, resurrecting power of God at work in Jesus. In the end, the one whom "no one could restrain" is seated, clothed, and in his right mind, and the demons destroy a herd of swine. Then the man delivered from his demons proclaims in the Decapolis what Jesus has done for him—arguably the beginning of the Gentile mission.

The latter half of Mark 5 continues the theme of Jesus' life-giving power. It also illustrates Mark's "sandwich" technique: the story of the healing of the hemorrhaging woman is sandwiched between the introduction and conclusion of the raising of Jairus's daughter. The sandwiching technique not only provides variety in the progress of the narrative but invites reflection on the relationship between the two sandwiched events.

All four miracles in this section illustrate Jesus' giving of life. The disciples are delivered from the threat of death at sea. The Gerasene demoniac is liberated from the demonic powers and restored to civil life. The woman with the hemorrhage is delivered from her shame and uncleanness after twelve years of suffering, and Jairus's twelve-year-old daughter is returned to life. When Jesus does battle with the powers of evil, he does so in order to give life, and the power he exercises is the power of the coming kingdom.

In all three stories in this chapter we find a supplicant at Jesus' feet: the demoniac (5:6), Jairus (5:22), and the woman with a hemorrhage (5:33). In addition, in each of the three stories Jesus crosses the boundary between clean and unclean. With the demoniac, he is surrounded by tombs, swine, and Gentiles. He is defiled by the touch of a woman with a hemorrhage, and then he takes the hand of a dead girl. Jesus is unconcerned about ritual impurity, however, and in each case restores the person to life and wholeness.

COMMENTARY

The Gerasene Demoniac, 5:1-20

The healing of the Gerasene demoniac is a vivid tale that unfolds in five acts. Modifying Vincent Taylor's division of the story into four parts (vv. 1-10, 11-13, 14-17, 18-20),[1] Robert Guelich proposed the following five-part division: (1) the setting (5:1-5), (2) Jesus and the demon(s) (5:6-10), (3) the swine (5:11-13), (4) the witnesses (5:14-17), and (5) the healed man's response (5:18-20).[2] We will follow this outline below.

Like many other passages in the Gospels, the healing of the demoniac resonates with a chorus of Old Testament passages. Isaiah 65:1-7 pronounces God's judgment on Israel for its disobedience and worship of pagan deities. The people "sit inside tombs" (65:4; cf. Ps 67:7 LXX), which suggests that they consulted the dead, which is condemned in Deuteronomy 18:11-12. They spend the night in "secret places" and "eat swine's flesh" (65:4), condemned in Deuteronomy 14:8. The people "reviled" the Lord "on the hills" (65:7), but he pledged to measure full payment into their laps (cf. Mark 4:24). [Isaiah 65:3-4] Jesus silenced "the roaring of the seas" and "the tumult of the peoples" (Ps 65:5-7). Less convincing are the parallels between the drowning of the pigs and the drowning of the Egyptians at the exodus, the deliverance of the demoniac and the deliverance of the Israelites (Exod 14:1–15:22).[3]

Isaiah 65:3-4

"A people who provoke me to my face continually . . .
who sit inside tombs,
and spend the night in secret places;
who eat swine's flesh. . . ."

The Setting, vv. 1-5

The "other side" is described as the "region" of the Gerasenes. Textual and geographical factors create an almost insoluble problem here. Gerasa (modern Jerash) was a prominent city in the Decapolis, but it lies some thirty miles from the Sea of Galilee, creating the unlikely image of a thirty-mile stampede to the sea! If this is the original reading, "region" must be taken in a general sense. Early on, scribes recognized the problem, so some manuscripts have "Gadarenes" and others "Gergesenes" [Gerasenes, Gadarenes, or Gergesenes?] Compounding the problem are the textual variants in the parallel passages in Matthew 8:28 (where the evidence favors "Gadarenes") and Luke 8:26 ("Gerasenes"). Although we cannot reconstruct the history of the tradition with any certainty, it is likely that an early place-name dropped out in favor of "Gerasenes" or even "Gadarenes" because these were better known locations.

Gerasenes, Gadarenes, or Gergesenes?

AΩ "Gerasenes" is supported by the strongest manuscript evidence: Codexes Sinaiticus (א, 4th c.), Vaticanus (B, 4th c.), and Bezae (D, 5th c.). Gerasa, modern Jerash, was one of the leading cities of the Decapolis, but it is located thirty miles southeast of the Sea of Galilee. "Gadarenes" is probably an accommodation to the parallel in Matthew 8:28, and is supported by Codex Alexandrinus (A, 5th c.), Ephraemi (C, 5th c.) and the majority texts. Gadara lies only six miles from the Sea of Galilee (modern Um Qeis). Bruce Metzger called "Gergystenes," which is supported by W, "a scribal idiosyncrasy." "Gergesenes," which is supported by א[2], L, X, Θ, family 1, and Coptic manuscripts, was (first?) proposed by Origen:

"But Gergesa, from which the name Gergesenes is taken, is an old town in the neighborhood of the lake now called Tiberias, and on the edge of it there is a steep place abutting on the lake, from which it is pointed out that the swine were cast down by the demons. Now, the meaning of Gergesa is 'dwelling of the casters-out,' and it contains a prophetic reference to the conduct towards the Saviour of the citizens of those places, who 'besought Him to depart out of their coasts.'" (*Commentary on John 6.24; ANF* 10:371)

Bruce M. Metzger, *A Textual Commentary on the Greek New Testament* (New York: United Bible Societies, 1971), 84.

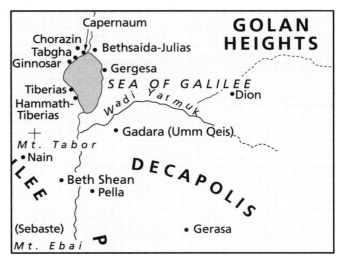

"Immediately" Jesus was met by a man "from the tombs," who had an unclean spirit (see above, commentary and connections on 1:21-28). Verses 3-5 set the scene by describing the man and establishing his desperate, violent condition. Tombs were located outside of a town so as not to defile it, and were often shallow caves carved in a hillside. The demoniac found shelter in the tombs. Mark's description of the man suggests implicitly that he is a Gentile: Jesus and the disciples had crossed the lake to a Gentile area; the man was staying in tombs; there were swine and swine herders in the vicinity, and at the end of the story he will go to "his own (people)" in the Decapolis (5:19).

Not only did he live in the tombs, but he was so wild that no one could restrain him (cf. the binding of the demon in Tob 8:3). Verse 3 ends with a string of negatives, which in Greek makes the point emphatically: "and neither with chains no longer no one was able to restrain him." The next verse details the point. Shackles and chains were used to restrain prisoners (Acts 12:6-7; Josephus, *Ant.* 19.295), but the demoniac "tore apart" (cf. Acts 23:10) the chains and smashed the shackles the way one would crush an alabaster flask (14:3) or break a reed (Matt 12:20). This "strong man" (cf. 3:27) could not be bound!

The first point of the description reports his surroundings (the tombs); the second suggests something of his history—"often" people had tried to restrain him—and his exceptional strength. The third point of the description characterizes his deranged and self-destructive behavior: continually howling (NRSV), or shrieking, and cutting himself with stones (5:5).

Jesus and the Demon(s), vv. 5:6-10

Following the extended description of the demoniac in vv. 3-5, the action resumes in v. 6. The demoniac takes the initiative, running to Jesus and then prostrating himself before him. The action of running itself, something no elder or person of rank or authority would do, demonstrated a lack of regard for dignity and propriety. The verb to "fall down before" him is jarring in this context. It is surprising following the description in vv. 3-5 and suggests nothing of the conflict that will follow. The verb *proskynein* is a compound verb ("to kiss" + "before") and means to fall on one's knees or face before a superior or a deity "to express in attitude or gesture one's complete dependence on or submission to a high authority figure" or "to welcome respectfully."[4] Interestingly enough, in the New Testament, where the term appears frequently in the Gospels and Revelation but almost never in the epistles, "the object is always something—truly or supposedly—divine."[5] Falling on one's face before one who has just stepped on your shores would be an appropriate way to welcome a conqueror.

Gustave Doré

Doré captures the demoniac kneeling and pleading with Jesus.

Gustave Doré (1832–1883). *Jesus Healing the Man Possessed with a Devil*. 19th C. Engraving. (Credit: Dover Pictorial Archives Series)

Then, in striking contrast to his gesture of submission, screaming "at the top of his voice" (NRSV; cf. 3:11, where Mark summarizes this sequence of actions), he challenges Jesus and begins to make demands of him. The Garazene demoniac's words echo those of the man with an unclean spirit in the synagogue at Capernaum (1:24), with interesting variations. Here the demoniac starts referring to himself in the singular ("to me") and moves to the plural in v. 9 and 10 (see below), whereas the demoniac at Capernaum begins using in the plural ("to us") and moves to the singular ("I know"). In both cases the use of the singular and the plural signals the conflict between the possessed man and the possessing spirits. The effect of the demoniac's question is to ask, "What business do you have with me?" He then proceeds to declare Jesus' identity—which is especially important in Mark because of the theme of the "Messianic secret." (See below, [Messianic Secret]). At this point in Mark no one but Jesus, the unclean spirits, and we, the readers, know who Jesus is. The demoniac in the synagogue addressed Jesus as "the holy one of God" (1:24), and in the Markan summary the acclamation is "the Son of God" (3:11). The Gerasene demoniac elevates the title to "Son of the Most High God" (5:7), an acclamation particularly suitable coming from a Gentile. In the Old Testament it typically occurs on the lips of Gentiles confessing the sovereignty of the God of Israel over all the nations (Gen 14:18-20; Num 24:16; Deut 32:8; Dan 3:26; 4:17). The God whose Son is Jesus, therefore, is "the Most High God," the God of Gentiles as well as Jews.

In almost burlesque fashion,[6] the demoniac at Jesus' feet "adjures" Jesus "by God" not to torment him. The language here would be expected from the exorcist, not from the possessed man, and he appeals to God when he has just acknowledged Jesus as the Son of God. The reader would have expected this command to come from Jesus, not the demoniac. When the itinerant Jewish exorcists tried to exorcise demons in the name of Jesus, they said, "I adjure you by the Jesus whom Paul proclaims" (Acts 19:13). To "adjure" is to "implore" or "command someone under oath."[7] The spirits that so savagely debased the possessed man now plead with Jesus not to "torment," "torture," "harass," or "punish" them.[8] They can give it out, but they cannot take it, so they cower before the threat of just retribution and try to bluff their way by talking loudly and authoritatively even though they know they are in the presence of a superior (see ["Son of God" in Mark]).

Verse 8 is an "analepsis"—a reference to an event that occurred earlier in the story. In this case it fills a gap the reader had been unaware of. Prior to the demoniac's outburst in v. 7, Jesus had commanded the unclean spirit to come out of the man (cf. 1:25). Knowing the name of one's opponent was crucial in any battle. By

---

The Demon's Name

"When I heard these things, I, Solomon, got up from my throne and saw the demon shuddering and trembling with fear. I said to him, 'Who are you? What is your name?' The demon replied, 'I am called Ornias. . . . I am descended from an archangel of the power of God, but I am thwarted by Ouriel, the archangel.'

"When I, Solomon, heard the archangel's name, I honored and glorified the God of heaven and earth. After I sealed (the demon) with my seal, I ordered him into the stone quarry to cut for the Temple stones which had been transported by way of the Arabian Sea and dumped along the seashore. But being terrified to touch iron, he said to me, 'I beg you, King Solomon, let me have a measure of freedom, and I shall bring up all the demons.' Since he did not want to be subject to me, I prayed that the archangel Ouriel would come to help me. Immediately I saw the archangel descending to me from heaven." (*Testament of Solomon* 2:1, 4-7)

James H. Charlesworth, ed., *The Old Testament Pseudepigrapha* (Garden City NY: Doubleday, 1983), 1:963–64.

Legion

The legions were the primary units of the Roman army. During most of the first century there were 25-28 Roman legions, with around 5,000 heavy infantry in each. The effectiveness of the legions can be attributed in large measure to their flexibility and internal organization. Each legion consisted of ten cohorts of 480. Each cohort was divided into six centuries of 80 men, under the command of a veteran centurion, and each century was divided into units of eight soldiers who lived and ate together. In addition, a legion was supported by about 120 scouts and messengers.

David Kennedy, "Roman Army," *ABD* 5:789–90.

using the opponent's name—which represented all they were, their essence—one could gain control or influence over one's opponent. [The Demon's Name] A legion was the largest unit of the Roman army. [Legion] The name is probably calculated to convey the power or the terrible number of the demons that had possessed the man. The comment that follows—"for we are many" (v. 9)—supports this interpretation. On the other hand, it may also signal a secondary political commentary, drawing a parallel between the demonic spirits that had possessed the Gerasene and the Roman army that had occupied their land.[9] If that is the case, the demoniac's request that the spirits not be sent "out of the country" (v. 10) can also be understood both as the spirits' bargaining with the exorcist not to be driven from their native area (cf. Tob 8:3; see the bargaining in the Testament of Solomon; also see [The Demon's Name]) and as the determination of the Roman troops not to be driven out of the region.

Swine

"The pig [is unclean], for even though it has divided hoofs and is cleft footed, it does not chew the cud; it is unclean for you. Of their flesh you shall not eat, and their carcasses you shall not touch; they are unclean for you." (Lev 11:7-8; Deut 14:8)

See Isa 65:4 (in [Isaiah 65:3-4] above).

"R. Eliezer used to say: He that eats the bread of the Samaritans is like one that eats the flesh of swine." (*m. Shebith* 8.6)

"None may rear swine anywhere." (*m. Baba Kamma* 7.7)

(Credit: Barclay Burns)

The Swine, vv. 11-13

Verse 11 is an aside or comment by the narrator that introduces a new element into the story: "Now there on the hillside a great herd of swine was feeding." Pigs of course were unclean according to Jewish law [Swine], and their presence in the region is another signal that Jesus is in a Gentile area. The unclean spirits (5:13) ask to go into the unclean swine, and when Jesus grants their request both are destroyed. The number "2,000" has no symbolic significance, but it would have been a large herd. The destruction of the pigs serves several functions in the story: (1) it confirms that the unclean spirits came out of the man and thus the exorcism was effective; (2) Jesus not only delivers the man from the unclean spirits, but he also delivers the land from the unclean swine;[10] (3) it suggests the destructive power of evil—in this case humorously self-destructive; (4) it would have occasioned glee among Jewish hearers and may point to an earlier setting for this story; (5) it establishes the irony that although Jesus grants their request to stay in the region, when the unclean spirits enter the swine they rush into the sea and are destroyed; and (6) it may suggest the political subplot in which the Roman legions are driven into the sea.

The Witnesses, vv. 14-17

Confirmation of the miracle is a standard feature of every miracle story. In this case, the herders whose swine are destroyed provide the confirmation. Undoubtedly, the herders are Gentiles. Herding was a despised trade, probably

Despised Trades

"A man should not teach his son to be an ass-driver or a camel-driver, or a barber or a sailor, or a herdsman or a shopkeeper, for their craft is the craft of robbers." (*m. Kiddushin* 4.14)

Herbert Danby, trans., *The Mishnah* (Oxford: Clarendon Press, 1931), 329.

because herders were regarded as dishonest drifters whose flocks grazed over other people's land and crops. [Despised Trades] Herding swine was even more reprehensible. Remember, the degradation of the prodigal son is complete when he ends up feeding pigs in the fields of the "far country" (Luke 15:15). Having witnessed the demonic phenomenon, the herders run off and tell everyone what happened—"in the city and in the country" (5:14). By contrast, at the end of the Gospel, the women who witness the empty tomb run off and tell no one (16:8).

The herders are effective witnesses. People come to see what has happened. The undertone of bearing witness is suggested by the report that the people come to Jesus. What they see is the restored demoniac. Three participles underscore the dramatic change in the man's condition: he is sitting, clothed, and in his right mind (5:15). His composure and soundness of mind are evidence of the power of something greater than a legion of demons.

Just as the disciples were afraid when Jesus stilled the storm (4:41), so now the people from the surrounding area are afraid (5:15). In both cases it is an example of the fascination and fear, attraction and repulsion that human beings feel when confronted with the divine, what Rudolf Otto called "mysterium tremendum."[11] In Mark, however, fear often conveys a lack of faith or an inadequate faith. Even when they are witnessed, God's mighty acts must be told. Those who saw what had happened told the others (5:16). The people cannot move beyond their fear, however. They beg Jesus to leave them. Begging or pleading characterizes several of the exchanges in this story: the demons beg Jesus not to send them out of the region (v. 10), then they beg him to send them into the swine, now the people beg Jesus to leave their region (v. 17), and the man delivered from the demons begs Jesus to let him go with him (v. 18).

The Healed Man's Response, vv. 18-20

The man's request echoes the commissioning of the disciples: he asks to "be with" Jesus (cf. 3:14). Jesus has other plans for the man, however. Having a Gentile disciple would no doubt have provoked further hostility when Jesus was in Jewish communities. Instead, Jesus sends the man to his home and to his "friends" (5:19 NRSV), or to his own people, to tell them "how much the Lord has done for you, and what mercy he has shown you." The title "Lord" sounds strange here on the lips of Jesus. It echoes the early Christian confession, "Jesus is Lord." The recounting of what the Lord has done and how great is God's mercy is a recurring theme in the Old Testament (Exod 33:19; Rom 9:15-18), suggesting the conclusion that Jesus' mighty acts reveal that he is the Lord and that the redemptive acts of God in the history of Israel are now continuing in him. The command to "go" is Jesus' characteristic instruction to those who have experienced his deliverance (1:44; 2:11; 5:34; 7:29; 10:21, 52; 16:7). The command to go and tell, however, is curiously inconsistent with Mark's emphasis on the "messianic secret," which is suggested by Jesus' pattern of telling others not to tell anyone about what he has done (e.g., 1:34, 44; 3:12; 7:36). Going and announcing what the Lord has done echoes the mission language of the early church (Acts 15:27; 26:20).[12] Verse 20 presents three significant differences in the language of v. 19: (1) having been sent to "tell" (*apangeilon*) he began to "proclaim" (*kēryssein*), which is one of the functions of a disciple (1:14, 38, 39, 45; 3:14; 6:12; 7:36; 13:10; 14:9); (2) having been sent to his home and his own, he went to the Decapolis, the region named for its ten prominent Gentile cities [The Decapolis]; and (3) having been instructed to tell what "the Lord" had done for him, he preached what Jesus had done. In effect, Mark justifies the Gentile mission by

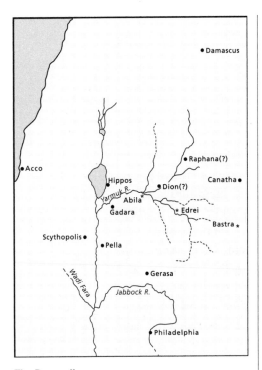

The Decapolis

The earliest listing of the ten cities of the Decapolis appears in Pliny's *Natural History* (5.74): "Adjoining Judaea on the side of Syria is the region of Decapolis, so called from the number of its towns, though not all writers keep to the same towns in the list; most however include Damascus, with its fertile water-meadows that drain the river Chrysorrhoë, Philadelphia, Raphana (all these three withdrawn towards Arabia), Scythopolis (formerly Nysa, after Father Liber's nurse, whom he buried there) where a colony of Scythians are settled; Gadara, past which flows the river Yarmak; Hippo [i.e., Hippos] mentioned already, Dion, Pella rich with its waters, Galasa [i.e., Gerasa], Canatha."

Pliny the Elder, Natural History (trans. H. Rackham; LCL; Cambridge MA: Harvard University Press, 1942), 277. S. Thomas Parker, "The Decapolis Reviewed," JBL 94/3 (1975): 437–41; Jean-Paul Rey-Coquais, "Decapolis," ABD 2:116–21.

tracing it to Jesus himself. If Mark's community was located in a Gentile area or was predominantly Gentile, one can understand the importance of this point. It gives his Gentile readers a place to find themselves in the "gospel of Jesus Christ, the Son of God" (1:1; cf. 13:10). Not only is the demoniac restored, but Jesus' great mercy also transforms the Gentiles from pigs and scorned outcasts to persons to be included in the good news of the kingdom.

Jairus's Daughter and the Woman with a Hemorrhage, 5:21-43

Two miracles involving giving life to females follow. Several verbal and thematic connections bind the two stories together: In both, the petitioner desires "salvation" (5:23, 28, 34) and falls at Jesus' feet (5:22, 33). In both, the person healed is called a "daughter" (5:23, 34, 35); in the one case the "daughter" has been ill for twelve years, and in the other she is twelve years old (5:25, 42). The condition of the two female sufferers, moreover, is similar in that both have been rendered ritually unclean, the one by a menstrual disorder, the other by death. Yet in both cases this uncleanness is boldly ignored, in the one case by the woman, who touches the garment of Jesus, in the other case by Jesus, who touches the girl's corpse. Fear, moreover, is mentioned in both healings (5:33, 36), and faith is a factor in both (5:34, 36).[13]

The story of the healing of the woman with a hemorrhage is sandwiched within the story of the raising of Jairus's daughter, yielding the following structure: (A) Jairus's request (5:21-24a), (B) the healing of the woman with a hemorrhage, and (A') the raising of Jairus's daughter (5:35-43). See [Markan Sandwiches].

The note that Jesus crossed again to the other side (5:21) not only connects the sequence of stories that follows with the preceding miracle but establishes that Jesus is once again on the west side of the Sea of Galilee, where he will be in Jewish surroundings. By now the gathering of a crowd is expected (see 4:1, 36), and "by the sea" is one of the stock settings in Mark (1:16; 2:13; 4:1). A "leader of the synagogue" (*archisynagōgos*; Acts 13:15; 18:8, 17) was a layperson appointed to look after the synagogue and take care of the arrangements for the services there. [Leader of the Synagogue]

Leader of the Synagogue

The direction of the congregation fell to the "chiefs" or elders of the synagogue. The leader of the synagogue "had accordingly nothing whatever to do with the direction of the congregation in general. Instead, his special responsibility was to attend to public worship. He is called *archisynagōgus* not as chief of the congregation, but as leader of its meetings for worship. As a rule, he was probably chosen from among the elders. It is said in particular of his functions that he had, for example, to decide who should read the Bible and the prayer, and to summon suitable persons to preach. He had, generally speaking, to insure that nothing improper took place in the synagogue (Lk. 13:14), and probably also had charge of the synagogue building."

Emil Schürer, *The History of the Jewish People in the Age of Jesus Christ* (175 BC–AD 135) (ed. Geza Vermes, Fergus Millar, and Matthew Black; Edinburgh: T. & T. Clark, 1979), 2:435; cf. Wolfgang Schrage, "archisynagōgos," *TDNT* 7:844–47.

The occurrence of a name in a miracle story is unusual but not without parallel (see "Bartimaeus" in 10:46). Later tradition often supplied names for unnamed personages. In this instance the name may have been preserved by tradition because of its etymology. "Jairus" can be traced to Hebrew names meaning "he enlightens" (Heb. *ya'îr*: Num 32:41; Judg 10:3-5; Esth 2:5) or "he awakes" (Heb. *ya'îr*: 1 Chr 20:5).[14] Like the Gerasene demoniac, he falls at Jesus' feet and begins to plead with him. A "leader of the synagogue" was a highly respected person, so his act of falling at Jesus' feet would have been all the more notable. His role in the story, however, is that of father, not his public function. He pleads for Jesus to come to his house and lay his hands on his daughter "so that she may be made well [Gk., *sōthē*; in other contexts, "be saved"] and live" (5:23). Laying hands on a person was typically an act of blessing, for it to have been regarded as an effective act of healing demonstrated that Jairus believed Jesus possessed special powers.[15] Healing by laying hands on the sick was not unknown in antiquity, however [Laying Hands on the Sick], and although Jesus at times healed at a distance, he also laid his hands on the sick person (6:5; 7:32; 8:23, 25). In the two sandwiched healing stories, both healings are accomplished by touching (5:27-31, 41). Jairus used a colloquial expression to report his daughter's condition. Cranfield suggests the translation "My little daughter is 'at death's door'" (5:23).[16] In Greek literature the verb *sōzō* can mean "cure," but it can also mean "deliver" or "save," from which its theological meaning developed.[17] Mark uses the term to mean both "healing" or "making well" (5:28, 34; 6:56; 10:52) and "saving one's life" or "living" (3:4; 8:35; 13:20; 15:30).[18]

Verse 24 provides a transition to the story of the healing of the hemorrhaging woman by noting that the crowd followed Jesus and pressed upon him (cf. 3:7, 9-10), a detail that has no relevance for the raising of Jairus's daughter.

In contrast to Jairus, the woman with a hemorrhage is nameless in Mark, though later tradition identifies her as Bernice (or Veronica). [Bernice] Furthermore, Eusebius claims to have visited her home in Caesarea Philippi. [The Home of the Woman with a Hemorrhage] Whereas he has position, distinction, family, and a house,

---

Laying Hands on the Sick

Both of the passages that mention laying hands on the sick in the *Genesis Apocryphon* found at Qumran also use the verb "live": "Then HRKNWS [the Pharaoh's friend] came to me [Abraham] and asked me to come and pray for the king and lay my hands upon him so that he would live. . . . and I laid my hands upon his head. The plague was removed from him; [the evil spirit] was banished [from him] and he lived." (1 QapGen 20.22, 29)

Florentino García Martínez, *The Dead Sea Scrolls* Translated (trans. Wilfred G. E. Watson; Leiden: E. J. Brill, 1994), 233-34. Cf. David Flusser, "Healing through the Laying on of Hands in a Dead Sea Scroll," *IEJ* 7 (1957): 107-108; Joseph A. Fitzmyer, *The Genesis Apocryphon of Qumran Cave I* (Biblica et Orientalia, 18a; 2d ed.; Rome: Biblical Institute Press, 1971), 140–41.

Bernice

Setting: an apocryphal account of the trial before Pilate.
"And a woman called Bernice [Lt: Veronica] crying out from a distance said: 'I had an issue of blood and I touched the hem of his garment, and the issue of blood, which had lasted twelve years, ceased' [Mk. 5:25ff.]. The Jews said: 'We have a law not to permit a woman to give testimony.'" (*Acts of Pilate* 7)

Wilhelm Schneelmelcher, ed., *New Testament Apocrypha* (rev. ed.; trans. R. McL. Wilson; Louisville: Westminster John Knox Press, 1991), 1:511.

The Home of the Woman with a Hemorrhage

"But since I have come to mention this city [Caesarea Philippi], I do not think it right to omit a story that is worthy to be recorded also for those that come after us. For they say that she who had an issue of blood, and who, as we learn from the sacred Gospels, found at the hands of our Saviour relief from her affliction, came from this place, and that her house was pointed out in the city, and that marvelous memorials of the good deed, which the Saviour wrought upon her, still remained. For [they said] that there stood on a lofty stone at the gates of her house a brazen figure in relief of a woman, bending on her knee and stretching forth her hands like a supplicant, while opposite to this there was another of the same material, an upright figure of a man, clothed in comely fashion in a double cloak and stretching out his hand to the woman; at his feet on the monument itself a strange species of herb was growing, which climbed up to the border of the double cloak of brass, and acted as an antidote to all kinds of diseases. This statue, they said, bore the likeness of Jesus. And it was in existence even to our day, so that we saw it with our own eyes when we stayed in the city. (Eusebius, *Ecclesiastical History* 7.18.1-3)

Eusebius: The Ecclesiastical History (trans. J. E. L. Oulton; LCL; Cambridge MA: Harvard University Press, 1932), 175, 177.

she is a ritually unclean outcast who has spent all she had on useless cures. But the last shall be first, and the first last (Matt 19:30; 20:16); she is cured, while Jairus's daughter dies because of Jesus' delay.

The Greek style changes dramatically. Rather than the simple "parat- actic style" (characterized by clauses joined by "and"), vv. 25-28 are one long sentence, and the woman's condition is described in a series of seven participles: (1) She "had been suffering from hemorrhages" for twelve years (5:25). The language echoes the Septuagint of Leviticus 15:25, which suggests that she was suffering from chronic menstrual bleeding, a condition that rendered her "unclean" (Lev 12:7; 15:19-30). An entire tractate of the Mishnah, tractate "Zabim" ("they that suffer a flux"), deals with the restrictions upon such persons and those who come in contact with them. Uncleanness could also be conveyed to bedding and clothing by touch. This legacy continued in the early church: Dionysius of Alexandria (third century) expressed his judgment that women "in the time of their separation," should not enter the church or approach the holy table (*Epistle to Basilides*, Canon 2).[19] The information that she had suffered this condition for twelve years con- firms that it is chronic, underlines the difficulty of any cure, and provides another parallel with the raising of Jairus's twelve-year-old daughter (5:42).

Continuing the sequence of participles, v. 26 describes the futility of her efforts to find a cure: she had (2) suffered greatly under many physicians, (3) spent all she had, (4) grew no better, but (5) became worse. This extended sequence of miseries, like the extended descrip- tion of the behavior of the Gerasene demoniac (5:3-5), dramatizes the wonder of the miracle that will follow. No human power or skill could cure her. It also subtly invites the reader to join in ridiculing physicians who take one's money but cannot make one any better. [Physicians] Parenthetically, when Alec McGowan performed the Gospel of Mark

Physicians

"I went to physicians to be healed, but the more they treated me with ointments the more my vision was obscured by the white films, until I became completely blind." (Tob 2:10)

"And he [the pharaoh] sent for all [the wise men] of Egypt to be called, and all the wizards as well as all the healers of Egypt, (to see) whether they could heal him of that disease. . . . However, all the healers and wizards and all the wise men were unable to rise up and heal him." (1 QapGen 20.20)

"The best among physicians is destined for Gehenna." (*m. Kiddushin* 4.14)

For a much more positive view of physicians, see Sir 38:1-15.

Florentino García Martínez, *The Dead Sea Scrolls Translated* (trans. Wilfred G. E. Watson; Leiden: E. J. Brill, 1994), 233; Herbert Danby, trans., *The Mishnah* (Oxford: Clarendon Press, 1931), 329.

on stage, the audience laughed at this point. Among the traditional cures the woman might have suffered, William Lane found the following: "drinking a goblet of wine containing a powder compounded from rubber, alum and garden crocuses," "a dose of Persian onions cooked in wine administered with the summons, 'Arise out of your flow of blood!'" and "sudden shock, or the carrying of the ash of an ostrich's egg in a certain cloth."[20]

The sixth and seventh participles report that the woman had heard of Jesus, presumably how he had healed others (cf. 1:28, 39, 45; 3:7-10). The language of seeing and hearing, given particular significance by Mark 4:10-12, is echoed in the two sandwiched miracles also: Jairus saw Jesus (5:22) and the woman had heard of him (5:27). Some do indeed hear and see and have faith!

Joel Marcus perceptively observes that the word "touched" "gains extraordinary intensity as the climax of the string of participles."[21] The woman shared Jairus's conviction that she could be healed by Jesus' touch, but she could not ask Jesus to touch her in her condition. It would have been her duty to avoid transmitting her uncleanness to others. Resolving her dilemma by a further step of faith, she decided that she would be cured if she could touch even his clothing. If uncleanness could be transmitted to clothing, then healing power could also be transmitted through Jesus' cloak (cf. 3:10; 6:56; Luke 6:19; Acts 5:15; 19:11-12). The imperfect tense of the verb "saying" in v. 28 implies that this is what she was saying over and over to herself: "If I touch even his clothes, I will be made well" (author's translation).

Confirmation of the miracle is a standard element in a healing story. In this case, of course, the confirmation is tricky and requires a longer than normal part of the story. Everything up to this point merely sets up the exchange between Jesus and the woman who touched him. In the first part of v. 29 the narrator reports the healing; in the second part the narrator reports that the woman knew she had been healed. The language is vivid. The first part of the verse translated literally says, "and immediately the spring [fountain, or flow] of her blood was dried up." The verb can be used of plants withering (4:6), but here, coupled with the noun meaning "spring" or "fountain," the image is that of a river drying up (cf. Rev 16:12). The woman feels the change instantly. She had been delivered from her "torment" (Gk. *Mastix*, lit., "whip" or "lash"; cf. 3:10; 5:34). Jesus also knows immediately "in himself," just as the woman knows "in her body," that power has gone forth from him. Literally, it is "the power from him" that has gone out. This is the first of ten occurrences of the word "power" in Mark. Elsewhere it refers to a miracle (6:2, 5; 9:39); here it is the divine power within Jesus by which the miracle is accomplished (cf. 6:14). It is hard to deny the overtones of magic in this story. The woman's faith is clearly evident as she presses forward to touch Jesus in spite of the cultural and religious restrictions placed on her. Still the cure is affected without Jesus' will to heal the woman. At best, one can argue that God was acting through Jesus and that it was God's intention to heal her.[22] Although Jesus does not know who touched him, he and the woman are privy to knowledge no one around them has.

It is important for Jesus that he make personal contact with the man or woman who touched him, so that the healing is not understood as simply a magical power. Jesus therefore turns around and begins asking. "Who touched my clothes?" The disciples, who have not been mentioned since 4:34, are incredulous because they do not know what has just happened. Accordingly, they become an obstacle to Jesus' desire to know who had touched him. The crowd was pressing around him; anyone could have touched him. Jesus' response is to look around searching for the person who received the "power." With the exception of Luke 6:10, Mark is the only New Testament writer to use the verb to "look around," and he uses it six times (3:5, 34; 5:32; 9:8; 10: 23; 11:11). Although the participle for "who had done it" is feminine, it is simply a grammatical accommodation to the story. The implication is that Jesus did not know who had touched him, not that he knew it was a woman.

In v. 33 "fear and trembling" are both participles, but they echo the combination of the two nouns elsewhere. In the New Testament, the noun "trembling" (*tromos*) only occurs when it follows "fear" (1 Cor 2:3; 2 Cor 7:15; Eph 6:5; Phil 2:12). In the Old Testament the combination of "trembling and fear" or "fear and trembling" is a common response to God's mighty acts (Exod 15:16; 4 Macc 4:10), to God's people (Deut 2:25; 11:25), or to an enemy (Ps 55:5; Isa 19:16). Although she had lesser reasons to fear, the language here suggests that her "fear and trembling" was a response to the divine power that she had experienced at work in her body.

When she stepped forward, she fell at Jesus' feet, just as the Gerasene demoniac (5:6) and Jairus (5:22) had before her, and told Jesus "the whole truth" (5:33). Marcus notes that this phrase occurs in secular literature in trial scenes ["The Whole Truth"], which may mean that it had particular significance for the persecuted Markan community (cf. 13:9-13).[23] Regardless of the consequences, the woman who had been healed told "the whole truth" about what Jesus had done for her. Here there is no hint of any effort to maintain secrecy.

Because of her courageous faith, Jesus claims her as a member of his new family (cf. 3:35; 10:29-30), calling her "daughter" (5:34; cf. 5:23 and 35, where the term reoccurs). Jesus then affirms that her faith has made her well, or delivered her. Jairus used the term *sōzein* (to make well, deliver, or save) earlier (5:23), but here, following the woman's healing and witness to the truth, the reader may understandably suspect that the term carries overtones of its theological meaning, "Your faith has saved you" (cf. 10:52). This pronouncement was later used as a baptismal formula in the early church (Tertullian, *Bapt.* 12.8). She has been made whole in body and spirit by her encounter with Jesus.

He sends her away with the traditional word of parting, "Go in peace" (where the Greek echoes the Hebrew "shalom"; Judg 18:6; 1 Sam 1:17; 2 Sam 15:9; Acts 16:36; Jas 2:16). As a farewell on the lips of Jesus, however, it is more than a goodwill wish (Luke 7:50). In the Old Testament *shalom* can carry the sense of "salvation which comes from God, especially the eschatological salvation."[24] When Jesus bids the woman healed by her faith farewell, therefore, he bids her go as one who "has been restored to a proper relationship with God."[25]

The story of the raising of Jairus's daughter resumes with v. 35. Dramatically, while Jesus is still speaking, a messenger from the leader of the synagogue's ["house" is understood] arrives with the devastating message, "Your daughter is dead." The second part of the message, "Why trouble the teacher any further?" sounds like gentle counsel, or an afterthought given on the spot rather than part of the message. The verb to "trouble" appears elsewhere in the Gospels in Matthew 9:36 and Luke 7:6 and 8:49. "Teacher" is the most common term of address used in the miracles stories in Mark (4:38; 9:17, cf. 9:38), but it is also used in other contexts by supplicants and skeptics (10:17, 20, 35; 12:14, 19, 32).

"The Whole Truth"

On trial, Socrates told "the whole truth," and when Simon ben Giora, the zealot, was captured, Josephus reports that he too told "the whole truth":

". . . from me you shall hear the whole truth: not, however, delivered after their manner in a set oration duly ornamented with words and phrases. No, by heaven! but I shall use the words and arguments which occur to me at the moment; for I am confident in the justice of my cause." (Plato, *Apology* 17b)

"He [Terentius Rufus, who had been left in command], after hearing from Simon the whole truth, kept him in chains and informed Caesar of the manner of his capture." (Josephus, *J.W.* 7.31)

B. Jowett, trans., *The Dialogues of Plato* (New York: Random House, 1937), 1:401.

Josephus, *J.W.* (trans. H. St. J. Thackeray; LCL; Cambridge MA: Harvard University Press, 1928), 513, 515.

Having been called "teacher," Jesus immediately begins to instruct Jairus on faith and death. The verb in v. 36 (*parakousas*) can mean either "overheard" or "ignored." The use of the term in the Septuagint and in Matthew 18:17 favors the latter translation. Jairus came to Jesus in faith that he could save his daughter's life. Now even in the face of the report that she has died, Jesus challenges Jairus to a further act of faith. Fear is a common element in this collection of miracle stories. Jesus told his disciples not to fear when they thought they were about to perish in the storm at sea (4:40), the herdsmen were afraid when they saw the demoniac restored to his right mind (5:15), and the hemorrhaging woman who had just been healed came in "fear and trembling" (5:33). To Jairus, Jesus says, "do not fear, only believe" (5:36). The present imperative carries the sense of continuing action: "Not a single act, but a steady attitude, of faith is called for. . . . the father has already shown faith by coming to Jesus—now he must go on believing."[26]

At this point Jesus instructs the crowd and his disciples to stay behind, taking with him only Peter, James, and John, who emerge now as the three disciples privileged to be with Jesus at the Transfiguration (9:2) and to be closest to him at Gethsemane (14:33). [Peter, James, and John] When Jesus gets to Jairus's house, he sees a "commotion" (cf. Mark 14:2; Matt 26:5; 27:24; Acts 20:1; 21:34; 24:18) and people "weeping and wailing loudly" (5:38). The verb "to wail" is vividly onomatopeic: *alalazein* (cf. 1 Cor 13:1). The commotion may have been noise and confusion of friends and neighbors gathering at the house, or it may be that we are to understand that the customary professional mourners had already come. [Mourning]

Peter, James, and John

"The Gospels record three scenes in which Jesus left the other nine disciples and took with him only Peter, James, and John: the raising of Jairus's daughter, the transfiguration, and the Garden of Gethsemane. The role of this group of disciples seems to have been more important for Mark than for either Matthew, who does not single them out at the raising of Jairus's daughter, or Luke, who does not separate them from the others at Gethsemane. Neither Matthew nor Luke introduces this group into any other scene."

R. Alan Culpepper, *John, the Son of Zebedee: The Life of a Legend* (Columbia: University of South Carolina Press, 1994), 31.

Mourning

The father of an unmarried girl was responsible for her burial. "Even the poorest in Israel should hire not less than two flutes and one wailing woman" (*m. Ketuboth* 4.4), but because of Jairus's status in the community one can imagine a larger number of mourners. The mourning began immediately after the death and continued through the internment. The period of consolation lasted for a week. The hired mourners, usually women, would "weep and wail" (cf. 5:28), play the flute (Jer 48:36; Josephus, *J.W.* 3.437), beat on musical instruments, and beat their breasts. They would be joined by members of the family, men and women. The gestures, including stamping their feet and wringing their hands, and the cries were violent and noisy because it was believed that the deceased witnessed everything until the internment was complete. The cries may also have been thought to frighten away evil spirits that might threaten the dead person's house. Mourning and lamentation accompanied the funeral procession, and especially during breaks in the procession, when the women could sit in the dust and beat their breasts and faces. In the ancient Near East, the wailing women also danced and beat their cheeks to the rhythm of a tambourine.

Herbert Danby, trans., *The Mishnah* (Oxford: Clarendon Press, 1931), 250; Gustav Stählin, "*kopetos*," *TDNT* 3:832, 842-44.

The Raising of Jairus's Daughter
This painting by Polenov portrays Jesus, the girl's parents, and the three disciples. The others have been sent out.
James Jacques Joseph Tissot (1836–1902). *Christ raising the daughter of Jairus, Governor of the Synagogue, from the dead.* 1897. Ann Ronan Picture Library, London, Great Britain. (Credit: HIP / Art Resource, NY)

The mourners were around the house, or in a courtyard. In any case, the leader of the synagogue apparently had more than a typical peasant's one-room house. When Jesus entered the house, he reproached the mourners, saying, "The child is not dead but sleeping" (5:39). Sleep was a common euphemism for death. If one takes the statement literally, then the miracle is not that Jesus raised the dead girl but that he knew (even before he saw her) that she was not dead. Luke removes the ambiguity by reporting that when Jesus commanded her to get up, "her spirit returned" (Luke 8:55). Mark no doubt understood the tradition in the same way. Death, for the girl as for all who have faith, "will be no more permanent than sleep."[27] The mourners responded by "laughing against" him or "ridiculing" him (5:40). Jesus was not deterred in the least by ridicule, however. He "threw" them all out and took only the girl's parents and the three disciples with him into the room where the girl lay.

The raising of the girl shares features with stories of resuscitations both by the prophets (1 Kgs 17:17-24; 2 Kgs 4:18-37) and by other ancient faith healers [Ancient Faith Healing], including the utterance of secret words. At several points in the Gospel, Mark preserves Aramaic words

Ancient Faith Healing

"A girl had died just in the hour of her marriage, and the bridegroom was following her bier lamenting as was natural, his marriage left unfulfilled, and the whole of Rome was mourning with him, for the maiden belonged to a consular family. Apollonius then witnessing their grief, said: 'Put down the bier, for I will stay the tears that you are shedding for this maiden.' And withal he asked what was her name. The crowd accordingly thought that he was about to deliver such an oration as is commonly delivered as much to grace the funeral as to stir up lamentation; but he did nothing of the kind, but merely touching her and whispering in secret some spell over her, at once woke up the maiden from her seeming death; and the girl spoke out loud, and returned to her father's house. . . . Now whether he detected some spark of life in her, which those who were nursing her had not noticed—or whether life was really extinct, and he restored it by the warmth of his touch, is a mysterious problem which neither I myself nor those who were present could decide."

Philostratus, *Life of Apollonius of Tyana* 4.45.

[Aramaic Words], which would have been foreign to Greek speakers but which ground the tradition in the language spoken by Jesus and his disciples. "*Talitha koum*" means "Little girl, get up!" Jesus often touched or took the hand of the one he was healing (1:31; 9:27), and the command to "rise" echoes both earlier healings (1:31; 2:11; 3:3) and, for the Christian reader, the resurrection of Jesus (16:6).

Confirmation of the miracle is immediate. The girl gets up and begins to walk around. Mark then adds the detail that may have originally led to the sandwiching of these two miracle stories: the girl was twelve years old. [Age in Antiquity] The deeper link between the two stories is the common theme of Jesus' power to give life. Blood, the life force, was restored to the hemorrhaging woman, and life ("her spirit"; Luke 8:55) was restored to the dead girl.

The response is great amazement (see the same expression in 2:12; 6:51). Jesus then gives two instructions: first that they tell no one, and then that they give the girl something to eat. The admonition to tell no one is consistent with the secrecy motif in Mark [Messianic Secret] but seems forced here because the resuscitation of the twelve-year-old girl could hardly be kept a secret. Eating could be a confirmation that the dead had actually been raised and was not a spirit or a vision (see Tob 12:19; Luke 24:43), but here Jesus' request seems to be a simple act of concern for a hungry twelve-year-old.

Aramaic Words

AΩ Aramaic is a Semitic language closely related to Hebrew. It originated among the Arameans in northern Syria. When the Assyrians conquered the area, Aramean scribes made Aramaic the common language of the Near East. It continued as the popular vernacular throughout the Persian, Greek, and Roman periods. Mark translates each of the following terms, except "Hosanna!"

Boanērges	"Sons of Thunder" (3:17)
talitha koum	"Little girl, get up!" (5:41)
korban	"an offering to God" (7:11)
ephphatha	"be opened" (7:34)
hōsanna	untranslated (11:9-10)
abba	"father" (14:36)
Golgotha	"the place of a skull" (15:22)
elōi elōi lema sabachthani	
	"My God, my God, why have you forsaken me? (15:34)

Age in Antiquity

"To imagine the significance of age in the first-century Mediterranean, note that a person of twelve was well along in his or her life span. In the cities of antiquity nearly a third of the live births were dead before age six. By the mid-teens 60 percent would have died, by the mid-twenties 75 percent, and 90 percent by the mid-forties. Perhaps 3 percent reached their sixties. Few ordinary people lived out their thirties. . . . much of Jesus' audience would have been younger than he, disease-ridden, and looking at a decade or less of life-expectancy."

Bruce J. Malina and Richard L. Rohrbaugh, *Social-Science Commentary on the Synoptic Gospels* (Minneapolis: Fortress, 1992), 211.

Messianic Secret

At the beginning of the 20th c., the prevailing view was that Mark provided an accurate historical reflection of the life of Jesus. In particular, scholars believed that Mark accurately portrays the gradual awakening of the recognition of Jesus' identity among his disciples, and their cooperation in keeping his identity secret from the general populace. William Wrede, who more than any other influenced the course of Markan scholarship in the last century, asked, "Did Jesus consider himself to be the Messiah?" and "Was Jesus regarded as the Messiah by others?" And if so, when? Wrede called attention to four lines of evidence that Jesus deliberately suppressed the messianic character of his ministry: (1) Jesus forbade the demons to make him known (1:25, 34); (2) he commanded secrecy to those who might have revealed the messianic character of his ministry—those whom he healed and his disciples (1:43-45; 5:43; 7:36; 8:30; 9:9); (3) Jesus withdrew from the crowds in order to give special or esoteric teachings (4:34; 7:17); and (4) according to Mark, Jesus taught in parables in order to conceal the mystery of the kingdom of God from outsiders (4:10-12).

From this evidence, Wrede made these conclusions: (1) The description Mark gives is historically impossible. The commands to remain silent when people were cured miraculously, and often in view of others, would have been pointless; and if the secret was revealed to the disciples, and they were taught about Jesus' death and resurrection, why were they discouraged when his prediction about his death came true? (2) Since the secrecy motif cannot be historically accurate, it must be a theological construct imposed on the account of Jesus' ministry. This conclusion was important because for the first time it raised the possibility that Mark was more theologian than historian and that he wrote the Gospel with theological and apologetic interests. (3) Mark 9:9 is an indication that, according to Mark, the messiahship of Jesus was a closely guarded secret during his earthly ministry; it was made known only after the resurrection. (4) The early church originally believed that Jesus became the Messiah through the resurrection (Acts 2:36; Rom 1:4). Gradually the belief that Jesus was the Messiah was thrust back into the period of the earthly ministry of Jesus. Mark lived in the period in which the two views were in tension. Mark resolved this tension by saying Jesus was the Messiah during his earthly life, but he did not want others to know. Thus, his messiahship was kept secret until after the resurrection. Mark therefore developed the secrecy motif to explain how it was that Jesus was not recognized as the Messiah during his lifetime but was proclaimed to be the Messiah after his death and resurrection. (5) Finally, Wrede concludes that Mark did not originate this conception but took it from his community and heightened it in his Gospel.

Most conservative New Testament scholars now argue that Wrede forced a false dichotomy between the mind of Jesus and the mind of Mark. The emphasis on secrecy probably originated with Jesus rather than with Mark. Jesus may well have commanded secrecy to avoid the misunderstanding that he was merely a wonder worker and to discourage further suspicion from the religious and political authorities. After all, secrecy was inherent in the nature of his mission—God in the form of a servant.

William Wrede, *Das Messiasgeheimnis in den Evangelien* (1901; Eng. trans., *The Messianic Secret* [trans. J. C. G. Grieg; Edinburgh: T. & T. Clark, 1971]).

CONNECTIONS

Mark 5:1-20

The story of the Gerasene demoniac conjures up stark images and deep feelings. It is set in a foreign territory, the almost primal surroundings are threatening, and it taps deep-seated impulses of flight and self-preservation. In a cemetery Jesus meets a deranged man, so wild no one could restrain him, so mad he shrieked and cut himself. The man has lost his identity to his madness. The only name he can give is that of a military unit, "Legion," which the Good News for Modern Man translation rendered as "Mob." He was an army of violent spirits.

As distant and foreign as this story is to our own experience, we can meet it on several levels. First, we recognize the revulsion we feel in the presence of another human being who has been ravaged by violent dehumanizing forces—those who are severely injured, incapacitated, or deformed and those who are psychologically ill and out of control. How can we love the homeless or institutionalized who have lost so much to deprivation, illness, and/or drug abuse? Jesus was not put off by the man's surroundings, his appearance, or his behavior. Instead, he met him as a unique individual and a person of value. "What is your name?" he asked. He desired to know who this other person was, his unique identity that made him infinitely lovable.

The response of the herdsmen and the political subplot of the story remind us that our encounters with others are never merely individual but always involve corporate dimensions. Jesus' effort to help one man hurt the livelihood of others. The Gospel records no joy at the restoration of the demoniac, only fear and the request that Jesus leave. Some have suspected that they were reacting to the loss of their swine: Jesus was bad for business. On the other hand, the implicit allusions to Roman occupation—"Legion" and driving the pigs into the sea—are a reminder that while Jesus was always concerned for the individual, his vision of the kingdom was corporate—a new community where destructive forces do not oppress, exploit, and dehumanize and where individuals can fulfill their God-given identity and calling.

One of the lines in this story that stays with the reader is the demoniac's initial question: "What have you to do with me?" Although the demoniac asked it defensively, attempting to avoid any interaction with Jesus, it is a question we may each ask of God: "What do you want from me? What in the world do you want with me?" In tone it is a skeptical, evasive question, but it is enough of an opening for God's mercy. The eventual answer, of course, is that Jesus wants the man's deliverance from the dehumanizing forces that have possessed him. Mark 5:1-20 is a story that may give hope to many as they struggle with family members who have been overcome by alcoholism, drug addiction, depression, or mental illness. What has happened to them matters to God. Every person, regardless of how unlovely he or she has become, is still loved by God as though he or she were the loveliest person in the world. Jesus wants the demoniac "seated, clothed, and in his right mind" (5:15). Within the demoniac was a potential that only Jesus' delivering and transforming power could bring out. In the course of the story, the man moves from being surrounded by tombs and swine to setting out to be reconciled with home and family.

Second, Jesus wanted the man to be his ambassador to his people in the Decapolis. The eventual result of every genuine encounter with the divine is the missionary imperative to go and tell others. Share your story. The same love that makes God care about us makes God care about others also, those who have not yet experienced God's liberating love. So the conclusion is always the same: be one of the cutting edges of kingdom growth. Go to those with whom you have a unique relationship, who may not experience what you have experienced unless you share God's great mercy with them. The mission of the church is to carry God's love to every person. The church's mission, therefore, is like the flame of a candle; it is where the transforming light meets the world around it. What does God have to do with you?

Mark 5:24b-34

Miracle stories are inherently optimistic, comedy rather than tragedy. They all end well. The most striking feature of the bleeding woman is not her physical condition, but her determination to get to Jesus and her unshakable conviction that she will be healed if she can touch even his cloak. She should be remembered not hiding momentarily in the crowd, nor kneeling at Jesus' feet, nor going away healed and affirmed, but pressing through the crowd, eyes fixed on Jesus, hand outstretched, reaching for his cloak. Her faith and determination to let her life be touched by Jesus' power can be an inspiration for the bleeding, broken, and ostracized regardless of their circumstances. Jesus can make you whole. All you have to do is reach out to him.

There were many others on the road with Jesus that day, many of them his disciples. Jesus was on a mission, to save a little girl. There was a good deal of jostling in the excitement as disciples and onlookers jockeyed for position near Jesus. They were astonished when he asked who had touched him; many people had touched him. But Jesus was so attuned to the needs of others that he sensed that someone hurting and

Bleeding Woman
The Canaanite Woman, from *the Tres Riches Heures du Duc de Berry*. MS 65, fol. 164. 15th century Book of Hours. Musée Condé, Chantilly, France. (Credit: R.G. Ojeda, Réunion des Musées Nationaux / Art Resource, NY)

in need had reached out to him. It was the difference between elbows and fingertips.[28] Many wanted to be near Jesus, to see if he could really save Jairus's daughter. Only the woman wanted to be made whole by his power. [Touching in Faith] On the other hand, just as the striking characteristic of the woman is not her physical condition but her faith and determination, so the most impressive thing about Jesus in this story may not be his power to heal but his sensitivity to need. Most of us would have been so focused on the important task at hand that we would not even have sensed the fingertips on our cloak.

Touching in Faith

"Few are they who by faith touch him; multitudes are they who throng about him." (Augustine, *Sermons* 12.5 [Benedictine ed. 62.5])

Thomas C. Oden and Christopher A. Hall, eds., *Ancient Christian Commentary on Scripture: New Testament II, Mark* (Downers Grove IL: InterVarsity Press, 1998), 75; NPNF, 1, 6:299.

Mark 5:21-24a, 35-43

Jairus's plea, "My little daughter is at the point of death" (5:23), opens a gap in the narrative. The question is whether Jesus will be able to save her from death. The intervening healing of the woman with a hemorrhage delays Jesus' arrival, builds suspense, and makes the situation all but hopeless when the report comes that Jairus's daughter has passed away. What can Jesus do for the dead? On that side of the resurrection, the raising of Jairus's daughter pointed to the divine power at work in Jesus. On this side of Jesus' resurrection, it is a promise of God's power to give life beyond death to those who have faith. Eduard Schweizer perceptively observed, "In this way the story points forcefully away from itself and asks the reader whether he considers God able to triumph over death in the hour of his own death when, presumably, no 'miracle' may be expected."[29] The existential question, therefore, is not whether Jesus raised Jairus's daughter but whether there will be life beyond the grave for you and me.

The question of life after death has troubled human beings at least since the development of the earliest burial practices, well before the beginnings of recorded history. Job lamented,

A mortal, born of woman,
few of days and full of trouble,
comes up like a flower and withers,
flees like a shadow and does not last. . . .
For there is hope for a tree,
if it is cut down, that it will sprout again,
and that its shoots will not cease. . . .
But mortals die, and are laid low;
humans expire, and where are they?. . . .
If mortals die, will they live again? (Job 14:1-2, 7, 10, 14a)

Job was troubled, but he could only raise the question; he had no answer. All he could do was plead with God to hide him in Sheol and "appoint me a set time and remember me" (Job 14:13). Perhaps he might live on in the memory of God.

Throughout history there have been troubled souls that brooded over the question of life after death. Miguel de Unamuno, the Spanish existentialist, was one of the great "agonizers." Roland Bainton placed him in an elite company of troubled souls: "If anyone would discover parallels to Luther as the wrestler with the Lord, then one must turn to Paul the Jew, Augustine the Latin, Pascal the Frenchman, Kierkegaard the Dane, Unamuno the Spaniard, Dostoievski the Russian, Bunyan the Englishman, and Edwards the American."[30] Immanuel Kant was concerned with the same problem: "I mean with the only vital problem, the problem that strikes at the very root of our being, the problem of our individual and personal destiny, of the immortality of the soul."[31]

Unamuno's life was a battleground for the struggle between the head that said there could be no reason to think there is life beyond death and the heart that demands that there must be. For Unamuno this was "the tragic sense of life." Because he did not grant the final verdict to reason, however, he did not despair. For Unamuno, there were only three possible solutions to the problem of death: "(a) I know that I shall die utterly, and then irremediable despair, or (b) I know that I shall not die utterly, and then resignation, or (c) I cannot know either one or the other, and then resignation in despair or despair in resignation . . . and hence conflict."[32]

Unamuno would not let either faith or reason triumph, perhaps because he feared that reason would prevail. He preferred for the war to continue, and he found meaning in struggling with the mystery. Moreover, rather than rendering ethics pointless, the tragic sense of life served as the basis of an ethic for life. His religion was struggle, whether he won or not. Indeed, the prize may be the struggle itself. Unamuno formulated his principle for action succinctly: "Act so that in your judgment, and in the judgment of others you may merit eternity, act so that you may become irreplaceable, act so that you may not merit death."[33] In other words, live in such a way that if there is nothing beyond death, it will be an injustice.

That was as far as the existentialist philosopher could go. To go further one must peer beyond the grave through the lens of the resurrection of Jesus. Paradoxically, the answer to the universal human question is found in Jesus' probing question: "I am the resurrection and the life. Those who believe in me, even though they die, will live, and everyone who lives and believes in me will never die. Do you believe this?" (John 11:25-26).

NOTES

[1] Vincent Taylor, *The Gospel according to St. Mark* (London: Macmillan and Co., 1952), 277.

[2] Robert A. Guelich, *Mark 1–8:26* (WBC 34a; Dallas: Word, 1989), 274.

[3] Joel Marcus, *Mark 1–8* (AB 27; New York: Doubleday, 2000), 349.

[4] BDAG, 882.

[5] Heinrich Greeven, *"proskyneō," TDNT* 6:763.

[6] Marcus, *Mark 1–8*, 350.

[7] BDAG, 723.

[8] BDAG, 168.

[9] Marcus, *Mark 1–8*, 351-52.

[10] Guelich, *Mark 1–8:26*, 283.

[11] Rudolf Otto, *The Idea of the Holy* (trans. John W. Harvey; New York: Oxford University Press, 1950), 12-40.

[12] Guelich, *Mark 1–8:26*, 285.

[13] Marcus, *Mark 1–8*, 364-65.

[14] Guelich, *Mark 1–8:26*, 295.

[15] Bruce J. Malina and Richard L. Rohrbaugh, *Social-Science Commentary on the Synoptic Gospels* (Minneapolis: Fortress, 1992), 210-11.

[16] C. E. B. Cranfield, *The Gospel according to Saint Mark* (CGTC; Cambridge: Cambridge University Press, 1959), 183.

[17] Werner Foerster, *"sōzō," TDNT* 7:989-92.

[18] Guelich, *Mark 1–8:26*, 296.

[19] *ANF* 6:96.

[20] William L. Lane, *The Gospel according to Mark* (NICNT; Grand Rapids: Wm. B. Eerdmans, 1974), 192 n. 46.

[21] Marcus, *Mark 1–8*, 367.

[22] Cranfield, *The Gospel according to Saint Mark*, 185; Lane, *The Gospel according to Mark*, 192-93.

[23] Marcus, *Mark 1–8*, 360.

[24] Werner Foerster, *"eirēnē," TDNT* 2:412.

[25] Eduard Schweizer, *The Good News according to Mark* (trans. Donald H. Madvig; Atlanta: John Knox Press, 1970), 118.

[26] Cranfield, *The Gospel according to Saint Mark*, 187.

[27] Ibid., 189.

[28] An insight I owe to a sermon John B. Howell preached at Crescent Hill Baptist Church, Louisville, Kentucky.

[29] Schweizer, *The Good News according to Mark*, 122.

[30] Roland H. Bainton, *Here I Stand: A Life of Martin Luther* (New York: Abingdon-Cokesbury Press, 1950), 385. The following section on Unamuno is excerpted from the summary of

Hugo H. Culpepper's dissertation in R. Alan Culpepper, *Eternity as a Sunrise: The Life of Hugo Culpepper* (Macon GA: Mercer University Press, 2002).

[31] Miguel de Unamuno, *Tragic Sense of Life* (trans. J. E. Crawford Flitch; New York: Dover Publications, Inc., 1954), 4.

[32] Ibid., 33.

[33] Ibid., 263.

THE MISUNDERSTOOD MESSIAH AND THE MARTYRDOM OF JOHN THE BAPTIST

Mark 6:1-56

If the sequence of miracles in the preceding chapter lulls the reader into a false sense of optimism, the rejection of Jesus in his hometown (6:1-6a) bursts this bubble. Jesus could do no miracle there and was amazed at their unbelief. Having been rejected in Nazareth, Jesus went elsewhere (6:6b) and sent the disciples out on mission in pairs (6:7-13). His instructions to them call itinerants to journey by faith and depend on hospitality wherever they go. Mark fills the interim during which the disciples are on mission with an account of the beheading of John the Baptist (6:14-27). The pattern is ominous. John preached, was arrested, and was put to death. Jesus preached but was rejected by the scribes from Jerusalem (3:22) and his own hometown. Those who follow Jesus in the work of the kingdom should therefore be prepared for a similar fate.

When the disciples return, Jesus' plans for a time of rest with them are frustrated by the crowd that follows them. After teaching them, Jesus uses the occasion to teach the disciples how to feed the multitude (6:30-44). After sending the crowd away and going up into the mountains to pray, Jesus comes to the disciples, walking on the sea—an epiphany, revealing his divinity (6:45-52). But the disciples' hearts are hardened, and they cannot understand even the lesson of the loaves. At Gennesaret, the crowds gather again, and Jesus continues his healing ministry (6:53-56), in stark contrast to his reception in his hometown.

COMMENTARY

Jesus' Rejection at Nazareth, 6:1-6a

Although Nazareth is not named, we assume that is what Mark means when it says that Jesus went to his own *patris*—his own part of the country, or his "home town." The use of the term here is probably due to its occurrence in the proverb in v. 4, since these are the only two contexts in which it occurs in the Gospels. Luke 4:16-30 describes a visit to Nazareth near the beginning of Jesus' public ministry. In both, Jesus teaches in the synagogue and is met by skepticism. Beyond that, the two accounts pursue different interests: Luke features Jesus' fulfillment of Isaiah 61:1-2, while Mark notes that because of their lack of faith Jesus could do no miracles there. While Luke says nothing about the disciples, Mark notes that they accompanied Jesus to his hometown. The disciples were with Jesus throughout Mark 5, and they will play a major role in events later in Mark 6.

In other respects Mark's account of Jesus' visit to his hometown resembles the account of his teaching in the synagogue in Capernaum in Mark 1:21-28. Joel Marcus observes that four elements of Mark 6:2 echo the earlier synagogue visit: Jesus' teaching on the Sabbath, the amazement of the people, and their remarks about his teaching, and his mighty works.[1]

Mark uses the verb "to be amazed" (*ekplēssesthai*) exclusively to describe the response to Jesus' teachings and miracles (1:22; 7:37; 10:26; 11:18). In this instance the amazement is skeptical, and their skepticism is related to his family and the source of his special powers. A series of questions follows. They ask not "how?" but "from where?" The second part of their question is also twofold: What is "this wisdom" and these "deeds of power"? Jesus' teachings reflected wisdom, and "powers" (cf. 5:30) here is a term for Jesus' miracles. The two are related, just as authoritative teaching and exorcism are related in the earlier synagogue appearance, when the people respond, "What is this? A new teaching—with authority! He commands even the unclean spirits, and they obey him" (1:27). Wisdom and mighty deeds were regarded as the inner and outer manifestations of inspiration or spirit possession. The two are also related in Paul's defense of the preaching of the gospel in 1 Corinthians:

> For Jews demand signs and Greeks desire wisdom, but we proclaim Christ crucified, a stumbling block to Jews and foolishness to Gentiles... Christ the power of God and the wisdom of God. For God's foolishness is wiser than human wisdom, and God's weakness is stronger than human strength. (1 Cor 1:22-25)

Perhaps also significant is the combination of wisdom and might in prophecy of the Davidic king in Isaiah 11:2.

The hometown folk ask where Jesus got his special powers. The wisdom had to be "given" to him (6:2). By what spirit was he possessed? Jesus understands their skepticism is unbelief—the last word in

Jesus the Carpenter

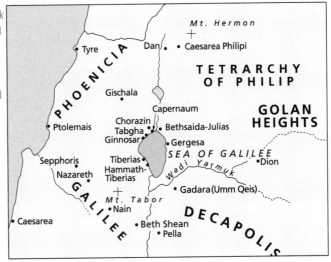

The term translated "carpenter" (Gk *tektōn*) is also used for masons and smiths. Justin Martyr records that Jesus made "ploughs and yokes; by which He taught the symbols of righteousness and an active life" (*Dialogue with Trypho* 88). Based on the discovery of the construction of Sepphoris, just three miles from Nazareth, Richard A. Batey suggests that Jesus probably worked on the construction of the new capital:

The construction of an influential Roman capital city near Jesus' home in Nazareth redefines the carpenter's occupation in central Galilee. In 4 BC Varus' army crushed the rebellion centered at Sepphoris, burned the old town, and sold the inhabitants into slavery. To erect Antipas' new capital, many skilled workers from surrounding towns and villages came to Sepphoris and found employment. Artisans from Nazareth would have been among those employed.

Nazareth and Sepphoris

The Greek word *tektōn*, translated "carpenter" in Mark 6:3, has the root meaning of "artisan," that is, a skilled worker who works on some hard material such as wood or stone or even horn or ivory. A metal smith also might be described as a *tektōn*. The preferred translation of *tektōn* in Mark 6:3 is "carpenter." In Jesus' day construction workers were not as highly specialized as in today's work force. For example, the tasks performed by carpenters and masons could easily overlap.

ANF 1:244. Richard A. Batey, *Jesus and the Forgotten City: New Light on Sepphoris and the Urban World of Jesus* (Grand Rapids: Baker, 1991), 76.

this pericope (6:6a). If not by God's spirit, then he must be possessed by a demonic spirit. In Capernaum (1:21-28), and in Gentile territory (5:1-20), Jesus cast out demonic spirits; in his hometown, his own people suspect him of being possessed by demonic spirits!

They then ask about Jesus' parentage and family. Strong manuscript evidence favors the reading: "Is this not the carpenter, the son of Mary" (6:3). This is the only place where Jesus, rather than Joseph, is called a carpenter. [Jesus the Carpenter] Matthew 13:55, where there is no debate about the text, reads, "Is not this the carpenter's son? Is not his mother called Mary?" The heretic Celsus mocked the interpretation of the "tree of life" in Genesis as a reference to resurrection, saying that it was interpreted in this way only because Jesus was nailed to a tree or because he was a carpenter. In response, Origen, the greatest biblical scholar of the early third century, replied, "in none of the Gospels current in the Churches is Jesus Himself ever described as being a carpenter" (Origen, *Against Celsus* 6.36).[2] Did Homer nod, thinking of Matthew but overlooking the reference in Mark, or did the great scholar have early texts in which Mark 6:3 agreed with Matthew 13:55? Compounding the issue is the question of whether the early scribes changed the text of

Jesus' Brothers and Sisters

The 4th-century church fathers advanced three views regarding those named in Mark 6:3 as Jesus' brothers and sisters: (1) Helvidius (c. AD 380) claimed they were blood brothers and sisters, (2) Epiphanius (c. AD 382) maintained they were Joseph's children by a former wife, and (3) Jerome (c. AD 383) said they were Jesus' cousins, the children of Mary the wife of Clopas, the sister of Jesus' mother.

Jerome's view, designed to refute Helvidius, is not found in earlier fathers, and Vincent Taylor rejects it on four grounds: (1) *adelphos* is not used for "cousin" (*adelphos*) in classical Greek, (2) the "brothers" are never associated with James the son of Alphaeus or Mary of Clopas, and (3) in John 19:25 there are four women; it is unlikely that Mary, the mother of Jesus, had a sister also named Mary: Mary the wife of Clopas. Neither is it clear that Alphaeus and Clopas were one and the same.

On the other hand, Taylor cites widespread early support for the Epiphanian view: Clement of Alexandria, Origen, Eusebius, Hilary, "Ambrosiaster," Gregory of Nyssa, Ambrose, Cyril of Alexandria, the Gospel of Peter, and the Protoevangelium of James (8:3; 9:2). Against this view, one may appeal to the implications of Luke 2:7 and Matt 1:25, that Joseph "knew" Mary after the birth of Jesus, and that she had other children.

The Helvidian view was also held by earlier writers: Tertullian, Bonosus, Jovinianus, and others. J. B. Lightfoot argued that the fact that Jesus entrusted the care of his mother to the Beloved Disciple rather than to his brothers defeats the Helvidian hypothesis. Other interpretations of John 19:26-27 may be advanced, however, and most Protestant scholars have held that the view that those named in Mark 6:3 were actually Mary's children is the simplest and most natural understanding.

Vincent Taylor, *The Gospel according to St. Mark* (London: Macmillan, 1952), 247–49.

Mark to agree with Matthew, the more familiar Gospel, or to protect the teaching of the Virgin Birth by not referring to "the carpenter" as Jesus' father. It was very unusual to trace one's genealogy through the mother rather than the father. The reference to Jesus as his mother's son may therefore imply questions about the legitimacy of his birth (as in John 8:41 and Origen, *Against Celsus* 1.28). Alternatively, the reference to Mary may mean that whereas she was well known in the community, Joseph had died, perhaps some years earlier, so it was natural to refer to her rather than her deceased husband.

The reference to Jesus' brothers and sisters was interpreted in various ways by the church concerned to defend the perpetual virginity of Mary, but most Protestant scholars regard them as Mary's children. [Jesus' Brothers and Sisters] James is listed among those to whom the risen Lord appeared (1 Cor 15:7). He soon became one of the "pillars" of the church (Gal 1:19; 2:9, 12) and eventually the leader of the Jerusalem church (Acts 12:17; 15:13; 21:18; cf. 1 Cor 9:5). James can also claim the distinction of being the church's third known martyr (Acts 12:2; after Stephen and James the son of Zebedee).[3] [The Martyrdom of James]

According to Eusebius, after James's martyrdom the church together with the surviving apostles and members of Jesus' family elected Simeon to succeed James as the head of the church in Jerusalem. Simeon is identified by Hegesippus and Eusebius as the son of Clopas and as a "cousin" of Jesus (*Ecclesiastical History* 3.11.1; 4.2.4). Since Hegesippus refers to Simeon as "another cousin of the Lord," it is probable that this Simeon, like James, was one of the brothers of Jesus. Simeon too was eventually accused of heresy by certain Jews, tortured, and martyred during the time of Trajan (around AD 106–107; see

The Martyrdom of James

When Festus, the governor, died in AD 62, the Sadducean high priest Ananus II seized the opportunity to kill James and others. Ananus assembled the judges of the Sanhedrin, had James condemned for transgressing the law, and delivered him to be stoned to death. For this rash action, Josephus records (*Ant.* 20.200), moderate Jews complained to King Agrippa, and the king deposed Ananus from the high priesthood. Citing now lost writings of Hegesippus (c. AD 180), Eusebius provides the following account of James's character and martyrdom. James was called "Just" because he took a Nazirite vow; that is, he drank no wine, ate no flesh, and did not shave, bathe, or anoint himself with oil. He was allowed to enter the sanctuary of the temple and spent so much time praying for the people that his knees became hard like a camel's. Many believed in Jesus because of him, so many that the scribes and Pharisees asked him to stand on the wall of the temple at the Passover and denounce Jesus. Instead of denouncing Jesus, James acclaimed him as the Son of Man.

"So they went up and threw down the Just, and they said to one another, 'Let us stone James the Just,' and they began to stone him since the fall had not killed him, but he turned and knelt saying, 'I beseech thee, O Lord God and Father, forgive them, for they know not what they do.' And while they were thus stoning him one of the priests of the sons of Rechab, the son of Rechabim, to whom Jeremiah the prophet bore witness, cried out saying, 'Stop! what are you doing? The Just is praying for you.' And a certain man among them, one of the laundrymen, took the club with which he used to beat out the clothes, and hit the Just on the head, and he suffered martyrdom. And they buried him on the spot by the temple, and his gravestone still remains by the temple." (Eusebius, *Ecclesiastical History* 2.23.16-18)

Eusebius, *The Ecclesiastical History* (trans. Kirsopp Lake; Cambridge MA: Harvard University Press, 1926), 1:175. R. Alan Culpepper, "Jesus' Earthly Family," *Biblical Illustrator* 6/2 (Winter 1980): 12-17.

The James Ossuary

An empty ossuary bearing the inscription "James, son of Joseph, brother of Jesus" in 1st-century Aramaic was discovered among the relics in a private collection in Jerusalem in 2002 but is now widely regarded as a fake. The James ossuary was on display at the Royal Ontario Museum from November 15, 2002 to January 5, 2003.

(Credit: http://en.wikipedia.com/wiki/James_Ossuary)

Eusebius, *Ecclesiastical History* 3.32.1-4). Two books of the New Testament are attributed to Jesus' brothers: James and Jude (Jas 1:1; Jude 1). Later tradition also supplies names for Jesus' sisters: Lysia and Lydia, or Mary (or Anna) and Salome.[4]

Because they know Jesus' family and regard him as one of themselves, they "take offense" (see 4:17) at him. Jesus responds with the telling proverb, "Prophets are not without honor except in their hometown, and among their own kin, and in their own house" (6:4, NRSV). With slight variations, the proverb appears in other traditions (Matt 13:57; Luke 4:24; John 4:44; *Gos. Thom.* 31; POxy 1:6). Significantly, however, Mark is the only Gospel that adds the phrase, "and among his own kin," clearly identifying his family among those who did not accept him. In Mark 3 Jesus' family appears in the same context as the scribes from Jerusalem who say, "He has Beelzebul" (3:22). Here they again appear in a bad light, with the hometown folk who question the source of his wisdom and power. Luke uses the term for "kin" (Greek *syngenēs*) in other contexts (Luke 1:58; 2:44; 14:12; 21:16), but Luke has no parallel to this passage. Mark's rejection of the family of Jesus, therefore, stands in sharp contrast to the more positive role Luke gives them (Luke 8:19-21; Acts 1:14).

The last two verses of this paragraph pick up language Mark used in the two sandwiched miracle stories that precede it. Because of their lack of faith (see Matt 13:58), Jesus could do no "deed of power" (Greek *dynamis*; cf. 5:30; 6:2 where the term means "power [to do miracles]"), except that he did lay his hands on a few sick people. For the laying on of hands in healing see the commentary on 5:23. The typical conclusion for a miracle story is for the witnesses to be amazed at what they have seen (5:20; 6:51), but here Jesus is amazed at their unbelief (cf. 9:24, where the father of the epileptic boy pleads, "help my unbelief!" The reversal is clear: Jesus comes, is confronted by suspicion, does no miracle, and is amazed at their lack of faith. Sadly, Mark reports Jesus' visit to his hometown as a "non-miracle" story.

The Mission of the Twelve, 6:6b-13

The brief summary in Mark 6:6b and the sending out of the Twelve introduce the third major section of the Gospel following the introduction. Similar features mark off these sections: each begins with a summary statement (1:14-15; 3:7-12; 6:6b) that is followed by a commissioning of the disciples (1:16-20; 3:13-19; 6:7-13), and each ends with a response to Jesus (3:1-6; 6:1-6a; 8:27-30). In each case, the summary statements have connections both with preceding and coming material. Mark 6:6b is the briefest of the summary statements, but it nevertheless summarizes Jesus' activities over an unspecified period of time. Mark 1:16-20 reports the calling of the first disciples, Mark 3:13-19 the appointment of the Twelve to be with Jesus and to be sent out on mission, and Mark 6:7-13 the sending out of the Twelve by twos. The first two sections end with the rejection of Jesus, first by the authorities (Mark 3:1-6) and then by his hometown (6:1-6a). Marcus finds the end of this third section at Mark 8:14-21, but in doing so violates the parallel structures of the two feeding sequels: the feeding of the 5,000 (6:35-7:37) and the feeding of the 4,000 (8:1-26) both of which end with a transitional healing story (7:31-37 and 8:22-26). It seems better, therefore, to mark the end of this third section with Peter's confession at Caesarea Philippi (8:27-30), which also introduces the passion predictions in the next section (Mark 8:31-10:52). See the outline in the introductory material.

The theme of the first major section (1:14–3:6) is Jesus' authority in relation to demons and the religious authorities. The second section (3:7–6:6) announces the coming of the kingdom through Jesus' teaching and his miracles, and the gathering of a new community of faith. The third section builds on the emphases of the first two, adding the exodus themes of sea crossings and wilderness feedings. The ministry of Jesus, therefore, fulfills the heritage of Israel with a new exodus, a new Moses gathering a new community of faith and embarking on a journey that will lead that community to new and strange lands of promise. The sending out of the Twelve establishes the journey motif for the coming section. All that they do from this point on will be an extension of this urgent mission. Sadly, it soon becomes clear that they have no understanding of what this mission is about.

All but one (11:2) of Mark's references to "villages" occur in the coming section (6:6, 36, 56; 8:23, 26, 27). Similarly, Mark refers to Jesus' teaching several times in the coming section (6:6, 30, 34; 7:7; 8:31; 9:31; 10:1). Having been rejected in his hometown, Jesus goes elsewhere, teaching, and then sends the Twelve to extend his mission even further. Prophetically, Jesus does not allow rejection to defeat the work of the kingdom.

Mark 6:7-13 can be divided into four sub-sections: (1) the commissioning of the disciples (6:7), (2) instruction regarding what to take and what not to take with them (6:8-9), (3) instruction regarding what to do when they are received and what to do when they are rejected (6:10-11), and (4) a summary of their mission activities (6:12-13).

The sending of the Twelve marks the beginning of a new era in the inauguration of the kingdom, but it is a beginning that Jesus has carefully prepared for. When he called the first disciples, he told them, "Follow me and I will make you fish for people" (1:17). When he appointed the Twelve, it was to "be with him" and to "be sent out to proclaim the message and to have authority to cast out demons" (3:14-15). In the previous section the disciples were apprenticed, hearing Jesus' teaching and witnessing his casting out of demons.

Although their apprenticeship is far from complete, they will now learn by doing, and the mission that began with this sending out will continue in the mission of the early church.

Jesus' act in calling the Twelve to him echoes the verb used to introduce the appointment of the Twelve in 3:13, but elsewhere Jesus calls both the disciples and the crowd (3:23; 7:14; 8:1, 34; 10:42). Mark often refers to the group of Jesus' disciples as "the Twelve" (see 3:14; 4:10; 9:35; 10:32, etc.). The construction of the verb "begin" followed by an infinitive occurs frequently in Mark. Although the verb "to send" (*apostellein*) can have the technical sense "to send as one's emissary," Mark uses it also in a general sense (3:31; 4:29; 5:10; 6:17). The practice of sending by twos can probably be traced to the Jewish law requiring testimony to be substantiated by two witnesses (Deut 17:6; 19:15; Num 35:30). Given the dangers of travel, two were safer than one (Eccl 4:9-12; Tob 5:4, 17, 22). Elsewhere in Mark Jesus sends two when there is a job to be done (11:1; 14:13), and the early church seems to have followed this practice also:

Peter and John—Acts 8:14
Paul and Barnabas—Acts 13:2; 1 Cor 9:6; 15:36-40
Barnabas and Mark—Acts 15:39
Paul and Timothy—Acts 16:3
Paul and Silas—Acts 16:25; 17:3, 10

The list of the Twelve in Matthew 10:2-4 is divided into pairs, perhaps preserving the traditional pairing of the disciples.

The granting of authority to cast out unclean spirits echoes the commissioning of the Twelve in Mark 3:15. Jesus has already demonstrated his authority in teaching and in exorcisms (1:22, 27; 2:10). Now he commissions the disciples as his emissaries, to carry his authority with them. In an era when business required that emissaries be able to travel and represent one's interests, the rabbinic ruling was that "a man's agent is like to himself" (*m. Berakoth* 5.5; cf. 2 Chr 17:7-9; John 13:16). See the discussion of "unclean spirits" in the commentary and connections on Mark 1:23 above.

Jesus' instructions regarding what the disciples should and should not take with them ensure that they will travel by faith, depending on God to provide for them through the hospitality and generosity of others. The clothing and equipment listed in vv. 8 and 9 provide a revealing glimpse of first-century dress and travel conditions. The prescriptions suggest some contact with contemporary itinerant Cynic philosophers [Cynic Philosophers] and with the descriptions of the Israelites hastily preparing to leave Egypt: "This is how you shall eat it: your loins girded, your sandals on your feet, and your staff in your hand"

Cynic Philosophers

Cynicism can be traced to Socrates' student Antisthenes in the 4th c. BC and found adherents throughout the period of the early church. The Cynics challenged the aristocratic ethos of the Greco-Roman society both in their teachings and in their style of life. The name "Cynic" was popularly linked with the Greek word for "dog" (*kyōn*). They were "doggish philosophers" who, like dogs, showed shocking disregard for social conventions, sleeping in storage jars, urinating, and engaging in sex in public. They claimed a strong consciousness of mission, being "sent by Zeus," to challenge conventional values and opinions and call the lost mass of humanity to live simply according to nature. Cynics therefore reduced their possessions to an absolute minimum, a poor man's cloak, a begging bag, and a staff (Diogenes Laertius 6.13, 22-23).

Generally they wore long, unkept hair and were often barefoot. Epictetus characterized the Cynics as having "neither property, nor house, nor wife, nor children, no, not even so much as a bed, or a shirt, or a piece of furniture" (*Discourses* 4.8.31 [trans. W. A. Oldfather; LCL; Cambridge MA: Harvard University Press, 1928], 387). Diogenes carried a cup until he saw a boy drinking water from his cupped hands. Immediately, "he cast away the cup from his wallet (Greek *pēra*) with the words, 'a child has beaten me in plainness of living'" (Diogenes Laertius 6.37 [trans. R. D. Hicks; LCL; Cambridge MA: Harvard University Press, 1925], 39).

Following this philosophy, the Cynics lived on edible plants that grew by the road and by begging.

Ronald F. Hock, "Cynics," *ABD* 1:1221–26; Karl Heinrich Rengstorf, "*apostolos*," *TDNT* 1:409–12.

(Exod 12:11; cf. Deut 8:4; 29:5-6).[5] If traveling with a staff and beggar's bag had become associated with the Cynic lifestyle in popular thought, Jesus may have been requiring his disciples to maintain an even more radical freedom from possessions.[6] His intent is that the disciples should trust in God's provision for their needs, lead lives consistent with their message, and cultivate community by depending on the provision of hospitality wherever they go. If this is the case, we may infer something of Jesus' dress and manner of life from these instructions. He apparently expected the disciples to continue to live and travel as he did (see the reference to the money bag in John 12:6) and repeat the teachings on the kingdom they had learned from him. Nevertheless, because Exodus parallels figure prominently in the rest of Mark 6, it is not inconceivable that Mark saw a parallel between the disciples and the Israelites, traveling by faith and depending on the provision of bread.

The synoptic traditions vary in details.

	Mark 6:8-9	**Matthew 10:9-10**	**Luke 9:3**	**Luke 10:4**
Allowed	staff, sandals			
Forbidden	bread, bag, copper coins, two tunics	gold, silver, copper, bag, two tunics, sandals, staff	staff, bag, bread, money, two tunics	purse, bag, sandals

The common term "road" or "way" (Gk., *hodos*) becomes a metaphor later in the Gospel for the "way" of suffering servanthood that leads to the cross (see 1:2, 3; 4:4, 15; 8:3, 27; 9:33, 34; 10:17, 32, 46, 52; 11:8;

12:14; Acts 9:2; 19:9, 23; 22:4; 24:14, 22). Given the overtones of this term, Mark evidently understands Jesus not merely as giving directions for a one-time mission of the original disciples but as setting the pattern for the church as it fulfills its mission. The rod or staff was used both as a weapon for defense and as a walking stick. The bag (Greek, *pēra*) was a leather pouch used by travelers, a knapsack.[7] Alternatively, it may have been a beggar's bag, in which case Jesus may have been forbidding the disciples to beg as the itinerant Cynic philosophers did. Nor were they to put copper coins (not even coins with the least value) into their belts. Sandals were permitted, but they were not to take, or perhaps to wear, two tunics. The Cynics folded their tunics double for greater warmth when they slept out in the open (Diogenes Laertius 6.13). The tunic was worn next to the skin, under the cloak. T. W. Manson noted an interesting connection between these instructions and the rabbinic injunction that one may not enter the Temple Mount "with his staff or his sandal or his wallet, or with dust upon his feet" (*m. Berakoth* 9.5).[8] On the basis of this reference, Cranfield comments, "perhaps the implication of the most primitive form of the charge [which he finds in Matthew and Luke] is that the mission is a sacred undertaking comparable with worship in the Temple."[9]

Verse 10 marks the beginning of a second set of instructions, regarding the disciples' response to hospitality or the lack thereof. Because they were to carry no provisions with them, they would be dependent on others to provide them with food and shelter wherever they went. When they entered a village, if someone invited them to stay with them, they were to stay there until they left. [Hospitality] The purpose of this instruction was to ensure that they did not embarrass anyone by moving to better quarters, which would have been a violation of the conventions of honor and shame in the ancient Near East.

Hospitality

The practice of hospitality is rooted in the Bedouin obligations to provide for traveling strangers (cf. Gen 18:1-8; Josephus, *Ant.* 1.250-51). The patriarch Abraham became the exemplar of hospitality in Jewish tradition, so that blessedness in the afterlife was imaged as receiving hospitality in "Abraham's bosom" (Matt 8:11; Luke 16:22-25). The Israelites even thought of God as host and hoped to dwell forever in "the house of the Lord" (Ps 23:5-6; cf. Ps 104; Isa 25:6-8). In Jesus' teachings also heaven is pictured as God's gracious hospitality (Luke 14:16-24; Matt 25:21-33; John 14:1-6). Hospitality demonstrates love. It is a spiritual gift (1 Pet 4:9). Those who hoped for eschatological hospitality were expected to show hospitality to others now, and one might even "entertain angels unawares" (Heb 13:2). Hospitality is therefore listed among the important virtues in the epistles (1 Tim 3:2; Rom 12:13). Moreover, the mission of the church depended upon itinerant preachers and evangelists finding hospitality. Therefore, it was a serious offense when Diotrephes refused to accept those sent by the Johannine elder (3 John 10). The traveling emissaries "began their journey for the sake of Christ, accepting no support from non-believers. Therefore we ought to support such people, so that we may become co-workers with the truth" (3 John 7-8). When itinerant evangelists abused the duty of hospitality, the early church responded with the rule that true prophets never stayed for more than three days or asked for money (*Didache* 11.5-6; 12.2). If he settled among them, he should earn his own bread, as Paul did (*Didache* 12.3; 1 Cor 9:15; 2 Cor 11-7:9; 1 Thess 2:9). Still, hospitality remains deeply rooted in Jewish and Christian practices. Christ himself was knocking on the door of the Laodiceans: "I am standing at the door, knocking; if you hear my voice and open the door, I will come in and eat with you, and you with me" (Rev 3:20).

John Koenig, "Hospitality," *ABD* 3:299–301; Gustav Stählin, "*xenos*," *TDNT* 5:17–25.

Rejecting the emissary was the same as rejecting the sender, and v. 10 explains rejection as refusing to hear the disciples (see the judgment on those who have ears but do not hear in 8:18; cf. 4:12, 33). As they leave this place of "bad soil" (cf. 4:13-20), the disciples are instructed to shake off the dust from their feet as a witness against them. This practice is attested in the Old Testament, where Nehemiah shook out his garments saying, "So may God shake out everyone from house and from property who does not perform this promise. Thus may they be shaken out and emptied" (Neh 5:13). Earth from a foreign country was deemed to be unclean (*m. Oholoth* 2.3; *m. Tohoroth* 4.5), so a Jew returning from a Gentile country would carefully shake off the dust from his feet. Paul also practiced this sign of judgment. When the Jews in Corinth opposed him, he shook out his clothes, saying, "Your blood be on your own heads! I am innocent. From now on I will go to the Gentiles" (Acts 18:6; cf. 13:51).

Mark explains the meaning of this sign with the words "as a testimony against them" (6:11). The Greek syntax would allow the interpretation "as a testimony to them," meaning that the prophetic sign was offered as a last appeal for them to repent, but the meaning here, as in Mark 1:44, is probably one of judgment. It was a sign that the proclamation of the kingdom and the call to repentance had been offered and rejected. The messengers had done all they could and were moving on.

Verses 12-13 provide a brief summary of the disciples' activities and their success. The appointment of the Twelve expressed two mission purposes: to preach the gospel and cast out demons (3:14-15). Jesus' instructions to the disciples for their mission gave them authority over the demons but did not mention preaching explicitly (cf. Matt 10:8), though it may be assumed in verb "send out" (*apostellein*). Mark's report of their work lists three activities: preaching, casting out demons, and anointing the sick with oil. Their success in the latter two is noted, but nothing is said about the response to their preaching. In general, however, the tone is positive. Indeed, this is the high point in the Gospel for the disciples. When they follow Jesus' instructions and undertake their mission, they are successful. From this point on, however, they appear in a much less positive light.

The note that the disciples preached repentance recalls the preaching of John the Baptist (1:7) and Mark's keynote statement in 1:14-15 (see the commentary there). The disciples' fledgling mission efforts were already part of the work of the kingdom (cf. 5:20; 13:10; 14:9). They contributed to Jesus' mission and the fulfillment of his inauguration of the kingdom. Casting out demons was also part of Jesus' ministry (cf. 1:34, 39; 3:22; 7:26-30—see the commentary and connections on

Mark 1:21-28). Mark provides no other account of the disciples casting out demons (Mark 9:18; cf. Matt 7:22; Luke 10:17), although they forbade another who cast out demons in Jesus' name (9:38). The unanticipated element is the report that the disciples were anointing the sick with oil and curing them. Olive oil was used medicinally to soften wounds and promote healing (Isa 1:6; Luke 10:34; cf. Josephus, *J. W.* 1.657). It was also used for various kinds of anointings (Luke 7:46; Heb 1:9/Ps 45:7). Although the anointing and the curing may be separate activities, the association of these two in this three-part list of activities suggests that the anointing with oil was medicinal, as in James 5:14-15.

This brief paragraph provides an apt summary of the mission and ministry that grew from Jesus' teachings and example. The disciples were sent to travel by faith, laying aside material possessions, relying on hospitality, preaching repentance, and caring for the spiritual and physical needs of others. In spite of their failures, they learned a valuable lesson—when they followed Jesus' instructions and authentically embodied the gospel they proclaimed, they experienced success. Whereas Jesus healed few (6:5), they healed many (6:13).

Following the report of the martyrdom of John the Baptist, the only section of the Gospel (apart from 1:2-8) in which Jesus is not the central character, Mark resumes the narrative of Jesus' ministry with a second report of the disciples' activities (6:30).

The Beheading of John the Baptist, 6:14-29

Mark strategically inserts an account of the death of John the Baptist at this point in the Gospel. The placement appears to be deliberate for several reasons. John the Baptist was the forerunner. He came preaching (1:2-8) and was arrested (1:14). Now we learn that he had been put to death. The pattern is set: Jesus preached; he too would be arrested and put to death. Now the disciples had been sent out to preach. In spite of their initial success, they should not be surprised when they too are arrested. The placement of the story of John's death at this point contributes to the subtheme of feasts and food in Mark 6–8. John's death occurs during a drunken feast at the court of a king, and in a macabre twist John's head is served on a platter to the king and his guests. Immediately following, Jesus will feed the multitude of 5,000, blessing, breaking, and giving bread in an act that foreshadows the Last Supper and the church's sacred meal. One meal results in death; the other gives life. But the life-celebrating meal is itself a commemoration of the death of Jesus that is anticipated by the death of John the forerunner.

Mark appears to have taken the account of John's death from prior sources. In style it differs noticeably from Mark's typical patterns. One notices in particular the four "for" clauses in vv. 14, 17, 18, and 20, and the use of the aorist tense throughout this section. Verses 14-16 serve as the transition from the sending of the Twelve to the death of John the Baptist by reporting that Herod Antipas heard reports (of Jesus, or of the disciples' activities) and said that John had come back to life. Verse 15 reports other popular explanations for Jesus' power. Verses 17-20 set the stage: Herod Antipas had sent his first wife, the daughter of a Nabatean prince, back to her father and married Herodias, who had been married to Herod Philip, one of his half brothers. Marrying a brother's wife was forbidden by Levitical law (Lev 18:13, 16; 20:21), unless the brother was deceased. John had preached against Herod's brazen violation of the law. Herod had arrested John, perhaps to prevent him from arousing further controversy and to protect him from Herodias. Verses 21-29 report the banquet at the court, Salome's dancing, Herod's oath, Herodias's instructions that Salome should ask for the head of John the Baptist, the gruesome presentation of his head on a platter, and the burial of the body by John's disciples.

The story of John's death evokes echoes of numerous other stories and themes from Jewish folklore. Among the stories of the martyrdom of the faithful, one can cite the deaths of Zechariah (2 Chr 24:20-22), Eleazar (2 Macc 6:18-31), and the seven brothers (2 Macc 7). John's death at the hands of Herod recalls other stories of the persecutions of a wicked king: Potiphar and Pharaoh (Gen 39; Exod 5), Nebuchadnezzar and Belshazzar (Dan 1–6; see Belshazzar's banquet in Dan 5), Antiochus (esp. 1 Macc 1:41-50; 2:15-28). Even more intriguing are the parallels with other stories of prophets and female adversaries, especially Elijah, Jezebel, and Ahab (1 Kgs 18:3-4, 11-13; 19:1-3; 21:23; 2 Kgs 9:30-37). In other stories the female killers kill the wicked kings. Jael drives a tent stake through the head of Sisera (Judg 5:24). Judith beheads Holofernes (following a banquet), puts his head in her food bag, and then hangs it on the parapet of the city wall (Judith 13:6-10; 14:1). As a variation on a theme, Mark's account of John's death follows the pattern of Judith's song of triumph over Holofernes:

> She anointed her face with perfume;
> she fastened her hair with a tiara
> and put on a linen gown to beguile him.
> Her sandal ravished his eyes,
> her beauty captivated his mind,
> and the sword severed his neck! (Jdt 16:6-9)

In the book of Esther, the heroine wins king Artaxerxes, who promises her half his kingdom (Esth 5:3, 6-7; 7:2-3), and Haman is executed.[10] The depiction of Herod Antipas as an impotent king who cannot control his own family is worthy of Shakespeare (*Macbeth, King Lear*) or a Greek tragedian (Sophocles or Euripedes).

While these themes and parallels are clear in Mark, they are absent from Josephus's account of John's death. [Josephus's Account of John's Death] Even a cursory comparison of the two accounts reveals their similarities and differences. In both John preaches eloquently, is arrested by Herod Antipas, and is put to death at his fortress. In Josephus, Herod fears John's preaching for its influence on the people; in Mark, Herod hears John gladly. The greatest difference between the two accounts lies in Herod's attitude toward John. In Josephus, Herod fears John and concludes that he must kill him. Herodias has no role except that Herod's divorce and remarriage are the circumstances (according to popular interpretation) for the divine retribution on Herod. In Mark, Herodias plots to force Herod to do what he does not want to do. Josephus reports that John was killed at Machaerus, Herod's fortress northeast of the Dead Sea. Mark does not identity the location, but the banquet for "the leading men of Galilee" suggests that the events took place at Tiberius. Mark's account of John's death, therefore, reflects historical tradition embellished by folklore and creatively integrated into Mark's themes and narrative context.

Verse 14 introduces Herod rather awkwardly. Herod is inaccurately called "king." [Herod Antipas and Herodias] His title was actually "tetrarch" or "ruler of a fourth part" (of Herod the Great's kingdom). Ironically

---

Josephus's Account of John's Death

"But to some of the Jews the destruction of Herod's army seemed to be divine vengeance, and certainly a just vengeance for his treatment of John, surnamed the Baptist. For Herod had put him to death, though he was a good man and had exhorted the Jews to lead righteous lives, to practice justice towards their fellows and piety towards God, and so doing to join in baptism. . . . When others too joined the crowds about him, because they were aroused to the highest degree by his sermons, Herod became alarmed. Eloquence that had so great an effect on mankind might lead to some form of sedition, for it looked as if they would be guided by John in everything that they did. Herod decided therefore that it would be much better to strike first and be rid of him before his work led to an uprising, than to wait for an upheaval, get involved in a difficult situation and see his mistake. Though John, because of Herod's suspicions, was brought in chains to Machaerus, the stronghold that we have previously mentioned, and there put to death, yet the verdict of the Jews was that the destruction visited upon Herod's army was a vindication of John, since God saw fit to inflict such a blow on Herod." (Josephus, *Ant.* 18.116-19)

Josephus: Jewish Antiquities (trans. Louis H. Feldman; LCL; Cambridge MA: Harvard University Press, 1965), 9:81–85.

Rembrandt Harmensz van Rijn (1606–1669). *Decapitation of St. John the Baptist.* 1628–1635. Pen & brown ink. Louvre, Paris, France. (Credit: Réunion des Musées Nationaux / Art Resource, NY)

Herod Antipas and Herodias

Herod Antipas, the son of Herod the Great by his Samaritan wife, Malthace, was made tetrarch of Galilee and Perea when his father died in 4 BC (Luke 3:1). Jesus called him "that fox" (Luke 13:32). He rebuilt Sepphoris, built a capital at Tiberius (the Jews condemned him for building it over an ancient cemetery; Josephus, *Ant.* 18.36-38), and formed a political alliance with the Nabateans by marrying the daughter of king Aretas. On the other hand, he complained about Pilate's erection of Roman shields in Jerusalem (Philo, *Leg. ad Gaium* 38).

While visiting his half brother, whom Mark identifies as Philip (erroneously unless there were two Herod Philips—as in the genealogical chart in [Herodians]), Antipas fell in love with and proposed marriage to Herodias, his half brother's wife (Josephus, *Ant.* 18.109). According to Josephus (*Ant.* 18.137), Philip was the husband rather than the father of Salome. Salome was the daughter of Herodias and Herod Antipas's half brother (Josephus, *Ant.* 18.136). Herodias had to divorce her husband, and Antipas divorced his Nabatean wife, deeply offending King Aretas. Aretas later attacked and defeated Antipas (AD 36). When Caligula succeeded Tiberius in AD 37, he appointed Agrippa (Herodias's brother) "king" of the territory that had been governed by Philip. Prompted by Herodias, Antipas sailed to Rome to request that he too be appointed "king." Antipas was surprised to find that Agrippa had sent emissaries at the same time, accusing Antipas of treasonous dealings with the Parthians and stockpiling weapons. As a result, Caligula deposed Antipas and banished him to Gaul or Spain (Josephus, *Ant.* 18.240–55; *J.W.* 2.183). Herodias followed Antipas into exile, and Caligula placed Galilee and Perea under Agrippa's control.

David C. Braund, "Herod Antipas," *ABD* 3:160; Gary A. Herion, "Herod Philip," ABD 3:160-61; Ben Witherington III, "Herodias," *ABD* 3:175–76; Emil Schürer, *The History of the Jewish People in the Age of Jesus Christ (175 B.C.–A.D. 135)* (rev. and ed. Geza Vermes and Fergus Millar; Edinburgh: T. & T. Clark, 1973), 1:340–53; H. W. Hoehner, *Herod Antipas* (SNTSMS 17; Cambridge: Cambridge University Press, 1980).

Herod's downfall occurred when, prompted by Herodias, he requested the title "king." The awkwardness of the transition is most obvious in the ambiguity of the reference to the report Herod heard. In context, it is presumably an account of the works the disciples were doing in Jesus' name. On the other hand, the report may have been of the works that Jesus had been doing. Some were saying that John had been raised from the dead (in Jesus) and that Jesus was able to do mighty works because of the spiritual power at work in him, either because he was John redivivus or simply because he was one who had returned from the dead. There is no reference in the Gospels to John having done mighty works (cf. John 10:41). From Mark's point of view, they were right in concluding that there was a relationship between John and Jesus but wrong in their assumption that Jesus was John redivivus. The speculations are named in reverse order both in standing and chronology: John, Elijah, one of the prophets. Elijah was the greatest of the prophets. Ironically, there are striking parallels between Elijah's struggle with Ahab and Jezebel, and John's own fate. Elijah was also expected to return before "the great and terrible day of the lord" (Mal 4:5; cf. 3:1), and Mark associates John with the fulfillment of this expectation (9:11-13). Although the identification of Jesus as a prophet (6:4) was not adequate for the Christian community, it was a significant claim in a time when it was widely believed that God had withdrawn the spirit of prophecy from Israel (see 1 Macc 4:46; 14:41). Verse 16 reports Herod's view, which now takes on greater significance because of the alternative speculations. It also dramatically introduces new and unexpected information: "John, whom I beheaded, has been raised." This is the first indication Mark gives to the reader of how John had died.

The second "for" statement (v. 17; cf. v. 14) begins to set the scene for the story of John's death. Perhaps anticipating the events of the Passion Narrative, Mark reports that John was "arrested" (14:1, 44, 46, 49) and "bound" (15:1, 7). The explanation that Herod arrested John "because of Herodias" (14:17) presumably means that Herodias had goaded Herod into arresting John. Herodias's vendetta against John is her defining attribute in this story and will be explained in the next two verses. Herodias's ability to get Herod to do what she wanted done also telegraphs the conclusion of the story (see Josephus, *Ant.* 18.136, 240-46). Alternatively, but less probably, one may interpret the arrest of John as Herod's ploy to secure John so that he could protect John from Herodias.[11] The scandalous identification of Herodias as "his brother Philip's wife, because Herod had married her" (6:17) reminds one of David's great sin: "David the father of Solomon by the wife of Uriah" (Matt 1:6; 2 Sam 11:3; 12:10).

The third explanatory "for" statement reports that, just as in Josephus's account of John's death, John's preaching is a factor (see 1:4; Luke 3:7-14). In Mark the specific issue is that John was publicly condemning Herod's marriage to Herodias (compare the debate over what is "lawful" in regard to divorce and marriage in 10:2). As a result, Herodias (literally) "had it in" for John—her constant motivation throughout this story—and wanted to kill him. The plot complication is that she was not able to kill John because Herod feared him and protected him.

As the fourth "for" statement (6:20) explains, Herod regarded John as "a righteous and holy man," which implies John's innocence of any wrongdoing. Herod's response to John's preaching was twofold, and there is a textual variant regarding the first response: either he "was greatly perplexed" (*ēporei*; NRSV; NIV) or "did many things" (*epoiei*; KJV, Guelich).[12] The stronger reading, that Herod was perplexed by John's preaching, reports Herod's inability to comprehend "the word," which the temptress will quickly snatch from him (4:15) through "the desire for other things" (4:19). Nevertheless, being a "double-minded man," as James might say (Jas 1:8; 4:8), he heard him gladly.

By this point the reader knows that John was beheaded (6:16) and that Herodias was determined to have him put to death (6:19), while Herod was protecting him (6:20). The plot, therefore, concerns how Herodias will get Herod to execute John against his wishes. A birthday banquet for Herod afforded Herodias the opportunity (*eukairos*) that she sought. Later Judas Iscariot would be the one seeking an opportunity (14:11). Earlier Mark said that after John was arrested the *kairos* was fulfilled (1:15).

Birthday celebrations for rulers can be traced to ancient Egypt (Gen 40:20) and were common among Persian kings (Plato, *Alc. Maj.* 1.121c) and the Herodian princes (Josephus, *Ant.* 19.321).[13] Against this background, Origen declared that he found "in no scripture that a birthday was kept by a righteous man" (*Comm. Matt.* 10.22).[14] Herod's feast provides a contrast for Jesus' feasts—meals with tax collectors (2:15-16), feeding multitudes (6:30-44; 8:1-10), and the Last Supper (14:12-25). Political magistrates (*megistasin*), Roman military commanders (*chiliarchois*), and prominent men (*prōtois*) came to Herod's banquet. It was an assembly of the powerful—all of whom were vassals or subordinates. Herod was their patron, and he himself was a client of the Roman emperor.

Three genitive constructions (when an opportune day came, when his daughter entered, and when she danced) lead up to the climactic "she pleased Herod and his guests" (6:22). Mark's account in v. 22 seems to suffer from confusion at two points: who danced (Herodias or Salome), and whose daughter was she? Matthew 14:6 says, "the daughter of Herodias danced," and according to Josephus, Salome was the daughter of Herodias (and Herod's half brother). Some scribes attempted to correct Mark's account by changing "his" (*autou*) daughter to an awkward construction that might be translated "the daughter of Herodias herself" (*autēs tēs*).[15] Although Salome's dance has often been interpreted as sensual, the text itself does not indicate whether the dance was innocent or erotic.[16] [Salome Dancing] Josephus uses the same verb for David's "unseemly behaviour in dancing—so great a king as he was—and in uncovering himself, as he danced" (*Ant.* 7.87; cf. 2 Sam 6:14, 16, 20) and records Herod Archelaus's "drinking to riotous

---

Salome Dancing

The following quotation from Ambrose illustrates both the condemnation of the luxury flaunted by the feast and embellishment of the account of Salome's dance: "Note how varied sins are interwoven in this one vicious action! A banquet of death is set out with royal luxury, and when a larger gathering than usual has come together, the daughter of the queen, sent for from within the private apartments, is brought forth to dance in the sight of all. What could she have learned from an adulteress but the loss of modesty? Is anything so conducive to lust as with unseemly movements to expose in nakedness those parts of the body which either nature has hidden or custom his veiled, to sport with looks, to turn the neck, to loosen the hair?" *(Concerning Virgins 3.6.27)*

Thomas C. Oden and Christopher A. Hall, eds., *Ancient Christian Commentary on Scripture: New Testament II, Mark* (Downers Grove IL: InterVarsity Press, 1998), 85.

Fra Filippo Lippi (1406–1469). *The Story of Saint John the Baptist: The Banquet of Herod.* Duomo, Prato, Italy. (Credit: Scala/Art Resource, NY)

The Beheading of John the Baptist
Monaco depicts the beheading of John the Baptist in three scenes: (1) the banquet with the headless body, hands folded in prayer, in the background; (2) a soldier presenting John's head (on a platter turned upright) to Herod; and (3) Salome presenting her grisly prize to Herodias.

Lorenzo Monaco (c. 1370–c. 1422). *Herod's Banquet*; Salome with the head of the Baptist. Left wing of a predella for an altar in Santa Maria degli Angeli, Florence. 1387–1388. Wood, gold foundation. Louvre, Paris, France. (Credit: Erich Lessing / Art Resource, NY)

excess" (*J. W.* 2.29).[17] The verb "pleased" can have an innocent meaning (Acts 6:5; Rom 8:8; 15:1-3, etc.), but it is also used in contexts where it means to arouse sexual interest (Judg 14:3, 7; Esth 2:4, 9). Because the girl had pleased Herod with her dancing, reciprocity demanded that he give her something in return. Jairus's daughter is also called a "little girl" (*korasion*; 5:41, 42). Herod's rash offer echoes the words of King Ahasuerus in Esther: "What is it, Queen Esther? What is your request? It shall be given you, even to the half of my kingdom" (Esth 5:3, 6; 7:2). Because Herod swore an oath in front of his guests, he was honor bound to grant Salome's request. Like a quickening dance, the pace of the story begins to accelerate. The girl goes to her mother with the question, "What should I ask for?" (6:24). The speed and decisiveness of Herodias's answer is communicated by its brevity: "She replied, 'The head of John the baptizer'" (6:24). Notice that she does not say, "on a platter." That is Salome's own contribution to the grisly request (6:25). The speed of the action becomes almost frenetic in v. 26: "Immediately she rushed back . . . give me at once." The trap has been sprung. Herodias has caught Herod in public in his own rash promise. Herod's relationships with "the leaders of Galilee" (v. 21) were based on promises. He could not suffer the public shame of refusing her request. Neither could he hold their loyalty if they thought that his promises were worthless. Jesus too will be "deeply grieved" (14:34) before his death. In spite of his distress, Herod "immediately" dispatched a guard (*spekoulatōr*) to carry out the execution. *Spekoulatōr* is a Latin loanword that is often used in other contexts for soldiers (at times officers) who carry out executions and other covert actions.[18] The prison was presumably in the dungeon of the palace or fortress where the banquet was held. Following the detail of Salome's request, the executioner brought John's head "on a platter" and gave it to Salome, who in turn gave it to her mother. The banquet scene in Herod's court ends with Salome serving her mother this gruesome dish.

John's Head on a Platter

Tiziano Vecellio Titian (c.1488–1576). *Salome with the head of John the Baptist.* Galleria Doria Pamphili, Rome, Italy. (Credit: Alinari / Art Resource, NY)

Mark adds one further detail that will later become significant. When John's disciples heard what had happened, in an act of great courage, they came [secured permission to take his body], and gave it a proper burial. At the end of the Gospel, upon reflection, the reader may ask why Jesus' disciples did not do the same for Jesus. John's disciples are mentioned in Mark 2:18; Matthew 11:2/Luke 7:18; Luke 11:1; and John 1:35, and his followers appear in Ephesus a quarter of a century later (Acts 18:24-19:7).

The Feeding of the 5,000, 6:30-44

Following the long parenthesis relating the death of John the Baptist (6:14-29), Mark reports the return of the Twelve and the feeding of the 5,000. Since Jesus and the disciples travel by boat in the coming scenes, they must have gathered at a site on the Sea of Galilee, presumably either Capernaum (1:21; 2:1; 9:33) or Bethsaida (6:45; 8:22). Except for the reference to Bethsaida in v. 45, however, Mark leaves the geography of this section rather vague. Commentators debate whether

6:30-33 or 6:30-34 should be treated as a separate unit, but it is so closely tied to the feeding story that it is best to regard all of 6:30-44 as one unit. [Outline of the Feeding of the 5,000]

The term "apostles" (lit., "the ones sent") appears only in v. 30 in Mark, since the reference in 3:14 seems to be a later harmonization with Luke 6:13. The term is particularly appropriate here since the disciples are returning from the mission on which Jesus had sent them. A translation rendering a non-technical meaning, such as "the missionaries," would be possible, but by the time Mark wrote Paul had already used the term in a technical sense (see esp. 1 Cor 1:1; 9:1, 2, 5) to claim equal authority with the Twelve, who are called "apostles" in Matthew 10:2 and Luke 6:13 (cf. Acts 1:26; 2:37). The role of an apostle in the early church was related to the Hebrew concept of a *shaliah*. An apostle was not greater than the one who sent him, but the commonly accepted principle was that "a man's agent is like to himself" (*m. Berakoth* 5.5; cf. 2 Chr 17:7-9; John 13:16).[19]

Having been sent out with explicit instructions, the disciples report to Jesus what they had done and what they had taught when they returned. Because they have successfully completed the first stage of their training, Jesus may already have been looking ahead to his need to teach the disciples the lessons of the self-denial and suffering servanthood that lay ahead (see 8:27-38). Jesus' plan to withdraw for a season with the Twelve may therefore have been for the purpose of teaching as well as rest (in Mark *kat' idian*, "by themselves," typically means a private place for rest and teaching: 4:34; 9:2, 28; 13:3). The following phrase "to a deserted place" (*erēmon topon*; cf. 6:32, 35) is characteristically redundant but evokes the wilderness (*erēmos*) overtones of the exodus experience that were also prominent with John the Baptist and the beginning of Jesus' ministry (1:3, 4, 12, 13, 35, 45). In Mark the term only appears in chapter 1 and in the present context.

The pace of activity throughout Mark's account of Jesus' ministry is frenetic. The crowds press about him (1:33; 2:2; 3:32; 4:1; 5:24) so that they cannot even eat (cf. 3:20). The feasting at Herod's court contrasts, therefore, with Jesus and the disciples' inability to eat and with the simple fare of bread and fish that he will set before the crowd. Herodias found an "opportune time" (*eukairos*; 6:21, 31) to betray John at Herod's feast, but Jesus' opportune time had not yet arrived.

Jesus and the disciples travel by boat (cf. 3:9; 4:1, 35-41; 5:1, 18; 6:45-52, 54; 8:10, 14). The traditional site of the feeding of the 5,000

Tabgha

"Tabgha" or "Et-Tabgha" is a corruption of the Greek *Heptapegon*, which means "Seven Springs." Located just south of Capernaum, there is no sign of habitation there in the time of Jesus. In the 4th c. Christians built three churches in the area, to commemorate the multiplication of the loaves, the beatitudes, and the appearance of the risen Lord by the Sea of Galilee (John 21). The church of the Multiplication was built over the foundation of an earlier church, over a slab of stone on which tradition held that Jesus placed the bread. A mosaic representing the basket of loaves and fish dates from perhaps the 5–6th century. All three churches were destroyed by the invasion of the Persians in 614 and the Arabs in 637. The Crusaders rebuilt the church of the Multiplication, and pilgrims can still see the ancient mosaic of the loaves and fish.

Basket with bread between two fish. Mosaic from the ancient church of the Multiplication of the Loaves in Tabgha, northern shore of Lake Genezareth, Israel. 6th CE. Church of the Multiplication, Tabgha, Israel. (Credit: Erich Lessing / Art Resource, NY)

Eugene Hoade, *Guide to the Holy Land* (8th ed.; Jerusalem: Franciscan Printing Press, n.d.), 742–47.

---

is Tabgha, two or three miles south of Capernaum. [Tabgha] The response of the crowds has grown to such a pitch that seeing Jesus and the disciples departing by boat and suspecting their destination, people "from all the cities" run ahead of them. When Jesus gets out of the boat and sees the crowd, he is moved with compassion. Compassion is also Jesus' motivation in the feeding of the 4,000 (8:2), and Mark uses the verb only of Jesus (1:41; 9:22). The Greek noun from which the verb is derived means "inward parts," specifically "the heart, liver, lungs, and kidneys, which are separated in the sacrifice and consumed by the participants."[20] In later Jewish and early Christian writings (esp. the *Testaments of the Twelve Patriarchs*) these organs become the seat of mercy. In the Gospels the verb appears in three parables to describe a human emotion (Matt 18:27; Luke 10:33; and 15:20). Elsewhere in the Gospels, the verb always describes the messianic character of Jesus' actions.[21] This characterization of Jesus is extended by the narrator's use of a quotation of Numbers 27:17 to describe the crowd. Technically, it is a rare "inside view" of why Jesus had compassion on the crowd. In this instance the context of the quotation is significant. Lacking such modern narrative devices as footnotes, parentheses, or even chapter and verse references, Mark quotes a familiar line of Scripture, evoking its context also as a means of commenting on the situation and placing Jesus' response to the crowd in a biblical context:

Moses spoke to the LORD, saying, "Let the LORD, the God of the spirits of all flesh, appoint someone over the congregation who shall go out before them and come in before them, who shall lead them out and bring them in, so that the congregation of the Lord may not be like sheep without a shepherd." (Num 27:15-17; cf. 1 Kgs 22:17; Ezek 34:5-10)

In response, God instructed Moses to appoint Joshua, "a man in whom is the spirit" (Num 27:18). In Ezekiel, God appoints David to be the shepherd: "I will set up over them one shepherd, my servant David, and he shall feed them: he shall feed them and be their shepherd" (Ezek 34:23; cf. Zech 11:7; John 10:11, 14-16, 27-28). By feeding the people, Jesus fulfills the roles of Moses and David, becoming the messianic Shepherd, Deliverer, and King. The nature of his kingship in relation to the hopes of a Davidic Messiah will be clarified later (10:47-48; 11:10; 12:35-37). Jesus' response to the crowd, teaching them and feeding them, are both cast in a significant light by familiar passages of Scripture. In response to Moses' request on Mount Horeb, God instructs him to tell the people, "I will raise up for them a prophet like you [Moses] from among their own people; I will put my words in the mouth of my prophet, who shall speak to them everything I command" (Deut 18:18). Jesus' compassion, his regard for the people as "sheep without a shepherd," his teaching, and feeding them are all fulfillments of Scripture that cast Jesus in the role of a messianic "prophet like Moses."

The same word (*polys*) is translated "many things" in v. 34 and "late" in v. 35. Cranfield proposes an attractive alternative to the translation of v. 34: "*polla* is used adverbially—'at length': the meaning is not that Jesus taught them a great number of different things, but that he taught the one message of the kingdom of God persistently."[22]

The feeding of the 5,000 is one of the foundations of the Gospel accounts of Jesus' ministry. It is the only miracle reported in all four Gospels, a doublet of the miracle occurs in Mark 8 with the feeding of the 4,000, it portrays Jesus as a Mosaic deliverer, it echoes Elisha's feeding miracle (2 Kgs 4:42-44), it fulfills the expectation of a messianic banquet in the wilderness (Isa 25:6-9; *2 Bar.* 29:4-8), and it resonates with the accounts of the Last Supper and its observance by the early church. The reader should therefore be alerted to listen closely for the portrayal of Jesus; his relation to Moses, the disciples, and the crowd; and echoes of the church's accounts of the Last Supper.

The disciples come to Jesus concerned about the welfare of the crowd. It is late, they are in a desolate place (cf. vv. 32, 35; Ps 107:4-9), and there are no provisions for the people. Their proposal is practical: send the people away before it gets any later so that they can make their way to the surrounding villages and provide for themselves. Jesus'

Two Hundred Denarii

A denarius was a Roman coin, minted of silver and bearing the image of the emperor. Bruce Malina and Richard Rohrbaugh estimate that two denarii (Luke 10:35) would provide a bread ration for a poor itinerant for 24 days.

Bruce J. Malina and Richard L. Rohrbaugh, *Social-Science Commentary on the Synoptic Gospels* (Minneapolis: Fortress Press, 1992), 219.

Denarius minted under Tiberius Caesar (AD 14–37). (Credit: Edgar Owen, EdgarLOwen.com)

response is emphatic and stunning: "You give them something to eat" (6:37). Matthew and Luke both abbreviate the account at this point, letting the disciples report that they have only five loaves of bread and two fish, but Mark and John amplify the disciples' response. While John reports Jesus' conversation with Philip and Andrew (John 6:5-7), Mark conveys the incomprehension of the disciples as a group, foreshadowing their hardness of heart and inability to understand the miracle of the loaves and the fish (see 6:52; 8:17-21). The participle and the two verbs in the disciples' question telegraph the difficulties they foresee: where are they to go in search of provisions for such a crowd? It would require two hundred denarii—two hundred days' wages (Matt 20:2)—to feed such a crowd, and how are they to go about giving it to them to eat? [Two Hundred Denarii] The neighbor requests three loaves for his surprise guest so that he can give him a meal (Luke 11:5). By this formula, the disciples would need to gather and distribute 15,000 loaves! When the New Testament speaks of bread, it means "a relatively small and generally round loaf of bread (considerably smaller than present-day typical loaves of bread and thus more like 'rolls' or 'buns')."[23] [Bread] John 6:9 identifies the bread as barley loaves, as in Elisha's feeding miracle (2 Kgs 4:42-44). Barley was coarser, half the value of wheat (*m. Ketuboth* 5.8), and hence used exclusively by the poor and for animal fodder.

Just as God had fed the Israelites with manna in the wilderness in the time of Moses, so Jesus fed the multitude in a desolate place. And while Elisha fed 100 with 20 loaves of barley, Jesus fed 5,000 with only 5 loaves and 2 fish ([Diet of Fish]; see also [Fish]). On the other hand, there is a subtle contrast between the commands given in the two adjacent meal scenes. With the same verb Mark reports Herod's command for his officer to bring the head of John the Baptist and Jesus' command

Bread

"There is a rich vocabulary related to the production of bread. Mention is made of mills, millstones, and grinding grain (Matt 24:41; Luke 17:2; Mark 9:42). The sound of the grinding of grain was a sound of normal everyday existence in a city (Rev 18:22). References are made to the sifting of flour (Luke 22:31), a batch of dough (1 Cor 5:6-7), yeast and the process of fermentation, regular flour (Matt 13:33), and fine wheat flour (Rev 18:13)."

Stephen A. Reed, "Bread," *ABD* 1:779.

The miracle of the Loaves and Fishes. Relief from the the Cathedral of St. John, s'Hertogenbosch, The Netherlands. Victoria and Albert Museum, London, Great Britain (Credit: Victoria & Albert Museum, London / Art Resource, NY)

for the disciples to seat the crowd (6:27, 39). Jesus instructed the disciples to have the people "recline," which normally meant to recline on a banqueting couch. Joachim Jeremias argued that the description of the disciples reclining at the Last Supper is evidence that it was a Passover meal.[24] If so, the reference to reclining here underscores the Passover overtones of the feeding of the 5,000 (cf. John 6:2), or it may cast the meal as a precursor of the messianic banquet (Isa 25:6-8; Matt 8:11; 13:29).

By translating the Greek with the bland phrase "in groups," in both vv. 39 and 40 the NRSV obscures that fact that the terms are different in the two verses and have different nuances. Jesus' instructions in v. 39 are to seat the people *symposia, symposia*. In classical Greek (e.g., the Platonic dialogues) the term designates a drinking party or banquet that served as a context for witty and serious conversation. Verse 40 reports that the people sat "*prasiai prasiai*." This term means literally "garden plot" or "garden bed," and Danker comments, "it is but a short step to . . .

Diet of Fish

"The frequent references to fish in the New Testament indicate that fish was an important part of the diet of the first-century Galileans and Judeans. They ate fish, fresh and processed, more than any other meat: 'Bread and fish with the addition of olive-oil and wine, formed in ancient times the most substantial parts of the diet of the people, rich and poor. Fish, fresh and salted, pickled and dried, was consumed in large quantities, the poor classes being almost entirely dependent for their *opson* [sustenance] on the cheaper qualities and especially on slated and dried fish' [Michael I. Rostovtzeff, *The Social and Economic History of the Hellenistic World* (Oxford: Clarendon Press, 1941), 2:1177]. A hungry boy might ask his father for fish (Matt. 7:10; Luke 11:11), or carry a lunch

of bread and fish [John 6:9]. Accounts of the appearances of the risen Lord relate that he ate broiled fish in Jerusalem (Luke 24:42) and fresh fish with the disciples in Galilee (John 21:9, 14). Galilee was the food basket of Palestine. Galilean farmers produced grain in the fertile soil of the plain of Gennesaret, and Galilean fishermen harvested fish from the lake. The population was so dependent upon the supply of fish that when the fishermen interrupted the supply by observing religious feast days, there were complaints [Salo Wittmayer Baron, *A Social and Religious History of the Jews* (New York: Columbia University Press, 1952), 1:254–55]."

R. Alan Culpepper, *John the Son of Zebedee: The Life of a Legend* (Columbia: University of South Carolina Press, 1994), 10.

picturing the groups of people contrasted w. the green grass."[25] Cranfield cites a rabbinic interpretation of Song of Solomon 8:13 that says, "When students sit arranged like garden-beds and are engaged in studying the Torah, then I come down to them and hearken to their voice and hear them."[26] While Matthew 14:19 and John 6:10 refer to the grass, Mark is the only Gospel to specify "green grass" (6:40). For there to be green grass means that the feeding took place in the spring, corroborating John's report that it was at the time of Passover (John 6:4). Beyond this chronological information, the reference may be an allusion to the familiar Twenty-third Psalm, "He makes me lie down in green pastures" (Ps 23:2), or to the vision of the bounty of the End, when Eden would be restored and the desert would bloom like a garden: "For the LORD will comfort Zion . . . and will make her wilderness like Eden, her desert like the garden of the LORD" (Isa 51:3; cf. Isa 27:6; 35:1-2; 41:18; 1QH 8:4).

Mark adds that the people sat in companies of hundreds and fifties, which evokes memories of the wilderness organization of the people of Israel (Exod 18:21, 25; Deut 1:15). In Jesus' time, however, such organization might have been interpreted politically. The apocalyptic community at Qumran also organized itself in companies in preparation for eschatological warfare (CD 13:1; 1QS 2:21-22; 1Qsa 1:14-15; 1QM 4:1-5). Zealot groups had organized themselves in the wilderness (Josephus, *Ant.* 18.4-10, 23; 20.97, 167, 188; *J. W.* 7.437), so it is scarcely surprising that John reports that the people perceived Jesus was a prophet (an eschatological prophet) and wanted to make him their king (John 6:14-15). Mark says nothing about any effort to make Jesus king—the charge that Jesus was the king of the Jews does not emerge until the trial of Jesus (15:2, 9, 12, 18, 26, 32).

Verses 41 and 42 are striking for their consistency in the Gospel traditions. In contrast to the variations in wording in the rest of the accounts, the Synoptic Gospels report the blessing, breaking, giving, and eating of the bread and fish with almost word-for-word agreement. The verb "took" (the bread) appears in all the accounts of the feeding of the 5,000 (including John 6:11), the feeding of the 4,000 (8:6; Matt 15:36), the Last Supper (14:22 par.), the meal at Emmaus (Luke 24:30), and the words of institution in the Pauline churches (1 Cor 11:23), either as a participle or a finite verb (see also the ordinary meal in Acts 27:35). In all the synoptic accounts, Jesus blesses the five loaves and two fish all at once. By contrast, "and looking up" appears only in the three synoptic accounts of the feeding of the 5,000. Looking up, eyes raised toward heaven, was the common posture for prayer (Job 22:26-27; Luke 18:13; John 17:1; see also 7:34; John 11:41). The rabbis, who said, "It is forbidden to man to enjoy anything belonging

Baruch 29.3-8

As the author of 2 Baruch, a pseudepigraphical writing from the latter part of the first century AD, demonstrates, when Jesus fed the multitude he recalled the provision of manna for the Israelites in the wilderness long ago and fulfilled the expectation of the provision of manna again in the last days.

"And it will happen that when all that which should come to pass in these parts has been accomplished, the Anointed One will begin to be revealed. And Behemoth will reveal itself from its place, and Leviathan will come from the sea, the two great monsters which I created on the fifth day of creation and which I shall have kept until that time. And they will be nourishment for all who are left. . . . And those who are hungry will enjoy themselves and they will, moreover, see marvels every day. For winds will go out in front of me every morning to bring this fragrance of aromatic fruits and clouds at the end of the day to distill the dew of health. And it will happen at that time that the treasury of manna will come down again from on high, and they will eat of it in those years because these are they who will have arrived at the consummation of time." (*2 Bar.* 29:3-4, 6-8)

Manna in the Last Days

Documenting the expectation of the return of the provision of manna in "the age to come," Cranfield cites the following rabbinic references:

"As the first Redeemer caused manna to descend, so shall also the last Redeemer cause manna to descend" (*Qoheleth Rabba* on Eccles. 1.9).

"For whom has it [i.e., the manna] now been prepared? For the righteous in the age that is coming: everyone who believeth is worthy and eateth of it" (*Tanhuma b^esallah 21*).

"Ye shall not find it [i.e., the manna] in this age, but ye shall find it in the age that is coming" (*Mekilta* on Exod 16:25).

James H. Charlesworth, ed., *The Old Testament Pseudepigrapha* (Garden City NY: Doubleday, 1983), 1:630–31; C. E. B. Cranfield, *The Gospel according to Saint Mark* (CGTC; Cambridge: Cambridge University Press, 1959), 222.

to this world without a blessing" (*b. Ber* 35a), based the practice of giving thanks to God before eating on Leviticus 19:24 and Deuteronomy 8:10.[27] The Jewish blessing over the bread is always "Blessed be Thou, Yahweh our God, king of the world, who hast caused bread to come forth out of the earth" (*m. Berakoth* 6.1).[28] The act of taking, blessing, breaking, and giving, which was based on everyday Jewish piety, becomes a kind of signature act for Jesus that evokes memories not only of the Last Supper but also of his meals in Galilee and feedings of the multitudes. In Luke the risen Lord is recognized by this act (Luke 24:30-31).

At this point Jesus draws the disciples into the miracle, giving them the bread to set before the people. The verb is in the imperfect tense, perhaps suggesting that Jesus kept on giving bread to the disciples to set before the people. By involving the disciples, Jesus may be using the miracle as an object lesson to teach the disciples. If so, it is a lesson they failed to learn (see 8:17-21). Later, according to the book of Acts, the disciples do provide bread for the people (Acts 4:32-37; 6:1-6; 11:27-30). The dividing of the two fish is added, almost as a secondary act here and in v. 43. All three Synoptics report, "And all ate and were filled" (6:42; cf. Deut 8:10). [*Baruch 29:3-8*] [Manna in the Last Days]

When the Lord provided manna in the wilderness, the Israelites were instructed to gather what they needed but not to keep any over for the next day, unless the next day was the Sabbath (Exod 16:13-26). When some tried to keep some of the manna for the next day, it turned foul. When Elisha fed 100 with 20 loaves of barley, the Lord instructed Elisha, "They shall eat and have some left" (2 Kgs 4:43), and when Elisha set it before them, "they ate, and had some left, according to the word of the LORD" (2 Kgs 4:44). The collecting of fragments, which underscores the magnitude of the miracle, picks up on the miracle of Elisha rather than the exodus. "Fragments" (*klasmata*) is also the word used for "the broken bread" of the Eucharist in the *Didache* 9.3-4—"As this broken bread [*klasma*] was scattered upon the mountains, but was brought together and became one, so let thy Church be gathered together from the ends of the earth into thy kingdom" (*Did.* 9.4).[29]

It is difficult to know how much credence to place on a symbolic interpretation of the number twelve. Obviously, it was associated with the number of the tribes of Israel, or the number of the disciples, but in this instance it can mean simply that each disciple collected a basket full. (See below the discussion of the number seven in Mark 8:8, 17-21). Although there is no way to determine the size of the baskets from the Greek term or parallel references (Judg 6:19 LXX B; Ps 80:7 LXX [79:7]), it is generally thought that they were large baskets used for produce. A basket was also standard equipment for the infantry in the Roman army (Josephus, *J. W.* 3.95). So characteristic of Jewish life was the basket that twice Juvenal uses it as a symbol for the Jew in his *Satires* (3.14; 6.542). The count of 5,000 men may be related to the Israelite practice of counting men only (Exod 12:37; Num 1:2, 20, 22), emphasizing either the exodus or the military overtones of the story. Matthew 14:21 adds "besides women and children."

By evoking echoes of the feeding of the Israelites in the wilderness, the multiplication miracles of the prophets, the image of the Lord as a shepherd who makes his sheep to lie down in green pastures, the words of institution, and the hope of an eschatological messianic banquet and age of plenty, the Gospel uses the story of the feeding of the 5,000 as a christological statement. It not only reports what Jesus did; it tells us who he is.

Walking on Water and Healing the Sick, 6:45-56

The sequence of feeding the multitude in a desolate place and then crossing the sea is reminiscent of the exodus, though the sequence is reversed. The fact that these two traditions also appear in the same order in John 6 probably indicates that they formed an early complex that predates both Gospels. Luke omits the account of Jesus walking on the water, but each of the other Gospels uses it in a distinctive manner: in Mark it is a mysterious epiphany, in Matthew it is a lesson on discipleship, and in John it is a disclosure of the incarnate Logos.[30]

The note of urgency returns to the narrative. Jesus "immediately" (6:45; cf. 6:50, 54) sends the disciples onto the boat (6:32) to cross the sea. The urgency of sending the disciples away even before he dismissed the crowd, while unexplained in Mark, makes sense when read in the light of John's report that the people perceived Jesus was a prophet and wanted to make him king (John 6:14-15). On this reading, Jesus may have sent the disciples away to prevent them from getting caught up in the crowd's enthusiasm. The geographical references are problematic. Starting from the west side of the Sea of Galilee, Jesus and the disciples went to a remote place (6:32), presumably on the same side of the lake, but perhaps across the lake. Now, Jesus sends the disciples to Bethsaida, the home of Peter and Andrew according to John 1:44, which lay at the north end of the lake. After crossing the lake, however, they land at Gennesaret, which is on the southwestern shore. One may postulate that the adverse winds forced them to change their plans, although the winds ceased when Jesus got into the boat. On the other hand, it may be either that the author did not have a clear grasp of Galilean geography (see below the comment on 7:31) or that he was trying to fit together geographical references already attached to independent traditions.

The scene is set when Jesus, having dismissed the crowd, goes up the mountain to pray. The mountains were places of revelation and proximity to God in Israel's history (Exod 19:3, 12, 18, 23; 1 Kgs 19:8; Ps 121:1; Heb 12:18-24). In contrast, the disciples were alone on the sea, which in the Hebrew Scriptures was often a place of terror (2 Sam 22:5; Pss 69:2; 107:23-25, 28-29; Jonah 2). Jesus' need for rest and prayer is a recurring motif in Mark (1:35; 9:2; 14:32-42), as is the adversity the disciples face when Jesus is not with them (2:20; 9:14-29; 14:32-42). No doubt Mark's persecuted community could easily identify with the disciples in danger at sea while Jesus was up on the mountain (see the connections below). The day stretched into evening (6:47) because it was "already late" (6:35) before Jesus fed the multitude.

Joel Marcus observes that "throughout the Gospel, Mark puts special emphasis on Jesus' 'seeing,' his piercing glance that is especially directed at disciples (1:16, 19; 2:14; 3:34; 8:33; 10:14, 23), potential disciples (10:21; 12:34), and other objects of his compassion (2:5; 5:32; 6:34 . . .)."[31] Even though it was dark and the disciples were several miles away, Jesus saw that "they were straining at the oars against an adverse wind" (6:48). The word translated as "straining" (NRSV; Gk. *basanizō*) is actually more colorful. In other contexts it means "torture," "harass," "torment," or "put to a test" (cf. 5:7). Subtly, it may suggest a further meaning of this scene for a persecuted Christian community experiencing harassment in a chaotic context and feeling acutely the absence of their Lord.

Here and in 13:35 Mark follows the Roman custom of dividing the night, from 6 p.m. to 6 a.m., into four "watches": evening, midnight, cockcrow, and dawn. The Jews and Greeks marked three night watches

(Luke 12:38; Josephus, *J. W.* 5.510). The Lord comes at dawn, walking on the water. Mark can hardly mean that Jesus was walking "by" the sea because when Jesus gets into the boat and the winds cease, they cross to the other side (6:53; cf. Matt 14:24). By walking on the water, Jesus was doing what God alone can do in the Hebrew Scriptures. ["God Walking on Water"] Demonstrating his sovereignty over the sea, Jesus revealed that he exercised the same divine power that had led the Israelites through the sea.

The overtones of divinity continue. Mark comments that Jesus "intended to pass them by" (6:48). This comment is absent from both Matthew and John. John adds only that Jesus was near the boat (6:19). What good would it do for Jesus simply to walk past the disciples while they fought the wind and the waves? Mark almost certainly intends the reader to hear an echo of well-known scriptural texts:

> **"God Walking on Water"**
>
> [God] who alone stretched out the heavens,
> and trampled the waves of the Sea. . . ." (Job 9:8; cf. Sir 24:5-6)
>
> "When the waters saw you, O God,
> when the waters saw you, they were afraid;
> the very deep trembled. . . .
> Your way was through the sea,
> your path, through the mighty waters;
> yet your footprints were unseen." (Ps 77:16, 19)

Moses said, "Show me your glory, I pray." And he said, "I will make all my goodness pass before you, and will proclaim before you the name, 'The Lord'. . . ." "But," he said, "you cannot see my face; for no one shall see me and live." And the LORD continued, "See, there is a place by me where you shall stand on the rock; and while my glory passes by I will put you in the cleft of the rock, and I will cover you with my hand until I have passed by; then I will take away my hand, and you shall see my back; but my face shall not be seen." (Exod 33:18-23; cf. 34:6)

"He said, 'Go and stand on the mountain before the LORD, for the LORD is about to pass by.'" (1 Kgs 19:11)

"Look, he passes by me, and I do not see him." (Job 9:11)

"The end has come upon my people Israel; I will never again pass them by." (Amos 8:2)

Yet, once again the Lord did pass by his people, and this time the disciples saw the face of God in Jesus.

Understandably, the disciples are terrified. They think they are seeing a ghost, a phantom (Gk. *phantasma*). Like the man with an unclean spirit in the synagogue, they cry out (1:23) at the appearance of Jesus. Fear is the typical human response to an epiphany (see Judg 13:21-22; Dan 10:12, 19; Luke 1:13, 30). The narrator's report that they all saw him affirms the credibility of the miracle, although they were at a loss to explain what they were seeing. Immediately Jesus speaks, but this time his words are not the catalyst for the miracle; they interpret the miracle. He speaks to reassure the frightened disciples. His first admonition is "take heart" or "be courageous." Second comes a self-disclosure: "It is I" or "I am" (*ego eimi*). The words echo the divine name revealed to Moses at the burning bush (Exod 3:14), suggesting again that the entire story declares that God was revealed in the person of Jesus and that God is indeed with the community of faith in times of distress.

As if to confirm Jesus' assurance to the disciples, Jesus got into the boat with them. This act, simple as it may be, is profoundly significant. Immediately the wind ceases and the waves grow calm, as in the stilling of the storm in Mark 4:35-41. Again, the disciples are amazed (cf. 2:12; 3:21; 5:42), but this time Mark adds the unsettling explanation that they did not understand about "the loaves" and that their hearts had been hardened. The explanation implies that if the disciples had understood the feeding miracle, they would not have been terrified by the appearance of Jesus walking on the water. Joel Marcus endorses the argument advanced by Quentin Quesnell that the issue is the disciples' lack of understanding of Jesus' presence with them.[32] The feeding of the 5,000 anticipates the Eucharist. Therefore, "the loaves" stand for the Eucharist, the means by which the risen Lord is present with the community. While "bread" might evoke associations with the Eucharist for Christian readers, one may well note that Mark regularly uses bread in contexts where there is no obvious association with the Eucharist (3:20; 6:8; 7:2, 5), and Mark does not use the more technical phrase "breaking of bread" here. The interpretation of one story by reference to another story is unusual, but it is consistent with Mark's technique of sandwiching one story within another, as in the healing of Jairus's daughter and the woman with the hemorrhage, or the cursing of the fig tree and the cleansing of the temple. If the disciples had understood the cleansing of the temple, they would not have been surprised by the cursing of the fig tree. Similarly in the case of these two exodus-related stories, if the disciples had understood the feeding's assurance that the Lord cares for the needs of the community, just as God provided for the Israelites in the wilderness, they would have been prepared to understand the disclosure of Jesus' divinity through his deliverance of them from the chaos of the sea. Beyond the question of the disciples' comprehension, one recognizes the real issue is whether Mark's readers understand that the miracle of the walking on water is really an assurance that the Lord cares about the community in crisis and will be present with them in the storm. He is still "I am," the Lord of wind and sea, the almighty Deliverer and Savior.

The hardening of the disciples' hearts again evokes exodus motifs, but now in a surprising and disturbing way. The hardening of the heart is an idiom that means not only one's stubbornness or recalcitrance but one's inability to see in dramatic events signs of God's redemptive activity, or worse, one's opposition to God's redeeming work (Exod 7:3, 13; John 12:40; Rom 11:25; see commentary on Mark 3:5). Instead of the pharaoh's or the Pharisees' hearts being hardened, it is the disciples' hearts that are hardened. It is an ominous omen that portends the eventual failure of the disciples (see 8:17-20, 33; 14:50).

Chapter 6 ends with another Markan summary statement (cf. 1:14-15; 3:7-12; 6:6b). As in other summary statements, Mark generalizes motifs from individual stories. The summary sections both introduce and conclude sections of the Gospel. In this case, however, its structural significance is secondary. It serves as a transition from the series of miracle stories that begins with the stilling of the storm in Mark 4:35-41 and ends with the walking on the water in 6:45-52. Surprisingly, it makes no reference to Jesus' teaching or exorcisms. In addition, Jesus no longer frequents the synagogues; the last reference to Jesus being in a synagogue in Mark is in 6:2.

The summary statements also serve to provide a sense of completeness to the Gospel story. By reporting individual events and then adding summary statements that report that Jesus did other similar things, the reader is led to surmise that he or she has been told all that is distinctive and typical of Jesus' ministry. Events that are unreported would have added nothing to the account.

The geographical reference in 6:53 is puzzling because although Jesus sent the disciples to cross to Bethsaida (6:45), they land at Gennesaret. [Gennesaret] One may explain the change of destination either by appealing to the effects of the adverse winds, or as an indication that the evangelist is here combining different sources. The report that follows is a compilation of elements from earlier passages. The landing and recognition of Jesus echoes 5:21. The gathering of a crowd from the whole region echoes 6:32-34. The bringing of the sick on mats reminds the reader of the healings in Capernaum (1:32) and the healing of the paralytic (2:1-12), where the mat is mentioned four times. After all, "those who are well have no need of a physician, but those who are sick" (2:17). The hearing of reports about where Jesus was underscores the excitement his ministry created (1:28, 45; 3:7-10,

Gennesaret

Gennesaret was a fertile plain about three and half miles long and a mile and a half wide that extended from Tiberias to Capernaum on the west shore of the Sea of Galilee. It was heavily populated during the Roman period, with Magdala (Taricheae), the home of Mary Magdalene, serving as its administrative center until that role passed to Tiberias. The name Taricheae, which means "Tower of (salted) Fish," indicates its importance as a center for processing and exporting fish. The Jewish fleet was destroyed by the Romans at Taricheae in AD 67 in the only sea battle between the Romans and the Jewish rebels.

Douglas R. Edwards, "Gennesaret," *ABD* 2:963; James F. Strange, "Magdala," *ABD* 4:463–64.

20; 4:1). Verse 56 describes the healing scenes, as the sick, laid in the marketplaces, plead with Jesus to let them touch even the fringes of his garment. Healing by touching recalls 3:10 and the healing of the woman with a hemorrhage (5:25-34). The fringes were the tassels on the four corners of the garments men wore that were to remind them of God's commandments (Num 15:37-41; Deut 22:12). Since this detail is part of the summary statement that follows the exodus miracles of the feeding in the wilderness and the crossing of the sea, it is interesting that the tassels were to remind the Israelites of their God: "I am the LORD your God, who brought you out of the land of Egypt, to be your God: I am the LORD your God" (Num 15:41).

CONNECTIONS

Mark 6:1-6a

Thomas Wolfe is famous for writing, "You can't go home again."[33] The story of Jesus' visit to his hometown illustrates a number of human foibles: the need to leave home in order to make one's mark, the suspicion and jealousy of one's peers when one achieves distinction, and the natural tendency to stereotype and jump to conclusions. Jesus' hometown folk thought they knew him. They knew his family. They therefore bound Jesus by their assumptions and expectations and would not let him achieve more than they expected from him. Grace may at times mean giving a person, a family, a church, or a community the chance to prove expectations wrong, to reserve or suspend judgment.

On the other hand, Jesus refused to be bound or diminished by the limitations his hometown placed upon him. He could do not miracles there, and he had to go elsewhere to fulfill God's purposes for him, but he refused to live down to the expectations of his family and his hometown. Faith may therefore at times mean rejecting the judgment of others in faithfulness to God's direction for one's life.

Mark 6:6b-13

Jesus' instructions to the disciples when he sent them out on mission are so far removed from us that we may be tempted to lay them aside and go on to more relevant passages. When we travel, we carry a cell phone rather than a staff, a credit card rather than a beggar's purse. We always carry a change of clothes, and cars and airplanes have replaced sandals. Nevertheless, these ancient instructions express principles that should still guide us as we seek to fulfill our role as people on mission.

The first principle is that those who are called into fellowship with God through Jesus Christ are always sent out to share God's grace and love with others. From God's calling of Abraham to be the father of a people through whom God could bless all peoples (Gen 12:1-3), through the formation of a covenant community at Mount Sinai and the prophetic challenges of the eighth-century prophets, to Jesus' self-giving for a kingdom not of one nation but of people drawn from all nations, God's redemptive purpose has been constant. Those who are called into God's fellowship are also called to participate in this world-redeeming mission. The disciples, therefore, were called to "be with him" and to "be sent out" (3:14-15; 6:7).

The second principle is that those who are sent out after having entered into fellowship with God are sent with authority. God authorizes them and empowers them for this mission. The disciples had been with Jesus, seen his mighty works, and heard his teachings. Later the disciples and those who would come after them would be authorized and empowered by the Holy Spirit for the tasks given to them. As authorized emissaries, those sent on mission represent the One who sent them. Those who accept or reject them accept or reject the One who sent them.

Third, those who are sent on mission to the world, to cross the boundary of belief and unbelief and share the knowledge of God, must authentically live out the life-changing revelation of God. For the first disciples, journeying by faith meant renouncing possessions and provisions and relying on hospitality wherever they went. Authentic embodiment of the gospel still requires journeying by faith, although the specific demands and expressions of faith will vary in different settings and circumstances. Nevertheless, radical trust and dependence on God for the success of what is ultimately not our mission but God's mission will always be an identifying characteristic of the church's mission when it is authentic.

Fourth, disciples representing a gracious Lord will be gracious to those with whom they seek to share God's love and the good news of the kingdom. For the disciples this meant not embarrassing a host by moving to better quarters or accepting the hospitality of a wealthier host. This practice of gracious consideration for one's host illustrates a basic principle regarding how those on mission relate to those to whom they are sent. The host is valued as a person with inherent value regardless of his or her background, status, or means. The host is not a statistic to be counted. The host is not to be manipulated. Instead, the disciple as guest must exercise great consideration in protecting the personhood, honor, and status of the host. How one carries out the mission reflects profoundly on why one goes out on mission and what that mission is.

Fifth, the disciples on mission will meet rejection as well as success, but they cannot allow rejection to deter them from their mission. Their mission is to share the knowledge of God that has come to them through Jesus. Many of their efforts may fail to bear fruit, just as much of the farmer's seed fails to germinate and grow. Even so, the disciple will persist, shake off the dust from his or her sandals, and go on to others who may be more receptive. Success is measured by the disciple's faithfulness rather than by the response he or she receives. Another characteristic of the authentic mission is the steadfast hope and confidence that because God has called us to this mission, God will eventually bring the kingdom to full fruition. For one with this hope, rejection, failure, is never the final result. The kingdom is coming just as surely as the seed grows night and day (4:26-29).

Mark 6:14-29

Dark and macabre, the story of the beheading of John the Baptist easily lends itself to moralizing against one's favorite sins, as the history of its interpretation illustrates. Early church fathers pointed to it as an illustration of the evils of birthday celebrations, luxury, drinking, dancing, and taking oaths: "We hear at the same time of three evil deeds done: the inauspicious celebration of a birthday, the lewd dancing of a girl, and the rash oath of a king" (Bede, *Homilies on the Gospels* 2.23).[34] Similarly, contemporary interpreters see in the story an illustration of "willingness to sacrifice others to maintain honor, prestige, and power" and "use of sexual attractiveness to gain access to power" in the workplace.[35] The Gospel of Mark does not use the story for such moralizing, however—though doubtless Mark condemned the immorality it depicts.

Head of John the Baptist

Michelangelo Merisi da Caravaggio (1573–1610). *Salome with the Head of John the Baptist*. National Gallery, London, Great Britain. (Credit: Nimatallah / Art Resource, NY)

Instead, the story is a tale of three kingdoms: Herod's (i.e., Rome's, or more broadly the kingdoms of the world), Satan's, and God's.[36] The choices it offers and the decisions it compels are ultimate ones. The basic opposition is between the kingdom of God and the power of Satan, and Jesus' militant attack on the powers of evil is a running sub-theme throughout Mark's account of Jesus' ministry. The kingdoms of this world do not represent a third power; they have fallen under the power of Satan. Parenthetically, we may note how quickly the civil authority resorts to violence to protect its honor. Like Jesus, his followers can expect that "they will hand you over to councils . . . and you will stand before governors and kings because of me, as a testimony to them" (13:9). In tasting martyrdom at the hands of imperial authorities, John was the forerunner of Jesus, of Jesus' disciples, and of the believers for whom Mark wrote. Mark's Gospel offers no cheap grace. Its call to faith comes with the warning, "If you choose to follow Jesus, you too will be persecuted." You too will be setting your life in opposition to the powers of self-interest, acquisitiveness, indulgence, and exploitation that drive the unredeemed world.

By placing the story of John's death where he does, the evangelist reminds the reader that success in carrying out the mission on which Jesus sends his disciples will always be tempered by opposition and defeats, that this was the experience of John and Jesus, but that the powers that oppose them will not have the last word. Although the story of the gospel leads to Golgotha, it does not end in death and defeat but in resurrection and life.

Mark 6:30-44

One afternoon Jesus and the disciples found themselves surrounded by a crowd of more than 5,000. The people had been listening to Jesus teach, and Jesus was concerned that they had nothing to eat, so he instructed the disciples to get food for the crowd. Aghast, they said, "Are we to go and buy two hundred denarii worth of bread?" He said, "How many loaves have you?" They said, "Five, and two fish."

What could Jesus do with five loaves and two fish? He could not send the people away hungry, and what he held in his hands was so little compared to the need he faced.[37]

What do you do when your resources are woefully inadequate to meet the needs you face? Perhaps you are a student and you want to be a lawyer, doctor, minister, teacher, or concert musician—but this week you have tests and papers due. You are a parent and you want your children to be happy, well adjusted, confident, and make a difference with their lives—but this week it is another round of ball practice, music

Miracle of the Loaves and Fish

Palma Giovane (1548–1628). *Miracle of the Loaves and Fishes*. S. Giacomo dell'Orio, Venice, Italy.
(Credit: Cameraphoto / Art Resource, NY)

lessons, and dentist appointments. You are a senior adult wanting to continue to be active, but it is getting harder and harder to get out and do things. What do you do when what you hold in your hands is so small, and the challenge before you is so great?

Jesus took the loaves that he had, lifted them up, offered them to God, and then gave them to the disciples to set before the others. What he put in was so much less than what came out. A little yeast leavened the whole lump (Luke 13:20-21). They all ate, and there were baskets full left over.

That act of taking, blessing, breaking, and giving was not unusual. In fact, it was characteristic of Jesus. On the night he was betrayed, Jesus took bread, blessed it, broke it, and gave it to the disciples. In Emmaus, the unrecognized stranger took bread, blessed it, and gave it to the two who had traveled with him from Jerusalem, and they recognized that the risen Lord had been with them.

But God has always been in the business of doing much with little. He promised to take Abraham and Sarah and make their descendants a great nation through whom he would bless all people. What could David do with a handful of stones, when the Israelites faced the powerful Philistines? What could Elijah do for the widow who had only a jar of oil, when the creditors were coming to take her two children as slaves? What could Barnabas do when the church in Jerusalem was suffering from a famine, and all he had was a field? What can we do when what we hold in our hands is so small and the need before us is so great?

In December 1931, Ted and Dorothy Hustead bought the only drug store in a little prairie town, fifty miles east of Rapid City, South Dakota. These were the days of the Great Depression. There were only 326 people in town, 326 poor people, and business was bad. Most were farmers who had been wiped out either by the Depression or by the drought. The winter winds were viciously cold, and in the summer it was blazing hot. Tin lizzies chugged along the two-lane highway on their way home for the holidays or over to Mount Rushmore, but nobody stopped in Wall, South Dakota.

Ted and Dorothy were devout Christians. They prayed and agreed that they would stick it out for five years to see if they could make a go of it. By the summer of the fifth year they were about to give up. There was no shade, no air conditioning, and no customers. Ted spent most of his time looking out the store windows, waiting for someone to come in. One afternoon Dorothy put the children down for a nap, but she could not sleep because of the noise of the jalopies making their way down the highway. Then, she had an idea. What the travelers really needed while they were driving across that hot prairie was water, ice cold water, and although she and Ted did not have much, they did have water and ice.

The next day they put up signs offering free ice water at Wall Drug. By the time they got back to the store, people had already started coming. For hours they poured water, sold ice cream, and gave directions. And the people kept coming. The next summer they had to hire eight girls to help them, and today the drug store has become a variety store that covers several square blocks. The café seats 520, and on a good summer day about 20,000 people turn off the highway for some free ice water and to browse through the store. Who would ever have imagined in 1931 what that drug store would become?[38]

What can we do when the needs around us are so great? There is a community wrestling with poverty and violence. There are young people looking for direction for their lives. There are elderly people needing companionship. There are families just trying to make it work and persons facing medical problems that threaten to overwhelm them. What do you do when what you hold in your hands is so small and the challenge is so great?

Jesus came to change the world, but after three years he had only twelve disciples. Time was running out, and still they did not understand. One of them had betrayed him, and the others would abandon him. What could he do? The Gospels say that Jesus took bread and blessed it, and broke it, and gave it to them.

Never underestimate the power of the good you can do. Sometimes the opposite of faith is not doubt but despair. Do not give up, and do not assume there is nothing you can do to make a difference. What you hold in your hands may seem to be so little, but offer it to God and see what happens.

Mark 6:45-56

Crises, whether personal or national, inevitably raise questions of faith and theology. Following the attacks of September 11, 2001, church attendance rose, and Americans all across the country called upon their personal faith and renewed their commitments to their families. Similarly, when we are shaken by unemployment, hospitalizations, or broken family relationships we naturally ask about God's role in our personal experience. Doesn't it make any difference that we are Christians? Does God care about our personal misfortunes and tragedies? Mark 6:45-52 speaks to believers who feel they are weathering storms alone.

The Lord sent the disciples out onto the sea and left them. When the wind and the waves rose against them, they may well have asked, where was Jesus, the miracle worker, when they needed him? Didn't he care what was happening to them? These questions probably also troubled Mark's community. Jesus had left the early Christians following the resurrection. He had sent them to carry the gospel across the Mediterranean to the Gentiles and to all the world. Now, with the persecution under Nero and the Jewish war, the dangers of worshiping a Jewish revolutionary put to death by the Romans while the Romans were at war with Jewish revolutionaries, life was difficult and dangerous. The Lord seemed absent just when they needed him most. Didn't he care what was happening? Why didn't he return and vindicate them as he had promised?

In the midst of this storm, Mark reached back into the life of Jesus for an event to use as a vehicle for the word the community needed to hear: the Lord did care, and he would come to them as they fought the storm. Jesus' walking on the water revealed that he was the master of the sea into which he had sent his disciples. Mark was assuring his community that the Lord cared about their distress and that in the darkest hour he would come and make himself known to them. The text does not explain how the Lord comes, but in this instance, once again, the Lord comes in an unexpected way. His coming is always mysterious, and his identity is often concealed.

Significantly, the Lord is revealed in the words that he spoke: "Take heart. It is I; do not be afraid" (6:50). Whenever the Word of God is heard in a crisis, this is the word that is heard: "You have no need for anxiety. Have courage. I am. I am still God. I continue to care for my creation. Stop being afraid."

On Thanksgiving night 1988, my father suffered a heart attack. He and my mother had driven to Tampa, Florida, to pick up a new Avion travel trailer. On the way back, they stopped at a camp ground near Adairsville, Georgia, for the night. After Dad had gone to bed, about 11:00 p.m., he felt severe pressure and pain in his chest. Mother ran to call for help. Fortunately there was an EMS station less than a half a mile away, and help came quickly. Dad was transported to the hospital in Cartersville, where he remained for the next six days, while his condition stabilized. Several weeks later Dad had heart bypass surgery. On the afternoon before his surgery, he said that he was not afraid of the surgery the next day, though no one could know what the outcome of it would be. The question of life after death had fascinated him for years and he had read all the great thinkers on the subject, but he said that in the final analysis all the theories of eschatology really did not matter. It all came down to a conviction that "God is," and if God is then one can face the unknown with every confidence. As he later said in an interview, "Because I have a confidence and trust in one ultimate conviction, 'God is,' I can say that at no time in my life have I experienced fear. If 'God is,' then that's enough."[39]

This is the same word the prophet Isaiah delivered to the believing community in his day:

> Do not fear, for I have redeemed you;
> I have called you by name, you are mine.
> When you pass through the waters I will be with you;
> and through the rivers, they will not overwhelm you;. . . .
> For I am the LORD, your God, the Holy One of Israel, your Savior. (Isa 43:1-3)

[Be Carried by the Wood]

Be Carried by the Wood

"But why was he crucified? Because the wood of his lowliness was necessary for you. For you had swollen with pride and had been cast forth far from your homeland. The way has been washed out by the waves of this world, and there is no way to cross over to the homeland unless you are carried by the wood. Ungrateful man, do you ridicule him who has come to you that you may return? He himself became the way, and this through the sea: that he might show you that there is a way upon the sea. But you, who cannot in any way yourself walk on the sea, let yourselves be carried by the ship, be carried by the wood." (Augustine, *Lectures or Tractates on the Gospel according to St. John* 2.4.3)

Thomas C. Oden and Christopher A. Hall, eds., *Ancient Christian Commentary on Scripture: New Testament II, Mark* (Downers Grove IL: InterVarsity Press, 1998), 95; *NPNF*, First Series, 7:15.

NOTES

[1] Joel Marcus, *Mark 1–8* (AB 27; New York: Doubleday, 2000), 378.

[2] *ANF* 4:589.

[3] See John Painter, *Just James: The Brother of Jesus in History and Tradition* (Columbia: University of South Carolina Press, 1997); Bruce Chilton and Jacob Neusner, eds., *The Brother of Jesus: James the Just and His Mission* (Louisville: Westminster John Knox Press, 2001).

[4] Wolfgang A. Bienert, "The Relatives of Jesus," in *New Testament Apocrypha* (rev. ed.; ed. Wilhelm Schneemelcher; trans. R. McL. Wilson; Louisville: Westminster John Knox, 1991), 1:472.

[5] See Marcus, *Mark 1–8*, 389.

[6] Martin Hengel, T*he Charismatic Leader and His Followers* (trans. J. Greig; New York: Crossroad, 1981), 28.

[7] BDAG, 811.

[8] T. W. Manson, *The Sayings of Jesus* (London, 1949), 181; Herbert Danby, trans., *The Mishnah* (Oxford: Oxford University Press, 1933), 10.

[9] C. E. B. Cranfield, *The Gospel according to Saint Mark* (CGTC; Cambridge: Cambridge University Press, 1959), 200.

[10] See the discussion of these parallels in Janice Capel Anderson, "Feminist Criticism: The Dancing Daughter," in *Mark and Method: New Approaches in Biblical Studies* (ed. Janice Capel Anderson and Stephen D. Moore; Minneapolis: Fortress, 1992), 127-30.

[11] So Marcus, *Mark 1–8*, 394.

[12] Robert A. Guelich, *Mark 1–8:26* (WBC 34A; Dallas: Word Books, 1989), 325; see Bruce M. Metzger, *A Textual Commentary on the Greek New Testament* (New York: United Bible Societies, 1971), 89.

[13] Emil Schürer, *The History of the Jewish People in the Age of Jesus Christ (175 B.C.–A.D. 135)* (rev. and ed. Geza Vermes and Fergus Millar; Edinburgh: T. & T. Clark, 1973), 1:346-48.

[14] *ANF* 10:429.

[15] Metzger, *A Textual Commentary on the Greek New Testament*, 89-90.

[16] Anderson, "Feminist Criticism: The Dancing Daughter," 122-26.

[17] Josephus, *Jewish Antiquities* (trans. H. St. J. Thackeray and Ralph Marcus; LCL; Cambridge: Harvard University Press, 1934), 5:405-07.

[18] Schürer, *The History of the Jewish People in the Age of Jesus Christ (175 B.C.–A.D. 135)*, 1:371.

[19] Karl Heinrich Rengstorf, "*apostolos*," *TDNT* 1:407-43.

[20] Hulmut Koester, "*splanchnon*," *TDNT* 7:548.

[21] Ibid., 553, 554.

[22] Cranfield, *The Gospel according to Saint Mark*, 217.

[23] Johannes P. Louw and Eugene A. Nida, *Greek-English Lexicon of the New Testament* (New York: United Bible Societies, 1988), 1:50.

[24] Joachim Jeremias, *The Eucharistic Words of Jesus* (trans. Norman Perrin; Philadelphia: Fortress Press, 1977), 48-49. Cf. Marcus, *Mark 1–8*, 407.

[25] BDAG, 860.

[26] Cranfield, *The Gospel according to Saint Mark*, 218.

[27] Beyer, *"eulogeō," TDNT* 2:760.

[28] Ibid.

[29] Kirsopp Lake, trans., *Apostolic Fathers* (LCL; Cambridge: Harvard University Press, 1912), 1:323.

[30] See Gail R. O'Day, "John 6:15-21: Jesus Walking on Water as Narrative Embodiment of Johannine Christology," in *Critical Readings of John 6* (ed. R. Alan Culpepper; Leiden: E. J. Brill, 1997), 149-59.

[31] Marcus, *Mark 1–8*, 423.

[32] Marcus, *Mark 1–8*, 434-35; Quentin Quesnell, T*he Mind of Mark: Interpretation and Method through the Exegesis of Mark 6,52* (AnBib 38; Rome: Pontifical Biblical Institute, 1969).

[33] Thomas Wolfe, *You Can't Go Home Again* (rpt. New York: HarperCollins, 1998).

[34] Thomas C. Oden and Christopher A. Hall, eds., *Ancient Christian Commentary on Scripture: New Testament II, Mark* (Downers Grove IL: InterVarsity Press, 1998), 85.

[35] Pheme Perkins, "The Gospel of Mark," *NIB* (Nashville: Abingdon, 1995), 8:599.

[36] See M. Eugene Boring, "The Gospel of Matthew," *NIB* (Nashville: Abingdon, 1995), 8:321-22.

[37] I owe this theme to a sermon Charles Bugg preached years ago.

[38] http://www.walldrug.com/history.htm

[39] Brian W. Burton, "Hugo H. Culpepper: Seeker of God," *The Philippine Baptist* 30 (June 1989): 9; cf. R. Alan Culpepper, *Eternity as a Sunrise: The Life of Hugo H. Culpepper* (Macon GA: Mercer University Press, 2002), 348-49.

JESUS' CHALLENGE TO FALSE VIEWS OF HOLINESS

Mark 7:1-37

Jesus' crossing of the sea and arrival on the west side, in the area of Gennesaret, opens a new section of the Gospel in which he confronts false notions of purity and holiness that had grown up in Jewish tradition. Readers today may be tempted to skip this section of the Gospel, but Jesus' response to the practices of the Pharisees actually exposes far-reaching distinctions between true and false piety that are relevant in every age.

In the course of his debate with the Pharisees about hand washing, "Qorban" (gifts offered to God), and dietary laws, Jesus articulates a principle with far-reaching implications: "There is nothing outside a person that by going in can defile, but the things that come out are what defile" (7:15). Taking sides in what was a divisive debate at the time, Mark adds, "Thus he declared all foods clean" (7:19). Observance of the food laws was part of a system of purity that required the Pharisees to avoid defiling contact with Gentiles and other ritually unclean persons. The next scene extends Jesus' challenge to the Pharisaic legislation on purity by reporting Jesus' response to the request of a Syrophoenician woman (7:24-30). Her persistence and wit prevails, and Jesus exorcizes an "unclean" spirit from her daughter. Following this scene, Jesus travels further through Gentile areas and restores hearing and speech to a Gentile (7:31-37). Throughout this chapter, therefore, Mark lays a foundation for the church's mission to the Gentiles.

COMMENTARY

Jesus' Rejection of the Tradition of the Elders, 7:1-23

This section reflects a complicated composition history. It is a controversy story that has been extended by several related but secondary additions. The original unit may be seen in vv. 1-8, in which the authorities challenge Jesus because his disciples were not washing their hands before they ate. The form is similar to Mark 2:15-17 (eating with tax collectors), 2:18-20 (fasting), and 2:23-28 (plucking grain on the Sabbath). The scene is set in vv. 1-2. Verses 3-4, which are placed in parentheses in the NRSV, as an aside or explanatory comment, explain the Pharisees' washings for a Gentile audience. Verse 5 reports the Pharisees' challenge. Jesus quotes Isaiah 29:13 in vv. 6-7 and draws this conclusion in v. 8: "You abandon the commandment of God and hold to human tradition."

Upon close examination, one can see that the rest of the section is composed of related units: vv. 9-13 deal with the issue of Qorban, vv. 14-15 overturn the traditional notion of uncleanness, v. 16 is a later gloss, vv. 17-19 and 20-23 contain interpretations of the principle articulated in v. 15, and v. 19c, "Thus he declared all foods clean," is a comment added by the evangelist.

The Pharisees, who last appeared in the controversies in 2:1–3:6 that culminated in the Pharisees taking counsel with the Herodians about how to kill Jesus (3:6), now reenter the Gospel narrative. With somewhat threatening overtones, Mark reports that they and the scribes who had come from Jerusalem—who interrogated Jesus in 3:22-30—gathered around Jesus again (7:1). This time their interrogation is sparked by their observation that "some" of Jesus' disciples did not observe the Pharisaic practice of washing their hands before they ate. The reference to "some" may reflect the situation in the Markan community as well as among the Twelve. Hand washing before eating is not actually commanded in the Hebrew Scriptures. One finds only that before the priests approached the altar and offered sacrifices, they were to wash their hands (Exod 30:18-21; 40:31-32). The Pharisees sought to live continually in a state of ritual purity and condemned others who did not do so. That is, they expected all Jews to maintain the same standards of purity that were commanded for the priests.

The issue of hand washing, however, merely provides the catalyst for Jesus to call into question the authority of the whole system of the "tradition of the elders." The Hellenistic challenges to the practice of Judaism from the period of the Maccabees (second century BC) on had made the sanctity of Jewish traditions a sensitive issue for many Jews. When Mattathias and his sons killed the king's officer who was forcing Jews to offer sacrifices to a pagan god, Mattathias called for all who lived by "the covenant of our ancestors" and who were "zealous for the law" to follow him (1 Macc 1:20, 27). The Pharisees held that Moses received the Law from Sinai and committed it to Joshua, and Joshua to the elders, and the elders to the Prophets; and the Prophets committed it to the men of the Great Synagogue. They said three things: "Be deliberate in judgment, raise up many disciples, and make a fence around the Law" (*m. Aboth* 1.1; Danby, 446).

The oral tradition served as "a fence around the Law," interpreting it in every situation so that it might not be violated inadvertently. It was this tradition that Jesus challenged.

One's hands were always assumed to be unclean. Unless they were washed, they could convey a lesser grade of uncleanness to foods and offerings, rendering the offerings invalid. The Pharisees debated the kind of washing that was required to cleanse one's hands:

> [To render the hands clean] a quarter-*log* or more [an amount equal to about an egg and a half] [of water] must be poured over the hands [to suffice] for one person or even for two; a half-*log* or more [suffices] for three persons or for four; and one *log* or more [suffices] for five or for ten or for a hundred. (*m. Yadim* 1.1)[1]

A whole tractate of the Mishnah is devoted to the traditions of the elders regarding the washing of hands.

Verse 3 contains an adverb whose meaning is uncertain. The manuscript evidence favors the reading *pykmē*, while other manuscripts have *pykna* (often, thoroughly). Martin Hengel examined four interpretations of the term: (1) "to the elbow," (2) "with the fist," (3) "to the wrist," and (4) "with a handful of water." While Hengel concluded that the term is a latinism best understood in the latter sense, "with a handful of water," others understand the term as meaning "with cupped hands."[2] The NRSV adopts the translation "thoroughly," and the NIV adds the adjective "ceremonial" to describe the washing. The washings are further described in v. 4: they wash "cups, pots, and bronze kettles," and some manuscripts add "and beds" or possibly "dining couches" (NIV). If beds were originally included (following Lev 15, which speaks of the purification of beds), the inclusion may signal hyperbole or satire— when they come from the market, the Pharisees wash not just hands and utensils but even beds. The theme throughout, however, is the keeping of the tradition of the elders (see vv. 3 and 5). The issue, moreover, is not Jesus' conduct but that of his followers (as in 2:18); some of them did not maintain the tradition by

Mikweh
A Mikweh or Jewish ritual bath found at Jericho.
(Credit: John McRay)

washing their hands before they ate. The idiom in v. 5, "why do your disciples not walk according to the tradition of the elders," is suggestive because the Hebrew word for the "law" (*halakah*) is derived from the verb "walk" (*halak*). Here "elders" seems to be used as a synonym for "scribes.[3] The question of the place of tradition may well have divided not just the Twelve but the Markan community also. Every generation must determine what it will preserve from the past and what it will accommodate to contemporary situations.

Jesus responds not by answering the question of hand washing but by addressing the underlying issue of tradition. He characterizes his critics as "hypocrites," which literally meant "actors" or those who wore masks. As the biblical basis for his charge, Jesus cites Isaiah 29:13, a verse that describes the spiritual condition of the people of Jerusalem prior to Sennacherib's attack on Judea in 701 BC. The quotation in Mark follows the Septuagint text closely but sharpens the contrast in the line to read, "teaching as teachings commandments of men" (cf. Col 2:22). Like actors, the words of their lips do not represent the attitudes of their hearts. True worship requires integrity and purity of heart. Consequently, their worship is vain. The quotation from Isaiah foreshadows Jesus' condemnation of the temple and warning of its destruction in Mark 11:15-17. Building his case from the last line of the quotation, Jesus returns to the issue of the place of tradition, charging that the religious authorities have abandoned God's commandment in favor of human tradition (v. 8). The next verse heightens the scandal further by escalating "abandon" (v. 8) to "reject" (v. 9) and shifting from "human tradition" to "your tradition" (v. 9). The Pharisees have effectively elevated their own precepts and traditions above God's commandment. Their hypocrisy is that they present their own traditions as though they were God's.

As an example to substantiate this charge, Jesus cites their practice of Qorban. Mark quotes the command to honor one's father and mother (Exod 20:12) and the penalty for "cursing" one's parents (Exod 21:17). Again, both quotations follow the Septuagint closely. The rhetoric is pointedly adversarial: "For Moses said . . ." (v. 10), "but you say . . ." (v. 11). The specific practice seems to be the swearing of an oath making one's property a gift to God—Qorban. Accordingly, if a son were to say to his parents that what they would have received in support from him was Qorban, he would then be released, indeed prohibited, from using his property or goods for their support. The Mosaic command was probably not originally intended as an admonition for small children, but rather was instruction for grown children. Support your parents in their old age so that your children will support you in turn and "your days may be long and that it may go well with you in the land that the Lord your God is giving you" (Deut 5:16; Sir 3:1-16).

Qorban

 Several ancient references illuminate the practice of Qorban.

"If a man was forbidden by vow to have any benefit from his fellow, and he had naught to eat, his fellow may give [the food] to another as a gift, and the first is permitted to use it. It once happened that a man at Beth Horon, whose father was forbidden by vow to have any benefit from him, was giving his son in marriage, and he said to his fellow, 'The courtyard and the banquet are given to thee as a gift, but they are thine only that my father may come and eat with us at the banquet.' His fellow said, 'If they are thine, they are dedicated to Heaven.' The other answered, 'I did not give thee what is mine that shouldst dedicate it to Heaven.' His fellow said, 'Thou didst give me what is thine only that thou and thy father might eat and drink and be reconciled one with the other, and that the sin should rest on his head!' When the case came before the Sages, they said: Any gift which, if a man would dedicate it, is not accounted dedicated, is not a [valid] gift." (*m. Nedarim* 5.6, Danby, *The Mishnah*, 271)

An Aramaic inscription on an ossuary found at Jebel Hallet et-Turi near Jerusalem reads, "Everything that a person will find to his profit in this ossuary is an offering (*qorban*) to God from the one within it" (Joseph A. Fitzmyer, "The Aramaic Qorban Inscription from Jebel Hallet et-Turi and Mk 7:11/Mt 15:5," in *Essays on the Semitic Background of the New Testament* [London: Geoffrey Chapman, 1971], 93-100). Josephus also provides evidence of such oaths: "Again, those who describe themselves as 'Corban' to God—meaning what the Greeks would call 'a gift'—when desirous to be relieved of this obligation must pay down to the priests a fixed sum" (Josephus, *Ant.* 4.73; LCL 4:511; cf. *Against Apion* 1.166-67).

Herbert Danby, *The Mishnah* (Oxford: Oxford University Press, 1933).

The quotation in v. 10 is actually a conflation of the command to honor father and mother (Exod 20:12; Deut 5:16) and the legislation that one who curses his father or mother shall be put to death (Exod 21:17; Lev 20:9). Although pronouncing one's goods Qorban [Qorban], whether in a rash oath or fit of spite, is not the same as cursing one's father and mother, the principle still applies: everyone has an obligation to care for his or her parents. It would be consistent for Jesus to speak in this way, since elsewhere he forbade not only murder but being angry with one's brother, and not just adultery but lust also (Matt 5:21-30). The legal situation that is envisioned is not entirely clear. Jesus may have been objecting to the practice of Qorban as a legal loophole for sheltering one's goods from the obligation of parental care, or he may have been calling attention to the further violation of the intent of the law if the Pharisees forbade a person from rescinding an oath of Qorban. This is implied by v. 12: "you no longer permit doing anything for a father or mother." The rabbis also debated the matter of when a vow could be rescinded and when it was binding:

R. Eliezer says: They may open for men the way [to repentance] by reason of the honour due to father and mother. But the Sages forbid it. R. Zadok said: Rather than open the way for a man by reason of the honour due to father and mother, they should open the way for him by reason of the honour due to God; but if so, there could be no vows. But the Sages agree with R. Eliezer that in a matter between a man and his father and mother, the way may be opened to him by reason of the honour due to his father and mother. (*m. Nedarim* 9.1)

Verse 13 concludes the argument by recapitulating Jesus' charge against the Pharisees stated in vv. 8 and 9: they have abandoned the word of God by holding to their traditions. The charge is deeply ironic because the traditions were developed to ensure that the faithful would not inadvertently or unknowingly violate God's commands.

The note that Jesus called the crowd to him (v. 14) signals a transition to a related but broader issue. He calls the crowd to "hear" and "understand"—actions that mark the transition from "outsiders" to "insiders" (see 4:9, 12; 6:52; 8:17, 21). The principle that "there is nothing outside a person that by going in can defile, but the things that come out are what defile" (7:15) has such broad implications that it challenged the very foundations on which much of the piety of the Pharisees was based. The issue is not just washing one's hands, and it is not just the practice of Qorban. The question is, what counts as holiness and righteousness before God? The question is framed negatively, however: what alienates or separates a person from God? The Pharisees believed that any contact with impurity defiled a person and alienated him or her from God. Therefore one could not eat unclean foods, foods prepared improperly, foods prepared in unclean utensils, or foods prepared by unclean persons. One could not have contact with unclean persons or eat with the ritually unclean. One could not go into a Gentile's home. Bodily fluids and discharges rendered one unclean. Skin diseases made one unclean, and uncleanness could be transferred by contact with unclean persons, objects, foods, or liquids. In an effort to live blamelessly and faithfully, the Pharisees had therefore developed a way of life based on purity. They only associated with others who lived by the commandments as they interpreted them, and they offered all of their lives to God by living in constant purity.

Jesus' challenge to Pharisaic piety was sweeping. Righteousness is not a matter of ritual purity, what one eats or does not eat, or what one touches. Righteousness is a matter of the heart, thought, will, desires, priorities, and speech. In this emphasis Jesus was actually returning to the piety of Israel's prophets. Amos called for justice: "I hate, I despise your festivals and I take no delight in your solemn assemblies. . . . But let justice roll down like waters, and righteousness like an ever-flowing stream" (Amos 5:21, 27). Hosea called for purity in love: "For I desire steadfast love and not sacrifice, the knowledge of God rather than burnt offerings" (Hos 6:6). Isaiah called for purity in actions: "Wash yourselves; make yourselves clean; remove the evil of your doings from before my eyes; cease to do evil, learn to do good; seek justice, rescue the oppressed, defend the orphan, plead for the widow" (Isa 1:16-17), and Micah called for humility: "He has told you, O mortal, what is good; and what does the LORD require of you but to do justice, and to

love kindness, and to walk humbly with your God?" (Mic 6:8). Jesus
called for a piety based on purity of heart and life rather than on the
distinction between common and holy, or clean and unclean, things
and substances. What then makes one unclean before God? Jesus gives
a list of such actions in his explanation of this pronouncement in the
scene that follows (7:17-23).

Entering into a house (v. 17) is a typical Markan transition that introduces a scene in which Jesus gives the disciples private instruction
concerning his public teaching (see 3:20; 9:28, 33; 10:10). The pattern
of private instruction in Mark allows for the interpretation of Jesus'
teachings on selected points, while underscoring both the special role of
the disciples and their striking lack of compre-
hension. The private teaching often, but not
always, focuses on a parable or specific saying.
[Private Teaching] Strictly speaking, the saying in
v. 15 is not a parable, but Mark treats it like a
riddle (*mashal*) that requires interpretation.
Jesus rebukes the disciples for their lack of comprehension, as he does elsewhere in Mark, with
no apparent effect (4:13; 7:18; 8:17-21; 10:38).
Although Jesus had exhorted the crowd to hear
and understand (*synete*, 7:14), the disciples had
not understood (*asynetos*, 7:18). This is the only
occurrence of the term *asynetos* (without understanding) in Mark, but it occurs several times in
Romans in connection with Gentile sinfulness
(Rom 1:21, 31; 10:19; cf. Deut 32:21). The
explanation that follows replicates the structure
of the saying in 7:15. Verses 18-19 explain the
meaning of the first part, what goes into a
person; while verses 20-23 interpret the second
part, what comes out of a person. The explanation for why that which enters a person does
not defile is based on the difference between the

Private Teaching

The pattern of private teaching is
explained in Mark 4:33-34. The motif of
the disciples' lack of comprehension and failure to
understand Jesus' teachings allows the evangelist
to provide interpretation and commentary on
selected topics:

4:10-12	The purpose of the parables
4:13-20	The parable of the sower
4:34	The parables
cf. 6:31-32	Retreating to a private place
7:17-23	Defilement: the importance of inner purity
9:2	The transfiguration
9:28	The disciples' inability to cast the demon from the epileptic boy: the importance of prayer
9:33	The disciples' argument about which of them was the greatest: the importance of humility and servanthood
10:10	Divorce
13:3-37	The destruction of Jerusalem and the coming of the Son of Man

heart and the stomach. The heart was the seat of one's will, affection,
and moral purity. The stomach merely processed food, which then
passed on to the latrine, never entering one's heart. By means of this
simple—and somewhat crass—explanation, Jesus set aside generations
of law that distinguished what one could eat from what one could not
eat. Certain foods defiled those who ate them (see Lev 11:2-47; Deut
14:3-21), so the Jews abstained from these foods. The food laws also
separated the Jews from non-Jews (Lev 20:24b-26). It is not surprising,
therefore, that when the early church began to work among Gentiles it

had to confront the question of the continuing validity of these prescriptions. Peter's vision of the sheet with all kinds of animals preceded his visit to the house of Cornelius and the revelation that "I should not call anyone profane or unclean" (Acts 10:28). Nevertheless, the issue of eating with Gentiles remained the most divisive issue the early church faced (see Gal 2:11-14; Acts 15:19-21). Many in the Roman church took the position of "the strong," who did not distinguish among foods (Rom 14:2-3, 14, 20), and the Gospel of Mark has traditionally been assigned to Rome. The debate over foods in Mark 7 may therefore reflect a debate in the Markan community.

The evangelist's comment at the end of v. 19, "Thus he declared all foods clean," does not occur in the parallel context in Matthew 15:17. The evangelist's comment offers a further level of interpretation of Jesus' words. The saying on what defiles (Mark 7:15) nullified the distinctions on which Jewish cultic law was based, and in so doing introduced a different understanding of what being "a holy people" requires. Food laws would no longer divide the pious from the pagan.

Not forbidden foods but immoral intentions defile a person. One of the accepted interpretations for why some persons were morally upright while others were wicked was the principle that two inclinations lurk in the human heart, one good (the *yetzer ha-tov*) and one evil (the *yetzer ha-rah*):

> He created man to rule the world and placed within him two spirits so that he would walk with them until the moment of his visitation: they are the spirits of truth and of deceit. . . . Until now the spirits of truth and of injustice feud in the heart of man and they walk in wisdom or in folly. (1QS 3.18-19, 4.23)[4]

From the human heart there comes unfathomable evil. The gravity of the fall, and the seriousness of human depravity, means that we cannot shift the blame for our inherent sinfulness to external influences or the violation of established codes of conduct.

Within the human heart there resides all manner of evil. Jesus lists twelve, "six nouns in the plural indicating evil acts and six nouns in the singular indicating moral defects or vices."[5] This list of vices has parallels elsewhere in the New Testament (e.g., Rom 1:29-31; Gal 5:19-21; 2 Tim 3:2-5) and in Jewish literature of the period (1QS 4.9-11). Leading the list of vices is a general term for forbidden sexual acts (*porneiai*), which can mean adultery (possibly Matt 5:32), fornication, or incestuous marriages (see Acts 15:29; 1 Cor 5:1). It also appears at the beginning of the lists of vices in Romans 1:29, Galatians 5:19, and Colossians 3:5, which reflects the early church's concern over pagan sexual practices. [Lists of Vices] Theft or stealing follows in Matthew 15:19

Lists of Vices

The list of vices in Mark 7:21-22 has close parallels in Matt 15:19 but also in Rom 1:29 and Col 3:5.

	Mark 7:21-22	Matt 15:19	Rom 1:29	Gal 5:19-21	Col 3:5
Fornication	x	x		x	x
Theft	x	x			
Murder	x	x	x		
Adultery	x	x			
Avarice	x		x		x
Wickedness	x		x		
Deceit	x		x		
Licentiousness	x			x	
Envy	x				
Slander	x	x			
Pride	x				
Folly	x				

---

also. Murder or killing is included in the list of vices in Romans 1:29 and Galatians 5:21. Adultery follows next in the list, indicating that *porneiai* at the beginning of the list had other meanings. Similarly, adultery is inserted into the list in Galatians 5:19, just ahead of *porneiai* in some manuscripts. Greediness or avarice does not occur in the parallel list in Matthew 15:19 but does appear in the lists in Romans 1:29 and Colossians 3:5. The term translated "wickedness" (*ponēriai*), which also occurs in Romans 1:29, indicates a general lack of moral or social values.

At this point the list changes from plural to singular terms. Like the previous term, deceit does not occur in Matthew 15:19 but does appear in Romans 1:29. Licentiousness (*aselgeia*) is a general term that denotes "lack of self-constraint which involves one in conduct that violates all bounds of what is socially acceptable."[6] To have an "evil eye" was a Semitic idiom that usually connoted stinginess or covetousness (see Deut 15:9 LXX; Prov 28:22; Sir 14:8-10; Matt 6:22; 20:15). Blasphemy can have the broader meaning of "speech that denigrates or defames, [meaning] reviling, denigration, disrespect, slander."[7] As Marcus observes, in this context all the other sins are social ones: "The focus thus shifts from the evil eye, which envies the neighbor, to the evil tongue, which reviles him or her."[8] Pride, haughtiness, or arrogance (*hyperēphania*, which occurs only here in the New Testament) derives from an inflated sense of one's own importance. Closely related is the vice of folly or foolishness, a term that Paul uses three times to characterize his boasting (2 Cor 11:1, 17, 21). These are a sample of the evil that comes from within a person and defiles him or her.

The radical reorientation that follows from this interpretation of Jesus' dictum in Mark 7:15 requires that we be more concerned about the pollution or defilement that we may cause than the foods or things that might defile us. The greater evil lies not outside but within each of us.

The Wit and Faith of the Syrophoenician Woman, 7:24-30

A geographical notice signals a change of scene and setting. ["On the Borders"] Tyre and Sidon were mentioned in the summary section in Mark 3:8, so it is not surprising that Tyre (or Tyre and Sidon) should reappear at this point in the narrative. Several strong manuscripts add "and Sidon" (Sinaiticus, Alexandrinus, and Vaticanus among them). The story turns on the woman's reinterpretation of Jesus' sharp aphorism about giving children's bread to dogs. The aphorism may have arisen out of the hostility between the Tyreans and the Jews.

Tyre was an island that enjoyed a strong economy, but it had to import its produce from Galilee, the breadbasket of the region. In times of plenty the exchange was mutually

"On the Borders"

Origen, in a classic example of spiritual or allegorical interpretation, found further significance in the geographical notice. On the meaning of the name "Tyre," he reports, "Among the Hebrews, then Tyre is called Sor, and it is interpreted 'anguish.'" The phrase "the region of Tyre" also pointed to a further meaning: "The Gentiles, those who dwell on the borders, can be saved if they believe. . . . Think of it this way: Each of us when he sins is living on the borders of Tyre or Sidon or of Pharaoh and Egypt. They are on the borders of those who are outside the inheritance of God."

Origen, *Commentary on Matthew*, 11.16; *ANF* 10:444–45. The latter is quoted by Thomas C. Oden and Christopher A. Hall, eds., *Ancient Christian Commentary on Scripture: New Testament II, Mark* (Downers Grove IL: InterVarsity Press, 1998), 101.

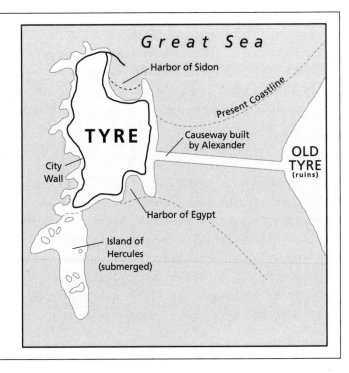

Tyre
Tyre was originally an island, but after Alexander the Great's army besieged the city in 322 BC, the ruins of the city were used to build a causeway that connects the island to the mainland. Cf. [Idumea, the Transjordan, Tyre, and Sidon]

beneficial, but in times of crisis or famine, the prosperous Tyreans were able, literally, to buy bread off of the tables of the Jews. [Famines] One such time of heightened tension between the Tyreans and the Jews is reported in the book of Acts: "Now Herod was angry with the people of Tyre and Sidon. So they came to him in a body; and after winning over Blastus, the king's chamberlain, they asked for a reconciliation, because their country depended on the king's country for food" (Acts 12:20). As a result, the Jews of the area resented the Gentile "dogs" for taking the bread of the children (of Israel). Josephus even places the Tyreans among the Jews' bitterest enemies (*Against Apion* 1.70).

Mark says, "he entered a house, and would not have any one know it; yet he could not be hid." Ironically, although the house is typically the place in Mark where Jesus teaches the disciples, in this instance he will be confronted and taught by a Gentile woman. The house also incidentally strengthens the parallels between Mark 7, with its sequence of Jesus' teaching on unclean foods and his meeting with the Gentile woman, and Acts 10, with its parallel sequence of Paul's vision of the sheet with the unclean foods and his meeting the Gentile Cornelius at his house (Acts 10:2, 22, 30). Mark's comment that Jesus did not want anyone to know that he was there signals either his continuing effort to avoid the press of crowds around him (see recently 5:21, 24; 6:31-33, 54-56), or possibly his effort to conceal the fact that he was in a Gentile area (which would set up his excursion through the Decapolis, reported in 7:31, as a dramatic change following his conversation with the Syrophoenician woman). Predictably, though, his efforts to conceal his presence were futile (6:33, 54).

The woman, whose little daughter had some malady that Mark speaks of as an unclean spirit (see [Evil Spirits]), heard of Jesus and came and fell before his feet. [Syrophoenician Woman] The reference to the "unclean" spirit invites reflection on the relationship between this story and Jesus' words on uncleanness and defilement in the preceding verses. By prostrating herself before Jesus, the woman echoes the actions of the Gadarene demoniac (5:6), Jairus (5:22), and the woman with a hemorrhage (5:33). Like Jairus, she came pleading for Jesus to cure her daughter. She was a Greek, a Syrophoenician by birth. In this instance "Greek" (*Hellēnis*) seems to mean "Gentile," and the label Syrophoenician identifies her more precisely as a native of the area Jesus

Famines

Galen (c. AD 129–199) described the difference in the hardships brought on by famine for city dwellers and country people:

"The city people who, as is customary, store up enough food in summer to last the whole year, take all the wheat from the fields together with the barley, beans and lentils, and leave for the country people nothing but the remaining pulses, although they themselves even take the greater part of that, too, into the cities. The country people then, when they have used up their winter supplies, have only unhealthy nourishment through the entire summer. In that period these country people eat the shoots and suckers of unhealthful plants."

Galen, *De probis pravisque alimentorum succis* 1.6.749–50; quoted by Gerd Theissen, *The Gospels in Context: Social and Political History in the Synoptic Tradition* (trans. Linda M. Maloney; Minneapolis: Fortress, 1991), 75.

Syrophoenician Woman

📖 Inevitably legends grew up around the identity of the unnamed Syrophoenician woman. Tatian recorded the following tradition about the Syrophoenician woman's home in his harmony of the Gospels: "And at (the same) time a woman, a Canaanite, (whose) daughter had had an unclean spirit, heard of him. And this woman was a believer from Homs in Syria."

The Pseudo-Clementine Homilies claim that the woman was named Justa and her daughter Bernice (2.19; 3.73), and further:

"She, therefore, having taken up a manner of life according to the law, was, with the daughter who had been healed,

driven out from her home by her husband, whose sentiments were opposed to ours. But she, being faithful to her engagements, and being in affluent circumstances, remained a widow herself, but gave her daughter in marriage to a certain man who as attached to the true faith, and who was poor. And, abstaining from marriage for the sake of her daughter, she bought two boys [Niceta and Aquila] and educated them, and had them in place of sons." (2.20; *ANF* 8:232)

Tatian, in Gerd Theissen, *The Gospels in Context: Social and Political History in the Synoptic Tradition* (trans. Linda M. Maloney; Minneapolis: Fortress, 1991), 247, citing E. Preuschen, *Tatians Diatessaron*, 127.

---

was visiting. The term "Syrophoenician" can be traced to the Latin term "Syrophoenix," which appears around the second century BC and was used first to distinguish Syrophoenicians from Libyphoenicians, but it was also used in a pejorative sense, as in the insult that appears in Lucilius, *Satires*: "that devil of a money-grubber, that Syrophoenician."[9] In other words, she was Gentile, probably a Greek-speaking woman born in southern Syria. For those familiar with the Hebrew Scriptures, the Syrophoenician woman also evokes echoes of Elijah's meeting with the widow in Zarephath, near Sidon (1 Kgs 17:8-16; Luke 4:25-26). For Jesus to have any contact with her would make him unclean in the eyes of the religious Jews of his time, and all the regional prejudices between the Galileans and the Syrophoenicians lay close beneath the surface.

When the woman pleads for Jesus to cast the demon out of her daughter, Jesus says the most shocking thing attributed to him in the Gospels: "Let the children be fed first, for it is not fair to take the children's food [lit. "bread"] and throw it to the dogs" (7:27). The implication is as clear as it is scandalous. On the other hand, one need not conclude that Jesus was calling the woman a dog. The saying is parabolic, drawing a picture of a home scene in which the children naturally take precedence over the dogs. Jesus was saying that his ministry was for the Jews, the children of God, and that it was not right to take what was theirs and give it to the Gentiles. The reference to "bread" reminds the reader of the theme of "bread" and feeding in Mark 6, where the 5,000 were fed, and 12 baskets of the leftover fragments were collected.

In the Sermon on the Mount, Jesus said, "Do not give what is holy to dogs, and do not throw your pearls before swine" (Matt 7:6). Swine and dogs are also linked in a revolting proverb in 2 Peter 2:22, "The dog turns back to its own vomit" (see Prov 26:11), and "the sow is washed only to wallow in the mud." The last chapter of Revelation says that outside the holy city are "the dogs and sorcerers and fornicators and murderers and idolaters" (Rev 22:15). [Dogs]

Some interpreters set this exchange in the context of the early church's mission to the Gentiles.[10] Paul said, "to the Jew first, then to the Gentile" (Rom 1:16; cf. Acts 13:46). If this is the case, the point of the story is that although the Jews retain their rightful priority in God's salvific plan, the Gentiles are included also. Perhaps significantly the parallel account in Matthew lacks the term "first" (Matt 15:26; compare Mark 7:27). The inclusion of "the nations" is implicit in Isaiah's view of salvation history (Isa 2:2-4; 42:1; 60:1-3; 66:18-20): "It is too light a thing that you should be my servant to raise up the tribes of Jacob and to restore the survivors of Israel; I will give you as a light to the nations, that my salvation may reach to the end of the earth" (Isa 49:6; cf. Acts 14:47, where Paul preaches in a Gentile area). The mission to the Gentiles remained a problematic issue for the early church, as Paul's excursus in Romans 9–11 amply illustrates. The use of the designation "children" to refer to Jews occurs in *Mishnah Aboth*, "Beloved are Israel for they were called children of God . . . as it is written, 'Ye are the children of the Lord your God'" (3.15).[11] Against this background, one can appreciate the importance of the debate over who could be counted among the "children" and therefore among the heirs of the promises. This debate can be traced in both the Pauline (Rom 4:11-12, 16; 8:15-17, 19; Gal 3:7-9) and the Johannine literature (John 1:12; 11:52). By adding the word "first," the Markan Jesus may signal that there will be a time for the feeding of the Gentiles, but it had not yet arrived.

The woman's response cleverly transposes Jesus' pronouncement. The term for dogs in v. 27 is the diminutive (*kynarion* rather than *kyōn*), which may indicate house dogs or lap dogs

Dogs

Dogs were generally regarded as wild and unclean in antiquity, so to call someone a dog, or a dead dog, was an insult:

"The Philistine said to David, 'Am I a dog, that you come to me with sticks?'" (1 Sam 17:43).

"He did obeisance and said, 'What is your servant, that you should look upon a dead dog such as I?'" (2 Sam 9:8; cf. 16:9).

"The dog is reckoned a kind of wild animal" (*m. Kilaim* 8.6; Danby, *The Mishnah*, 37).

"And Aseneth took her royal dinner and the fatlings and the fish and the flesh of the heifer and all the sacrifices of her gods and the vessels of their wine of libation and threw everything through the window looking north, and gave everything to the strange dogs. For Aseneth said to herself, 'By no means must my dogs eat from my dinner and from the sacrifice of the idols, but let the strange dogs eat those.'" (Joseph and Aseneth 10:14, in James H. Charlesworth, *The Old Testament Pseudepigrapha* [Garden City NY: Doubleday, 1985], 2:216)

Dogs are also listed among the enemies of the sheep (Israel) in *1 En.* 89:41-50.

Herbert Danby, *The Mishnah* (Oxford: Oxford University Press, 1933).

"Cave Canem," Roman dog mosaic from threshold of house in Pompeii. Museo Archeologico Nazionale, Naples, Italy. (Credit: Erich Lessing / Art Resource, NY)

rather than yard dogs. Whether Jesus' use of the diminutive signaled this distinction or not, the woman picked up on it. Her reply is filled with diminutives, literally, "Lord, even the little dogs under the table eat the little crumbs from the little children." The address, "Lord," in this context may be a confession rather than a mere term of respect (cf. Mark 10:51). She took no offense at the implied slur. She did not ask for the whole loaf or that her child be fed first. She merely took the potential inherent in Jesus' saying and turned it to her advantage. Certainly the bread is for the children, but even so there are crumbs left for the dogs under the table. Her persistence is like that of the four who took up the roof over Jesus' head (2:1-12) or of the hemorrhaging woman who pressed to touch Jesus' garment (5:25-34). The Syrophoenician woman's faith also contrasts dramatically with the disciples' lack of understanding (6:52) and the Pharisees' misplaced piety (7:1-15).

Responding to the woman, Jesus announces that because of what she said the demon had gone out of her daughter. In Matthew, Jesus' response is different, probably as a result of Matthean redaction: "Woman, great is your faith! Let it be done for you as you wish" (Matt 15:28; cf. Matt 8:13). The reference to the girl's bed reminds the reader of the raising of Jairus's daughter (5:40-42) and the paralytic taking up his pallet (2:11-12). There are three other Gospel accounts of healings at a distance. All involve Gentiles. In Matthew 8:13 and John 4:50, Jesus sends the petitioner home with the command, "Go" (7:29). Each of the stories typically ends with praise of the faith of the Gentile petitioner (Matt 8:10; 15:28; Luke 7:9). Mark leaves this element relatively understated and implicit. Nevertheless, the point is clear, and the Syrophoenician woman serves as yet another Markan minor character whose persistent faith is ultimately rewarded.

This experience may have been a turning point for Jesus' ministry. Whereas he had worked only among the Jews before this incident (with the notable exception of the exorcism of the Gadarene demoniac, 5:1-20), this courageous and witty Gentile woman may have convinced Jesus that God's mercy could not be limited to the Jews only. In the next paragraph Mark reports Jesus' travel through the Decapolis, and at the beginning of the next chapter Jesus feeds a multitude of 4,000, just as earlier he had fed the 5,000, but this time the feeding takes place on the other side of the Sea of Galilee, in a Gentile area. What Jesus had done for the Jewish crowd, he now did for the Gentile crowd—he gave them bread.

The Miracle of Hearing for the Deaf, 7:31-37

The account of Jesus' healing of the deaf mute carries much more significance than one may see in it on first reading. It is strategically located following Jesus' conversation with the Syrophoenician woman and just before his feeding of the 4,000. Symbolically it announces that through Jesus the ears of the Gentiles can be opened to hear the good news of God and their tongues can be loosed to proclaim God's glory.

The story opens with a geographical notice, just as did the story of the Syrophoenician woman. Mark 7:31 therefore balances 7:24, as each contains a reference to "the region of Tyre." The geographical references in v. 31 have played a significant role in the debate over the authorship and provenance of the Gospel. Taken at face value, the report is confusing and improbable. From Tyre Jesus went "by way of Sidon," twenty miles north of Tyre, "towards" the Sea of Galilee, which lay to the southeast, "in the region of" the Decapolis, ten Hellenistic cities, nine of which lay east of the Sea of Galilee. Scholars skeptical of the tradition that this Gospel was written by John Mark have contended that the evangelist's lack of precise geographical knowledge of the region suggests that the Gospel was not written by someone familiar with this area.[12] On the other hand, advocates of a Galilean or Syrian provenance have turned the argument on its head, contending that Mark 7:31 reflects the evangelist's interest in naming the sites of Christian communities in the area in which it was written.[13] Without necessarily reflecting on the Gospel's provenance, the references to Gentile areas signal that the coming kingdom will embrace the Gentile world also.[14]

Unnamed friends brought a deaf mute to Jesus and asked him to lay his hands on the man. The context of this scene, with the story of the Syrophoenician woman preceding it, the references to Gentile areas introducing it, and the story of the feeding of the 4,000 following it, suggests a continuing Gentile theme. The text does not specify explicitly that the man was a Gentile, but the implication that he was lends the story added significance. The unnamed associates who bring the man to Jesus remind the reader of the anonymous friends who appear in other

The Healing of the Deaf Man

Jesus healing the deaf man. Byzantine, 14th c. Mosaic in the narthex. Hora Church (Kariye Camii), Istanbul, Turkey. (Credit: Erich Lessing / Art Resource, NY)

passages: neighbors in Capernaum (1:32), the four who carried the paralytic (2:3), the people of Gennesraet (6:55-56), the people of Bethsaida who brought a blind man to him (8:22), and those who brought children to Jesus (10:13-16). In contrast, there were others who sought to prevent the sick from reaching Jesus or who were offended by his healing (the Pharisees, 3:2; the swineherds, 5:15-17; the messengers from Jairus's house, 5:35; and those on the road in Jericho who sought to silence Bartimaeus, 10:48).

The healing of the deaf is more prominent in Matthew, where it is evidence of fulfillment of the Scriptures (see Matt 9:32-33; 11:5; 12:22; 15:30-31). The man's speech was also affected. He may not have been mute, but "had an impediment in his speech." The Greek term *mogilalon* appears nowhere else in the New Testament, and only in Isaiah 35:6 in the Septuagint. Isaiah 35:5-6, which is evoked by Matthew 11:5 and Luke 7:22, prophesies the opening of the eyes of the blind, unstopping the ears of the deaf, and releasing the tongue of the speechless. Commentators have noted the impressive parallels between this healing miracle and the giving of sight to the blind man of Bethsaida in the next section, suggesting that the two may have been drawn from the same source.[15]

Mark 7:31-37	**Mark 8:22-26**
Geographical location noted:	*Geographical location noted:*
The Decapolis	Bethsaida
Unnamed friends bring the man	Unnamed friends bring the man
to Jesus and beg Jesus	to Jesus and beg Jesus
to lay his hand on him	to touch him
He took him aside in private	He took the blind man . . . and led him out of the village
He spat	He put saliva on his eyes
and touched his tongue	and laid his hands on him
Details of the healing follow:	*Details of the healing follow:*
Jesus looked up	the man looked up
Command to secrecy: Jesus ordered them to tell no one.	*Command to secrecy:* "Do not even go into the village."

Taken together these two miracle accounts affirm that Jesus fulfilled the expectations of Isaiah 35:5-6, that the Messiah would give hearing to the deaf and sight to the blind.

Both of these stories report the healing in considerable detail. They are also the only two miracle stories in Mark that are omitted by both

Matthew and Luke, perhaps because they report a number of actions that could have been understood as magic.[16] In this instance, the man's companions beg Jesus to touch him—a means Jesus used on other occasions (1:41; 5:23; 6:2, 5). The idiom "in private" (*kat' idian*) occurs frequently in Mark in scenes where the disciples are "in private" with Jesus (4:34; 6:31, 32; 9: 2, 28; 13:3), but this is the only time the phrase is used when Jesus takes someone else aside. He did not just touch, or lay his hands, on the man. He thrust his fingers into the man's ears, mimetically acting out the opening of his ears that he intended. Then he spat and touched the man's tongue. Spittle was commonly thought to have healing power (Pliny, *Nat. Hist.* 28.4.7; Tacitus, *Hist.* 4.81; 6.18; Suetonius, *Vesp.* 7; John 9:1-7). Mark does not say where he spat, but the meaning is most likely that he spat on his hands and then touched the man's tongue. The spittle from his own (free) tongue was applied to the man's (bound) tongue, thereby freeing it. Touching and applying spittle seem to be merely preparatory steps. Jesus then looked up into heaven (cf. 6:41; John 11:41), as if asking for power or giving recognition that the healing was being done by the power of God. Next, Jesus sighed or groaned. Although sighing appears in ancient magic, Jesus transformed it into something quite different. In Judaism, sighing expressed deep distress of spirit and often led to prayer (Tob 3:1). Johannes Schneider notes, "God hears the sighing of his people" (Exod 2:24; 6:5), and interprets the reference in Mark 7:34 as "a prayer-sigh" (cf. Rom 8:22-27): "It establishes the inner relation with God and represents explicit prayer for the power of healing."[17] After this elaborate process, the healing actually occurs when Jesus says, "Ephphatha," which means "Be opened." Scholars debate whether Jesus was speaking Hebrew or Aramaic and have proposed various terms Jesus may have used.[18] Whether Hebrew or Aramaic, the term is not a magical formula; it was understood by the first hearers, and when the story was translated into Greek a translation was supplied (see [Aramaic Words]).

The effects of Jesus' healing actions and the response to the healing are also reported in great detail. Although the manuscript evidence is divided, the favored reading declares that "immediately" the man's ears were opened, his tongue was loosed, and he began to speak clearly. Jesus' command that they tell no one what they had seen is part of Mark's secrecy motif (see 1:25, 44; 3:12; 5:43) and complements the earlier report that he took the man aside, "in private." Nevertheless, the more he sought to maintain the secrecy, the more they proclaimed what Jesus had done. Just as on other occasions, neither Jesus' presence (6:33, 54; 7:24) nor his work (1:28, 45) could be hidden. The technical term for preaching is used in v. 36, so Mark may have intended an implicit exhortation for his community in a time of persecution: be like the witnesses who preached their confession all the more zealously regardless of how much they were commanded not to preach! Their amazement conveys awareness that something out of the ordinary had occurred, the full meaning of which still lies beyond their comprehension (cf. 1:22; 6:2; 10:26; 11:18). Their message echoes the words of Scripture in Genesis 1:31: "He has done everything well." The inbreaking of the kingdom through Jesus' work signaled a restoration of the creation to its original goodness. Their joyful exclamation was, "He even makes the deaf to hear and the mute to speak" (7:37). Jesus was fulfilling the expectations of Isaiah (Isa 35:5-6) for a time when

> the ransomed of the LORD shall return,
> and come to Zion with singing;
> everlasting joy shall be upon their heads;
> they shall obtain joy and gladness,
> and sorrow and sighing shall flee away. (Isa 35:10)

Even among the Gentiles, Jesus was able to open ears to hear and loose tongues to declare the glory of God. It was a new day indeed!

CONNECTIONS

Mark 7:1-23

The outbreak of a contagious disease, such as SARS, leads to measures designed to prevent its spread. In the case of SARS, thousands of people in the most affected areas began to wear masks as they went about their daily tasks, roadblocks were set up to prevent travel from one village in China to another, and those who were diagnosed with SARS were placed in quarantine. The measures differed according to whether one had the disease and needed to protect others from contracting it, or whether one was free of it and feared contact with those who had it. In the absence of a vaccine or other measures, the options were a mask or quarantine.

Jesus' response to the practices of the Pharisees, "there is nothing outside a person that by going in can defile, but the things that come out are what defile" (7:15), called for those whose religion required wearing spiritual masks to take measures to deal with the evil within them instead. The problem was not that they might be defiled; they were already corrupt to the core (*couer,* heart). Until they dealt with their own spiritual condition, they did not need masks; they needed to be quarantined so they would not pollute their communities. Like those concerned about the splinter in their neighbor's eye, they were unaware of the beam in their own (Matt 7:3-5; Luke 6:41-42).

A similar difference in perspective is reflected by the disciples' responses to Jesus' announcement that one of them would betray him. In John the disciples looked at one another, uncertain of whom he was speaking, and the Beloved Disciple asked Jesus, "Lord, who is it?" (John 13:21-25). In Luke the disciples asked him "which one of them it could be who would do this" (Luke 22:23). In Matthew and Mark, the disciples began to say one after the other, "Surely not I, Lord?" (Matt 26:22; Mark 14:19)—each one recognized that he might be capable of this heinous betrayal.

Jesus' challenge to Pharisaic understandings of purity and defilement directs our attention to the impurity that lies within each of us and to our awful capacity to pollute, abuse, and corrupt the communities around us with our "evil eyes" and wicked tongues. Like "Pig Pen" in the Peanuts cartoon, we carry our dirt wherever we go.

So what can we do? Characteristically, Jesus, whose preferred form of teaching was the parable, leaves it for the hearer to act once he or she has understood the parable or aphorism. At this point, we must look elsewhere for guidance. Jesus' argument turns on the distinction between heart and stomach; it is not what goes into the stomach but what comes out of the heart that defiles a person. The problem is one's "heart condition." Quoting Isaiah 29:13, Jesus said, "their hearts are far from me; in vain do they worship me" (7:7-7). On various occasions both Jesus' critics (3:5) and his disciples (6:52; 8:17) gave evidence that "their hearts were hardened," meaning that they could not or would not recognize how God was acting through Jesus. In contrast, one who has faith will not harbor skepticism (11:23; cf. 2:6, 8) but will love God with heart and soul, with mind and strength, and one's neighbor as one's self (12:30, 33). Such love will make one's heart pure and keep it from the kind of pollution that leads to the destructive tendencies and actions itemized in the list of vices in Mark 7:20-23. For most of us, it is past time that we paid attention to the condition of our hearts.

Mark 7:24-30

A short story titled "The Crumb" caught the author's attention initially because its central character is named Haber Hill Culpepper. The name evokes the character's pampered, privileged life—Virginia aristocracy, a fifty-seven-year-old retired law professor living with his aging mother, responding to her demanding whims, and spending his days reading Scripture, poetry, and philosophy as he seeks some divine disclosure.

Emily Dickinson

"Emily Dickinson (December 10, 1830 – May 15, 1886) was an American poet. Though virtually unknown in her lifetime, Dickinson has come to be regarded, along with Walt Whitman, as one of the two quintessential American poets of the 19th century. Dickinson lived an introverted and hermetic life. Although she wrote, at the last count, 1,789 poems, only a handful of them were published during her lifetime. All of these were published anonymously and some may have been published without her knowledge."

(Credit: http://en.wikipedia.org/wiki/Emily_Dickinson)

He is as close to royalty as Virginia aristocracy can get. On this particular day, his birthday, Haber Hill reads Emily Dickinson's poem:

God gave a loaf to every Bird—
But just a Crumb—to Me—
I dare not eat it—tho' I starve—
My poignant luxury—

. . . .

I wonder how the Rich—may feel—
An Indiaman—An Earl—
I deem that I—with but a Crumb—
Am Sovereign of them all—

Because it is his birthday, they invite the parson over for tea. Adele, the housekeeper, is working in the kitchen when they hear a clatter. When Haber Hill goes to investigate, he finds that she has broken the teapot and burned her foot. When he scolds her for being barefooted, the housekeeper replies, "But if I wore shoes when I cooked, the food wouldn't taste the same." Because it is obvious that she is in pain, Haber Hill asks where he could find something to put some water in, fills a plastic dishpan with cold water and ice cubes, and tells Adele to sit down. Every time he speaks, he feels that he is "emotionally all thumbs." After she has soaked her foot for a few minutes, he kneels in front of her and says, "Here, let's have a look," lifts her foot out of the pan, and cups it in his hand. It is a poor old workingwoman's foot. The toenails are brittle, yellow as old parchment paper. There is a large bunion at the side of the big toe and corns on the second and third toes. It has the coarse texture of an oyster shell.

Just at that moment, the parson comes in and says, "Ah, washing the disciples' feet, are we?" Later, Haber Hill reflects that he has never been cold or hungry or poor, and that instead of seeking something from God, as he always had, perhaps he should offer some prayer or sign that he does indeed know how fortunate he is. The story ends with Haber Hill realizing that in the act of washing the housekeeper's foot he has at last received his "but a Crumb"—not in his reading of philosophy and poetry but in caring for an old, working woman's hurt foot—and that if it is not a true epiphany, at least it is more than he deserved.[19]

In Matthew 25, Jesus tells the parable of the sheep and the goats. The determining question at the Judgment is not what your theology is or how many church committees you served on but whether you fed the hungry and clothed the poor: "As you did it not to the least of these, you did it not for me." The lesson of these Gospel texts came home to the author several years ago when he had the privilege of attending a small meeting of scholars concerned over Jewish-Christian relations.

Martin Hengel, a professor at Tübingen in Germany, told us how his father's factory had been seized by the Nazis, how as a teenager he had been sent to the eastern front to serve as an anti-aircraft gunner in the German army, and how he did not learn of the atrocities against the Jews until after the war. Directly across the table from him sat Professor Shemaryahu Talmon, from Israel. Talmon told us how difficult it had been for him to return to Frankfort, Germany, where he had grown up, and to be received with honor and esteem, because he remembered how it had been. As children going to school, the Jewish boys and girls walked in a group, with the girls on the inside for their protection. People ridiculed them and threw things at them. Then, he and his family were taken to a concentration camp in Poland. Near the camp lived some Polish miners, simple hard-working people who were called "Bibel Lesern" because they had grown up reading the Bible and had little formal education. Professor Talmon said that he had never known that Christians were not taught to hate Jews until some of the Bibel Lesern began to slip across the lines and into the camp at night to bring the Jewish prisoners bread from their own tables. They too believed that "even the little dogs" should get the crumbs that fell from their tables.

Mark 7:31-37

Gospel stories were preserved and told for a purpose. It was not just historical curiosity that led the evangelist to include the story of Jesus' healing of the deaf mute. It contains several embedded messages for the church: (1) Jesus worked among Gentiles also, therefore the Gentile mission is a legitimate extension of the church's mission; (2) the Gentile mission fulfills the redemptive purposes of God that are clear even among the Old Testament prophets (such as Isaiah); the mission of the church is to declare the glory of God to all people; (3) just as God empowered Jesus to heal the deaf mute, so God empowers the church on mission to bring hearing and speech to those who have never heard

Be Opened

the gospel or worshiped the Lord; (4) be zealous in sharing the good news of God's goodness and the gospel of Jesus Christ, in spite of opposition, prejudice, and efforts to silence you; and (5) sharing in God's mission in the world brings great joy when one sees ears, hearts, and minds opened and tongues loosed.

Note that Jesus did not just open the man's ears. Hearing, in the biblical sense, requires obedience, doing. The work would have been only half done if Jesus had enabled the man to hear but done nothing to allow him to speak. Nevertheless, there are many today who live as if that were their condition—they hear but they do not speak. Jesus' healing of the deaf mute ties the two together: his command "be opened," which addresses primarily his inability to hear, carries with it the effect of releasing his tongue so that he can speak. Perhaps those of us who hear but do not speak are like the blind man who could see, but not clearly (see 8:22-26). When we really understand the mission of the church as God's mission in the world, conducted through the church, then we too will be able to speak. To us he says still, groaning, "Ephphatha," be opened! [Be Opened]

NOTES

[1] Herbert Danby, *The Mishnah* (Oxford: Oxford University Press, 1933), 778.

[2] Martin Hengel, "Mk 7.3 *pygmē*: Der Geschichte einer exegetischen Aporie und der Versuch ihrer Lösung," *ZNW* 60 (1969): 182-98; S. M. Reynolds, "*pygmē* (Mark 7:3) as 'Cupped Hand,'" *JBL* 85 (1966): 87-88; Robert A. Guelich, *Mark 1–8:26* (WBC 34A; Dallas: Word, 1989), 364-65.

[3] Günther Bornkamm, "*presbys*," *TDNT* 6:661-62.

[4] Florentino García Martínez, *The Dead Sea Scrolls Translated* (trans. Wilfred G. E. Watson; Leiden: E. J. Brill, 1994), 6-7.

[5] C. E. B. Cranfield, *The Gospel according to St. Mark* (CGTC; Cambridge: Cambridge University Press, 1959), 241.

[6] BDAG, 141.

[7] Ibid., 178.

[8] Joel Marcus, *Mark 1–8* (AB 27; New York: Doubleday, 2000), 456.

[9] Lucilius, *Satires*, frag. 540-41, quoted by Gerd Theissen, *The Gospels in Context: Social and Political History in the Synoptic Tradition* (trans. Linda M. Maloney; Minneapolis: Fortress, 1991), 246.

[10] E.g., Guelich, *Mark 1–8:26*, 386-87.

[11] Danby, *The Mishnah*, 452.

[12] C. Clifton Black, *Mark: Images of an Apostolic Interpreter* (Columbia: University of South Carolina Press, 1994), 5.

[13] Theissen, *The Gospels in Context*, 243-45; Marcus, *Mark 1–8*, 472.

[14] Eduard Schweizer, *The Good News According to Mark* (trans. Donald H. Madvig; Atlanta: John Knox Press, 1970), 154; Howard Clark Kee, *Community of the New Age: Studies in Mark's Gospel* (Philadelphia: Westminster Press, 1977), 171.

[15] Cranfield, *The Gospel according to St. Mark*, 253-54; Marcus, *Mark 1–8*, 476.

[16] So John P. Meier, *A Marginal Jew: Rethinking the Historical Jesus* (New York: Doubleday, 1994), 2:712.

[17] Johannes Schneider, *"stenazō," TDNT* 7:600, 603.

[18] See the summaries of this debate in Guelich, *Mark 1–8:26*, 395-96, and Meier, *A Marginal Jew*, 2:759 n. 159.

[19] Sunny Rogers, "The Crumb," *New Stories from the South: The Year's Best 1988* (ed. Shannon Ravenel; Chapel Hill NC: Algonquin Books of Chapel Hill, 1988), 177-90.

OPENING EYES TO
RECOGNIZE THE MESSIAH

Mark 8:1-38

Mark 8 holds a strategic place in the literary structure of the Gospel. It contains a second feeding cycle, advances the theme of ministry among the Gentiles, and deepens the disciples' failure to comprehend what Jesus was doing. At the same time, the first half of the Gospel reaches its christological climax with Peter's confession at Caesarea Philippi, "You are the Messiah" (8:29).

The feeding of the 4,000 introduces the second feeding cycle:

A. Mark 6:35-7:37

1. Feeding of the 5,000 (6:35-44)

2. Crossing and Landing (6:45-56)

3. Controversy with the Pharisees about Defilement (7:1-23)

4. The Syrophoenician Woman (the children's bread) (7:24-30)

5. The Healing of the Deaf Mute (7:31-37)

B. Mark 8:1-26

1. Feeding of the 4,000 (8:1-9)

2. Crossing and Landing (8:10)

3. Controversy with the Pharisees about Signs (8:11-13)

4. The Mystery of the Loaves (the leaven of the Pharisees) (8:14-21)

5. The Healing of the Blind Man (8:22-26)[1]

The parallels are strongest in the two feedings (A1 and B1), but the parallels between the two healings (A5 and B5) have also been noted (see the commentary on 7:31-37). Between the first and the last stories in each cycle, one finds a crossing and landing, a controversy with the Pharisees, and a dialogue concerning bread. A reason for such duplication of sequence begins to emerge when one notices that the Gospel of John, which most scholars believe drew from an independent line of tradition, contains the same structure:[2]

Feeding the multitude	John 6:1-15	Mark 6:30-44	Mark 8:1-9
Sea crossing	John 6:16-21	Mark 6:45-56	Mark 8:10
	————(Walking on the sea)————		
Request for a Sign	John 6:25-34		Mark 8:11-13
Discussion about bread	John 6:35-59	(Mark 7:24-30)	Mark 8:14-21
Peter's confession	John 6:60-69		Mark 8:27-30
Passion theme; betrayal	John 6:70-71		Mark 8:31-33

This parallel structure becomes all the more striking in view of the fact that the feeding of the multitude is the only miracle found in all four Gospels. In these cycles we may have the earliest core of the Gospel traditions regarding Jesus' ministry in Galilee, and, significantly, they are informed by exodus motifs, with a feeding in the wilderness and crossing of the sea.

The retreat to Caesarea Philippi and Peter's confession that Jesus is the Christ (8:29) bring the first half of the Gospel to a close. Jesus' attention turns toward Jerusalem and preparing the disciples for the fate that awaits him there. At the end of this chapter, and introducing the next section of the Gospel, we find the first of Mark's three passion predictions (8:31; 9:31; 10:32-34) and the first of a set of three collections of teachings on discipleship (8:32-9:1; 9:33-37; 10:35-45).

COMMENTARY

The Feeding of the 4,000, 8:1-9

No change of setting introduces the second feeding, leading to the assumption that Jesus was still in a largely Gentile area. The assumption that this feeding involves a Gentile multitude on the eastern side of the Sea of Galilee, across from Dalmanutha (see 8:10), seems to be implied.

The similarities and differences between the feeding of the 4,000 and the earlier feeding of the 5,000 reveal interesting nuances in the account. Although crowds were present in Mark 7 (vv. 14, 17, 33), the adverb "again" is probably intended to remind the reader of the crowd at the first feeding (6:34, 45). One may also note the double reference to "a great crowd" in John 6:2 and 5. The narrator reports the problem: they had nothing to eat (*mē echontōn ti phagōsin*). In Mark 6, by contrast, they were "like sheep without a shepherd" (*mē echonta poimena*;

The Feeding of the Multitudes

Feeding of the multitudes, baskets of bread. Byzantine, 14th c. Mosaic in exonarthex, Hora Church (Kariye Camii), Istanbul, Turkey. (Credit: Erich Lessing / Art Resource, NY)

6:34). Again, Jesus had compassion on them (6:34; 8:2). In this instance Mark does not report that Jesus had been teaching the crowd, but we may assume so from the report that they had been with him for three days. The period of "three days" immediately reminds the Christian reader of the coming passion predictions and the time between the crucifixion and the resurrection of Jesus. While the phrase may indicate nothing more than a brief period to time (Hos 6:2), in a post-Easter confessional context it may have suggested overtones of the expected messianic banquet (Isa 25:6-10).

The setting suggests teachings on discipleship, or instructions for the church. The crowd had been with Jesus (cf. the role of a disciple in Mark 3:14), or literally "continuing" with him (cf. the theological use of the same verb in Acts 11:23; 13:43). They were in the wilderness, and the phrase "bread in the wilderness" in the disciples' question (8:4) clearly suggests connections with the exodus experience (note the repeated references to "the wilderness," symbolically the place of testing, in Exod 16:1-3). They had nothing to eat, they were far from home, and without something to eat they would faint "on the way" (a phrase Mark often uses to mean the "way" or path of discipleship [4:4, 15; 6:8; 8:27; 9:33-34; 10:32, 46, 52]). The verb "to faint" is also used elsewhere in the New Testament with the meaning to grow weary in doing good or slack in one's resolve or faithfulness (Gal 6:9; Heb 12:3, 5; cf. Deut 20:3; Prov 3:11). How can the church find sustenance for the journey? Where can one find provisions in the wilderness? How can ministry (feeding the hungry) take place in the wilderness? (8:4)

The note that many in the crowd had come "a great distance" (KJV "from far"; Gk. *apo makrothen*) resonates with descriptions of the Gentiles elsewhere, who were seen as far off, while Israel was near (Deut 28:49; 29:22; Josh 9:6; 1 Kgs 8:41; Ps 148:14; Acts 2:39; 22:21; Eph 2:13; so also the description of the prodigal son going to the "far" country, where he ends up tending swine, Luke 15:13). This detail in the description offers another reason for assuming that the feeding of the 4,000 is primarily a feeding of Gentiles, which may explain why Mark found it significant to include two similar feeding accounts— Jesus was now doing among Gentiles what he had earlier done among Jews.

The disciples' question, "How can one . . ." (*pothen toutous dynēsetai tis*), has overtones that anticipate Jesus' response to the disciples in 10:27, "For mortals it is impossible (*adynatan*), but not for God; for God all things are possible (*dynata*)." When Jesus asks the disciples how many loaves of bread they have, they answer, "seven."

Jesus initiates the action in this account (see 8:1, 5, 6; contrast Mark 6:35, where the disciples initiate the action). Jesus' actions and words in the various feeding accounts, moreover, are reported with remarkable consistency at this point, which makes the variations in the accounts all the more significant. In Mark 8 (and Matt 15:35 and 14:19), he orders the crowd to sit on the ground. In Mark 6 Jesus involves the disciples, instructing them to seat the crowd in groups. Jesus then took the loaves, gave thanks, broke them, and gave them to the disciples to distribute to the people. The difference in verbs in Mark 6 and 8 is significant: in Mark 6, Jesus looked up to heaven (compare 7:34) and "blessed" (*eulogēsen*) the bread and the fish; in Mark 8, Jesus "gave thanks" (*eucharistēsas*) for the bread only. This change of verbs probably reflects the influence of the practice of the Eucharist in the early church. The same verb (*eucharistēsas*) appears in 1 Corinthians 11:24 and Luke 22:19. The next two verbs complete Jesus' eucharistic act: he broke the loaves and gave them to the disciples (compare the parallel accounts and John 6:11 [in which he does not "break" the loaves], 1 Cor 11:24 [in which he does not "give" them], and Luke 24:30). The disciples, who have not been mentioned since 7:17, have an active role in this feeding (8:1, 4, 6), which makes their lack of comprehension about its meaning (see 8:14-21) all the more devastating. The fish are separated from the bread in this account and relegated to a secondary role (see [Diet of Fish]), which again probably reflects the influence of the observance of the Eucharist in the early church.[3] They are small fish, their number is not specified, and Mark returns to the alternative verb; Jesus "blessed" (*eulogēsas* rather than *eucharistēsas*) them.

The feeding is completed with a minimum of fanfare. The people "ate and were filled" (8:8, as in Matt 15:37 and the synoptic parallels of the feeding of the 5,000). Then, the disciples took up seven baskets of fragments. Those fed were about 4,000, and Jesus sent them home. The numbers have seemed to many interpreters to be significant. Is there a special meaning to the number 7 here, is the number 4,000 significant, and are the two connected? The number 7 is significant in other biblical contexts, but need not carry such special significance here. Interpreters have also noted that the 12 baskets of fragments following the feeding of the 5,000 and the 7 baskets of fragments following the feeding of the 4,000 correspond to the 12 disciples and the 7 Hellenists in Acts 6:1-6, but again the connection is elusive and presumes the evangelist's (or the tradition's) knowledge of Acts 6 or the tradition behind it. Moreover, the Hellenists in Acts 6 were not Gentiles but Greek-speaking Jews in Jerusalem. Robert Guelich suggests a more mundane but more likely solution: the 7 baskets of fragments mean that each of the 7 loaves produced a basket of fragments—1 basket per loaf.[4] The word for basket is different from the one used in Mark 6 and lacks the earlier term's symbolic connection with Jews (see the commentary on Mark 6:43), but this kind of basket could be large enough to hold a person (Acts 9:25). Neither are the associations between 4 or 4,000 and the Gentiles strong enough to be convincing. The Gentile character of this feeding is still evident, but it is based on the context, the geographical notices, and the comment that some of the people had come "a great distance" (see 8:3 and the commentary there).

Sea Crossings and Sign Seeking, 8:10-13

The next scene, a controversy with the Pharisees about signs, is framed by sea crossings. Following each of the accounts of a feeding, Jesus crosses the sea. The boat was introduced in the summary section in Mark 3:9 and was used in Mark 4, 5, and 6. In this instance, he and the disciples cross to the area of Dalmanutha—a name that does not occur elsewhere. Some manuscripts, therefore, harmonize the text with Matthew 15:39, which reads "Magadan," or "Magdala." [Dalmanutha]

The significance of the geographical notice lies not in the precise location of this obscure site but in the pattern of sea crossings in Mark.

Dalmanutha

"In 1970, when the shores of the Sea of Galilee were exceptionally low, it became possible to investigate several ancient anchorages below the modern surface of the lake. These were walled enclosures built of stone blocks in the water near the shore. There is one at Capernaum and another at Magdala, among others. A possible third is to be found N of and near Magdala and W of Capernaum. This may be ancient Dalmanutha. If so, Dalmanutha was a small anchorage, likely in the district of Magdala. On the other hand, it is also possible that the Aramaic word meant 'enclosure, anchorage' and came to be understood as a proper name. Thus the oral tradition may have had either '. . . the anchorage of the district of Magdala' or 'Dalmanutha of the district of Magdala.' There is no scholarly consensus."

James F. Strange, "Dalmanutha," *ABD* (New York: Doubleday, 1992), 2:4.

Jesus has been on the eastern side of the Sea of Galilee, in a Gentile area (see 7:31), but now crosses to the western side. As soon as he does so, he is confronted again by the Pharisees, who last appeared in the narrative in 7:1-13. In Mark's symbolic geography, when Jesus is on the western side of the Sea of Galilee, he is always among Jews. When he is on the eastern side, he is among Gentiles. The sea therefore becomes the symbolic barrier between the two, which Jesus crosses repeatedly as he announces the coming of the kingdom in Galilee.[5]

The Pharisees begin to argue with Jesus (cf. 1:27; 9:10, 14, 16; 12:28), challenging him to do a sign "from heaven." In Mark 13, the disciples ask to know the sign that the destruction of Jerusalem is at hand (13:4), and Jesus warns them that false messiahs and false prophets will do "signs and wonders" (13:22). The request for a sign "from heaven" probably meant that they were asking for a sign of unequivocal meaning, not a healing, for there were other healers, but something that clearly demonstrated Jesus' access to divine power. This interpretation is supported by the occurrence of the divine passive in Jesus' response: "no sign will be given to this generation" means "God will not give this generation a sign" (8:12).

The authentication of prophets by signs was a matter of dispute in ancient Israel (Deut 13:1-3; 18:18-22; 2 Kgs 20:8-11; Isa 7:10-14). The Pharisees asked Jesus for a sign, testing or tempting (*peirazontes*) him, which evokes other contexts. Following the feeding in the Gospel of John, the crowd asked for a sign, reminding Jesus that Moses had given the people bread in the wilderness, and Jesus answered that it was not Moses who had given them bread "from heaven" (John 6:30-32). The sequence of feeding and testing in the wilderness is rooted in Exodus 16–17, where the people quarreled with Moses, and he answered, "Why do you quarrel with me? Why do you test the LORD?" (Exod 17:2). So Moses called the place Massa and Meribah, "because the Israelites quarreled and tested the LORD" (Exod 17:7; cf. Deut 6:16; Ps 95:7-11). Testing God later became the trademark of Satan, the tempter (Job 1:6-12; Zech 3:1-2). Satan tempted Jesus in the wilderness (Mark 1:13), and Matthew calls him "the tempter" (4:3; cf. 1 Thess 3:5). By testing Jesus, asking for a sign, ironically just after Jesus has fed the multitude in the wilderness, the Pharisees place themselves in the role of the faithless Israelites who tested God and were therefore forbidden to enter the promised land: "'They are a people whose hearts go astray, and they do not regard my ways.' Therefore in my anger I swore, 'They shall not enter my rest'" (Ps 95:10-11) (see [Peirazein, To "Tempt" or "Test," in Mark]).

The focus of this section, of course, is Jesus' response in v. 12. The word for groaning or sighing occurs only here in the New Testament, but it is an intensive form of the verb that occurred in 7:34. Here, it seems to express his emotion, disappointment or anger, in response to the Pharisees' demand for a sign (cf. 1:41; 3:5). In context, their quarreling with Jesus stands in marked contrast to the faith Jesus encountered in the Syrophoenician woman and those who brought the deaf mute to Jesus. Jesus' rhetorical question brands the Pharisees as "this generation," which he later describes as "adulterous and sinful" (8:38) and "faithless" (9:19; cf. 13:30; Deut 32:5, 20). The echoes from Deuteronomy again connect Jesus' response to the Pharisees with the exodus background, for the Lord swore: "Not one of these—not one of this evil generation—shall see the good land I swore to give to your ancestors" (Deut 1:35). Alternatively, the saying may evoke allusions to the faithless in Noah's day (as in Matt 24:37-38; Luke 17:26-27; 1 Pet 3:20; 2 Pet 2:5), but the exodus typology is much stronger in the Gospels than the allusions to Noah.

The solemn formula, "Truly I tell you," in which "truly" translates the word *amēn*, occurs thirty-one times in Matthew, thirteen times in Mark, and six times in Luke. John always uses the double amen, "Truly, truly, I tell you"—twenty-five times. There is no parallel to this formula outside the New Testament, and within the New Testament this usage is confined to the sayings of Jesus. The formula may have been connected with prophetic utterances, and served to validate the truth of the pronouncement that followed. See the commentary on 3:28 above. In the present context this solemn formula is followed by another, a curse formula found in the Old Testament and Jewish writings (Num 32:11; Deut 1:35; 2 Kgs 6:31; Ps 95:11), but only here in the New Testament. It is elliptical, and literally it would be translated, "If a sign shall be given to this generation, [then may]. . . ." The omitted apodosis would contain a curse on oneself.

The saying in Mark 8:12 occurs in Q in a different form: "An evil and adulterous generation asks for a sign, but no sign will be given to it except the sign of the prophet Jonah" (Matt 12:39//Luke 11:29).[6] Matthew interprets Jonah as a foreshadowing of Jesus' three days in the tomb, but Luke says nothing of this interpretation. For Luke the sign of Jonah was his call to repentance, and no other sign would be given to that generation except Jesus' call for them to hear the word of God and obey it (Luke 11:28). The thought is similar, if more absolute, in Mark. Jesus himself and his declaration of the kingdom is the only sign that generation would receive.

Because they rejected him, there was no further recourse for them. Ironically, his action can be seen as a sign: Jesus left them and went across to the other side of the lake once more. From this point forward, Jesus devotes himself to his disciples, and he will soon leave Galilee and make his way to the fate that awaits him in Jerusalem. At least symbolically, therefore, this moment in the Gospel parallels Paul's repeated declaration in Acts, "It was necessary that the word of God should be spoken first to you. Since you reject it and judge yourselves to be unworthy of eternal life, we are now turning to the Gentiles" (Acts 13:46; cf. 18:6; 28:28). Nevertheless, the focus in the coming scenes and chapters is on Jesus' work with his disciples rather than the Gentiles.

The Lesson of the Leaven and the Loaves, 8:14-21

Jesus uses the sea crossings as teaching moments in the Gospel of Mark. On the first sea crossing, Jesus stilled the storm and challenged the disciples, "Why are you afraid? Have you still no faith?" (4:40). The return journey is uneventful (5:21). After feeding the 5,000, Jesus sent the disciples on ahead, then came to them walking on the water. The second sea-crossing scene ends with the evangelist's comment, "And they were utterly astounded, for they did not understand about the loaves, but their hearts were hardened" (6:52). The related themes of teaching, loaves, and faith are present again in this third sea-crossing scene.

The scene begins somewhat abruptly and awkwardly with the report that the disciples had forgotten to bring bread. Even so, they had one loaf with them in the boat (8:14). The relationship between the two parts of this verse has raised questions about the meaning of the reference to "one loaf." One's first thought might well be that Mark is preparing to narrate a third feeding miracle—one loaf for the disciples and Jesus. Others see a christological or eucharistic significance in this awkward qualification of the initial assertion that they had no bread for their journey.[7] The eucharistic overtones are further strengthened if the reference to the boat is a symbolic allusion to the church (see [The Ship as the Church]), but the discussion of the loaves and the feeding that follows is less pointedly eucharistic.

Verse 15 breaks the continuity between vv. 14 and 16, as Jesus warns the disciples to beware of "the leaven" of the Pharisees and of Herod. A similar warning appears in Luke 12:1. Throughout Mark, the Pharisees are critical of Jesus, and the Herodians appear only in association with the Pharisees (cf. 3:6; 12:13). Earlier, when Herod heard of the healing being done by Jesus' disciples, he concluded that John the Baptist had been raised (6:14-16). Leaven is the old dough that is used to leaven the new. It was often associated with corruption and evil (1 Cor 5:6-8; Gal 6:9).[8] The meaning of the image may therefore have been: "Beware of the corrupting influence of the Pharisees and of Herod." Neither one understood who Jesus was or what his works meant. The warning is

The Leaven of the Pharisees and of Herod

Commentators have offered the following interpretations of the leaven in this passage:

"A false messianic hope and/or a narrow nationalism" (Ernst Lohmeyer, 157).

"The figure of leaven thus describes the disposition to believe only if signs which compel faith are produced" (William Lane, *Mark*, 281).

"In short, the 'leaven of the Pharisees and the leaven of Herod' is unbelief" (Guelich, *Mark 1–8:26*, 423).

"Jesus, then, is warning his disciples against being infected by the same evil impulse that has hardened the hearts of his enemies, the Pharisees and Herodians" (Marcus, *Mark 1–8*, 510).

Robert A. Guelich, *Mark 1–8:26* (WBC 34A; Dallas, Texas: Word, 1989); William L. Lane, *The Gospel according to Mark* (NICNT; Grand Rapids: Wm. B. Eerdmans, 1974); Ernst Lohmeyer, *Das Evangelium des Markus* (Meyer Kommentar 2; Göttingen: Vandenhoeck & Ruprecht, 1963); Joel Marcus, *Mark 1–8* (AB 27; New York: Doubleday, 2000).

---

appropriate, at least as an anticipation of the lack of understanding the disciples demonstrate in the ensuing conversation. Commentators have sought in various ways to render a more precise interpretation on the figurative significance of the leaven in this passage. [The Leaven of the Pharisees and of Herod]

The report that the disciples were debating among themselves echoes Mark's report of the scribes debating Jesus' words to the paralytic (see *dialogizomai* in 2:6, 8; 9:33; and 11:31). It signals yet again their lack of understanding. The report casts the disciples in the role of helpless stooges. Either they disregard or completely miss the seriousness of Jesus' warning and continue to discuss the fact that they had forgotten to bring bread, or, less likely, their response to Jesus' warning is that they need not be concerned about "the leaven" of the Pharisees and Herod because they have no bread at all.

As on other occasions, Jesus is aware of what they were discussing (cf. 2:8; 5:30; 6:2-4; 9:33-35). This time he responds directly to their immediate situation—that they had no bread—but his response addresses five pointed questions to the disciples that call for them to recognize their own danger of falling into the lack of understanding and hardheartedness of the Pharisees and Herod. First, their preoccupation with lack of bread reflects an astounding lack of reflection on their own experience of the two recent feedings. Do they not yet "perceive or understand"? The verb to "perceive" was used in Jesus' challenge to the disciples in 7:18, and the verb to "understand" occurs in 4:9, 12; 6:52; 7:14, and at the end of this scene (8:21). In 4:12 it occurs in the quotation of the pronouncement of judgment in Isaiah 6:9-10, and in 6:52 the disciples' lack of understanding "about the loaves" leads Jesus to question whether their hearts have been hardened. The question, "are your hearts hardened?" is particularly appropriate in light of the exodus typology of the wilderness feedings; it evokes memories of Pharaoh's hardness of heart in Exodus (7:3, 13, 22; 8:15, 19, 32) and Israel's hardness of heart in response to the prophets (Jer 7:24; 9:14; 13:10; 16:12). Hardness of heart means willful rejection of God's redemptive work, or the inability to grasp the significance of God's activity (see Isa 6:10; Mark 3:5). The meaning of having one's heart hardened is explained parenthetically by the allusion to Scripture in v. 18. In this instance, hardness of heart means dullness or lack of comprehension.

Although the question resonates disturbingly with Jesus' words about those "outside" to whom everything is in riddles (4:10-12), the quotation here is not from Isaiah 6:9-10 but from Jeremiah 5:21 and/or Ezekiel 12:2 (cf. Isa 42:18-21). In beautiful literary artistry, the healing miracles that bracket this section report Jesus' power to bring sight to the blind (8:22-26) and hearing to the deaf (7:31-37). By reporting Jesus' question to the disciples, with this scriptural allusion, Mark ties together the healing miracles, the figurative meaning of opening eyes and ears, and the obtuseness or hardheartedness of the disciples. The disciples are in grave danger of being so hardhearted that they become like the Pharisees and Herod, but the bracketing healing miracles remind the reader that Jesus can bring sight even to the blind and hearing even to the deaf. The implication is that there is hope for the disciples, regardless of how little they have grasped to this point.

Jesus follows with a further question about the feedings, suggesting that the feedings are an important key to further understanding. Just as Jesus had said, "Do you not understand this parable [the parable of the sower]? Then how will you understand all the parables?" (4:13), so here he seems to be saying, "Do you not understand the feedings? Then how will you understand all the miracles?" Jesus asks the disciples to recall the details, the exact quantities involved in the two feedings, and even uses the distinct words for basket in the two accounts (*kophinous* and *spyridōn*, 8:19-20). The question of whether the numbers are symbolic has been discussed in the commentary on each feeding episode. If the numbers do not carry symbolism in the feedings, then it is unlikely that they do so here. The significance is not in the symbolic meaning of the numbers but in Jesus' repeated demonstrations of God's bounty and provision for the needs of the people. God provides in times of need and crisis, even more than is needed. In view of the announcement of the coming of the kingdom of God at the outset of Jesus' ministry (1:14-15), one need not find eschatological overtones in the numbers twelve and seven to agree with Joel Marcus's conclusion, "What the Pharisees and Herod do not realize, then, and what the disciples are in danger of forgetting, is that in Jesus God is bringing the new age into being."[9] The disciples had eyes but did not see and ears but did not hear. As William Lane observes, they knew the right answers but still did not understand: "The disciples remembered the facts perfectly and responded to Jesus' questions without hesitation. Nevertheless, they failed to understand the significance of what had taken place before their eyes."[10] Jesus' final question is both damning and hopeful: "Do you not yet understand?" (8:21). What more could he do? Is the twice-given miracle of feeding not amply clear? On the other hand, the qualifier "yet" cuts both forward and backward and holds forth the possibility that the disciples may yet understand. [Seeing, Hearing, and Understanding]

Seeing, Hearing, and Understanding

"You have seen all that the LORD did before your eyes in the land of Egypt . . . the signs, and those great wonders. But to this day the LORD has not given you a mind to understand, or eyes to see, or ears to hear." (Deut 29:2-4)

Cited by C. Myers, *Binding the Strong Man: A Political Reading of Mark's Story of Jesus* (Maryknoll NY: Orbis, 1988), 225; and Joel Marcus, *Mark 1–8* (AB 27; New York: Doubleday, 2000), 513.

Healing the Blind Man, 8:22-26

The healing of the blind man at Bethsaida occupies a significant position in the Gospel, bringing to a close the third large section of the first half of the Gospel (6:6b–8:26), marking the end of the second feeding cycle (8:1-26), standing as the second of the twin healing narratives (along with 7:31-37), and serving as the first blind man healing, which complements the healing of the blind Bartimaeus (10:46-52). The structural parallels in the beginning and ending of these three large sections of the first half of the Gospel have often been noted:

Summary statement	1:4-15	3:7-12	6:6b
Calling/sending disciples	1:16-20	3:13-19	6:7-13
Conclusion (foreshadowing rejection)	3:1-6	6:1-6a	8:14-21

The scenes of rejection at the end of each of these sections move progressively from rejection by the authorities (3:1-6, which marks the end of Jesus' conflict with the authorities in 2:1–3:6), Jesus' hometown (6:1-6, which marks the end of a section that deals with the distinction between insiders and outsiders, in 3:20–6:6), and finally Jesus' disciples (8:14-21, which picks up the theme of the disciples' hardness of heart that appears in 6:52 and 7:17-18 in preparation for the concentration on the disciples' lack of understanding in 8:27–10:52). This next section is framed by the two accounts of the healing of a blind man (8:22-26 and 10:46-52). For the parallel structure of the two feeding cycles, see the introduction to Mark 8 above, and for the parallels with Mark 7:31-37 see the commentary on that scene.

Like its twin (7:31-37), this healing begins with the report of Jesus' travel to a new location. This time, he and the disciples sail across the Sea of Galilee, from Dalmanutha to Bethsaida, probably a journey from the southwest side of the lake to a location near its tributary at the northern end of the lake. [Bethsaida]

Bethsaida

"Bethsaida was a fishing village located on the east side of the
Jordan, two kilometers from where it flows into the Sea of Galilee.
Josephus tells us that Philip had recently rebuilt Bethsaida and renamed it
Julias: 'He [Philip] also raised the village of Bethsaida on Lake Gennesaritis
to the status of city by adding residents and strengthening the fortifications.
He named it after Julia, the emperor's daughter' (*Ant.* 18.28; LCL 9:25). . . .
Debate as to the exact location of Bethsaida continued until recently with
three sites in contention: et-Tell, a prominent hill two and a half kilometers
north of the lake; khirbet el-Araj, at the edge of the lake about a thousand
meters east of the current river bed; and khirbet el-Mesadiyeh, a ruin one
kilometer southeast of el-Araj that is too small to have been a city.
Excavations in 1987 revealed only one level of occupation (fourth to fifth c.
AD) at el-Araj, leaving et-Tell as the only reasonable site for Bethsaida."

R. Alan Culpepper, *John the Son of Zebedee: The Life of a Legend* (Columbia: University of
South Carolina Press, 1994), 15–16; cf. Heinz-Wolfgang Kuhn and Rami Arav, "The Bethsaida
Excavations: Historical and Archaeological Approaches," in *The Future of Early Christianity: Essays
in Honor of Helmut Koester* (ed. Birger A. Pierson; Minneapolis: Fortress Press, 1991), esp. 87–90;
and Rami Arav and John J. Rosseau, "Elusive Bethsaida Recovered," *The Fourth R* 4 (1991): 1–4.

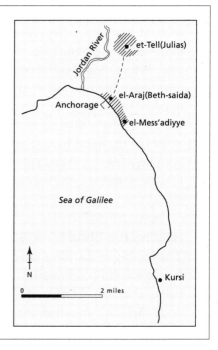

The phrases "they brought to him" (*kai pherousin autō*) and "they
begged him" (*kai parakalousin auton hina*) are the same in 7:32 and
8:22. For the role of the unnamed friends, see the commentary on
7:32. In this instance the reference to laying hands on the man ("to
touch him") is less specific than in 7:32, but it is clear nevertheless that
they are asking Jesus to heal the blind man. Because the man cannot
see, Jesus leads him out of the village. This action again parallels Jesus'
taking the deaf mute aside (7:33), and both may be connected to the
secrecy motif in Mark, which is explicit in the command to secrecy in
7:36 and may be implied by Jesus' order that the man not go back to
the village in 8:26. In both of these healing stories Jesus spits. In this
instance he spits into the man's eyes, which is delicately translated by
the NRSV as "when he had put saliva on his eyes" (8:23) and lays his
hands on him (as in 1:41; 5:23; 6:2, 5; 7:32; 8:25).

The distinctive feature of this healing story is that it is the only
miracle in the Gospels that is not immediately successful. This, along
with the references to Jesus spitting, may explain why both Matthew
and Luke omit this story and the healing of the deaf mute. The man
recovers his sight in stages. There is no parallel to the Aramaic "*ephphatha*" in 7:34. Instead, Jesus asks the man if he can see anything. The
use of the Greek particle (*ei*) to introduce a direct question is not
typical of Classical Greek but is common in the Septuagint, where it
probably reflects the use of the Hebrew "*h*" to introduce a question.[11]
Such devices were needed because question marks had not yet been
developed. Five different verbs for "to see" occur in this scene. In

response to Jesus' question, the man "looked up" (the same verb is used in 10:51, where it means Bartimaeus regained his sight). The grammar of the man's response has challenged the copyists, some of whom altered the text, and commentators, some of whom have suggested mistranslation of the earlier Aramaic. At best, the man's statement is elliptical, meaning, "I see people, because I see [something] like trees walking."

John Meier comments on the "Janus-like quality" of this story;[12] it looks both backward and forward. Janus was the god of gates and doorways in Roman mythology. The man can see, but not clearly. In this state, he reflects the condition of the disciples, who follow Jesus but do not understand. They are on the way from blindness to sight, but they do not yet see clearly. The story stands appropriately between Jesus' warning to the disciples about their blindness in 8:14-21 and Peter's confession in 8:27-29 that reflects not clear sight but a beginning at least. Although we may presume that the disciples will eventually understand clearly (see 16:7; 13:9), they will not really understand who Jesus is until after the resurrection. As followers of Jesus, they also serve as stand-ins for the readers, who understand something but do not yet grasp fully the good news Mark writes to convey to them—and to us.

The blind man, like the disciples and the readers, requires a second touch. Jesus again laid his hands on the man's eyes, and this time he "looked intently," his sight was restored, and he could see clearly. The word for "clearly" (*tēlaugōs*) is the adverbial form of the adjective that means literally "far-shining" and can be used metaphorically for intellectual understanding.[13] Both the adverb and the reference to "everything" emphasize the successful effect of the second touch. The reference to everything may also echo the occurrence of "everything" in 7:37, "He has done everything well," which in turn is an allusion to Genesis 1:31. In this scene, however, there is no response to the miracle. Jesus sends the man home (as in 5:19-20), admonishing him not to return to the village.

Peter's Confession at Caesarea Philippi, 8:27-30

Peter's confession that Jesus is the Christ brings the first half of the Gospel to a climax. In the first verse of the Gospel, the reader is told that Jesus is "the Christ, the Son of God" (1:1—see the commentary on this verse). Throughout the first half, however, Jesus' identity has been recognized only by the voice from heaven at Jesus' baptism, which may have been audible only to Jesus (1:11), and by the demons (1:24; 3:11; 5:7). The scribes from Jerusalem said that he had Beelzebul (3:22). The people of Jesus' hometown asked, "Is not this the carpenter?" (6:3).

When Herod heard of the healings being done by Jesus' disciples, and that the people were speculating that Jesus was John the Baptist redivivus, or Elijah, or one of the prophets, he declared that Jesus was John the Baptist (6:14-16). The disciples, on the other hand, have asked, "Who then is this, that even the wind and the sea obey him?" (4:41), and they have failed to understand the parables (4:13; 7:17), the walking on the water (6:52), and the feedings (6:52; 8:14-21). Like the blind man of Bethsaida, they are blind to Jesus' identity. Jesus' conversation with the disciples on the way to Caesarea Philippi takes up the question of his identity, and for the first time their blindness begins to abate. As if in answer to Jesus' question, "Do you not yet understand?" (8:21), Peter, answering for the disciples, says, "You are the Messiah" (8:29).[14] As the exchange between Jesus and Peter following the confession shows, like the blind man following Jesus' first touch, Peter sees,

---

Caesarea Philippi

Sacred centers were located in the area of Caesarea Philippi from antiquity, as the Canaanite names Baal-gad (Josh 11:17; 12:7; 13:5) and Baal-hermon (Judg 3:3; 1 Chr 5:23) indicate. The surroundings were dramatic—a cave and a pool of water located on the slopes of Mount Hermon, on a terrace 1,150 feet above sea level. The nature god Pan was worshiped there, and miracles were associated with the place (Eusebius, *Ecclesiastical History*, 7.17). Its history may be outlined as follows:

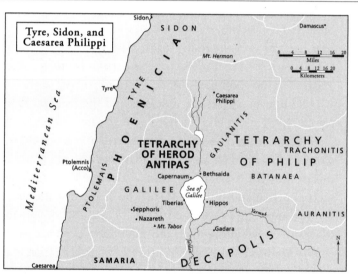

2d century BC—The site, called Paneion, was the scene of a significant battle in which Antiochus the Great defeated the Egyptian army and took control of Palestine (Polybius 16.18.2).

20 BC—Caesar Augustus gave the area to Herod the Great, "and when he [Herod] returned home after escorting Caesar to the sea, he erected to him a very beautiful temple of white stone in the territory of Zenodorus, near the place called Paneion. In the mountains here there is a beautiful cave, and below it the earth slopes steeply to a precipitous and inaccessible depth, which is filled with still water, while above it there is a very high mountain. Below the cave rise the sources of the river Jordan. It was this most celebrated place that Herod further adorned with the temple which he consecrated to Caesar" (Josephus, *Ant.* 15.363-64; LCL 8:175-77; cf. Josephus, *J.W.*, 3:509-14).

4 BC—At Herod's death, this area was passed to his son, Herod Philip (4 BC–AD 34), who enlarged the city and named it Caesarea. The name Caesarea Philippi was used to distinguish it from other Caesareas.

AD 66–70—Caesarea Philippi was used as a retreat for the Roman general Vespasian and Titus, and the latter held a celebration there at the end of the Jewish Revolt (Josephus, *J.W.* 3.444; 7.23-24).

Emil Schürer, *The History of the Jewish People in the Age of Jesus Christ (175 B.C.–A.D. 135)* (rev. and ed. Geza Vermes et al.; Edinburgh: T. & T. Clark, 1979), 2:169–71; John Kusko, "Caesarea Philippi," *ABD* 1:803.

but not clearly. He does not yet fully grasp who Jesus is or what his role will be.

Like other recent scenes, this one begins with the report of Jesus' travel to a new location (cf. 7:24, 31; 8:22). In this instance, however, the location may be significant because the confession that occurs there stands in sharp contrast to its history and its current associations. Caesarea Philippi was a center for the worship of false gods[15] and had more recently been dedicated to the honor of Caesar.[16] [Caesarea Philippi] Mark's reference to "the villages of Caesarea Philippi" (8:27) is precise because it means not only the villages in the area of Caesarea Philippi but the villages under the administrative control of Caesarea Philippi.[17]

The motif of "the way" becomes prominent at this point. It has perhaps been foreshadowed by earlier references (1:2-3; 4:4, 15; 6:8; 8:3), but the events of the next two chapters (Mark 9–10) take place on "the way" to Jerusalem and the cross that awaits Jesus there (9:33-34; 10:17, 32, 46, 52; 11:8; 12:14). "The way" becomes symbolically the path of discipleship, self-sacrifice, and suffering servanthood. Ethical teachings regarding the "two ways" were common (1QS 3.13-4.26; 9.18; Didache 1-6), and early readers of the Gospel may also have known that before the followers of Jesus were called Christians they were known as "followers of the way" (Acts 9:2; 18:25; 19:9, 23; 22:4; 24:14, 22).

In this politically and thematically significant setting, Jesus asks the disciples who the people say he is. In an ancient Near Eastern culture, one's identity was determined in community. One looked to significant others, not inward, to find one's identity.[18] Nevertheless, one need not assume that Jesus does not know who he is and is trying to find out from the disciples, because the voice from heaven at his baptism definitively declared, "You are my son" (1:11). The secrecy motif in Mark also implies that Jesus knows who he is and tries to keep his identity a secret until it can be understood in light of the cross (9:9). On the contrary, Jesus is once again testing and teaching the disciples, taking an opportune moment to prod them one step further along the path of understanding. Simultaneously, of course, the evangelist moves the reader, who both identifies with the disciples and watches them from the elevated position of the inside knowledge disclosed by the superscript in Mark 1:1, the divine voice in 1:11, and the narrator's comments in passages such as 3:7-12 and 6:52. Having heard who Jesus is and seen and heard (through the evangelist) what Jesus did and said, the reader is ready to identify with the confession of Jesus as the Messiah.

William Lane observed that in Mark, "the term 'men' is usually shaded to mean those from whom revelation remains veiled."[19] Jesus calls the first disciples to be "fishers of men," to gather those who need to be drawn into the kingdom of God (1:17). In the quotation of Isaiah 29:13 in Mark 7:7, "human precepts" (literally, precepts of men) are said to be vain, and the tradition of men is set over against the commandment of God (7:8). When Jesus is betrayed into the hands of men, they will kill him (9:31). Men cannot bring about salvation, but God can (10:27). Finally, human and divine authority is juxtaposed in the question about John's baptism in 11:30. Given this pattern, the question Jesus asks the disciples is already framed in such a way as to imply that the answers will be false, or partial at best.

In fact, the answers the disciples report rehearse the speculation that the evangelist reports in Mark 6, where the implication seems to be that these were the rumors Herod heard:

6:14	John the Baptist	8:28a
6:15a	Elijah	8:28b
6:15b	a prophet, like one of the prophets of old	8:28c

Although readers of the Gospel naturally regard these answers as the groping speculation of those who are still blind, they already signal that the role of Jesus was extraordinary. John is introduced in the opening verses of the Gospel as the one about whom the prophet Isaiah wrote (1:2-3), who would prepare the way of the Lord. Herod claims that "the powers are at work" in Jesus because he is John who has been raised from the dead (6:14). In Matthew, Jesus declares that "among those born of women no one has arisen greater than John the Baptist" (11:11), and identifies him with the expected Elijah (11:14). Luke, on the other hand, elevates Jesus by praising John and then holding Jesus as one greater than John (Luke 1:15-17). In the Gospel of John, John the Baptist is a true witness to Jesus (John 1:29-34; 3:28-30; 10:41). Elijah was the foremost of the prophets, and the Old Testament closes with the announcement that Elijah will come again "before the great and terrible day of the LORD comes" (Mal 4:5) [Elijah]; cf. [Elijah's Coming] Each of the Gospels develops the connection between John the Baptist and Elijah in its own way. Matthew explicitly claims that John fulfilled the role of Elijah (Matt 17:10-13), while John seems to rely on a source that denied the connection in order to allow Jesus to fulfill that expectation also (John 1:21, 25).[20] Elijah returns to the

Elijah

J. Louis Martyn summarizes the expectations concerning Elijah in the Jewish sources as follows: "In the traditions about his eschatological coming, Elijah is expected to do many things, such as make peace, whether within families or in the whole world; reassemble the members of the people who have been taken away; determine which are the genuine Israelites, thus, re-establishing the purity of corpus Israel; restore to Israel the manna, the sprinkling water, and the anointing oil; raise the dead, thus vanquishing death as he once vanquished the prophets of Baal."

Louis Martyn, "'We Have Found Elijah,'" in *The Gospel of John in Christian History* (New York: Paulist Press, 1978), 18.

Gospel narrative at two climactic moments, the transfiguration and the death of Jesus (9:4-5, 11-13; 15:35-36).

The reference to "one of the prophets" is vague, yet still connects Jesus with the tradition of the prophets. To say that Jesus was a prophet, however, was to make a significant eschatological claim because it was widely held that the spirit of prophecy had been quenched and would not return to Israel until the coming of the end times. When the Maccabees retook Jerusalem during the Maccabean revolt, they tore down the altar that had been defiled by the Gentiles and "stored the stones in a convenient place on the temple hill until a prophet should come to tell what to do with them" (1 Macc 4:46). The Essenes and others looked forward to the coming of a prophet, sometimes identified as the prophet like Moses (1QS 9.11; see Deut 18:15, 18). Similarly, *4 Ezra* 2:18 promises the return of the prophets Isaiah and Jeremiah. The recognition that Jesus was a prophet (6:4), while inadequate from a Christian perspective, would still have carried with it significant eschatological implications.

In the earlier context (Mark 6:14-16) this sequence of conjectures about Jesus' identity sets up Herod's declaration, "John, whom I beheaded, has been raised" (6:16). Here, it adds drama to Jesus' turning the question to his disciples. If the earlier question implied that the response would be false or inadequate, the contrast, literally, "but you, who do you say that I am?" challenges the disciples to be more perceptive than others.

Peter answers without hesitation, "You are the Messiah." Peter is called Simon until Jesus gives him the name "Peter" at the appointment of the Twelve (3:16; see 1:16, 29-30, 36). Thereafter he is called Peter (5:37; 8:32; 9:2, 5, etc.). Peter's role as spokesman for the disciples and foil for Jesus begins with this scene and continues at the transfiguration (9:5), in Peter's question about rewards for the disciples (10:28), in the cursing of the fig tree (11:21), in the prophecy of Peter's denial of Jesus (14:29), and at the Garden of Gethsemane (14:37).

Peter confesses that Jesus is the Messiah, the "Anointed One." In the Old Testament, kings and priests were anointed. The most frequent references are to the anointing of a king, especially David. Oil was poured from a horn or vessel on the head of the person being anointed (1 Sam 10:1; 16:13; 1 Kgs 1:39; 2 Kgs 9:3, 6). The promise that the house of David would rule over Israel forever (2 Sam 7:11-16; Isa 55:3) led to the expectation of a coming Davidic king (Isa 9:6-7; 11:1; Jer 23:5; cf. 4Q174 3.11-12). As the *Psalms of Solomon* written in the first century BC confirm, Israel's hope for the future often included the coming of a Messiah, a king who would free Israel from bondage:

> Undergird him with the strength to destroy the unrighteous rulers,
>   to purge Jerusalem from gentiles . . .
> to destroy the unlawful nations with the word of his mouth.
> (*Pss. Sol.* 17:22, 24; cf. CD 19.10-11)

This warrior king would be the anointed one, the Messiah:

> And he will be a righteous king over them, taught by God.
> There will be no unrighteousness among them in his days,
>   for all shall be holy,
>   and their king shall be the Lord Messiah. (*Pss. Sol.* 17:32)[21]

By the first century, however, there were various messianic expectations. The Essenes at Qumran expected a royal messiah, a priestly messiah, and a prophet (1QS 9.11; 1Qsa 2.11-17). In the Gospel of Mark the term is used as a messianic title (9:41; 12:35; 13:21; 14:61; 15:32), but it is little wonder that Jesus himself seems to have avoided claiming this politically charged title. Because the messianic sense of "the anointed one" derives from Jewish eschatological expectations, the term did not have the same currency among Gentiles, for whom it would have resonated with the claims of the Roman emperors. In Paul's writings, therefore, one finds common use of the term almost as a second name for Jesus: Jesus Christ. Walter Grundmann explains:

> The Gentile churches formed as a result of Paul's ministry, however, do not take this in the same way as the apostle. For them the Messiah-Christ is not related to the divine promise which makes Him God's supreme proxy. When *Christos* is used with the name Jesus they regard it as a double name. Caesar Augustus is a parallel. He styled himself Imperator Caesar Augustus. *Kyrios Iēsous Christos* has a similar ring.[22]

In a sense, therefore, while Jesus gives Simon the name by which we know him (Peter), Peter gives Jesus the name by which he is commonly confessed (Christ).[23] In Mark the title is used in the absolute, "the Messiah," whereas Luke has "the Messiah of God" (9:20) and Matthew, "the Messiah, the Son of the living God" (16:16).

In contrast to Jesus' response in Matthew, in Mark and Luke Jesus neither accepts nor rejects Peter's confession. His response is a stern command that they tell no one (8:30). Elsewhere in Mark, the evangelist uses this verb to describe Jesus' commands to the demons (1:25; 3:12; 9:25), the storm at sea (4:39), and Peter (8:33). The command does not relate specifically to the confession "Messiah" but is a comprehensive command not to say anything to anyone about him.

The First Passion Prediction, 8:31-33

Peter's confession that Jesus is the Messiah serves as both a conclusion to the first half of the Gospel and an introduction to the second half. Everything changes. Jesus immediately begins to prepare the disciples for the journey to Jerusalem and his coming death and resurrection. The distinctive feature of the coming section is the threefold repetition of Jesus' "passion predictions," his announcement to the disciples that they are going to Jerusalem, and that he will be rejected there, crucified, and raised on the third day. These predictions have been the focus of a great deal of debate. If Jesus predicted his death and resurrection repeatedly and so clearly, why were the disciples unprepared for these events? Were Jesus' warnings more veiled, while the evangelist sharpened them as part of his theme of the disciples' blindness and lack of understanding? One may also ask what the term "the son of man" and the reference to "three days" would have meant in this context.

We may notice first the role of the three passion predictions in the structure of Mark 8:27–10:52. Following each prediction there is a scene that indicates the disciples still do not understand what he is saying, and this scene introduces a new series of teachings on discipleship. [Structure of Mark 8:31–10:52] The effect of this repeated structure is that it prepares the reader for Jesus' death while deepening the theme of the disciples' failure.

Mark has noted the growing opposition toward Jesus along the way. The authorities question Jesus and his disciples (2:6-7, 16, 24). They watch for an opportunity to accuse him,

Structure of Mark 8:31–10:52			
Passion prediction	8:31	9:31	10:32-34
Disciples' lack of understanding	8:32-33	9:32	10:35-40
Teachings on discipleship	8:34–9:1	9:33-50	10:41-45

Norman Perrin, *The New Testament: An Introduction* (New York: Harcourt Brace Jovanovich, 1974), 155.

and then they plot to put him to death (3:1-6). The scribes from Jerusalem charge that Jesus acts in the power of Beelzebul (3:22), and his family comes to take him home, apparently fearing for his safety (3:31-35). Jesus speaks in riddles and withdraws periodically to Gentile areas across the Sea of Galilee, or to the north. Even in his hometown he is not received with faith (6:1-6). In Mark 7 Jesus attacks the foundation of Pharisaic piety—the importance of ritual purity. It would not require supernatural perception for Jesus to be aware that his present course was leading him to a conflict with the Jerusalem authorities from which there would be no escape.

While it does not appear that there was any expectation of a messiah who would suffer an atoning death,[24] the suffering servant passage in Isaiah 52:13–53:12 and the role of the righteous sufferer in the wisdom tradition [The Righteous Sufferer] laid a foundation for understanding the suffering of the righteous as atoning for the sins of their persecutors, as

The Righteous Sufferer

The Wisdom of Solomon describes the plotting of the wicked against the righteous one:

Let us lie in wait for the righteous man,
because he is inconvenient to us and opposes our actions;
he reproaches us for sins against the law,
and accuses us of sins against our training.
He professes to have knowledge of God,
and he calls himself a child of the Lord.
He became to us a reproof of our thoughts;
the very sight of him is a burden to us,
because his manner of life is unlike that of others,
and his ways are strange.
We are considered by him as something base,
and he avoids our ways as unclean;
he calls the last end of the righteous happy,
and boasts that God is his father.
Let us see if his words are true,
and let us test what will happen at the end of his life;
for if the righteous man is God's child, he will help him,
and will deliver him from the hand of his adversaries.
Let us test him with insult and torture,
so that we may find out how gentle he is,
and make trial of his forbearance.
Let us condemn him to a shameful death,
for, according to what he says, he will be protected. (Wis 2:12-20)

The Maccabean Martyrs

Evidence of reflection on the atoning significance of the suffering of the righteous:

The last of the seven brothers: "I, like my brothers, give up body and life for the laws of our ancestors, appealing to God to show mercy soon to our nation and by trials and plagues to make you confess that he alone is God, and through me and my brothers to bring to an end the wrath of the Almighty that has justly fallen on our whole nation." (2 Macc 7:37-39)

Eleazar: "Make my blood their purification, and take my life in exchange for theirs." (4 Macc 6:29).

The martyrs became "a ransom for the sin of our nation. And through the blood of those devout ones, and their death as an atoning sacrifice, divine Providence preserved Israel that previously had been mistreated." (4 Macc 17:21-22)

we find in the tributes to the Maccabean martyrs. [The Maccabean Martyrs] Against this background, it would have been surprising if Jesus had not been aware that his life was in danger, or reflected on the significance of his death in light of his awareness of his sonship and his role as agent of the kingdom. The prophets and martyrs also looked forward to divine vindication, as for example when the Maccabean martyrs declare, "the king of the universe will raise us up to an everlasting renewal of life, because we have died for his laws" (2 Macc 7:9; cf. 7:14). The extent to which Jesus' words at this point have been shaped by the church in light of his death and resurrection is a matter of great debate. Nevertheless, the echoes of allusions to the son of man and the suffering servant may well go back to Jesus himself.

Jesus' announcement of his coming death and resurrection, with its reference to the Son of Man, appears to be a direct response to Peter's declaration that Jesus is the Messiah. While not repudiating the title "Messiah," therefore, Jesus substitutes for it the term "Son of Man" and interprets his role in terms that contradicted popular expectations for the Messiah.

The fact that the suffering of the Son of Man is "necessary" (*dei*) implies that it is part of God's eternal plan, an event of eschatological significance (see also 9:11; 13:7, 10, 14).[25] Secondarily, the term may also suggest that the events of Jesus' death and resurrection are "necessary" because they are foretold in Scripture. For the background of the Son of Man sayings, see [The Son of Man] and the commentary on 2:10. The passion predictions stand in ironic contrast to the splendor evoked by Daniel's vision of "one like a son of man" coming in the clouds of heaven and being presented before the "Ancient One" (Dan 7:13-14). Instead of dominion, glory, and kingship, the Son of Man will undergo great suffering, be rejected, and ultimately be killed. Instead of being served by "all peoples, nations, and languages" (Dan 7:14), the Son of Man will be rejected by the elders, chief priests, and scribes. Whereas in the Danielic vision his dominion "shall not pass away," the Son of Man will be killed and after three days rise again. Like the suffering servant, he will be "despised and rejected by others" (Isa 53:3). The verb "to be rejected" echoes one of the Hallel psalms that is quoted often in the New Testament: "The stone that the builders rejected has become the chief cornerstone" (Ps 118:22; cf. Mark 12:10; Matt 21:42; Luke 20:17; Acts 4:11; 1 Pet 2:7). The connection between this verse from the psalms and the passion prediction is confirmed pointedly when Jesus quotes it while responding to the chief priests, scribes, and elders in the temple in Jerusalem (12:10; cf. 11:27). Later, Jesus is arrested by the same three groups mentioned in the passion prediction (see 14:43).

The reference to three days may be an echo of Hosea 6:2—"After two days he will revive us; on the third day he will raise us up, that we may live before him." There is some variation in the New Testament passages regarding whether Jesus would be raised "on" the third day or "after" three days probably because of efforts to match the prediction with the actual events, when Jesus was raised early on the third day. ["After Three Days"] The formula "after three days" in the passion predictions argues that the saying has not been shaped after the fact.[26] If it were a reference to Jesus' resurrection after the fact, it would probably read "on the third day" rather than "after three days," as in Matthew and Luke. The phrase "three days," however, can mean merely a short time. Matthew and Luke also change the verb "to rise" to the passive, emphasizing by the divine passive that God raised Jesus from the dead. The preaching of the apostles in

"After Three Days"

Note the variations in the New Testament references to "three days and nights," "after three days," and "on the third day":

"For just as Jonah was three days and three nights in the belly of the sea monster, so for *three days and three nights* the Son of Man will be in the heart of the earth." (Matt 12:40)

"This fellow said, 'I am able to destroy the temple of God and to build it *in three days*.'" (Matt 26:61; cf. 27:40; Mark 14:58; 15:29; John 2:19-20)

"Sir, we remember what that impostor said while he was alive, '*After three days* I will rise again.'" (Matt 27:63)

"The Son of Man is to be betrayed into human hands, and they will kill him, and *three days after* being killed, he will rise again." (Mark 9:31; cf. 10:34)

". . . and *on the third day* be raised" (Matt 16:21; 17:23; 20:19; Luke 9:22; 18:33; 24:7, 46)

". . . but God raised him *on the third day*" (Acts 10:40)

". . . and that he was raised *on the third day* in accordance with the scriptures" (1 Cor 15:4)

Acts makes this same point (Acts 2:24, 32; 3:26; 17:31), whereas the Gospel of John gives Jesus an active role in laying down his life and taking it up again (John 10:18).

For all that is said and implied by allusion in the passion prediction, it is also important to recognize what is not said. Ben Witherington offers the following four observations in favor of the authenticity of at least some form of the prediction: (1) "there is no reference to the crucifixion, only that Jesus is killed"; (2) "Each of these passion predictions speaks of the Son of Man, and we know that this was not the preferred terminology of the early church or even of Mark for Jesus"; (3) "the concluding clause does not match up exactly with the passion narrative account of a death on Friday and a resurrection on Sunday"; and (4) "we do not find here the later atonement theology of the church; rather, at most Jesus is portrayed as a martyr to the cause."[27]

Jesus was speaking "quite openly" (*parrēsia*), which stands in contrast to Jesus' speaking "in parables" (or "riddles," *en parabolais*; 3:23; 4:2, 11, 33-34; 12:1). Jesus was lifting the veil of secrecy and speaking plainly to his disciples. Even so, they did not understand or were not ready to hear what he was saying. Peter, having confessed that Jesus was the Christ, which in Mark seems to be the equivalent of seeing but not clearly, now stumbles again into opposing Jesus. Taking Jesus aside, Peter began to "rebuke" (*epitiman*) Jesus. Mark uses the same verb here as in v. 30 and v. 33. At a minimum the implication is that Peter presumes to order or command Jesus with the same authority that Jesus exercises in response to the demons and the unbelieving disciples. A natural inference is that Peter was pressing his case that Jesus should be the conquering Messiah rather than suffering Son of Man.

The alternatives are reduced to two: either one follows Jesus or one opposes him. Either one takes the role of Satan or the role of a disciple. Either one sets his or her mind on the things of God or on the things of man. See above the commentary on 8:11 on Satan, the tempter, and the commentary on 8:27 on "man" or human things in Mark. Jesus' rebuke of Peter confirms that Peter has moved from blindness and incomprehension to opposition. He was playing out the role of the tempter, who in the temptation stories in Matthew and Luke offers to give Jesus all the kingdoms of the world if he will worship him (Matt 4:9; Luke 4:6-7). Peter was tempting Jesus to take the human, and Satanic, path of the exercise of power and violence to achieve his ends rather than the path of suffering and self-surrender. In response, Jesus orders Peter to "get back in line," to get "behind me." There may be a double entendre here, to get behind in the sense of get away from him, and get behind in the sense of taking up his proper place again with the other disciples.[28] The note that Jesus turned and saw the other disciples may imply that he feared that Peter's error might spread to them also, or that he was making an object lesson of Peter for the sake of all the disciples.

Teachings on Discipleship, 8:34-38

This collection of five teachings on discipleship follows thematically from the first passion prediction and Peter's misguided effort to get Jesus to embrace Peter's hopes for Jesus rather than his own self-understanding. The theme of suffering is extended. Not only Jesus but his followers also must be prepared to make the ultimate sacrifice. The path of reward is paradoxically the path of sacrifice and self-denial for the sake of the gospel, because gains and losses must be measured not in the short term but in an eschatological context.

The six sayings in 8:34–9:1 are related by topic, theme, and form. Verse 34 introduces the collection with a call for the disciples to take up the cross. The next four sayings begin with the postpositive *gar*, "for," explaining and providing a rationale for the call to sacrifice in v. 34. Verses 35 and 38 begin with the formula *hos gar ean*, literally, "for whoever," and bracket two questions that begin with *ti gar*, "for what?" Thematically, all four sayings address the issue of how one gains (or loses) one's life in the new order of the kingdom. Verses 35-37 are also linked by the catchword "soul" (*psyche*). Mark 9:1 concludes the collection, adding urgency to the demands of discipleship by announcing that some of those hearing Jesus would live to see the kingdom come in power. Taken together, these sayings provide the Gospel's most definitive teachings on what it means to follow Jesus in discipleship.

The note that Jesus calls the crowd sits awkwardly here because the previous scene featured Jesus with the disciples, and the last mention of a crowd came in 8:1-10. Presumably the reader is to understand by this point that wherever Jesus went he attracted a crowd. By addressing the sayings that follow not only to the disciples but to the crowd as well, Mark makes it clear that there is only one standard of discipleship for all, not one for the people and a higher one for their leaders. The only standard is an absolute demand: lay down your life and devote all you have to following Christ.

Verse 34 makes this demand in stark terms. Discipleship is open to anyone and everyone. There is no hint of election here; literally: "If anyone desires to be my disciple. . . ." The verb "to follow" is used in the Gospels with this technical sense (see, e.g., 1:18; 2:14-15). The phrase "behind me" (*opisō mou*) in v. 34 links this saying with Jesus' warning for Peter to get "behind me" in the previous verse. The "if" clause of a conditional sentence is called the protasis, and the "then" clause the apodosis. Three imperatives follow in the apodosis: deny oneself, take up the cross, and follow me. The Greek tenses are important here because the first two verbs are in the aorist tense, while the last is in the present tense, which emphasizes continuous action. Therefore, the sense is deny yourself, take up the cross, and go on following me. Luke carries this emphasis a step further by altering the second command so that it reads "take up the cross *daily*" (Luke 9:24).

For the early church this saying would have an obvious reference to imitating the death of Jesus on the cross, but scholars have debated whether Jesus could have used this image and what it would have meant to the crowd before Jesus' death.[29] Crucifixion was a common form of execution [Crucifixion], used by both the Hasmonean rulers and the Romans: Alexander Jannaeus crucified 800 Pharisees on one occasion (Josephus, *J.W.* 1.97; *Ant.* 13.380), and the Roman governor Varus crucified 2,000 rebels (Josephus, *Ant.* 17.295).[30] Joachim Jeremias proposed that Jesus was figuratively pointing to the moment a criminal was condemned to death:

Crucifixion

"I see crosses there, not just of one kind but made in many different ways: some have their victims with head down to the ground; some impale their private parts; others stretch out their arms on the gibbet." (Seneca, *Dialogue* 6 [*De consolatione ad Marciam*] 20.3)

"And additional derision accompanied their end: they were covered with wild beasts' skins and torn to death by dogs; or they were fastened on crosses and, when daylight faded, were burned to serve as lamps by night." (Tacitus, *Annals* 15.44.4)

Martin Hengel, *Crucifixion* (Philadelphia: Fortress Press, 1977), 25–26.

a particular point in time is envisaged: the beginning of the way to execution when the victim takes the *patibulum* [i.e., the cross bar] on his shoulder and goes from the judgment hall into the street to face the howling, hostile mob. . . . To agree to follow Jesus means to venture on a life as hard as the last walk of a man condemned to death.[31]

Frank Stagg took a similar view: "To take up one's cross for the gospel is to tread a lonely road and to bear men's hatred."[32] In support of the authenticity of this saying, one may cite Jesus' figurative references to his death in Mark 10:38, where he questions whether the disciples can "drink the cup" or "be baptized" with the baptism with which he will be baptized.

The saying in Mark 8:35 shifts from the figurative image of taking up one's cross to the language of losing one's life. Partial parallels can be found in the sayings of the rabbis and philosophers (*b. Tamid* 32a; Epictetus 4.1.165),[33] but Jesus sharpens the paradox of saving what you desire by giving it up. The Greek term *psychē* ("life") does not mean "soul" as distinct from body or one's physical being, but rather the totality of one's physical being. This life is not inherently immortal. Hence the New Testament never speaks of our eternal *psychē*. Rather, as Eduard Schweizer explains: "*Psychē* is the life which is given to man by God and which through man's attitude towards God receives its

Mark 8:35 and Parallels

Mark 8:35—"For those who want to save their life will *lose* it, and those who lose their life for my sake, and for the sake of the gospel will save it."

Matt 10:39—"For those who find their life will *lose* it, and those who lose their life for my sake will find it."

Luke 17:33—"Those who try to make their life secure will *lose* it, but those who lose their life will keep it."

John 12:25—"Those who love their life will *lose* it, and those who hate their life in this world will keep it for eternal life."

---

character as either mortal or eternal," and again, "death is not a frontier which makes God's truth untrue. Resurrection is the final actualization of the fact that man receives his life wholly as a gift from the hands of God."[34]

The saying comes down to us in four forms. [Mark 8:35 and Parallels] All have the verb "lose," but the other elements reflect adaptations during the period of oral transmission. The words "for my sake and for the sake of the gospel" in Mark 8:35 explain what is meant by losing one's life (see Luke 17:33) and may therefore be a later addition. John 12:25 converts saving and losing to loving and hating and adds the reference to "this world" that is characteristic of John's dualism. In each of the Gospels, however, the import is the same: by seeking to secure our physical lives, or by becoming absorbed in them to the exclusion of eternal concerns, we ultimately lose the real essence of life, the capacity to live in fellowship with God. On the other hand, by devoting our lives to cultivating God's fellowship through the pursuit of the values and aims of the kingdom, God is able to give one's *psychē* an eternal quality and character. Hope lies not in what the human *psychē* already and naturally is but in what it is capable of becoming.

Verses 36 and 37 are rhetorical questions that draw out the implications of the view of human life articulated in v. 35. Life is the most precious thing we have, but it is not just precious because of its natural or temporal quality but because it is God's gift. The language of gain and forfeit are drawn from commerce or gaming. "Gain" (*kerdainō*) typically means procuring profit or advantage (Jas 4:13; cf. also Titus 1:11; Phil 1:21; 3:7-8). "Profit" (*ōpheleō*) means to provide assistance, benefit, or be of use to. Ignatius asks the Smyrneans, "For what does anyone profit me if he praise me but blaspheme my Lord?" (*Smyrneans* 5.2).[35] The term "forfeit" (*zēmioē*) continues the commercial imagery but can also connote loss from hardship, punishment, or suffering (cf. Phil 3:8),[36] apparently a real threat for the Markan community. "To gain the whole world" may refer to the objective of the church's missionary enterprise,[37] but Jesus warns that the disciples can forfeit their lives in this work. What have you gained at the end of the day, if you have gained the whole world but lost the only thing that has eternal significance? Again, this reflection on life can be found in the background literature (Ps 49:7-9; *2 Bar.* 51:15). "Give in return for" (*antallagma*) completes the commercial analogy. In some forms of contemporaneous Judaism, humanity was viewed as being in debt to God. Here the thought is related but different. If one forfeits not just one's physical life but one's life with God, what could one possibly give in exchange for it? The question calls disciples to weigh life's decisions and choices not just in a momentary context but in an eternal one. Seen in this context, "it makes ridiculous the avaricious desire of man for possession and enjoyment."[38]

Verse 38 ends this unit of related sayings by asserting a law of just retribution. Earlier Jesus declared, "the measure you give will be the measure you get" (4:24). Now the warning implicit in the future tense of the earlier saying is made explicit. Verse 38 also spells out what is meant by losing or forfeiting one's life in the previous verses. Being ashamed of the gospel or of the name of the Lord is an idiom found elsewhere in the New Testament (Rom 1:16; 2 Tim 1:8) and the Shepherd of Hermas (*Similitudes* 9.14.6; 9.21.3), where it has particular relevance to denying the faith in the face of persecution. The phrase "and my words" is similar to the references to "for the sake of the gospel" in 8:35 and 10:29. Moreover, a shorter form of this saying, lacking the words "in this sinful and adulterous generation," appears in Luke 9:26. The description evokes what is implied in Jesus' earlier reference to "this generation" in 8:12.[39] The description of "this generation" as "adulterous and sinful" is reminiscent of the language of the Old Testament prophets, where the idolatry of Israel is condemned as adultery (Ezek 16:32; Hos 2:4).

The latter half of the saying makes significant connections between "me and my words" in the first half and "the Son of Man" and "his father" in the second half. Such a connection between the Son of Man and the Son of God is rare in the Synoptic Gospels. Jesus uses the term "Son of Man" to refer to his own role in the future, thereby inviting the hearers to make the connection between his present role as suffering servant and his future coming in judgment as the Son of Man. This is the first clear reference to the parousia in Mark (cf. 4:22-25),[40] and it therefore casts a reflective light on the earlier references to the work of the Son of Man on earth (2:10, 28; 8:31). George Beasley-Murray commends I. Howard Marshall's contention that

> the expression "Son of Man" was a perfect vehicle for Jesus' proclamation of the message of the kingdom of God; it is a humble term with associations of divine glory that preserves "the secrecy of self-revelation from those who had blinded their eyes and closed their ears to it."[41]

The descriptive statements "in the glory of his Father" and "with the holy angels" and the reference to judgment evoke the setting of Daniel 7:13 (cf. 13:26):

> As I watched, thrones were set in place,
> and an Ancient One took his throne,
> his clothing was white as snow,
> and the hair of his head like pure wool;
> his throne was fiery flames,
> and its wheels were burning fire.
> A stream of fire issued
> and flowed out from his presence.
> A thousand thousands served him,
> and ten thousand times ten thousand stood attending him
> The court sat in judgment,
> and the books were opened. (Dan 7:9-10)

The Father of Jesus Christ, therefore, is "the Ancient One." Although the saying points to the danger of condemnation, the exhortation to the disciples is the same as that found in 1 John 2:28, "Abide in him, so that when he is revealed we may have confidence (*parrēsia*) and not be put to shame before him at his coming (*parousia*)."

CONNECTIONS

Mark 8:1-9

The feeding of the 4,000 often stands in the shadow of the more familiar feeding of the 5,000, as an unnecessary doublet of the earlier story. This neglect is unfortunate because the less prominent story has a distinctive message for the contemporary church. First, this is a lesson for the post-Easter church. Jesus is in a Gentile area, some of the people have come from "afar," and they have been with Jesus for three days. The danger is that unless they are nourished, they may fall out while they are "on the way" (a term that suggests discipleship in Mark). The issue, then, is how we can find sustenance "in the wilderness," a place that has strong exodus overtones and is therefore symbolically the place of testing. What do you do when following Jesus has led you to the end of your physical and spiritual resources? What do you do when you don't have what you will need to sustain you on the way home? Or, translating the situation to the context of the church, where can the church find what it needs to survive in "the wilderness"—on mission, in uncharted territory, with people who do not have roots in Israel?

The good news starts with the notice that Jesus had compassion on the people. He saw their need and moved to respond to it. When we find ourselves in the wilderness, we are not alone. Jesus will do for his followers what they cannot do for themselves. Faith is important for most people because it provides them with truth, meaning, and help: truth about God and the meaning of life, and the assurance of God's help and presence in times of crisis and need. The truth is that Jesus revealed a God who is compassionate and loving, who cares for the needs of all people. Meaning and purpose are to be found in discipleship, being on the way, being about our Lord's redemptive work, but mission is no guarantee of ease or freedom from distress. In fact, the opposite is true. Because the church moves in counter-cultural ways to rescue the neglected, liberate the oppressed, give voice to the disenfranchised, care for weak, empower the excluded, and heal the broken, it is constantly challenging the powers of oppression and exploitation. For this reason, it is always taking on challenges for which it does not have ready resources.

What do you do when you find yourself in the wilderness, a long way from home? What do you do when the challenges you face are greater than your resources for meeting them? What you hold in your hands is so meager, and the need is so great! The first thing Jesus did was to ask the disciples what they had. Often we have more than we realize, if we will only offer it to God. Then, Jesus prepared the people for the meal that was to come. He ordered them to sit on the ground. He took the loaves and gave thanks for them. The term Mark uses here (*eucharistēsas*) echoes the liturgy of the early church as it celebrated the Lord's Supper. The people were being connected to a heritage that stretched back to the provision of manna in the wilderness, that recalled Jesus' feeding of the 5,000, that would reach its revelatory pinnacle at the Last Supper, that would be celebrated ever after by the church, and that points ahead to the great messianic banquet at the end of time. Just seven loaves, but when they were offered to God in thanksgiving they became part of an unlimited treasury of blessing— enough to sustain the people in wilderness, with plenty left over. When we celebrate the Lord's Supper, therefore, we recall this great tradition of blessing, and we testify that even in a few loaves of bread there is more than enough for our needs. They are God's gift, they carry the life of our Savior, and they remind us that He has always provided for the needs of the faithful in times of crisis and distress.

Mark 8:10-13

There is irony in the Pharisees' request for a sign. In the Gospel of John also, after the feeding of the 5,000, the people follow Jesus across the Sea of Galilee, asking for a sign (John 6:30). Jesus had just given them what they were asking for, and they did not recognize it. Signs are revelatory only for those with eyes to see and ears to hear. In the Gospel of John there is a voice from heaven, but some said it thundered, while others said they heard the voice of an angel (John 12:28-29). God's ways are simply beyond human comprehension: "What no eye has seen, nor ear heard, nor the human heart conceived, what God has prepared for those who love him" (1 Cor 2:9).

Still, it is natural for us to want signs to confirm our faith, to offer security when life offers only mystery. Signs can scarcely replace faith, however. Faith is "the assurance of things hoped for, the conviction of things not seen" (Heb 11:1). Such assurance and conviction is not based on things that can be seen or on proofs that can make faith unnecessary. Rather, faith is always forward looking. It is based on the character of God already revealed in what God has done in history. What more can God do? The deficiency lies not in the historical evidence of the reality and character of God but in our willingness to stake our lives on the good news of what God has already done. At the end of Jesus' parable of the rich man and Lazarus, after it is clear that there is no longer any remedy for the rich man who neglected the beggar at his gate while he feasted day after day, the rich man asks Abraham to send Lazarus back to warn his brothers. Abraham replies, "If they do not listen to Moses and the prophets, neither will they be convinced even if someone rises from the dead" (Luke 16:31). We don't need more signs; what we need is the gift of open eyes and ears, hearts and minds, to receive the good news of what God has already done in Christ. Let us pray not for signs but for greater openness, understanding, courage, trust, and faith.

Mark 8:14-21

Jesus' warning to the disciples about the leaven of the Pharisees and of Herod, and the scathing questions that follow, should call readers of the Gospel into deep introspection and self-examination. No one is more blind than the one who sees only the blindness of others. The disciples' problem was not that they did not have enough light or that they had not experienced enough of the revelation in Jesus. Their problem was that they had been so preoccupied, or so focused on other things, that they had missed the revelation that had been given to them. What have we missed? What has God been showing us, trying to get us to see, but having eyes we have not seen and ears we have not heard?

The following story about the experience of a twelve-year-old blind boy was published years ago in *Theology Today*.[42]

I've heard on the radio all this talk about integration in the schools. To give all children a chance to go to school together. And there seems to be such a fuss about it because some of the children are different. And I can't understand at all what this great difference is.

They say it's their color. And what is color? I guess I am lucky that I cannot see differences in color because it seems to me that the kind of hate these people put in their minds must chase out all chance to grow in understanding.

"I noticed the other day when I had an earache and had cotton in one of my ears, that I was always veering to one side and bumping into the wall. I have not realized before how much I depend on my hearing—the sound of my steps, the bounce-back of the sound, to keep me in time with my sense of direction.

Then, another time, I was walking down the hall and I passed a door and inside that other room was a lot noise. So much noise that I lost all my clues—and I lost completely my sense of direction.

It was an awful, bottomless feeling. Afraid I'd bump into something. You never know whether you are going toward good things or toward trouble. Because you never know right off if it is something you like and need and want. Or something that is just in the way.

That is why I would not kick it, or blame it, or shove it aside. I would not make up my mind ahead of time, because if I did I could be so very wrong. I could destroy something that might be one of the most important and valuable aids to me. Destroy it in ignorance. Without giving either it or me a chance. That's like prejudice.

I walked down the path towards the woods by the school. And all of a sudden a dog and another boy rushed by. They threw a branch of a tree in front of me. I was startled and I jumped back and fell into some bushes. When I untangled myself and got up on my feet I couldn't find the path. I couldn't tell which direction was which. I couldn't hear any telltale sounds as a guide.

I called. Nobody answered. I was surrounded by silence and confusion. Then after a lot of trying and a lot of falls and scratches and bumps into the bushes, I heard the chimes on the old church that is north of the school. I knew then where I was. And I got back all right. But that awful feeling of not knowing where I was, which way to turn, which way to go. It was a terrible feeling.

And suddenly I thought of Campy [Roy Campanella, former Brooklyn Dodger catcher]. All of a sudden he finds himself paralyzed. All of his life suddenly has to change. He can't turn around any more. He can't even walk. . . . He had been a great ball player, one of the greatest. Now all of a sudden that was over. What was he thinking about now? Probably wondering what he would do now. Probably wondering which way he would turn. And I decided the worst thing that can happen to a person isn't being blind or being paralyzed. The worst thing is to lose all sense of direction in your life. And feel that you haven't got any place to go.

I have often wondered what it must be like to see. I have never seen light. But if I have darkness all around me all the time, I must learn to know that darkness. I think I do know it very well. Sometimes as a friend. Sometimes as an enemy.

But then it isn't the darkness that I should blame. Because darkness can be either friend or enemy. If wishes could come true, I'd wish I could see. But if I only had one wish, I wouldn't waste it on wishing I could see. I'd wish instead that everybody could understand one another and how a person feels inside."

"Then he said to them, 'Do you not yet understand?'" (8:21).

Mark 8:22-26

The blind man of Mark 8:22-26 is a figure with whom every reader can identify. He can see, but not clearly. He understands, but only in part. In the Gospel he evokes the experience of the disciples who follow Jesus but do not yet understand his mission or the ways of the kingdom he came to inaugurate. They are still bound by the traditional expectations of their heritage and culture—an earthly, political, nationalistic kingdom in which a strong man will use violence to expel foreign oppressors and then exercise authority over his followers (see 10:42-43). [Jesus Heals the Blind Man]

Like the blind man and the disciples, most Christian readers of the Gospel find themselves in the position of being believers who see and understand only in part. In a sense we know more than the disciples because we stand on this side of Easter, looking back at Jesus from the perspective of the resurrection. On the other hand, we are still limited by our own blindness, by the

Jesus Heals the Blind Man

The Healing of the Blind Man by El Greco (Dominikos Theotokopoulos; 1541–1614). One of El Greco's early works, painted in Venice between 1566–1570. While he was employed in the workshop of Titian, El Greco was also strongly influenced by Tintoretto. His *The Healing of the Blind Man* demonstrates his assimilation of Titianesque color and Tintoretto's figural compositions and use of deep spatial recesses.

El Greco (1541–1614). *The Healing of the Blind Man*. Galleria Nazionale, Parma, Italy. (Credit: Scala / Art Resource, NY)

grip of traditional, cultural values and expectations, and by our human limitations. Who knows how much more we are capable of understanding, or how much more faithfully we might be able to follow our Lord?

The blind man reports that he can see because he sees something like trees walking. It must be people that he is seeing. He sees, but he has to guess at what he is seeing. Although this miracle account is unique in that the healer's touch does not immediately restore the man to perfect sight, as one would expect of a divine miracle worker, it is true to human experience. Not many things change or resolve themselves immediately. We do not instantly achieve maturity. Insight and wisdom develop slowly. Raising children, building a strong marriage, finding one's vocation, and most of the important processes of life take time, sometimes a lifetime, to achieve.

We live in a culture that demands instant solutions and changes. Lose weight in three weeks, solve your credit problems in one painless fix, become financially secure in six months, find the right products and they will solve all your desires for health and beauty! But life usually does not respond so quickly to our demands. Like the blind man we need Jesus' second touch. Unlike the blind man, that second touch usually does not come immediately. We live our lives in the middle state of seeing but not clearly.

Perhaps we should give more attention to how to live in this twilight. At least the man recognized that he could not see clearly. Jesus saved his greatest condemnation for those who did not recognize their own blindness—those who saw the speck in their neighbor's eye but not the beam in their own (Luke 6:41-42), and the Pharisees who thought they could see but were blind (John 9:41). Partial sight requires that we recognize our limitations and live within them. We may live hopefully toward the time when we shall see clearly, but for now we know only in part and we see only as in a dim mirror (1 Cor 13:9, 12).

Twilight disciples need a healthy dose of humility. If we know that we do not see clearly, then we need to test our understanding against that of fellow travelers. Do you see what I see? Are those trees or men? You may have a clearer view than I do, and there is much that we might learn from each other. Such humility and openness to truth from others is especially important when we are talking about religious beliefs, values, and expectations that are often culturally related. We may easily assume that our ways are the right ways or the only ways just because they are the ways we are accustomed to. Living in the twilight and shadows means that we ought always to be ready to test old perceptions and learn new truth, because we know that we do not see clearly.

We are a band of the half blind, traveling together along the way as best we can while we pray and wait for the clarity of future light.

Mark 8:27-30

Jesus was concerned about who people thought he was and who the disciples thought he was. On the most human level, that concern is common to all people. What are others thinking about me? One wag commented that we would not worry so much about what others think of us if we realized how seldom they did! Jesus had a mission, however, and his work depended on what others thought of him. Were they beginning to understand what he was doing and who he was?

The confessions of the people and of the disciples were important—as are those of the contemporary church because there is a direct relationship between lordship and discipleship. Who we believe Jesus was has a direct bearing on what it means to be his disciple. If Jesus was a political, nationalist, zealot out to launch a holy war against Roman domination, as some of the disciples apparently hoped, then being his disciple would mean joining in the cause and being ready to lay down one's life in the revolution. On the other hand, if Jesus was an apocalyptic prophet announcing the end of the world, then being his disciple would mean renouncing all worldly pursuits (including marriage? see 1 Cor 7:26-31). If Jesus sought to found an ascetic, monastic movement, then his followers should go to the wilderness to live in isolation and purity, like the Essenes. If Jesus was a nonviolent pacifist, then his disciples should renounce all violence (see Rev 13:9-10). The point is that it makes a difference who we think Jesus is. The titles and language we use in our confessions matter. Most of them are functional (Savior, Redeemer, Lord, the Lamb of God [who takes away the sin of the world], even Son of Man) rather than ontological titles (Son of God), so they express our understanding of what Jesus has done. Many of the titles we use for Jesus are rooted in the ancient world, when the Ptolemaic, Hasmonean, and Roman rulers were given titles such as Euergetes (benefactor or worker of good deeds), Epiphanes (God manifest), Soter (savior), and Son of Zeus (son of God). The early church's titles made an important point. They reminded people that their ultimate hope lay not with kings and emperors but with God. The claims of human authorities are limited, while the majesty of God exceeds our capacity to grasp it. All the expectations of the Hebrew Scriptures are fulfilled in Jesus. He is the Prophet like Moses, the Prince of Peace, the son of David, Emmanuel, the Suffering Servant, the Son of Man, the Messiah, and on and on. Yet none of these titles exhausts the scope or meaning of who he is and what he has done.

The Sanctuary of Pan at Caesarea Philippi
The excavated foundations of the sanctuary of Pan at Caesarea Philippi.

(Credit: R. Alan Culpepper)

The titles we use are therefore deeply rooted in Scripture and tradition. Still, we need to be aware of what they communicate, especially to those who come from backgrounds or cultures in which they were not exposed to the "language of Zion." We also need to be aware of the need to recognize the overtones and implicit meanings of our theological language so that it does not limit or distort our theology in ways that make it difficult for the secular world to grasp or appropriate. The confessional language of the church, for example, is heavily oriented toward the political, authoritarian, and military, at a time when we are discovering the need to express Jesus' work as reconciler, caregiver, nurturer, sustainer, counselor, and guide. The political language of our titles is also thoroughly masculine, when again we are recognizing that the "feminine" functions are not limited to women. Children graphically and literally imagine kings and "soldiers of Christ," but our language for Jesus and for the church does not give them vivid titles based on new metaphors. Without abandoning the old, it is time that we reflected on the language we use and find new terms when we answer the question, "but who do you say that I am?" (8:29).

Mark 8:31-33

Jesus' rebuke of Peter, "Get behind me, Satan! For you are setting your mind not on divine things but on human things" (8:33), should be a reminder for all of how quickly we can move from the pinnacle of scintillating success to the shame of public failure. The light was beginning to dawn for Peter when he confessed that Jesus was the Messiah. Recognizing Jesus as the Messiah, however, Peter assumed that he also knew what the Messiah was to do. His error shows how difficult it is for us ever to fathom the mind of God. All our understanding is limited by our humanity and corrupted by our sinfulness.

Peter probably assumed that Jesus would bring vindication, advantage, and privilege to him, to the disciples, to their families, and to the Jewish people. His vision was limited, provincial. It was tinged with self-interest. If Jesus were really the long-awaited Messiah, then the long-anticipated restoration of Israel must also be at hand. The disciples would be carried along to power on Jesus' coattails.

Jesus saw an alternate reality. He saw that oppression and injustice will never be rooted out by the exercise of greater force. One kingdom may displace another, but only the power of love, even at the cost of one's life if necessary, can break the domination of the evil powers. His way would be the way of the cross, not the way of the sword or the throne. The way of the Son of Man requires self-sacrifice, whereas the way of the Messiah, as popularly understood, promises rewards of power and privilege.

Peter was thinking more about what benefit Jesus' messianic role might have for him than about what he might do to support Jesus in his messianic work. Just that quickly he had moved from setting his mind on divine things to preoccupation with human concerns. Jesus was concerned not just about the disciples but about all people—the scribes and Pharisees, his hometown, the women and children, and even the Gentiles. Jesus was concerned not with the restoration of Israel as a kingdom but with the inauguration of the kingdom of God. Jesus was intent on breaking not just Roman domination in Israel, but all oppression and domination. He was focused on breaking the power of evil in all its forms. Peter sought blessing for himself and his own; Jesus sought to usher in an era of blessing and peace for all people.

Jesus' rebuke of Peter should stand, therefore, as a continual reminder of the ease with which we turn from the divine to the self-centered. To confess Jesus as Lord, on the other hand, means that we pledge our lives to Jesus' mission as the suffering Son of Man, being ready to suffer rejection for the sake of divine purposes that transcend our own self-interests and indeed our limited understandings.

Mark 8:34-38

Jesus' challenge to the disciples to "take up the cross" and follow him has become so much a part of popular religious language that its meaning has been lost. One regularly hears such things as "that is just my cross to bear" when the speaker is referring to some daily inconvenience—there is no money to fix the air conditioner, or a close relative is a source of constant aggravation. While we may endure such inconveniences or aggravations with a Christian spirit, they hardly fit the voluntary element of choosing to take up the cross.

More appropriate is the interpretation that taking up the cross refers to all that we do for the sake of Christ and the gospel. It is a way of speaking of the commitment and sacrifice that grows out of our discipleship to Christ. Luke's addition of the qualifier "daily" tends in this direction. From this perspective, the disciples' leaving of the nets to follow Jesus would be an act of "taking up the cross." This is often the way this saying is interpreted, and there is an element of truth to this broad, general interpretation of it. On the other hand, the cross has a particular meaning that lends the saying a further sense. The cross was the result of Jesus' opposition to the corruption of religion, the oppression of the poor, and the perversion of justice. It was precisely Jesus' challenge to these evils and his identification with the outcast, the forgotten, and the oppressed that led the coalition of religious and political powers to put him to death. From this perspective, to take up the cross means to step forward, regardless of the sacrifice required, to join in the work of confrontation of the powers and identification with the excluded and persecuted. Taking up the cross means being at work where God is at work in the world to relieve suffering and injustice, to rescue the weak, and to bring peace and justice to bear in the human community. Each person has a unique opportunity to participate in God's redemptive work in the world—Jesus said not just "the cross" but "his cross" or "her cross." [A Cross for Everyone]

A Cross for Everyone

"Must Jesus bear the cross alone, and all the world go free? No, there's a cross for everyone, and there's a cross for me."

Thomas Shepherd, 1665–1739

The sayings in Mark 8:34-38 challenge everyone to consider their ultimate commitments, those things that define the values that orient their lives. Are our decisions the result of the impulse to acquire personal gain and recognition, or are they the expression of our commitment to serving others in the name of Jesus? Ben Witherington reminds of a grim witness from the distant past:

Some years ago archaeologists discovered the tomb of Emperor Charlemagne of France. When it was opened for the first time in many centuries, the usual treasures of the kingdom were found, but in the center of the vault was a great throne, and upon it sat the skeleton of the ruler himself with an open Bible in his lap. His bony finger had been made to point to a certain verse of Scripture—in fact, the one just referred to: "For what shall it profit a person if he shall gain the whole world and lose his own soul?" It is a timely reminder that our Western society needs to hear over and over again.[43]

NOTES

[1] Vincent Taylor, *The Gospel according to St. Mark* (London: Macmillan, 1952), 628-32. For an alternative proposal, see Paul J. Achtemeier, "Toward the Isolation to Pre-Markan Miracle Catenae," *JBL* 89 (1970): 265-91. See [Pre-Markan Miracle Catenae].

[2] Raymond E. Brown, *The Gospel according to John, I-XII* (AB 29; Garden City NY: Doubleday, 1966), 238; Joel Marcus, *Mark 1–8* (AB 27; New York: Doubleday, 2000), 486.

[3] So Robert A. Guelich, *Mark 1–8:26* (WBC 34A; Dallas, Texas: Word, 1989), 407; and Marcus, *Mark 1–8*, 497.

[4] Guelich, *Mark 1–8:26*, 408.

[5] Werner Kelber, *The Kingdom in Mark: A New Place and a New Time* (Philadelphia: Fortress Press, 1974), 60-63.

[6] For a discussion of the various forms of this saying, see Joseph A. Fitzmeyer, *The Gospel according to Luke (Z-XXIV)* (AB 28A; Garden City NY: Doubleday, 1985), 930; R. Alan Culpepper, "The Gospel of Luke," *NIB* (Nashville: Abingdon, 1995), 9:243.

[7] Ben Witherington III, *The Gospel of Mark* (Grand Rapids: Wm. B. Eerdmans, 2001), 238, contends, "It may be doubted that there are any Eucharistic overtones to this story"; while Marcus, *Mark 1–8*, 509, argues, "This otherwise superfluous clause, which highlights the one loaf, probably has symbolic significance" and "It is likely that the symbolism is Eucharistic; we know from 1 Cor 10:17 that 'one loaf' could be used of the bread at the Lord's Supper."

[8] Hans Windisch, "*zymē*," *TDNT* 2:902-06.

[9] Marcus, *Mark 1–8*, 514.

[10] William L. Lane, *The Gospel of Mark* (NICNT; Grand Rapids: Wm. B. Eerdmans, 1974), 282.

[11] A. T. Robertson, *A Grammar of the Greek New Testament in the Light of Historical Research* (5th ed.; New York: Harper & Brothers, 1914), 916.

[12] John P. Meier, *A Marginal Jew: Rethinking the Historical Jesus, vol. 2: Mentor, Message, and Miracles* (New York: Doubleday, 1994), 691.

[13] BDAG, 1001.

[14] Lane, *The Gospel of Mark*, 288.

[15] Witherington, *The Gospel of Mark*, 240.

[16] Lane, *The Gospel of Mark*, 289. See also Craig A. Evans, *Mark 8:27–16:20* (WBC 34B; Nashville: Thomas Nelson Publishers, 2001), lxxxi-xciii. Evans proposes that "the markan evangelist presents Jesus as the true son of God and in doing so deliberately presents Jesus in opposition to Rome's candidates for a suitable emperor, savior, and lord" (lxxxix).

[17] Emil Schürer, T*he History of the Jewish People in the Age of Jesus Christ (175 B.C.–A.D. 135)* (rev. and ed. Geza Vermes et al.; Edinburgh: T. & T. Clark, 1979), 2:171.

[18] Bruce J. Malina and Richard L. Rohrbaugh, *Social-Science Commentary on the Synoptic Gospels* (Minneapolis: Fortress Press, 1992), 229-31.

[19] Lane, *The Gospel of Mark*, 289.

[20] See J. Louis Martyn, "We Have Found Elijah," in *The Gospel of John in Christian History* (New York: Paulist Press, 1978), 9-54.

[21] James H. Charlesworth, ed., *The Old Testament Pseudepigrapha* (Garden City NY: Doubleday, 1985), 2:667.

[22] Walter Grundmann, "*chriō*," *TDNT* 9:542.

[23] Evans, *Mark 8:27–16:20*, 15.

[24] See, however, Joachim Jeremias, "*pais theou*," *TDNT* 5:686-97; George Eldon Ladd, *A Theology of the New Testament* (Grand Rapids: Wm. B. Eerdmans, 1974), 156.

[25] Walter Grundmann, "*dei*," *TDNT* 2:21-25.

[26] So Joachim Jeremias, "*pais theou*," *TDNT* 5:715.

27 Witherington, *The Gospel of Mark*, 242-43.

28 See Evans, *Mark 8:27–16:20*, 19.

29 Johannes Schneider, "*stauros*," *TDNT* 7:578.

30 See Martin Hengel, *Crucifixion* (Philadelphia: Fortress Press, 1977), for a definitive account of crucifixion in antiquity.

31 Joachim Jeremias, *New Testament Theology: The Proclamation of Jesus* (trans. John Bowden; New York: Charles Scribner's Sons, 1971), 242.

32 Frank Stagg, *Polarities of Man's Existence in Biblical Perspective* (Philadelphia: Westminster Press, 1973), 183.

33 See Eduard Schweizer, "*psychē*," *TDNT* 9:643.

34 Schweizer, " *psychē*," *TDNT* 9:643-44.

35 Kirsopp Lake, trans., *The Apostolic Fathers* (LCL; Cambridge: Harvard University Press, 1970), 1:257.

36 BDAG, 428.

37 Albrecht Stumpff, "*zēmia*," *TDNT* 2:891.

38 Friedrich Büchsel, "*allassō, antallagma*," *TDNT* 1:252.

39 On the question of the relationship between the Markan and the Q versions of this saying, see George R. Beasley-Murray, *Jesus and the Kingdom of God* (Grand Rapids: Wm. B. Eerdmans, 1986), 291-96.

40 C. E. B. Cranfield, *The Gospel according to St. Mark* (CGTC; Cambridge: Cambridge University Press, 1959), 285.

41 Ibid., 229, citing I. Howard Marshall, "The Synoptic Son of Man Sayings in Recent Discussion," *NTS* 12 (1966): 350-51.

42 "Light in the Darkness," *Theology Today* 16 (1959–1960): 15-16; the quotations in it are taken from an article by Howard A. Rusk, M.D., which appeared in *The New York Times*, 4 January 1959, p. 71. They come from a verbatim transcript of a therapeutic interview with a twelve-year-old boy, blind from birth, who was having trouble at school because he was said to be "out of touch with reality."

43 Witherington, *The Gospel of Mark*, 254.

FOLLOWING A GLORIFIED YET SUFFERING MESSIAH

Mark 9:1-50

The paradox of the gospel is that Jesus is both the exalted Son of God and the suffering Messiah. In Mark 9 Jesus is transfigured before the disciples (9:2-8), yet later calls them to be servants of all. Jesus is the long-awaited Messiah, announced by John the Baptist, who fulfilled the role of Elijah (9:9-13). Nevertheless, John was rejected and killed, foreshadowing Jesus' own death. From the Mount of Transfiguration the scene quickly shifts to the plight of a father whose son is tormented by a demon in the valley below (9:14-29). The disciples are powerless to help the boy. Jesus challenges the father of the boy with the demonic spirit, and the father replies, "I believe; help my unbelief" (9:24), a cry that has echoed from believers ever since.

Following the second passion prediction in 9:31, the disciples again show that they do not understand what Jesus is telling them. Along the way they debate which of them is the greatest. In response, Jesus calls them to the kingdom's radical inversion of the standards of greatness. The one who is least of all and servant of all will be the greatest (9:33-37). To illustrate the point, he takes a child in his arms and then rebukes John for attempting to forbid the work of an exorcist who was casting out demons in Jesus' name (9:38-41). The chapter closes with a series of related sayings linked by catchwords (9:42-50).

COMMENTARY

The Transfiguration, 9:1-8

Mark records admonitions for the church both through what Jesus said and through what he did. The sayings, particularly Mark 8:38 and 9:1, point toward the transfiguration, which is a kind of parable of the coming parousia, or "second coming." Parenthetically, the more technical term, "parousia," is preferred because the term "second coming" does not occur in the New Testament. Just as Jesus warned his disciples about his death, so Mark 8:38 functions as a prediction of the parousia. Mark 9:1 proceeds to assure the disciples of Mark's day that the coming of the kingdom, the theme of Jesus' ministry (see 1:15), will indeed occur imminently.

The saying has been interpreted in a variety of ways, in part at least in an effort to alleviate the implication that Jesus was mistaken about the time of the coming of the kingdom. The interpretations that have been advanced include (1) the saying predicts the transfiguration, a sign of the power of the kingdom; (2) the coming of the kingdom is fulfilled in the age of the church; (3) the grammar of the perfect tense allows for the meaning that some will not pass away until they see that the kingdom has come in the resurrection of Jesus; or (4) Mark 9:1 should be interpreted in light of Mark 13:30 and 13:32, as an intensification of Mark 13:30, affirming the imminent coming of the kingdom, even though Jesus did not know the time of its coming.[1] A brief review of these alternative interpretations sheds light on some of the saying's nuances.

Commentators agree that there is a close relationship between Mark 9:1 and the transfiguration that follows. Indeed, the sequence suggests that Mark saw such a connection, and Matthew and Luke follow the same sequence. On the other hand, the saying seems to envision a period of years before the coming of the kingdom, yet not more than the lifetime of some of those present with Jesus. The fulfillment of Jesus' saying by the transfiguration a mere six days later would be jarring. It is hardly significant that some standing there lived another week! Moreover, the transfiguration has a proleptic sense; it points ahead to the parousia. By itself, it hardly qualifies as a stronger candidate than the resurrection or the parousia to be the definitive event marking the coming of the kingdom.

Beasley-Murray traces to Gregory the Great the view that the kingdom spoken of in Mark 9:1 is to be equated with the church, an interpretation endorsed by many Lutheran and Catholic scholars.[2] The Gospel of Mark, however, nowhere suggests such a direct connection between kingdom and church. Jesus did not come to announce the coming of the church, but the coming of the kingdom of God! The emphasis on the verb "come" suggests something more dramatic than the beginning of the age of the church.

C. H. Dodd based his interpretation of the saying on his view that Jesus announced not the imminent coming of the kingdom but the fact that it had arrived in his person and work (a view commonly termed "realized eschatology"). The verb in 9:1 is perfect, allowing for the interpretation that the time will come soon when some will see that the kingdom had already come in Jesus and his resurrection from the dead.[3] Mark 9:1 must be interpreted not as an isolated saying, however, but in the context of related sayings in the Gospels that deal with the coming parousia.

Beasley-Murray himself points out the relationship between Mark 9:1, Mark 13:30, and Matthew 16:28, suggesting that they are developments of one core saying. Note the similarities in the three sayings:

"Truly I tell you, this generation will not pass away until all these things have taken place." (Mark 13:30)

"Truly I tell you, there are some standing here who will not taste death until they see that the kingdom of God has come with power." (Mark 9:1)

"Truly I tell you, there are some standing here who will not taste death before they see the Son of Man coming in his kingdom." (Matt 16:28)

All three begin with the solemn formula "Amen, I tell you," followed by a temporal reference to that generation. "Tasting death" is a Semitic idiom that may also have suggested the prospect of a violent death (John 8:52; Heb 2:9; *4 Ezra* 6:26).[4] In steps, one can see that Mark 9:1 intensifies "this generation" to "some standing here" and clarifies "all these things" as "the kingdom of God [come] with power." Matthew 16:28 removes the ambiguity in the latter phrase by substituting for it "before they see the Son of Man coming in his kingdom."[5]

The account of the transfiguration of Jesus is so distinctive some interpreters contend that it is a displaced account of a resurrection appearance, but differences in form militate against this interpretation.[6] The transfiguration is more profoundly influenced by the exodus traditions, as a fulfillment of the Sinai theophany. Craig Evans lists the following parallels between the transfiguration and the exodus events:

(1) the reference to "six days" (Mark 9:2; Exod 24:16), (2) the cloud that covers the mountain (Mark 9:7; Exod 24:16), (3) God's voice from the cloud (Mark 9:7; Exod 24:16), (4) three companions (Mark 9:2; Exod 24:1, 9), (5) a transformed appearance (Mark 9:3; Exod 34:30), and (6) the reaction of fear (Mark 9:6; Exod 34:30).[7]

Beyond the exodus parallels, however, the transfiguration is a synthesis scene that gathers threads from various climactic events in sacred history. In Mark it stands in parallel with the baptism of Jesus, which opens the first half of the Gospel, just as the transfiguration introduces the second half. In each the divine voice speaks and affirms Jesus' role as the Son of God (cf. 1:11). Following the first of the passion predictions, the transfiguration dramatically confirms that the one who will suffer is also the one who will be glorified; it prefigures the resurrection.

Similarly, following the sayings in Mark 8:38 and 9:1, the transfiguration foreshadows the parousia (see 2 Pet 1:16-18): The Son of Man will come "with the clouds of heaven" (Dan 7:13; Mark 8:38; 13:26; 14:62; cf. 1 Thess 4:17; Rev 1:7). The transfiguration, therefore, reveals the glory of Jesus as the Son of Man in a secret theophany in the midst of his ministry, just as he begins his journey to Jerusalem.

The reference to "six days" is unusual, since Mark notes specific intervals of time only in 1:35 (in the morning), 8:3 (three days), 11:12 (the following day), 11:20 (in the morning), 14:1 (two days before the Passover), 14:12 (the first day of the Unleavened Bread), 15:25, 33, 34 (the third, the sixth, and the ninth hour), 15:42 (when evening had come), and 16:1 (when the Sabbath was over). The connection with the reference to six days in Exodus 24:16 probably explains the presence of the temporal reference here, and efforts to find further symbolism in it are probably misguided.

Peter, James, and John constitute the "inner three" within the group of the Twelve, and Mark gives the three greater prominence than the other Gospels (see [The Inner Three]). They are with Jesus at the raising of Jairus's daughter (5:37), the transfiguration, and the Garden of Gethsemane (14:33), each of which has the character of a secret revelation of Jesus' power, glory, or suffering.

Mount Tabor

"Mount Tabor's primary fame rests on its traditional identification as the mount of transfiguration. But whether it is the actual site of the transfiguration cannot be determined with certainty since the mountain is not named in the gospel narratives (Matt. 17:1-8; Mark 9:2-8; Luke 9:28-36). On the strength of this identification, Helena the mother of Constantine built a church on Mount Tabor in AD 326, and by the seventh century there were three shrines on its summit, dedicated to Jesus, Moses, and Elijah. Other churches and monasteries were built during the next four centuries, and all these structures were destroyed in 1187 by Saladin, whose brother in turn erected a fortress on the hill in 1212. By the end of the thirteenth century, this structure had also been destroyed, and the summit was abandoned for six hundred years."

G. W. Van Beek, "Tabor, Mount," *IDB* 4:508.

Mount Tabor, the center of Galilee. View from the crusader castle Belvoir. Place of the Transfiguration of Christ. Height above sea level: 568 M. Mount, Tabor, Israel. (Credit: Erich Lessing / Art Resource, NY)

The "high mountain" is not identified. It is generally thought that since Jesus and the disciples were in the area of Caesarea Philippi, he went further up on Mount Hermon, a massive mountain range that reaches 9,000 feet elevation. An alternate tradition identifies Mount Tabor, near Nazareth, as the Mount of Transfiguration, but there is nothing to support this tradition. [Mount Tabor] In its canonical context, the "high mountain" recalls not only Moses on Mount Sinai (Exod 24:15-18; Heb 12:18-24) but also Elijah on Mount Horeb (1 Kgs 19:11).

Mark emphasizes the remoteness of the location, appropriate for the mystical revelatory experience that followed, by adding that they were "apart, by themselves"

(9:2). Jesus does not speak at all until they are coming down from the mountain (9:9), adding to the haunting, liminal atmosphere of the scene. The emphasis throughout is on what the disciples saw: "he was transfigured before them" (9:2), "his clothes became dazzling white" (9:3), "and there appeared to them Elijah and Moses" (9:4), "then a cloud overshadowed them" (9:7), and "suddenly when they looked around, they saw no one with them any more, but only Jesus" (9:8). By reporting in such detail what the disciples saw, the evangelist draws the reader into the scene, allowing the reader to experience the transfiguration through the eyes of the disciples.

The transfiguration of Jesus must be understood in the context of Jewish apocalyptic, in which "a change of form is one of the gifts of eschatological salvation which the blessed receive after the resurrection."[8] According to *2 Baruch*, the righteous "will then be glorified by transformations, and the shape of their face will be changed into the

Transfiguration

Raphael's untimely death occurred on his thirty-seventh birthday as he was working on *The Transfiguration*. The painting introduces elements of the Mannerist style with its grace, poise, and sophistication.

Raphael Sanzio (1483–1520). *Transfiguration*. Pinacoteca, Vatican Museums, Vatican State. (Credit: Scala / Art Resource, NY)

light of their beauty so that they may acquire and receive the undying world which is promised to them" (51:3), and "they will be changed into any shape which they wished, from beauty to loveliness, and from light to the splendor of glory" (51:10). According to Paul, all of us "are being transformed into the same image from one degree of glory to another" (2 Cor 3:18; cf. Dan 12:3). Just as angels appear in white clothing (Mark 16:5; Rev 4:4; 7:9), so the clothing of the righteous will shine. *First Enoch* promises that "the righteous and elect ones shall rise from the earth and shall cease being of downcast face. They shall wear the garments of glory" (62:15). Similarly, Enoch describes the garments of "the Great Glory" as "shining more brightly than the sun, it was whiter than any snow" (14:20; cf. Dan 7:9). Therefore, "what is promised to the righteous in the new aeon (cf. also 1 Cor 15:51f.) happens already to Jesus in this world."[9]

Fuller

"Along with the craft of the weaver went that of the *fuller*, who had to render the cloth from the looms watertight by teasing together the fibres. The north-east corner of the northernmost wall formed the so-called 'fuller's tomb' ([Josephus,] *BJ* 5.147). It was a fuller with his mallet who gave the death-blow to James the Just, brother of Jesus, when in AD 62 he was thrown by the Jews from the pinnacle of the Temple."

Joachim Jeremias, *Jerusalem in the Time of Jesus* (trans. F. H. and C. H. Cave; Philadelphia: Fortress Press, 1969), 5.

Jesus' clothes, that have been the conduit of healing power (5:27-30; 6:56), now become dazzling white. The term "dazzling" (*stilbō*) is used elsewhere to describe the radiance of stars or eyes.[10] Although the context in Mark focuses on the bleaching or dyeing of cloth, the translation "fuller" may be too narrow since the term (*gnapheus*) can refer to "a specialist in one or more of the processes in the treatment of cloth, incl. fulling, carding, cleaning, bleaching. Since the Eng. term 'fuller' refers to one who shrinks and thickens cloth, a more general rendering such as cloth refiner is required to cover the various components."[11] [Fuller]

The passive verb (*ōphthē*) is often used in the New Testament for appearances of angels (Luke 1:11; 22:43) or of the risen Lord (Luke 24:34; 1 Cor 15:5-8; 1 Tim 3:16). Moses and Elijah may represent "the Law and the Prophets," but they were associated in other ways also. Both had eschatological roles. Moses promised that the Lord would raise up "a prophet like me" and admonished the people, "you shall heed such a prophet" (Deut 18:15). Elijah would return "before the great and terrible day of the LORD comes" (Mal 4:5). Elijah "ascended in a whirlwind into heaven" (2 Kgs 2:11), and at least according to legend, while Moses was talking with Eleazar and Joshua after having bid farewell to the people, "a cloud of a sudden descended upon him and he disappeared" (Josephus, *Ant.* 4.326; LCL 4:633). The *Lives of the Prophets* records that when Elijah was born, "his father Sobacha saw that men of shining white appearance were greeting him and wrapping him in fire" (21:2).[12] Mark lists Elijah first, but Matthew and Luke place the names in the customary and chronological order, "Moses and Elijah" (see [Elijah]). Whereas Mark heightens the emphasis on the visual aspect of this event by reporting merely that the two were talking with Jesus, Luke adds that "they were speaking of his departure (*exodon*), which he was about to accomplish at Jerusalem" (Luke 9:31).

Peter, who had just confessed Jesus as the Messiah, now addresses him as "rabbi." The return to a more common title may seem strange in the Christology of the Gospel, but in fact Jesus was probably regularly addressed in this way. In pre-AD 70 Judaism, the term "rabbi" was used loosely for any teacher or scribe. It was a term of honor meaning "great one." Only later did a formal credentialing process develop, leading to the installation of pharisaic teachers of rank being recognized as rabbis. The distribution of the term in the Gospels reveals interesting patterns. In Mark and John, Jesus is addressed as rabbi by his disciples and others (see Mark 10:51; 11:21; 14:45). In Matthew the disciples

Rabbi

Rudolf Bultmann emphasized the similarities between Jesus and other teachers of his day, saying, "But if the gospel record is worthy of credence, it is at least clear that *Jesus actually lived as a Jewish rabbi*. As such he takes his place as a teacher in the synagogue. As such he gathers around him a circle of pupils. As such he disputes over questions of the Law with pupils and opponents or with people seeking knowledge who turn to him as the celebrated rabbi. He disputes along the same lines as Jewish rabbis, uses the same methods of argument, the same turns of speech; like them he coins proverbs and teaches in parables. Jesus' teaching shows in content also a close relationship with that of the rabbis."

Rudolf Bultmann, *Jesus and the Word* (trans. L. P. Smith and E. H. Lantero; New York: Charles Scribner's Sons, 1958), 58.

---

use "Lord" (*kyrie*) instead of "rabbi," suggesting that Matthew "is obviously seeking to emphasise that Jesus is not a *didaskalos* [teacher] in the Jewish sense but Lord of His people."[13] Similarly, Luke never uses the term, perhaps because his Greco-Roman readers would not have been familiar with it. [Rabbi]

Peter volunteers that the disciples should build "booths" (*skēnas*) there, one for Jesus, one for Moses, and one for Elijah (9:5). It is good that the disciples are there, he says, so that they can build booths for the other three. The term can mean tents, or tabernacles, but here indicates "booths or huts whose walls and roofs were made of thickly entwined leaves."[14] At the Feast of Tabernacles (or Booths) each year, the Jews built booths to commemorate the period of Israel's wandering in the wilderness (Lev 23:40-43; Neh 8:15). There is no apparent connection between the transfiguration and this celebration, but the choice of the term "booths" may suggest that some thought that in the Messianic age the people would again live in booths, with God dwelling in their midst.[15]

Booths

A Sukkah for the observance of the Feast of Booths.

(Credit: Courtesy of Bruce Okkema, Executive Director, En-Gedi Resource Center, www.egrc.net)

Mark reports that Peter spoke as he did because "they were terrified" (9:6). The term "terrified" (*ekphobos*) appears only one other place in the New Testament, Hebrews 12:21 (see the context in Hebrews), "Indeed, so terrifying was the sight that Moses said, 'I tremble with fear (*ekphobos*),'" which quotes Deuteronomy 9:19 LXX, the only place the term is used in the Septuagint (except 1 Macc 13:2). The occurrence of

The Tent of the Spirit

"It seems to me that this cloud is the grace of the Holy Spirit. Naturally, a tent gives shelter and overshadows those who are within; the cloud, therefore, serves the purpose of the tents. O Peter, you who want to set up three tents, have regard for the one tent of the Holy Spirit who shelters us equally." (Jerome, *Homily* 80)

Thomas C. Oden and Christopher A. Hall, eds., *Ancient Christian Commentary on Scripture: New Testament II, Mark* (Downers Grove IL: InterVarsity Press, 1998), 120.

the term in this parallel context may be entirely coincidental, but it adds yet one more connection between Mark's account of the transfiguration and the Sinai scene. Matthew omits the narrator's comment, while Luke says, "not knowing what he said" (Luke 9:33).

The cloud is associated with Divine presence in biblical symbolism. [The Tent of the Spirit] The Lord went before the people of Israel in a cloud by day and a pillar of fire by night (Exod 14:19-20, 24). At Sinai, the Lord said to Moses, "I am going to come to you in a dense cloud" (Exod 19:9), and on the third day there was a thick cloud on the mountain (Exod 19:16; cf. 20:21; 34:5). Later, "the cloud covered the tent of meeting, and the glory of the LORD filled the tabernacle" (Exod 40:34-35; cf. 40:38). Clouds are also associated with the Son of Man (Dan 7:13).

According to Exodus 24:16, God "called to Moses out of the cloud." Similarly, at the transfiguration, God spoke from the cloud, saying, "This is my Son, the Beloved; listen to him" (9:7). The voice from heaven reminds the reader that God spoke from heaven at the baptism of Jesus at the beginning of the first half of the Gospel. The phrase "from the cloud" in 9:7 is parallel to "from heaven" in 1:11. There, the voice confirmed for Jesus that he was God's Son (see the commentary on 1:11) (see ["Son of God" in Mark]). Here, it is an announcement to the disciples. Both passages echo the coronation formula in Psalm 2:7, "You are my son; today I have begotten you," and as at the baptism of Jesus, the term "beloved" may echo Genesis 22:2 and Isaiah 42:1. The injunction "hear him" (*akouete autou*) recalls Deuteronomy 18:15, the prediction of the coming of a prophet like Moses, where Moses adds, "you shall heed such a prophet" (LXX: *autou akousesthe*). The implication is that the authority of Moses and Elijah has passed to Jesus; he is the one they are to hear. In the context of the transfiguration, Jesus had just been telling the disciples that he would suffer and die as the Son of Man and that they too should take up their cross and follow him. The voice from heaven, therefore, serves to underline the imperative significance of Jesus' core teachings about his own role and his teachings on discipleship. [The Voice of God]

The scene ends with the report that suddenly they saw no one with them except Jesus. Fittingly, the focus at the end of the scene is on Jesus alone. Both Moses and Elijah and the voice of God have borne witness to him. The divine voice admonished the disciples to "hear him," and at the end Jesus alone is with them. At least for the disciples, the veil of secrecy around his identity has been pulled aside.

The Voice of God

Oracles were a common feature in Greek religion, where at Delphi the Pythia mediated the voice of God. In the Old Testament, God typically speaks through thunder (Amos 1:2; Isa 29:6; 30:30-31), and the rustling of the wings of the cherubim is like the voice of the Almighty (Ezek 10:5). An entire psalm (29) is devoted to the praise of God's voice, which is like a storm from the west. The waters of the primal flood were chased from the earth by God's voice of thunder (Ps 104:7), and at Sinai God's presence was signaled by the claps of thunder, lightning, and the sound of the ram's horn (Exod 19:16-20; 20:18-21). There, the congregation of Israel "saw his glorious majesty, and their ears heard the glory of his voice" (Sir 17:13). By contrast, the Johannine Jesus charges, "You have never heard his voice or seen his form" (John 5:37). Sirach adds that God allowed Moses in particular "to hear his voice, and led him into the dark cloud" (45:5).

The rabbis spoke of a heavenly voice (Bath Qol), which was the echo of God's voice, audible on earth. God spoke to Moses directly at Sinai, not in a Bath Qol. A Bath Qol might guide the rabbis in their work, instruct them in calendar matters, or show them the solution to a difficult legal matter, but it was not to be regarded as a continuation of the revelation of God in the Law and the prophets.

When the voice from heaven speaks in the Gospel of John, the crowd says it thundered, while others say they heard the voice of an angel (12:29). In the book of Acts, Peter sees the heaven opened, a sheet lowered, and hears a voice instructing him to kill and eat (Acts 10:13), and according to 2 Peter, Peter purportedly claims "we ourselves heard this voice come from heaven, while we were with him on the holy mountain" (1:18). Finally, in the book of Revelation the voice of God rings out in heaven (Rev 10:8; 11:12; 14:13).

See Otto Betz, *"phōnē," TDNT* 9:278–99, esp. 288.

The Coming of Elijah, 9:9-13

As they were coming down from the mountain, Jesus gave the disciples strict orders that they were to tell no one what they had seen. Mark uses the verb "to give strict orders" (*diastellō*) more frequently than any other New Testament writer (see 5:43; 7:36; 8:15). The phrase "to tell no one what they had seen" is similar to Mark's description of the report of the witnesses to the healing of the Gadarene demoniac (5:16). The distinctive feature of Jesus' command to silence in this context is that for the first time it has a time limit, "until after the Son of Man had risen from the dead" (9:9) (see [Messianic Secret]). The reference to the rising of the Son of Man from the dead echoes and recalls the first passion prediction in Mark 8:31. The disciples, however, miss the connection to the passion prediction, apparently hearing the statement in the context of the tradition of the coming of the Son of Man in glory (Dan 7:13; Mark 8:38). They "kept" (*ekratēsan*) the matter, that is they told no one but discussed it among themselves. The teaching of the resurrection was common among the Pharisees (cf. 6:14, 16; 12:18-27), so Mark's report may be a bit elliptical. In context, the apparent sense is that what troubled and puzzled the disciples was not the general matter of the resurrection of the dead but the resurrection of the Son of Man, since there was no expectation that the Son of Man would die. By having the disciples question the connection between the Son of Man and the resurrection of the dead, Mark allows Jesus' response to serve as an explanation not only of his command that they tell no one about

Heuristic Questions

The Socratic method of teaching involves posing questions and then challenging facile or traditional answers until students arrive at new insights in their efforts to offer a more cogent answer to the question. The Gospel of Mark illustrates that Jesus often used questions in his debates with the authorities and in his teaching of the disciples. In contrast to the Socratic use of questions, which in Plato's dialogues usually lead to extended examinations of definitions, Jesus posed heuristic questions in order to lead his hearers to make an association or see the issue in a new context. Jesus' question in Mark 9:12 is a particularly good example because it seems unrelated to the issue under discussion, but the answer to the question will shed new light on it. Compare the heuristic questions elsewhere in Mark:

"Which is easier, to say to the paralytic, 'Your sins are forgiven,' or to say, 'Stand up and take up your mat and walk'?" (2:9)

"The wedding guests cannot fast while the bridegroom is with them, can they?" (2:19)

"Is it lawful to do good or to do harm on the Sabbath, to save life or to kill?" (3:4)

"Who are my mother and my brothers?" (3:33)

"Is a lamp brought in to be put under the bushel basket, or under the bed, and not on the lampstand?" (4:21)

"Do you not see that whatever goes into a person from outside cannot defile, since it enters not the heart but the stomach, and goes out into the sewer?" (7:18-19)

"When I broke the five loaves for the five thousand, how many baskets full of broken pieces did you collect? . . . And the seven for the four thousand, how many baskets full of broken pieces did you collect?" (8:19-20)

"Who do people say that I am? . . . But, who do you say that I am?" (8:27, 29)

"Are you able to drink the cup that I drink, or be baptized with the baptism that I am baptized with?" (10:38)

"Whose head is this, and whose title?" (12:16)

---

the transfiguration (9:9), but also as an explanation of the passion prediction (8:31).

Jesus often asks heuristic or teaching questions. [Heuristic Questions] Here the disciples ask, "Why do the scribes say that Elijah must come first?" (9:11). Malachi's announcement of the coming of Elijah was taken up by various writers during the New Testament period and later. Elijah was to call people to repentance and prepare the way for the eschatological events, but there was no expectation that Elijah would suffer and die [Elijah's Coming]; cf. [Elijah].[16] Jesus' question assumes the answer he intends to lead the disciples to see: John the Baptist was Elijah. Jesus validates the expectation of Elijah, affirming that he will "restore all things." Elijah was expected to "restore" the tribes of Israel by leading them to repentance, expelling those families that do not belong to Israel, and gathering those that do (see Sir 48:10). Jesus' question is, how then is the suffering of the Son of Man to be understood? Jesus was radically reorienting the tradition of the coming of Elijah. Rather than being recognized by Israel, Elijah came unrecognized and was rejected and killed. Walter Wink comments incisively: "What is expressed is the quite offensive paradox that the heavenly Elijah should be this captive, murdered prophet: a *dead* prophet."[17] Consequently, just as Jesus recast the traditional expectations regarding the role of the

---

Elijah's Coming

"At the appointed time, it is written, you [Elijah] are destined to calm the wrath of God before it breaks out in fury, to turn the hearts of parents to their children, and to restore the tribes of Jacob." (Sir 48:10; cf. Luke 1:17)

"R. Joshua said: I have received as a tradition from Rabban Johannan b. Zakkai . . . as a *Halakah* given to Moses from Sinai, that Elijah will not come to declare unclean or clean, to remove afar or to bring nigh, but to remove afar those [families] that were brought nigh by violence and to bring nigh those [families] that were removed afar by violence." (*m. Eduyoth* 8.7; Danby, 436)

"And the resurrection of the dead shall come through Elijah of blessed memory." (*m. Sotah* 9.15; Danby, 307)

"Then [Elijah] the Thesbite, driving a heavenly chariot at full stretch from heaven, will come on earth and then display three signs to the whole world, as life perishes." (Sibylline Oracles 2.187-89; Charlesworth, *OTP* 1:349)

"And they shall see the men who were taken up, who from their birth have not tasted death." (*4 Ezra* 6:26; Charlesworth, *OTP* 1:535)

"But Christ—if He has indeed been born, and exists anywhere—is unknown, and does not even know Himself, and has no power until Elijah comes to anoint Him, and make Him manifest to all." (Justin Martyr, *Dialogue with Trypho* 8; *ANF* 1:199, adapted; cf. 49)

Herbert Danby, *The Mishnah* (Oxford: Oxford University Press, 1933).
James H. Charlesworth, ed., *The Old Testament Pseudepigrapha* (Garden City NY: Doubleday, 1985).

Messiah, so also the traditional expectations regarding Elijah were recast in John the Baptist. As William Lane comments, Jesus insisted "that his sonship is misunderstood unless it is perceived that his exaltation is inseparably bound up with his humiliation."[18]

The Son of Man will "suffer many things and be treated with contempt" (9:12). The verb "to be rejected" or "treated with contempt" (*exoudeneō*) occurs in some versions of Isaiah 53:3 and Psalm 118:22 (cf. Acts 4:11),[19] and therefore it may have been part of the early Christian vocabulary concerning the suffering of Jesus. Elijah had come, but he had been rejected and murdered. The Gospel of Matthew, which characteristically places the disciples in a better light than Mark, adds, "Then the disciples understood that he was speaking to them about John the Baptist" (Matt 17:13).

Healing a Boy with an Evil Spirit, 9:14-29

The story of the exorcism of the boy with a demonic spirit is in many respects parallel to the account of the exorcism of the Gadarene demoniac in the first half of the Gospel: both are relatively long, detailed, and vivid accounts. In both, the unusual power of the spirit is emphasized. The differences are also significant, however. In the present story the issue of faith is much more prominent, the disciples' lack of faith is once again exposed, and the lesson for the church is suggested by the disciples' lack of power in Jesus' absence, the father's pleas of "help my unbelief," and the emphasis on the power of prayer. In the exorcism of the Gadarene demoniac, Jesus converses with the demon; in this story the demon is silent and Jesus converses with the boy's father. One may also detect parallels with the story of the raising of Jairus's daughter: both feature a father petitioning Jesus on behalf of his child, and in the present story the boy becomes "like a corpse" (v. 26), some say he is dead (cf. 5:39-40), and Jesus takes him by the hand and lifts him up (cf. 5:41). The complication in the first story is that Jesus is delayed by the woman with a hemorrhage; in this story the exorcism is delayed by the disciples' inability to accomplish it. Both stories also make an issue of the father's faith (compare 5:36, "do not fear, only believe" and 9:24, "I believe; help my unbelief").

The story falls into four parts: (1) introduction of the scene (9:14-16), (2) description of the problem, and the power of the demonic spirit (9:17-24), (3) exorcism of the spirit and restoration of the boy (9:25-27), and (4) conclusion: private teaching of the disciples, in a house (9:28-29). Missing from the usual pattern of a healing miracle is the response of the father or the crowd following the exorcism, which one would expect following v. 27. Instead, the praise of the crowd comes early in the story, before the miracle is performed (v. 15).[20] Matthew and Luke both abbreviate Mark's account, omitting vv. 14b-16, 21-24, and 26-27.[21]

Introduction of the Scene, vv. 14-16

The introduction is reported from the viewpoint of the three disciples who had been with Jesus at the transfiguration. Mark has reported a "great crowd" around Jesus on other occasions (5:21, 24; 6:34; 8:1; 12:37). The scribes have been his constant critics (2:6, 16; 3:22; 7:1, 5; 8:31), and the disciples' question in 9:11 serves to link this story with the previous scene.

The amazement of the crowd when they saw Jesus has suggested to some interpreters that there was something out of the ordinary about Jesus' appearance, just as Moses continued to have a radiance when he descended from Sinai (Exod 34:29-30; cf. 2 Cor 3:13). The verb that describes the crowd's reaction to Jesus is *ekthambeō*. Mark is the only New Testament writer to use this verb: in Mark 14:33 it describes Jesus' emotional state in the Garden of Gethsemane, and in Mark 16:5, 6 it describes the reaction of the women to the appearance of the angel at the empty tomb. The NRSV translates it "overcome with awe," but it generally means "to be moved to a relatively intense emotional state because of something causing great surprise or perplexity, *be very excited.*"[22]

The pronouns in v. 16 are ambiguous. Did Jesus ask the disciples what they were arguing about with the scribes (or the crowd), or did he ask the scribes (or the crowd) what they were arguing about with the

Demon Exorcism

Solomon was widely held to be the authority on demons because of his wisdom regarding all things (1 Kgs 4:29-34). According to the Wisdom of Solomon, he had unerring knowledge of "the powers of spirits" (7:20). Josephus claims to have witnessed the effectiveness of rites of exorcism attributed to Solomon:

"I have seen a certain Eleazar, a countryman of mine, in the presence of Vespasian, his sons, his tribunes and a number of other soldiers, free men possessed by demons, and this was the manner of the cure: he put to the nose of the possessed man a ring which had under its seal one of the roots [possibly Baaras; see Josephus, *J.W.* 7.185, quoted in [Evil Spirits]] prescribed by Solomon, and then, as the man smelled it, drew out the demon through his nostrils, and, when the man at once fell down, adjured the demon never to come back into him, speaking Solomon's name and reciting the incantations which he had composed. Then, wishing to convince the bystanders and prove to them that he had this power, Eleazar placed a cup or foot-basin full of water a little way off and commanded the demon, as it went out of the man, to overturn it and make known to the spectators that he had left the man. And when this was done, the understanding and wisdom of Solomon were clearly revealed." (*Ant.* 8.46–49; LCL 5:595-97)

In the *Testament of Solomon*, Solomon interrogates, exorcizes, and subdues various demons, often with the aid of a ring.

---

disciples? The second pronoun could also be reflexive, meaning "among themselves." Verse 14 reports that they came "to the disciples," but it goes on to say "some of the scribes were arguing with them." Both the grammar and the context allow for various interpretations. Commentators are divided on the issue,[23] but little hangs on it either way. No answer is given because the father of the boy immediately comes forward and addresses Jesus. The fact that the scribes were debating with the disciples implies, however, that a legal matter was at issue, and in view of the situation it may have concerned the proper procedure for exorcising demons [Demon Exorcism]; see also the connections on Mark 1:23 and [Evil Spirits]; [Exorcist].

Description of the Problem, and the Power of the Demonic Spirit, vv. 17-24

Jesus is referred to as "teacher" twelve times in Mark, and he is addressed as "teacher" by the disciples (4:38; 9:38; 10:35; 13:1; 14:14), the Pharisees and Herodians (12:14), the Sadducees (12:19), a scribe (12:32), and others (5:35; 9:17; 10:17, 20). See the comment on "rabbi" above (9:5).

The father of the boy does not care about the debate between the disciples and the scribes. He is simply seeking help for his son, who has a "dumb spirit," which probably means that the boy is unable to speak. The manifestations of the demon possession have often been interpreted as symptoms of epilepsy: the spirit throws him down, causes him to foam at the mouth and grind his teeth, and makes him rigid. The verb that in this context means to grow rigid or stiff (*xēraino*) usually means to dry up or wither (3:1; 4:6; 5:29; 11:20-21).

Impairment of speech, however, is not normally caused by epilepsy. The father intended to bring his son to Jesus, but when he was not available he asked Jesus' disciples. The rabbinic principle was that "the one sent is as the sender," but the disciples were unable (*ischyō*) to cast the spirit out. No one had been able to subdue the Gadarene demoniac (5:4), and later the disciples were unable to watch with Jesus in the Garden of Gethsemane (14:37).

Jesus' emotional response expresses his exasperation and disappointment with the disciples. They are representative of their "faithless generation." Jesus condemned the faithlessness of that generation earlier (8:12, 38) and predicted that it would not pass away before God's judgment came upon it (13:30). Here he looks ahead to the time when he would be delivered from them and their faithlessness. How long would he have to endure, or "put up with" them? There is no hint that the disciples had not tried to help the boy. They had tried, but they had been unable to help him. Earlier, Jesus had commissioned them to cast out unclean spirits, and they had done so successfully (6:7, 13). Jesus' insistence on the need for prayer in his private teaching to the disciples (10:28-29) implies in retrospect that the problem was that the disciples had presumed that they had the power to exorcise the spirit because they had exorcised other spirits. If this is the case, then their faithlessness lies in their presumption or their trust in their own ability rather than turning to God for the power to help the boy. Jesus would therefore do what the disciples had been unable to do.

When the evil spirit saw Jesus, it convulsed the boy, and the boy fell to the ground and rolled about foaming at the mouth (9:20). On other occasions when Jesus confronted a demon, the demon cried out, identifying Jesus (1:24; 3:11; 5:6-7). In this instance, it is a "dumb spirit," so it is appropriate that it acts rather than speaks.

Like a doctor gathering information about a patient, Jesus asks the father how long the boy has been having such convulsions. "From childhood," the father answers, using a term (*paidiothen*) that normally means from infancy, or a very early age. His possession has lasted for a considerable period of time, and hence presumably will be all the more difficult to break. Moreover, so malicious is the spirit that it often cast the boy into fire or water in an effort to destroy him. Ironically, the unclean spirits fear (correctly) that Jesus has come to destroy them (1:24; cf. 12:9), and the authorities have conspired to destroy Jesus (3:6; 11:18). On the other hand, Jesus cared that his disciples not perish (i.e., be destroyed; 4:38), and that no one lose their life (i.e., perish; 8:35).

Pleading, the father asks Jesus, "If you are able to do anything, have pity on us and help us" (9:22). Perhaps other exorcists had tried and failed. Since Jesus' own disciples (presumably acting in his name) had failed, the father's confidence that Jesus could help his son may have been shaken. Still, perhaps Jesus could do something—"if you are able." The reader knows that on three previous occasions Jesus has responded in mercy: healing the leper (1:41), teaching the 5,000 (6:34), and feeding the 4,000 (8:2). In Mark, Jesus can always be trusted to act with compassion (see the commentary on 6:34).

The note of uncertainty in the father's plea, "if you are able," provokes Jesus' immediate response, not unlike Jesus' response to the disciples when they questioned whether Jesus cared that they were perishing in the storm (4:38): "All things are possible for one who believes" (9:23). The man's desperation becomes the occasion for a lesson in faith for the disciples, and for the Markan community. The affirmation has the succinct ring of a mantra—*panta dynata*: "all things are possible, all things are possible." After all, Jesus had just been transfigured, his garments becoming whiter than any fuller could have made them (9:3). ["All Things Are Possible" (*panta dynata*)]

> ### "All Things Are Possible" (*panta dynata*)
>
> The claim, "All things are possible" (*panta dynata*) occurs three times in Mark, but only once elsewhere in the New Testament.
>
> Mark 9:23   "All things can be done for the one who believes."
>
> Mark 10:27   "For mortals it is impossible, but not for God; for God all things are possible." (par. Matt 19:26)
>
> Mark 14:36   "Abba, Father, for you all things are possible, remove this cup from me; yet, not what I want, but what you want."

Jesus' theme in Mark is believing in the gospel (1:15). Jesus admonishes Jairus, the leader of the synagogue, "do not fear, only believe" (5:36). Fear, hopelessness, and doubt are all antitheses of faith. One who places a stumbling block in the way of the faith of another has much to fear (9:42). On the other hand, one who has faith will be able to move mountains (11:22-24), but Jesus' enemies did not believe in John's baptism (11:31). False prophets also call for belief (13:21), and the chief priests and scribes demand that Jesus come down from the cross and they will believe (15:32).

The father replies with a plea that captures the fallenness of humanity, even among the faithful: "I believe; help my unbelief!" (9:24). His plea has shifted from asking Jesus to do something for his son to a plea to do something about his unbelief. William Lane comments, "His cry expresses humanity and distress at being asked to manifest radical faith when unbelief is the form of human existence."[24] In response, and paradoxically in response to both pleas simultaneously, Jesus exorcises the spirit from the man's son, thereby removing any doubt as to whether he could do anything to help him. [Unbelief (*apistia*) in Mark]

> ### Unbelief (*apistia*) in Mark
>
>
>
> Mark 6:6   "And he was amazed at their unbelief."
> Mark 9:24   "I believe; help my unbelief."
>
> Unbelief and doubt are also prominent in the longer ending of Mark
>
> Mark 16:14   "and he upbraided them for their lack of faith and stubbornness, because they had not believed those who saw him after he had risen."

Exorcism of the Spirit and Restoration of the Boy, vv. 25-27

Jesus' conversation with the boy's father is cut short by the gathering of a crowd. The reference is obscure because it is unclear how this crowd is different from the crowd that greeted Jesus in v. 15, or whether we are to understand that other onlookers came to gawk at the boy, or because word spread of Jesus' presence (see 1:28, 37; 3:7-8; 6:31). There is no command to secrecy in this story, so it is also unclear why the gathering of a crowd spurred Jesus to act. Compassion for the boy, desire to avoid as much public attention as possible, or because the crowd might interfere with the exorcism are all possible explanations. As on other occasions, Jesus performs the exorcism by categorically commanding the demon to leave the boy and not to enter into him again. When Jesus was confronted by a man with an unclean spirit in the synagogue, he commanded, "Be silent, and come out of him" (1:25), and to the Legion that possessed the Gadarene demoniac, he commanded, "Come out of the man, you unclean spirit!" (5:8). This time he identifies the spirit as, literally, "The dumb and deaf spirit," and his command is, "come out of him and never enter him again!" (9:25).

Illumination of Healing of the Epileptic Boy

Gladzor Gospel, from the *Bound Manuscripts Collection* (Collection 170/466, page 108). Department of Special Collections, Charles E. Young Research Library, UCLA.

In one last act of resistant malice, the spirit cries out (although it is a dumb spirit) and convulses the boy once more before leaving him. Demons are often characterized as "crying out" (3:11; 5:5, 7), but others cry out also: the boy's father (9:24), Bartimaeus (10:47, 48), the crowd cheering Jesus' entrance into Jerusalem (11:9), the crowd calling for Jesus' death (15:13-14), and Jesus himself as he is dying (15:39). The spirit that Jesus expelled from the man in the synagogue had also convulsed his victim before leaving him (1:26).

When the demon leaves the boy, he becomes so still that "most of them" (NRSV) or perhaps "all" said, "he is dead."[25] Interestingly, Mark left the death of Jairus's daughter somewhat ambiguous also by having Jesus say that she was not dead but just sleeping, when others had already started mourning her death (see 5:39). The act of taking the boy's hand and raising him up is reminiscent of Jesus' act in healing Peter's mother-in-law (1:31) and raising Jairus's daughter (5:41). William Lane notes "the accumulation of the vocabulary of death and resurrection in vv. 26-27."[26] The English translations miss or suppress the overtones of resurrection by translating the report as "Jesus . . . lifted him up, and he was able to stand" (9:27 NRSV) and "Jesus . . . lifted him to his feet, and he stood up" (NIV). The verb to raise or lift up, which can mean merely to stand on one's feet (2:9, 11, 12; 3:3), also occurs in 5:41 (raising Jairus's daughter), Herod's speculation that John has come back to life (6:14, 16), in the Sadducees' question about the resurrection (12:26), and in reference to Jesus' resurrection (14:28; 16:6). The report that the boy "arose" or "stood up" (9:27) also echoes the report that Jairus's daughter "got up" (5:42). The overtones of resurrection in this scene, anticipating Jesus' resurrection (that was announced in 8:31), more subtly parallel the way the raising of Lazarus foreshadows the discovery of the empty tomb in the Gospel of John.

Conclusion: Private Teaching of the Disciples, in a House, vv. 28-29

The scene shifts abruptly, with no response from the boy's father or the crowd that had gathered, to Jesus' private conversation with the disciples. "The house" is often the setting for private instruction in the Gospel (7:17; 9:33; 10:10; cf. 7:24), and Jesus instructs the disciples privately on other occasions also (4:10, 34; 13:3). [House as Narrative Space in Mark]

This story has two open issues, the father's need to find help for his son, which slides into the father's need for faith in Jesus, and the disciples' inability to cast out the demon. Jesus' response to the father and the exorcism of the demon resolve the first issue. Jesus' response to the disciples in private resolves the second. The disciples may naturally have assumed that because Jesus had commissioned them to cast out demons (3:15; 6:7) and because they had done so successfully (6:13, 30), they would be able to cast the demon out of the boy. Jesus' answer, "This kind can come out only through prayer" (9:29), underscores not only the power

House as Narrative Space in Mark

"The initial architectural mode of the Gospel of Mark is 'in the synagogue.' Jesus teaches, heals, and sparks controversy in the synagogue. But the dominant architectural marker of the Gospel of Mark is house. Jesus is often reported to be in his home or in a house teaching or healing; those with him there are sometimes crowds, sometimes all his disciples, sometimes a few of his disciples. Also Jesus often sends people back to their own homes, frequently after a healing. A synagogue, of course, is a religious space, a sacred space; in relation to it a house, a residential space, is profane. On this basis, the two architectural terms are in opposition." (p. 131)

"To summarize the architectural schema, one may say that as SACRED is to PROFANE, so is SYNAGOGUE—AND TEMPLE to HOUSE, COURTYARD to ROOM, and TEMPLE to TOMB. And it must be noted that, contrary to what one might expect of 'religious literature,' the positively valued pole of this Markan schema, the pole manifested by the architectural spaces most closely associated with Jesus, is the PROFANE pole. But even more significant is the observation that, as the narrative progresses, both the sacred and the profane architectural spaces of Mark's Gospel are abandoned by Jesus. . . ." (p. 140)

"By the close of the Gospel of Mark, no architectural space functions in its normal, expected way any longer. A house is no longer a family dwelling but has become a gathering place for a new community. . . . Empty tomb, ruined temple, house of gathering—Jesus' death, the destruction of the temple, the new community—all are, according to Mark's Gospel, witnesses to the breakdown of the opposition of the sacred and the profane and the breakthrough to a new reality." (p. 140).

Elizabeth Struthers Malbon, *Narrative Space and Mythic Meaning in Mark* (San Francisco: Harper & Row, 1986), 131, 140.

of this particular demon and the importance of prayer for the disciples generally. It also teaches the disciples (and Mark's community) that they are not to presume on past successes but to seek God's help in every situation. Cranfield puts the matter this way:

> They [the disciples] had to learn that God's power is not given to men in that way. It has rather ever to be asked for afresh (*en proseuchē* ["in prayer"]) and received afresh. To trust in God's power in the sense that we imagine that we have it in our control and at our disposal is tantamount to unbelief; for it is really to trust in ourselves instead of in God.[27]

The scribes who added the phrase "and fasting" in 9:29 (see the KJV) did not understand that true discipleship "does not result from the effectiveness of one's own piety but only from the action of God."[28] Those who would follow Jesus must abandon any presumption that their faith can ever be adequate for the demands they will face: they must learn to pray.

The Second Passion Prediction, 9:30-32

At last report Jesus and the disciples were in the area of Caesarea Philippi (8:27) and from there went up on a high mountain (9:2). The note that "they went on from there and passed through Galilee" probably traces their movement from Gaulanitis back into Galilee, rather than meaning that they went from the house (9:28) through Galilee. Jesus was not returning to Galilee to resume his ministry there, however. He was on his way to Jerusalem, teaching his disciples as he went. For this reason, he sought to avoid public notice.

The second of the passion predictions is the shortest, and is generally held to be the earliest or most primitive, of the three (see the commentary on 8:31). Mark 9:31 lacks the claim of divine necessity (*dei*), the prediction of suffering and rejection, and the list of specific groups (elders, chief priests, and scribes) in 8:31. On the other hand, the latter part of the prediction is stated more briefly in 8:31.

Mark 8:31	Mark 9:31
"The Son of Man must undergo great suffering, and be rejected by the elders, the chief priests, and the scribes,	"The Son of Man is to be betrayed into human hands,
and be killed,	and they will kill him,
and after three days	and three days after being killed,
rise again."	he will rise again."

The new elements in 9:31 are (1) the introduction of "handing over" or betrayal, (2) the change to the present tense, and (3) the theological significance of "human hands" rather than the lists of the Jewish groups, as in 8:31 and 10:32-34. The Greek verb *paradidōmi* can be used in the general sense of "hand over" tradition, authority, or a person. It also acquired the more specific sense of "betray." Both are found in the passion material:

> The word occurs frequently in the passion story, being used for the betrayal of Jesus by Judas (Mk. 14:10 and par. etc.); for His handing over to Pilate by the Sanhedrin (Mk. 15:1 and par.); and for His delivering up by Pilate to the will of the people (Lk. 23:25) or to the soldiers for execution (Mk. 15:15 and par.).[29]

Indeed, Paul shows that the verb was so closely related to the tradition of the last supper, arrest, and trial of Jesus that it could be referred to as "the night when he was betrayed" (1 Cor 11:23). The idiom to hand over "into the hands of" also occurs in the Septuagint (Jer 26:24 [33:24 LXX]).

Noting that the verb occurs in Daniel 7:25 and that Daniel 12:2 refers to the resurrection of the righteous, Ben Witherington suggests that Jesus "read his own destiny out of some of the stories in Daniel."[30] More likely, however, is the influence of the suffering servant passages in Isaiah. The occurrence of the verb in the Septuagint in two passages that differ significantly from the Hebrew is particularly significant: Isaiah 53:6 LXX, "and the LORD handed him over for our sins," and 53:12 LXX, "and because of their sins he was handed over."[31] These passages relate to the second and third of the distinctive elements noted above. Mark 9:31 uses the present tense rather than the future, emphasizing the certainty of the event, which can be viewed as though it were already accomplished. Moreover, the sense of Mark 9:31 may well be not merely that Judas will betray Jesus (see 3:19; 14:10, 11, 18, 21, 41-44) but that God will deliver the Son of Man into the hands of men. For this reason, Jeremias suggested that a Semitic *mashal* or riddle, "God will (soon) deliver up the man to men," lies behind the passion predictions.[32] The events that are about to transpire are therefore more than the result of human depravity. On the contrary, they are God's liberating response to human sinfulness.

Once again, however, the disciples do not understand what Jesus is telling them, whether because he used a *mashal* that was capable of various interpretations or because they did not want him to confirm what they feared he was saying. See the commentary on 8:31 for the significance of the pattern of passion prediction, misunderstanding, and teachings on discipleship in 8:31–10:45.

Opposing Perspectives on Greatness and Discipleship, 9:33-37

The conversation in the house in Capernaum that begins in v. 33 extends through v. 50. While it is typically divided into three subsections—greatness and discipleship (9:33-37), the unauthorized exorcist (9:38-41), and stumbling blocks and salt (9:42-50)—the linkages within the larger unit should not be missed. It begins with an argument among the disciples over rank and ends with Jesus' admonition to "be at peace with one another" (9:50). The sayings within the larger unit are related by means of "catchword linkage," a mnemonic device in which words or phrases from one saying recur in the next saying. The following pattern of linkages can be seen in vv. 33-50.

"a little child" (v. 36)
"in my name" (vv. 37, 38, 39, 41)
"a stumbling block" (v. 42)
"one of these little ones" (v. 42; cf. v. 36)
"it would be better" (v. 42)
"if your . . . causes you to stumble, . . . it is better" (vv. 43, 45, 47)
"hell . . . fire" (vv. 47-48)
"salted with fire" (v. 49)
"salt (three times in v. 50).

Alongside these catchwords, one finds other, sometimes more subtle connections. The Aramaic word *talya* can mean both "servant" and "child," so Jesus' act of taking a child (v. 36) serves as an acted out parable supporting his call for the disciples to be servants (v. 35). "Welcoming" a child then segues into welcoming Jesus and the one who sent him (v. 37). Following immediately, the apostle John recalls an incident in which they did not welcome but forbade an exorcist from using Jesus' name because he was not following them, but Jesus places acting in his name above adherence to their group. Because what they have done is tantamount to placing a stumbling block in the way of the unauthorized exorcist, the transition to the series of sayings on removing stumbling blocks (vv. 42-48) follows naturally enough. The reference to hell evokes the image of fire, which attracts the concluding sayings on salt (vv. 49-50). Finally, the call for peace among the disciples serves as an "inclusio" that recalls the opening verses of the section and voices Jesus' response to the disciples' argument among themselves.[33]

Continuing their southward journey, Jesus and the disciples return to Capernaum, where they are once more "in the house" (cf. 1:21; 2:1). See the comment on 2:1; Jesus apparently stayed in the house of Simon and Andrew when he was in Capernaum. The setting, "in the house," also introduces a new section of private teachings to the disciples on the meaning of discipleship (see 4:34; 7:17; 9:28). Jesus opens the teaching session by asking the disciples a question (see [Heuristic Questions]): "What were you arguing about on the way?" (9:33). He may have been concerned about their argument, but he would have been more concerned that they understood what it really meant to follow him. The reference to "the way" quite naturally refers to their conversation among themselves on the road to Capernaum, but as we have noted, Mark uses the term as a motif for "the way" of suffering servanthood (see above 8:3, 27 and the commentary on these verses). The motif is repeated by the narrator in v. 34.

The disciples are silent (cf. 3:4; 14:61). Earlier they feared to ask Jesus what his second passion prediction meant (9:32). Now they remain silent because they are embarrassed by Jesus' question; they had been arguing about which of them was greatest. Rank and status were important in antiquity, and social order depended on establishing one's position and that of others. [Rank and Status]

Mark's report that Jesus sat down is more than an idle detail. Sitting was the customary posture for teaching (cf. 4:1-2; 13:3; Matt 5:1; 23:2-3; Luke 4:20-21; 5:3).[34] The last time "the Twelve" were mentioned as a group was in Mark 6:7 (cf. 3:14; 4:10; 10:32; 11:11, etc.), but Mark seems to use this term interchangeably with "the disciples" (9:14, 28, 31). This time Jesus chides the disciples, saying that whoever would be

---

Rank and Status

The community at Qumran was rigidly hierarchical. Rank was assigned annually, and penalties were assigned for failing to maintain one's proper place:

"And they shall be recorded in the Rule, each one before his fellow, according to his insight and his deeds, in such a way that each one obeys his fellow, junior under senior. And their spirit and their deeds must be tested, year after year, in order to upgrade each one to the extent of his insight and the perfection of his path, or to demote him according to his failings." (1QS 5.23-24)

"This is the Rule for the session of the Many. Each one by his rank: the priests will sit down first, the elders next and the remainder of all the people will sit down in order of rank. And following the same system they shall be questioned. . . . And neither should he speak before one whose rank is listed before his own." (1QS 6.8-11)

In Greco-Roman society at large, one's social position also determined both one's legal rights and one's privileges and obligations. Pliny the Younger records the following description of a meal:

"Some very elegant dishes were served up to himself [the host] and a few more of the company; while those which were placed before the rest were cheap and paltry. He had apportioned in small flagons three different sorts of wine; but you are not to suppose it was that the guests might take their choice: on the contrary, that they might not choose at all. One was for himself and me; the next for his friends of lower status (for you must know that he measures out his friendship according to the degrees of quality); and the third for his own freed-men and mine." (Pliny, the Younger, *Letters* 2.6)

Florentino García Martínez, *The Dead Sea Scrolls Translated* (trans. Wilfred G. E. Watson; Leiden: E. J. Brill, 1994), 9–10; *Pliny: Letters* (trans. William Melmoth; rev. W. M. L. Hutchinson, LCL; Cambridge MA: Harvard University Press, 1915), 109–11.

first must be servant of all (9:35). The formula "if anyone . . ." (*ei tis*) extends an open invitation followed by instruction in the form of an imperative. Jesus also uses this formula in the following sayings in Mark: "If anyone has ears to hear, listen" (4:23; 7:16—author's translation); "If anyone wants to follow me, let him deny himself, take up the cross, and follow me" (8:34—author's translation; see also Luke 14:26). Another version of this saying occurs in 10:43-45, where it is grounded in the example of Jesus. "First" (*prōtos*), when applied to persons, designates a status of preeminence, power, or privilege, as in "the leaders (*prōtois*) of Galilee" (6:21), "and not a few of the leading (*prōtōn*) women" (Acts 17:4), and "the leaders (*prōtoi*) of the Jews" (Acts 25:2; cf. 28:17). In contrast, "the last" are "the people living in the most extreme misery."[35] Closely related in the catalog of Jesus' sayings are those that promise an eschatological reversal: "But many who are first will be last, and the last will be first" (10:31; Matt 19:30), and "So the last will be first, and the first will be last" (Matt 20:16). This reversal is depicted in a dramatic form in the parable of Lazarus and the rich man when the rich man goes to Hades and Lazarus to the bosom of Abraham (Luke 16:19-31). The theme of reversal is particularly important in Luke: "He has brought down the powerful from their thrones, and lifted up the lowly" (1:52), and "For all who exalt themselves will be humbled, and those who humble themselves will be exalted" (Luke 14:11). The thought is the same here. If the disciples are so intent on being first, let them be servants of all. This is the new economy of the kingdom.

To drive home the point, Jesus took a small child in his arms (9:36). A doublet of this tradition occurs in 10:13-16, where the same rare verb (*enagkalizesthai*) is used. Jesus put the child among the disciples (cf. 3:3; 14:60), and then embraced the child. While this simple act might not attract notice today, it was revolutionary in first-century Galilee. [Children in Antiquity] Far more than a sentimental scene with gentle Jesus blessing the children, Mark presents Jesus as at once challenging the proud who shunned children and confronting his disciples (who sought positions of honor) by embracing a child. Elsewhere Jesus challenges the disciples to receive the kingdom as a child (10:15; Matt 18:3; John 3:3, 5).

The Aramaic term *talya* and the Greek term *pais* can both mean either "child" or "servant." Jesus plays on the term, speaking of

Children in Antiquity

Ancient Judaism seems to have had little regard for the individuality of a child. Children were generally thought to be self-willed, lacking in understanding, and in need of stern discipline (Isa 3:4; Eccl 10:16; Wis 12:24; 15:14). The same might be said of Greco-Roman society except that with Hellenism one can trace a rising regard for the place of children, as both the art and literature of the period attest. Rabbis, in particular, did not associate with children: Rabbi Dosa ben Harkinas, "Morning sleep, mid-day wine, chattering with children, and tarrying in places where men of the common people assemble destroy a man" (*m. Aboth* 3.11); R. Johanan, "Since the day the temple was destroyed prophecy has been taken from the prophets and given to fools and children" (*b. Baba Batra* 12b).

Albrecht Oepke, "*pais*," *TDNT* 5:646.

a servant while holding a child. Neither had any pretense or claim to power or status. Therefore, one who would be great in the kingdom must become like a child and be a servant to all. Verse 37 moves the relationship one step further. A servant to all will receive even a child. Therefore, whoever receives a child in Jesus' name receives Jesus, and since "the one sent is like the sender" (b. Ber. 5.5), whoever receives Jesus receives the one who sent him (9:37; John 13:20). "To receive" (in Mark only here and in 6:11 and 10:15) means to accept, welcome, or approve. Extending hospitality to traveling evangelists and teachers was especially important for the mission of the early church (see the commentary on 6:10-11).

Let the Children Come Unto Me
Enrico Scuri (1805–1884). *Let the Children Come Unto Me* ("Suffer Little Children..."). Private Collection, Milan, Italy. (Credit: Scala / Art Resource, NY)

The Unauthorized Exorcist, 9:38-41

The apostle John appears in the Gospels and Acts as one of the Twelve, one of the inner three (Peter, James, and John), with his brother James, or with Peter, but this is the only scene in the Gospels that features him alone or records something he said.[36] In context it functions as a second illustration of the principle that Jesus' disciples are to be least of all and servants of all. There is no place for turf battles or exclusive privileges. One who receives a child will also celebrate the release of others from the demonic powers, even if it does not come about by his or her own hands.

John addresses Jesus as "teacher," a title the disciples (4:38; cf. 9:5) and the father of the possessed boy (9:17) had used earlier. John speaks for himself and others of the disciples. They had seen someone casting out demons in Jesus' name, and they had sought to prevent him from doing so. Ironically, the disciples, who had not been able to cast the demon out of the boy, now seek to prevent someone else from doing what they themselves had been unable to do. Worse, they were doing so "because he was not following us" (9:38). The plural here moves the issue from whether the unauthorized exorcist was following Jesus to the fact that he was not one of the Twelve, or perhaps one sanctioned by the Twelve. To cast out demons "in your name" suggests first that the man was invoking the power of Jesus' name in the rite of exorcism (see

[Evil Spirits] and [Demon Exorcism]). Beyond this, to act in the name of another was to claim his authority for one's actions, or to make one's actions an extension of the one in whose name one acted. The phrase also serves as a verbal link with the preceding scene: one who welcomes a child in Jesus' name will not then seek to prevent others from acting in his name also.

The verb translated "tried to stop" (*kōlyō*) means to hinder, prevent, or forbid. Here, in the imperfect tense, it implies that they attempted to stop the exorcist from using Jesus' name but were not able to do so. The scene is similar to Joshua's protest, when Eldad and Medad were prophesying, "My lord Moses, stop them!" and Moses responded, "Are you jealous for my sake? Would that all the LORD's people were prophets, and that the LORD would put his spirit on them!" (Num 11:28-29). The book of Acts seems to take a less tolerant view of the use of Jesus' name by exorcists; the man with the evil spirit attacks the seven sons of Sceva and chases them out of the house naked (Acts 19:13-16).

The issue is whether the disciples can act as brokers of Jesus' power. Jesus had given them the authority to cast out demons (3:15; 6:7), and they apparently interpreted this as an exclusive prerogative. According to the prevailing social pattern, the unauthorized exorcist was therefore infringing on their role and rights as brokers of Jesus' power. [Patrons, Brokers, and Clients] Jesus, however, announced an unbrokered kingdom in which none have prerogatives over others and the grace of God is available to all—children, women, Gentiles, the poor, and the outcasts.[37] It is not the place of the disciples to decide who may and who may not call on Jesus' name.

One who claims Jesus' power will not soon speak evil of him (9:39). Even the conventions of patronage assured loyalty and a commitment to honor the patron. Jesus' open-spirited saying in v. 40 has an interesting parallel in Cicero. In defense of the Pompeiani, Cicero says to Caesar, "Let that maxim of yours, which won you your victory, hold good. For we have often heard you say that, while we considered all who were not with us as our enemies, you considered all who were not

---

Patrons, Brokers, and Clients

 Bruce Malina and Richard Rohrbaugh describe the patronage system:

As the Roman style of patronage spread to provinces such as Syria (Palestine), its formal and hereditary character changed. The newly rich, seeking to aggrandize family position in a community, competed to add dependants. Formal, mutual obligations degenerated into petty favor seeking and manipulation. Clients competed for patrons just as patrons competed for clients in an often desperate struggle to gain economic or political advantage. . . .

Patrons were powerful individuals who controlled resources and were expected to use their positions to hand out favors to inferiors based on friendship, personal knowledge, and favoritism. . . .

Brokers mediated between patrons above and clients below. First-order resources—land, jobs, goods, funds, power—were all controlled by patrons. Second-order resources—strategic contact with or access to patrons—were controlled by brokers who mediated the goods and services a patron had to offer. . . .

Clients were those dependent on the largesse of patrons or brokers to survive well in the system. They owed loyalty and public acknowledgment of honor in return. Patronage was voluntary but ideally lifelong. . . .

Bruce J. Malina and Richard L. Rohrbaugh, *Social Science Commentary on the Synoptic Gospels* (Minneapolis: Fortress Press, 1992), 236.

against you your friends" (Cicero, *Or. Pro Lig.* 11).[38] The saying is also found in the parallel in Luke 9:50 and in another version in POxy 1224.2. Elsewhere, the Gospels also attribute to Jesus the narrower form of this saying: "Whoever is not with me is against me" (Matt 12:30; Luke 11:23).

Verse 41 appears to be an isolated saying that Mark added here because of the catchword "in the name." In its present form it reflects the editorial hand of a Christian scribe who altered something like "in my name" to, literally, "in the name that you are Christ's." The saying asserts that no service, even giving a cup of water, will go unnoticed or unrewarded. Although this is the only occurrence of the term "reward" (*misthos*) in Mark (cf. Matt 5:12, 46; 6:1, 2, 5; 10:41-42; 20:8), the thought lies behind Peter's question in Mark 10:28-30. While the disciples think of the reward they are due, Jesus promises that anyone who gives even a cup of water will be rewarded. Again, the subtle implication is that while the disciples may have their reward if they serve others in Jesus' name, they have no exclusive claim to a reward. By implication, the unauthorized exorcist, far from needing to be stopped, will receive his reward also.

Stumbling Blocks and Salt, 9:42-50

A series of sayings constructed by catchword linkage may or may not be unified topically. The sayings in vv. 42-50 are linked by the words "stumbling block," or "cause to stumble," and "salt." The reference to "one of these little ones" in v. 42 is open to various interpretations: it may mean a child, like the one Jesus took in his arms (vv. 36-37), the unauthorized exorcist (v. 38), or any weaker member of the Christian community. The warning against causing one of these weaker or marginal members of the community to abandon the faith takes the form of an ancient proverb. It would be better to suffer a quick and sure death by drowning than to suffer the sort of punishment that is reserved for those who cause "one of these little ones" to stumble.

Millstones were common in Galilean villages, and many of them have been found in the excavation of Capernaum. [Millstones] The upper stone has a funnel-shaped opening in the top through which the grain sifted down and was ground as the upper stone was turned around a stationary lower stone (Num 11:8; Isa 47:2). Animals were used to turn the larger millstones, and Mark 9:42 literally says a millstone of a donkey, in other words one of the larger millstones. Josephus records the drowning of some of Herod's men (*Ant.* 14.450). In Judges 9:53 a woman crushes Abimelech's head with a millstone (cf. 2 Sam 11:21), and in Revelation 18:21 an angel throws a millstone into the sea as a sign of how Babylon will be overthrown.

Millstones

Millstones at Capernaum. The upper millstone, broken, upside down, and sitting to the right of the lower millstone, fits over the top of the lower millstone as shown in the photo on the left. The square hole in the side of the upper millstone is for a beam of wood that served as a lever for rotating the upper millstone over the stationary lower millstone. Grain poured in the funnel at the top of the upper millstone was ground between the surfaces of the two stones and sifted out at the base of the lower millstone.

(Credit: R. Alan Culpepper)

Jesus turns from the danger of causing others to lose their faith to warnings against losing one's own faith. The chain of sayings that follows continues to make use of hyperboles. Just as earlier Jesus called the disciples to take up a cross (8:34), and painted an image of being drowned with a millstone hung around one's neck (9:42), so now he calls for disciples who are tempted to cut off the offending member of their body. The exaggerated image is used to underscore the seriousness of entertaining temptations, but of course should not be taken literally. In a typically Semitic fashion, Jesus concretizes the temptations, speaking of them in terms of the parts of the body with which they are associated. With one's hand one may steal or do violence. With one's foot one may be led into temptation, trespass, or stumble, and with one's eye one may lust or covet. The point is that the goal of entering into "life" (vv. 43. 45) or "the kingdom of God" (v. 47) is so great that one should readily sacrifice even a part of one's body if it interferes with achieving that goal. The logic of these sayings is an example of the rabbinic principle of *Qal wahomer:* "what applies in a less important case will certainly apply in a more important case."[39] If one would sacrifice a limb or an eye to preserve one's life, how much more is it the case that one should make whatever sacrifice is called for to ensure that one is not barred from entering the kingdom of God? The image of cutting off limbs and gouging out eyes may also have spoken directly to the

Markan community, if it was in danger of persecution. The account of the martyrdom of the seven brothers in 2 Maccabees speaks of just this kind of torture. [Torture]

The alternative to life is hell, "the unquenchable fire" (v. 43). The term for hell is "Gehenna," which literally means "the land of Hinnom," a valley south of Jerusalem. [Gehenna] The only other references to unquenchable fire in the New Testament are in the sayings of John the Baptist (Matt 3:12; Luke 3:17). Mark 9:44 and 46 are quotations of Isaiah 66:24 that anticipate the quotation in Mark 9:48, "where their worm never dies and the fire is never quenched." Because these verses are not present in the best manuscripts, and because their addition by an early scribe is more easily explained than their omission, they are omitted from most contemporary translations (compare the KJV). The apocryphal book Judith envisions a similar fate for the nations that rise up against Israel: God "will send fire and worms into their flesh; and they shall weep in pain forever" (Jdt 16:17; cf. Sir 7:17).

The catchword "fire" has attracted the sayings on salt that conclude the chapter. Salt was an important preservative in all eras before refrigeration. Salt was used for religious purposes also. It was mixed with sacrifices (Lev 2:13) and incense (Exod 30:35). Newborn children were

Torture

While his mother and brothers watched, the king gave orders that his officers cut out the tongue of the first brother, scalp him, and "cut off his hands and feet" (2 Macc 7:4). The second brother was asked whether he would concede his faith rather than "have your body punished limb by limb" (2 Macc 7:7). He replied that the king of the universe "will raise us up to an everlasting renewal of life, because we have died for his laws" (2 Macc 7:9). The third brother stretched out his hands, and said, "I got these from Heaven, and because of his laws I disdain them, and from him I hope to get them back again" (2 Macc 7:11).

Gehenna

AΩ The New Testament distinguishes between Hades and Gehenna. Hades receives the souls of the dead until the resurrection and judgment. After the judgment, the reunited bodies and souls of the wicked are consigned to eternal torment in Gehenna.

The Valley of Hinnom, known as Wadi er-Rababeh, south of Jerusalem, was the site of child sacrifices to the pagan god Moloch in the time of Ahaz and Manasseh, who sacrificed their own sons, by fire, to this god (2 Kgs 16:3; 21:6). It became known as the place of eschatological torment. In *1 Enoch* (2d c. BC), the angel Uriel explains to Enoch, "This accursed valley is for those accursed forever. . . . here shall be their judgment in the last days" (*1 En* 27:2; *OTP* 1:27). It is "a valley, deep and burning with fire" (*1 En* 54:1; *OTP* 1:38). The torments of the wicked in Gehenna are described in the *Sybilline Oracles* (1:103; 2:290-310; 4:179-91), *4 Ezra* 7:36, and *2 Bar.* 59:10; 85:13. R. Judah said, "the best among physicians is destined for Gehenna" (*m. Kiddushin* 4.14; Danby, 329). A similar fate awaits one who "talks much with womankind" and neglects the study of the Law (*m. Aboth* 1.5; Danby, 446; cf. 5.20; *m. Eduyoth* 2.10).

Joachim Jeremias, "geenan," *TDNT* 1:657–58; Duane F. Watson, "Gehenna," *ABD* 2:926-28; Herbert Danby, *The Mishnah* (Oxford: Oxford University Press, 1933).

Hinnom Valley Tomb

View of a very fragmentary unexcavated Iron Age tomb on the southern slope of the Hinnom Valley. Only a partial burial bench remains. Note the decorative cornice where the wall meets the ceiling of this chamber.

This tomb is located to the east of St. Andrew's Church on the southern slope of the Hinnom Valley.

(Credit: Image courtesy of www.holylandphotos.org)

rubbed with salt, either for health purposes or to drive evil spirits away (Ezek 16:4). Vanquished cities were sown with salt so that they would be barren (Judg 9:45). But salt also had life-giving functions: Elisha purified the spring at Jericho by throwing salt into it so that "neither death nor miscarriage shall come from it" (2 Kgs 2:21). A "covenant of salt" was a permanent one (Num 18:19; 2 Chr 13:5). Eating or "taking salt" with someone bound one to him in loyalty (Ezra 4:14; cf. Acts 1:4). Jesus' disciples were to be "the salt of the earth" (Matt 5:13), and their speech should be "seasoned with salt" (Col 4:6).[40]

The references to fire in the preceding verses probably prompted the reminder for Mark's community that they would have to endure fiery trials (1 Pet 4:12). They would be "salted with fire" (9:49), which probably means that they would be purified and preserved by the ordeal they faced.

Pure salt does not lose its potency, but the salt found around the Dead Sea was mixed with gypsum and other minerals and often became stale (cf. Pliny, *Natural History* 31.34.67). Accordingly, the notion of salt losing its flavor was common (cf. Luke 14:34-35). The rabbis warned, "the wisdom of the Scribes shall become insipid" (*m. Sotah* 9.15).[41] To "have salt in yourselves" probably meant that the disciples were to serve as preservative agents, like salt, to be "the salt of the earth" (Matt 5:13). Therefore, because this is their calling, and because they have been warned about putting any stumbling block in another's path (vv.42-48), they should "be at peace with one another" (v. 50). The end of this section neatly returns to the original setting—the disciples' argument among themselves as to which of them was the greatest (9:33-34) and their dispute with the unauthorized exorcist (9:38).

CONNECTIONS

Mark 9:1-8

The transfiguration has received surprisingly little attention in Christian worship. It does not have a prominent celebration, like Christmas, Easter, or Pentecost. [The Feast of the Transfiguration] Its significance is less obvious, and for most preachers it would never rate

The Feast of the Transfiguration

"The Feast of the Transfiguration is observed on 6 Aug. It originated in the E. Church, where it appears to have been at first a local and unofficial feast, but had become widely adopted before AD 1000. In the W., where the feast was not introduced till a much later date, its general observance goes back to 1457, when Callistus III ordered its universal celebration in commemoration of the victory gained over the Turks at Belgrade on 6 Au. 1456."

F. L. Cross, ed., *The Oxford Dictionary of the Christian Church* (2d ed.; Oxford: Oxford University Press, 1983), 1390.

as a favorite preaching text. Like the disciples, we stand speechless before it.

Through the centuries mystics have quested for a beatific vision, often by long vigils of prayer, fasting, and ascetic living. Many people, however, can point to events in their lives when the veil of the ordinary seemed to part for a moment revealing and confirming spiritual realities that lie beyond our mundane experience. For some it was a conversion or call experience, for others a dramatic event in which their life was spared. Whatever the event, it changes life, marking a permanent divide. Forever after one will know that life is played out on an eternal stage. The content of such an experience may vary from person to person, but the transfiguration, with its announcement of the divinity of Christ, is the norm. When God's divine presence breaks into our common experience, it is in the person of Jesus. Such transcendent experiences may occur with less intensity on a more or less regular basis in worship, but they can never be programmed or orchestrated.

Like Peter, we may want to camp out in the places of our greatest spiritual experiences. Our temptation may be to want to stay on the mountaintop, but the kingdom is not about creating private, spiritual highs for believers. It is about bringing the reign of God to all persons and to all of life. We cannot tarry; there are people in the valley below who need us.

Mark 9:9-13

Jesus' conversation with the disciples as they descend from the mountain offers a poignant reflection on the limitations of our understanding. The disciples had just been privileged to have an experience no other human beings, not even the other disciples, would have. They had seen Jesus transfigured and talking with Moses and Elijah, and they had heard God's voice speaking from the cloud. No others would have such firsthand experience of Jesus' divinity. Nevertheless, their understanding was still limited. They were not yet prepared to tell others what they had seen. Then, Mark makes it clear that they do not understand the meaning of Jesus' resurrection from the dead or that John the Baptist had fulfilled the role of Elijah.

At least in reference to the resurrection and the role of John the Baptist, it appears that the disciples' inability to understand is rooted in the false expectations they harbored. The contemporaneous expectations regarding the coming of the Messiah, which formed their frame of reference, called for the coming of a powerful national leader who would root out Roman oppression and restore the throne of David. So strong was this misunderstanding that it clouded the disciples' sight even when Jesus charted a radically different vision of the kingdom for them.

Similarly, they had come to think that the Messiah's forerunner, Elijah, would "restore the tribes of Jacob." He would come, "driving a heavenly chariot at full stretch from heaven," "to remove afar those [families] that were brought nigh by violence and to bring nigh those [families] that were removed afar by violence" (see the texts cited in [Elijah's Coming]). With such expectations, the disciples were totally unprepared to see Elijah in the camel-haired prophet, calling the people to repentance and suffering death for his preaching.

False expectations prevented the disciples from seeing the mighty acts of God being done by John and Jesus. Jesus' vision of the kingdom required a radical reorientation of concepts of holiness, the role of God's people, the nature of community, and the shape of the future. The church has re-minted that vision in a succession of strikingly different versions: the early community of the persecuted, Constantine's imperial church, Augustine's "City of God," the medieval church of monasteries and Machiavellian pontiffs, the reformers' Geneva, the Puritans' Massachusetts Bay colony, the missionary societies of the nineteenth century, and the mega-churches of the late twentieth and early twenty-first centuries. Perhaps God is doing a new thing, and we are missing it because our vision is clouded by past practices and false expectations.

Mark 9:14-29

The story of Jesus casting out the "dumb" spirit from the boy is a study in power and faith. Four persons or groups surround the boy: the father, the disciples, the scribes (and the crowd), and Jesus. The father is unable to help his son, knows that he needs help, and trusts that Jesus can help him. The disciples, who earlier were commissioned to cast out demons and did so successfully, apparently assume they will be able to help the boy but are unable to do so. The scribes, who make no effort to help, argue with the disciples, presumably because they feel it necessary to ensure that any efforts on the boy's behalf be in accord with their understanding of the Law. [Controversy and Praise]

In this instance, Jesus responds not to the scribes—who are ignored—but to the needs of the disciples, the boy, and the boy's father. He

Controversy and Praise

Augustine's observation speaks as incisively now as it did in his day: "Look now, blessed Jesus, from your holy hill. See your true believers with a throng about them who delight in nothing but to question and contradict and perpetually dispute. Open their eyes, O Lord, that they may see you, and being amazed at the beauty of your truth, come running to adore you." (Augustine, *Sermons* 234)

But sometimes it is also the true believers "who delight in nothing but to question and contradict and perpetually dispute" and who need to have their eyes opened!

Thomas C. Oden and Christopher A. Hall, eds., *Ancient Christian Commentary on Scripture: New Testament II, Mark* (Downers Grove IL: InterVarsity Press, 1998), 123.

leads the boy's father to see his need for a steadfast faith: "help my unbelief." He casts the dumb spirit out of the boy, and he teaches the disciples on their constant need for prayer.

The father plays a supporting role to the disciples in the theme of the need for constant faith. The framing of the story within the accounts of Jesus' approach to the disciples and his teaching of the disciples in the house at the end turn this exorcism into a lesson on discipleship. Faith is seldom pure or constant. The father becomes a model for the disciples. Like the blind man who could see but not clearly (8:22-26), he believes but still struggles with unbelief. The disciples follow Jesus and attempt to cast out the demon, presumably in Jesus' name, but are unable to do so. Jesus' admonition that they need to pray leads readers to fill the gap in the story regarding why they were unsuccessful by concluding that they relied on their own entitlement rather than seeking again the power that comes only from God.

In the connections for Mark 9:9-13, I suggested that the disciples' false expectations kept them from recognizing that John the Baptist had fulfilled the role of Elijah. Now Mark shows that the disciples' misplaced confidence in their own ability to help the boy robs them of the power to do so. Perhaps nothing leads to a false sense of confidence more quickly than a track record of success. Those who are most effective, and those who are called to full-time ministry, are therefore most at risk of falling into this trap. Success breeds confidence, but ministry in Jesus' name requires the constant renewal of humility that acknowledges that disciples can do nothing of their own accord.

In the polar-opposite standards of the kingdom, therefore, success can lead to the kind of self-confidence that renders one ineffective, while failure can throw one back on God's power, thereby creating the conditions for future successes. The disciples were open to learning from their failure: "Why could we not cast it out?" (9:28). Are we?

Mark 9:30-32

The passion predictions in Mark go to the heart of the matter. They speak of what God is doing (handing Jesus over to humanity), what Judas will do (betray Jesus), what Jesus will do (accept his death), what the authorities will do (kill him), and the outcome of these events (he will rise again). The language of the passion predictions also reminds us that Jesus fulfilled the role of the suffering servant, foreseen by Isaiah generations earlier.

The mysteries here defy human understanding. The events are at once the result of human actions and divine intent. God takes the events, choices, and decisions of human beings and works through them seamlessly to accomplish redemptive purposes. In rural Galilee, through a Jewish carpenter turned teacher and prophet, God was preparing the way for the salvation of all humanity through the death of this one man. That salvation would be effected not by the exercise of power or coercion but through love and self-sacrifice.

The cross is therefore the clearest revelation of God's love for humanity. Paradoxically, that clearest revelation takes the form of a love so profound that it defies human understanding. We are left with the mystery of divine love, forgiving us and calling us into fellowship with God.

Like the disciples we may shrink from this mystery. We may never understand it fully, but the important thing is that we keep following, as they did on the way to Jerusalem, until we are transformed by the power of God's love for us. That transformation, however, is not a momentary experience, though we may be able to identify the moment when we became aware of it. The power of the cross continues its transforming effect on us daily. So, look daily to the cross and remember Christ's sacrifice on our behalf. What do you see there?

Mark 9:33-37

It must be rooted in our culture, but many of us have the notion that it is wrong to aspire to distinction, to want to be first. It may be all right in sports; but even in school, teachers are making learning more cooperative and less competitive. Being one of the group is often more socially acceptable than aspiring to being a leader. Lessons on pride and humility also lead us to take the lesser position and to avoid presuming that we are better than others.

It comes as some surprise, therefore, that Jesus does not rebuke the disciples for wanting to be first. Instead, he actually tells them how to be first. In the kingdom conventional standards are overturned. Jesus' followers will be rewarded not for their achievement of positions of power and preeminence but for their service to others. Years ago Jesse Jackson prophetically painted a picture of heaven in which he saw Jesus, the patriarchs and prophets of old, and the freedom fighters of the Civil Rights era sitting around together:

> They all will be discussing hard trials and tribulations and the angels will be flocking around them because they'll be freedom heroes. And every time one of you break into the conversation, with no scars on you, dying on a pension plan—what will you have to contribute to the conversation?[42]

Mark 9:38-41

Jesus' response to John, correcting him for attempting to stop an exorcist from casting out evil spirits in Jesus' name, speaks to the petty desire for control, recognition, and reward in each of us. Because Jesus had called them to be apostles and given them authority to cast out demons, the disciples thought they had been given an exclusive prerogative. The assumed they had been given the status of brokers in Jesus' coming kingdom. They would choose his clients and grant privileges. Rather than seeing the unauthorized exorcist as an ally in the larger context of the battle against evil, the disciples saw him as a threat to their own status as brokers of Jesus' power.

Envy and jealousy are near-sighted sins. They limit our vision, focusing all our attention on ourselves and our status, which cannot be the first response of one who would be "servant of all." John Claypool told the story of a farmer to whom God granted three wishes. The only condition was that whatever he was given, his neighbor would receive double. First, he asked for more cattle, and he was proud of his herd, but then he became jealous that his neighbor's herd was twice as large as his. For his second wish he asked for more land, and he was proud of his spread until he looked across the fence at the size of his neighbor's farm. So, for his third wish he asked to have one of his eyes put out, and God wept.

The gospel call to self-denial, however, is not merely a call to asceticism for its own sake. The call to discipleship requires us to examine our innermost motivations and lay aside all self-centeredness for the sake of serving Christ and serving others in a cause that makes our own sacrifices inconsequential. One of the ironies of contemporary American culture is that those who have so much in the way of material goods often find life so meaningless. We are privileged to be able to entertain questions about how we will spend our lives and what will make our lives meaningful. The American dream of owning a house, building a 401K, retiring early, and living out our days on a golf course often seems empty. There must be something greater for which one can give his or her life.

At the same time, the gospel challenges our every attempt to set limits on who can and cannot receive God's mercy. What do we do when the Spirit moves in ways beyond our control, when the church down the road flourishes while ours plods along? It may be hard for us to see the big picture, precisely because we have such a small part in it. Jesus did not establish exclusive franchises. Instead, "there is a wideness in God's mercy" that constantly challenges us to remove the limitations we would place in the path of others who come to receive the same love by which we live.

Mark 9:42-50

These verses have a cruel history of literal interpretation. More often, however, they are ignored as quaint moralizing. Because we know these words are not meant to be taken literally, we feel free to ignore them entirely. Jesus meant for his followers to take seriously both the impediments they might place in the way of another's faith and the offenses they tolerate that pose a danger to their own faith. In context, the two are related. The disciples had placed a stumbling block before the unauthorized exorcist by forbidding him to use Jesus' name, and they had done so because of their concern for their own positions and entitlements. [Augustine on Judgmental Excess]

The saying "a little knowledge is a dangerous thing" is particularly true in matters of faith. Those who have a measure of understanding often assume an attitude of sophistication and expertise that is offensive to others. Jesus gave no bonus points to the disciples for knowing the sources of the Pentateuch, form criticism, or process theology. Understanding something of the theology of worship should therefore never become a license to be critical of another's sincere but unstructured worship. Nor should having studied theology free one from maintaining the highest ethical standards.

In these permissive times students all too often assume that education confers entitlement on them. The logic is "we don't have to do *x* any longer because we know *y*." On the other hand, Jesus turned from the relationship between knowledge and privilege to the responsibility that knowledge confers on those who acquire it. The more one knows, and the more mature one's faith, the larger the circle of "these little ones" becomes. At the beginning we are all "little ones." Then, the more one grows, the greater the number of those who are smaller or weaker becomes, and the more people there are who will be hurt if we stumble. In this respect also, therefore, the ways of the kingdom are the opposite of the ways of culture: growth and advancement bring not greater privilege but greater responsibility. Jesus asks not only what do you know but what have you done with what you know.

Augustine on Judgmental Excess

"Some who are intent on severe disciplinary principles which admonish us to rebuke the restless, not to give what is holy to dogs, to consider a despiser of the church as a heathen, to cut off from the unified structure of the body the member which causes scandal, so disturb the peace of the church that they try to separate the wheat from the chaff before the proper time. Blinded by this error, they are themselves separated instead from the unity of Christ." (*Faith and Works* 4.6)

Thomas C. Oden and Christopher A. Hall, eds., *Ancient Christian Commentary on Scripture: New Testament II, Mark* (Downers Grove IL: InterVarsity Press, 1998), 129.

NOTES

[1] For a full discussion of these alternatives, see George R. Beasley-Murray, *Jesus and the Kingdom of God* (Grand Rapids: Wm. B. Eerdmans, 1986), 187-93.

[2] Ibid., 189.

[3] Ibid., citing C. H. Dodd, *The Parables of the Kingdom* (New York: Charles Scribner's Sons, 1935), 53-54.

[4] Ben Witherington III, *The Gospel of Mark: A Socio-Rhetorical Commentary* (Grand Rapids: Wm. B. Eerdmans, 2001), 262.

[5] Beasley-Murray, *Jesus and the Kingdom of God*, 191-92.

[6] See Robert H. Stein, "Is the Transfiguration (Mark 9:2-8) a Misplaced Resurrection Account?" *JBL* 95 (1976): 79-96.

[7] Craig A. Evans, *Mark 8:27–16:20* (WBC 34B; Nashville: Thomas Nelson, 2001), 34.

[8] J. Behm, "*metamorphoō*," *TDNT* 4:757.

[9] Ibid., 4:758.

[10] BDAG, 945.

[11] BDAG, 202.

[12] James H. Charlesworth, ed., *The Old Testament Pseudepigrapha* (Garden City NY: Doubleday, 1985), 2:396.

[13] Eduard Lohse, "*rabbi*," *TDNT* 6:965.

[14] Wilhelm Michaelis, "*skēnē*," *TDNT* 7:371.

[15] Witherington, *The Gospel of Mark*, 264.

[16] Contrary to Joachim Jeremias, "*el(e)ias*," *TDNT* 2:939-41, who argues for the expectation that Elijah would suffer on the basis of Rev 11:3ff.

[17] See Walter Wink, *John the Baptist in the Gospel Tradition* (Cambridge: Cambridge University Press, 1968), 15.

[18] William L. Lane, *The Gospel according to Mark* (NICNT; Grand Rapids: Wm. B. Eerdmans, 1974), 326.

[19] See C. E. B. Cranfield, *The Gospel according to St. Mark* (Cambridge: Cambridge University Press, 1959), 298; Joachim Jeremias, *New Testament Theology: The Proclamation of Jesus* (New York: Charles Scribner's Sons, 1971), 295.

[20] Witherington, *The Gospel of Mark*, 266, who cites Morna Hooker, *The Gospel according to Mark* (Peabody MA: Hendrickson, 1991), 222.

[21] Lane, *The Gospel according to Mark*, 329.

[22] BDAG, 303.

[23] Lane, *The Gospel according to Mark*, 331 (scribes); Cranfield, *The Gospel according to St. Mark*, 300 (the crowd); and Evans, *Mark 8:27–16:20*, 50 (the disciples).

[24] Lane, *The Gospel according to Mark*, 334.

[25] Cranfield, *The Gospel according to St. Mark*, 304, points out that *tous pollous* may mean "all."

[26] Lane, *The Gospel according to Mark*, 334.

[27] Cranfield, *The Gospel according to St. Mark*, 305.

[28] Eduard Schweizer, *The Good News according to Mark* (trans. Donald H. Madvig; Atlanta: John Knox Press, 1970), 190.

[29] Friedrich Büchsel, *"didōmi," TDNT* 2:169.

[30] Witherington, *The Gospel of Mark*, 269.

[31] Evans, *Mark 8:27–16:20*, 57.

[32] Jeremias, *New Testament Theology*, 282.

[33] Lane, *The Gospel according to Mark*, 338-39.

[34] W. D. Davies, *The Setting of the Sermon on the Mount* (Cambridge: Cambridge University Press, 1963), 423.

[35] BDAG, 398.

[36] See R. Alan Culpepper, *John the Son of Zebedee: The Life of a Legend* (Columbia: University of South Carolina Press, 1994), esp. ch. 2, "Son of Thunder: The Apostle in the Synoptic Gospels and Acts."

[37] See John Dominic Crossan, *The Historical Jesus: The Life of a Mediterranean Jewish Peasant* (San Francisco: HarperSanFrancisco, 1991).

[38] Cranfield, *The Gospel according to St. Mark*, 310, who credits W. Nestle, "Wer nicht mit mir ist, ist wider mich," *ZNW* 13 (1912): 85, with citing this reference.

[39] John Bowker, *The Targums and Rabbinic Literature: An Introduction to Jewish Interpretations of Scripture* (Cambridge: At the University Press, 1969), 315.

[40] See Friedrich Hauck, *"halas," TDNT* 1:228-29; J. F. Ross, "Salt," *IDB* 1:167.

[41] Herbert Danby, *The Mishnah* (Oxford: Oxford University Press, 1933), 306.

[42] Jesse L. Jackson, "Chastising the Rich Young Ruler," *Home Missions* (July 1969): 25.

CONDITIONS FOR ENTERING THE KINGDOM

Mark 10:1-52

With the beginning of Mark 10 Jesus leaves Galilee and makes his way across the Jordan on his way to Judea. As he does so, he is questioned about divorce (10:1-12) and rebukes the disciples for preventing people from bringing their children to him (10:13-16). In both instances Jesus offers teachings that call for a reordering of relationships in the kingdom. It is also possible to see in these scenes a continuation of the theme of Jesus' teaching on "these little ones" in 9:33-37 and 9:42. Prohibiting divorce protected women from being cast aside with no means of support. The new order of the kingdom, therefore, protects women and children in a patriarchal society.

Similarly, the kingdom ethic requires the distribution of material possessions to care for the poor (10:17-22). When the disciples respond in amazement to the stringency of these teachings, Jesus reminds them that only God can save a person; it lies beyond our human capacities to effect the change that salvation requires (10:23-27). When Peter objects that they have left everything to follow Jesus, implying that they deserve to be rewarded, Jesus promises that they will indeed receive rewards, though not the rewards they have in mind (10:28-31).

The third passion prediction is the longest and most detailed of the three (10:32-34). Like the first two, it is followed by a scene that confirms that the disciples still do not understand what Jesus is saying, or what it means for them. James and John ask for the places of honor in the kingdom, and Jesus' reply implies that these are reserved for those who follow him in self-sacrifice even to the point of suffering and martyrdom. If the disciples want to be first, they should reject the authoritarian practices of the culture and follow him in giving their lives in service to all (10:35-45).

As they are leaving Jericho, Bartimaeus, a blind beggar, calls out to Jesus. When Jesus restores his sight, Mark says that he followed Jesus "on the way" (10:46-52), which is Mark's way of saying that in contrast to the disciples Bartimaeus followed Jesus on the path of servanthood that would lead Jesus to the cross that awaited him in Jerusalem.

COMMENTARY

Teachings on Divorce, 10:1-12

A geographical notice introduces chapter 10. Mark uses such notices periodically to move the narrative along (e.g., 7:24, 31; 8:22, 27; 9:30, 33). As Jesus continues his journey southward, he follows the route from Galilee across the Jordan into Perea with the intention of making his way to Jericho and from there up to Jerusalem. He would not actually enter Judea until he crossed the Jordan again on his way to Jericho. The reference to Judea in 10:1 is at best an indication of his destination rather than his location at that point in the journey.

The language of v. 1 is thoroughly Markan, leaving no doubt that the verse is a Markan seam or transitional verse: "Characteristic vocabulary includes *kai ekeithen*, 'and from there' (6:1; 9:30), *anastas*, 'arising,' (1:35), *erchetai*, 'he goes' (1:40; 2:3; 3:20), and *eis ta oria*, 'into the region' (5:17; 7:31)."[1] This is the only place where Mark uses the plural, "crowds," perhaps suggesting that in the following scenes various crowds gathered around Jesus. The term *eiōthei*, in context meaning "as was his custom," occurs only here in Mark, but Luke notes that it was Jesus' custom to go to the synagogue on the Sabbath (Luke 4:16). If v. 1 introduces not just the following scene but the blessing of the children (10:13-16) and the conversation with the rich man also (10:17-22), then the imperfect tense is iterative, following the plural "crowds."

The Pharisees, who conspired with the Herodians to kill Jesus in 3:6, last approached Jesus in 8:11, seeking a sign, testing him. Once again they come, again testing Jesus (10:2). The Herodians test Jesus in 12:15, and the only other occurrence of this verb in Mark is its initial occurrence in 1:13, which links testing with Satan. Why would a question about divorce pose a test for Jesus? Although there is some evidence that there was a division of opinion between the Pharisees, who allowed divorce and debated the conditions under which a divorce might be justified, and the Essenes, who did not allow divorce, it is doubtful that the Pharisees were trying to impugn Jesus by exposing his agreement with the Essenes on this issue. [Divorce among First-century Jews] More likely, they were hoping to lead Jesus to make a statement on divorce that might be construed as a criticism of the Herods. John the Baptist had been arrested by Herod because he said, "It is not lawful (*exestin*) for you to have your brother's wife" (6:18). Herod Antipas had sent his first wife, the daughter of a Nabatean prince, back to her father so that he could marry Herodias, who had been married to Herod Philip, one of his half brothers. As a result, the Nabateans had made

Divorce among First-century Jews

An entire tractate of the Mishnah is devoted to "Bills of Divorce" (*m. Gittin*). Extended debate concerned who could write a bill of divorce, its content, the witnessing of the bill, its delivery, and provisions for rescinding it. The essential formula in the bill of divorce was "Lo, thou art free to marry any man" (*m. Gittin* 9.3; Danby, 319). The schools of Hillel and Shammai differed on the interpretation of the phrase in Deut 24:1 regarding permissible grounds for a divorce: "The School of Shammai say: A man may not divorce his wife unless he has found unchastity in her, for it is written, *Because he hath found in her* indecency *in anything*. And the School of Hillel say: [He may divorce her] even if she spoiled a dish for him, for it is written, *Because he hath found in her indecency* in anything. R. Akiba says: Even if he found another fairer than she, for it is written, *And it shall be if she find no favour in his eyes* . . ." (*m. Gittin* 9.10; Danby, 321).

The Essenes, in contrast, held that a man could remarry only if his wife died: "He shall take no other wife apart from her because only she will be with him all the days of her life. If she dies, he shall take for himself another from his father's house, from his family" (11Q19 57.17-19; Martínez, 174).

Their opponents (which included the Pharisees) were therefore guilty of fornication "by taking two wives in their lives, even though the principle of creation is *Gen 1:27* 'male and female he created them.' And the ones that went into the ark *Gen 7:9* 'went in two by two into the ark.' And about the prince it is written: *Deut 17:17* 'He should not multiply wives to himself'" (CD 4.20-5.2; Martínez, 36).

A Jewish woman could not divorce her husband: "The man that divorces is not like to the woman that is divorced; for a woman is put away with her consent or without it, but a husband can put away his wife only with his own consent" (*m. Yebamoth* 14.1; Danby, 240). Moreover, a Jewish woman could not remarry without her husband's permission (Josephus, *Ant.* 15.259). Nevertheless, if a man had boils or worked at certain trades that defiled him (such as a coppersmith or a tanner), the wife would force him to give her a divorce (*m. Ketuboth* 7.10). Furthermore, there were apparently instances, such as Salome's divorce of her husband, when powerful women acted in defiance of the law.

Herbert Danby, *The Mishnah* (Oxford: Oxford University Press, 1933). Florentino García Martínez, *The Dead Sea Scrolls Translated* (trans. Wilfred G. E. Watson; Leiden: E. J. Brill, 1994).

war on the Galileans, inflicting heavy losses on them. Divorce was therefore a sensitive political and social issue.

The Hebrew Scriptures contain two passages that allow for differing interpretations of whether and when divorce is permissible. According to Genesis 2:22-24, God created woman from man to be man's companion: "Therefore a man leaves his father and his mother and clings to his wife, and they become one flesh" (Gen 2:24). The union of husband and wife creates a new entity ("one flesh") that is indissoluble. For this reason, if a man divorces his wife and she marries another, he cannot later remarry her because to do so would be like marrying a close relative (Deut 24:4; Jer 3:1; cf. Lev 18:6). On the other hand, Deuteronomy 24:1-4 allows for an Israelite man to divorce his wife if "he finds something objectionable about her." The only requirement is that he must write her "a certificate of divorce," which would enable her to remarry. The Pharisees followed Deuteronomy 24:1-4, allowing divorce, while debating the conditions under which a man could divorce his wife. The Essenes, on the other hand, forbade divorce and considered remarriage to be fornication.

Jesus' response to the Pharisees' question set a trap for them. His view on the issue of divorce was shaped by God's intention in creating human beings male and female rather than by the provisions in

Deuteronomy 24. By asking the Pharisees, "What did Moses command you?" he was soliciting an answer that he would reject. He knew the Pharisees' position and invited them to state it, knowing that it was not his view. One can almost detect a note of triumph or satisfaction in the Pharisees' response: "Moses allowed a man . . ." (10:4). Jesus' response to their appeal to Moses is surprisingly sharp: "Because of your hardness of heart he wrote this commandment for you" (10:5). Hardness of heart, which implies willful disobedience or resistance to God's commands, again evokes echoes of the exodus (see the comment on the disciples' hardness of heart in 6:52). Moses and the prophets had condemned Israel for its hardness of heart (Deut 10:16; Ezek 3:7).

By setting up the antithesis between "Moses wrote this commandment" and "God made them male and female" (a quotation of Gen 1:27 or 5:2), Jesus subtly claims a higher authority for the ideal of marriage without divorce. The divine intent for marriage is reflected from creation in the contrasting and complementing roles of males and females. Moses had granted the husband the right to initiate divorce, but Jesus recalls the man's God-given responsibility from the creation: "For this reason *a man* shall leave his father and mother and be joined to his wife" (10:7; Gen 2:24). Leaving father and mother meant establishing a new family, being joined to his wife meant the priority of the marriage relationship over all others, and becoming one flesh meant the creation of a new entity that had not existed before and could not be dissolved thereafter. The verb "join" (*suzeugnymi*) literally means to "yoke together" (see Paul's reference to "true yoke fellow" in Phil 4:3) or "make a pair" (Ezek 1:11, 23 LXX), and was a common metaphor for marriage (Josephus, *Ant.* 6.309). The often-quoted prohibition of divorce, "Therefore, what God has joined together, let no one separate" (10:9), is expressed in Greek in the form of a third person imperative.

The change of scene, "in the house," is a familiar introduction to private teaching for the disciples (cf. 7:17; 9:28, 33; cf. 7:24). In this setting Mark introduces the related but separate teaching on divorce that has parallels in Luke 16:18 and Matthew 5:32; 19:9, where Matthew adds the except clause, "except in case of *porneia*," which is commonly translated "adultery" but may have other meanings (cf. Acts 15:20, 29). At this point Jesus moves beyond the position of the Essenes by making the husband guilty of adultery if he divorces his wife and remarries. This prohibition is more ambiguous than is commonly thought. First, the implication, "one who divorces in order to marry another," may be implied but is not explicit. Second, the last phrase may be translated "commits adultery against her" or perhaps "with her," depending on whether it means against his first wife or with his second wife.[2] The radically new concept here is that in a culture in

Adultery

In the Old Testament, "the Decalogue numbers the inviolability of marriage among the fundamental commandments for the community life of the people of Israel, Ex. 20:14(13); Dt. 5:18(17). But adultery is possible only if there is carnal intercourse between a married man and a married or betrothed Israelitess, Dt. 22:22ff.; Lv.20:10. Adultery is the violation of the marriage of another, Gn., 39:10ff. . . . Unconditional fidelity is demanded only of the woman, who in marriage becomes the possession of her husband."

According to the Mishnah, "only adultery with an Israelitess is to be punished. There is no penalty for intercourse with the wife of a non-Israelite. . . . Only the wife, who is set apart for her husband alone . . . and not the husband . . . is exposed to the full threat of the penalties. In the Roman period the death penalty drops away. The husband is simply forced to divorce an adulterous wife, who forfeits the money assigned her under the marriage contract (Sota, IV, 3), and is not permitted to marry her lover (Sota, 5, 1)."

Under Greek and Roman law, "a mark of the ancient view of marriage is that unconditional fidelity is demanded of the wife alone. The married man is not forbidden to have intercourse with an unmarried woman. . . . In Roman law up to the time of the Republic the husband has, in a case of *adulterium*, the one-sided right of private revenge against the guilty wife even to putting to death, whereas the wife must accept the adultery of her husband."

In the New Testament, however, the concept of adultery is sharply intensified: "the right of a man to sexual freedom is denied. Like the wife, the husband is under obligation of fidelity. . . . adultery does not consist merely in physical intercourse with a strange woman; it is present already in the desire which negates fidelity (Mt. 5:28). . . . The OT prohibition of adultery is not confined to the negative avoidance of the sinful act. It finds its true fulfillment only in the love of spouses who are joined together by God (R. 13:9)."

F. Hauck, "*moicheuō*," *TDNT* 4:730–34.

Giambattista Tiepolo (1696–1770). *Christ and the Adulteress*. Louvre, Paris, France. (Credit: Erich Lessing / Art Resource, NY)

which a woman could commit adultery against her husband (Sir 23:22-26), and a man could commit adultery against another man by having intercourse with the other man's wife, Jesus introduced the notion that a man could commit adultery against his wife by having intercourse with any other woman. The wife is thereby elevated to a position of equal partnership and rights in the marriage and entitled to the same fidelity that the husband could expect from the wife. [Adultery] Because the marriage bond ("one flesh") cannot be dissolved, for either partner to marry another was tantamount to committing adultery.

Verse 12 forbids a woman from divorcing her husband, something that was not allowed by Jewish law but was allowed under Roman law. Luke includes this provision (Luke 16:18), while Matthew omits it (Matt 19:9).

The New Testament passages that deal with divorce probably reflect an extended tradition history as the early church struggled to be both faithful to Jesus' teachings on the matter and pastorally sensitive, especially in situations in which Christian women were married to pagan husbands. Mark records the most stringent, and hence probably the

Divorce in the Early Church

"In the first two centuries Hermas and Clement of Alexandria seem to reflect the common position. Both allowed for separation but both came out strongly against second marriage. Thus Hermas argued that one may put away a wife for adultery but must take her back if she repents (Mand. 4.1.4-8). The question was urgent for Christians in the world of pagan antiquity, since divorce was common. With increasing evangelization male converts in particular tried to maintain the right to end their marriages, but Augustine strongly championed the position of women in opposing remarriage after divorce and bringing husbands under the common rule. The Council of Carthage in 407, which also took a stand against marriage with pagans, plainly disallowed remarriage after divorce (canon 8), and thus stated what became, or continued to be, the Western position. Later the Eastern Church took a less stringent attitude under the Justinian Code (6th cent.), although this code maintained strong control over the granting of divorces."

G. W. Bromiley, "Divorce," *ISBE* (rev. ed., ed. Geoffrey W. Bromiley; Grand Rapids: Wm. B. Eerdmans, 1979), 1:978–79.

earliest form of the tradition—a man may not divorce his wife (Mark 10:11), which is extended in a Greco-Roman setting to the prohibition of a woman divorcing her husband (10:12). Matthew (5:32; 19:9) adds the except clause, allowing for divorce in situations of adultery or other sexual offenses, perhaps including polygamy or marriages within forbidden degrees of relationship. Paul then allows divorce in cases in which the unbelieving partner desires to separate from the believer (1 Cor 7:15). [Divorce in the Early Church]

Blessing the Children, 10:13-16

The sequence of material here may be less random than it appears on first reading. In 9:36-37 Jesus took a child in his arms and spoke to the disciples about receiving such children. The transition from speaking of marriage in the preceding verses to speaking of children is also a natural connection, as is the connection between women and children as powerless persons. Hence to be servant of all (9:35), Jesus' disciples must protect women from being victimized by divorce and receive and bless children. Similarly, just as Jesus corrected the disciples for attempting to forbid the unauthorized exorcist by saying, "do not stop him" (*mē kōluete auton*; 9:39), so now he says, "do not stop them" (*mē kōluete auta*; 10:14). In this scene the disciples again show that they do not understand; as Painter observes, "The disciples did not remember the lesson about receiving the little children in Jesus' name."[3] And Jesus continues to teach the disciples what it means to be a "servant of all."

Verse 13 provides a minimal setting for the scene. We are not told where they are or who was bringing the children—presumably the parents. The term for children normally means young children up to the age of twelve (see [Age in Antiquity]). Jesus attends to children remarkably frequently in Mark. He raises the daughter of Jairus (5:21-24, 35-43), casts the demon out of the Syrophoenician woman's daughter (7:24-30), casts the unclean spirit out of the epileptic boy (9:14-29), takes a child in his arms (9:36-37), and blesses the children (10:13-16).

The fact that children were being brought so that Jesus might touch them indicates that people recognized Jesus as a distinguished person, a prophet, or a teacher whose touch could confer a blessing or heal (see

3:10; 5:28; 6:56; 8:22). By preventing the children from being brought to Jesus, the disciples were again acting as brokers, protecting Jesus from unworthy clients (see the commentary on 9:38-41 and [Patrons, Brokers, and Clients] and [Children in Antiquity]). The term translated "spoke sternly" (*epitimēsan*) is a strong verb meaning to rebuke, reprove, censure, or warn (1:25; 3:12; 4:39; 8:30, 32, 33; 10:48).[4] Jesus' response is equally strong. He became indignant, angry (10:41; 14:4) with the disciples. Both Matthew and Luke omit the term (Matt 19:14; Luke 18:16), just as they omit the reference to Jesus' anger in Mark 3:5. The reference to Jesus' anger probably indicates a significant escalation in Jesus' disapproval of the disciples since there are no such references in the earlier scenes in which Jesus takes a child in his arms (9:36-37) or responds to their attempt to stop the unauthorized exorcist (9:38-41). Jesus never approves of efforts to keep people from coming to him. He searched for the woman who had touched him when the disciples dismissed the incident (5:30-33); he had compassion on the crowd that followed them, even when they had no time to eat (6:31-34); when he tried to withdraw to Tyre, he still cast the demon out of the Syrophoenician woman's daughter (7:24-30); and later he will heal Bartimaeus when the crowd seeks to keep him from calling out to Jesus (10:46-52).

In this instance, Jesus explains, "it is to such as these that the kingdom of God belongs" (10:14). Even if v. 15 once circulated independently, the logic of the two verses is the same: the kingdom belongs to those who do not presume to merit, deserve, or be entitled to it. Therefore, one must receive the kingdom with the same delight and humility that a child shows when given a gift. The nature of the kingdom itself determines who can enter it. Verse 15 is related to Matthew 18:3 and John 3:3, 5. All of these sayings have the same elements:

"Truly (*amēn*), I say to you,
   whoever does not receive the kingdom of God as a child (Mark
      10:15),
   unless you change and become like children (Matt 18:3),
   unless you are born from above (again) (John 3:3),
   unless you are born of water and Spirit (John 3:5),
      (you) cannot enter the kingdom of God."

The syntax of v. 15 is such that it is possible that "receive . . . as a child" might mean unless one receives the kingdom as one would receive a child (gladly, openly), but the more natural and more likely meaning is unless one receives the kingdom as a child receives it (without presumption, or with delight).

Driving home the point, Jesus (1) takes the children in his arms (the same verb that occurs in 9:36, but nowhere else in the New Testament), (2) lays his hands on them (fulfilling the desire that he might touch them, v. 13), and (3) blesses them (*kateulogei,* a rare verb that occurs only here in the New Testament and in Tob 11:1, 17 in the Septuagint).[5] As a lesson for the church, this story is double-edged, with a twist: the children are presented as role models, while the disciples are presented as a warning.[6]

The Rich Man, the Camel, and the Eye of a Needle, 10:17-31

The next three scenes can be treated separately or together because they are closely related. Following Jesus' response to the rich man's question (10:17-22), he comments to the disciples about the difficulty of entering the kingdom with wealth (10:23-27), and Peter reminds Jesus that they have left everything to follow him (10:28-31).

Earlier Jesus spoke of the urgency of removing stumbling blocks that keep one from entering life (or the kingdom of God, 9:47). The previous scene also addressed the requirements for entering the kingdom—receive it as a child (10:15). Jesus' response to the rich man calls attention to the impediment of "cares of the world and the lure of riches" (4:19) that choke the seed sown among the thorns. Jesus' encounter with the rich man also completes the sequence of the "little ones" for whom the disciple must care: women (who could be put aside by divorce), children, and now the poor.

As a result of harmonizing the Gospels, the man in this story is often called "the rich young ruler," but only Matthew says he is young (19:20), and only Luke calls him a ruler (18:18). In Mark he is neither young nor a ruler. Mark sets the scene with significant details: (1) Jesus was setting out "on the way," (2) the man ran to him, (3) knelt before him, and (4) addressed him as "good teacher." Matthew (19:16) omits all of these details, and Luke (18:18) retains only the last. Because the motif of "the way" is prominent throughout this section of the Gospel (8:27; 9:33-34; 10:32, 46, 52), its presence here should not be overlooked. Riches are a stumbling block to any who would follow Jesus "on the way" to the cross. The detail that the man ran to Jesus should be taken with his kneeling before him and his address "good teacher." All communicate extravagance. It was considered undignified or shameful for a man to run (pulling up his robe, exposing his legs, sandals flapping) except in an emergency (cf. the father running in Luke 15:20).[7] Kneeling before Jesus, the man assumed the posture of a supplicant, in contrast to those who engaged Jesus in legal debates (cf. the scribes in 12:28). The address, "good teacher," is surprisingly unusual: "There are no examples from the first century or earlier of anyone being called 'good teacher' as we have here."[8] The man's question is interesting both for what it requests and for what it assumes. "What must I do" assumes that by *doing* something he can gain eternal life. The term "inherit," likewise, is loaded with connotations deeply rooted in Scripture. Israel looked back to the covenant between God and Abraham in which God called Abraham to be the father of a people through whom God could bless all the peoples of the earth, and in return promised to make Abraham the father of a great nation and give his descendants land. Those who were descended from Abraham were therefore heirs of the covenant (cf. Paul's interpretation of this important concept in Rom 4 and Gal 3–4).[9] The scribe in Luke 10:25 asks the same question. The phrase "to inherit eternal life" is well established in Jewish writings from the period: "the devout of the Lord will inherit life in happiness" (*Pss. Sol.* 14:10, *OTP* 2:664), and ". . . the hope of those who would inherit eternal life" (*1 En* 40:9; *OTP* 1:32; cf. 4 Macc 15:3).[10] Surprisingly, though, eternal life is a much greater concern in modern preaching than it is in the Gospel of Mark, where it is mentioned only in this passage and in 10:30.

Initially, Jesus responds not to the question but to the address "good teacher." Jesus' response, saying there is none good but God alone, raised interesting christological questions for the early interpreters. [In Defense of Jesus' Goodness] Some, however, interpreted Jesus' response as a test of the man's faith (Hilary of Poitiers, *On the Trinity* 9.2). If so, it is similar to Jesus' response to the Syrophoenician woman, or his question to the disciples, "who do you say that I am?" (8:29). In this instance, however, Jesus moves on to a recitation of the commandments, thereby addressing the man's question. The intent therefore seems to be to deflect acclamation from himself to God. Jesus' mission was not to win acclaim for his works or his wisdom but to call the people to the kingdom—the reign, the Lordship—of God (1:15). Eduard Schweizer observes that "Jesus merely intended to say it is not fitting to exchange compliments when discussing a matter which concerns God and no other."[11] Jesus' response to the man is also subtly related to the answer to which he is directing the man, however. Eternal life lies not in doing, not in keeping commandments, but in complete

In Defense of Jesus' Goodness

Hilary of Poitiers said, "the Lord rejected this declaration of a spurious faith because the question was put to him as if he were merely a teacher of the law. . . . He would not have rejected the attribute of goodness if it had been attributed to him as God" (*On the Trinity* 9.16). Origen saw a different purpose in Jesus' response: "The purpose of this statement is to make it understood that the Son is not of some other ancillary 'goodness,' but of that alone which is in the Father" (*On First Principles* 1.2.13).

Thomas C. Oden and Christopher A. Hall, eds., *Ancient Christian Commentary on Scripture: New Testament II, Mark* (Downers Grove IL: InterVarsity Press, 1998), 139–40.

abandonment of oneself to faith in God. God alone is good and hence worthy of such faith. The kingdom must be received as a gift from God (10:15).[12]

Jesus' recitation of the commandments is not his definitive answer but rather a further test of the man's understanding. The assurance that one who obeys the Law will live is rooted in the Hebrew Scriptures (Exod 20:12; Deut 30:16; Ezek 33:15). The commandments Jesus lists, significantly, are those that deal with one's obligation to others rather than one's relationship to God (having no other gods, not making graven images, not taking the Lord's name in vain, keeping the Sabbath). Instead of these, Jesus lists the prohibitions against murder, adultery, stealing, bearing false witness, and defrauding, and the obligation to honor father and mother. One is left to assume, like the man himself, either that one can inherit eternal life by observing the commandments that deal with loving one's neighbor, or that Jesus has deliberately omitted the first commandments, those dealing with one's relationship to God, in order to test the man's understanding. Jesus' initial response, that God alone is good, should be a clue.

Commentators have noted further that "you shall not defraud" (10:19) is not one of the Ten Commandments, and that Jesus omitted the commandment, "you shall not covet" (Exod 20:17). One plausible explanation for this substitution is that the man was rich and hence more likely to be guilty of having defrauded others than of coveting (cf. Zacchaeus's pledge to Jesus, Luke 19:8).[13] It is possible, however, that defrauding is understood here as the result of coveting; covetousness leads to defrauding.

The man's response, "Teacher, I have kept all these since my youth" (10:20; cf. Acts 26:4), may communicate either pride or disappointment that Jesus had offered him such a predictable answer. Asking a question that elicited a novel or sophisticated response would bring honor on the questioner, but asking a question that elicited an answer anyone might have given would shame the questioner. The man had kept the commandments from the time he became an adult and embraced the Torah for himself. He was Torah observant, but surely there must be more to it than this. To "guard" in the sense of keeping or observing the law also occurs in Acts 7:53; 21:24; Romans 2:26; and Galatians 6:13; cf. Luke 11:28.

The man's response communicates a sincerity to which Jesus is drawn. Mark reports that he looked at the man intently (cf. 8:25; 10:27; 14:67) and loved him. This is the only person in the Gospel of Mark whom Jesus is said to love; the only other occurrences of the verb are in 12:30-33. Mark's report of Jesus' love for the man is important because it means that the radical demand that follows flows from Jesus' love; it is in no way meant to discourage the man or turn him away. It is not a test; it is what the man needs to do in order to inherit eternal life.

Jesus says that the man lacks one thing, then gives a command with five verbs (*deuro*, "come," is technically an adverb that functions imperatively). The five imperatives are meant to be taken together as one act: Go, sell what you have, give to the poor, and come, follow me. Jesus' invitations to discipleship are tailored to each individual's needs. This is the only instance in Mark where he instructs a would-be disciple to sell everything and give to the poor. Giving everything to the community briefly became the pattern of the first believers in Jerusalem (Acts 2:44-45; 4:32-37), as it was among the Essenes (1QS 1.12-13; 6.19-20, 24-25; Josephus, *J. W.* 2.122), but this pattern is not attested elsewhere in the New Testament. Nevertheless, concern for the poor continued to be a sign of faithfulness in the church (Rom 15:26; Gal 2:10; Jas 1:27; 2:1-8; 1 John 3:17). Peter will claim shortly that the disciples had left everything to follow Jesus (10:28), but the command "follow me" was not accompanied earlier by the command to sell everything (1:16-20; 2:14), and the poor appear in only two other passages (the poor widow, 12:42-43, and the anointing of Jesus, 14:5-7). In contrast, the poor are featured much more prominently in Jesus' teachings in Luke, where the term occurs ten times.[14]

For this man at least, selling his possessions and giving to the poor were bound up with what it would mean for him to follow Jesus. The important element, however, is the last, that he follow Jesus. If he will follow Jesus, he will inherit eternal life. By implication, therefore, this scene is consistent with the voice from heaven at the transfiguration: "This is my Son, the Beloved; listen to him" (9:7). The answer to the man's question is that he will find eternal life not in the commandments (Moses and Elijah) but in following Jesus. What he must do to inherit eternal life is to follow Jesus on the way to the cross, and for him that way will require divesting himself of his possessions. [Giving up Everything]

Giving up Everything

"One who gives up both what one owns and what one desires to own, gives up the whole world." (Augustine, *Letters*, 157, to *Hilarius*)

Thomas C. Oden and Christopher A. Hall, eds., *Ancient Christian Commentary on Scripture: New Testament II, Mark* (Downers Grove IL: InterVarsity Press, 1998), 142–43.

Jesus' assurance, "and you will have treasure in heaven" (10:21), is functionally parallel to the man's question about inheriting "eternal life" (10:17). His "doing" is reduced to the decision regarding whether he will follow Jesus or not. The phrase "treasure in heaven," which is found only in the Gospels in the New Testament (Matt 6:20; 19:21; Luke 12:33; 18:22), also occurs in the Jewish literature of the period, where it is often associated with giving up one's possessions now:

Do not turn your face away from anyone who is poor, and the face of God will not be turned away from you. If you have many possessions, make your gift from them in proportion; if few, do not be afraid to give according to the little you have. So you will be laying up a good treasure for yourself against the day of necessity. (Tob 4:7-9; cf. *Pss. Sol.* 9:5; *2 Bar.* 24:1; Sir 29:10-12).[15]

On the command "follow me," see the commentary on the call of the first disciples in 1:16-20 and 2:14.

The man's response stands in dramatic contrast to his extravagant approach to Jesus (v. 17). Whereas he had come on the scene running, kneeling before Jesus, and hailing him, "good teacher," he left shaken and grieving. When he heard Jesus' challenge to him, he was dismayed, shocked, appalled (*stygnazein*).[16] As Augustine observed, "'he went away sad,' carrying a great burden of possessiveness upon his shoulders" (*Tractate on John* 34.8).[17] Jesus had said, "If your hand causes you to stumble, cut it off" (9:43), but this man would not give up his possessions.

The fact that the man had many possessions is suppressed until the last possible moment, causing the reader to replay the entire scene with this new information in mind. Jesus' comment to the disciples as the man leaves seizes on this point: "How hard it will be for those who have wealth to enter the kingdom of God" (10:23). The adverb "hard" or "difficult" (*dyskolōs*) is rare, but does not mean "impossible." Josephus uses it for the difficulty of scaling a wall: "to contend with difficulties [*dyskolois*] best becomes those who aspire to heroism" (*J. W.* 6.36, LCL 3:387).

The conditions for entering the kingdom of God are a motif that runs through this section of the Gospel: "It is better for you to enter the kingdom of God with one eye than to have two eyes and be thrown into hell" (9:47), and to enter the kingdom one must receive it as a child (10:15). Jesus' conversation with the rich man about what he must do to "inherit eternal life" (10:17) was really about what he needed to do to "enter the kingdom of God" (10:23). The disciples are astonished (*thambeomai*, 1:27; 10:32—a word that occurs only in Mark in the New Testament, and in variant readings in Acts 3:11; 9:6). The disciples are as astonished by Jesus' statement here as the crowds in Capernaum were by his exorcism of a demon.[18] They are astonished because wealth was generally viewed as a sign of God's blessing. A just God rewarded the righteous and punished the wicked. Therefore wealth was a sign of God's favor. If the wealthy will have a hard time entering the kingdom, then how much more difficult will it be for everyone else? This view was rooted in Deuteronomic theology:

Then you shall again obey the LORD, observing all his commandments that I am commanding you today, and the LORD your God will make you abundantly prosperous in all your undertakings. . . . For the LORD will again take delight in prospering you . . . when you obey the LORD your God by observing his commandments and decrees. . . . (Deut 30:8-10)

In contrast to this theology, Jesus prophetically affirmed the view that God embraced the poor (see especially Jesus' teachings in Luke—4:18; 6:20; 7:22; etc.). [God Favors the Poor]

Jesus' observation on the difficulty the rich will have in entering the kingdom was shocking not only because it overturned common assumptions about the relationship between wealth and blessing but because it removed the matter of salvation from human control. If the rich and powerful cannot assure their salvation, then what chance do the poor have?

> **God Favors the Poor**
>
> 📖 Liberation theologians have seized on this theme of Jesus' teaching, reading the Bible as "the historical memory of the poor." Gustavo Gutierrez comments incisively: "God has a preferential love for the poor not because they are necessarily better than others, morally or religiously, but simply because they are poor and living in an inhuman situation that is contrary to God's will."
>
> Gustavo Gutierrez, "Song and Deliverance," *Voices from the Margin: Interpreting the Bible in the Third World* (ed. R. S. Sugirtharajah; Maryknoll NY: Orbis, 1991), 131; cf. 63.

Jesus repeats the shocking assertion, but this time it applies to all, not just the rich: "Children, how hard it is to enter the kingdom of God!" (10:24). This is the only time in the Gospels that Jesus addresses the disciples as "children" (but see 1 John 2:1, 12, 28, etc., 2 John 1), but ironically it follows the recent scene in which the disciples were preventing others from bringing children to Jesus (10:13-16). The connection is not as clear as it may appear in translation, however, because in that scene and in 9:36-37 Mark uses *paidia* for "children" rather than *tekna*, which is the term used in 10:24. Jesus drives home the point of the danger that wealth poses for discipleship with a vivid hyperbole that involves the largest animal in Palestine and the smallest opening: "It is easier for a camel to go through the eye of a needle than for someone who is rich to enter the kingdom of God" (10:25). The popular notion that there was a narrow gate in Jerusalem through which a camel could pass only after all its burdens were removed can be traced back no further than the ninth century. Origen suggested that with the change of just one letter the image would change from a camel (*kamēlos*) threading the eye of a needle to threading a needle with a rope (*kamilos*).[19] No attempt to diminish the incongruity of Jesus' image is warranted, however. Jesus used such hyperboles elsewhere: remove the beam in your own eye before attempting to remove the speck in your brother's eye (Luke 6:42), and the scribes and Pharisees "strain out a gnat but swallow a camel" (Matt 23:24), which contrasts the smallest insect and the largest animal in Palestine.

When the disciples ask who then can be saved, Jesus affirms that for human beings it is impossible, but "for God all things are possible"

(10:27). Salvation is not a matter of human virtue or effort; it is solely and entirely a gift of God's grace. This principle can be traced to the Hebrew Scriptures in the Lord's response to Sarah's laughing (Gen 18:14 LXX) and in Job's acclamation of God's power (Job 10:13; 42:2 LXX). Philo affirms, "What is impossible to all created beings is possible to [God] only" (*Moses* 1.174).[20]

Entering the kingdom, inheriting eternal life, or gaining salvation is therefore a paradoxical matter. It requires abandoning all pretense and proof of one's virtue, abandoning every other pursuit besides the kingdom of God and everything that might offer one security, remove every temptation, and receive the kingdom in childlike simplicity, and still nothing one can do ensures one's salvation. It is entirely a matter of God's goodness, a free gift from God. But there is hope—God can save even people like us.

One should probably not read too much into the statement that Peter "began" to remind Jesus that the disciples had left everything to follow him. Mark is fond of introducing new scenes by using "began" as a helping verb. The verb "to begin" (*archesthai*) occurs twenty-six times in Mark: e.g., 4:1; 5:17; 6:2, 34; 8:31. Peter again serves as the spokesman for the Twelve, as he does in 8:29, 32; 9:5; 11:21. Peter is transparently hinting that they have done exactly what Jesus instructed the rich man to do; they have left everything to follow Jesus (recall 1:18, "and immediately they left their nets and followed him," and 1:20 "and they left their father Zebedee . . . and followed him"). The repetition of categorical conditions here prompts further reflection on the demands of the kingdom:

Commandments: "Teacher, I have kept all these since my youth" (10:20)
Possessions: "You lack one thing; go, sell what you have . . . then come, follow me" (10:21)
Family and home: "Look, we have left everything and followed you" (10:28)

Peter's claim that they have done what Jesus commanded implies that their reward is now due. It is a matter of honor. Jesus therefore solemnly assures Peter that everyone who forsakes everything on his account will be rewarded. The formula "truly (*amēn*) I tell you" occurs thirteen times in Mark, and in many cases the statement that follows concerns reward or punishment (see 3:28; 8:12; 9:1, 41; 10:15; 13:30; 14:9, 25). Jesus picks up the verb "left" (1:18, 20; 10:28) and begins to itemize what may be involved when a disciple leaves "everything" to follow him: house, brothers, sisters, mother, father, children, fields. In first-century society, security and identity were closely tied to place, home, and family. Eduard Schweizer points out that "wife" is not included in the list, and that according to 1 Corinthians 9:5 Peter was accompanied by his wife.[21] "Wife" may also have been omitted from the list to avoid the awkwardness of the following assurance that he would receive wives a hundredfold! Not to be missed, however, is the importance of this assurance for Mark's understanding of the eschatological community. Sacrifices now will be rewarded in "the age to come."

The concept of time as divided between "this age" (Heb., *ha-olam ha-zeh*) and "the age to come" (Heb., *ha-olam ha-bah*) was the foundation of Jewish eschatology. This pericope is the counterpart of Mark 3:31-35, where Jesus says, "Here are my mother and my brothers! Whoever does the will of God is my brother and sister and mother" (3:35). Those for whom family implied kin who were honor bound to defend and support family members would find that they had a whole host of family members. The early church modeled this new reality when in time of famine one sold what he had to provide for the needs of the community of believers, and all things were held in common (Acts 2:44; 4:32-37). The community of the new age was also foreshadowed in the practice of extending hospitality to traveling apostles and emissaries (Mark 6:7-11; cf. 3 John). The phrase "for my sake and for the sake of the good news" (10:29) occurs also in 8:35, where some suspect that it is a Markan addition, and is echoed in 13:9 ("for my sake"). Similarly, the promise of a "hundredfold" reward echoes with the parable of a hundredfold harvest (4:8, 20), which also warned of "persecution" (4:17, *diōgmou*; 10:30, *diōgmōn*), an ominous reminder that would not have been lost on Mark's community. The promise of the kingdom was no promise of freedom from trials and hardships, at least not in "this age." In the blessed "age to come," however, they could expect eternal life, precisely what the rich man had sought (10:17; cf. 9:43, 45).

The coming of the kingdom, therefore, will bring an unexpected reversal: "many who are first will be last, and the last will be first" (10:31; cf. Matt 19:30; 20:16; Luke 13:30). In this context, this free-floating saying gathers up the theme of most of this chapter. Those who put themselves first, such as the disciples who sought to stop the unauthorized exorcist (9:38-39) and those who were bringing children to Jesus (10:13-16), those who divorce their wives (10:1-12), and the rich who rely on the security of their possessions (10:17-22) will be last, while those who give a cup of water (9:41), the servants of all (9:35), the children and those who are like them (9:36-37; 10:13-16), and those who sacrifice all for Jesus and the good news (10:28-30) will be first.

The Third Passion Prediction, 10:32-34

The third passion prediction underscores the climactic significance of the death and resurrection of Jesus. The threefold repetition is a literary device that builds suspense while alerting the reader to the importance of the coming events. This third passion prediction is the most detailed of the three, and despite the special pleading of some commentators, the specificity of this prediction shows that it has been influenced by the account of Jesus' death that was known to Mark.[22]

Mark 10:32-34	Mark 8:31	Mark 9:31	Passion Narrative
The Son of Man will be handed over		X	14:41-44
to the chief priests and the scribes,	X		14:1, 10, 43, 53
and they will condemn him to death;			14:64
then they will hand him over to the Gentiles			15:1, 10
they will mock him, and spit upon him;			15:15-20
and kill him;	X	X	15:25-39
and after three days he will rise again.	X	X	16:1-8

This passion prediction is set explicitly "on the way" (see 8:27; 9:33, 34; 10:17, 46, 52) to Jerusalem. This is first time that Mark has identified Jesus' destination as Jerusalem, which has earlier been introduced in Mark as the place from which the scribes and Pharisees were sent (3:8, 22; 7:1). Jerusalem is spelled in two ways in the New Testament. Mark consistently uses the spelling *Ierosolyma* (ten times), never *Ierosalēm*. Matthew favors *Ierosolyma* also, whereas Luke favors *Ierosalēm*. Mark wrote, as was customary, of "going up" to Jerusalem both because one traveled up to the city regardless of which approach to it was used and because it was the center of Jewish religious life (see Matt 20:17; Luke 2:42; 18:31; 19:28; John 2:13; 5:1; 11:55; 12:20; Acts 11:2; 15:2; 18:22; 21:12; 24:11; 25:1, 9).

Jesus was leading, or "going ahead of," the disciples, which would be expected for the teacher, whom the disciples "followed." The verb will recur in 14:28 and 16:7, however, where it is used for Jesus' going ahead of the disciples to Galilee. Mark's comments that the disciples were "amazed" (*ethambounto*, see 1:27; 10:24) and that those who followed him were "afraid" heighten the sense of drama. Both the reason for these strong emotions and the syntax of the statements are open to various interpretations, however. Were they amazed and fearful because of Jesus himself, because of what he had just said, because he was in danger, or because he was going to Jerusalem? Similarly, the syntax of the statement that "those who followed him were afraid" can be interpreted as meaning either that all of those who followed him were afraid or that only some of them were afraid (cf. Matt 28:17).

Fear in Mark usually denotes a defective response to Jesus, setting up the alternative of fear or faith.[23] Fear characterizes the disciples' defective response when Jesus stilled the storm: Jesus asks, "'Why are you afraid? Have you no faith?' And they were filled with great awe" (4:40-41, literally, "they feared a great fear"). Fear keeps others from coming to Jesus: when the swineherds saw the demoniac sitting, clothed, and in his right mind, they were afraid (5:15), and the woman who touched Jesus' clothes and was healed, "knowing what had happened to her, came in fear and trembling" (5:33). To Jairus, Jesus said, "do not fear, only believe" (5:36); when Jesus walked on the water, he reassured the disciples, saying, "Take heart, it is I; do not be afraid" (6:50). The disciples were afraid to ask him about his death (9:32), and the chief priests and scribes were afraid of him because of the crowd (11:18, 32; 12:12). Fear is therefore an inadequate response, an obstacle to greater faith (5:36; 16:8).

The reference to the Twelve in the next verse can be taken as synonymous with "those who followed him" or as singling the Twelve out from the others who accompanied them, which is more likely in view of the comment in Mark 15:41 that "there were many other women who had come up with him to Jerusalem." Jesus takes the Twelve aside for another session of private instruction (cf. 5:40; 9:2; 14:33).

The chief priests [Chief Priests] and scribes (see [Scribes]) were mentioned in the first passion prediction (8:31), and they figure prominently in the Passion Narratives in all the Gospels. Together the chief priests and the scribes formed the religious aristocracy of Judaism and the temple cult. The combination of this reference to the religious leadership that was closely associated with the Sanhedrin and the verb *katakrinein*, which means to "pronounce a sentence after determination of guilt," implies that Jesus will be condemned in a legal proceeding.[24] In the Passion Narrative, Mark reports that "all the chief priests, the elders, and the scribes were assembled" (14:53), and "all of them condemned him as deserving death" (*katekrinan*, 14:64). Neither of the previous passion predictions said anything about a legal proceeding or Jesus' condemnation to death. The second passion prediction said simply that the Son of Man would be "handed over" (*paradidotai*) into the hands of men (9:31). The term is used in the third prediction not for the

Chief Priests

AΩ The numerous plural references to "the chief priests" in the New Testament (a surprising sixty-four times) have sparked debate over the usage of this term. Emil Schürer advanced a broad interpretation. Because the high priesthood was passed down for generations among a few priestly families, Schürer contended, "the mere fact of belonging to one of the privileged families must have conferred a particular distinction." The "chief priests" in the New Testament and Josephus would have included "high Priests in the strict sense, i.e. the High Priest in office and his predecessors, and secondly, members of the noble families from which the High Priests were selected." The chief critic of this view was Joachim Jeremias, who offered a narrower interpretation. The chief priests were defined not by genealogy but only by rank: "They were the permanent chief priests of the Temple, who by virtue of their office had seats and votes in the Sanhedrin where they formed a well-defined group. . . . The minimum number of this chief priestly group . . . amounted to one high priest, one captain of the Temple, and one Temple overseer (a priest), and three treasurers—six in all, to which were added the retired high priests, and those priests who were employed as overseers and treasurers." Gottlob Schrenk followed Jeremias, explaining the frequency of the occurrence of the term as emphasizing that "when opposition arose against Jesus, it was not the work of a single individual . . . but of the religious authorities in general." Geza Vermes, who edited the revised edition of Schürer, offered a mediating view, saying that "the real difference between the two theories may be smaller than Jeremias and his followers believe." The "priestly aristocracy on the one hand and the present and past High Priests and their heirs on the other are bound to have been substantially the same."

Emil Schürer, *The History of the Jewish People in the Age of Jesus Christ* (rev. and ed. Geza Vermes et al.; Edinburgh: T. & T. Clark, 1979), 2:234–36; Joachim Jeremias, *Jerusalem in the Time of Jesus* (trans. F. H. and C. H. Cave; Philadelphia: Fortress Press, 1979), 179; Gottlob Schrenk, "archiereus," *TDNT* 3:271–72; cf. BDAG 139.

arrest of Jesus by the Jewish authorities but for their action in delivering Jesus to the Roman authorities. It is also used in 15:1, 10, and 15, where this event is recorded. By calling the Roman authorities "Gentiles," Mark adopts a Jewish perspective but identifies the Roman authorities as those who would ultimately be drawn to the temple, "a house of prayer for all nations" (11:17), and those to whom the gospel must be proclaimed (13:10). The point could not have been missed by Mark's first readers.

The references to the abuse of Jesus in the passion prediction also foreshadow specific elements of Mark's account of Jesus' death. The abuse of Jesus is described in 14:65, following his condemnation by the Jewish authorities; 15:16-20, following his trial before Pilate; and 15:29-32, while he was on the cross. Jesus himself probably understood his suffering in light of the description of the suffering servant in Isaiah: "I did not hide my face from insult and spitting" (Isa 50:6). The verb to mock (*empaizein*, 10:34) recurs in 15:20 and 15:31, and the verb to spit (*emptuein*, 10:34) appears in 14:65 and 15:19. Jesus was flogged, or whipped, by the Roman soldiers, but the term in 15:15 is a Latin loanword (*phragelloun*) instead of the term *mastigoun* in 10:34.

That Jesus will die is clear, but there is no mention of crucifixion in the passion predictions. On the other hand, the final clause, "and after three days he will rise again," is remarkably similar in all three predictions (8:31; 9:31; 10:34). See the commentary on 8:31 and ["After Three Days"].

The Places of Honor in Jesus' Kingdom, 10:35-45

Following each of the three passion predictions, the disciples say something that confirms they do not understand what Jesus is trying to tell them. Following the first prediction, Peter took Jesus aside to try to get him to follow a different course (8:32-33). Following the second prediction, the disciples argued about who was the greatest (9:32-34). Just as the third prediction is the most detailed of the three, so the scene of discipleship misunderstanding that follows it is the longest and most detailed of the three. James and John ask Jesus for the right- and left-hand seats when Jesus comes into his glory.

James and John were given the name "Sons of Thunder" (see the commentary on 3:14 and [*"Boanerges, the Sons of Thunder"*]). The two brothers were among the first disciples (1:16-20), and they along with Peter composed the group of three who are with Jesus at the raising of Jairus's daughter (5:37), the transfiguration (9:2-8), and at Gethsemane (14:33). Jesus is addressed with the title "teacher" ten times in Mark, four times by the disciples (4:38; 9:38; 10:35; 13:1), and six times by others (9:17; 10:17, 20; 12:14, 19, 32), and referred to as "teacher" on two other occasions (5:35; 14:14). Their question is open-ended and suggests that they were trying to

Christ and the Family of Zebedee

Bonifacio de' Pitati (1487–1553). *Christ and the Family of Zebedee*. Galleria Borghese, Rome, Italy. (Credit: Scala / Art Resource, NY)

manipulate Jesus into making a commitment to them before he knew what they were asking for. The clumsiness of their request, their concern for status when Jesus has said he is going to be put to death, and their effort to outmaneuver the other disciples all reflect poorly on them, and by association on the other disciples also.

The motif of asking is developed in an interesting way in Mark. The disciples' request, "we want you to do for us whatever we ask of you" (10:35), is the counterpart of Herod's rash promise, "Ask me whatever you wish, and I will give it" (6:22). The disciples did not know what they were asking, and Herod did not know what he was promising. On the other hand, in the context of prayer, where trust and faithfulness are assumed, Jesus could say, "whatever you ask for in prayer, believe that you have received it, and it will be yours" (11:24).

What James and John ask for are the places of honor in Jesus' glory. "Glory" in Mark is always associated with the Parousia (8:38; 13:26), but commentators have debated whether these were thrones at the Parousia or places of honor at the messianic banquet. Lane raises the intriguing question, "were James and John asking for a confirmation that the places they occupied in the fellowship meals which the Twelve shared with Jesus would be their seats when his glory was openly unveiled?"[25] According to John 13:23, the Beloved Disciple was reclining on Jesus' right. Alternatively, according to Matthew 19:28 and Luke 22:28-30, Jesus promised the disciples that they would sit on twelve thrones, judging the twelve tribes of Israel. Thrones are part of the Old Testament imagery associated with the Son of Man (Dan 7:9) and the coming judgment (Ps 122:5).

The seat to the right of the king, or the host, was the seat of honor, with the seat to the left ranking second in honor (1 Kgs 2:19; Ps 110:1; 1 Esd 4:29; Sir 12:12; Josephus, *Ant.* 6.235).[26] Dubious tradition, based on conflating the report in Matthew 27:55-56 that the mother of the sons of Zebedee was among the women at the cross with Mark 15:40 that names Salome in the list of the women, and John 19:25, identifies James and John as Jesus' cousins.[27] [Were James and John Jesus' Cousins?] If this were the case, their request for the places of honor may have been based on their familial connections with Jesus.

Jesus responds with a question designed to lead the disciples to a clearer understanding of discipleship (see [Heuristic Questions]). The effectiveness of the question, however, depends on their being able to connect the imagery of drinking the cup and baptism with Jesus' predictions of his future and the expectations on which their question was based. Clearly, they expected that when they reached Jerusalem either Jesus would establish an earthly kingdom or the Parousia would occur (see 9:1). In either case, they expected Jesus to rule in power.

The image of drinking the cup represents God's judgment in the Old Testament and ancient Judaism. The judgment of the nations in Jeremiah is introduced with the declaration, "for thus the LORD, the God of Israel, said to me: Take from my hand this cup of wine of wrath, and make all the nations to whom I send you drink it. They shall drink and stagger and go out of their minds because of the sword that I am sending among them" (Jer 25:15-16). Leonhard Goppelt explained the image:

> Like an intoxicating drink, this robs the one who must drink it of his sense, and causes him to stagger and fall, so that they cannot stand up again. Hence in Ez. and Dt. Is. the cup is expressly called the cup of astonishment and stupefaction (Ez. 23:33), or the cup of staggering (. . .) or cup of fury (. . .), Is. 51:17, 22.[28]

Were James and John Jesus' Cousins?

📖 "Many women were also there, looking on from a distance; they had followed Jesus from Galilee and had provided for them. Among them were Mary Magdalene, and Mary the mother of James and Joseph, *and the mother of the sons of Zebedee.*" (Matt 27:55-56)

"There were also women looking on from a distance; among them were Mary Magdalene, and Mary the mother of James the younger and of Joses, *and Salome.*" (Mark 15:40)

"Meanwhile, standing near the cross of Jesus were his mother, *and his mother's sister,* Mary the wife of Clopas, and Mary Magdalene." (John 19:25)

If the mother of the sons of Zebedee (Matthew), was Salome (Mark) and Jesus' mother's sister (John), then the sons of Zebedee were Jesus' cousins.

In Jesus' response to the sons of Zebedee, the cup represents the suffering and death that lies ahead of him, and by extension the persecution and martyrdom that the church would experience in Mark's day. The places of honor are reserved for those who follow in the path that Jesus trod before them. For example, the dying Polycarp prays, "I bless thee in that thou hast deemed me worthy . . . that I might take a portion among the martyrs in the cup of thy Christ" (*Martyrdom of Polycarp* 14.2; *TDNT* 6:153). The question is whether there is a material connection between Jesus' use of the image (suffering and martyrdom; cf. Mark 14:36; John 18:11) and its meaning in the Old Testament (God's judgment).

The companion image of baptism, dipping, or washing is at least equally perplexing. The Greek verb *baptizein* can mean to drown or perish, but this meaning is absent from its use in Jewish Greek and in the Hebrew and Aramaic term that it translates.[29] Therefore, comparisons with references to being "overwhelmed by disaster or danger" are less convincing, even though the Greek translations by Symmachus and/or Aquila use *baptizein* in Psalm 49:3 (48:3 LXX) and 69:2 (68:2 LXX).[30] The "cup" and "baptism" metaphors appear to be parallel or synonymous, but some interpreters find different meaning in the two metaphors. Edward Burrows suggests that Jesus was reflecting on the baptism of John the Baptist that signified a new beginning.[31] Reflection on Jesus' death might have suggested the connection between baptism and death (e.g., "therefore we have been buried with him by baptism into death," Rom 6:4), but it is difficult to see how this metaphorical use could have developed apart from such a context.[32]

Jesus' prophecy to the two disciples that they will indeed drink the cup and be baptized with the baptism with which he would be baptized led to the development of a late tradition that John as well as James was martyred. The martyrdom of James is firmly attested in Acts 12:2, while the most commonly accepted tradition concerning John is that he became a leader of the church in Ephesus and lived to an old age there. On the other hand, Philip of Side (fifth century) reported that Papias, bishop of Hierapolis in the second century and the author of a five-volume work on "The Lord's Gospel," wrote that "John the Evangelist and his brother James were slain by the Jews."[33] A similar report of the death of John at the hands of the Jews appears in one manuscript of the *Chronicle of George the Sinner* (c. AD 840), which says:

> John has been deemed worthy of martyrdom. For Papias, the Bishop of Hierapolis, having been eyewitness of him (or "of it"), says in the second book of his "Dominical Oracles," that he was killed by Jews,

having evidently fulfilled, with his brother the prediction of Christ concerning them.[34]

This tradition has been rejected by most Johannine scholars as late and probably based on Mark 10:38 and the parallel in Matthew 20:23. Nevertheless, it has attracted some significant advocates, notably B. W. Bacon and Martin Hengel.[35]

The notion that rewards and punishments are prepared for the faithful and the wicked can also be found elsewhere in the New Testament. In the parable of the sheep and the goats, the king says to the sheep at his right hand, "Come, you that are blessed by my Father, inherit the kingdom *prepared* for you from the foundation of the world" (Matt 25:34), and to the goats on his left hand he says, "depart from me into the eternal fire *prepared* for the devil and his angels" (Matt 25:41). At the beginning of the farewell discourse in the Gospel of John, Jesus assures the disciples, "In my Father's house there are many dwelling places. If it were not so, would I have told you that I go to *prepare* a place for you?" (John 14:2). Paul quotes from an unknown source in 1 Corinthians, saying, "What no eye has seen, nor ear heard, nor the human heart conceived, what God has *prepared* for those who love him" (1 Cor 2:9). The Seer of Revelation adds that he saw "the new Jerusalem, coming down out of heaven from God, prepared as a bride adorned for her husband" (Rev 21:2). Persecuted believers can take heart; their rewards are already prepared for them. Still, just as Jesus did not claim to know the time of the Parousia (13:32), neither was it his place to assign the seats of honor.

When the other ten heard the conversation, they were angry with James and John. The sons of Zebedee had sought their own advantage at the expense of the status of the others. The division among the disciples provokes Jesus' second response. The order of the kingdom will not be like the agonistic system of the world they know. In Mark, Jesus summons the disciples for important teachings (10:42; cf. 3:13, 23; 6:7; 8:1; 12:43).

Among the Gentiles, those who are recognized as rulers exercise authority over them (10:42). The irony was that the disciples were imitating those whom they despised.[36] Jesus could have said the same about the Jewish leaders (the Maccabees, the Hasmoneans, and the chief priests), but by pointing to the Gentiles he turned their attention to the Herods and the Romans. The construction "*hoi dokountes archein*" means "those who are recognized as rulers" rather than the more wooden sense, "those who seem to rule."[37] Compounding the irony, Paul uses the verb *dokein* in a similar fashion in Galatians 2:2, 6, 9 for Peter, James (Jesus' brother), and John: "those who were supposed to be acknowledged leaders (what they were makes no difference to me)." The author of 1 Peter later admonishes the elders of the church, "do not lord it over those in your charge, but be examples to the flock" (1 Pet 5:3). Jesus' reference to "their great ones" (*hoi megaloi*, 10:42) reminds the reader of Herod's entertaining his "courtiers" (*megistasin*, 6:21). Maneuvering for the places of honor has no place in the kingdom.

A number of Jesus' teachings on discipleship in Mark take the form "whoever wishes . . . will . . ." (8:35; 10:43, 44; cf. 8:34; 9:35). Verses 43 and 44 reiterate the kingdom principle that the one who is servant of all will be the greatest among them (see 9:35). Here, Jesus offers the principle as an inversion of the commonly accepted norms. The great serve; they do not oppress, manipulate, or coerce. Verse 44 repeats and heightens v. 43: "whoever wishes to be great/first among you must be your servant/slave of all." The heightening of the earlier saying is apparent at three points: "great" is heightened to "first," "servant" (*diakonos*) is heightened to "slave" (*doulos*), and finally "your" is elevated to "of all." ["Serve" and "Servant"]

Mark 10:45 is a crucial verse because it has implications for Jesus' self-understanding, Jesus' and/or Mark's use of the suffering servant passages in Isaiah, and Mark's understanding of Jesus' death. The saying also belongs to a group of sayings in the Synoptic Gospels in which Jesus voices the purpose of his ministry using the formula "I have come" (see 2:17; and 1:38; 4:21) (see ["I Have Come"]). Mark 10:45 blends the concept of the Son of Man (from Dan 7:13-14) with reflection on the role of the suffering servant, especially Isaiah 52–53. Whereas Daniel 7:14 says, "all peoples, nations, and languages should serve him [the son of man in 7:13]," Jesus says, "the Son of Man came not to be served but to serve" (10:45). Thematically, this verse serves as an appropriate climax to Jesus' instruction to the Twelve on the kingdom's reversal of the relationships between power, servanthood, and greatness. Jesus will lay down his own life as a sacrifice for all humanity. The verse is connected to its context both thematically and linguistically, since the verb "to serve" (*diakonein*) follows naturally from the reference to "servant" (*diakonos*) in v. 43 (see the truncated parallel in Luke 22:27).

"Serve" and "Servant"

AΩ "The concept of serving is expressed in Greek by many words which are often hard to differentiate even though each has its own basic emphasis. *douleuō* means to serve as a slave, with a stress on subjection. . . . *diakoneō* has the special quality of indicating very personally the service rendered to another. . . . Fundamental to an understanding of *diakoneō* in all its uses is the fact that it has an original concrete sense which is still echoed in its figurative meanings. In secular Greek *diakoneō* . . . means: a. 'to wait at table,' . . . b. Rather more generally it means 'to provide or care for,' . . . . On the basis of these original senses it has c. the comprehensive meaning 'to serve.' . . . The reversal of all human ideas of greatness and rank was accomplished when the Son of Man came not to be ministered unto, but to minister. . . . *diakonein* is now much more than a comprehensive term for any loving assistance rendered to the neighbour. It is understood as full and perfect sacrifice, as the offering of life which is the very essence of service, of being for others, whether in life or death."

Hermann W. Beyer, "*diakoneō*," *TDNT* 2:81–86.

The connections between this verse and Isaiah 52–53 can be displayed as follows:

"to serve"—"*diakonein*" does not appear in the servant songs, or anywhere else in the Septuagint, but "my servant" appears in Isaiah 52:13; 53:11, and the verb "to serve" (*douleuō*) occurs in Isaiah 53:11.

"to give his life"—"When you make his life an offering for sin . . ." (Isa 53:10; cf. Lev 5:14-6:7; 7:1-7; Num 5:5-8); ". . . he poured out himself to death" (Isa 53:12)

"a ransom"—does not appear in Isaiah 53 (cf. Isa 43:3-4), but the metaphorical sense of ransom in Mark 10:45 is not far from "upon him was the punishment that made us whole . . . and the LORD laid on him the iniquity of us all" (Isa 53:5-6)

"for many"—"The righteous one, my servant, shall make many righteous" (Isa 53:11) "yet he bore the sin of many" (Isa 53:12)[38]

The concept that a martyr's death could atone for the sins of the nation is well established in the histories of the deaths of the Maccabean martyrs (see the commentary on 8:31, and [The Righteous Sufferer] and [The Maccabean Martyrs]). "Ransom" appears only here in the New Testament and in the parallel in Matthew 20:28, yet it has given rise to the "ransom theory" of the atonement, which held that the ransom was paid to the devil, and to the "satisfaction theory" offered by Anselm of Canterbury (1033–1109), according to which Jesus' death served as a reparation paid to God. Mark 10:45 says nothing about who receives the "ransom." The term, however, is used in secular Greek for money paid to redeem or purchase the freedom of slaves or captives. ["Ransom"] The term "many" in Mark 10:45 probably carries the sense of "all" rather than "some but not others," as it does in Romans 5:15.[39] In Mark 14:24, Jesus declares in the words of institution that his blood is the blood of the covenant, "which is poured out for many," and the more hellenized confession in 1 Timothy 2:5-6 acclaims Christ Jesus, "who gave himself a ransom for all." Of course, although Jesus died for all, not all accept his death on their behalf.

"Ransom"

AΩ "Etymologically *lytron* denotes 'a means of release,' or, more specifically, 'money paid as a means of release.' It was used especially of payment for the release of prisoners of war, of slaves, and of debtors. It was also applied in the cultic sphere to payment made to a deity to which an individual incurred indebtedness, and thus it was extended to denote expiation or compensation."

In ancient Judaism one finds the idea of human beings as debtors before God (cf. the Lord's Prayer in Matt 6:12; Luke 11:4).

George R. Beasley-Murray, *Jesus and the Kingdom of God* (Grand Rapids: Wm. B. Eerdmans, 1986), 281; see also the full discussion of the wider issues in Friedrich Büchsel, "*lytron*," *TDNT* 4:340–49. For the concept of human beings being in debt to God, see Friedrich Hauck, "*opheilō*," *TDNT* 5:561–63.

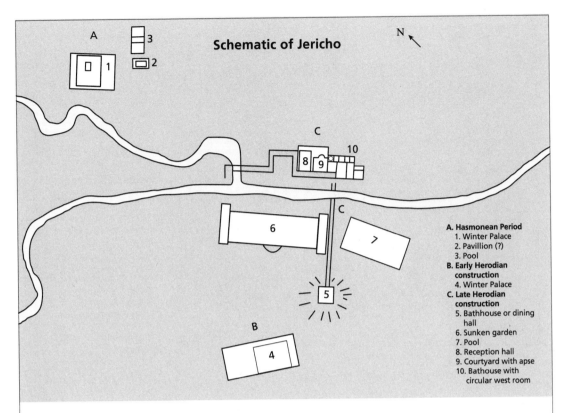

Schematic of Jericho

A. **Hasmonean Period**
  1. Winter Palace
  2. Pavillion (?)
  3. Pool
B. **Early Herodian construction**
  4. Winter Palace
C. **Late Herodian construction**
  5. Bathhouse or dining hall
  6. Sunken garden
  7. Pool
  8. Reception hall
  9. Courtyard with apse
  10. Bathhouse with circular west room

Jericho

Jericho claims two distinctions: it is located at the lowest point on the earth, 825 feet below sea level, and it is the world's oldest city, continuously inhabited since 9,000 BC. Just west of the modern town, along the Wadi Qelt, the Hasmoneans built an impressive winter palace, and Herod the Great later built several palaces there. Three mounds comprise the so-called New Testament Jericho.

For a brief period (c. 35–30 BC) Jericho was taken from Herod and given to Cleopatra. Herod also built a racetrack and theater for the city. Jericho was known for its fruit and its roses, but it was also the site of several high-profile murders and deaths that shaped the history of the period: the murders of Simon and his sons (134 BC; 1 Macc 16:11-17), the drowning of the high priest Aristobulus III in the palace swimming pool, ordered by Herod the Great (35 BC; Josephus, *Ant.* 15.53-56; *J.W.* 1.437), the murder of Antipater, ordered by his father, Herod the Great (4 BC; Josephus, *Ant.* 17.187–90), and five days later the death of Herod the Great himself (4 BC; Josephus, *Ant.* 17.173–79, 190).

The Healing of Bartimaeus, 10:46-52

The story of the healing of Bartimaeus forms the closing bracket for Mark 8:22–10:52, a section of the gospel that opens with the healing of the blind man in Bethsaida (8:22-26) and closes with the healing of the blind man in Jericho (10:46-52). Between these two healings Mark presents Peter's confession at Caesarea Philippi and the three passion predictions (8:31; 9:31; 10:32-34). The story also blends elements of a healing miracle and a call story, as will be clear below.

Jericho is mentioned twice in v. 46, perhaps because the first statement is Mark's editorial addition, marking Jesus' progress toward

Bartimaeus

On the left, Christ and Peter stand against a background of gold over green. On the right, against an ultramarine background, a young disciple holds his left hand extended diagonally and with his right hand takes the right hand of the seated blind beggar Bartimaeus. Bartimaeus holds his eyes tightly closed and wears a purse over the left shoulder, and a hat, which is falling off his head.

T'oros Taronec'i. *Christ's Cure of Blind Bartimaeus.* Drawing on vellum. Gladzor Gospel, from the Bound Manuscripts Collection (Collection 170/466). Department of Special Collections, Charles E. Young Research Library, UCLA.

Jerusalem, while the second is part of the tradition. Jericho was located just west of the Jordan River on a fertile plain about fifteen miles east of Jerusalem. [Jericho] The story of Jesus surrounded by an excited crowd yet stopping to help one individual who persistently reached out to him is reminiscent of the healing of the paralytic (2:1-12) and the healing of the bleeding woman (5:25-34).

Verse 46 sets the scene. Jesus, his disciples, and a considerable crowd were leaving Jericho on their way to Jerusalem. Meanwhile, the son of Timaeus, Bartimaeus, was sitting by the roadside, begging. In a departure from his normal practice, Mark introduces him in Greek first and then gives his name in Aramaic (contrast 5:41; 7:34; 15:22). The mention of the name is also distinctive because Bartimaeus is the only named character in a miracle story in Mark, except for Jairus (5:22). Bartimaeus probably had his outer garment spread out before him to receive alms. [Beggars]

The action of the scene begins when Bartimaeus hears that Jesus of Nazareth is coming. The term *Nazarēnos,* which is found only in Mark (1:24; 10:47; 14:67;

Beggars

Beggars congregated along thoroughfares and around markets and temples. Jerusalem was therefore "a centre for mendicancy," "a city of idlers." Giving alms atoned for the sins of the donor (Dan 4:27; Sir 3:30), and "righteousness" came to be a synonym for "almsgiving" (Prov 11:4; Matt 6:1). According to the Damascus Document, one who entered the covenant was expected to give at least two days' wages each month for alms. From this fund, "they shall give to the orphans and with it they shall strengthen the hand of the needy and the poor, and to the elder who [is dy]ing, and to the vagabond, and to the prisoner of a foreign people, and to the girl who has no protector, and to the unma[rried woman] who has no suitor" (CD 14.14-16).

G. Hinton Davies, "Alms," *IDB* 1:87–88; Joachim Jeremias, *Jerusalem in the Time of Jesus* (trans. F. H. Cave and C. H. Cave; Philadelphia: Fortress Press, 1969), 116–18; Florentino García Martínez, *The Dead Sea Scrolls Translated* (Leiden: E. J. Brill, 1994), 44.

16:6) and Luke (4:34; 24:19) in the New Testament, is probably associated with Nazareth. An alternative explanation for the meaning of "the Nazarene" links it to the reference in Isaiah 11:1 (see Matt 2:23), "a shoot shall come out from the stump of Jesse, and a branch [Hebrew *nazir*] shall grow out of his roots," which is particularly relevant in this context, where Bartimaeus immediately addresses Jesus as "Son of David." This association, however, requires that the meaning of the Greek term be determined by its Hebrew homonym. Other explanations—for example, that it means Jesus was a Nazirite, like Samson (Judg 13:5, 7), or that it is related to the sect of the Nasarenes mentioned by Epiphanius in the fourth century—have less to commend them.[40]

Having been told that Jesus is "the Nazarene," Bartimaeus calls out, "Son of David, have mercy on me!" (10:47). The title "Son of David" foreshadows the reference to David in the entry into Jerusalem (11:10) and Jesus' denial that he is the "Son of David" in 12:35-37. Solomon is the only king to be called by this title in the Old Testament (1 Chr 29:22; 2 Chr 1:1; 13:6; etc.). By the first century, however, the title had acquired other associations. It appears in the *Psalms of Solomon* 17:21 and 4Q Patriarchal Blessings 1.3-4 as a messianic title (cf. Isa 11:1; Jer 23:5-6; Ezek 34:23-24).[41] Elsewhere, Solomon is regarded as an exorcist, healer, and magician (see [The Demon's Name] and [Demon Exorcism]).[42] These associations suggest interesting interpretations for the blind man's address to Jesus. At the conclusion of the section introduced by the healing of the blind man at Bethsaida (8:22-26), which seems to use blindness as a metaphor for the disciples' lack of comprehension, Bartimaeus sees, even before he is healed, that Jesus is "the son of David." If the title was associated with Solomon, or at a minimum one known for his mercy and healing (Isa 29:18; 32:1-3; 35:1-10; 61:1-4),[43] it would be quite natural for a blind beggar to use it to attract the attention of one who might be able to help him. [4Q Messianic Apocalypse] On the other hand, if it also had messianic connotations, then Bartimaeus was either confessing more than he knew or he serves as an ironic contrast to the disciples, who though they see still have difficulty comprehending who Jesus is.

4Q Messianic Apocalypse

The following fragment from Qumran (4Q521) provides evidence of the expectation of a Messiah who would usher in an era of blessing, healing, and acts of mercy:

". . . [for the heav]ens and the earth will listen to his Messiah, [and all] that is in them will not turn away from the holy precepts. Be encouraged, you who are seeking the Lord in his service! *Blank* Will you not, perhaps, encounter the Lord in it, all those who hope in their heart? For the Lord will observe the devout, and call the just by name, and upon the poor he will place his spirit, and the faithful he will renew with his strength. For he will honour the devout upon the throne of eternal royalty, freeing prisoners, giving sight to the blind, straightening the twisted. Ever shall I cling to those who hope. In his mercy he will jud[ge,] and from no-one shall the fruit [of] good [deeds] be delayed, and the Lord will perform marvelous acts such as have not existed, just as he sa[id] for he will heal the badly wounded and will make the dead live, he will proclaim good news to the meek, give lavishly [to the need]y, lead the exiled and enrich the hungry."

Florentino García Martínez, *The Dead Sea Scrolls Translated* (Leiden: E. J. Brill, 1994), 394.

Bartimaeus's cry, "have mercy on me!" echoes that of the psalmist (Pss 6:2; 9:13; etc.). The crowd, here identified as "many" (ironically, those for whom Jesus would lay down his life! See 10:45), ordered Bartimaeus to be silent, just as Jesus had earlier ordered the demons to be silent (cf. 1:25; 4:39; 9:25). Bartimaeus, however, demonstrates his persistent faith by calling out to Jesus all the more. In doing so, he assures his place among those in Mark's Gospel who serve as examples of faith under duress—the four who brought the paralytic to Jesus, the woman with a hemorrhage, Jairus, the Syrophoenician woman, and the father of the epileptic boy. Bartimaeus's faith is demonstrated not so much by his correct confession, however, as by his persistence in the face of efforts to silence him and stop him from reaching Jesus.

Jesus stopped, or stood still, and said, "Call him" (10:49). The repetition of the verb "to call" three times in v. 49 suggests that like the calling of the first disciples (1:16-20; 2:14), this healing miracle serves also as a call story, even though the verb to call (*phōnein*) does not appear in the earlier stories. The unidentified "they" call Bartimaeus, saying, "take heart, get up, he is calling you" (10:49). Jesus used the verb "take heart" when he spoke to the terrified disciples in 6:50. In Mark, Jesus is continually raising people: he lifts up Peter's mother-in-law (1:31), the paralytic (2:9, 11, 12), the man with the withered hand (3:3), Jairus's daughter (5:41), the epileptic boy (9:27), and now Bartimaeus.

Bartimaeus responded by throwing aside his garment, springing up, and coming to Jesus (10:50). If Bartimaeus had spread his garment in front of him to receive alms, throwing it aside allowed him free mobility of his feet (cf. Heb 12:1), but more may be suggested. His outer garment may have been virtually all he had. Like the disciples (1:16-20; 10:28), and in contrast to the man with many possessions (10:17-22), Bartimaeus left his garment behind. Simon and Andrew had left their nets (1:18); James and John left their father as well (1:20). Perhaps analogously, the widow gave all she had (12:44). The garment, therefore, may represent that which the disciple leaves behind to follow Jesus.[44] Metaphorically at least, Bartimaeus would have no further need of the garment: no one can sew a new patch on an old garment (2:21). In the next scene, Jesus' followers will throw their garments on the road in front of him (11:7-8).

Jesus asks Bartimaeus the same thing he had asked James and John: "What do you want me to do for you?" (cf. 10:36, 51). Bartimaeus, however, wants only one thing: that he might see again. Parenthetically, he had apparently not been born blind, like the man in John 9. Like Mary Magdalene in John 20:16, he addresses Jesus as *rabbouni*. His response to Jesus is clipped, like a beggar's urgent plea, just three words in Greek, literally, "rabbi, that I might see again," or we might render it, "rabbi, my sight" (cf. Isa 61:1 LXX).[45] First-century inscriptions "indicate that the title *rabbi* should be thought of as an honorific address roughly equivalent to 'sir,' with no explicit connection to either teaching or adjudication."[46] Where the disciples address Jesus as teacher (4:38; 9:38; 10:35; 13:1), they use the term *didaskalos*, as do non-disciples (9:17; 10:17, 20; 12:14, 19, 32).

Jesus' response to Bartimaeus's request echoes his words to the woman with the hemorrhage, "Go, your faith has made you well" (cf. 5:34). "Immediately" (*euthys*—forty or forty-one times in Mark), his sight was restored. Mark adds, pointedly, "and he followed him on the way" (10:52). Readers who have paid close attention to Mark's language recognize that "followed" (*akolouthei*) is a term that connotes discipleship. More specifically, it is a term Mark has used in the call stories (1:18; 2:14-15; cf. 3:7; 6:1; 8:34; 9:38; 10:21, 28, 32). Jesus specifically called the rich man to follow him (10:21), but he would not. In contrast, Bartimaeus's faith, demonstrated by his persistence in the face of opposition, leads to the granting of his request, and seeing, he begins to follow Jesus "on the way." "The way" is also a loaded term that Mark has used as a metaphor for the way of discipleship, or the way to the cross (4:4, 15; 6:8; 8:3, 27; 9:33-34; 10:17, 32, 46). If the story of the healing of the blind man at Bethsaida illustrates the condition of the disciples, who see but not clearly, the story of the calling of Bartimaeus serves as a paradigm for Jesus' power to heal, restore, and give sight to those who respond to his call to follow him on the way to the cross.

CONNECTIONS

Mark 10:1-12

The divorce teachings in the New Testament are difficult, not because the texts are obscure or ambiguous—their meaning is clear—nor because of the differences among them. They are difficult because they give us little guidance on how to deal with unhealthy or failed marriages and divorced persons. Unfortunately, divorce is common in our society. No one promotes divorce, least of all those who have been divorced. Simply prohibiting divorce, however, makes the church irrelevant and insensitive, judgmental and unhelpful, just when hurting couples need a supportive community the most. The dilemma, therefore, is how to be faithful to Jesus' teachings on divorce and compassionate at the same time.

In some ways the issue is similar to the struggle Christians face on the issues of women in ministry and homosexuality. These are issues that are from one perspective social and cultural, and from another perspective rooted in the created order. Culturally, the situation has changed in that there are many more opportunities for women to work and be independent today than there were in the first century. These are also issues on which one can either consider the Scripture passages that speak to these issues in isolation, or place them in the larger context of Jesus' example in dealing with women, outcasts, or the woman taken in adultery, and Jesus' teachings on grace and forgiveness. The question is not what the divorce passages say, but how to interpret them in the context of the rest of the Gospel. How can one affirm the ideal of the sanctity of marriage without being judgmental and insensitive? On the other hand, how can one allow divorce (and remarriage) when Jesus forbade it?

Did Jesus forbid divorce because of the sanctity and permanence of marriage or to protect women from being cast aside with no means of support? While the answer may be "both," and the context in Mark lends support to the consideration that Jesus forbade divorce in order to protect those who would be hurt most by it, Jesus based the argument against divorce on the scriptural support for the indissolubility of marriage.

The New Testament itself gives evidence of the development of interpretations and qualifications of Jesus' prohibition of divorce that respond to specific situations. If one partner is unfaithful, surely that can be a situation in which divorce should be allowed. Matthew agrees, adding the "except" clause that allows divorce in such situations. What if one partner is an unbeliever and demands divorce from the believing partner, perhaps specifically because of the believing partner's faith and new way of life? Is the believing partner bound to an unbeliever who may be abusing the believer? Paul says no. In such instances divorce is allowed (1 Cor 7:15). Taking all the passages on divorce together, therefore, one can see both a call to God's intention for a holy and indissoluble union between husband and wife and a pastoral response of compassion for those who find themselves in intolerable relationships or failed marriages. In such instances divorce is allowed and compassion and love should be unstinting. There is no contradiction between holding up the ideal of lifelong marriages, requiring premarital counseling for couples before marriage and regular attention to healthy marriages through marriage enrichment retreats or classes on the one hand, and support for separated and divorced persons or blessing appropriate second marriages on the other. We live in the tension between the ideal and the actual, and in all areas of life we are called to strive for the ideal while accepting Christ's love and forgiveness when we fail and extending it to others when they fail.

Mark 10:13-16

This scene is really not about children; it is about the kind of attitude a disciple should have. Jesus' pronouncement is a response to the disciples' attempt to keep children away from him. In doing so, they demonstrated a presumption, self-importance, and sense of entitlement that is alien to the kingdom of God. Such self-importance is also alien to childhood. Grace is freely given and should never be assumed or expected, but received with surprise, delight, and gratitude. Repentance (see 1:15) leads to an acknowledgment that one is not worthy to enter the kingdom. Therefore, one who does not receive the kingdom as a child receives an unexpected delight cannot enter it. This warning should call us all to deep introspection regarding whether we approach life with a sense of entitlement or with humility. Do we assume that we have a right to whatever we want or need, or are we grateful for all we have that we did not earn? Presumption can lead to an inert state of self-satisfaction, while gratitude leads to wonder, delight, and a desire to give back to others. ["Enlarge the Door"]

Children can be wonderful and disarming models for those who seek to control the kingdom. Because Jesus pointed out that how we treat children reveals a lot about our character, it would serve the church well to consider how it treats children. Are children treated as a vital part of the community of faith, one that enriches its experience, or as a necessary inconvenience? Is the worship made accessible to children, or does the church design worship for adults only? Are children given opportunities to lead in worship, or is their leadership in worship treated as entertainment for the congregation? The church also needs to be careful to nurture the faith of children and avoid manipulating children, either by leading them to do something they are not ready to do or by blocking their childish efforts to own their faith and identify with their community of faith. "Let the little children come to me" (10:14) means do not put obstacles or impediments in their path—don't keep them from coming to Jesus. On

---

"Enlarge the Door"

A brief verse written by Miguel de Unamuno shortly before his death is not far off the mark:

Enlarge the door, Father,
Because I can not pass;
You made it for children,
And I have grown heavy.

If you do not enlarge the door for me
Make me smaller, for pity's sake,
Return me to the blessed age
When to live is to dream.

Jesus says the kingdom belongs "to such as these" (10:14). The irony is that those who think they deserve it and can control it cannot get in, while those who stand in wonder at it actually own it.

Hugo H. Culpepper, "The Christian Faith and Modern Man in the Thought of Miguel de Unamuno" (Th.D. dissertation; Southern Baptist Theological Seminary, 1961), 22, citing Hernán Benítez, *El drama religioso de Unamuno* (Buenos Aires: Universidad de Buenos Aires, Instituto de Publicaciones, 1949), 193.

Children in the Church

Resources for ministry to and with children:

Kathryn Chapman, "Communicating with Children," in *The Ministry of Childhood Education* (comp. Ray F. Evette; Nashville: Convention Press, 1985).

William L. Hendricks, *A Theology for Children* (Nashville: Broadman, 1980).

Andrew D. Lester, ed., *When Children Suffer: A Sourcebook for Ministry with Children in Crisis* (Philadelphia: Westminster Press, 1987).

G. Wade Rowatt, *Pastoral Care with Adolescents in Crisis* (Louisville: Westminster/John Knox, 1989).

———, *Today's Youth: A Profile for Teachers, Leaders and Parents* (Nashville: Convention Press, 1993).

the other hand, it does not mean "drag" them or force them to come to Jesus. Those who brought the children to Jesus are like the other anonymous helpers who bring people to Jesus all through the Gospel of Mark (see the commentary on 7:32).

Children offer themselves to us openly. They bring joy, delight, and simplicity because they trust implicitly. For a child every day is a new adventure in learning, play, and exploration. The world is a place of endless wonder. Even if we who are adults think we understand the world and have grown cynical and hardened by it, the kingdom is certainly strange and unexplored territory for us—a place where mercy takes precedence over justice, where the least of all, children and servants, lead the way, where the demons are driven from our lives, the broken are restored, and the boundaries that divide us are transcended. What a place! How else could we receive it except to receive it as though we were children again? [Children in the Church]

Mark 10:17-31

The story of the rich man's question to Jesus about how he might inherit eternal life strikes modern American readers at two sensitive points, our preoccupation with the question of eternal life and our runaway materialism. How can we live in a culture whose entire way of life is built around capitalism and consumerism and still have eternal life? Miguel de Unamuno, quoted earlier, is best known for his book *Tragic Sense of Life*, which ends with his statement that he took up his pen "to distract you for a while from your distractions."[47] He meant that the question of whether or not there is life after death is such a distressing question for us that we spend our lives, working or playing, distracting ourselves from it. There is something within us that demands that there must be more to life than this physical existence—our spirits demand that it must be so, yet we cannot know that there is anything beyond death. Therefore, we spend our lives distracting ourselves from this ultimate question. Unamuno's eventual answer, as an agnostic, was that we should live in such a way that if there is nothing beyond death it will be an injustice.[48] Unamuno accepts both the uncertainty and the assumption that is implicit in the rich man's question, but on different grounds. The rich man assumed without question the reality of life beyond death, whereas Unamuno could not.

The rich man also assumed that there might be something he could do to assure that he would enter this eternal life, whereas Unamuno could only offer the nobility and virtue of living in such a way that one would merit eternal life, if there is life beyond death. In a survey of religious beliefs in America, George Gallup, Jr., found that more Americans share the rich man's questions than are concerned with Unamuno's. Two-thirds of those surveyed believe there is life after death and believe that the quality of existence after death will be different for different people. Still, only 29

Americans Believe in Afterlife

Two-Thirds Affirm Life after Death
Do you believe you will exist in some form after your death?

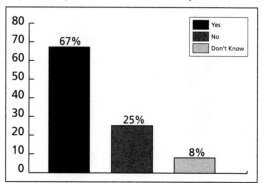

(Credit: Gallup Institute survey conducted for the Nathan Cummings Foundation and the Fetzer Institute in May, 1997.)

percent of those surveyed think their chances of going to heaven are excellent.[49] Hence the importance we attach to the question, "What must I do to inherit eternal life?"

The other nerve this story pricks is our preoccupation with material possessions. Living in the United States requires a high level of consumption of consumer goods: housing, energy, transportation, clothes, food, medical care, and insurance. Things that were once luxuries have become necessities: second cars, televisions, computers, cell phones, and the list goes on. Beyond those things we regard as necessities, the media reinforce our desire for more and better things. As a result, most Americans live beyond their means and carry a heavy load of credit debt that cripples them financially, inflicts a heavy toll in stress and marital conflict, and limits their ability to be generous to the church, to charities, and others. Americans consume a disproportionately large share of the world's resources, yet poverty and homelessness in America—and in countries whose goods and labor we consume—have become a national and global crisis.

Jesus' call for those who would follow him to deny themselves (8:34), leave homes and fields (10:29-30), sell everything, give to the poor, and follow him (10:21) sets a requirement no one can follow unless they too become homeless and dependent on the generosity of others for their survival. What might have worked for an individual in an agrarian society that placed a high value on almsgiving is now out of the question. Imagine the chaos that would be created if every Christian in America followed Jesus' challenge to the rich man literally. WWJD is not a bad approach to this issue, if one recognizes that Jesus' teaching and example was tied to its cultural context in the first century and must surely be adapted to various cultural contexts in the twenty-first

More Americans Believe in Heaven than Hell

Is heaven something you believe in, something you're not sure about, or something you don't believe in?

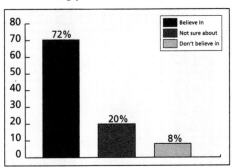

(Credit: Gallup Institute survey conducted for the Nathan Cummings Foundation and the Fetzer Institute in May, 1997.)

Is hell something you believe in, something you're not sure about, or something you don't believe in?

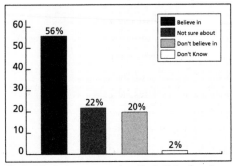

(Credit: Gallup Institute survey conducted for the Nathan Cummings Foundation and the Fetzer Institute in May, 1997.)

century. What would Jesus do to change our appetite for materialism? What would Jesus do to turn our attention from our own needs and desires to those of others with far less means and far harder lives? How would the quality of our lives—spiritually, emotionally, and materially—be improved if we took strong steps toward living by the priorities and values implicit in Jesus' teachings? Who knows, a camel might yet make it through the eye of a needle! God is still changing lives and redeeming humanity.

Mark 10:32-34

Mark's comment that the disciples were afraid as they followed Jesus on the road to Jerusalem is intriguing. The commentary suggests several reasons why they might have been afraid, and observes that fear in Mark is often a sign of defective faith or lack of faith. Whatever the specific reason for their fear, following Jesus had drawn the disciples well outside their comfort zone. First, they had left their homes and work to follow Jesus. Then, they had traveled around most of Galilee and even ventured into neighboring territories. Now, they were going to Jerusalem, where they knew the authorities were plotting against Jesus.

Although Mark makes it clear that there was much the disciples did not understand, they were still following Jesus—even though doing so made them afraid. We all want to be in control of our lives, but here is a perspective on discipleship that warns us that a significant step in faith is giving up control and following in faith even when what lies ahead is not clear to us, or scares us. Fear is the impulse to act self-defensively; faith is trust in God's purposes and God's protection. Fear says turn back and go home; faith says go on to Jerusalem, for God will use whatever happens there for good.

Some have not followed Jesus far enough to be afraid. Some will indeed turn back (the rich man, Judas). The way ahead may be costly for some (James and John), but God's call is the call to surrender all self-interest (8:34) and to devote ourselves completely to God's redemptive work. Those who press on, in spite of their fear, will find in their service to Jesus a quality of life and a family of fellow travelers they could scarcely have imagined: "houses, brothers and sisters, mothers and children, and fields [a hundredfold] with persecutions—and in the age to come eternal life" (10:30).

Mark 10:35-45

Most of us can identify with the urge to find an inside track, to get ahead of the crowd. If the line is long, we look for a friend up at the head of the line. If traffic is tied up, we switch lanes or take the frontage road to get around it. Perhaps others have worked for the company faithfully for years, but we would be happy to be promoted ahead of them on the basis of friendship or a family connection. Ambition is not a bad thing, but it is dangerous—hence the commonplace, "blind ambition." Unchecked, ambition does not count the cost, or consider the consequences, or anything else. It becomes so focused on the goal that other persons, principles, or priorities are forgotten in the single-minded drive to achieve the prize we covet. Financiers create accounts or whole companies to hide money, athletes take drugs, and coaches violate NCAA regulations.

James and John were just playing the game, coming to Jesus on the side in an effort to secure places of honor for themselves. Their actions in doing so were simply an extension and confirmation of the assumptions implicit in their request: that the world operates by the exercise of power and that one gets ahead by securing status. As a result, James and John clearly demonstrate that they have not yet understood or committed themselves to the kingdom of God.

The disciples also represent a great many modern Christians in that they were following Jesus, but they had little understanding of the nature of the kingdom of God. Their hopes and ambitions were not conformed to the mission of the one whom they followed. Their values and their ways of relating to others did not yet mirror the transformation that participation in God's redemptive purposes requires. The kingdom is oriented not toward power but toward service. Greatness is therefore measured not by one's status or power but by one's commitment to serving others in Jesus' name. The same dichotomy—the quest to control or the desire to serve—can also be used as a measure of denominations and religious movements. Every church, school, business, and denomination has its own "institutional culture," its own history, values, and goals, and its own peculiar ways of doing things.

Embarrassing moments are often revealing. We are caught off guard, and our true nature is exposed. James and John's question showed Jesus that they still had a long way to go; they were still thinking like "the Gentiles" rather than like children of God. Perhaps we ought to stop at intervals along the way and measure our progress. Which pursuit shapes our dreams and guides our actions, power or service?

Mark 10:46-52

The observation is sometimes made that Americans have become a nation of spectators. Rather than playing sports, we watch sports; and rather than going to the ballpark or the stadium, we prefer to stay at home and watch the game on the television. Worse still, we often bring the same preferences to our faith and worship. Televised worship may be a blessing for those who cannot go to church to worship with others, but it is more like watching others eat than enjoying a meal with family and friends. Then, when we do go to church to worship, many prefer to sit back and watch others "perform" rather than to participate actively in singing, praying, reading, and responding. Similarly, we pay others to do ministry, evangelism, and missions for us rather than embracing these as the tasks to which every follower of Christ is called.

The story of Bartimaeus is the story of one who moved from the sidelines to the playing field. His blindness reduced him to a life of begging, sitting by the roadside with his garment spread before him, waiting for others to do for him what he could not do for himself. Even his blindness, however, did not rob him of his awareness of his surroundings or his will to free himself from his disability. What is it that keeps us on the sidelines, and what is robbing us of the quality of life and faith we might enjoy?

Bartimaeus called out to Jesus. He would not let others keep him from getting the help he needed. He asked Jesus directly to free him from that which kept him sitting "by the roadside." For most of us, what keeps us on the sidelines is something far less difficult to deal with than blindness. Jesus assured Bartimaeus, "your faith has made you well." Faith itself has a healing power! The change in Bartimaeus was immediate, and he followed Jesus "on the way." He moved from the sidelines to the most thrilling experience of his life—following Jesus on his journey up to Jerusalem.

The story of Bartimaeus, therefore, should be the story that we read daily to remind ourselves never to be content to be spectators, simply watching others live, worship, or do ministry. The call to discipleship is a call to active participation: "You follow me." (See the commentary on 1:16-20 and the connections for 8:14-21 and 8:22-26.)

NOTES

[1] Craig A. Evans, *Mark 8:27–16:20* (WBC 34B; Nashville: Thomas Nelson, 2001), 81-82.

[2] Ben Witherington III, *The Gospel of Mark: A Socio-Rhetorical Commentary* (Grand Rapids: Wm. B. Eerdmans, 2001), 277-78.

[3] John Painter, *Mark's Gospel* (London and New York: Routledge, 1997), 143.

[4] BDAG, 384.

[5] Evans, *Mark 8:27–16:20*, 94.

[6] Painter, *Mark's Gospel*, 143.

[7] Bruce J. Malina and Richard L. Rohrbaugh, *Social Science Commentary on the Synoptic Gospels* (Minneapolis: Fortress, 1992), 372.

[8] Evans, *Mark 8:27–16:20*, 95.

[9] See James D. Hester, *Paul's Concept of Inheritance: A Contribution to the Understanding of Heilsgeschichte* (Scottish Journal of Theology Occasional Papers 14; Edinburgh: Oliver and Boyd, 1968).

[10] William L. Lane, *The Gospel according to Mark* (Grand Rapids: Wm. B. Eerdmans, 1974), 365 n 42.

[11] Eduard Schweizer, *The Good News according to Mark* (trans. Donad H. Madvig; Atlanta: John Knox Press, 1970), 210.

[12] Lane, *The Gospel according to Mark*, 365.

[13] Evans, *Mark 8:27–16:20*, 96.

[14] Craig Evans's claim, "there is no indication that care for the poor was a distinctive feature of Jesus' agenda" (*Mark 8:27–16:20*, 98), overstates the case even for Mark.

[15] Evans, *Mark 8:27–16:20*, 99.

[16] BDAG, 949.

[17] Thomas C. Oden and Christopher A. Hall, eds., *Ancient Christian Commentary on Scripture: New Testament II, Mark* (Downers Grove IL: InterVarsity Press, 1998), 144; NPNF1 7:202.

[18] Evans, *Mark 8:27–16:20*, 101.

[19] Origen, *Catena, frgs. in Matt.* 19.24 (GCS 41.166), cited by Joseph A. Fitzmyer, *The Gospel according to Luke X-XXIV* (AB 28A; Garden City NY: Doubleday, 1985), 1204.

[20] Evans, *Mark 8:27–16:20*, 102.

[21] Schweizer, *The Good News according to Mark*, 214.

[22] Vincent Taylor, *The Gospel according to St. Mark* (London: Macmillan, 1952), 436; Lane, *The Gospel according to Mark*, 375; and Evans, *Mark 8:27–16:20*, 106, have similar tables.

[23] See Robert Wayne Stacy, "Fear in the Gospel of Mark" (Ph.D. dissertation, Southern Baptist Theological Seminary, 1979), 255-56.

[24] BDAG, 519.

[25] Lane, *The Gospel according to Mark*, 379 n 77.

[26] Ibid., 379.

[27] R. Alan Culpepper, *John the Son of Zebedee: The Life of a Legend* (Columbia: University of South Carolina Press, 1994), 8-9.

[28] Leonhard Goppelt, *"potērion,"* *TDNT* 6:149.

[29] Albrecht Oepke, " *baptō*," *TDNT* 1:536; George R. Beasley-Murray, *Baptism in the New Testament* (Grand Rapids: Wm. B. Eerdmans, 1962), 72-77.

[30] Lane, *The Gospel according to Mark*, 380 n. 85. See Edward W. Burrows, "Baptism in Mark and Luke," in *Baptism, the New Testament and the Church* (ed. Stanley E. Porter and Anthony R. Cross; JSNTSup 171; Sheffield: Sheffield Academic Press, 1999), 110-11.

[31] Burrows, "Baptism in Mark and Luke," 112-13.

[32] Oepke, "*baptō*," *TDNT* 1:538-39.

[33] Culpepper, *John the Son of Zebedee*, 171.

[34] Ibid.

[35] B. W. Bacon, "John and the Pseudo-Johns," *ZNW* 31 (1932): 137-39; Martin Hengel, *The Johannine Question* (trans. John Bowden; Philadelphia: Trinity Press International, 1989), 21, 158 n. 121; and Culpepper, *John the Son of Zebedee*, 170-74.

[36] Lane, *The Gospel according to Mark*, 382.

[37] BDAG, 255.

[38] Evans, *Mark 8:27–16:20*, 119-25. For the debate over the influence of Isa 53 on Mark 10:45, see C. K. Barrett, "The Background of Mark 10:45," in *New Testament Essays* (Festschrift for T. W. Manson; ed. A. J. B. Higgins; Manchester: Manchester University Press, 1959), 1-18, who dismisses the parallels with Isa 53; George R. Beasley-Murray, *Jesus and the Kingdom of God* (Grand Rapids: Wm. B. Eerdmans, 1986), 278-83, who affirms that "the concept in Mark 10:45 [of 'the vicarious nature of the martyr's death'] most surely reflects Isaiah 53:10-12"; Witherington, *The Gospel of Mark*, 288-90, who concludes that "at several points Isa. 53 stands in the background of this saying and informs its semantic field."

[39] See C. E. B. Cranfield, *The Gospel according to Saint Mark* (Cambridge: Cambridge University Press, 1959), 343; Beasley-Murray, *Jesus and the Kingdom of God*, 282.

[40] See H. H. Schaeder, "*Nazarēnos*," *TDNT* 4:874-79; Stephen Goranson, "Nazarenes," *ABD* 4:1049-50.

[41] Lane, *The Gospel according to Mark*, 387; A. Dupont-Sommer, *The Essene Writings from Qumran* (trans. G. Vermes; Cleveland: World, 1961), 314-15.

[42] John P. Meier, *A Marginal Jew*, vol. 2: *Mentor, Message, and Miracles* (New York: Doubleday, 1994), 689-90.

[43] Painter, *Mark's Gospel*, 151.

[44] I suggested this interpretation in "Mark 10:50: Why Mention the Garment?" *JBL* 101 (1982): 131-32.

[45] David Rhoads and Donald Michie, *Mark as Story: An Introduction to the Narrative of a Gospel* (Philadelphia: Fortress Press, 1982), 24.

[46] Hayim Lapin, "Rabbi," *ABD* 5:601.

[47] Miguel de Unamuno, *Tragic Sense of Life* (trans. J. Crawford Flitch; New York: Dover Publications, 1954), 330.

[48] Ibid., 263, 269.

[49] George Gallup, Jr., and D. Michael Lindsay, *Surveying the Religious Landscape: Trends in U. S. Beliefs* (Harrisburg PA: Morehouse Publishing, 1999), 27-31.

JESUS' ENTRY INTO JERUSALEM

Mark 11:1-33

In the Gospel of Luke, Jesus "sets his face to go to Jerusalem" at Luke 9:51, shortly after his transfiguration and the second passion prediction. His journey to Jerusalem then stretches over the next ten chapters. In contrast, in Mark Jesus does not mention his destination until 10:32, so there is far less text devoted to the journey, and Jesus arrives in Jerusalem at the beginning of Mark 11. Still, after ten chapters devoted to Jesus' ministry in Galilee, and Jesus' repeated prediction that he was going to be handed over to the authorities and put to death, the reader naturally experiences a heightened sense of excitement and anticipation as Jesus approaches the Holy City.

Mark 11–13 forms a section of teaching and confrontation with the authorities that prepares for the Passion Narrative (Mark 14–16). The preparation for Jesus' entry into the city anticipates the preparation for the Passover meal that follows in Mark 14:12-16. As the commentary points out, the entry conforms to the pattern of ceremonial entrances in antiquity, but with striking variations. Jesus rides into the city humbly, on a donkey, looks around, and then anticlimactically withdraws from the city for the evening. The next day, in a typical Markan sandwich construction, Jesus curses the fig tree on the way into the city, carries out a demonstration in the temple, and then withdraws again. The next morning Peter notices that the fig tree has withered away to its roots. Jesus seizes the moment to teach the disciples another lesson on faith and prayer. When they enter the temple, the authorities challenge Jesus to tell them by what authority he is acting. It is the first of a series of pronouncement stories that extends through Mark 12 in which one group after another approaches Jesus with a question only to be trumped by his wit and wisdom.

COMMENTARY

The Triumphal Entry, 11:1-11

Mark's account of Jesus' entry into Jerusalem begins with an ironic account of the preparation for Jesus' entry into the city. The story of Jesus' sending of two of his disciples to secure a colt for him has

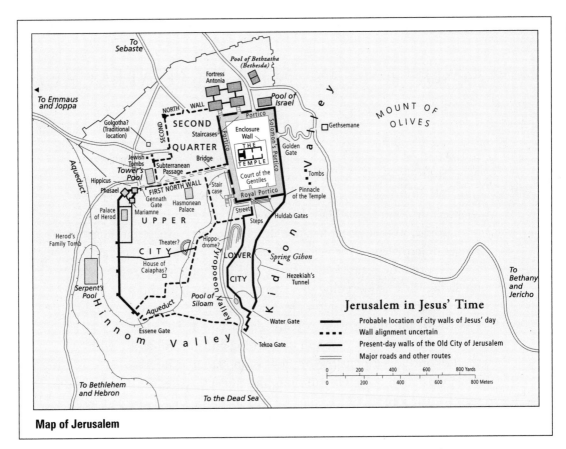

Map of Jerusalem

parallels with his sending of two of his disciples to make preparations for the Passover meal. The question is why Mark would give so much attention to these preparations. Craig Evans argues that the story is "a fragment of an authentic story, which the tradents and eventually the evangelist himself passed on but without being in full possession of the facts."[1] In other words, the point of the story had been lost by the time it came to Mark, but he included it because it came to him as historical tradition. Elsewhere, however, the Gospel is so tightly written that this explanation is inconsistent with Mark's literary work and apparent motives.

Nevertheless, the scene remains puzzling, unless Mark intended it to introduce the ironic incongruities that follow. Scripture is fulfilled in the course of everyday, inconsequential acts and by disciples who do not understand what they are doing. The Son of God enters the Holy City on a colt, acclaimed by a crowd, but by the end of the week another crowd will call for his death. The temple appears to be full of activity, but it is like a barren fig tree. The Messiah will be anointed, but he will be anointed not by the high priest but by a woman. When he is acknowledged as Son of God, it is again not the high priest but a Gentile, the Roman centurion, who voices the confession. Throughout,

Mark's account of Jesus' death is filled with pathos and irony. Just as the Easter message will be announced by women who say nothing because they are afraid, so the account of Jesus' last days in Jerusalem is introduced by a report of the mundane activities of disciples and bystanders who did not know the meaning of what they were doing.

Jesus' entry into the city follows the well-established pattern of accounts of entrance processions. Numerous kings and conquerors had entered Jerusalem over the years. Although the welcoming ceremony of a conqueror and the celebration of the return of a victorious general can be distinguished from each other, they share similar features. Paul Brooks Duff has summarized the characteristic elements of an entrance procession as follows:

(1) The conqueror/ruler is escorted into the city by the citizenry or the army of the conqueror.
(2) The procession is accompanied by hymns and/or acclamations.
(3) The Roman triumph has shown us that various elements in the procession . . .
symbolically depict the authority of the ruler.
(4) The entrance is followed by a ritual of appropriation, such as sacrifice, which takes place in the temple, whereby the ruler symbolically appropriates the city.[2] [Entrance Processions]

Entrance Processions

Alexander the Great's entrance into Jerusalem: "Then all the Jews together greeted Alexander with one voice and surrounded him . . . [then] he gave his hand to the high priest and with the Jews running beside him, entered the city. Then he went up to the temple where he sacrificed to God under the direction of the high priest. (Josephus, *Ant.* 11.332–36 [trans. Ralph Marcus; LCL; Cambridge MA: Harvard University Press, 1937], 475, 477.)

Antony's entrance into Ephesus: "When Antony made his entrance into Ephesus, women arrayed like Baccanals, and men and boys like satyrs and Pans, led the way before him, and the city was full of ivy and thyrsus-wands and harps and pipes and flutes, the people hailing him as Dionysus Giver of Joy and Beneficent. For he was such undoubtedly, to some." (Plutarch, *Antonius*, 24.3–4 [trans. Bernadotte Perrin; LCL; Cambridge MA: Harvard University Press, 1920], 187–89.

Each of these elements is present in Mark, even though it is hardly a "triumphal" entry. Jesus has yet to win the ultimate victory on the cross, and Mark's description of Jesus' entry into the city in imitation of an entrance procession establishes the irony of the servant Messiah whose victory is achieved by his death.[3] Jesus is escorted into the city by his followers, but they are not an army. They are a band of fishermen and tax collectors, disciples who don't really know who they are following, a once blind beggar from Jericho, and some women from Galilee. They acclaim Jesus, chanting words from one of the processional psalms (Ps 118:25-26). Elements of the procession symbolically depict Jesus' authority: the colt, which shows that Jesus fulfilled the Scriptures (Zech 9:9), the branches, and the cloaks thrown on the road (2 Kgs 9:13). Finally, Jesus appropriates the temple and curses the fig tree, announcing God's judgment on the city and its leaders. Jesus was not the nationalistic Messiah that many expected, however, and Mark's use of irony forces the reader to reflect on the ultimate irony of a Messiah who triumphed not by killing but by dying.

Mount of Olives

The Mount of Olives is part of the central mountain range that runs north-south through Palestine, and is actually three summits. The northernmost, rising nearly 3000 feet above sea level, has been identified with Nob, or Mount Scopus. The middle peak, at 2700 feet above sea level, stands opposite the site of the temple and rises about 100 feet above the city. The southern summit is the smallest of the three.

The Mount of Olives is mentioned explicitly only twice in the Old Testament (2 Sam 15:30 and Zech 14:4-5), but may be intended in other references: the high places Solomon built for his foreign wives (1 Kgs 11:7-8; 2 Kgs 23:13) and the mountain east of the city where Ezekiel saw the glory of God (Ezek 11:23).

(Credit: R. Alan Culpepper)

Numerous chapels and shrines have been erected on the Mount of Olives to commemorate events reported in the Gospels and Acts.

Warren J. Heard, Jr., "Olives, Mount of," *ABD* 5:13–14.

The story of Jesus' entry into Jerusalem begins when he arrives at Bethphage and Bethany on the Mount of Olives, signaling the fulfillment of Israel's eschatological expectations: "On that day his [the Lord's] feet shall stand on the Mount of Olives, which lies before Jerusalem on the East" (Zech 14:4). Bethphage is named before Bethany either because it was closer to Jerusalem[4] or because a traveler from Jericho would pass through Bethphage before reaching Bethany. [Bethphage and Bethany]

The sending of two disciples to make preparations for Jesus' entry into Jerusalem is strikingly similar to the later report of sending two disciples to make preparations for the Passover meal (14:12-16), with verbatim repetition of some of phrases:

Mark 11:1-4	Mark 14:12-16
"He sent two of his disciples and said to them, 'Go into the village'"	"He sent two of his disciples and said to them, 'Go into the city'"
What the disciples would find there	What the disciples would see there
What the disciples were to say	What the disciples were to say
"They went away and found. . . ."	"So the disciples set out and went into the city and found everything as he had told them."

Bethphage and Bethany

In Aramaic Bethphage means "House of Figs." The location of Bethphage is uncertain. A location west of Bethany, about one kilometer east of the top of the Mount of Olives, was accepted by the crusaders and marked by frescoes and inscriptions, but there is no evidence of an ancient village there. Others accept the modern village of Abu Dis, southeast of Bethany, as the site of Bethphage.

Bethany, which may mean "House of Dates" or "House of the Poor," was located less than two miles east of Jerusalem, on the southeast slopes of the Mount of Olives. The Gospels report that it was the home of Mary, Martha, and Lazarus (John 11:1, 18; cf. Luke 10:38-42) and of Simon the leper (Mark 14:3). Luke reports that the ascension took place at Bethany (Luke 24:50-51), although churches on the top of the Mount of Olives mark traditional sites where the ascension was believed to have occurred. Today Bethany is called in Arabic El-'Aziriyeh, a corrupt form of Lazarus, and tourists are shown what is purported to be the home of Mary and Martha and the tomb of Lazarus. The location is dubious but can be traced to the 4th century: "The traditional crypt of Lazarus was reported by the Bordeaux pilgrim in AD 333. The 'spot where Mary met the Lord' was enclosed in a church before 385. Another church was built over the crypt by that date (Jerome *Onomasticon*), and a monastery was added later (according to Arculf, *c.* AD 670). In the eleventh century a basilica was erected to mark a site for the anointing of Jesus' feet by Mary. . . . All these and other traditional sites reveal a confusing conflation of different gospel stories. Although an underground chamber is still honored as the crypt of Lazarus, all other ancient structures have suffered decay" (K. W. Clark, "Bethany," *IDB* 1:388).

K. W. Clark, "Bethphage," *IDB* 1:396; and K. W. Clark, "Bethany," *IDB* 1:387–88; cf. Scott T. Carroll, "Bethphage," *ABD* 1:715; R. Earle, "Bethany," ISBE, rev. ed., 1:463–64.

In Mark 14 the implication is that Jesus has made arrangements with the man carrying the jug of water. He knows Jesus as "the teacher" and has provided Jesus with a guest room. In Mark 11 it is not clear whether Jesus has made prior arrangements to purchase or borrow the colt, or whether Jesus' knowledge that the disciples would see a colt there that had never been ridden is meant to be a sign of Jesus' supernatural knowledge.

Luke identifies the two disciples sent to prepare the Passover meal as Peter and John (Luke 22:8), but none of the Gospels names the two who were sent to retrieve the colt. Similarly, the village is not named, and hence may be either Bethany or Bethphage. The word *pōlos* signifies a young animal, here probably a colt or a young donkey (as in Zech 9:9). The significance of the fact that no one had ridden the colt is probably to be explained either as an echo of Zechariah 9:9, which describes the animal as "a new colt" (*pōlon neon*), or as an indication that the animal was suitable for a consecrated task since it had not been used for ordinary purposes (Num 19:2; Deut 21:3; 1 Sam 6:7; 2 Sam 6:3). The attention given to securing the proper animal for Jesus to ride as he entered Jerusalem is reminiscent of David's provision of his own mule for Solomon to ride to his coronation (1 Kgs 1:33, 38), and the untying of the colt may evoke associations with Jacob's prediction that Judah would bind his colt to the choice vine (Gen 49:11) and that the scepter would not depart from him. This passage was linked to Zechariah 9:9 and read as a messianic prophecy by the church fathers because the verse continues, "he washes his garments in wine and his robe in the blood of grapes" (Gen 49:11; cf. Justin Martyr, *Apology*

1.32). Matthew mistook the poetic parallelism of Zechariah's prediction that the king would come "riding on a donkey, on a colt, the foal of a donkey" (Zech 9:9) and therefore has Jesus riding on two animals (Matt 21:2-7). Justin Martyr extended the symbolism further, commenting that Jesus requested "His disciples to bring both beasts; [this fact] was a prediction that you of the synagogue, along with the Gentiles would believe in Him. For as the unharnessed colt was a symbol of the Gentiles, even so the harnessed ass was a symbol of your nation [i.e., Israel]" (*Dialogue with Trypho* 53).

The instructions that if they were asked about what they were doing, the disciples were to say, "The Lord needs it," is open to various interpretations. The term "Lord" (*kyrios*) is used of God and Jesus, and in ordinary usage means "sir" or "master." It is unlikely that Jesus used it to refer to himself in its elevated sense, though for parallels one might consider 2:28 and 5:19. Neither is it likely that it is a reference to God in this instance.[5] Vincent Taylor, therefore, proposed that "the lord" is the colt's owner. The response is directed not to the colt's owner but to bystanders, and the owner may have been with Jesus.[6] Nevertheless, it is hard to avoid the impression that Mark is playing on the overtones or elevated meaning of the term.

When the disciples enter the village, they find the colt and are challenged, just as Jesus had said, and their response satisfies the bystanders. When the two disciples bring the colt to Jesus, the others place their garments upon it, for a saddle for Jesus. Others throw their garments on the road before Jesus. The two references to the garments here echo the report that Bartimaeus cast his garment aside to make his way to Jesus (10:50). In 2 Kings 9:13, the people spread their garments on the steps before Jehu and hail him, "Jehu is king!" According to Plutarch, when Cato the Younger left his troops, the soldiers "spread their garments at his feet and kissed his hand as he passed, an honour which the Romans at that time scarcely paid even to a very few of their generals and commanders-in-chief" (*Cato Minor* 7).[7]

Others spread *stibadas* on the road before him. The translation of this term is debated, with Craig Evans favoring "tall grass"[8] and the Bauer-Danker lexicon rendering it "leafy branches," while noting that the term appears only here in the New Testament and does not occur in the Septuagint or Philo.[9] Perhaps because the word is unusual and imprecise, Matthew changes it to "branches from the trees" (Matt 21:8) and John to "branches of palm trees" (John 12:13). Carrying on the metaphorical significance of "the way" from earlier references (see 10:52), the road into Jerusalem is still the way that will lead Jesus to the cross.

Like other processions of pilgrims entering Jerusalem, Jesus' followers sing and chant the words of one of the hallel psalms (Ps 118:25-26), perhaps antiphonally. Mark has carefully adapted the text of the psalm, however. Mark retains the Semitic "Hosanna" rather than translating it into Greek as the Septuagint does, rendering it "Save us now" (Ps 117:25 LXX). Omitting the second half of v. 25, Mark quotes the first part of v. 26, "Blessed is the one who comes in the name of the Lord," and then adds the line, "Blessed is the coming kingdom of our ancestor David" (11:10). The closing line, "Hosanna in the highest heaven!" echoes Psalm 148:1. The cry to God, "Hosanna," "save us," was later adopted through repeated use as a liturgical formula. Jerome said it was Hebrew for "O Lord, grant salvation!" (*Homilies* 94).[10] In context, however, the cheering crowd was probably calling out to God, in the presence of this one whom they recognized as the Messiah, to inaugurate the events that would restore the kingdom of their forefather David, an understanding of Jesus and the kingdom that neither Jesus nor Mark shared.[11]

Roman readers might well have contrasted Jesus' ironically humble entry into Jerusalem with Vespasian's triumphal procession into Rome after the destruction of Jerusalem in AD 70.[12] Josephus describes it at length and in great detail (*J. W.* 7.123-157). Vespasian was "crowned with laurel and clad in the traditional purple robes." The senate and chief magistrates awaited him. Josephus declares, "it is impossible adequately to describe the multitude of those spectacles and their magnificence," but notes in particular the rare works of art, the treasures of silver and gold, the massive moving stages on which the progress of the war was rehearsed for all to see, and the spoils of war, including a copy of the Jewish Law. By contrast Jesus' procession is pitiful—a motley band of Galileans, fishermen, beggars, and women, hailing a Messiah riding on a donkey and calling out to God for deliverance.

The conclusion to the entrance procession is surprisingly anticlimactic. Nothing more is said of those who went before him and followed him, and the subject changes from the plural to the singular: Jesus entered into Jerusalem, went to the temple and looked around, and then went out to Bethany with the Twelve. Jesus is not greeted at the temple, nor does he do anything except look around. Sensing the uneasiness with which this conclusion follows the joyful entrance procession, Matthew adds a comment that the whole city was abuzz with speculation about Jesus (Matt 21:10), and Matthew and Luke both place the cleansing of the temple immediately after Jesus' entry into the city.

C. E. B. Cranfield notes that Mark says nothing about a great crowd following Jesus into Jerusalem. It was unusual for a pilgrim to ride into

Overnight in Bethany

According to Joachim Jeremias, it would not have been unusual for Jesus and his followers to spend the nights outside of Jerusalem.

"Where did the mass of the pilgrims stay? It is one of the ten wonders of God in the Holy Place, that all found shelter and none said to another: 'The crowd is too great, I cannot find shelter in Jerusalem' (M. Ab. V.5). . . . Some might stay in near-by places like Bethphage or Bethany. . . . The majority of the pilgrims, however, had to have tents in the immediate neighbourhood of the city, since at Passover it was still very cold at night and there could be no question of sleeping out in the open. . . . However, the participants in the Passover feast were obliged to spend the Passover night (14-15 Nisan) in Jerusalem. The city itself could not take the crowd of pilgrims, and so that they could fulfil the law the boundaries of Jerusalem were extended to take in even Bethphage (M. Men. xi.2)."

Joachim Jeremias, *Jerusalem in the Time of Jesus* (trans. F. H. and C. H. Cave; Philadelphia: Fortress, 1969), 60–61.

the city, but apparently neither the Romans nor the temple authorities took note of Jesus' riding into the city on a donkey: "It was a veiled assertion of his Messiahship."[13] Mark's understated report that Jesus "looked around" does not say what he saw. It therefore opens a gap in the narrative that will not be filled until the next day when Jesus drives out the merchants and money-changers. Although Mark does not make note of it, Jesus' action fulfills the warning in Malachi. The first part of Malachi 3:1 was quoted in reference to John the Baptist: "See, I am sending my messenger to prepare the way before me" (Mal 3:1a; Mark 1:2). Now the second part has been fulfilled: "and the Lord whom you seek will suddenly come to his temple. . . . and who can stand when he appears?" (Mal 3:1-2). [Overnight in Bethany]

The Fig Tree and the Temple, 11:12-25

The cursing of the fig tree is intercalated with the demonstration in the temple in Mark, creating a typical "Markan sandwich" in which the two events are to be considered together, each providing a context for interpreting the other (see [Markan Sandwiches]). Matthew and Luke both smooth out the chronology. Luke omits the cursing of the fig tree altogether, while Matthew places it on the day after Jesus' prophetic action in the temple. By doing so, however, the effect of the cursing on the tree must be immediate, and its association with Jesus' action in the temple is diminished.

Cursing the fig tree, vv. 12-14

The next morning, following the night at Bethany, while they were on their way back to Jerusalem, Jesus was hungry. Nothing is said about whether they had eaten or whether the disciples were hungry also. Mark omits all extraneous details. Problems arise with the next verse. Seeing a fig tree in leaf, Jesus goes to it to see if it has any edible fruit. Finding none, he curses the tree, saying, "May no one ever eat fruit from you again" (11:14). Jesus' action seems inappropriate and petty, all the more so since, as Mark reports, "it was not the season for figs" (11:13).

Fig trees were common in Judea and bore fruit twice each year, the early figs in May and June and the late figs from late August into October. At the time of Passover, in later March or early April, one could have expected to find only figs left over from the previous season or unripe early figs. According to some accounts, these unripe early figs could be eaten even though they were not sweet. In the Old Testament the fig tree is "a proverbial sign of peace and security" (1 Kgs 4:25; Mic 4:4; Zech 3:10);[14] being able to sit under one's fig tree or grapevine represented peace in the land. The barren fig tree, like the unproductive vineyard (Isa 5:1-7), came to be associated with Israel's failure in the imagery of the prophets: "When I wanted to gather them, says the LORD, there are no grapes on the vine, nor figs on the fig tree" (Jer 8:13), and "Woe is me! For I have become like one who . . . finds no cluster to eat; there is no first-ripe fig for which I hunger" (Mic 7:1).

Mark's report that the disciples heard what Jesus said serves as a bridge to Peter's observation the next day that the fig tree had withered (11:20). The connection between the fig tree and the temple is not explained, but the association is apparently based on the metaphor of the fig tree in the prophetic passages cited above, where Israel is condemned for its barrenness. Like the barren fig tree that had leaves and appeared to be healthy, the temple was full of activity but bore no fruit of holiness, righteousness, or justice.

The most problematic aspect of this already difficult passage is Mark's comment that it was not the time for figs. Craig Evans suggests plausibly that the explanatory "for" clause is misplaced here as in Mark 16:4, where the clause, "for it was very large" (author's translation), should naturally follow the women's question, "Who will roll away the stone for us from the entrance to the tomb?" in 16:3 rather than the report that when they looked up they saw that the stone had been rolled back in 16:4a.[15] The NRSV translation obscures the problem of the misplaced "for" clause by inserting it as an appositional clause in 16:4a. Following this suggestion, the comment, "for it was not the season for figs," in 11:13 should serve as an explanation for why Jesus went to see if the tree had figs rather than as an explanation for why it had nothing but leaves: "Thus, Mark's *gar* clause explains why Jesus had doubts about whether he might find figs rather than why the tree did not have figs."[16] While this rearrangement relieves some of the incongruity of Jesus' looking for figs when it was not the season for figs, it still does not lessen the difficulty of Jesus' cursing the fig tree when it did not bear figs out of season.

Alternatively, Mark's comment can be seen as "a signal that the story is to be read for its symbolic meaning."[17] The word "season" translates the significant Greek term *kairos* that denotes not the chronological passing of time but a particularly significant period of time. Mark uses the term in Jesus' thematic announcement of the coming of the kingdom in 1:15. Jesus assures the disciples that they will receive a hundredfold "now in this age (*kairos*)" (10:30). In the parable of the wicked tenants that follows shortly, the owner of the vineyard sends a servant to collect his share of the produce of the vineyard "when the season came" (12:2). And in the eschatological discourse in Mark 13 Jesus warns the disciples to be alert because "you do not know when the time (*kairos*) will come" (13:33). Read in the context of these other occurrences of the term in Mark, the comment that "it was not the season for figs" carries at least the implication that the real point is not about the time for the harvest of figs but about the suddenness of Jesus' appearance in the temple, when it was not yet the time for the eschatological judgment. The point is eschatological rather than agricultural.

Cleansing the Temple, vv. 15-19

Both the cursing of the fig tree and the demonstration in the temple were acted out parables that placed Jesus in the tradition of Israel's prophets. Isaiah walked naked and barefoot through Jerusalem for three years (Isa 20:2-4); Jeremiah hid a linen loincloth at the Euphrates until it was ruined (Jer 13:1-11) and then broke an earthen jug as a sign of God's coming judgment (Jer 19:1-13). Ezekiel dramatized the siege of Jerusalem (Ezek 4:1-15), and Hosea married Gomer, named her children Jezreel ("God sows"), Lo-ruhamah ("Not pitied"), and Lo-ammi ("Not my people"), and then took Gomer back. The destruction of the fig tree, similarly, symbolized the coming judgment on Israel: "I will waste her vines and her fig trees" (Hos 2:12; cf. Isa 34:4).[18] Similarly, Jesus' prophetic demonstration in the temple pointed to its commercial corruption, recalled the warning of destruction from Jeremiah, brought to a halt the temple activities by prohibiting people from carrying vessels through it, and in the words of Isaiah reminded its leaders of its true purpose—to be "a house of prayer for all nations."

The quantity of animals and goods consumed by the offerings in the temple during a festival was staggering. Josephus records that during Passover of AD 66, worshipers required an estimated 255,600 lambs (*J. W.* 6.9.3). Blood flowed from the altar in such quantity that it was carried by a channel to two holes, like two narrow nostrils, in the southwestern corner of the temple wall. From these openings it poured out into the Kidron valley where it was collected and sold to gardeners and farmers as fertilizer (*m. Yoma* 5.6; *m. Middoth* 3.2; *m. Meilah* 3.3). The animals had to be without blemish or broken bones, and if they were quadrupeds they had to be male. Every offering had to be accompanied by salt (Lev 2:13; Ezek 43:24), and libations of wine usually accompanied the sacrifice of animals and bread (Hos 9:4; Jer 7:18). Only red wine could be used for this purpose, however. Since thousands of pilgrims came to Jerusalem each year to participate in the three great pilgrimage festivals, Passover, Pentecost, and Tabernacles, there was a great demand for animals and goods fit for use as offerings.[19]

The origin of trade in the temple is difficult to trace. According to the Mishnah, the written code of the oral law of the Pharisees, the holiness of the temple meant that one "may not enter into the Temple Mount with his staff or his sandal or his wallet, or with the dust upon his feet, nor may he make of it a short by-path; still less may he spit there" (*m. Berakoth* 9.5; cf. Mark 11:16). Such veneration of the temple makes it difficult to conceive of cattle being sold there. Zechariah, a late prophetic writing, claims that in the "day of the LORD," when his reign is established, "there shall no longer be a trader in the house of the LORD of hosts" (Zech 14:21). This prophetic statement can be taken as evidence that the practice of commerce in the temple existed prior to the New Testament period and that the prophet, and presumably others, felt that it was inappropriate there.

The next references to buying and selling in the temple are those in the Gospels. It has been suggested, however, that the admission of merchants to the Court of the Gentiles was an innovation of the high priest Caiaphas. If so, the presence of merchants in the temple would have been a recent development, and Jesus may have been protesting this corruption of the temple by the current high priest. This is the thesis of Victor Eppstein. The key to his argument is that apparently just prior to Jesus' cleansing of the temple "the Sanhedrin departed or was expelled from its place in the Chamber of Hewn Stone in the temple to a place on the Mount of Olives called Hanuth."[20] References in the Talmud say this departure took place forty years before the destruction of the temple, in other words in AD 30, and Eppstein suggests that this development occurred just before Passover of that year.

On the Mount of Olives there were four markets called *hanuyoth* that were controlled by the "sons of Hanan." Here visitors to the temple could purchase the doves and other goods they would need. The whole area was regarded as sharing in the holiness of the temple, and stringent precautions guarded it from contamination. The high priesthood controlled the temple but had no authority over the Mount of Olives. The Sanhedrin probably resided in the temple because they served as advisers and instructors for the priests when they came in for their period of priestly service. With the approval of the high priest, priests and levites collaborated to insure that temple worship was conducted properly. The reason for the removal of the Sanhedrin from the temple to the Mount of Olives is unknown. Presumably they were either

Money-changers

The clearest evidence we have about money-changers in the temple links them to the payment of the "shekel of the sanctuary" commanded by Exod 30:13-16. Half a shekel was due from every male Israelite twenty years old and over. Women, minors, and slaves were exempted. Roman coins could not be used for this purpose, since they bore the images of men. Instead, they were exchanged for the Tyrian shekel, which was the coin closest in value to the old Hebrew shekel. A surcharge of half a silver *maah*, which was equal to one twenty-fourth of a shekel, was added. This surcharge was used to compensate the money-changers, to cover any loss incurred in the exchange, and to cover losses due to the wear of coins in circulation. The temple tax was due on the first of the month of Nisan each year, two weeks before Passover (Nisan 15). In order to facilitate the payment, a warning was read on the first of the previous month (Adar), reminding the people that the tax would soon be collected. On the fifteenth of Adar tables were erected for money-changers in the provinces, and on the twenty-fifth tables were set up in the temple (*m. Shekalim* 1.1-7). The tables were apparently taken down on the twenty-fifth in the provinces and on the first of Nisan in the temple. Some provision was made for late payment of the shekel tax. The tax was used to purchase the public offerings and for the support of the temple, but the coins collected late could not be used for the holiest purposes. The most intense money-changing activity, therefore, took place about two weeks before the Passover. There is some reason for dating the "cleansing of the temple" between the twenty-fifth of Adar and the first of Nisan on this basis, but there may have been tables for money-changers in the temple at other times of the year also. It is unclear whether ordinary coinage could be used to purchase the sacrificial animals in the temple. If it could not be used, money-changers would be required all year; but there is no reference to their presence for this purpose. Since there were regulations regarding the use of late payments of the temple tax, some tables may have remained in the temple after the first of Nisan for those who still needed to pay the shekel.

Alternatively, it has been suggested that the tables were those of bankers. Ancient temples, including the temple in Jerusalem, were used as banks. The deities were thought to protect them, so temples were considered to be the safest places for money. The second book of Maccabees records an attempt by Heliodorus to confiscate temple funds for the Syrian King. Simon, the captain of the temple, reported that there were both sacred and secular accounts: "the treasury in Jerusalem was full of untold sums of money, so that the amount of the funds could not be reckoned, and that they did not belong to the account of the sacrifices, but that it was possible for them to fall under the control of the king" (2 Macc 3:6). On this occasion, the priests also prayed "to him who had given the law about deposits that he should keep them safe for those who had deposited them" (2 Macc 3:15). In addition to the temple captain, the temple staff included three treasurers, seven supervisors, and two persons who held office "over the public in aught concerning property" (*m. Shekalim* 5.2). Surpluses and revenues accrued to the temple fund, which was used for the construction of public buildings, walls, aqueducts, scholarships for students, support of the sages, and loans. By upsetting the tables Jesus may have been attacking the banking operations and economic functions of the temple.

See Neil Q. Hamilton, "Temple Cleansing and Temple Bank," *JBL* 83 (1964): 365–72.

---

ordered to leave by the high priest, Caiaphas, or they left in protest. Eppstein suggests that in a further act of vindictiveness against the Sanhedrin, which had made a place for itself among the markets on the Mount of Olives, Caiaphas opened the Court of the Gentiles to merchants for the sale of items to be used in the temple. [Money-changers]

Doves were the prescribed offering for the purification of women (Lev 12:6-8; 15:29), lepers (Lev 14:21-22), and uncleanness (Lev 15:14). Luke records that Mary and Joseph offered the sacrifice of "a pair of turtledoves, or two young pigeons" following Jesus' birth (Luke 2:24). Doves, or young pigeons, were the common offering of the poor. Sheep, oxen, wine, oil, and salt were also used in the temple. The opportunity to buy doves and other animals within the temple precincts was probably welcomed by many, since there was always the possibility that the animals could be damaged or defiled even in the course of the short walk from the Mount of Olives across to the temple. [Bird Offerings]

If the sale of animals in the temple was a recent development, it casts fresh light on Jesus' dramatic action in the temple. He was fulfilling the vision of Zechariah, driving traders from the temple, and by implication showing that the kingdom of God had come, at least in a preliminary way (Mal 3:1). He was further opposing the corruption of the temple by Caiaphas, who in an effort to protect the temple and the nation said, "it is expedient for you that one man should die for the people, and that the whole nation should not perish" (John 11:50; cf. v. 48).

Jesus Drives the Merchants from the Temple

Bernardo Bellotto (1720–1780). *Jesus driving the moneychangers and merchants from the Temple.* Oil on canvas. National Museum, Warsaw, Poland. (Credit: Erich Lessing / Art Resource, NY)

The question put to Jesus in the temple may also be interpreted in this context. Eppstein suggests that when the chief priests asked him "By what authority are you doing these things, or who gave you this authority to do them?" they were probing to see whether he was acting under the authority of the Sanhedrin.[21]

As fascinating as the implications of Eppstein's proposal are, the force of Jesus' act in the temple does not depend upon it. For understanding Jesus' ministry and his motives for journeying to Jerusalem, much depends on whether he intended to "cleanse" the temple so that it (and by implication Israel) could achieve its true purpose or whether he was condemning the temple (and its religious leadership) and foreshadowing its coming destruction. E. P. Sanders has argued that Jesus' demonstration was not intended to purify the worship offered there but to announce that its end had come and that God was about to raise up a new temple in its place. [E. P. Sanders's Thesis] Far from cleansing the temple for future use, Jesus was condemning it as corrupt, no longer the place where God would dwell, no longer the place where people

Bird Offerings

There were strict and complicated laws regarding the consequences of a pigeon breaking loose and mingling with others which had been assigned for a different offering or with birds designated as unfit for sacred use. There could be no confusion among the birds that were assigned for obligatory offerings and those that were for voluntary offerings. A whole tractate of the Mishnah is devoted to regulations concerning the bird offerings (*m. Kinnim*). One section illustrates the potential difficulties:

"Thus if two women had each two pairs and the one that belonged to the first woman flew among them that belonged to the second, by its flying away it renders invalid one [of the birds from which it flew]; if it flew back, by its

flying back it renders invalid yet another. If it again flew away and then flew back, and yet again flew away and then flew back, it can effect no further loss, since even if they were all confused together, there are never less than two pairs [which may validly be offered]." (*m. Kinnim* 2.2)

In view of the liability loose pigeons could inflict on their owners, it would not be surprising if buyers of these sacrificial animals desired to get them to the altar as quickly as possible!

R. Alan Culpepper, "Mark 11:15-19," *Int* 34 (April 1980): 176–81.

would find the spirit of God. Jesus' judgment on the temple was confirmed by the rending of the veil from top to bottom at his death (15:38). Jesus' death and resurrection marked the beginning of a new temple, however, a temple "not made with hands," the church (14:58).

Jesus' act of prohibiting anyone from carrying vessels through the temple may be interpreted either as forbidding the people from profaning the court of the Gentiles by using it as a shortcut from one side of the temple to the other, in keeping with the Mishnah's injunction, "nor may he make of it a short by-path" (*m. Berakoth* 9.5) and Josephus's recollection that "no vessel whatever might be carried into the temple . . . nothing of the nature of food or drink is brought within the temple" (*Against Apion* 2.106, 109; LCL 1:335). Alternatively, in context with the overall significance of Jesus' prophetic announcement of the end of the temple, by stopping anyone from carrying vessels through the temple Jesus effectively, if temporarily, brought an end to its sacrifices and sacral functions.

Jesus' appeal to Scripture with the question, "Is it not written . . . ," is consistent with the authority accorded Scripture in this Gospel. Mark begins with an appeal to Isaiah (1:2), and the next time Mark refers to what is written it is also to Isaiah (7:6). The references to the sufferings of the Son of Man in Mark 9:13 and 14:21 are probably also references to the suffering servant in Isaiah, but the allusions to Moses (10:4-5; 12:19) and Zechariah (14:27) break the pattern.

E. P. Sanders's Thesis

"On the hypothesis presented here the action and the saying [Mark 14:58; 15:29] form a unity. Jesus predicted (or threatened) the destruction of the temple and carried out an action symbolic of its destruction by demonstrating against the performance of sacrifices. He did not wish to purify the temple, either of dishonest trading or of trading in contrast to 'pure' worship. Nor was he opposed to the temple sacrifices which God commanded to Israel. He intended, rather, to indicate that the end was at hand and that the temple would be destroyed, so that the new and perfect temple might arise."

E. P. Sanders, *Jesus and Judaism* (Philadelphia: Fortress, 1985), 75. For a response to Sanders, see Craig A. Evans, *Mark 8:27–16:20* (WBC 34B; Nashville: Thomas Nelson, 2001), 170–71, 181–82.

It is appropriate, therefore, that Jesus quoted part of the following passage from Isaiah while he condemned the temple. In order to grasp the full significance of the quotation, one must remember that in the first century there were no chapter and verse divisions in the Hebrew Scriptures, and that quotation marks, footnotes, and cross references were not yet in use. Therefore, brief quotations of key phrases were often used to evoke the larger context of a familiar passage of Scripture. Note the context of the phrase "a house of prayer for all nations" in Isaiah's vision of a time when the nations would come to Jerusalem to worship:

> And the foreigners who join themselves to the LORD, to minister to him, to love the name of the LORD, and to be his servants, all who keep the sabbath, and do not profane it, and hold fast my covenant—these I will bring to my holy mountain, and make them joyful in my house of prayer; their burnt offerings and their sacrifices will be accepted on my altar; for *my house shall be called a house of prayer for all peoples.* Thus says the Lord GOD, who gathers the outcasts of Israel, I will gather others to them besides those already gathered. (Isa 56:6-8; my emphasis)

For the temple, God intended a place where peoples from all nations would be welcome. This passage is linked to Jeremiah's temple sermon by the phrase "this house" or "my house" in the immediate context of the phrase "a den of robbers":

> Stand in the gate of the LORD's house, and proclaim there this word, and say, Hear the word of the LORD, all you people of Judah, you that enter these gates to worship the LORD. Thus says the LORD of hosts, the God of Israel: Amend your ways and your doings, and let me dwell with you in this place. Do not trust in these deceptive words: "This is the temple of the LORD, the temple of the LORD, the temple of the LORD." . . . Here you are, trusting in deceptive words to no avail. Will you steal, murder, commit adultery, swear falsely, make offerings to Baal, and go after other gods that you have not known, and then come and stand before me in this house, which is called by my name, and say, "We are safe!'—only to go on doing all these abominations? Has *this house,* which is called by my name, become *a den of robbers* in your eyes? You know, I too am watching, says the LORD. Go now to my place that was in Shiloh, where I made my name dwell at first, and see what I did to it for the wickedness of my people Israel. And now . . . I will do to the house which is called by my name, in which you trust, and to the place that I gave to you and to your ancestors, just what I did to Shiloh. (Jer 7:2-4, 8-14; my emphasis)

The warning from Jeremiah should stand as a reminder to the leaders of the people that if God did not spare Shiloh, neither would God spare Jerusalem (see [*Peirazein*, To "Tempt" or "Test," in Mark]).

The phrase "den of robbers" would have had added significance for Mark's readers after the destruction of the temple in AD 70, when the rebels held the temple until the destruction of the city by the Romans. Josephus uses the same term found in the Septuagint translation of Jeremiah 7:11 for the rebels: *lēstai*.[22] [Revolutionaries] Josephus also reports that one Jesus ben Ananias (c. AD 62–69) cried out condemnations of the temple at one of the festivals, quoted Jeremiah 7, and was arrested by the Romans (*J.W.* 6.300-309).[23]

Revolutionaries

AΩ Josephus used the term *lēstai* for the insurrectionists, especially during the latter stages of the war of 66–70:

"But while the country was thus cleared of these pests, a new species of banditti [*lēstōn*] was springing up in Jerusalem, the so-called sicarii, who committed murders in broad daylight in the heart of the city." (*J.W.* 2.254; LCL, 2:423)

"In the end, satiated with their pillage of the country, the brigand chiefs [*archilēstai*] of all these scattered bands joined forces and, now merged into one pack of villainy, stole into poor Jerusalem." (*J.W.* 4.135; LCL 3:41)

"Simon, son of Gioras . . . joined the brigands [*lēstas*] who had seized Masada." (*J.W.* 4.504; LCL 3:151)

Just as the disciples heard Jesus' cursing of the fig tree (11:14), so the chief priests (see [Chief Priests]) and scribes (see [Scribes]) heard Jesus' recitation of the words of Isaiah and Jeremiah (11:18). The reference here is all the more ominous since the only earlier references to these two groups together have been in the predictions of Jesus' death (8:31; 10:33). In keeping with these earlier predictions, the chief priests and scribes were "looking for a way to kill him" (11:18). Earlier references to seeking Jesus have been neutral (1:37; 3:32; 8:11-12; cf. 16:6), but from this point on they typically signal a hostile motive (11:18; 12:12; 14:1, 11, 55). Literally, the verb translated "to kill" means "to destroy" (*apollymi*). Ironically, the demons feared that Jesus had come to destroy them (1:24), but the authorities conspired to destroy Jesus (3:6). Those who seek to save their lives will destroy them (8:35). Then, in the next chapter, in the paradigmatic parable of the wicked tenants, which Jesus will tell about the chief priests and scribes, the owner of the vineyard will destroy the wicked tenants (12:9) and give the vineyard to others.

The reason they seek to kill Jesus, Mark explains, is that they feared him (11:18). In this case, however, fear is not a defective faith but a misguided response that arises from concern to protect their own positions and leads ultimately to a murderous miscarriage of justice (see the commentary on 10:32). The crowd, on the other hand, was "spellbound" (NRSV) by his teaching. Mark uses this verb (*ekplēssomai*), which typically means to "be amazed, overwhelmed,"[24] exclusively to characterize the response to Jesus' teaching and healing on various occasions—in the synagogue (1:22), in his home-town (6:2), following the healing of the deaf man (7:37), and following his teaching on the difficulty the wealthy have in entering the kingdom (10:26).

The report that Jesus and the disciples left the city when it became late fits the setting established earlier, in which Jesus and the disciples were staying at Bethany and coming into Jerusalem during the day (11:11-12). It also sets up the discovery of the withered fig tree as they were coming back to Jerusalem the next morning (11:20). The gates of ancient cities were locked at night for the protection of the elite who lived inside the city walls. [The Preindustrial City]

The Fig Tree Withered, vv. 20-25

Having left the city late (11:19), Jesus and the disciples return early (11:20) the next day, and as they pass by they see that the tree that Jesus cursed had withered "to its roots." The expression is found in the Old Testament (Hos 9:16; Job 18:16; 31:12). It means that the tree had dried up completely, confirming Jesus' curse: that no one would ever eat fruit from it again. The fig tree was a symbol for Israel (Jer 8:13; Hos 9:10; Joel 1:7; Mic 7:1-6), and the destruction of a fig tree was a sign of God's judgment on the nation (Isa 34:4; Hos 2:12).[25] Finding the fig tree withered not only confirms that Jesus' condemnation of the tree was fulfilled, but by virtue of its symbolism and its sandwiching with Jesus' condemnation of the corruption of the temple it also confirms that the temple too will soon be withered "to its roots"—not one stone will be left on another (13:2).

Parenthetically, the reader may note that the next time Peter remembers something Jesus had said it will be an even more painful memory (see 14:72).

Jesus' response addresses the issue of the power of faith, implicit in Peter's surprise. As Sharyn Dowd observes, "'faith' in the Gospel of Mark is unswerving confidence that the power of God at work in Jesus is able to heal and transform those who seek God's help."[26] Faith is foundational for Mark, even though the term does not occur frequently in the Gospel. When Jesus sees the faith of those who bring the paralytic to him, he heals the man (2:5). Similarly, faith leads to healing for the woman with a hemorrhage (5:34) and for Bartimaeus (10:52). Jesus

The Preindustrial City

"Temple and palace dominated the center of the city, often with fortifications of their own. Around them, in the center, lived the elite populations, which controlled cult, coinage, writing, and taxation for the entire society. At the outer limits of the city lived the poorest occupants, frequently in walled-off sections of the city in which occupational and ethnic groups lived/worked together. (Note that the configuration of an industrial city is just the opposite: the poorest people live in the center, while the richest live in the suburbs.) Outside the city walls lived beggars, prostitutes, persons in undesirable occupations, traders (often wealthy), and landless peasants who drifted toward the city in search of day-laboring opportunities. They required access to the city during the day, but were locked out at night. Gates in internal city walls could also be locked at night to prevent access to elite areas by non-elite persons."

Bruce J. Malina and Richard L. Rohrbaugh, *Social-Science Commentary on the Synoptic Gospels* (Minneapolis: Fortress, 1992), 368.

Moving a Mountain

The four forms of this saying occur in two contexts: Matt 17:20 and Luke 17:6 in Q, and Mark 11:23 and Matt 21:21 following the withering of the fig tree. All four are connected with having faith, and all are followed by an assurance. Parallels to the Markan form of the saying are in italics. Following the theory of Markan priority, Matthew used Mark as a source.

"For *truly I tell you, if you* have faith the size of a mustard seed, you will *say to this mountain,* 'Move from here to there,' and it will move; and nothing will be impossible for you." (Matt 17:20)

"*If you* had faith the size of a mustard seed, you could *say to this* mulberry tree, 'Be uprooted and planted in the sea,' and it would obey you." (Luke 17:6)

"*Truly I tell you, if you say to this moun-tain, 'Be taken* [Greek *arthēti*] *up and thrown into the sea,' and if you do not doubt* in your heart, but believe that what you say will come to pass, *it will be done* for you." (Mark 11:23)

"*Truly I tell you, if you* have faith and *do not doubt*, not only will you do what has been done to the fig tree, but even *if you say to this mountain, 'Be lifted* [Greek *arthēti*] *up and thrown into the sea,' it will be done.*" (Matt 21:21)

A succinct form of the saying can be constructed from the common elements of the four forms that have come down to us: "Truly I tell you, if you have faith the size of a mustard seed, you could say to this mountain, 'Be taken up and thrown into the sea,' and it would be done." Alternatively, the four forms may reflect the mixing of elements that were originally paired as follows in two separate sayings: (A) faith the size of a *mustard seed*—move *mulberry tree* from here to there; (B) say to this *mountain*—be cast into the *sea*; do not doubt and it will be done.

---

marvels that the disciples do not have faith (4:40), and now admonishes them (plural): "Have faith in God" (11:22). Before any other issue—the destruction of the temple, prayer, or the coming of the kingdom—there is the issue of faith in God. Only when that issue is settled do the others become relevant (cf. 1:15; 5:36; 9:23-24).

Having said that the temple should be a "house of prayer for all nations" (11:17; Isa 56:7), Jesus turns directly to the place of prayer in the new temple, not made with hands. The assurance of power to move mountains occurs in four forms in the Gospels [Moving a Mountain], and is echoed in 1 Corinthians 13:2 and the *Gospel of Thomas* (48 and 106). Statements about moving mountains may have circulated in various contexts, but Jesus' assurance echoes Zechariah 14:4: "On that day his feet shall stand on the Mount of Olives, which lies before Jerusalem on the East; and the Mount of Olives shall be split in two from east to west by a very wide valley; so that one half of the Mount shall withdraw northward and the other half southward." The appeal of this verse for Mark is clear: the eschatological day had come (cf. Isa 40:3-5; 45:2), Jesus was standing on the Mount of Olives, and his action in the temple had foreshadowed its destruction. Moreover, Jesus did not say that the disciples could move any mountain; probably gesturing or pointing, he said, "this mountain." The question of whether Jesus meant the Mount of Olives, in fulfillment of the statement in Zechariah, or the temple mount, in a further allusion to its destruction, has been widely debated.[27] In either case, the saying announces the arrival of the eschatological conditions that will usher in the new age of the kingdom. In this age the temple (and perhaps even the mountain on which it stands) will pass away, and a new temple not made with hands will arise, open for all peoples seeking God and characterized by faith, prayer, and forgiveness.

A discussion of the effectiveness of prayer following Jesus' prophetic warning of the coming judgment on the temple makes sense given the ancient practice of offering prayers in holy places or facing the temple in Jerusalem (see *m. Berakoth* 4.5).[28] [Praying Toward the Temple] The anti-temple polemic can be traced in Greek as well as in Jewish materials, as Sharyn Dowd has shown. Seneca declared, "We do not need to uplift our hands towards heaven, or to beg the keeper of a temple to let us approach his idol's ear, as if in this way our prayers were more likely to be heard. God is near you, he is with you, he is within you" (*Epistles* 41.1, LCL).[29]

The effectiveness of prayer, Jesus insisted, was not determined by the posture of the petitioner, where one prayed, or which direction one faced, but by one's faith in God. Do not fear, only believe (5:36); with God all things are possible (10:27). William Lane's comment is worth repeating: "When prayer is the source of faith's power and the means of its strength, God's sovereignty is its only restriction."[30] Authentic prayer is the expression of unwavering confidence in the sovereignty of God, a confidence that is affirmed by the prophets (Isa 65:24) and by Jesus (Matt 7:7-11; 18:19). The second condition essential for effective prayer is forgiveness. At this point Jesus echoes a well-established principle: "Forgive your neighbor the wrong he has done, and then your sins will be pardoned when you pray. Does anyone harbor anger against another, and expect healing from the Lord?" (Sir 28:2-3). What can block one's prayers, therefore, is not the destruction of a holy place but an unholy refusal to forgive one's brother or sister (cf. Matt 5:23-24).

The language of Mark 11:25 echoes Jesus' instructions on prayer in Matthew 6:14-15. Although Mark's form of the saying is shorter, it echoes the address in the Matthean form of the Lord's Prayer: "[your/our] father who is in heaven" (cf. Matt 6:9). Nevertheless, the

Praying Toward the Temple

"In Judith 4:9-15 the people prostrate themselves in front of the temple when they pray for protection from Holofernes. In 3 Maccabees the priest and people rush to the temple to pray in the face of the threat to the Holy of Holies by Ptolemy Philopator (3 Macc 1:20-24). The high priest prays, 'thou didst promise that if . . . we should come to this place and make our supplication, thou wouldst hear our prayer.' The enemy is struck down (3 Macc 2:1-22). In 2 Maccabees 3:15 the priests pray before the altar as Heliodorus prepares to sack the temple treasury. In response to the prayer, Heliodorus is flattened by a divine apparition and subsequently converted (2 Macc 3:24-40). After Judas and his men pray before the altar (2 Macc 10:25-26), the Lord gives them victory over Timotheus by sending angels into battle with them. . . .

"Given this background, it is not hard to see why the destruction of the second temple would cause some rabbis to question whether prayer were any longer possible: 'R. Eleazar said: From the day on which the Temple was destroyed, the gates of prayer have been closed. . . . *b. Ber* 32b.'"

Sharyn Dowd, *Reading Mark* (Macon: Smyth & Helwys, 2000), 120–21.

emphasis on faith, prayer, and its corollary, forgiveness, is an important part of Mark's concept of the new community that will replace the fallen temple.

The Question about Jesus' Authority, 11:27-33

Mark 11:27–12:34 contains a series of controversy dialogues that are set in the temple. The series of controversy dialogues, beginning with the question of Jesus' authority, is reminiscent of the series of pronouncement stories in Mark 2:1–3:6. Each question is put to Jesus by a group of the authorities critical of his activities:

- The Question about Jesus' Authority (the chief priests, the scribes, and the elders), 11:27-33
- The Parable of the Wicked Tenants (addressed to those who had questioned Jesus' authority—see 12:12), 12:1-12
- The Question about Paying Taxes (the Pharisees and the Herodians), 12:13-17
- The Question about the Resurrection (the Sadducees), 12:18-27
- The Question about the Greatest Commandment (one of the scribes), 12:28-34

Following this series, Jesus teaches on the son of David (12:35-37), condemns the scribes (12:38-40), and then comments on the generosity of the widow who puts her two coins in the treasury (12:41-44). When Jesus enters the temple in Mark 11:27, therefore, he does not leave it until the end of this section (13:1).

Jesus' entry into Jerusalem punctuates Mark 11. He enters the city three times in this chapter (11:11, 15, and 27), the first time in triumphal procession, the second time to condemn the corruption of the temple, and the third time, presumably, to teach in the temple. While he was walking in the temple, probably in one of its porticoes, he is approached by a group of the temple authorities—chief priests (see [Chief Priests]), scribes (see [Scribes]), and elders [Elders]—ominously, the same three groups mentioned in the first passion prediction (8:31; cf. 10:33). The same three groups will play a lead role in the arrest and trial of Jesus (14:43, 53; 15:1).

Elders

AΩ "Only gradually does it [*presbyteroi*] become the special term for lay members [of the *gerousia* or Sanhedrin] as distinct from the representatives of the priestly families, from whom the high-priest and president of the Sanhedrin was chosen, and also from the theological group of the *grammateis* [i.e., scribes]. It is obvious that the direction of the Sanhedrin never lay in the hands of the *presbyteroi*. Yet one may assume that the elders, as representatives of the privileged patrician families in Jerusalem, usually followed the lead of the priestly Sadducees."

Günther Bornkamm, *"presbys," TDNT* 6:659.

The authorities were presumably investigating Jesus' disturbance of the temple activities on the previous day. Authority for direction of the temple lay in the hands of the chief priests.[31] The authorities may therefore have been informally seeking to determine whether there were grounds for bringing Jesus to trial. Craig Evans captures the force of their question: "Either Jesus admitted his conduct was unauthorized, which would have made him publicly vulnerable, or he claimed a right superseding that of the ruling priests, a claim that would have made him politically vulnerable."[32]

The authorities actually pose two questions, the second an extension of the first: "By what authority are you doing these things? Who gave you this authority to do them?" (NRSV). In context, the referent of "these things" must be Jesus' demonstration in the temple (11:15-19). Authority (*exousia*) was understood as a prerogative to act or speak that was given or handed on by one's teacher or predecessor. The chief priests exercised the authority of the Sanhedrin with the blessing of the Roman procurator, who was appointed by the Roman emperor himself. By what authority did Jesus presume to disrupt the temple activities? Their question is reminiscent of the reaction of Jesus' hometown when he taught in the synagogue there. The NRSV translates the three-word Greek question (lit., "Whence these [things] [to] this [one]?") as "Where did this man get all this?" (6:2).

Jesus' authority was an issue throughout his ministry. The narrator commented in Mark 1:22 that Jesus "taught as one having authority, and not as the scribes." The authority of his teaching was confirmed by his exorcism of the unclean spirit while he was teaching, so that those who witnessed the event commented, "What is this? A new teaching—with authority!" (1:27). Later, Jesus gave authority over the unclean spirits to his disciples (3:15; 6:7). The most interesting reference to Jesus' authority, however, arises in the first of the controversy stories in Mark 2:1–3:6. After Jesus forgave the paralytic, he responded to the questioning scribes, "But so that you may know that the Son of Man has authority on earth to forgive sins—. . ." (2:10). The recurrence of the issue of Jesus' authority in this series of controversy dialogues in the temple recalls the earlier series of challenges to Jesus from the religious authorities. At the same time, the reader now understands Jesus' role as Son of Man differently because of the occurrence of this title in the three passion predictions (8:31; 9:31; 10:32-34). The Son of Man who has authority to forgive sins on earth is also the Son of Man who will give his life as a ransom for many (10:45).

Ironically, Jesus, whose authority has just been challenged, responds by dictating terms to the temple authorities: "I will ask you one question; answer me, and I will tell you by what authority I do these things" (11:29). Jesus uses this technique of debate elsewhere when responding to the authorities: when the scribes ask, "who can forgive sins but God alone?" Jesus responds, "Which is easier . . . ?" (2:7-9). When the people ask why his disciples do not fast like those of the Pharisees and John the Baptist, Jesus answers, "The wedding guests cannot fast while the bridegroom is with them, can they?" (2:18-19). When the Pharisees ask why he allows the disciples to do what is not lawful on the Sabbath, he responds, "Have you never read what David did . . . ?" (2:24-25). When the Pharisees ask if it is lawful for a man to divorce his wife, Jesus again responds with a question: "What did Moses command you?" (10:2-3), and he will use the same technique in response to the question about paying taxes (12:14-16). A contest of wits, which often took the form of a challenge of questions, was a common feature of ancient debate. By asking a question in return, and especially by demanding an answer from the authorities before he will answer their question, Jesus issues a challenge to their honor. If they fail to answer his question, they lose honor and by implication the right to question his authority (see [Honor and Shame]).

Jesus' syntax in v. 30 is abrupt and commanding, with a force lost in translation. Literally, he says, "The baptism of John—from heaven was it or from man? Answer me!" The question is a shrewd one, and once again Jesus' response, demanding an answer, exhibits unimpeachable authority. The reader knows that John was a prophet, that Jesus was baptized by John, and that at Jesus' baptism "the heavens [were] torn apart" and the voice from heaven spoke to Jesus (1:9-11). Both John's and Jesus' authority come from God. If the temple authorities will not recognize John's authority, neither will they recognize Jesus'. On the other hand, Jesus' counter question forces his interrogators into an awkward position, which Mark communicates by reporting their discussion of the alternatives. The authorities "argued (*dialogizonto*) with one another" (v. 31), an activity once again reminiscent of the scribes at the healing of the paralytic (cf. *dialogizomenoi* in 2:6 and 2:8, but also 8:16, 17; 9:33). If they acknowledge that John's authority was from God, Jesus will ask why they did not believe him—and by extension why they did not believe Jesus. If they say he acted on merely human authority, they might provoke a hostile reaction from the crowd. At this point the narrator adds an explanatory aside to the reader in the form of another "for" (*gar*) statement: "for all regarded John as truly a prophet" (see esp. 16:8 and the commentary there). By reporting their deliberations, Mark also allows the reader to see that their response to Jesus is disingenuous. It does not reflect their discussion. Instead, they claim not to know. The implication, however, is that this is an expedient answer that does not fully reflect what they cannot deny. Those who normally speak authoritatively on temple matters, instruct the priests, and sit on the Sanhedrin have been reduced to saying, "We do not know." Jesus' parting shot again implies an authority above that of the chief priests, scribes, and Pharisees: "Neither will I tell you . . ." (11:33), while at the same time unveiling the truth that they had sought to mask. [Knowing and Confessing] It is not that they did not know; it is rather that they would not say. The authority of the master who entered the city on a donkey is in the process of being fully established.

Knowing and Confessing

"It is as if Jesus had said: 'I will not tell you what I know, since you will not confess what you know.'" (Bede, *Homilies on the Gospels*, 2.22)

Thomas C. Oden and Christopher A. Hall, eds., *Ancient Christian Commentary on Scripture: New Testament II, Mark* (Downers Grove IL: InterVarsity Press, 1998), 164.

CONNECTIONS

Mark 11:1-11

This Sunday is special. There is an elevated buzz, more bustle and activity. Attendance is up—there are more children, and the choir is larger. Parents and Sunday school teachers hand out great, leafy branches to the children and rehearse with them how they will come down the aisles waving the branches while the choir sings.

Palm Sunday observances are just about right as long as we do not make them too formal or elaborate. The excitement recalls the celebration of a pilgrim's entrance into Jerusalem, and our improvised preparations are a fitting reminder of the disciples' mission to retrieve a donkey for Jesus. The challenge for us is how to create the spirit of anticipation, joy, and celebration, while maintaining the irony of Jesus' unpretentious entry into Jerusalem. We celebrate the coming of our king, but he comes riding on a donkey. Those who have cared for farm animals will not miss the irony. Jesus enters the city as its true Lord, but not as a conqueror. Another crowd will drive Jesus out of the city with a different chant: "Crucify, crucify him!" This king came not to be served, "but to serve, and to give his life a ransom for many" (10:45).

Perhaps it is right, then, that Palm Sunday is a confusing day, and that we don't quite know whether to be joyful in celebrating Jesus' coming to deliver us or reflective and repentant, knowing that within days we will be observing Maundy Thursday and Good Friday. There is great irony in the gospel of the donkey-riding king, the life-surrendering Son of Man, and the dying and rising Son of God. The triumph of love over hate and life over death allows for there to be humor in the incongruity of the Palm Sunday events. Let it delight and excite: "Hosanna! Blessed is the one who comes in the name of the Lord!" (11:9)—even the Galilean riding on a donkey, hailed by fishermen, women, and children waving palm branches in improvised celebration.

Mark 11:12-25

The ecology of worship is a central concern of every minister. The proper setting, music, liturgy, word, and spirit are all vital if the drama of worship is to lead to a true encounter with the divine. But even when the details have been attended to, worship may not occur and the drama may be merely playacting. For every worship leader, then, the threat that worship may be rejected is profoundly disconcerting. Imagine the Lord appearing in his temple and rejecting the worship of his people! It is tempting to read this text as a limited judgment directed only at Jewish worship, but if the "temple not made with hands" is not free from the offenses that led to the condemnation of the Jerusalem temple, will it fare any better? While this question may not have been consciously intended by Mark, the Gospel continuously communicates "thou shalt not be like those whom Jesus rejects."

From the beginning, Jesus' ministry threatened the wineskins of Jewish worship. The conflict is launched by a scene in the synagogue at Capernaum (1:21-28) that is structurally similar to the temple cleansing. He casts out those who defile the temple and he exorcizes the unclean spirit from the man in the synagogue. In both scenes he teaches, and the crowd marvels at his teaching (cf. *exeplēssonto* [*-seto*] *epi tē didachē autou* in both 1:22 and 11:18). In the synagogue Jesus' teaching is contrasted with that of the scribes, and in the temple the scribes react hostilely (cf. 11:18 and 3:6). In both synagogue and temple, the new wine of Jesus' teaching and presence cleanses corrupt worship and threatens its structures.

The conflict continues with Jesus forgiving sins (2:1-12), eating with outcasts (2:15-17), plucking grain and healing on the Sabbath (2:23–3:5), and rejecting the tradition of the elders (7:1-23). Dramatically the tension builds as Jesus makes his way to Jerusalem and repeatedly tries to tell his disciples what will happen there. The scene at the temple, therefore, is the climax of Jesus' conflict with the structures of worship in his day.

The Son of God has appeared at his Father's house (Mal 3:1-2). The opponent of ritual and tradition has entered the sanctuary of the ritual observers and ceremony makers. Mysteriously Jesus looks around and leaves without a recorded word, but it is clear to Mark that the evening of the temple has come (11:11). On the morrow it will be condemned and within a generation it will be destroyed.

The temple cult, like the fig tree, appeared to be healthy. Yet, the message of Palm Sunday is not that the people rejected their king, but that the king rejected the worship of his people. Why was their worship rejected? It might not be wrong to observe that we have become more sensitive to the ecology of the world than the ecology of worship. In many churches it is easier to arouse interest and indignation over the ways we poison our world than the ways we poison our worship. We know what we have done to our physical space. What have we done to the spiritual space in which we live? What poisons led Jesus to reject the temple? The text does not say why Jesus condemned the temple, but the offenses that led to the condemnation may be inferred from what Jesus said and did in the temple.

First, there was the poison of using worship as a means to something else. The merchants of piety were buying and selling inside the temple. They found worship to be a reliable means to prosperity. Pilgrims came from faraway places with their foreign currency, currency with human images that had to be exchanged before the pilgrims could buy a sacrificial animal. Then too, because it was so difficult to bring an animal in sacrificial condition, most pilgrims bought their animals in Jerusalem. The laws regulating worship, therefore, ensured the merchants a lucrative trade. Moreover, since the most direct paths through Jerusalem from east to west went through the temple, people took the shortcut through it and carried their vessels through the temple on their way to other places. The sacred area was treated like any other place when its space was used as a means to something else. When he cleansed the temple, therefore, Jesus purged it of the poison of worship for profit, for convenience, or for any other end besides the praise of God.

We have long since ceased to buy and sell in the church, but we are still using it as a means to inappropriate ends. A new breed of chief priests hypes the gospel on national television every Sunday to build their own reputations and evangelistic associations. Pop music groups are also cashing in on the gospel. But most people use worship for their own ends in other ways: by going to church to enhance their social status in the community or so their children will receive religious training. These pursuits may not be bad in themselves, but when one attends church for any reason other than the desire to worship, he or she uses it as a means to something else rather than as the essential activity for maintaining one's spiritual life. Like the people who carried vessels through the temple, many have profaned the sacred space of life by trampling through it on the way to other places. Treating worship as a

Court of the Gentiles

The Court of the Gentiles and the Fortress of Antonia in the Model of Jerusalem.

(Credit: R. Alan Culpepper)

means poisons it and leaves it as barren as polluted waters or a fruitless fig tree.

The second poison that led to the condemnation of the temple was the poison of observing social distinctions in God's presence. The temple itself was designed to enforce social exclusivism. Most of its forty-two-acre area was designated as the Court of the Gentiles. This outer area was the only part of the temple in which Gentiles were permitted. Yet, the Jews had taken the only area in which the Gentiles could worship and turned it into a place of commerce (see [The Temple]).

In contrast to the distance enforced upon Gentiles by the temple architecture, Jesus sought them out and brought them near (cf. Eph 2:13-18). He crossed the Sea of Galilee, restored the Gadarene demoniac to his right mind, and launched the Gentile mission by sending him to preach throughout the Decapolis (5:1-20). In contrast to Matthew (10:5-6), Mark (6:6b-13) does not limit the mission of the Twelve to Israel only. In the next chapter Mark tells of Jesus' ministry in Tyre and Sidon; he found faith in Tyre and opened the ears of a Gentile in Sidon (7:24-37). The feeding of the 4,000 follows immediately. Well before the explicit command in Mark 13:10, therefore, it is clear that the kingdom, the family of faith, the temple not made with hands, will embrace Gentiles as well as Israelites.

Mark says Jesus saw the fig tree (representing Israel) "from afar" (*apo makrothen*). The evangelist has used this phrase just twice to this point. The Gadarene demoniac, who by all implications was a Gentile living in an unclean area, saw Jesus "from afar" (5:6). Likewise, Mark's account of the feeding of the 4,000, which seems to take place on the eastern shore of the Sea of Galilee as a feeding of Gentiles following the feeding of the 5,000 in Jewish environs, states that some of those present came "from afar" (8:3). Mark's use of this phrase in 11:13 allows an extended meaning—that Jesus viewed the fig tree (representing Israel) from the perspective of a Gentile and found it fruitless.

The Beautiful Gate led from the court of the Gentiles to the court of the women. Jewish women were allowed into this area but could not ascend the thirteen steps leading to the Nicanor Gate. Jesus' acceptance of women is also clear in Mark. He healed Peter's mother-in-law (1:30-31), addressed the woman with the flow of blood as "daughter" (5:34), and raised the daughter of Jairus (5:35-43). Jesus rewarded the Syrophoenician woman's persistence and wit (7:24-30) and made a noble example of the poor widow (12:41-44). Mark 13:17 may also be a note of special concern for women: "And alas for those who are with child and those giving suck in those days!" In return, Jesus was anointed by a woman (14:3-9) and followed to his grave by women (15:40-41, 47; 16:1-8). There would be room for "mothers" and "sisters" as well as "brothers" in the kingdom (3:35).

Diagram of the Inner Courts of the Temple

Key:
1. Holy of Holies
2. Holy Place
3. Porch
4. Altar of Burnt Offering
5. Court of Priests
6. Court of Israel
7. Sanctuary Gates
8. Beautiful Gate (or Nicanor Gate?)
9. Nicanor Gate

Source: W. F. Stinespring, "Temple, Jerusalem," *Interpreter's Dictionary of the Bible* (Nashville: Abingdon Press, 1962), 4:556.

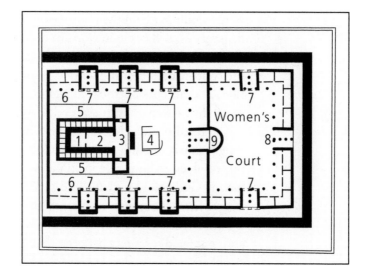

The Nicanor Gate led to the court of Israel. Jewish men of non-priestly ancestry could go this far, but no farther. Only the priests were allowed into the court of the priests, and only the high priest could enter the holy of holies, and he did so only on the Day of Atonement. Jesus cut the ground from beneath the superiority of clergy over laity.

Conflict with the religious authorities builds throughout the Gospel. For pronouncing forgiveness the scribes charged Jesus with blasphemy (2:6). He claimed authority over the sabbath, and scribes who came from Jerusalem charged that he had Beelzebub (3:22). Again, scribes from Jerusalem challenged Jesus because his disciples did not observe the traditions of the elders (7:1ff). The scribes continued to engage the disciples in controversy (9:11, 14), so it is hardly surprising that Jesus announced that he would lose his life at the hands of the chief priests and scribes (8:31; 10:33; cf. 14:1, 43, 53; 15:1, 31). Clearly, the scene in the temple is also the climax of the conflict between Jesus and the religious authorities.

The entire structure of the temple was therefore calculated to enforce social distinctions of race, sex, and family status. Jesus viewed the observance of such distinctions in the presence of God as obscene. The Jews took pride in their heritage as Israel and trusted in their birth within the elect for their hope for the future, but Jesus refused to recognize privilege based on birth (cf. John 3:3).

Today the poisons of social distinctions are named but not neutralized. People of other races are still frequently kept at a distance, though often in subtle rather than official ways. Women are admitted, but in some churches it is still only the men who have access to the court of Israel, the deacon council. And we have only begun to be aware of the effects that tearing down the dividing wall of hostility between lay and clergy would have on the ministry of the laity and the priesthood of the believer. We still come to worship to watch the priests whom we pay to do our ministry for us while we sit and watch. Part of the message of the condemnation of the temple, as of all the rest of Jesus' ministry, is that God accepts persons as persons apart from any of our labels or social distinctions. Yet, social exclusivism still poisons worship.

The third poison that permeated the temple was hypocrisy. People sought to use worship to appease God. They recognized their sinfulness but resolved to continue in it. They worshiped merely to attempt to placate God and so perhaps find sanctuary for their sinfulness in God's house. Jesus consequently charged that they had made God's house "a den of robbers." A den or cave was the place to which bandits and brigands retreated for safety between their assaults, so by calling the temple a robber's den Jesus condemned the people's failure to repent.

For this failure God had destroyed the ancient places of worship. God destroyed Shiloh, God condemned the temple, and God destroyed Jerusalem. Shall we dare say, while we poison our worship with the age-old poisons, that God will not destroy our temples also? God demands worship with a broken and contrite heart and a firm resolve to rid ourselves of the poisons that have polluted our lives, our world, and our worship. The choices are clear: purge the temple or be destroyed. The chief priests and scribes chose the second option (11:18; 14:1). What will we do about the ecology of worship?[33]

Mark 11:27-33

Questioning authority has moved from the adolescent trademark of the 1960s baby-boomer generation to the cultural badge of post-modernism. Religious authority, institutional authority, and tradition of all sorts are subject to the question, "By what authority do you do these things?" No longer is it sufficient to have authority or to act and speak with authority. Popular culture demands to know the basis of one's authority—where does it come from? At the same time, while many glibly question all authority, others quietly crave authoritative direction—hence the popularity of authoritative pastoral leadership, dogmatic certainty, and directive, didactic preaching. Behind the cynical questioning of all authority, therefore, one suspects there often lies a secret hope to find genuine authority somewhere.

The temple authorities' evasive response to Jesus is also one that most people can spot instantly, and one that all of us have resorted to at times. We know or suspect more than we are willing to say, so we profess ignorance. The other side of demanding transparency in our authorities (parents, teachers, pastors, politicians, and business and civic leaders) is that we be willing to be equally transparent, honest, and forthcoming. The opposite of acting on presumed authority one does not have is disregarding authority one knows to be genuine. Cynically dismissing all authority as baseless is no better than presumptuously acting on authority one does not have. The implication of Jesus' response to the temple authorities is that if one is going to question authority, one should be ready to acknowledge authority that is well founded.

On the other hand, if we are open to honest searching and willing to accept the answers we find, questioning authority while searching for a solid foundation for our lives is a wholesome exercise. Typically we all begin by accepting parental authority as the highest authority in our lives. As children, we learn to respect authority figures: teachers, ministers, and other adult authorities. From our parents and Christian teachers we may learn to respect the Bible as authoritative. In adolescence, our peer group often replaces adult authorities and we begin to question authority. What makes Christianity true? Why should we believe the Bible is more authoritative than the Koran or the Book of the Mormon? Various religions claim authority for their scriptures. The Christian Scriptures are authoritative for Christians, however, because they point to Jesus Christ, and we can experience the living presence of the Christ through the Spirit. Even Jesus is not the ultimate basis of religious authority, however—God is.[34] But it is through Jesus that we come to know God most fully. The two questions in this controversy dialogue are therefore two facets of the same quest, the human quest for ultimate authority that ends with God: "By what authority do you do these things? . . . Did the baptism of John come from heaven, or was it of human origin?" And Jesus' demand, "answer me!" is addressed to each of us.

NOTES

[1] Craig A. Evans, *Mark 8:27–16:20* (WBC 34B; Nashville: Thomas Nelson, 2001), 139.

[2] Paul Brooks Duff, "The March of the Divine Warrior and the Advent of the Greco-Roman King: Mark's Account of Jesus' entry into Jerusalem," *JBL* 111 (1992): 66. David R. Catchpole, "The Triumphal Entry," in *Jesus and the Politics of His Day* (ed. Ernst Bammel and C. F. D. Moule; Cambridge: Cambridge University Press, 1984), 319-21, observed a similar pattern. This material is cited in R. Alan Culpepper, "The Gospel of Luke," *NIB* (Nashville: Abingdon, 1995), 9:366.

[3] Werner Kelber, *Mark's Story of Jesus* (Philadelphia: Fortress, 1979), 57-59; and Duff, "The March of the Divine Warrior and the Advent of the Greco-Roman King," 70-71, agree that Mark's account of Jesus' entry is ironic.

[4] William L. Lane, *The Gospel according to Mark* (NICNT; Grand Rapids: Wm. B. Eerdmans, 1974), 394.

[5] See, however, Bas M. F. van Iersel, *Mark: A Reader-Response Commentary* (trans. W. H. Bisscheroux; JSNTSup 164; Sheffield: Sheffield Academic Press, 1998), 353.

[6] Vincent Taylor, *The Gospel according to St. Mark* (London: Macmillan, 1952), 455.

[7] *Plutarch: The Lives of the Noble Grecians and Romans* (The Dryden Translation; Great Books of the Western World; Chicago: Encyclopedia Britannica, 1952), 624.

[8] Evans, *Mark 8:27–16:20*, 144.

[9] BDAG, 945.

[10] Thomas C. Oden and Christopher A. Hall, eds., *Ancient Christian Commentary on Scripture: New Testament II, Mark* (Downers Grove IL: InterVarsity Press, 1998), 156.

[11] Evans, *Mark 8:27–16:20*, 145.

[12] See van Iersel, *Mark*, 354.

[13] C. E. B. Cranfield, *The Gospel according to Saint Mark* (Cambridge: Cambridge University Press, 1959), 354.

[14] Claus-Hunno Hunzinger, "*sukē*," *TDNT* 7:752.

[15] Evans, *Mark 8:27–16:20*, 156-57.

[16] Ibid., 157.

[17] John Painter, *Mark's Gospel: Worlds in Conflict* (London: Routledge, 1997), 157.

[18] Lane, *The Gospel according to Mark*, 400.

[19] See Joachim Jeremias, *Jerusalem in the Time of Jesus* (trans. F. H. and C. H. Cave; Philadelphia: Fortress, 1969), esp. 21-27, 77-84; and K. C. Hanson and Douglas E. Oakman, *Palestine in the Time of Jesus* (Minneapolis: Fortress, 1998), 131-57.

[20] Victor Eppstein, "The Historicity of the Gospel Account of the Cleansing of the Temple," *ZNW* 55 (1964): 48. Bruce Chilton, "Caiaphas," *ABD* 1:805-06, agrees that Caiaphas probably did permit the installation of vendors in the temple.

[21] Ibid., 57.

[22] BDAG, 594, gives the two meanings of *lēstēs*: (1) robber, highwayman, bandit, and (2) revolutionary, insurrectionist, guerrilla.

[23] See the detailed comparison on this account in Josephus and Mark 11:15-19 in Evans, *Mark 8:27–16:20*, 176-77.

[24] BDAG, 308.

[25] Edwin K. Broadhead, *Mark* (Sheffield: Sheffield Academic Press, 2001), 94.

[26] Sharyn Dowd, *Reading Mark* (Macon: Smyth & Helwys, 2000), 123.

[27] Favoring the Mount of Olives: Lane, *The Gospel according to Mark*, 410; van Iersel, *Mark*, 359-60. Favoring the temple mount: Edwin K. Broadhead, "Which Mountain Is 'This Mountain'? A Critical Note on Mark 11:22-25," *Paradigms* 2 (1986): 33-38; Ben Witherington III, *The Gospel of Mark* (Grand Rapids: Wm. E. Eerdmans, 2001), 318. See further, Evans, *Mark 8:27–16:20*, 188-89.

[28] For this insight I am indebted to Sharyn Dowd, *Reading Mark*, 120-22.

[29] Cited by Dowd, *Reading Mark*, 122.

[30] Lane, *The Gospel according to Mark*, 410.

[31] Jeremias, *Jerusalem in the Time of Jesus*, 175.

[32] Evans, *Mark 8:27–16:20*, 200.

[33] This material was originally published as "Mark 11:15-19," *Interpretation* 34 (April 1980): 176-81.

[34] See further Hugo H. Culpepper, "The Bible and Religious Authority," in R. Alan Culpepper, *Eternity as a Sunrise: The Life of Hugo H. Culpepper* (Macon: Mercer University Press, 2002), 329-34.

DEBATING WITH THE
AUTHORITIES IN THE TEMPLE

Mark 12:1-44

Jesus' debates with the authorities continue in Mark 12, and all of the action in this chapter takes place in the temple (11:27; 12:35, 41). The temple will also be the focus of the following chapter, in which Jesus leaves the temple (13:1), sits on the Mount of Olives opposite the temple (13:3), and predicts its destruction (13:2).

The parable of the wicked tenants (12:1-12) is one of the programmatic parables in Mark because it provides a lens through which the reader can interpret Jesus' confrontation with the authorities and his subsequent death. Jesus' response to the question put to him by the Pharisees and the Herodians regarding the payment of taxes (12:13-17) subtly declares that one owes ultimate allegiance only to God, while cleverly avoiding giving a treasonous answer. Next, the Sadducees pose an elaborate question designed to discredit the Pharisaic belief in resurrection (12:18-27), but Jesus again wins the contest of wits by an appeal to Scripture. Jesus' use of the Scriptures prepares the way for one of the scribes to raise a classic question regarding which of the commandments should be regarded as the most important (12:28-34). When no one dares to ask him another question, Jesus raises a question about one of the pronouncements of the scribes, and in standard debating style offers a response that discredits the cogency of their pronouncement (12:35-37). Jesus is on a roll, and the references to the scribes (12:28, 32, 35, 38) serve as a catchword linking the preceding stories with Jesus' denunciation of the scribes for their false piety and their extortion of widows. On cue, a widow comes forward and with striking absence of self-regard places all she has in the temple treasury (12:41-44). The chapter ends with the temple authorities discredited and silenced before Jesus' greater wit and authority.

COMMENTARY

The Parable of the Wicked Tenants, 12:1-12

Because the parable of the wicked tenants opens important glimpses into Jesus' self-understanding, the history of the synoptic tradition, and Mark's use of the parables, it warrants an extended treatment.[1] The parable also offers an intriguing opportunity for reflecting on interpretive processes and some of the functions of a Gospel text. A host of questions have troubled interpreters: Does the parable come from Jesus or the early church? If it comes from Jesus, what does it tell us about Jesus' self-understanding? What is its tradition history, which Gospel reproduces the parable in its earliest form, and is the parable inherently allegorical, or has an originally nonallegorical story been allegorized by the church? In a different vein, how does the parable function in the Gospels, and what is its theological significance? Like most Gospel texts, this one needs to be read in various ways: (1) historically, within the context of its first-century socioeconomic setting; (2) canonically, within the context of the whole biblical story; (3) as narrative, within the context of the gospel story; and (4) theologically, within the context of God's self-disclosure.

Although the story is a familiar one, it has been called the "most difficult of the parables."[2] Part of its difficulty is posed by the puzzling variations among the extant versions of the parable. According to Mark, a vineyard owner leaves his vineyard in the hands of tenants while he is away. When he sends a servant to receive the owner's portion of the harvest, the tenants beat him and send him away empty handed. The owner sends a second servant, whom they beat about the head and insult. The third servant they kill, "and so it was with many others" (12:5). Finally, he sends his own son. Thinking they will inherit the vineyard if they kill the heir, the wicked tenants kill the owner's son. Jesus then poses the question, what will the owner do? He will come and destroy those tenants and give the vineyard to others. The quotation from Psalm 118 that follows, which looks beyond the death of the son, may not have been part of the original parable.

The *Gospel of Thomas* contains a simpler, and hence possibly more primitive, form of this parable that lacks many of the allegorical features found in the Synoptics. [*Gospel of Thomas* 65] In Thomas, there is no reference to Isaiah 5,

Gospel of Thomas 65

He said, "There was a good man who owned a vineyard. He leased it to tenant farmers so that they might work it and he might collect the produce from them. He sent his servant so that the tenants might give him the produce of the vineyard. They seized his servant and beat him, all but killing him. The servant went back and told his master. The master said, 'Perhaps [they] did not recognize [him].' He sent another servant. The tenants beat this one as well. Then the owner sent his son and said, 'Perhaps they will show respect to my son.' Because the tenants knew that it was he who was the heir to the vineyard, they seized him and killed him. Let him who has ears hear."

Robert W. Funk, ed., *New Gospel Parallels* (Philadelphia: Fortress, 1985), 2:154.

only two servants are sent before the son, neither of the servants is killed, there is no interior monologue or question, "what shall I do?" (as in Luke), the son is not called "beloved," the owner says "perhaps" they will respect his son, and the parable ends immediately following the report of the killing of the son.

Reconstructing the Parable's Own Story

The tradition history of the parable has been reconstructed in different ways. It is generally agreed that the Markan text reflects an allegorical understanding of the story and that the description of the vineyard in Mark 12:1 is drawn from the "Song of the Vineyard" in Isaiah 5. Matthew depends on Mark and extends the allegory by (1) reporting the sending of many servants, some of whom they stoned; (2) changing the sequence of actions so that the tenants throw the son out of the vineyard before they kill him; (3) underscoring the significance of the owner's "coming"; and (4) extending the owner's judgment on the tenants by adding that they would die a miserable death and reporting that the other tenants to whom he would give the vineyard "will give him the produce at the harvest time."

Luke has always been difficult for interpreters because it generally follows Mark but is somewhat less allegorical: (1) it omits the Isaianic description of the vineyard; (2) only three servants are sent, none of them is killed, and Luke has no reference to stoning or beating on the head; and (3) Luke softens the owner's decision to send his son by saying "*perhaps* they will respect him." On the other hand, Luke adds (1) that the owner went to another country "for a long time"; (2) the owner's interior monologue with its question, "What shall I do?" that echoes Isaiah 5:4, 5; and (3) that the tenants threw the son out of the vineyard before they killed him (as in Matthew, but contrary to Mark). The similarities between Luke and Thomas (and their differences from Matthew and Mark) form a crux for interpreters: (1) Luke and Thomas lack the description of the preparation of the vineyard that echoes Isaiah 5. (2) The owner sent a servant so that the tenants "might give him" (Greek *dōsousin autō*) the produce of the vineyard. (3) No servants are killed before the sending of the son. (4) The owner says, "*Perhaps* they will respect him."

Although it is difficult to proceed with confidence on the basis of this evidence, the alternatives are (1) that both the differences between Mark and Luke and the similarities between Luke and Thomas are due to Luke's own redaction of the parable,[3] (2) that Luke knows an independent form of the parable (similar to Thomas),[4] or (3) that Thomas is dependent on Luke.[5] The allusion to Isaiah 5, while present in Luke and Thomas, is heightened in Mark and Matthew. The first and third elements above are simplifications of the story. The third heightens the effect of the killing of the son. The second element may be a minor stylistic variation, but the verb *dōsousin* ("they might give") is found in contracts from the period (see below). Likewise, the addition of "perhaps" appears to be more than stylistic. On balance, it appears likely that Luke used both Mark and an independent source that had similarities with Thomas.

Tied to the problem of the parable's tradition history are the related questions of whether it is inherently allegorical or depends on a nonallegorical parable, and whether it is authentic to Jesus or the creation of the early church. [Authenticity and Allegorical Character] Adolf Jülicher and Rudolf Bultmann set the prevailing judgment for German scholarship by contending that the parable was thoroughly allegorical and therefore the work of the early church.[6] Prior to the discovery of Thomas, both C. H. Dodd and Joachim Jeremias posited an original parable that was nonallegorical and therefore authentic—a theory that seemed to be confirmed by the discovery of the *Gospel of Thomas*.[7] John Dominic Crossan argued that the story in the synoptic account strains to construct an allegory from a nonallegorical story, and concludes that the account in Thomas "quite accurately" represents "the original version of the parable" that was nonallegorical and devoid of Old Testament allusions.[8] Others have argued that the version of the parable in Thomas is actually later and that Thomas deallegorized the parable.[9] Brandon Scott questions whether the parable in the Thomas tradition is superior to the synoptic version, but reconstructs an "originating structure" similar to the version in Thomas.[10] The Jesus Seminar followed this line of argument, judging that Thomas preserves an early version of the parable "without allegorical traits."[11] It therefore printed the parable in Thomas in pink, saying, "it appears that a simple, nonallegorical version can be ascribed to Jesus,"[12] but in the Synoptics the parable is gray (not from Jesus). Here the issue of interpretation again plays an interesting role in that if the Jesus Seminar had not been convinced that the version of the parable in Thomas is nonallegorical, they would no doubt have printed Thomas 65 in gray or black also. To my

Authenticity and Allegorical Character

Scholarship on the Authenticity and Allegorical Character of the Parable		
	Authentic	**Inauthentic**
Non-allegorical	Dodd and Jeremias Hengel Crossan, Scott, and the Jesus Seminar (Thomas: pink; Synoptics: gray)	
Allegorical	Lohmeyer Black Derrett Via Snodgrass Charlesworth	Jülicher Bultmann Kümmel

knowledge, no one has suggested that the original version of the parable was nonallegorical but the creation of the early church. From the beginning, the theory of a nonallegorical original has served as a means of defending the authenticity of the parable.

Scholars have debated whether the parable was originally nonallegorical and authentic to Jesus, or allegorical and a creation of the early church. Recently, however, some critical scholars have been charting a middle course, which is actually a return to the position of traditional Catholic and conservative Protestant scholarship: that the parable is authentic but that it was allegorical from the beginning.[13] Dan Via, for example, concludes that:

> . . . just the allusive reference to the vineyard and the beating of the servants must have referred subsidiarily to Israel and her rejection of God's messengers. And the "son" possibly refers to the climactic coming of Jesus but without specific christological implications. Thus this parable is more nearly allegorical than (most of) Jesus' other narrative parables.[14]

Before turning to the issue of whether the parable was originally allegorical or not, it will be helpful to set the story in its historical context.

Reading the Parable's Socioeconomic Setting

The system of absentee landlords can be traced back nearly 300 years, to the time of the Ptolemies. J. Duncan M. Derrett collected and surveyed numerous contracts from the period, but found no vinedresser's tenancy agreement from Israel.[15] The system of tenancy is well documented, however, in letters and contracts from the period. [Pliny, *Letters*, X.8] A contract for the lease of land in Egypt, which can be dated to 11 April 184 BC, in which Petebenetitis, a desert-guard, leases land to two tenants, specifies the payment of grain and the consequences for failure to pay. ["Lease of Land"]

Pliny, *Letters*, X.8

"It is absolutely necessary I should not defer any longer the letting of my lands in that province, for besides that they amount to above four hundred thousand sesterces annually, the time for dressing the vineyards is approaching, and *that* care must fall upon my new tenants. Moreover, the badness of the vintage for several years past obliges me to think of making some abatements in my rents; which I cannot possibly settle unless I am present."

Pliny, *Letters*, X.8 (trans. William Melmoth, rev. W. M. L. Hutchinson, LCL; Cambridge: Harvard University Press, 1915), 2:289.

"Lease of Land"

April 11, 184 BC

The tenants, Agathokles and Herakles, will pay (*dōsousin*, line 8) rents "yearly at the end of the year or whenever the release of the crop is granted, as grain, new, clean, and unadulterated, by just measure and with just measurement, bringing it at their own expense to Kerkesoucha wherever Petebenetitis shall decide, and if they do not pay the grain as it is written above, let Agathokles and Herakles pay to Petebenetitis for each artab for which they do not pay -x- drachmas of bronze money or whatever is the greatest fine in. . . . Petebenetitis shall control the crop until he gets the rent."

John F. Oates, Alan E. Samuel, C. Bradford Welles, eds., *Yale Papyri in the Beineck Rare Book and Manuscript Library*, I, American Studies in Papyrology, vol. 2 (New Haven: American Society of Papyrologists, 1967), 148.

By the first century, relatively little land remained free for individual peasant ownership. Some of the land was controlled by Gentile cities, and large estates were controlled by Jewish elites or Roman agents.[16] Herod the Great raised taxes for his building projects, confiscated land from his enemies, and turned it into royal estates.[17] As debt increased, creditors seized lands, and more and more of the land was taken from the farmers. Martin Goodman describes the situation in terms that bear directly on the situation portrayed by the parable: "The spark which set off each family's crisis came probably either from the effect of a bad year and the prospect of immediate starvation or from the death of the farm's owner and the prospect of dividing up the plot between his heirs, usually his sons."[18] The new landowners in turn reduced the number of tenants to the smallest number to increase their own profits. From the produce of the land, peasants paid religious and civic taxes that ranged anywhere from 35 to 50 percent. For those who raised grain, as much as one-third of the seed would have been needed for the next planting, and an additional one-fourth of it would have been used in feed for livestock. Only about 20 percent of the yield would have been left, and tenant farmers would have paid the absentee landlord from this narrow margin.[19] The result was a grim struggle for subsistence, hard agrarian labor, heavy taxation, and recurring conflict between peasants and land-lords.

Yet, there was little commonly accepted warrant for such a system. Again, Goodman provides illuminating insights:

> No ties of loyalty, no feudal oath, no sanction of long custom existed to coax the tenant into believing that his payment of rent to his supervisor was part of the natural order of things; on the contrary the peasant will have known that the divinely ordained ideal in the Torah required each man to own his own land as a free and equal citizen (cf. Micah 4:4, etc.).[20]

The Shape of the Story: Parable or Allegory?

Although the story fits well in the first-century context, as Dodd and Jeremias argued, that fit in itself does not answer the question whether the story was originally a parable or an allegory, and neither its congru-ence with first-century socioeconomic conditions nor the resolution of the issue of whether it was originally a parable or an allegory is neces-sarily determinative of whether the story originated with Jesus or the early church. The questions of whether the story was originally parable or allegory and whether it is authentic to Jesus or not need to be treated separately.

The former question (parable or allegory?) can only be settled by considering the effects of its plot and echoes of other texts, not by appeal to its congruity with what is known of tenancy in the first century, since an allegory can reflect that system as well as a parable. Both its structure or plot and its intertextual echoes require that the story be understood as an allegory of God's forbearance and judgment in response to Israel's rebelliousness.

The weakness of the argument that the parable was originally nonallegorical is evident in the attempts to read the story in this way. Responding to Dodd, Matthew Black charged that while Dodd claimed the story was nonallegorical, he read it as allegory. His witty language has often been quoted:

> While thus showing allegory firmly to the door, one cannot but wonder if Dr. Dodd has not surreptitiously smuggled it in again by the window. . . . Dodd manages to get the benefit of allegory while denying that it is allegory—to run with the allegorical hare, as it were, and still hunt with the Jülicher hounds. This will not do. The straightforward answer is that the parable was first and last allegory and that its main characters are to be understood allegorically.[21]

Jeremias commits the same fallacy as Dodd, reasoning that because the story draws upon "a definite situation" it is parable rather than allegory.[22] According to Jeremias, the parable "vindicates the offer of the gospel to the poor," but then he turns again to an allegorical reading of the story in which the vineyard is Israel and the tenants represent the leaders of Israel.[23]

Crossan and Scott are more rigorous in their nonallegorical readings of the parable, but the result is so reductive as to render the parable pointless. When Crossan asks why Jeremias slips both Isaiah and the punishment back into his interpretation, the answer he offers is that "otherwise Jesus is telling a most disedifying and immoral story," a "deliberately shocking story."[24] Scott's reading is more nuanced, but just as reductive. The reconstructed parable "frustrates not only allegory but also any effort to make sense of it."[25] The result for the audience is defamiliarization that blocks any closure or resolution: "In the plot the kingdom fails and the inheritance is in doubt."[26] Such a reductive and post-modern reading of the parable, however, serves only to confirm that the parable does not work apart from its allegorical sense.

Intertextual echoes reinforce the story's allegorical sense. Among these are (1) the vineyard, (2) the inheritance, (3) the exhortation "let us kill him," and (4) the judgment of coming and destroying the tenants.

(1) The reference to the planting of the vineyard evokes Old Testament allusions to Israel as a vine or vineyard [Israel as a Vine or Vineyard] The echoes of Isaiah 5 are significantly more pronounced in

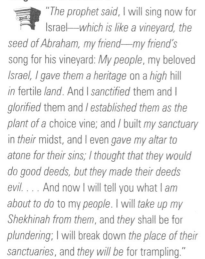

Israel as a Vine or Vineyard

Isa 5:1-2—Let me sing for my beloved my love-song concerning his vineyard: my beloved had a vineyard on a very fertile hill. He dug it and cleared it of stones, and *planted* it with choice vines.

Isa 27:2-3—A pleasant vineyard, sing about it! I, the Lᴏʀᴅ, am its keeper.

Ps 80:8—You brought a vine out of Egypt; you drove out the nations and *planted* it.

Jer 2:21—Yet I *planted* you as a choice vine, from the purest stock. How then did you turn degenerate and become a wild vine?

Ezek 19:10—Your mother was like a vine in a vineyard.

Hos 10:1—Israel is a luxuriant vine that yields its fruit.

Targum of Isaiah 5:1-7

"The prophet said, I will sing now for Israel—*which is like a vineyard, the seed of Abraham, my friend*—my friend's song for his vineyard: *My people*, my beloved *Israel, I gave them a heritage* on a *high* hill in *fertile land*. And I *sanctified* them and I *glorified* them and I *established them as the plant of a* choice vine; and I built *my sanctuary* in *their* midst, and I even *gave my altar to atone for their sins; I thought that they would do good deeds, but they made their deeds evil*. . . . *And now I will tell you what I am about to do* to my *people*. I will *take up my Shekhinah from them*, and *they* shall be for *plundering*; I will break down *the place of their sanctuaries*, and *they will be* for trampling."

B. D. Chilton, *The Isaiah Targum* (ArBib 11; Wilmington DE: Glazier, 1987), 10–11, quoted by Craig A. Evans, *Mark 8:27–16:20* (WBC 34B; Nashville: Thomas Nelson, 2001), 226.

Mark than in Luke. Mark adds three descriptive statements from Isaiah 5:2 (the first of which is present in the LXX but not in the Masoretic Text): the owner "put a fence around it, dug a pit for the wine press, built a watchtower" (12:1). Following a careful analysis of the relationships between the Markan text, the (Hebrew) Masoretic Text, the (Greek) Septuagint, and the (Aramaic) Targum of Isaiah 5:1-7 [Targum of Isaiah 5:1-7], Craig Evans concludes that the allusion to Isaiah 5 "(*a*) is consistent with the parable; indeed the parable grows out of it; (*b*) is more easily explained as originating in a pre-Christian, synagogue related context (in which the Isaiah Targum developed); and (*c*) probably derives from Jesus."[27] His findings, therefore, are consistent with the interpretation of the parable being developed here.

(2) The concept of inheritance and the concern for the rightful heir also play an important role in Israel's history. In Genesis 12, God promises Abraham a son who will become the father of a great people, and land. The land becomes the inheritance of God's people (Num 26:53; Deut 21:23). Moreover, Israel is God's own inheritance (Deut 4:20; Pss 33:12; 78:62). In the New Testament the promise of the land becomes the promise of the kingdom of God, and the promise of a people is applied not to Israel but to the church (Gal 3:15-18; Col 3:24).[28]

(3) The importance of the inheritance leads to repeated conflicts and intrigue between brothers in the Old Testament. Esau was the first-born, but he sold his birthright to Jacob for a pot of stew (Gen 25:29-34). The line of succession thereafter was traced through Jacob (Israel) and his sons, and ultimately Israel's inheritance is God (Jer 10:16).[29]

When the tenants plot to kill the son, they ironically echo the words of Joseph's brothers, "Come now, let us kill him" (Gen. 37:20). Brandon Scott interprets this echo to mean that

> The parable frustrates not only allegory but also any effort to make sense of it! . . . By alluding to the patriarchal story the parable questions whether the kingdom will surely go to the promised heirs. Since the parable provides no ready identification models, no clear metaphorical referencing, an audience is left in a precarious position: *In the plot the kingdom fails and the inheritance is in doubt.*[30]

This interpretation, however, misrepresents both the patriarchal narrative and the parable. The story of Joseph and his brothers does not leave the inheritance in doubt but moves to affirm that the promises to Abraham are secure because God is able to work through whatever Abraham's rebellious descendants may do. Likewise, the parable affirms that the owner is still in control regardless of what the tenants may do. The owner will give the vineyard to others. We may not presume on the line of succession, only on God's sovereign determination to deliver the promised inheritance.

(4) The parable ends with the affirmation that the owner "will come and destroy the tenants and give the vineyard to others" (12:9). This warning recalls various passages in which the prophets announce that the Lord, or the day of the Lord, is coming and that God will bring destruction either on Israel or on her enemies (Joel 1:15; Isa 13:6, 9). The coming of the Lord, moreover, will bring grief to the vineyards: "In all the vineyards there shall be wailing, for I will pass through the midst of you, says the LORD" (Amos 5:17).

Cumulatively, these echoes and intertextual allusions construct a subtext for the parable. They complement the narrative structure of covenant, rebellion, emissaries, violence, and warning of coming judgment that suggests an allegorical interpretation. The vineyard serves as a symbol for Israel, so the parable resonates with Isaiah's song of the vineyard and other prophetic warnings. It hauntingly depicts the self-serving rebellion of Israel (or Israel's leaders) against God's authority and God's repeated overtures toward Israel. The essence of sin is humanity's failure to take its place in covenant with God, alternately overreaching and underachieving that which is peculiarly human. In this story, the tenants who have been given charge of the vineyard reject the owner's authority and plot to take it from the owner. They reject their role as tenants and aspire to be owners. Neither Jesus nor the early church could have told such a story about a vineyard, its owner, the rejection of the owner's servants, and the sending of the owner's son without it being understood allegorically.

If the efforts to identify an original, nonallegorical story are unconvincing, then the alternatives are either that the parable is entirely a construction of the early church, or that it belongs to the authentic Jesus material, even given its allegorical sense. Unless one is

Occurrences of "Son" in Early Judaism

A. 2d or early 1st c. BC
1. Sir 4:10
   Hebrew: "and God will call you son"
   Greek: "You will then be like a son of the Most High"
2. *1 En.* 105:2
   "I and my son are united with them forever in the upright
   paths"
3. Ezekiel the Tragedian
   Moses is called by God "my son"
4. *T. Levi* 4:2 Levi is or will be a son of God

B. Late 1st c. BC
5. Wis 2:18 The righteous one shall be called "God's son."
6. 4QpsDan Aª
   "Son of God" and "Son of the Most High" (=4Q246)
7. 4Q Florilegium
   "I will be his father, he shall be my son" (interpreting
   2 Sam 7:14)

C. 1st c. AD
8. *b. Zera'im Berakot* 17a
   An early tradition in a later document regarding Hanina
   ben Dosa: "The whole world is sustained for the sake of
   My son Hanina, and Hanina My son has to subsist on a
   Kab of carobs from one weekend to the next."

9. Prayer of Joseph
   Jacob is an "angel of God," the supreme commander
   among "the sons of God"
10. Testament of Abraham
    Abel is one like a son of God

D. AD 75–125
11. *4 Ezra* 7:28
    "For my son the Messiah shall be revealed with those
    who are with him"
    4 Ezra 13:37 "Something like a figure of a man" (13:3) is
    "my son"
    4 Ezra 13:52 The son remains unseen until his day.
12. Josephus, *Ant.* 2.232
    Josephus describes Moses as a son in the likeness of
    God
13. Joseph and Asenath 6:3, 5
    Joseph is "the son of God"
14. Apocalypse of Elijah 5:25
    "the judgment of the Son of God"
15. Memar Marqah
    Moses is "the servant of God, the son of the house of
    God"

James H. Charlesworth, *Jesus within Judaism* (New York: Doubleday,
1988), 149–51.

---

predisposed, categorically, to disallow that Jesus used allegory or any
self-reference in his teachings, a decision about the authenticity of the
parable will rest heavily on whether the reference to "a son" reflects
Jesus' own self-understanding or grows out of early Christian
confessions.

The designation "son" for an ideal or redeemer figure was current in
first-century Judaism [Occurrences of "Son" in Early Judaism], so the reference
to the "son" in the parable need not indicate that it originated in
Gentile Christianity. The parable also coheres well with other evidences
of Jesus' self-understanding. Jesus' parables often reflect his understanding of his agency in bringing the kingdom,[31] and his use of
"*abba*" gives evidence of his sense of sonship before God.[32] In the
parable the sending of the son is parallel to the sending of the servants,
the term "beloved" does not occur in Thomas or in Matthew, and there
is no prediction of the resurrection in the parable itself. The parable of
the wicked tenants belongs, therefore, to a small group of sayings in the
Synoptics in which Jesus speaks of "the son" in a self-referential sense
(Mark 13:32; Matt 11:27).

In the Gospel of John, the sayings in 3:35; 5:19; and 8:35-36 bear
some resemblance to these synoptic sayings. John 8:35-36, like the

parable, contrasts the son and the slave. The other Johannine sayings deal with the relationship between the Father and the Son and the special knowledge that relationship conveys to the Son. The parable of the wicked tenants stands alone in the Synoptics, however, as a saying in which Jesus refers to his role as the Son (1) in a parable, (2) as following in the line of the prophets, and (3) predicting that he would die a violent death. If authentic, therefore, the parable provides valuable evidence of Jesus' self-understanding and his awareness that his activities would ultimately lead to his death by violence.

The Jewish version of the story in Sifre to Deuteronomy 32:9 §312 (134b) from the third century raises the possibility that the story was already current in Jewish circles and that Jesus adapted it for different purposes.[33] [Sifre to Deuteronomy 32:9 §312 (134b)] This story works in the same way as the synoptic parable, though, through the assignment of the vineyard to a succession of tenant farmers rather than through the sending of a succession of servants. "The son" plays a determinative role, but Jesus' story ends tragically when the son is killed. The Jewish story validates the giving of the vineyard to Israel rather than to Ishmael or Esau, while the synoptic parable ends with the removal of the vineyard from Israel (or her leaders) and the giving of the vineyard to others.

In sum, the storyline, the intertextual references, the critique of Jewish leadership, and the use of "son" in the parable all correspond with what we know of Jesus, the socioeconomic conditions in Palestine, and terminology current in first-century Judaism. There is good reason, therefore, to accept the parable as authentic and as allegorical from the beginning. As a result, the parable serves as significant evidence that Jesus understood his role in the context of the history of the prophets and God's appeal to Israel and her leaders. Jesus understood himself to be the "son" in relation to God as Father, and yet he saw that in the end his opponents would kill him, just as they had the prophets. The tragic result would be a coming judgment in which the vineyard would be given to others.

Sifre to Deuteronomy 32:9 §312 (134b)

 A. For the Lord's portion is his people [Jacob and his own allotment]

B. The matter may be compared to a king who had a field, which he handed over to tenant-farmers.

C. The tenant-farmers began to steal [the produce of the field that was owing to the king, so] he took it from them and handed it over to the children.

D. They began to conduct themselves worse than the earlier ones.

E. He took it from their children and handed it over to the children of the children.

F. They began to conduct themselves even worse than the earlier ones.

G. He had a son. He said to them, "Get out of what is mine. I don't want you in it. Give me my portion, which I may get it back."

H. So when our father, Abraham, came into the world, chaff came forth from him, Ishamael and all the children of Keturah.

I. When Isaac came into the world, chaff came forth from him, Esau and all the nobles of Edom.

J. They began to conduct themselves worse than the earlier ones.

K. When Jacob came along, no chaff came forth from him. All the sons that were born to him were proper people, as it is said, "And Jacob was a perfect man, dwelling in tents" [Gen 25:27].

L. Whence will the Omnipresent regain his share? It will be from Jacob: "For the Lord's portion is his people, Jacob his own allotment."

M. And further: "For the Lord has chosen Jacob to himself" [Ps 135:4].

Neusner, *Sifre to Deuteronomy*, quoted in Eugene Boring, Klaus Berger, Carsten Colpe, eds., *Hellenistic Commentary to the New Testament* (Nashville: Abingdon Press, 1995), 124.

The Gospel Story

Next we turn from the origin and history of the parable to its role and functions in the Gospel. Mark situates the parable strategically at the beginning of Jesus' ministry in Jerusalem, where it functions as a commentary on Jesus' ministry and an introduction to the events leading to his death. The parable provides an important perspective on the events of the last week of Jesus' life. Mary Ann Tolbert aptly calls it "a parabolic plot synopsis."[34] Jesus, the protagonist and a reliable voice in the Gospel narrative, tells a story whose plot and characters mirror and interpret elements of the larger narrative in which the parable is embedded. Mark sets the parable in the context of the growing opposition of the religious leaders against Jesus. Various elements in the parable either resonate with earlier parts of the Gospel story or foreshadow coming events: (1) the owner's departure to another country and entrusting of property; (2) the beating of the servants; (3) the reference to the "beloved son"; (4) the killing of the son and casting him out of the vineyard; and (5) the destruction of the tenants and the giving of the vineyard to others. Each of these elements takes on added meaning because of the parable's narrative context.

(1) *The owner's departure to another country and entrusting of his property* echoes the story of the householder who went away and left his servants in charge (13:34-37). In each case, the owner "went to another country" (12:1; 13:34). When the *kairos* came, however, the owner sent servants to claim his portion of the produce. Mark is keenly aware of the importance of the *kairos* (see 1:15; 10:30; 11:13; 13:33).

(2) *The beating of the servants.* The verb "to beat" (*derein*) recurs in 13:9, where Jesus warns the disciples that they will be handed over to councils and beaten in synagogues. The verbs "beat over the head" (*kephalioun*) and "insult" (*atimazein*) occur nowhere else in Mark. Before his crucifixion, Jesus is beaten following his "trial" before the chief priests, elders, and scribes, but the verbs used in this scene are different ("strike," *perikalyptein*, and "beat," *hrapismasin elabon*, 14:65).

(3) *The reference to the "beloved son."* In the Gospel of Mark, Jesus is addressed as the "beloved son" at his baptism (1:11) and at his transfiguration (9:7). The meaning is clear. The owner's decision to send his beloved son is also a parabolic response to the question posed to Jesus by the chief priests, scribes, and elders: "By what authority are you doing these things?" (11:28). By telling the story of the killing of the vineyard owner's beloved son, Mark is also foreshadowing Jesus' imminent death.

(4) *Killing the son outside the vineyard.* According to Mark, the wicked tenants kill some of the servants (12:5). When the vineyard owner sends his son, they kill him too, reasoning that by doing so they may inherit the vineyard. Mark says that they "killed him, and threw him

out of the vineyard" (12:8). Luke reverses the sequences, apparently to reflect the fact that Jesus was crucified outside the city (Luke 20:15).

(5) *The destruction of the wicked tenants and the giving of the vineyard to others* symbolically but graphically predict the destruction of Jerusalem and the temple and the passing of the mantle of leadership from Israel's leaders to the leaders of the church. In the next chapter, Jesus warns the disciples that armies will come and destroy Jerusalem (13:14). Then, the Son of Man will come (13:24-29). Against the backdrop of the parable, the reader understands that the destruction of Jerusalem is God's judgment on the wicked tenants who rejected God's messengers and killed God's Son.

Attention has rightly been called to the fact that the parable itself ends in unresolved tragedy. The owner's son is killed, and the narrator declares that he will come and destroy the tenants and give the vineyard to others. The parable functions as a miniature that dramatically depicts that because the leaders of Israel have rejected God's servants and killed God's Son, destruction will come upon Jerusalem and the gospel will be carried to the Gentiles.

In various details and in its overall theme, therefore, the parable of the wicked tenants has close connections with the larger narrative in which it is embedded. Jesus, an authoritative character in the narrative, tells a story to clarify the course of events in the Gospel narrative and to comment on key elements of that story. The parable, in its narrative context, therefore, functions as commentary that tells the reader how to read the Gospel. Israel has rejected the prophets who were God's servants, Jesus is God's beloved Son, and his death will be followed by sure judgment, destruction, and forfeiture of the vineyard to others.

This odyssey of interpretation has ranged across a wide variety of interpretive issues, but it suggests several observations about the text: (1) Efforts to distill from it a nonallegorical story are futile. The story is allegorical to the core. One could not tell a story about a vineyard, its owner, rebellious tenants, and the repeated sending of servants without it being understood allegorically. (2) The parable goes back to Jesus and therefore tells us a great deal about him. The parable draws on significant Old Testament themes and passages, it interprets Jesus' conflict with the religious authorities, it situates Jesus in the succession of Israel's prophets, and it predicts that he will die a violent death. The allusion to sonship is credible in the context of the use of "son" in early Jewish literature, Jesus' references to God as "abba," and the recognition of his role as agent of the kingdom that is reflected in his sayings and parables. Moreover, the reference to sonship in the parable is remarkably restrained. At most it is underscored by the addition of "beloved" in Mark and Luke. There is no reflection on preexistence, vicarious suffering, or hope of resurrection. (3) The Gospels use the parable as narrative commentary. It is an embedded story that comments on the larger story—a device that orients the reader and interprets the larger narrative. (4) The parable is filled with theological significance. It depicts God's patience and persistence in response to Israel's disobedience. The parable also starkly exposes the depravity of human sinfulness and its tragic consequences. (5) The parable is double sided. It calls for readers to recognize their own disobedience and yet allows for identification with the "others" to whom the vineyard will be given. As a parable, however, it still fascinates and withholds, inviting further reflection and interpretation.

The origin of the quotation of Psalm 118:22-23 in vv. 10-11 has been sharply debated. The majority view has been that the quotation is not part of the parable but is a later addition because it expresses a post-Easter perspective on Jesus' vindication. Others have argued that there is a Hebrew wordplay between "son" (*bēn*) and "stone" (*'eben*) that indicates that the link between the quotation and the parable goes back to an early Aramaic stage and therefore probably to Jesus himself.[35]

Psalm 118 is one of the Hallel psalms traditionally chanted by pilgrims entering Jerusalem. The stone that the builders rejected but that has become the cornerstone may be either Israel, scorned by the nations but destined for prominence in God's kingdom, or David, rejected as a youth but then chosen to be king. The Davidic allusion is particularly suggestive for its connections with Jesus' entry into Jerusalem, where Psalm 118:25-26 is quoted by Jesus' followers in 11:9-10, "Blessed is the coming kingdom of our ancestor David." The Davidic theme will also reappear in 12:35, "How can the scribes say that the Messiah is the son of David?"

The argument that the quotation represents a post-Easter perspective is buttressed by the quotation of these verses in other New Testament contexts (Acts 4:11; 1 Pet 2:4, 7; cf. Eph 2:20; *Barnabas* 6.4). On the other hand, the psalm says nothing about resurrection; it only affirms that the one rejected will be vindicated—a conviction Jesus would surely have shared. The term "builders" is used in the Jewish literature of the period in reference to the religious leaders: "But all these things the builders of the wall or those who daub with whitewash, have not understood" (CD 8:12), "and in my hatred for the builders of the wall his anger is kindled" (CD 8:18). Paul too appropriates the image: "like a skilled master builder I laid a foundation, and someone else is building on it. Each builder must choose with care how to build on it" (1 Cor 3:10). Ultimately, however, no stone will be left standing on another where the temple was (13:2), and Jesus will build "a temple not made with hands" (14:58; cf. 15:29; 2 Cor 5:1). To become the "cornerstone" may also have meant to become the "keystone" of an arch, or the "capstone" of a column.

The quotation makes the same point as the parable: Jesus was acting by God's authority and direction, whether the religious authorities recognized it or not: "This is the Lord's doing, and it is amazing in our eyes" (Ps 118:23; Mark 12:11). Of course the authorities had read this familiar passage, and everyone who heard him recognized the point he was making (contrast the secrecy motif in 4:11). The authorities, who had talked of killing Jesus even while he was in Galilee (3:6), want to arrest him immediately, but they still fear the crowd (cf. 11:32), so they leave, biding their time. Jesus' first confrontation with the authorities in the temple ends, therefore, on an ominous note, leaving the reader in suspense, knowing that eventually the authorities will arrest Jesus (see 14:1, 10-11, 43-50).

The Question Concerning Taxes, 12:13-17

Jesus' aphorism, to "render to Caesar the things that are Caesar's, and to God the things that are God's" (12:17 KJV), has become one of the most widely known and quoted of Jesus' teachings. It has also become the basis (along with Rom 13:1-7) for most Christian teachings on the Christian's civic responsibilities. The tradition also appears widely in non-canonical writings from the second century. [Parallels to Mark 12:13-17]

This pericope begins much like the question concerning Jesus' authority (11:27), and the next two pericopae (12:18, 28) follow the same pattern: authorities come to Jesus and pose a question designed to trap him. In this instance Mark says that "they" sent some of the Pharisees and Herodians to Jesus. Although the senders are not identified, the implication is that it is the same group referred to in 11:27; 12:1, and in the previous verse. The combination of Pharisees (see

---

Parallels to Mark 12:13-17

"They showed Jesus a gold coin and said to Him, "Caesar's men demand taxes from us." He said to them, "Give Caesar what belongs to Caesar, give God what belongs to God, and give Me what is Mine." (*Gospel of Thomas* 100)

". . . [ca]me to him to put him to the pro[of] and to tempt him, whilst [they said]: 'Master Jesus we know that thou art come [from God], for what thou doest bears a test[imony] (to thee which goes) beyond (that) of all the prophets. [Wherefore tell] us: is it admissible [to p]ay to the kings the (charges) appertaining to their rule? [Should we] pay [th]em or not?' But Jesus saw through their [in]tention, became [angry] and said to them: 'Why call ye me with yo[ur mou]th

Master and yet [do] not what I say? Well has Is[aiah] proph-esied [concerning y]ou saying: This [people honours] me with the[ir li]ps but their heart is far from me; [their worship is] vain. [They teach] precepts [of me].'" (Egerton Papyrus 2, recto, lines 43-59; cf. John 3:2; Mark 7:6-8)

". . . for at that time some came to Him and asked Him, if one ought to pay tribute to Caesar; and He answered, 'Tell Me, whose image does the coin bear?' And they said, 'Caesar's.' And again He answered them, 'Render therefore to Caesar the things that are Caesar's, and to God the things that are God's.'" (Justin Martyr, *First Apology* 17; *ANF* 1:168)

Egerton Papyrus 2, in Robert W. Funk, ed., *New Gospel Parallels* (Philadelphia: Fortress Press, 1985), 1:243.

commentary on 2:16) and Herodians is important for three reasons: (1) the two groups plotted to kill Jesus earlier (3:6); (2) Jesus had warned the disciples to "beware of the leaven of the Pharisees and of the leaven of Herod" (8:15 RSV); and (3) the two groups probably held divergent views on the issue of Roman taxation, with the Pharisees opposing it (see [Tax Collectors]) and the Herodians supporting the Romans. Mark reports that the Pharisees and Herodians intended to catch (*agreuein*) Jesus "unawares" or "in an unguarded statement."[36] It is a term used for trapping or ensnaring animals or fish.[37]

Their opening gambit is to flatter Jesus with false praise in hopes of enticing him to make an unguarded or ill-considered response. The Pharisees and Herodians address Jesus as "teacher" (12:14). Frank Moloney observes that "without exception, every prior use of this salutation shows a poor understanding of Jesus and limited belief in him" (see 4:38; 5:35; 9:17, 38; 10:17, 20, 35).[38] Their words are similar to those of Nicodemus in John 3:2, but Nicodemus's flattery is not so transparently insincere. In the present context, there is an ironic ring to the authorities' words since the chief priests, scribes, and elders had said, "we do not know" (11:33). Moreover, they praise Jesus for not making distinctions among people when "the scribes of the Pharisees" in Galilee had criticized him for not discriminating about those with whom he ate (2:16). Their praise of Jesus for teaching "the way of God" also echoes the early Christian designation of believers as followers of "the Way" (Acts 9:2; 19:9, 23; 24:14, 22) and the use of "the way" in Mark to mean the road to the cross, or suffering servanthood (8:27; 9:33-34; 10:32, 46, 52; see commentary on 8:27).

The question about taxation was set in the context of political and economic oppression. K. C. Hanson and Douglas E. Oakman cite Gerhard Lenski's estimate that the top 5 percent of the society controlled 50-65 percent of the goods and services.[39] They add the following illuminating description of the Roman system of taxation:

> Taxation in Roman Palestine was extractive, that is, designed to assert elite control over agrarian production. . . . Caesar's agents collected taxes and redistributed them to clients. The priests and the Jerusalem temple collected offerings and redistributed them. Redistribution exchanges were replicated throughout society. Their major impact was to remove most goods from the control and enjoyment of most people. The terms "extraction," "redistribution," and "tribute" reflect the political nature of these distributive mechanisms. All of the terms emphasize that the benefits in ancient economy flowed "upward" to the advantage of the elites.[40]

The Greek term *kēnsos* ("taxes") is a Latin loanword that means "census."[41] Josephus describes the disastrous effects of Herod the

Great's abusive administration. [Taxation under Herod the Great] Josephus also traces the origin of the Zealots to the revolt led by Judas the Galilean during the administration of Archelaus: "a Galilean, named Judas, incited his countrymen to revolt, upbraiding them as cowards for consenting to pay tribute to the Romans and tolerating mortal masters, after having God for their lord" (Josephus, *J. W.* 2.118; LCL 2:367-69). The question put to Jesus turns on this point: "Is it lawful to pay taxes to the emperor, or not?" (12:14). Obviously it was lawful under Roman law; was it lawful under God's law? Malina and Rohrbaugh caution us that in antiquity there was no concept of the separation of church and state.[42] The question of taxation, therefore, touched the raw nerves of political oppression, economic exploitation, and religious duty.

Taxation under Herod the Great

Josephus, the first-century historian, described the burden of taxation imposed by Herod.

"He had indeed reduced the entire nation to helpless poverty after taking it over in as flourishing a condition as few ever know, and he was wont to kill members of the nobility upon absurd pretexts and then take their property for himself; and if he did permit any of them to have the doubtful pleasure of living, he would condemn them to be stripped of their possessions. In addition to the collecting of the tribute that was imposed on everyone each year, lavish extra contributions had to be made to him and to his household and friends and those of his slaves who were sent out to collect the tribute because there was no immunity at all from outrage unless bribes were paid."

Josephus, Ant. 17.307–08; LCL 8:513–15.

In v. 15 the narrator reports that Jesus recognized their "hypocrisy." The English term "hypocrisy" is actually a loanword from the Greek *hypokrisis*, which is a term drawn from the theater that means to play a role or "create a public impression that is at odds with one's real purposes or motivations."[43] Jesus responds, "Why do you put me to the test?" The term "test" can also mean "tempt" but does not seem to have that meaning here (see [*Peirazein,* To "Tempt" or "Test," in Mark]). Jesus then resorts to some theater of his own. Just as he had asked the chief priests, scribes, and elders if they had read Psalm 118 (12:10), when surely they had, now he asks the Pharisees and Herodians to bring him a Roman denarius, the common silver coin of the day and the only one accepted for the payment of taxes. William Lane explains,

> The denarius of Tiberius portrayed the emperor as the semi-divine son of the god Augustus and the goddess Livia and bore the (abbreviated) inscription "Tiberius Caesar Augustus, Son of the Divine Augustus" on the obverse and "Pontifex Maximus" on the reverse. Both the representations and the inscriptions were rooted in the imperial cult and constituted a claim to divine honors.[44]

The Pharisees in particular may have been embarrassed at having to produce a Roman coin bearing an idolatrous inscription. Having seized the advantage, Jesus continues to make the most of it. His inquisitors had attempted to play the role of an *eiron* or ironist, plying Jesus with false praise and pretending to defer to his greater wisdom on a difficult

Caesar's Image and God's Image

"That means render the image of Caesar, which is on the coin, to Caesar, and the image of God, which is imprinted on the person, to God. You give to Caesar only money. But to God, give yourself." (Tertullian, *On Idolatry* 15)

"The image of the Emperor appears differently in his son and in a piece of coin. The coin has no knowledge of its bearing the image of the prince. But you are the coin of God, and so far highly superior, as possessing mind and even life, so as to know the One whose image you bear." (Augustine, *Sermons on New Testament Lessons* 43)

"... to Caesar his coins, to God your very selves." (Augustine, *Tractates on John* 40.9)

"Caesar seeks his image; render it. God seeks His image; render it." (Augustine, *On the Psalms* 58.8)

Thomas C. Oden and Christopher A. Hall, eds., *Ancient Christian Commentary on Scripture: New Testament II, Mark* (Downers Grove IL: InterVarsity Press, 1998), 167–68.

Roman coin with portrait of Julius Caesar. Bibliotheque Nationale, Paris, France. (Credit: Snark / Art Resource, NY)

question. Now Jesus becomes the ironist, disdainfully making them produce a coin and asking them whose image and inscription it bore. Publicly chagrined, they answer as briefly as possible: "Caesar's."

The climax of this contest of wit and wisdom is Jesus' pronouncement in v. 17. The Pharisees and Herodians assumed that Jesus would either have to endorse or oppose the payment of taxes to the Romans. If he approved paying taxes, he would lose favor with the crowd (just as the chief priests, scribes, and elders were faced with this prospect in 11:32). On the other hand, if he maintained that paying taxes was not "lawful," he could be charged with treason. Evading the horns of this dilemma, Jesus' response is sufficiently ambiguous to require the hearers to judge his meaning for themselves, while implying that they should pay their taxes but not treat the emperor as divine. The pronouncement, "Give to the emperor the things that are the emperor's, and to God the things that are God's," draws a sharp distinction between the emperor and God. It also reminds the hearer that just as one owes taxes to the emperor, there is also that which is due to God (and God alone). Early on, interpreters grasped the contrast between that which bore the image of Caesar (the denarius) and that which is made in the image of God. [Caesar's Image and God's Image] Give the coin to Caesar, but people belong to God, and therefore owe their ultimate allegiance to God.

Jesus' answer "utterly amazed" (*exethaumazon*) them. This intensive form of the verb "to amaze" (*thaumazein*) occurs nowhere else in the New Testament, but Mark notes the amazement of others in response to Jesus' words and actions several times (5:20; 6:51; 15:5, 44).

The Question about the Resurrection, 12:18-27

The parade of interrogators continues with the coming of a group of Sadducees to pose a question to Jesus. [Sadducees] Significantly, the

---

Sadducees

Little is known about the Sadducees, and nothing written by Sadducees has survived. They are mentioned fifteen times in the Gospels and Acts, where they are a Jewish group in Jerusalem, named alongside the Pharisees (particularly in Matthew), with whom they disagree on the matter of resurrection of the dead, angels, and "spirit" (Acts 23:8). Josephus identifies the Sadducees as the second of four Jewish schools, analogous to the Greek philosophical schools. They denied personal immortality (*Ant.* 18.16; *J.W.* 2.165), affirmed free will and denied determinism (*Ant.* 13.173; *J.W.* 2.164), and held only to the law, denying the validity of oral tradition (Ant. 13. 297; 18.17). In the rabbinic sources the disagreements between the Pharisees and the Sadducees concern matters of purity.

The origin of the name "Sadducee" is generally traced to Zadok, the high priest at the time of David and Solomon (1 Sam 8:17; 15:24; 1 Kgs 1:34; 1 Chr 12:29), but the group does not appear until the time of John Hyrcanus in the 2d century BC (135–104 BC; Josephus, *Ant.* 13.293, 297). On the basis of Josephus's statement that the Sadducees had "the confidence of the wealthy alone but no following among the populace" (*Ant.* 13.297; cf. 18.17) and the contexts in which they appear in the Gospels and Acts, the Sadducees are generally connected with the Jewish aristocracy, the temple, and the priesthood. Consequently, they may have been more open to Hellenistic influences and Roman authority, but these generalizations quickly move beyond the slender evidence of their social status provided by Josephus. With the emergence of the Pharisees as the dominant Jewish group following the war of AD 66–70, the Sadducees seem to have lost ground quickly, although they continue to be mentioned in the rabbinic materials for several centuries.

Rudolf Meyer, *"Saddoukaios,"* *TDNT* 7:35–54; Gary G. Parton, *"Sadducees,"* *ABD* 5:892–95; Emil Schürer, *The History of the Jewish People in the Age of Jesus Christ* (rev. Geza Vermes et al.; Edinburgh: T. & T. Clark, 1979), 404–14.

---

narrator in Mark identifies the Sadducees in an aside in v. 18 as those "who say there is no resurrection." This explanation implies that the intended reader of the Gospel may not know who the Sadducees were. The narrator's comment identifies the group in terms of what appears to have been the element of their theology that set them apart from other Jews (particularly the Pharisees, see Acts 23:8), and it sets up the question they will pose, which was designed to discredit those who believed in the resurrection. In contrast to the previous question, which involved sensitive political issues and could have placed Jesus in jeopardy from Roman authority, the Sadducees' question focuses on a theological issue debated by the Pharisees, Sadducees, and Essenes. Significantly, the resurrection had of course become a central tenet of Christian theology by the time Mark was written, so Jesus' refutation of the Sadducees' dismissal of belief in the resurrection functions for the Gospel's Christian readers as an authoritative endorsement of their hope for resurrection, and ironically this defense of resurrection comes from the one whom they knew had himself been raised from the dead.

The structure of this pronouncement story is more involved than is typically the case: (1) introduction of the challengers by name and interpretive comment (v. 18), (2) statement of a biblical premise: the laws of levirate marriage (v. 19), (3) description of a case (real or hypothetical) of levirate marriage: seven brothers each in succession take a woman as their wife; none leave an heir (vv. 20-22), (4) the question: whose wife will she be in the resurrection (v. 22)? (5) Jesus' first question, followed by a general statement about the nature of the resurrection (vv. 24-25), and (6) Jesus' second question, with an appeal to the Torah, followed by a general statement about the nature of God (vv. 26-27).

The Sadducees address Jesus as "Teacher" (see the commentary on Mark 5:35; 9:17, 38; 10:35; and 12:14), an address that is used in Mark by those who want something from Jesus (4:38; 5:35; 9:17; 10:17, 20, 35; 12:14). Because the Sadducees regarded only the Torah, the books of Moses, as Scripture, it is entirely in character for them to appeal to Moses. Jesus himself referred to "Moses" earlier in his conversation with the man with leprosy in Mark 1:44, in his debate with the Pharisees over Qorban (7:10), and in his response to the Pharisees' question regarding divorce (10:3-4). At the end of this scene Jesus will drive home his rejoinder to the Sadducees by questioning whether they had really read Moses (in 12:26).

The Sadducees approach Jesus indirectly, offering nothing at the outset that telegraphs the direction of their attack. They quote the law regarding levirate marriage (Deut 25:5 and Gen 38:8). Because the only supported positions for women in ancient Hebrew society were either as an unmarried virgin in her father's family or as a wife in her husband's family, Hebrew law required a man to marry his brother's widow, to provide her with support and to procreate children for his brother by her. [Levirate Marriage] Mark does not quote Deuteronomy verbatim, but summarizes the command using key words from Deuteronomy 25:5 and 7 adding, "and raise up offspring for your/his brother" from Genesis 38:8.

The reference to seven brothers echoes other stories of seven brothers (the seven martyrs of 2 Macc 7) or seven bridegrooms (Tob 3:8, 15) elsewhere in the Jewish literature of the period. The point of the Sadducees' tale, however, is to pose a situation that exposes the folly of belief in "the resurrection," which means the resurrection of the dead at the end of time.

Jesus' first response is direct and unsparing. The Sadducees, he charged, were mistaken because they knew neither the Scriptures nor "the power of God" (v. 24). The verb translated "wrong" (NRSV) or "in error" (NIV) literally means to "go astray" or "be misled."[45] The

Levirate Marriage

Lev 18:16 and 20:21 unconditionally forbid sexual intercourse with one's sister-in-law. Nevertheless, Deut 25:5-10 requires that if one's brother dies childless, one must marry his brother's widow. The Levitical law must therefore have been framed when the Deuteronomic practice was no longer followed, or Deuteronomy states an exception to the general principle stated in Leviticus. The practice is referred to in Gen 38:8, when Judah instructs Onan to fulfill the law with Tamar, and then subsequently violates the law by refusing to allow his third son, Shelah, to take Tamar as his wife. The story of Ruth and Boaz is probably related, but extends the practice of levirate marriage since Boaz was a kinsman of Ruth's deceased husband, not his brother. The Deuteronomic law may have been written to insure that the practice of levirate marriage, which was also practiced by the Assyrians, the Hittites, and the Canaanites, would continue to be practiced by the Israelites. Josephus interprets the law as having the following purposes: "[It is] profitable to the public welfare, houses not dying out and property remaining with the relatives, and it will moreover bring the women an alleviation of their misfortune to live with the nearest kinsman of their former husbands" (*Ant.* 4.254; LCL 4:599). The practice of marrying within the extended family is also maintained in Tobit (6:11-13). If the brother-in-law refused to do his duty, the widow removed his sandal and spat in his face. She was then free to marry someone else (Deut 25:9).

O. J. Baab, *"Marriage," IDB* 3:282–83; Mark E. Biddle, *Deuteronomy* (Smyth & Helwys Bible Commentary; Macon GA: Smyth & Helwys, 2003), 369–75; Victor P. Hamilton, "Marriage (OT and ANE)," *ABD* 4:567–68.

response that the scribes do not know the Scriptures is relevant because the scribes had just quoted the Scriptures to Jesus, making the case that there cannot be a resurrection of the dead because it would be inconsistent with the requirements of levirate marriage. It is surprising that there are so few references to "the scriptures" in Mark because of the scriptural background of so much of the Gospel and the quotations of Scripture that are sprinkled through it. Earlier, however, Jesus had challenged the authorities, asking, "Have you not read this scripture?" (12:10). The Scriptures will be fulfilled in the events that lead to Jesus' death: "in order that the scriptures might be fulfilled" (14:49; cf. 15:28, which is omitted in the best manuscripts). In the Old Testament God is personal and God's power is evident both in God's creation and in God's mighty acts in history:

"O Lord GOD, you have only begun to show your servant your greatness and your might; what god in heaven or on earth can perform deeds and mighty acts like yours!" (Deut 3:24)

"Who is the King of glory?
The LORD, strong and mighty,
the LORD mighty in battle." (Ps 24:8)

"The voice of the LORD is powerful;
the voice of the LORD is full of majesty." (Ps 29:4)

In the experience of Israel the power of God was decisively revealed in the exodus, the plagues, and the deliverance of the people from the hand of Pharaoh. The power of God is definitively revealed, therefore, in God's saving activity in history. In the New Testament, the term "the power of God" is found primarily in Paul's writings (Rom 1:16; 1 Cor 1:18, 24; 2:5; 2 Cor 6:7; 13:4; 2 Tim 1:8; cf. Acts 8:10; 1 Pet 1:5; Rev 19:1). The closest parallel in Mark occurs in Jesus' response to the high priest, where power is used as a circumlocution for the divine name: "you will see the Son of Man seated at the right hand of Power" (14:62). In the parallel passage Luke has "of the power of God" (22:69). The force of Jesus' retort to the Sadducees is that if they knew the Scriptures and the power of God revealed in his saving acts, they would have no problem in grasping the reality of the resurrection. The Old Testament Scriptures speak of the resurrection explicitly only in Daniel 12:2, but the hope of resurrection is an extension of the steadfast love and mercy of God expressed throughout the Scriptures. Mark has also noted that the power of God was exercised by Jesus in his mighty acts (5:30; 6:2; 9:39).

The explanation that follows this reminder of God's power is the most troublesome of the New Testament pronouncements regarding the resurrection: "For when they rise from the dead, they neither marry nor are given in marriage, but are like angels in heaven" (12:25). The popular belief was that angels dwelt in the presence of God, were arrayed in dazzling garments, and did not eat or drink. Part of the eschatological hope of various groups was that they would become like the angels (*1 En.* 39:4). Legend had it that Enoch dwelt with the angels for six jubilees of years (*Jub.* 4:21), and the Essenes at Qumran believed that the community of the new covenant there enjoyed communion with the angels (1QS 11.7-8; 1QH 3.21-22). It was natural, therefore, to understand the nature of the resurrection in terms of becoming like the angels. [Becoming like Angels] The basic argument is that the power of God can transform and preserve life. The extent to which the resurrection would involve continuation of life as we know it or transformation in ways we cannot yet comprehend was debated.

Having affirmed the power of God, Jesus turns again to the argument from Scripture. Perhaps because the Sadducees held the authority of the books of Moses above that of the prophets, Jesus staked his argument on the divine disclosure to Moses rather than on passages in the prophets that speak more explicitly of the resurrection hope (e.g., Job 19:26; Ps 16:9-11; Isa 26:19; Dan 12:2;).[46] The books of the Pentateuch do not mention the resurrection. Nevertheless, arguing in typical rabbinic fashion, Jesus appeals to God's self-designation as "the God of Abraham, the God of Isaac, and the God of Jacob" (Exod 3:6, 15). The argument is not forced but subtle. The assumption was that

---

Becoming like Angels

"You are about to be making a great rejoicing like the angels of heaven" (*1 En.* 104:4; Charlesworth, *OTP* 1:85)

". . . then both these and those will be changed, these into the splendor of angels. . . . For they will live in the heights of that world and they will be like the angels. . . ." (*2 Bar.* 51:5, 10; Charlesworth, *OTP* 1:638)

"You shall be like an angel of the face in the holy residence for the glory of the God of Hosts . . . sharing the lot with the angels of the face and the Council of the Community [. . . .] for eternal time and for all the perpetual periods." (1QRule of the Blessings [1Q28b or 1QSb] 4.24-26; Martínez, *The Dead Sea Scrolls Translated*, 433)

". . . inasmuch as they [martyrs] were no longer men, but had already become angels." (*Martyrdom of Polycarp* 2; *ANF* 1:39)

James H. Charlesworth, ed., *OTP* (Garden City, N.Y.: Doubleday, 1985).

Florentino García Martínez, *The Dead Sea Scrolls Translated* (Leiden: E. J. Brill, 1994).

Francesco Mochi (1580–1654). *Angel Annunciate*. Sculpture. Museo dell'Opera del Duomo, Orvieto, Italy. (Credit: Scala / Art Resource, NY)

God is not God of the dead but of the living, and that God would not have appealed to dead patriarchs. The patriarchs must therefore have been alive. In support of this argument, Evans cites two passages from 4 Maccabees:[47]

> "But as many as attend to religion with a whole heart, these alone are able to control the passions of the flesh, since they believe that they, like our patriarchs Abraham and Isaac and Jacob, do not die to God, but live to God." (4 Macc 7:18-19)

> "They knew also that those who die for the sake of God live to God, as do Abraham and Isaac and Jacob and all the patriarchs." (4 Macc 16:25)

There is a further point to be made, however. God spoke to Moses in the context of the deliverance of the Hebrew people from their bondage in Egypt saying, "I am the God of Abraham, Isaac, and Jacob." God's covenant faithfulness had preserved the patriarchs, and God would deliver the Israelites from their bondage. God delivers and preserves all who trust in God. God is therefore the God of the living, not the dead.[48] Those who know God's power to deliver, revealed in the Scriptures, do not question the resurrection. Jesus sharply reprimanded the Sadducees for their misguided thinking: "Have you not read?" (12:26; cf. 12:10); "you are quite wrong" (cf. 12:24).

The First Commandment, 12:28-34

The contest of wit and wisdom between Jesus and representatives of the various groups and leaders of the people reaches its climax with the question posed by one of the scribes (see [Scribes] and [Challenge-Riposte]). In contrast to the previous questions, however, the scribe's question is not overtly hostile. Mark explains that he is motivated by having heard Jesus' debates with the others. The verb "to debate" (*syzēteō*, translated "answered" them in the NRSV) occurs only in Mark (1:27; 8:11; 9:10, 14, 16; 12:28) and in Luke-Acts in the New Testament.

The scribe's question is typical of issues debated by the scribes and teachers of the law. Because they counted 613 commands in the Torah, they often looked for ways to summarize the essence of the Torah. When a Gentile challenged Hillel, saying that he would become a proselyte if Hillel could teach him the whole Law while he stood on one foot, Hillel replied, "What you yourself hate, do not do to your neighbor: this is the whole Law, the rest is commentary. Go and learn it" (*b. Shabbath* 31a).[49] Similarly, the oral tradition of the Pharisees records that Simeon the Just used to say, "By three things is the world sustained: by the Law, by the [Temple-]service, and by deeds of loving-kindness" (*m. Aboth* 1.2).

The scribe asks, "Which commandment is the first of all?" (v. 28). The use of "first" meaning "chief" or "preeminent" occurs elsewhere in Mark: the "first" men of Galilee (6:21) and the "first" among the disciples (9:35; 10:31, 44). Jesus responds by quoting Deuteronomy 6:4-5 in a form that is close to the Septuagint (and the Masoretic Text) but that adds a fourth qualifier, "and with all your mind," and changes the word for "strength" from *dynameōs* to *ischyos*. When the scribe repeats the command, he omits two of the qualifiers (soul and mind) and adds another (understanding), thereby returning to the form of three qualifiers as found in the biblical text. "Understanding" may also be a combination of "soul" and "mind." Matthew and Luke both omit Deuteronmy 6:4 and move directly to 6:5. Matthew omits the fourth qualifier (strength; Matt 22:37) and Luke reverses the last two qualifiers, reading "strength" then "mind." The form of the text was therefore still fluid even though it was the beginning of the Shema (Deut 6:4-9; 11:13-21; Num 15:37-41), which was recited twice each day by the faithful. [The Shema] From these variations in the synoptic texts Joachim Jeremias concluded that "the Greek *Shema* was not a regularly recited liturgical text for any of the three synoptic evangelists."[50]

The Shema, known by the first word of the Hebrew text of Deuteronomy 6:4, is the foundational confession of ancient Israel, a call for complete and exclusive devotion to Yahweh. The command to "hear" is not passive but active. To "hear" means to give heed to and obey. The affirmation that follows may emphasize either the oneness of Yahweh or the exclusivity of Yahweh's claim on Israel's devotion.[51] God demands our complete devotion; we are to serve no other God. Therefore, the affirmation of God's exclusive right to worship is followed by the command to love God with all one's being. William Lane comments: "The love which determines the whole disposition of one's life and places one's whole personality in the service of God reflects a commitment to God which springs from divine sonship."[52] For ancient anthropology the heart was the center of the will and volition, the center of one's inner life, the epitome of the person.[53] When one loves God with one's whole heart, there can be no hypocrisy. Like "heart," "soul" (*psychē*) denoted the whole person (see

---

The Shema

Although the practice of reciting the Shema each day probably originated much earlier, the earliest reference to it is in the *Letter of Aristeas* 160 (2d c. BC). Josephus writes, "Twice each day, at the dawn thereof and when the hour comes for turning to repose, let all acknowledge before God the bounties which He had bestowed on them through their deliverance from the land of Egypt" (*Ant.* 4.212; LCL 4:577). All men and boys above the age of twelve were expected to observe this practice, which was later followed by the recitation of the eighteen benedictions. Women, children, and slaves were free from this obligation (M. *Berakoth* 3.3).

Joachim Jeremias, *The Prayers of Jesus* (Philadelphia: Fortress Press, 1967), 67–69. See also Mark E. Biddle, *Deuteronomy* (Smyth & Helwys Bible Commentary; Macon GA: Smyth & Helwys, 2003), 124–28; Birger Gerhardsson, *The Ethos of the Bible* (trans. Stephen Westerholm; Philadelphia: Fortress Press, 1981).

commentary on 8:35). Behind the New Testament usage of *psychē* lies the Hebrew understanding of the human being as a living, breathing *nephesh*. James castigates the "double-minded" (*dipsychos*; Jas 1:8; 4:8) by which he means those whose loyalties are divided, or whose commitments vacillate. When one loves God with one's whole soul or life (*psychē*), one's ultimate allegiance is clear and uncompromised. "Mind" or "understanding" (*dianoia*) denoted one's moral consciousness. Paul characterizes the unbelieving Gentiles as "darkened in their understanding, alienated from the life of God" (Eph 4:18). When one loves God with one's whole mind, therefore, there can be no confusion about what is right before God. "Strength" (*ischys*) denotes all human energy and vitality. Ephesians 6:10 admonishes, "Finally, be strong in the Lord and in the strength of his power." Birger Gerhardsson extends the meaning of "strength" to encompass "external resources, power, mammon"—all of one's possessions, property, and resources.[54] When one loves God with one's whole strength, one neither squanders life on lesser pursuits nor allows material goods to become false gods. The call to love God therefore claims all that defines our lives.

To this greatest commandment Jesus adds a second: Leviticus 19:18, "and you shall love your neighbor as yourself." Mark 12:31 reproduces the Septuagint text of this command verbatim. Originally, "neighbor" meant one's fellow Israelite, but by the first century the question of who should be counted as a neighbor was in debate,[55] and in Luke Jesus responds to the question with the parable of the good Samaritan (Luke 10:29-37; cf. Matt 5:43; Rom 13:9-10; Gal 5:14; Jas 2:8). The elder of 1 John asks pointed questions about the love command: how can God's love abide in one who sees a brother or sister in need and yet refuses to help (3:17), and how can one love God, whom he has not seen, if he does not love a brother or sister, whom he has seen? (4:20). The two commands appear already to have been joined (*T. Iss.* 5:2, "Love the Lord and your neighbor"; see also 7:6, where Issachar says he has loved God and "every human being," and *T. Dan* 5:3). Nevertheless, there is no earlier text in which Deuteronomy 6:5 and Leviticus 19:18 are specifically linked.[56]

Mark's interest is neither in the definition of "neighbor" nor in the nature of the love that is commanded but in the inseparability of love of God and love of neighbor. The love command does not occur outside this passage in Mark, and the noun *agapē* does not appear in this Gospel. Instead, Mark insists that true belief in God is not expressed through participation in the cultic practices (purity, feasts, or sacrifices) but in keeping the moral law, that is, by loving one's fellow human being.[57]

The qualifier "as yourself" introduces a complexity to the command because it requires us to ask how we love ourselves and how we can love others in this way. While many have interpreted this phrase as an implicit third command (love God, neighbor, and self), Karl Barth denied that it has this meaning and said rather that love of neighbor places a necessary limitation on self-love. [Karl Barth on Love of Self]

Karl Barth on Love of Self

"It is true that this self-love is the visible and tangible reality of the one who loves his neighbour. The commandment itself recognises and establishes it to be true. But the commandment: Thou shalt love thy neighbour, is not a legitimation but a limitation of this reality. If I love my neighbour, that is the judgment on my self-love and not its indirect justification. When I love my neighbour I do not apply to him the same good thing as I do to myself when I love myself. Far from it. When I love my neighbour I confess that my self-love is not a good thing, that it is not love at all. I begin to love at all when I love my neighbour. The only positive meaning of 'as thyself' is, then, that we are commanded to love our neighbour as those who love themselves, i.e., as those in reality do not love, as the sinners we are."

Karl Barth, *The Doctrine of the Word of God*, in vol. 1 of *Church Dogmatics* (trans. G. T. Thomson and Harold Knight; Edinburgh: T. & T. Clark, 1956), 1.2: 450.

Matthew and Luke have no parallel to vv. 32-34. The scribe responds, approving Jesus' answer, repeating the two commands with slight variations, and adding these commands are "much more important than all whole burnt offerings and sacrifices" (12:33). Whole burnt offerings (*holokautōmatōn*) were the sacrifices that were not eaten; the whole sacrifice was burnt. Other sacrifices were offered and then the flesh was eaten by the worshipers.[58] The scribe's affirmation of the superiority of the love commands over the ceremonies and sacrifices echoes a sentiment that can be traced to the prophets (1 Sam 15:22; Hos 6:6), but here it reverberates with Jesus' cursing of the fig tree and condemnation of the temple (11:12-21) and the parable of the wicked tenants (12:1-12). Having condemned the temple, Jesus now displaces the sacrifices as unnecessary. Francis Moloney perceptively suggests that Jesus' response—or at least Mark's interpretation of it—points "to the end of the need for the detailed legislation that governed the life of a practicing Jew," and quotes Grundmann's comment: "Thereby a new position is established over against the whole pre-Christian concept of religious righteousness and interpersonal relations."[59]

Verse 34 draws the scene to a close by reporting first Jesus' response and then that of the bystanders. The narrator provides an inside view of Jesus' thoughts. When Jesus saw that the scribe answered "wisely," he said that he was "not far" from the kingdom of God. The term "wisely" (*nounechōs*), which is a combination of two words that means "having a mind" or "having understanding," does not occur elsewhere in the New Testament or the Septuagint. By seeing what true religion really involved—love of God and love for others—this scribe had moved close to Jesus, and therefore he was near to the kingdom. The terms "far" and "near" were generally used to contrast Gentiles and Jews (Eph 2:13, 17; cf. Mark 5:6; 8:3; 11:13), but here the metaphor of distance is applied in a new way—a Jewish scribe is "not far" from the kingdom.

The kingdom has come near; he has only to "repent and believe in the gospel" (1:15).

The scribe is the last of Jesus' interrogators. Mark comments that after that no one dared ask him any further questions. Jesus has turned aside the chief priests, scribes and elders (11:27-33), the Pharisees and Herodians (12:13-17), the Sadducees (12:18-27), and the scribe (12:28-34), and at this point the Pharisees, Herodians, and Sadducees all disappear from the Gospel narrative.

Although Jesus has silenced his opponents, he continues teaching in the temple, correcting their expectations of the Messiah (12:35-37), castigating the scribes for their abuse of their position (12:38-40), and elevating the generous widow in opposition to the scribes (12:41-44).

The Messiah and David's Son, 12:35-37

This pericope is attached to the preceding by the reference to the scribes (12:28, 32, 35). (See [Scribes]). The question concerns the expectation that the Messiah would be a royal messiah, a descendant of David, who would restore the kingdom of Israel. This expectation was cherished by many who chafed under Roman rule in the first century, and it is vividly reflected in the *Psalms of Solomon* (first century BC). [*Psalms of Solomon* 17]

The opening is puzzling because it is framed as Jesus' answer when no question is recorded, and in fact the previous sentence declares that no one dared ask him anything. It has been suggested, therefore, that Mark has recorded only the ending of a conflict story that opened with a question being posed to Jesus, perhaps a question designed to draw Jesus into the dangerous waters of Messianism and the people's hopes for one who would purge Israel of Gentile domination.[60]

Jesus introduces a new topic with a question directed to the scribes, the experts in biblical interpretation: "How can the scribes say that the Messiah is the son of David?" Anyone hearing the challenge would have thought that Jesus was woefully uninformed. The expectation of a coming descendant of David, which by the first century was understood as a messianic prediction, is well established in the Jewish Scriptures. Second Samuel 7 records God's covenant with David, that God would raise up descendants of David who would establish his kingdom forever (2 Sam 7:11-13, 16; cf. 23:1-7). The

Psalms of Solomon 17

"See, Lord, and raise up for them
   their king,
  the son of David, to rule over your servant Israel
  in the time known to you, O God.
Undergird him with the strength to destroy the unrighteous rulers,
  to purge Jerusalem from gentiles
  who trample her to destruction; . . . .
And he will purge Jerusalem
  (and make it) holy as it was even from the beginning. . . .
And he will be a righteous king over them, taught by God.
There will be no unrighteousness among them in his days,
  for all shall be holy,
  and their king shall be the Lord Messiah."
(*Pss. Sol* 17:21-22, 30, 32)

  James H. Charlesworth, ed., *OTP* (Garden City NY: Doubleday, 1985), 2:667.

prophets took up this promise also: "a shoot shall come out from the stump of Jesse" (Isa 11:1; cf. 9:2-7), "The days are surely coming, says the LORD, when I will raise up for David a righteous Branch, and he shall reign as king and deal wisely, and shall execute justice and righteousness in the land" (Jer 23:5; cf. 30:9; 33:15, 17; Ezek 34:23-24; 37:24-25; Amos 9:11). How could the scribes not expect that the Messiah would be the son of David?

Jesus follows the question with a quotation of Psalm 110:1 that follows the Septuagint text closely. Mark omits the article before "(the) Lord" and substitutes "under" your feet for "a footstool for" your feet. The force of the quotation rests on the assumption that the psalm was written by David himself, that it spoke of the coming Messiah, and that David would not refer to his son as "my Lord." Jesus underscores the importance of this quotation by affirming that the psalm was inspired: David said it "by the Holy Spirit" (12:36).

Jesus was hailed as "son of David" by the blind Bartimaeus in Jericho (10:47-48), and the excited crowd blessed "the coming kingdom of our ancestor David" as he entered Jerusalem (11:10). See the commentary on 10:47-48 for the connections between Jesus' healings and exorcisms and Solomon. On the way to Jerusalem his disciples looked forward to holding places of power and honor in Jesus' kingdom, but Jesus now rejects their expectations by denying the expectations of a Davidic messiah. Elsewhere the New Testament affirms that Jesus came from the Davidic lineage, as part of its affirmation that Jesus was the expected Messiah (Matt 1:1, 6, 17, 20; Luke 1:27, 32, 69; 2:4, 11; 3:31; Rom 1:3; 2 Tim 2:8). Matthew and Luke both include this pericope, so we need not think Mark denied that Jesus was from the line of David.

How is the Messiah David's son? More than physical descent is meant here. The Messiah would transcend the expectation of the coming of one who would restore an earthly kingdom. Jesus had come announcing not the kingdom of David (11:10) but the kingdom of God (1:15), and this would be accomplished by his death on the cross rather than by establishing an earthly, nationalistic kingdom. Then, through the resurrection, Jesus would be exalted to the right hand of God (14:62), fulfilling the promise of the perpetual reign of the house of David. Jesus' understanding of his role was influenced far more by the suffering servant of Isaiah and the son of man of Daniel than by the scribes' expectation of the son of David.

The "great crowd" (see 5:21, 24; 6:34; 8:1; 9:14) that had gathered to hear Jesus debate the authorities heard him "gladly" (6:20) because of the skill with which he bested them.

Jesus' Condemnation of the Scribes, 12:38-40

When Jesus taught, the people compared his teaching with that of the scribes (1:22). The scribes appear in Mark to be more closely associated with Jerusalem than with Galilee, and recent scholarship suggests that they were more often priests or Levites than Pharisees.[61] Still, they were probably not a unified group, although at times the Gospels convey the impression that they were. The term seems to have covered a number of functions. Originally, a scribe was one who could read and write (Judg 5:14). Then, the scribe became one who was trained in the Torah (Ezra 7:6), who could read and interpret the Scriptures. Sirach (38:24–39:11) praises the scribe as one who devotes himself to the study of the Law and the wisdom of the ancients, who preserves the sayings of the famous, and who penetrates the meaning of riddles and parables. By the New Testament period they were the respected stewards of a sacred lore—the Scriptures, esoteric teachings, and the oral traditions. They handled legal matters, produced documents, advised priests and civil authorities, and were recognized as teachers. The people greeted them in deference when they passed.

Jesus warned the people about the scribes, citing six characteristic behaviors in a sequence that moves from love of public recognition to oppression of the powerless to cavalier disregard for the sacred. The general picture that emerges from this list is one of self-centered exploitation of their position for their own benefit.

First, the scribes loved to "walk around in long robes" (12:38). The probable meaning is that the scribes wore the long ceremonial robes that were worn by priests at times of prayer and for formal religious functions. [Ceremonial Robes] They wore these robes so that they would be instantly recognized wherever they went.

Second, they liked "to be greeted with respect in the marketplaces" (12:38). Joachim Jeremias cites the requirement that the people rise in respect when a scribe passed, excepting only tradesmen at their work (*b. Kidd* 33a), and the typical greetings, "Rabbi," "Father," and "Master" (Matt 23:7-9; *b. Makk* 24a).[62]

Third, the scribes sought the seats of honor in the synagogues (12:39), which would have been elevated seats in full view of the people, with their backs to the ark that contained the Torah scrolls. Jesus' condemnation of the scribes for

Ceremonial Robes

 Josephus describes the robes of the priests as follows:

"Over this he wears a linen robe, of a double texture of fine *byssus*. . . . This robe is a tunic descending to the ankles, enveloping the body with long sleeves tightly laced round the arms; they gird it at the breast, winding to a little above the armpits the sash, which is of a breadth of about four fingers and has an open texture giving it the appearance of a serpent's skin. Therein are woven flowers of divers hues, of crimson and purple, blue and fine linen, but the warp is purely of fine linen. Wound a first time at the breast, after passing round it once again, it is tied and then hangs at length, sweeping to the ankles, that is so long as the priest has no task at hand, for so its beauty is displayed to the beholders' advantage; but when it behoves [sic] him to attend to the sacrifices and perform his ministry, in order that the movements of the sash may not impede his actions, he throws it back over his left shoulder."

Josephus, *Jewish Antiquities* 3.153–55; LCL 4:387–89.

seeking the seats of honor in the synagogue reminds the reader that two of the disciples, James and John, had similarly sought places of honor for themselves (10:35-45). The scribes, therefore, were exemplifying behavior that Jesus condemned in his disciples.[63] Fourth, the scribes enjoyed having the best seats at banquets, where their attendance added luster to the occasion. The rabbis were given precedence over the aged, and even over one's parents.[64]

The fifth characteristic bitingly charges the scribes with "devouring" widows' houses. They love banquets—and what they eat are widow's houses. For the relationship between this charge and the example of the generous widow, see the commentary on Mark 12:41-44. James 1:27 defines "pure religion" as "to care for orphans and widows in their distress," and the Old Testament is filled with reminders of the duty to care for widows (Exod 22:22-24; Deut 14:29; 24:17, 19-22; 27:19; Ps 146:9; Prov 15:25; Isa 1:17; Jer 7:6; 22:3; Zech 7:10; Mal 3:5).

Joseph A. Fitzmyer compiled a list of six ways in which scribes could have taken advantage of impoverished widows:

(a) Scribes accepted payment for legal aid to widows even though such payment was forbidden.
(b) Scribes cheated widows of what was rightly theirs; as lawyers, they were acting as guardians appointed by a husband's will to care for the widow's estate.
(c) Scribes sponged on the hospitality of these women of limited means.
(d) Scribes mismanaged the property of widows like Anna who dedicated themselves to the service of the Temple.
(e) Scribes took large sums of money from trusting old women as a reward for the prolonged prayer which they professed to make on their behalf.
(f) Scribes took the houses as pledges for debts which could not be paid.[65]

Any of these means is possible, and Jesus' saying does not allow us to be specific about how the scribes defrauded widows.

Sixth, the scribes offered long prayers "for the sake of appearance" (12:40). The offense was not that they offered long prayers but that their prayers were yet another way in which they paraded their pretended piety before others.

This scene is framed in a form reminiscent of a legal brief, specifically a judge's ruling. The offenses form the "whereas" portion, showing cause for the decision that comes in Jesus' last statement: therefore "they will receive the greater condemnation" (12:40). In God's court, the severest sentences are reserved for those to whom much has been entrusted, to those who know better, to those who are trusted by others, and to those who have been called to minister in God's name.

The Widow's Offering, 12:41-44

The pronouncement story about the widow who gave all she had closes Jesus' public ministry in the Gospel of Mark. It is the last thing he says before withdrawing to be with his disciples before his arrest. It brings to a close the section of the Gospel in which Jesus cursed the fig tree, condemned the temple, and debated the authorities in the temple. It also follows immediately after Jesus' judgment on the scribes, who "devour widows' houses" (12:38-40). The placement of this story, therefore, sets up a number of possible contrasts: the elite scribes vs. the destitute widow, the scribes' pretentious piety vs. the widow's wholehearted devotion to God, and the scribes' self-centeredness vs. the widow's generosity.

Interpreters have often presented the widow as a model to be imitated, but an opposing interpretation has recently gained favor. Jesus does not praise the widow. Rather, he points her out as a victim of the temple system, one whose house the scribes have devoured.[66] Earlier Jesus placed human need above cultic obligations: it is permissible to gather food on the Sabbath if one is hungry (2:23-28) and to heal on the Sabbath (3:1-5); one should not invoke Qorban and leave one's parents in need (7:9-13), and loving one's neighbor is more important than whole burnt offerings and sacrifices (12:28-34). Widows were supposed to receive a portion of the tithes (Deut 14:29; 26:12-13), but this widow had given all she had. [Widows] Without

Widows

"From early times the fate most feared and bewailed by a woman was that she should become a widow. When her husband died she could return to her own family if the purchase price was paid back to the husband's heirs or the dowry to the wife's family. Otherwise she had to remain in the husband's family, where she took an even more subordinate and often humiliating position. In many cases she was not allowed to remarry."

Gustav Stählin, *"chēra," TDNT* 9:441–42.

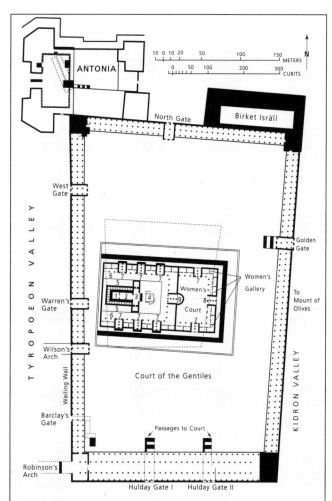

The Temple

finding fault with her sincerity or generosity, Jesus could not have been pleased that by putting all she had into the temple treasury the widow had left herself with nothing to live on. Not only did the temple cult bear no fruit; it preyed on pious widows. In the next chapter the anti-temple theme moves to center stage as Jesus warns his disciples about the coming destruction of the temple and the holy city.

Jesus had been teaching in the temple, perhaps in one of its outer stoas. Now he moves into the court of the women, where the treasury was located. The Mishnah records that there were thirteen "shofar-chests," or trumpet-shaped receptacles there, marked for various kinds of offerings (*m. Shekalim* 6.5). Josephus describes the beauty of this setting: "The porticoes between the gates, on the inner side of the wall in front of the treasury chambers, were supported by exceedingly beautiful and lofty columns; these porticoes were single, but, except in point of size, in no way inferior to those in the lower court" (*J.W.* 5.200; LCL 3:261). Josephus also comments on the wealth that was accumulated there when Jerusalem was destroyed in AD 70: "They further burnt the treasury-chambers, in which lay vast sums of money, vast piles of raiment, and other valuables; for this, in short, was the general repository of Jewish wealth, to which the rich had consigned the contents of their dismantled homes" (*J.W.* 6.282; LCL 3:459).

Jesus saw that the crowd was putting money into the receptacles, and "many rich people put in large sums" (12:41). The term for "money" (*chalkon*) literally means "copper" but was used for coins in general. The temple was the major industry of Jerusalem. Pilgrims came to pray, to offer sacrifices, and to pay their tithes. In a sense, temples functioned like national treasuries. They were also similar to banks in that the treasuries included private deposits (2 Macc 3:6, 10-11), and the temple in Jerusalem, like other temples, had been raided for its wealth on several occasions (2 Macc 3:13-28). In contrast to the "many" rich people, one widow came. In contrast to the "large sums" they contributed, she put in "two small copper coins." The "widow's mite" (KJV), as it has come to be known, was probably a Greek *lepton*. It was "the smallest coin then in circulation. It was half a Roman *quadrans* or Jewish *peruta*, and in diameter would have been smaller than any modern U.S. coin."[67] In value, it was one sixty-fourth of a denarius, a day's wage. [The Widow's Mite]

Jesus frequently calls the disciples (and at times the crowd) to teach them (3:13, 23; 6:7; 7:14; 8:1, 34; 10:42). This pericope is a pronouncement story that frames Jesus' saying in 12:43-44. Thirteen times in Mark Jesus begins a saying with the solemn formula, "Amen, I say to you" (see the commentary on 3:28). Jesus identifies the woman as poor and a widow, probably from her dress. The designation "poor" carried

The Widow's Mite

Minted from the time of Alexander Jannaeus (103–76 BC), the *lepton* was the smallest coin in circulation. It was made of bronze (not copper), and depicted the Seleucid anchor on one side and an eight-pointed star on the other.

Bronze coin of Alexander Jannaeus, Hasmonean king of Judah (103–76 BC), with symbols and Hebrew inscription. Israel Museum (IDAM), Jerusalem, Israel. (Credit: Erich Lessing / Art Resource, NY)

with it not only socioeconomic status; at times it also carried with it the connotation of piety (cf. Matt 5:3; Luke 6:20; Jas 2:1-7; and see the commentary on 10:21; 14:5, 7). [God Favors the Poor] Jesus' pronouncement may be understood either as a commendation of the widow for her giving with no thought for herself or as a keen observation of what has just taken place—and perhaps it is both. Jesus does not explicitly commend the widow or say that she is blessed. Instead, he points out that measured by what one has left after making an offering, she gave far more than the wealthy who made large gifts. She gave all she had. They gave out of their abundance, excess, or overflow. She gave out of her lack or need. Jesus describes her gift in two ways: "everything she had," and, literally, "her whole livelihood/life." The term *bios* can have both meanings. Francis Moloney comments, "The double meaning is intended, for in doing one she had done the other."[68] In contrast to the disciples who have been seeking personal gain (9:34; 10:23-31, 35-45), the widow has fulfilled Jesus' teachings on discipleship (8:35-37; 10:45). Like other minor characters in Mark (the paralytic's friends, the woman with the hemorrhage, the father of the epileptic boy, and Bartimaeus), the widow is an exemplary figure.

She is also a tragic figure. In her devotion, she has left herself destitute. Seen from this perspective, she is the final witness in the case against the temple. The chief priests and the Jerusalem scribes "devour widows' houses" (12:40). They have made the temple a "den of robbers" (11:17; cf. 11:18). Now, God will destroy *their* "house."

CONNECTIONS

Mark 12:1-12

The story of the vineyard is not merely a parable about the history of Israel or the death of Jesus. It spreads before us questions of God's nature, God's plan for humanity, and the frustration or fulfillment of God's redemptive purposes.

The parable focuses on the actions of the vineyard owner. First, Mark details his care in preparing the vineyard: he planted it, put a fence around it, dug a pit for a winepress, built a watchtower, and then leased it to tenants. When the tenants refused to receive those whom he sent to collect his portion of the produce, he sent a succession of servants. Even after the tenants had killed some of the servants and beaten others, the owner sent his beloved son, reasoning that they would respect him. The full extent of God's hope for the redemption of Israel, and therefore the full tragedy of its rejection, is expressed in the owner's intent: "they will respect him."

Watchtower
A tower at Nazareth Village. (Credit: R. Alan Culpepper)

The parable also reflects the corrupting power of human sinfulness. The wicked tenants did not start out to take the vineyard from its owner; they only wanted to keep its harvest for themselves. They did not set out to commit murder; they only beat the first servant and sent him away empty-handed. Once committed to this path, however, they were led to its consequences. Wanting to keep all the harvest for themselves, they ended up losing the vineyard. Sin is not only dynamic; it is also inherently destructive. Greed leads to rebellion, which leads to violence, which escalates to murder, which results in loss of the vineyard.

The tenants see an opportunity to secure the vineyard for themselves. The real significance of the contest over inheritance lies in the importance of the covenants with Israel and their appropriation by the early church. Isaac was the child of the covenant, Abraham's beloved son, his heir. Israel itself was considered to be God's beloved son (Isa 42:1; Jer 31:20), but the New Testament writers reflect a shift in the Christian understanding (cf. Gal 3:15-18; 4:7, 30; Rom 4:13-25; 8:14-17). Jesus will inherit the throne of David, and Gentile believers have become fellow heirs of God's promises to Israel. Therefore, one receives the inheritance not by killing the heir but by having faith in the Beloved Son.

The misguided plan of the wicked tenants leads to violence and then to loss of the vineyard. Foreshadowing the crucifixion of Jesus, the tenants of the parable kill the son and cast him out of the vineyard. Later, Pilate will hand Jesus over to the chief priests, the leaders, and the people, and they will lead Jesus out of the city to the place set aside for crucifixions. Through the parable, therefore, Jesus' death is set in the twin contexts of the rejection of the prophets and God's redemptive hope.

The wicked tenants thought they could determine the outcome of the story, but they were wrong. They could not secure the vineyard for themselves by killing the heir. The vineyard still belongs to the owner, and he will determine what will become of it—not the wicked tenants.

Earlier, the owner had pondered what he would do. Now Jesus poses a question to his audience: "What then will the owner of the vineyard do?" The owner had a decision to make: he sent his beloved son. The tenants had a decision to make: they killed him. Now the audience is drawn into the parable: what will the vineyard owner do in response to the murder of his beloved son? The question reminds the audience that the owner still holds the initiative for determining the ending of the story. Viewed historically, Jesus invites the audience,

Wine Press

An ancient wine press cut in the rocks at Nazareth Village. Grapes are mashed on the flat surface, and the juice runs off a trough in the ledge, where it can be caught. (Credit: R. Alan Culpepper)

which includes the chief priests, the scribes, and the elders (11:27; 12:12), to consider what God will do with them for their failed stewardship over Israel. Theologically, the question invites the reader to consider what God might have done in response to the crucifixion. Here we see once again the depth of God's commitment to the redemption of the vineyard.

Jesus supplies the answer with three future tense verbs, and here the future in the parable coincides with the future in the Gospel story. First, the owner will come; second, he will destroy the wicked tenants; and third, he will give the vineyard to others. The coming of the owner resonates with Old Testament prophecies of the coming of the Lord (Mal 3:1-2), Jesus' arrival in Jerusalem, and the future coming of the risen Lord. Mark says the chief priests, the scribes, and the elders got the point of the parable—they "realized that he had told this parable against them" (12:12). The authorities wanted to arrest Jesus right then, but they feared the crowd's reaction.

Such profound tragedy calls for soul-searching reflection. The parable is a mirror in which each reader can see his or her own repeated rejections of God's grace. How often, by word or by circumstance, has God called for us to respond to his claim on our lives and we have responded instead with calculations spawned by our own desires or ambitions? Where do we fit in the parable? Certainly we are not the vineyard owner or the beloved son. In a sense, we are the wicked tenants. We too have rejected God's calls to us. But the parable's effect is double-sided. We are also the others to whom the vineyard is entrusted at the end of the parable.

The parable then is a warning. Privilege and responsibility, grace and stewardship, are inescapably joined. When the tissue that binds responsibility and privilege is torn, the whole fabric of society will soon be destroyed. Grace rejected becomes condemnation. But the parable illuminates the character of God. It says that God is sovereign, and God will prevail, not human sinfulness. As Scripture, the parable speaks to each new generation. We are the tenants, but we are also the others to whom the vineyard has been given. We have received as a free gift what others killed for. By God's grace the vineyard is twice given. God would not give up on humankind. By calling it "the parable of the wicked tenants," we miss its double-sided meaning and the hope expressed in giving the vineyard to others; it is "the parable of the twice-given vineyard."[69]

But if we are the others to whom the vineyard has been given, will we be any more responsive to God's will and purposes than the first tenants? The vineyard is now in our hands.

Mark 12:13-17

There are three ways in which one may fail to follow Jesus' admonition to "render to Caesar the things that are Caesar's, and to God the things that are God's" (12:17 KJV). First, one may fail to carry out one's duties as a citizen. Second, one may fail in one's devotion and worship of God, and third, and clearly implied by this pronouncement story, one may offer to Caesar things that properly belong only to God. The third issue quite naturally attracts the lion's share of the attention of interpreters and preachers, but one should not overlook the first two, which are the two explicitly stated admonitions.

In a highly charged political atmosphere, in which he might easily have sided with those who advocated radical and militant efforts to overthrow Roman oppression, Jesus recognized the authority of the state to collect taxes. Paul would extend Jesus' line of thought by reminding the Roman Christians that they were to be subject to the state because it was established to maintain order and justice (Rom 13:1-7). Therefore, one ought to "be subject to governing authorities" (Rom 13:1) and "pay to all what is due to them" (Rom 13:7). The Pastoral Epistles "urge that supplications, prayers, intercessions, and thanksgivings be made for everyone, for kings and all who are in high positions" (1 Tim 2:1-2). First Peter balances admonitions to "accept the authority of every human institution," both that of the emperor and that of the governor, yet to "live as free people" (1 Pet 2:13-17), while Revelation calls for a radical rejection of the empire and its authority as demonic.

Without facilely attempting to harmonize Revelation's perspective on the state with those of the other New Testament witnesses, the church can and should teach the responsibilities of citizenship, the God-ordained role of the state, and the limits of the state's authority. Those who cheat on their taxes, fail to vote, or break the law fail to carry out Jesus' admonition to "render to Caesar the things that are Caesar's." The question of military service was difficult for the early church, and Christians generally refused to serve in the army during the first three centuries of the church's history. Today, the church needs to continue to serve as a prophetic voice in times of war.

The second part of the saying, the reminder to "render to God the things that are God's," echoes the Decalogue and foreshadows the extended treatment of this obligation in Jesus' response to the scribe's question regarding the first of the commandments in Mark 12:28-34. According to the commentary on the Shema, which was repeated daily by faithful Jews, "the LORD your God you shall fear; him you shall serve, and by his name alone you shall swear" (Deut 6:13). The insistence that God's claim is and should be unrivaled is consistent throughout the Scriptures. As people of faith, we worship and serve God and God alone.

This command, especially when it follows the injunction to "render to Caesar . . . ," implies that one should be careful not to confuse one's obligations or allow the claims of the state to usurp God's authority. The church has wrestled with the question of the relationship between these claims at least since Martin Luther's struggle with the church and the German princes led to the articulation of his "two-kingdoms" view of the roles of church and state.

Baptists began as a dissenting community. John Smyth (c. 1570–1612) declared, "the magistrate is not by virtue of his office to meddle with religion, or matters of conscience, to force or to compel men to this or that form of religion, or doctrine: but to leave religion free, to every man's conscience."[70] Likewise, Thomas Helwys (c. 1550–1615) demanded freedom of religion not only for those who believed as he did but for all people. [Excerpt from Thomas Helwys' Letter to the King] He insisted that all must be free to make their own religious commitments: "Let them be heretikes," he said, "Turcks, Jewes, or whatsoever, it appertynes not the earthly power to punish them in the least measure."[71]

Dissent and persecution also marked early Baptist life in the colonies. When the pilgrims came to this country, their vision was much more limited than that of Helwys. They sought freedom from the Church of England to practice their Puritan beliefs, but they gave no thought to granting others the same freedom. Roger Williams emigrated to Massachusetts in 1631 but was exiled from that colony in 1636 because of his views on religious liberty, freedom of conscience, and the rights

---

Excerpt from Thomas Helwys' Letter to the King

"Will our lord the K. being him self but a subject of Christs Kingdome, take upon him by his Kingly power to make Primates, Metropolitans, Arch Bishops, and lord Bishops to the lords in the Kingdome of Christ, and over the heritage of God! And will our lord the K. do this against the whole rule of Gods word wherein this is no one tittle to warrant our lord the K. thertoo. Will not our lord the K. be supplicated by the humble petition of his servants to examine his power & authority herein! Farr is it from the harts of us the Kings servants to move the King to depart from the least tittle of his right that belongs to his Royall Crowne & dignity: and farr be it from the King to take from Christ Jesus anie one part of that power & honor which belongs to Christ in his Kingdome.

Wee still pray our lord the King that wee may be free from suspect, for having anie thoughts of provoking evil against them of the Romish religion in regard to their profession, if they be true & faithfull subjects to the King, for wee do freely professe, that our lord the King hath no more power over their consciences then ours, and that is none at all: for our lord the King is but an earthly King, and if the Kings people be obedient & true subjects, obeying all humane lawes made by the King, our lord the King can require no more. For mens religion to God, is betwixt God and themselves; the King shall not answer for it, neither may the King be judg betwene God and man.

Let them be heretikes, Turks, Jewes, or whatsoever, it apperteynes not to the earthly power to punish them in the least measure."

H. Leon McBeth, *A Sourcebook for Baptist Heritage* (Nashville: Broadman Press, 1990), 72.

of Native Americans.[72] Although he was a Baptist only briefly, his call for religious liberty was an enduring one. He said, "government could do nothing with its whips and scourges and prisons to make men Christians," but he did not therefore discount the importance of government: "There was one thing government could do, though few governments had ever done it: government could protect the free exercise of conscience in religion."[73] Throughout the early history of Baptists, therefore, freedom was a cardinal principle they would not compromise. For the sake of freedom, Baptists fled England and then New England. In Virginia, Baptists were persecuted because they refused to submit to the state church's control of ordination and education in the eighteenth century. Baptists led in the fight for the adoption of the first amendment with its freedom of religion and anti-establishment clauses. In recent years the first amendment issues have become more and more complicated, but the principle of separation of church and state remains one of the distinguishing marks of Baptists who are faithful to their heritage and one of the most important witnesses that Baptists can offer in the public arena.

"Render to Caesar the things that are Caesar's, and to God the things that are God's"—the principle is all the more important because the image of Caesar and the image of God are not as clear, or as clearly distinguished, as they once were.

Mark 12:18-27

Many readers feel that this passage offers good news and bad news. The good news is that there is a resurrection of the dead! Because we know God to be a delivering God who preserves those who trust in God, we have every reason to hold to the hope of resurrection. (See the connections for Mark 5:21-24a, 35-43.) The bad news is that this passage seems to deny the continuation of even our closest earthly relationships and therefore creates uncertainty and distress regarding the nature of the resurrection life. Yet, when Jesus speaks of the resurrection in the parable of the rich man and Lazarus (Luke 19:19-31), the rich man recognizes Lazarus and is concerned for his five brothers. Similarly, Paul exhorts the Thessalonians to comfort one another with the hope that the dead in Christ will be raised and that they will be reunited with their loved ones at the coming of Jesus (1 Thess 4:16-18).

Obviously, none of us really knows what life after death holds for us: "For now we see through a glass, darkly" (1 Cor 13:12 KJV). Both the argument regarding angels and the promise of a feast are analogies, metaphors. We can only speak of what we have not experienced in terms of what we have. The point of Jesus' argument is primarily to affirm the power of God to transform human beings. God can provide eternal life even for those who are made of dust—we shall be like the angels. We shall also be free of sin, suffering, and bondage. For those who had been placed in marriages against their will and who found marriage a daily trial, as perhaps a woman who had been given in marriage to seven brothers, Jesus promised deliverance—in the resurrection they would be free, like the angels.

Nevertheless, arguing, as Jesus did, on the basis of the nature of God as we have experienced God's providence and blessing in this life, one would be inclined to believe that God has placed such great importance in creating and preserving faithful, loving relationships that God will not allow death to bring such relationships to an end. [Spiritual Partnership] The hope of the resurrection, then, is justifiably a hope that we shall once again share in the fellowship and love of those who have been closest to us in this life. The Hebrew hope for the future was always corporate—never radically individual. God will preserve the families of the covenant people. Therefore, one of the most common biblical images for the future is that of a banquet in which the whole family, guests and outsiders also, all celebrate together (Isa 25:6-8; Matt 8:11; Luke 13:29; 14:15-24; Rev 19:17). Clearly, there will be plenty of food in heaven! Feasting at a banquet is a metaphor also, of course, but it affirms celebration, plenty, joy, and fellowship with others in the praise of God. It is a hope we can all live for and live by.

Spiritual Partnership

"All the more shall we be bound to them [our departed spouses], because we are destined to a better estate, destined to rise to a spiritual partnership. We will recognize both our own selves and those to whom we belong. Else how shall we sing thanks to God to eternity, if there shall remain in us no sense and memory of this relationship? . . . Consequently, we who are together with God shall remain together. . . . In eternal life God will no more separate those whom he has joined together than in this life where he forbids them to be separated."

Tertullian, *On Monogamy*, 10 (*ANF* 4.67), in Thomas C. Oden and Christopher A. Hall, eds., *Ancient Christian Commentary on Scripture: New Testament II, Mark* (Downers Grove IL: InterVarsity Press, 1998), 170.

Mark 12:28-34

The genius of Judaism is that it is singularly focused on the love of God—God's covenant love (*hesed*) and the obligation of the faithful to live out their love for God. Love here is not a feeling; it is the expression of one's defining commitments. The lover devotes his whole life to his beloved, the musician to his music, the poet to her poetry. In the same way, the faithful are called to live out of the covenant knowledge of God so fully that all of life becomes an expression of their love of God. Such love encompasses one's whole person (what we do with our time, our mind, our possessions, our relationships), so that it actually comes to define who we are (our soul, our psyche, our self).

By combining the Shema with the command to love one's neighbor (Lev 19:18), Jesus underscored the principle that loving God invariably compels us to love our fellow human beings. The simplest defining statement about God is one every child raised in church learns from an early age: "God is love" (1 John 4:8, 16). One who has so experienced God's love as to be transformed by it will love others as naturally as if loving others were programmed into his or her genes. Those who are continually closed, hostile, suspicious, jealous, or resentful of others show that they have never really experienced love themselves. The seed parables, with their contrast between insignificant beginnings and bountiful harvests, express this axiom in another way. The coming of Jesus, through whom the love of God was revealed in his embrace of the outcasts, his exorcism of demons, and healing of the sick, was therefore the advent of the kingdom of God. Now it is a matter of whether those who bear Jesus' name can teach others to love before they learn to hate. The hope and expectant promise of the prophets is just this: that "the earth will be filled with the knowledge of the glory of the LORD as the waters cover the sea" (Hab 2:14).

Mark 12:35-37

The scribes had embraced the popular theology that looked forward to the coming of a Messiah who would deliver the Jews from Roman oppression and reestablish the glory of the kingdom of David. Based on indisputable biblical references, their theology fueled the self-interests of the people and the fantasies of the disciples. Others, including Judas Maccabeus, had sought to overthrow the foreign oppressors, but Jesus would not be that kind of Messiah. Instead, he chose the way of the cross—the scandal that the Anointed One of God would die as a common criminal.

The Gospel—with its call to deny oneself, take up the cross, and follow Jesus (8:34) in the way of love and self-surrender—is so radical that even those who have sought to follow Jesus have struggled with it. The sequence of this pericope in Mark is appropriate not just because it is connected to the question of the greatest command by the references to the scribes but because one who loves God with one's whole being, and loves one's neighbor as oneself, will not then be looking for God to establish a kingdom that will vindicate his or her self-interests. The question this text addresses to each of us, therefore, is whether we have pinned our hopes on Jesus because we believe he can help us achieve what we want or because through Jesus our self-seeking has been left behind and what we want has been transformed by the love of God.

Mark 12:38-40

The connections suggested by Jesus' denunciation of the scribes are clear and painful. On the one hand it speaks to everyone about the dangers of parading our piety and religion before others. T. S. Eliot has Thomas Beckett say, "The last temptation is the greatest treason: To do the right deed for the wrong reason."[74] After one has fought off the allures of other sins and devoted oneself to the worship of God, the final temptation is to worship God for ulterior motives and to be sure that others see how religious we are. The issue is motive and one's ultimate intent. Is it directed toward worshiping God and serving others, or has even what we do for others and for God been corrupted by our self-centeredness? Eduard Schweizer put it clearly: "the new principle will not permit the devout person to cherish any desire for special honor."[75]

Beyond the general warning, however, this passage speaks pointedly to the greater responsibility of those who hold positions of service and ministry. Because they have special training, because they are trusted, and because they handle holy things (the Scriptures, worship, the faith of others), when they sin the damage to others can be devastating. The community has a right to expect more from those who hold positions in the church—God does.

Mark 12:41-44

One of Jesus' most striking qualities was that he was a shrewd observer of human nature. At times he had breathtaking insight into those around him. He knew what the scribes were grumbling about (2:6-8; 3:2). He knew when a woman reached out to him in desperation (5:30-31) and what the disciples were quietly arguing about on the road (9:33-34). This scene begins with Jesus sitting in the temple, watching people come and go, making their gifts in the temple treasury. How people handle their money reveals a great deal about their character. Perhaps Jesus was fascinated by what he saw there. Some made a great show of dumping large amounts of coins into the trumpet-shaped coffers. Others hurriedly slipped their offerings into the vessels and moved on. There was no connection between the amount of the gift and the devotion of the giver.

Jesus took note of the widow who quietly gave all she had. She was one of the "little people" no one else noticed. The chief priests and scribes paid no attention to her gift. Neither, we may assume, did the disciples. Others simply looked on her with pity, but Jesus seized the moment to teach the disciples a lesson they desperately needed to learn. He had found a jewel in an unlikely cave, a ruby in a "den of robbers."

How do you measure personal worth? Investment counselors have elaborate formulas. Others determine how much they can give by how much they have. Jesus assessed what the widow was worth by how much she had left after she gave. From this perspective, her gift—and she herself—were greater than any other that day.

Little gifts can mean far more in the eyes of Jesus than we realize. Who notices the faithful janitor who cleans the sanctuary and the class-rooms every week? Who thanks the colleague who sends everyone a card on their birthday? Who rewards the neighbor who picks up litter around the neighborhood? Or the person who regularly brings canned goods for the food pantry? Jesus noticed those who served and gave of themselves in quiet and unassuming ways.

NOTES

[1] The following interpretation of the parable is adapted from my article, "Parable as Commentary: The Twice-Given Vineyard (Luke 20:9-16)," *PRSt* 26/2 (1999): 147-68.

[2] C. H. Dodd, *The Parables of the Kingdom* (New York: Charles Scribner's Sons, 1935), 124; Martin Hengel, "Das Gleichnis von den Weingärtnern Mc 12:1-12 im Lichte der Zenonpapyri und der rabbinischen Gleichnisse," *ZNW* 59 (1968): 9.

[3] Joseph A. Fitzmyer, *The Gospel According to Luke* (AB 28A; Garden City NY: Doubleday, 1985), 1280.

[4] John Nolland, *Luke 18:35–24:53* (WBC 35c; Dallas: Word, 1993), 948.

[5] See note 9 below.

[6] Adolf Jülicher, *Die Gleichnisse Jesu* (1899 rpt.: Darmstadt: Wissenschaftliche Buchgesellschaft, 1963), 385-406; Rudolf Bultmann, *The History of the Synoptic Tradition* (trans. John Marsh; New York: Harper & Row, 1963), 177, 205; W. G. Kümmel, *Promise and Fulfillment* (SBT 23; Naperville IL: Alec R. Allenson, 1957), 83.

[7] Dodd, *The Parables of the Kingdom*, 124; Joachim Jeremias, *The Parables of Jesus* (rev. ed., trans. S. H. Hooke; New York: Charles Scribner's Sons, 1963), 76.

[8] John Dominic Crossan, "The Parable of the Wicked Husbandmen," *JBL* 90 (1971): 451-65, esp. 465.

[9] W. Schrage, *Das Verhältnis des Thomas-Evangeliums zur synoptischen Tradition und zu den koptischen Evangelienübersetzungen* (BZNW 29; Berlin: A. Topelmann, 1964), 137ff.; Hengel, "Das Gleichnis von den Weingärtnern," 5; and Klyne R. Snodgrass, "The Parable of the Wicked Husbandmen: Is the Gospel of Thomas Version the Original?" *NTS* 21(1974): 142-44, who argues that elements of the parable in Thomas point to Thomas's dependence on the synoptic tradition.

[10] Bernard Brandon Scott, *Hear Then the Parable: A Commentary on the Parables of Jesus* (Minneapolis: Fortress, 1989), 245: Thomas's "so-called simplicity could result from its wisdom ideology."

[11] Robert W. Funk, Bernard Brandon Scott, and James R. Butts, *The Parables of Jesus* (Sonoma CA: Polebridge, 1988), 51.

[12] Robert W. Funk, Roy W. Hoover et al., *The Five Gospels* (New York: Macmillan, 1993), 510-11.

[13] Hengel, "Das Gleichnis von den Weingärtnern," 33 n. 106 cites Ernst Lohmeyer, *Urchristliche Mystik*, 2. Aufl. (Darmstadt: Wissenschaftliche Buchgesellschaft, 1958), 161-81; Matthew Black, "The Parables as Allegory," *BJRL* 42 (1960): 273-87; J. Duncan M. Derrett, *Law in the New Testament* (London: Darton, Longman & Todd, 1970), 286-312; Dan O. Via, Jr., *The Parables* (Philadelphia: Fortress, 1967), 134; James H. Charlesworth, *Jesus within Judaism* (New York: Doubleday, 1988), 139-56.

[14] Via, *The Parables*, 134.

[15] Derrett, *Law in the New Testament*, 292.

[16] Douglas E. Oakman, "The Countryside in Luke-Acts," in *The Social World of Luke-Acts* (ed. Jerome H. Neyrey; Peabody MA: Hendrickson, 1991), 162.

[17] See Charlesworth, *Jesus within Judaism*, 146.

[18] Martin Goodman, *The Ruling Class of Judaea: The Origins of the Jewish Revolt against Rome (A.D. 66–70)* (Cambridge: Cambridge University Press, 1987), 62.

[19] Bruce Malina and Richard L. Rohrbaugh, *Social-Science Commentary on the Synoptic Gospels* (Minneapolis: Fortress, 1992), 375-76.

[20] Goodman, *The Ruling Class of Judaea*, 67.

[21] Black, "The Parable as Allegory," 283.

[22] Jeremias, *The Parables of Jesus*, 76.

[23] Ibid.

[24] Crossan, "The Parable of the Wicked Husbandmen," 464-65.

[25] Scott, *Hear Then the Parable*, 252.

[26] Ibid., 253.

[27] Craig A. Evans, *Mark 8:27–16:20* (WBC 34B; Nashville: Thomas Nelson, 2001), 228.

[28] James D. Hester, *Paul's Concept of Inheritance: A Contribution to the Understanding of Heilsgeschichte* (SJT Occasional Papers, no. 14; Edinburgh: Oliver and Boyd, 1968), esp. viii.

[29] Quoted by Scott, *Hear Then the Parable*, 252.

[30] Ibid., 252-53.

[31] See esp. George R. Beasley-Murray, *Jesus and the Kingdom of God* (Grand Rapids: Wm. B. Eerdmans, 1986), 144-46.

[32] James D. G. Dunn, *Jesus and the Spirit* (Philadelphia: Westminster, 1975), 67, posits the centrality of Jesus' awareness of his sonship and the power of the spirit for his self-understanding: "Jesus thought of himself as God's son and as anointed by the eschatological Spirit, because in prayer he experienced God as Father and in ministry he experienced a power to heal which he could only understand as the power of the end-time. . . ." See also Dunn's discussion of this parable on pp. 35-36.

[33] See David Flusser, *Jesus* (trans. Ronald Walls; New York: Herder and Herder, 1969), 97-98.

[34] Mary Ann Tolbert, *Sowing the Gospel: Mark's World in Literary-Historical Perspective* (Minneapolis: Fortress, 1989), 232.

[35] For this perspective, and a full review of scholarship on this point, see Klyne R. Snodgrass, *The Parable of the Wicked Tenants: An Inquiry into Parable Interpretation* (WUNT 27; Tübingen: Mohr-Siebeck, 1983); Snodgrass, "Recent Research on the Parable of the

Wicked Tenants: An Assessment," *BBR* 8 (1998): 187-215; and Evans, *Mark 8:27–16:20*, 228-30.

[36] BDAG, 15.

[37] Joseph Henry Thayer, *A Greek-English Lexicon of the New Testament* (New York: American Book Company, 1886), 9; Joseph P. Louw and Eugene A. Nida, *Greek-English Lexicon of the New Testament Based on Semantic Domains* (2nd ed.; New York: United Bible Societies, 1989), 1:330.

[38] Francis J. Moloney, *The Gospel of Mark* (Peabody MA: Hendrickson, 2002), 235 n. 107.

[39] K. C. Hanson and Douglas E. Oakman, *Palestine in the Time of Jesus* (Minneapolis: Augsburg Fortress, 1998), 113, citing Gerhard E. Lenski, *Power and Privilege: A Theory of Social Stratification* (2nd ed.; Chapel Hill: University of North Carolina Press, 1984), 228.

[40] Hanson and Oakman, *Palestine in the Time of Jesus*, 116.

[41] BDAG, 542.

[42] Bruce J. Malina and Richard L. Rohrbaugh, *Social-Science Commentary on the Synoptic Gospels* (Minneapolis: Fortress, 1992), 257.

[43] BDAG, 1038.

[44] William L. Lane, *The Gospel according to Mark* (NICNT; Grand Rapids: Wm. B. Eerdmans, 1974), 424.

[45] BDAG, 821.

[46] Evans, *Mark 8:27–16:20*, 255-56.

[47] Ibid., 257.

[48] Lane, *The Gospel according to Mark*, 429-30.

[49] Ibid., 432.

[50] Joachim Jeremias, *The Prayers of Jesus* (Philadelphia: Fortress Press, 1967), 80.

[51] Mark E. Biddle, *Deuteronomy* (Smyth & Helwys Bible Commentary; Macon: Smyth & Helwys, 2003), 124-25.

[52] Lane, *The Gospel according to Mark*, 433.

[53] Edmond Jacob, "*psychē*," *TDNT* 9:626.

[54] Birger Gerhardsson, *The Ethos of the Bible* (trans. Stephen Westerholm; Philadelphia: Fortress Press, 1981), 47.

[55] Johannes Fichtner and Heinrich Greeven, "*plēsion*," *TDNT* 6:315-16.

[56] Victor Paul Furnish, *The Love Command in the New Testament* (Nashville: Abingdon Press, 1972), 62.

[57] Ibid., 29-30.

[58] C. E. B. Cranfield, *The Gospel according to St. Mark* (CGTC; Cambridge: Cambridge University Press, 1959), 379-80.

[59] Moloney, *The Gospel of Mark*, 240-41 and 241 n. 137, citing W. Grundmann, *Das Evanglium nach Markus* (6th ed.; THKNT 2; Berlin: Evangelische Verlagsanstalt, 1973), 252.

[60] Cranfield, *The Gospel according to St. Mark*, 381, who cites R. P. Gagg, "Jesus und die Davidssohnfrage: Zur Exegese von Markus 12.35-37," *Theologisches Zeitschrift* 7 (1951): 18-30.

[61] Joel Marcus, *Mark 1–8* (AB 27; New York: Doubleday, 2000), 524, who cites E. P. Sanders, *Judaism: Practice and Belief 63 BCE–66 CE* (Philadelphia: Trinity Press

International, 1992), 170-82; and D. R. Schwartz, "'Scribes and Pharisees, Hypocrites': Who are the 'Scribes' in the New Testament," in S*tudies in the Jewish Background of Christianity* (WUNT 60; Tübingen: J. C. B. Mohr, 1992), 89-101.

[62] Joachim Jeremias, *Jerusalem in the Time of Jesus* (trans. F. H. and C. H. Cave; Philadelphia: Fortress Press, 1969), 244.

[63] Harry Fleddermann, "A Warning about the Scribes (Mark 12:37b-40)," *CBQ* 44 (1982): 66-67.

[64] Jeremias, *Jerusalem in the Time of Jesus*, 244.

[65] Joseph A. Fitzmyer, *The Gospel according to Luke X-XXIV* (AB 28A; Garden City NY: Doubleday, 1985), 1318.

[66] This interpretation was advanced by Addison G. Wright, "The Widow's Mites: Praise or Lament?" *CBQ* 44 (1982): 256-65, and has been accepted by Fitzmyer, *The Gospel according to Luke X-XXIV*, 1320-21, and Evans, *Mark 8:27–16:20*, 282.

[67] John W. Betlyon, "Coinage," *ABD* 1:1086; cf. Emil Schürer, *The History of the Jewish People in the Age of Jesus Christ* (rev. Geza Vermes et al.; Edinburgh: T. & T. Clark, 1979), 2:66.

[68] Moloney, *The Gospel of Mark*, 247.

[69] See "The Gospel of Luke," *NIB* 9:384.

[70] H. Leon McBeth, *The Baptist Heritage* (Nashville: Broadman Press, 1987), 102.

[71] Ibid., 103.

[72] Bill J. Leonard, "What Can the Baptist Tradition Contribute to Christian Higher Education?" unpublished manuscript, p. 5.

[73] Edmund S. Morgan, quoted by Harold Bloom, *The American Religion: The Emergence of the Post-Christian Nation* (New York: Simon & Schuster, 1992), 192.

[74] T. S. Eliot, "Murder in the Cathedral," in *The Complete Poems and Plays, 1909–1950* (New York: Harcourt, Brace, & World, 1971), 196.

[75] Eduard Schweizer, *The Good News according to Mark* (trans. Donald H. Madvig; Atlanta: John Knox Press, 1970), 258.

THE DESTRUCTION OF JERUSALEM AND THE COMING OF THE SON OF MAN

Mark 13:1-37

Mark 11–12 deal with Jesus' teachings in the temple and his debates with the authorities. As a sign of the true meaning of the "cleansing of the temple," Mark sandwiched his account of that event between Jesus' cursing of the fig tree and the discovery of the tree withered to the root (11:12-14, 20-21). Mark's account of Jesus' teaching in the temple ends with the denunciation of the scribes for devouring the widows' houses (12:38-40) and his observation of the widow putting all she had into the temple coffers (12:41-44). Building on Jesus' prophetic condemnation of the temple in the preceding chapters, Mark 13 warns of the deceptions that will accompany the destruction of the temple and the city, and looks on to the coming of the Son of Man.

Mark 13 is one of the most debated chapters in the New Testament. Virtually every aspect of it has troubled interpreters: its genre—apocalyptic discourse, admonitions, or farewell discourse; its authenticity—a prophetic pronouncement from Jesus or a *vaticinium ex eventu* (declaration after the fact); its evidence for the date of the Gospel—before or after the destruction of the city in AD 70; and the extent of Mark's role in the composition of the chapter—light editing of a preexistent unit of tradition or composition of the discourse from isolated sayings and prophetic motifs.

The discourse in Mark 13 is "eschatological" or "apocalyptic" in the sense that it deals with the signs and events that will signal the coming of the Son of Man and the end times. The intent of the discourse, however, might better be termed "anti-apocalyptic" because it repeatedly warns against mistaking events, whether ordinary (rumors of war, famines, or persecution) or cataclysmic (the desolating sacrilege and the destruction of the temple), as signs of the end. Building on Jesus' prophetic condemnation of the temple in Mark 11 and 12, the discourse affirms that it will soon be destroyed. Its destruction should be anticipated and understood as God's judgment on its corruption. Believers should not be misled by these terrible events, by the persecution they would suffer, or by the false prophets who would arise at that time. The discourse therefore shares some of the characteristics of a "farewell discourse." The Bible contains farewell discourses attributed to patriarchs and prophets, Jesus and the apostles: Jacob (Gen 49), Moses (Deut 33), Joshua (Josh 23), Samuel (1 Sam 12), Jesus (John 14–17), Paul (Acts 20:17-35; 2 Tim), and Peter (2 Pet). Later, the tradition of farewell discourses evolved into a collection of the "Testaments of the Twelve Patriarchs."[1] Characteristically, the farewell discourses warn the coming generation(s) of the trials they will face and exhort them to be faithful to God by maintaining the covenant or the traditions they have received. Accordingly, William Lane observes that "the primary function of Ch. 13 is not to disclose esoteric information but to promote faith and obedience in a time of distress and upheaval. With profound pastoral concern, Jesus prepared his disciples and the Church for a future period which would entail both persecution and mission."[2] This mix of warning and exhortation is clearly evident in the structure of the discourse. (See below [The Structure of Mark 13].) The reader may hear first the predictions: the temple will be destroyed (v. 2), false prophets will arise (vv. 5-6, 21-22), there will be wars and famines (vv. 7-8), Jesus' followers will be betrayed by family members, arrested, and put on trial (vv. 9-13), the desolating sacrilege will be set up in the temple (v. 14), the suffering will be great (vv. 17-20), and then the Son of Man will come to gather the elect (vv. 24-27). Interlaced with these predictions, however, is a steady refrain of exhortation and encouragement: "Beware that no one leads you astray" (v. 5), "do not be alarmed" (v. 7), "as for yourselves, beware" (v. 9), "the good news must first be proclaimed to all nations" (v. 10), "do not worry beforehand what you are to say; but say whatever is given to you at that time" (v. 11), "the one who endures to the end will be saved," (v. 13), "flee to the mountains," (v. 14), do not "go down or enter the house" and do not "turn back" (vv. 15-16), "pray that it may not be in winter" (v. 18), "do not believe it" (v. 21), "be alert" (v. 23), "from the fig tree learn its lesson" (v. 28), "know that he is near" (v. 29), "beware, keep alert" (v. 33), "therefore, keep awake" (v. 35), "and what I say to you I say to all: Keep awake" (v. 37). The tone is urgent; the intent is to safeguard and encourage.

The sources and composition of the discourse are also sharply debated. William Lane contends that "Mark received this discourse pre-formed, as the teaching of Jesus, and that he incorporated it into his Gospel without substantial alteration."[3] George Beasley-Murray, who also takes a conservative approach to such questions and spent much of his career studying this chapter, concludes, "it is difficult for me not to acknowledge Mark's hand throughout the length of the discourse. 'Conservative redactor' he may have been, but the whole discourse bears the imprint of his style."[4] The stages in the composition of Mark 13 will continue to be debated, but in general one might postulate an initial question and answer such as we find in v. 2, vv. 3-4, and vv. 14-20. Individual units of the tradition circulated independently, as their parallel but different formulations in Q attest. We may compare, for example, Luke 12:11-12 with Mark 13:9 and 11, which split the Q saying into two parts. Similarly, the conclusion of the discourse is composed of parables of the fig tree (13:28) and the doorkeeper (13:34) that have been compiled with independent sayings (vv. 30, 31, 32) and exhortations that may have been added by Mark (vv. 29, 33, 35-36). Catchwords help to link together the traditional sayings and the exhortations ("know" in vv. 28, 29, 32, 33, 35; "keep alert/awake" in vv. 33, 35, 37), lending continuity and a sense of unity to the whole.

Mark 13 is generally seen as the key to the date and social location of the Gospel. The destruction of the temple and the persecution of believers loom as dominant concerns. Evidence of the persecution of the early Christians in Rome during the reign of Nero is well known (see the introduction and [Nero's Persecution of Christians]) and favors a Roman setting over Galilee or Syria. More difficult is the question of chronology. Nevertheless, it is easier to explain the differences between Josephus's account of the destruction of Jerusalem and Mark 13, and the absence of significant events, such as the burning of the city, on the assumption that Mark was written during the war of AD 66–70, and probably in 68 or 69. Nothing in the discourse demands a date after 70.[5]

COMMENTARY

Introduction: The Disciples' Questions, 13:1-4

The introduction of a new section of the Gospel is signaled by Jesus' movement away from the temple for the first time since Mark 11:27, the absence (at least temporarily) of the temple authorities, the introduction of a new set of interlocutors—the four disciples, and the setting—on the Mount of Olives. Mark 13:1-4 is the narrative introduction to the discourse in the rest of the chapter, but this introduction itself contains two parallel parts (vv. 1-2 and vv. 3-4):

Jesus' movement out of the temple (a)
   The unnamed disciple's comment (b)
   Jesus' response (c)

Jesus' movement to the Mount of Olives (a')
The four disciples' questions (b')

Jesus' response to their questions (c') will comprise the rest of the chapter. Verses 3-4 require vv. 1 and 2, however, because without them the antecedent of "these things" in v. 4 would be unclear.

The Temple Stones
A Jewish man praying at the Western Wall. Note the size of the stones and their carefully chiseled borders.
(Credit: R. Alan Culpepper)

Mark uses the verb (*ekporeuomai*) in verse 1 to note Jesus' movements often enough (see 10:17, 46; 11:19) that it is characteristic of his style. The Greek word *hieron* (11:11, 15, 16, 27; 12:35; 13:1, 3; 14:49) generally denotes the temple complex, while *naos* (14:58; 15:29, 38) means the sanctuary. It is also characteristic of Mark that those who address Jesus as teacher, especially the disciples, do not understand what they are talking about or asking for (see esp. 4:38; 9:38; 10:17, 20, 35; 12:14, 19). The unnamed disciple's comment does not really call for a response. It would have been the typical reaction of visitors to Jerusalem to marvel at the construction of the temple: "What large stones, and what large buildings" (13:1). The temple was one of the architectural wonders of the ancient world, and its stones were carefully prepared with borders that can still be seen on the portions of its walls that remain intact.

Josephus records that "the Temple was built of hard, white stones, each of which was about 25 cubits in length, 8 in height and 12 in width" (*Ant.* 15.392).[6] Located on the highest point in Jerusalem, it dazzled visitors and pilgrims as they approached the ancient city.

Jesus surprises the unnamed disciple by asking a question that adds dramatic emphasis to the pronouncement that follows (see [Heuristic Questions]). As in Mark 2:11, 20; 3:5, 34; 7:20; 10:39-40, Jesus follows the question with a categorical declaration or a command. In this instance Jesus' pronouncement prophesies the complete destruction of the temple. The inclusion of two double negatives in his pronouncement adds further emphasis to it. Translating the double negative as "certainly," one might render the statement in English as "Certainly not one stone will be left here upon another that will not certainly be cast down." Jesus uses the same vivid expression in Luke 19:44, where he weeps over Jerusalem.[7] Ironically, the idiom "stone upon stone" occurs in Haggai's call for the Jews to rebuild the temple (Hag 2:15). Jesus' words echo prophetic warnings about the destruction of the temple that can be traced to the Old Testament (Amos 9:1 [the temple at

Bethel]; Mic 3:12; Jer 7:14; 26:6, 18), but others too had prophesied the destruction of the temple.[8] Josephus himself claimed to have foreseen its destruction:

> But as . . . Josephus overheard the threats of the hostile crowd, suddenly there came back into his mind those nightly dreams, in which God had foretold to him the impending fate of the Jews and the destinies of the Roman sovereigns. . . . he was not ignorant of the prophecies in the sacred books. (*J. W.* 3.351-52, LCL 2:675)

The Mount of Olives offered a vantage point from which Jesus and the disciples could view the temple and the city of Jerusalem, and Mark notes that it lies "opposite the temple" (13:3). The setting is significant for the discourse that follows, however, because of the reference to the Mount of Olives in Zechariah 14:4-5. Zechariah 12–14 foretells the coming of the day of the Lord, when the Lord will make Jerusalem "a cup of reeling . . . in the siege against Jerusalem" (Zech 12:2), when the Lord will "gather all the nations against Jerusalem to battle, and the city shall be taken" (Zech 14:2). "On that day" (a motif that occurs repeatedly in Zech 12–14) the Lord will stand on the Mount of Olives, and the mountain shall be split in two (Zech 14:4-5). Similarly, Ezekiel saw the glory of God on the mountain east of the city (Ezek 11:23; cf. 43:2).

Sitting was the normal posture for a teacher,[9] and Jesus sat to teach the disciples (see 4:1; 9:35; 12:41). This is the only occasion on which Mark records the presence of the group of four disciples, and Mark is the only Gospel that provides a list of names at this point. They are the first four who were called (1:16-20), but Andrew is listed last, not following Peter as one would expect if the list were meant to serve as a reference to the calling of the disciples. Instead, his name follows the list of the three disciples who were with Jesus at the raising of Jairus's daughter and at the transfiguration, and who will be with Jesus in Gethsemane (5:37; 9:2; 14:33). The four names occur in the same order in Mark's list of the Twelve (3:16-18).[10]

The note that the disciples asked Jesus "privately" (*kat' idian*) signals that this is another of the scenes of private teaching that Mark intersperses throughout the Gospel (4:10-12, 34; 7:17-23; 9:2, 28; 10:10; see [Private Teaching]). The disciples ask the questions that connect the discourse that follows with the narrative. Then, they do not speak again in the rest of the chapter. Interpreters find in v. 4 one, two, or three questions. William L. Lane treats v. 4 as "a single question expressed in two parallel clauses."[11] Most interpreters treat the two clauses as separate questions, but Francis J. Moloney finds three questions in the verse by dividing the latter clause into two separate questions: a description of the signs and an indication of the time when "all these things" will be accomplished.[12]

Jesus has said that the temple would be utterly destroyed. The disciples, therefore, ask when "these things" will occur and what will be the signs when "all these things" will come about. These terms will all recur later in the discourse (see esp. vv. 29, 30, and 35).[13] The repetition of this phrase and the addition of "all" may signal the two parts of Jesus' response to their questions: the false signs that will accompany the destruction of the temple and the cosmic signs that will accompany the coming of the Son of Man. This repetition, therefore, is the reader's first clue that while the discourse that follows responds to the question of signs of the coming destruction of the temple, it "proceeds on the assumption that the really important event is not the temple's ruin but the coming of the Son of man."[14]

George Beasley-Murray perceptively notes that "the question 'when' is not intended to extricate a date, but a knowledge of events that will warn the faithful when the catastrophe may be expected."[15] Paul commented that seeking signs was characteristic of the Jews (1 Cor 1:22). The Pharisees had asked Jesus for a sign, but he responded that no sign would be given to that generation (8:11-12). Jewish and early Christian apocalyptic literature include two motifs that stand in tension with one another: the description of signs that will precede the events of the end time (2 Thess 2:1-12) and the warning that the end will come suddenly and unexpectedly (1 Thess 5:2-3). Jesus responds to the disciples' desire to know the time and the sign of the end time by warning them first about the false signs that will mislead others (vv. 5-23). The "desolating sacrilege" will be a sign for them to flee from Jerusalem (v. 14), but the main emphasis of the first part of the discourse is that they should not be misled by the social chaos and apocalyptic speculation that will accompany the destruction of Jerusalem. Jesus gives no "sign" of the destruction of the temple. In a sense all of Mark 11–12 has been his interpretation of the signs of God's coming judgment on it and on the religious leaders. Jesus interprets the coming destruction not as the result of Roman imperialism but as God's judgment. His concern, however, is that his followers in Mark's time not misinterpret these events as a sign that the coming of the Son of Man was at hand. Jesus' message throughout the Gospel is that "the kingdom of God is at hand" (1:15), but the destruction of Jerusalem is not the sign that the kingdom was coming. Jesus himself and his death and resurrection were the signs that the kingdom had come and that its full manifestation was imminent. Verses 24-27 describe the unmistakable cosmic signs that will accompany the coming of the Son of Man, and vv. 28-37 offer parables and admonitions to watch and be ready because "about that day or hour no one knows" (13:32). Jesus' response to the disciples' questions about signs, therefore, is a warning not to be misled by events others see as signs but to be vigilant and keep awake because the coming of the Son of Man will be sudden.

Misleading Signs that Will Accompany the Fall of Jerusalem, 13:5-23

In this section Jesus warns the disciples about the perils of the period of the Jewish revolt and the destruction of Jerusalem (AD 66–70). During this time of social upheaval and distress both in Judea and in Rome, many would be misled into thinking that the end was at hand. Mark 13, therefore, offers words from the tradition of Jesus' sayings as admonitions to the Markan community at the time of the writing of the Gospel. Verses 5-8 warn of the coming of false prophets and events that were often interpreted as having apocalyptic meaning: wars, earthquakes, and famines. Verses 9-13 warn of the coming persecution of Jesus' followers. Verses 14-23 identify the "desolating sacrilege" as the signal that the believers should flee from Jerusalem, and warn of the horrors that will accompany its destruction.

The evangelist marks the beginning of Jesus' discourse with the note that "Jesus began to say to them" (v. 5), a construction that is common in Mark (see esp. 4:1; 6:2, 34; 8:31; 12:1). The disciples had remarked, "Look . . ." (13:1), and Jesus had responded, "Do you see (*blepeis*) . . . ?" (13:2). Now, "Beware" (*blepete*) becomes the watchword of the discourse (vv. 9, 23, 33). The first warning concerns those who would seek to deceive or mislead (*planaō*). In the New Testament this verb often carries the transferred sense of leading to religious error, and it was used in connection with eschatology.[16] Jesus charged that the Sadducees were misled (12:24, 27). Elsewhere some of the people charged that Jesus himself was misleading the crowd (John 7:12). Paul warns the Corinthians not to be misled (1 Cor 6:9; 15:33; cf. Gal 6:7; 2 Tim 3:13). The Johannine elder warns his community not to be misled by false prophets (1 John 1:8; 2:26; 3:7), and the Seer uses the term in connection with the deceptions of the end time (Rev 2:20; 12:6; 13:14; 18:23; 19:20; 20:3, 8, 10).

"Many" false prophets were expected in the last days (see 2 Tim 4:3-4; 2 Pet 2:1-3; 1 John 2:18; 4:1; 2 John 7). Those who will mislead are identified in two ways: they will "come in my name," and they will say "I am he!" (v. 6). While the sense of these descriptions is clear enough, both are open to multiple interpretations. The Old Testament prophets ministered and spoke in the name of the Lord (Deut 18:5, 7, 20, 22). To "come in my name" may mean that they will come as his emissaries, sent by him and carrying his authority (see the discussion of 9:37-39, 41 above; cf. 1 Sam 25:9, where David's men act in his name).

False Messiahs

Josephus describes the activities of the following false prophets, false messiahs, and revolutionary leaders in Galilee and Judea:

• Judas, son of the "brigand-chief" Hezekiah; ambitious "for royal rank" (*Ant.* 17.271–72; *J.W.* 2.56; Acts 5:37)
• Simon of Perea, "he was bold enough to place the diadem on his head . . . he was himself also proclaimed king . . . in their madness" (*Ant.* 17.273–76; *J.W.* 2.57–59)
• Athronges the Shepherd of Judea, "remarkable for his great stature and feats of strength. This man had the temerity to aspire to the kingship" (*Ant.* 17.278–84; *J.W.* 2.60–65)
• Theudas, "persuaded the majority of the masses to . . . follow him to the Jordan River. He stated he was a prophet." (*Ant.* 20.97–98; Acts 5:36)
• An Egyptian false prophet, "collected a following of about thirty thousand dupes, and led them . . . to the mount called the mount of Olives. From there he proposed to force an entrance into Jerusalem." (Ant. 20.169–70; *J.W.* 2.261–63)
• Menahem son of Judas of Galilee, plundered Herod's armory at Masada and "returned like a veritable king to Jerusalem, became the leader of the revolution" (*J.W.* 2.433–48)
• John of Gischala, "carried in his breast a dire passion for despotic power" (*J.W.* 4.106–11, 126–28, 208, passim)
• Simon bar-Giora, "by proclaiming liberty for slaves and rewards for the free, he gathered around him the villains from every quarter" (*J.W.* 4.503–44, 556–65, passim)

Craig A. Evans, *Mark 8:2–16:20* (WBC 34B; Nashville: Thomas Nelson, 2001), 306; David Rhoads, *Israel in Revolution* (Philadelphia: Fortress, 1976).

Alternatively, it may mean that the deceivers will claim not that they have been sent by Jesus but that they have the authority that properly belongs to Jesus.[17] Similarly, the deceivers' claim, "I am he" may mean (1) that they will claim to be Jesus, (2) that they will act as though there were no god (cf. Isa 47:8, 10), or more likely (3) they will claim to be messiahs, acting in the authority of the divine name (Exod 3:14; see 6:50 above). Matthew interprets it in the latter sense: "For many will come in my name, saying, 'I am the Messiah'" (24:5). Mark 13:5-6 are closely related to vv. 21-22, where the deceivers are explicitly called false messiahs and false prophets. In the decades preceding the Jewish revolt, there was a succession of messianic pretenders. [False Messiahs]

Verse 7 shifts from the deceivers who will come to the historical events that will be misinterpreted as apocalyptic signs: wars, earthquakes, and famines. The description of the same three occurrences in Revelation 6 and in various Old Testament passages probably indicates that they were "a stock list of disasters and travails"[18]—"sword, famine, and pestilence" (Jer 14:12; 24:10; 32:24; Ezek 14:21; Bar 2:25). Then as now, anxiety and apocalyptic speculation accompanied war (Isa 17:14; 19:2; Jer 4:16-26; 51:46; Dan 11:44; Joel 2:1-11; Nah 2:11; *2 Bar.* 27:3, 5). Jeremiah 51:46 offers a close parallel: "Do not be fainthearted or fearful at the rumors heard in the land—one year one rumor comes, the next year another, rumors of violence in the land and of ruler against ruler."

In a culture in which news traveled by word of mouth, and especially in anxious times, rumors were rampant and excitement ran high, but people never knew which rumors were reliable.[19] There were no great wars during the years preceding the Jewish revolt, but there were constant uprisings, and the period of the war itself, following the death of Nero, was one of the most unsettled periods in Rome's history. Josephus says "every quarter of the world beneath their [the Romans'] sway was seething and quivering with excitement" (*J. W.* 7.79, LCL 3:529). Three would-be emperors (Galba, Otho, and Vitellius) claimed and lost the throne in a matter of months

(AD 68–69) before the senate recalled Vespasian from the war in Judea to bring order to Rome. The mention of war would therefore have been heard by Mark's community as far more than just an item in a traditional list of travails. [War as a Sign of the End]

Jesus' admonition for the community is "do not be alarmed" (13:7). The same verb occurs in a similar context in 2 Thessalonians 2:2. William Lane notes that in Mark 13 imperative exhortations are normally followed by indicative statements of consolation. Supporting this pattern, he cites Lloyd Gaston's observation regarding the role of *gar* ("for") in this chapter:

> The importance of this word would have been noticed long ago were it not for the unfortunate fact that it is missing in several places from the Nestle text, even though it is required by a synoptic comparison and is well attested. *Gar* appears at the beginning of v. 6, 7b, 8, 9b, 11b, 19, 22, 33, and 35. With the exception, therefore, of the longer sections 14-18 and 24-27, every apocalyptic element is attached to its context by a *gar*.[20]

War as a Sign of the End

"As to wars, when has the earth not been scourged by them at different periods and places? To pass over remote history, when the barbarians were everywhere invading Roman provinces in the reign of Gallienus [AD 260–268], how many of our brothers who were then alive do we think could have believed that the end was near, since this happened long after the ascension of the Lord! Thus, we do not know what the nature of those signs will be when the end is really near at hand."

Augustine, *Letters*, 199 to Hesychius 35, in Thomas C. Oden and Christopher A. Hall, eds., *Ancient Christian Commentary on Scripture: New Testament II, Mark* (Downers Grove IL: InterVarsity Press, 1998), 181–82.

The Structure of Mark 13

Exhortation	Explanation
v. 5 "Beware . . ."	v. 6 "[For] Many will come . . ."
v. 7a "Do not be alarmed"	v. 7b "[For] This must take place . . ." v. 8 "For nation will rise against nation . . ."
v. 9 "Beware"	v. 9b "For they will hand you over to councils"
v. 11 "Do not worry beforehand about what you are to say"	v. 11b "For it is not you who speak, but the Holy Spirit."
v. 14 "Flee to the mountains"	
v. 18 "Pray that it may not be in winter"	v. 19 "For in those days there will be suffering . . ."
v. 21 "Do not believe it."	v. 22 "For false messiahs and false prophets will appear . . ."
v. 23 "But be alert"	v. 23 "[Behold] I have already told you everything."
v. 33 "Beware, keep alert"	v. 33 "For you do not know when the time will come."
v. 35 "Therefore, keep awake"	v. 35 "For you do not know when the master of the house will come."
v. 37 "Keep awake"	

Whether the word *gar* originally stood in the text or not, the fact that some manuscripts include it confirms that the text develops a pattern of exhortation followed by consolation or explanation. [The Structure of Mark 13]

The explanation that follows the admonition not to be alarmed about wars is that these things "must" take place. This expression occurs elsewhere in Mark (8:31; 9:11; 13:10, 14) and in other New Testament writings (e.g., Matt 16:21; 26:54; Luke 2:49; 4:43; 13:16, 33; 19:5; John 3:14; 4:4; 20:9) to convey the conviction of divine necessity: God is in control of history regardless of the travails the community is experiencing, and God is leading all things to a purposeful end. History is neither cyclical nor random; it has both its beginning and end in God. The suffering community can therefore take hope that even the present travail does not threaten the fulfillment of God's divine purpose, which will lead to the coming of the Son of Man and the fulfillment of the kingdom of God. The Greek word *telos* conveys the fulfillment of purpose, which in the New Testament means God's foreordained end of all things (1 Cor 15:24; 1 Pet 4:7; Rev 21:6; 22:13).

Wars do not mean that the end is at hand. Mark's idiom, "Nation will rise against nation, and kingdom against kingdom" (13:8), echoes Isaiah 19:2, "Egyptians against Egyptians . . . neighbor against neighbor, city against city, kingdom against kingdom" (cf. 2 Chr 15:6; *4 Ezra* 13:31; 15:15). Similarly, earthquakes do not signal that the end is at hand, even though the prophets predicted that when the Lord came, striding upon the mountains, they would break under his feet (Judg 5:4-5; Pss 18:7; 68:8; 77:18; 114:3-7; Isa 13:13; 24:18-20; 29:6; 64:1, 3; Mic 1:3-4; Hab 3:6, 10; Zech 14:4; Rev 6:12, 14; cf. *2 Bar.* 27:2, 7; *4 Ezra* 6:13-15; 9:3; *T. Mos.* 10:4). [Earthquakes]

In antiquity famines were a constant threat to human life, and war and calamities such as earthquakes could disrupt agriculture, food production, and trade

Earthquakes

Israel, Syria, Greece, and Italy all lie in an active earthquake zone. Major earthquakes in this region during the New Testament period include the following:

Date	Place	Documentation
31 BC	Galilee, Qumran	Josephus, *Ant.* 15.5.2
AD 30 or 33	Jerusalem	Matt 27:54; 28:2
AD 49	Philippi	Acts 16:26
AD 60	Laodicea, Colossae (?)	
AD 63	Achaea, Macedonia	Tacitus, *Annals* 14.27
AD 68	Pompeii	Tacitus, *Annals* 15.22
AD 68	Rome	Dio Cassius, *Roman History* 63.28.1
AD 68	Rome	
	Marrucini (east coast of central Italy)	Suetonius, *Galba* 18.1 Pliny the Elder, *Natural History* 2.199

D. H. Kallner Amiran, "A Revised Earthquake-Catalogue of Palestine," *IEJ* 1 (1950–51): 223–46; *IEJ* 2 (1952): 48–62; Kenneth W. Russell, "The Earthquake Chronology of Palestine and Northwest Arabia from the 2nd through the Mid-8th Century A.D.," *BASOR* 260 (Nov 1985): 37–59; Martin Hengel, *Studies in the Gospel of Mark* (Philadelphia: Fortress, 1985), 23, 132 n. 129.

resulting in great uncertainty and suffering. Famines were therefore included among the apocalyptic signs by Old Testament prophets (Isa 14:30; Jer 11:22; 18:21; 24:10; 32:24; Ezek 5:16-17; Amos 4:6-9; *2 Bar.* 27:6), but famines persisted in the New Testament period also. [Famines in Judea]

Famines in Judea

Date	Documentation
25–24 BC	Josephus, *Ant.* 15.299-316
Fourth year of the	Orosius, *History* 7.6
reign of Claudius	
AD 46–47	Acts 11:28-30; cf. Acts 4:35;
	6:1; Gal 2:10; Josephus *Ant.*
	20.51–53, 101

Rome also had famines during the reign of Claudius (AD 41–54; Suetonius, *Claudius* 18.2; Tacitus, *Annals* 12.43; Dio Cassius, *Roman History* 60.11; Orosius, *History* 7.6).

Because the terrible, present sufferings would lead to God's redemptive intervention, they would soon be forgotten in the joy of the day of the Lord. One of the common motifs of the prophets was therefore the description of the present sufferings as birth pangs, either because of their intensity or their transience (Isa 13:8; 21:3; 26:17; 66:8-9; Jer 4:31; 6:24; 13:21; 22:23; Hos 13:13; Mic 4:9-10; see also 1QH 3.7-12; 1 Thess 5:3). The Gospel of John employs the same motif when it speaks of the travail of the community as "a little while" (John 14:19; 16:16-19). Jesus warns the disciples that "these things"—wars, earthquakes, and famines are not signs that the end is at hand: they are just the beginning of their travail!

Verse 9 shifts from warning the disciples to beware of the false prophets (vv. 5-6) to a warning to prepare themselves for persecution. Verses 9 and 11 are the Markan parallel to the Q saying in Luke 12:11-12. However one reconstructs the history of this saying, it is clear that Mark has inserted v. 10 in this context.[21] Mark has subtly developed the pattern of preaching, arrest, martyrdom. John the Baptist preached and was "handed over" (1:4-8, 14-15; 6:14-29). Jesus will soon be "handed over" (1:14-15; 8:31; 9:31; 10:32-34). Now it becomes clear that the disciples too will be "handed over" for their preaching (1:16-20; 6:7-13; 8:34-35; 10:29-30, 38-39). They will share Jesus' fate. In the time of persecution, the disciples should steel themselves to be ready to carry out their mission of bearing witness to the gospel. Mark 13, therefore, also serves as an introduction to the Passion Narrative that follows, where some of the same terms and themes recur: "hand you over" (*paradidōmi*: 14:10, 11, 18, 21, 41, 42, 44; 15:1, 10, 15), "councils" (*synedria*: 14:55; 15:1).

The early believers would be persecuted by both Jewish (councils and synagogues) and Gentile authorities (governors and kings). The book of Acts records just such experiences of persecution, and Paul reports, "Five times I have received from the Jews the forty lashes minus one. Three times I was beaten with rods. Once I received a stoning" (2 Cor 11:24-25; cf. Acts 5:40; 16:19-23, 37). [Forty Lashes Less One] In order to

Forty Lashes Less One

The Deuteronomic law prescribes a maximum of forty lashes: "If the one in the wrong deserves to be flogged, the judge shall make that person lie down and be beaten in his presence with the number of lashes proportionate to the offense. Forty lashes may be given" (Deut 25:2-3). Praising the virtues of the Jewish laws, Josephus adds: "But let him who acts contrary to these precepts receive forty stripes save one from the public lash. . . ." (*Ant.* 4.238, LCL 4:589–91).

An entire tractate of the *Mishnah* is devoted to "stripes." It includes the following prescriptions:

"How many stripes do they inflict on a man? Forty save one, for it is written, *By number forty*; [that is to say] a number near to forty. . . When they estimate the number of stripes that he can bear, it must be a number divisible by three. . . . How do they scourge him? They bind his hands to a pillar on either side, and the minister of the synagogue lays hold on his garments . . . so that he bares his chest. A stone is set down behind him on which the minister of the synagogue stands with a strap of calf-hide in his hand, doubled and re-doubled. . . . He gives him one-third of the stripes in front and two-thirds behind; and he may not

strike him when he is standing or when he is sitting, but only when he is bending low, for it is written, *The judge shall cause him to lie down.* And he that smites, smites with his one hand with all his might. . . . If he dies under his hand, the scourger is not culpable. But if he gave him one stripe too many and he died, he must escape into exile because of him." (*m. Makkoth* 3.10–14; Danby, *The Mishnah*, 407–08).

Women as well as men were subject to such beatings.

Roman beatings could be even more severe: "Acc. to Roman law the *verberatio* always accompanied a capital sentence, *condemnation ad metalla*, and other degrading punishments with the loss of freedom and civil rights. In many cases it was itself fatal. It usually preceded crucifixion. It was so terrible that even Domitian was horrified by it. Women were exempted. We know little about the details. The number of strokes was not prescribed. It continued until the flesh hung down in bloody shreds. Slaves administered it, and the condemned person was tied to a pillar." (Carl Schneider, "*mastigoō*," *TDNT* 4:517)

inflict a lashing, three (or twenty-three) judges were required according to later Jewish law (*m. Sanhedrin* 1.2). The reference to "councils" (*synedria*) in v. 9 refers generally to local courts or councils. [Councils] The pattern of Paul's mission in Acts reveals that he always made contact with the synagogue in every new city or town he entered (Acts 13:5, 14; 14:1; 17:1-2, 10, 17; 18:4, 19, 26; 19:8), and he often met opposition there. [Synagogues] In this verse, to "stand before" is an idiom meaning to be brought to trial or to be called to answer charges before an official (see Acts 24:20; 25:10). John the Baptist was imprisoned by Herod Antipas (6:14-29). Jesus was interrogated by the Jewish authorities (14:53-65) before being tried by Pilate, the Roman prefect or governor (15:1-15). The book of Acts records that Paul was tried before the Sanhedrin (Acts 22:30-23:10), before governors (Felix and Festus—Acts 24:10-27; 25:1-12; and 26:24-32), and before King Agrippa (Acts 25:23–26:32) before appealing his case to Caesar.

Like Paul, the disciples would be brought to trial precisely because they were preaching the gospel of Jesus Christ. Mark 13:9-13 is closely connected to 8:34–9:1.[22] Mark 8:35 promises salvation to those who lose their lives "for my sake and for the sake of the gospel" (*heneken emou kai tou euangeliou*), and the same phrase recurs in 10:29. The reference to persecution "because of me" (*heneken emou*) in 13:9 prepares the way, therefore, for the command to preach the gospel (*to euange-*

Councils

The role of the courts in Judea in the period before AD 70 is interpreted variously depending on which sources one follows. Josephus (*J.W.* 1.537; 2.25; 6.243; *Ant.* 14.167–80; 20.216–17) and the New Testament (Acts 4-6; esp. 5:34; 22:30; 23:6) use "Sanhedrin" to refer to various legislative, judicial, and advisory bodies, some formal, some ad hoc. The Roman governor Gabinius (57–55 BC) divided Palestine into five "sanhedrins" (Josephus, *Ant.* 14.91). Later, under the Roman procurators, the Sanhedrin condemned James, the brother of Jesus to death (*Ant.* 20.200). After the destruction of Jerusalem, the Sanhedrin was reconstituted at Jamnia, but it could no longer exercise political functions. Anthony J. Saldarini, summarizes the court system envisioned by the rabbinic sources as follows:

"*M. Sahendrin* (1.1–6; 3:1) defines the competences of courts with three, twenty-three, and seventy-one judges. The rabbis envisioned courts in every city and a Sanhedrin (of twenty-three) with power to try capital cases in any city with 120 men. In Jerusalem, according to the mishnaic system, there were three courts at the temple . . . (*m. Sanh.* 11.2). The center of the system was the Great Court of seventy-one members which met in the Chamber of Hewn Stone in Jerusalem. It tried tribes, false prophets, and high priests; sent people forth to voluntary wars; approved additions to Jerusalem and the temple; set up tribal sanhedrins; and declared cities apostate (*m. Sanh.* 1.5-6). It was also the final court of appeals concerning legitimacy of laws (11.2), and it executed rebellious elders (11.4). It had to be composed of Israelites with pure descent (*m. Qidd.* 4.5) and in the rabbinic ideal all were scholars (*m. Sanh.* 4.4)."

This system was an ideal, and clearly does not describe the situation in pre-70 Judea or Galilee. Nevertheless, while its membership and powers are not clear, a central council of priests and elders, Pharisees and Sadducees, functioned in Jerusalem during this period.

Anthony J. Saldarini, "Sanhedrin," *ABD* 5:975–80, esp. 978; Eduard Lohse, "*synedrion*," *TDNT* 7:860–71.

lion) in v. 10. The last phrase in v. 9, "as a testimony to them" (*eis martyrion autois*), occurred earlier in 1:44, where Jesus instructed the leper to show himself to the priests "as a testimony to them." In Mark 1:44 and 6:11 the phrase may be read negatively, i.e., as testimony against them, but Beasley-Murray cautions that the phrase should be allowed to carry the positive sense in 13:9, saying, "Mark's addition of v. 10

Synagogues

The term "synagogue" can refer to a group of people, an institution, or a building. The post-exilic origins of the synagogue are shrouded in mystery, but the existence of synagogues in the Fayyum in Egypt is confirmed by local inscriptions from the 3rd C. BC. A synagogue on the island of Delos has been traced to the 1st C. BC. Synagogues were therefore well established by the 1st century, but their number grew rapidly after the destruction of Jerusalem in AD 70. Eric Meyers has identified fifty-five synagogues in Judea and Galilee, but only three of these date from before AD 70 (Gamla, Masada, and Herodium). Meyers explains:

"The dearth of early Second Temple synagogue remains stands in striking contrast to the large number of synagogues referred to in ancient literary sources; but such an anomaly derives from our modern misunderstanding of the synagogue as a social and religious institution and the synagogue as a distinct and discrete architectural entity. This apparent contradiction disappears if we assume that, in the first centuries, large private houses were used as places of worship alongside other buildings that came to be utilized for worship and other matters requiring public assembly. In Palestine, it would seem, it was about a hundred years after the destruction of the Temple that the synagogue *as building* began to emerge as a central feature of Jewish communal life." (*ABD* 6:255)

The implications of this discovery for understanding the origins of New Testament "house churches" are obvious: the early Christians may have simply followed the pattern of the gathering of Jewish "synagogues" in homes, and the difference between synagogues and churches may not have been immediately clear to Gentiles.

Eric M. Meyers, "Synagogue," *ABD* 6:251–60.

shows that he must have viewed the *martyrion* as having positive as well as negative import, depending on the response of the hearers."[23]

Verse 10 seems to have been inserted in its present context by the evangelist; it interrupts the continuity of vv. 9 and 11, which are found together in Luke 12:11-12. Its effect is to further dampen enthusiasm regarding the imminence of the coming of the Son of Man. It does not mean that the gospel must be preached to all nations before the destruction of Jerusalem. The saying echoes the mission charge given to the disciples by the risen Lord in other contexts (Matt 28:19; Mark 16:15; Luke 24:47). The phrase "all the nations" (*panta ta ethnē*) occurs in these commissioning statements, but it also occurs in various other contexts (Acts 14:16; Rom 15:11 [Ps 117:1]; 16:26; Gal 3:8 [Gen 12:3]), especially in Revelation (12:5; 14:8; 15:4; 18:3, 23). The immediate context, however, is the earlier reference to the nations in Mark 11:17, where Jesus says that the temple is to be a "house of prayer for all nations" (Isa 56:7). The Gentile mission has been in view in Mark since the report that the Gadarene demoniac preached throughout the Decapolis (5:20). Now, the disciples are sent to preach "the gospel" to all nations. While Mark seems to insist that the Gentile mission was authorized by Jesus, it is also true, as William Lane observes, that "the thought of a mission to the Gentiles is firmly grounded in the OT (e.g. Isa. 42:6; 49:6, 12; 52:10; 60:6; Ps. 96) and is found in early Pharisaic Judaism as well (e.g. Psalms of Solomon 11:1; 8:17, 43)."[24] See the discussion of "gospel" in Mark 1:1. Significantly, it also occurs in conjunction with the verb to preach (*kēryssein*) in 1:14 and 14:9. If "gospel" (*euangelion*) commonly designated a royal or imperial decree of good news, then it carries a particular force in Mark 13. The governors and kings before whom the disciples will be made to stand do not proclaim good news; the disciples do.

Verse 11 continues the thought of v. 9. If the disciples are to bear witness, what are they to say? In addition to being anxious about their arrest, they may have been anxious that they would fail in their mission. Jesus relieves these fears. The translation "when they bring you to trial" renders the sense of the verb "to lead" (*agein*), but it is an extrapolation from the context. The verb to "hand over" (*paradidōmi*), meaning to arrest, echoes v. 9. The concern therefore is primarily with the disciples' defense rather than their preaching of the gospel. Anxiety in such a moment might seem inevitable, but it is a lack of trust in the power of God. Throughout Israel's history God empowered the faithful in their hours of trial. When Moses protested that he was not eloquent, God replied, "Who gives speech to mortals? Is it not I, the LORD? Now go, and I will be with your mouth and teach you what you are to speak" (Exod 4:11-12). God would put words in the mouth of the prophet like Moses who would arise (Deut 18:18). God touched

Jeremiah and said, "Now I have put my words in your mouth" and appointed him over nations and kingdoms (Jer 1:9). Ezekiel ate the scroll the Lord gave him (Ezek 3:1-4; cf. Jer 15:16; Rev 10:8-11), and the Lord commanded him to go and speak to Israel. The role of the Spirit of God in empowering the speech of those who are brought to trial is also attested in the New Testament. John 15:26-27 assured the disciples that the Paraclete would be with them to testify on Jesus' behalf (cf. John 16:8). When Peter and John testified before the council, the council could not refute them even though they were "uneducated and ordinary men" (Acts 4:13). Acts records the speeches of Stephen (Acts 7:1-53) and Paul (Acts 17:22-31; 18:9-10; 23:1-9; 24:10-21; 25:8-11; 26:2-29) when they were brought to trial. In Mark, this promise to the disciples also prepares the reader to pay particular attention to the words Jesus will speak when he is put on trial (14:62).

Mark uses the term "the hour" from this point forward to designate the hour of the coming of the Son of Man (13:32), the hour of Jesus' arrest and trial (14:35, 37, 41), and the hour(s) of Jesus' crucifixion (15:25, 33-34). In this regard, Mark anticipates the use of "the hour" in the Gospel of John (2:4; 5:25, 28; 7:30; 8:20; 12:23, 27; 13:1; etc.).

The only other references to "the Holy Spirit" in Mark are in 1:8, where John declares that the Messiah will baptize them in the Holy Spirit, in 3:29, where Jesus warns against blaspheming the Holy Spirit, and in 12:36, where David speaks "by the Holy Spirit." The Spirit also descends on Jesus at his baptism (1:12) and drives him into the wilderness (1:12). Now Jesus instructs the disciples that the Holy Spirit will speak through them when they are brought to trial.

Verses 12-13 remove any false hope that the intervention of the Holy Spirit will spare the early Christians from the terrors of persecution. Jewish society was built on family solidarity. The division of families was therefore particularly terrifying because it removed any hope of stability or any recourse to human resources. The earlier references to the "handing over" of the disciples have been impersonal: "they will hand you over" (13:9), "when they bring you to trial and hand you over" (13:11). The persecutors are not some anonymous "they," however. Jesus warns that brother will hand over (*paradōsei*) brother to death, and fathers their children. Children will rise up against parents and kill them. These verses evoke the tradition of Isaiah 1:2 and Micah 7:6. The latter is intensified by interpretation in the Septuagint, which renders the verse "a man's enemies are all the men in his house," and in Targum Jonathan, "A man delivers up his brother to destruction."[25] Evans traces the later development of this tradition in *1 Enoch* 100:1-2; *Jubilees* 23:19; *4 Ezra* 6:24; *3 Baruch* 4:17; Josephus, *Jewish War* 6.109; and *m. Sotah* 9.15.[26] Matthew places these warnings in the commissioning of the Twelve (Matt 10:16-22, esp. 21, and 10:35-36). In

Nero's Persecution of Christians

"But all the endeavours of men, all the emperor's largesse and the propitiations of the gods, did not suffice to allay the scandal or banish the belief that the fire had been ordered. And so, to get rid of this rumour, Nero set up as the culprits and punished with the utmost refinement of cruelty a class hated for their abominations, who are commonly called Christians. Christus, from whom their name is derived, was executed at the hands of the procurator Pontius Pilate in the reign of Tiberius. Checked for the moment, this pernicious superstition again broke out, not only in Judaea, the source of the evil, but even in Rome, that receptacle for everything that is sordid and degrading from every quarter of the globe, which there finds a following. Accordingly, arrest was first made of those who confessed [sc. *to being Christians*]; then, on their evidence, an immense multitude was convicted, not so much on the charge of arson as because of hatred of the human race. Besides being put to death they were made to serve as objects of amusement; they were clad in the hides of beasts and torn to death by dogs; others were crucified, others set on fire to serve to illuminate the night when daylight failed. Nero had thrown open his grounds for the display, and was putting on a show in the circus, where he mingled with the people in the dress of a charioteer or drove about in his chariot. All this gave rise to a feeling of pity, even towards men whose guilt merited the most exemplary punishment; for it was felt that they were being destroyed not for the public good but to gratify the cruelty of an individual."

Tacitus, *Annals* 15.44, in Henry Bettenson, ed., *Documents of the Christian Church* (2nd ed.; London: Oxford University Press, 1963), 1–2.

Rome these warnings were not merely part of a Jewish apocalyptic tradition of the terrors of the end time; they had become the commonplace result of Nero's persecution of the Christians. [Nero's Persecution of Christians]

Commenting on Tacitus's description of Christians as *odium humani generis,* the object of universal hatred, Martin Hengel notes the parallel with Mark 13:13, "you will be hated by all because of my name" (13:10; cf. John 15:18-19) and adds, "Mark is the first person in the New Testament to speak in this way of universal hatred against Christians."[27] From this observation Hengel draws further conclusions about the life setting of the Gospel:

> The emphatic theology of suffering and the cross in the Gospel has its very specific *Sitz im Leben* here. . . . in the years after this fearful event the Christians in Rome—and not only there—must have feared new bloody mass persecutions. . . . Thus despite its framework of traditional stereotyped apocalyptic formulae, the text in Mark refers to very specific events.[28]

The phrase "because of my name" (*dia to onoma mou*) is equivalent to "because of me" (*heneken emou* in v. 9), but it also evokes echoes of the references to receiving a child, casting out demons, doing deeds of power, and receiving a cup of water in the name of Christ. The apocalyptic and mission sayings in Mark are therefore closely related. In times of persecution and speculation that the end of time is near, the church should renew its faithfulness to its primary mission—proclaiming the good news of Jesus Christ. Those who remain faithful and endure in such times will be "saved." Does Mark mean that they will be spared from the persecution, or does he have the theological sense of this term in mind? Ben Witherington opts for the former,[29] but Craig Evans argues for the latter, citing *4 Ezra* 6:25, "whoever remains after all that I have foretold to you shall be saved and shall see my salvation and the end of my world."[30] In Mark 10:29-30 Jesus offers a similar assurance to the disciples; they will experience persecutions—"and in the age to come eternal life."

Mark 13:14 is ironically one of the most enigmatic verses in the Gospel. Technically, it is a narrative aside, where the narrator interrupts the narrative to make a comment to the reader/hearer. Even if the Gospel was written in order to be read in public by a reader or lector, the comment is a signal that something is being communicated that cannot be expressed more openly or that gains significance by being communicated in this way. The irony is that this intrusive comment—inserted for clarity—has sparked vigorous debate and numerous interpretations.

The reference to "the desolating sacrilege" standing where *he* ought not to be is the clearest response in the discourse to the disciples' request to know the sign when "these things" will occur. The reference is grammatically odd because the masculine participle "standing" (*estēkota*) follows the neuter noun "sacrilege" (*to bdelygma*). The NEB fittingly renders the verse "when you see 'the abomination of desolation' usurping a place that is not *his*." The starting point for interpreting the reference is the recognition that it is an echo of Daniel 9:27; 11:31; 12:11. In a vision, Gabriel revealed to Daniel that Jerusalem and the temple would be destroyed and that "the prince" would bring an end to the sacrifices in the temple, "and in their place shall be an abomination that desolates, until the decreed end is poured out upon the desolator" (Dan 9:27; LXX *bdelygma tōn erēmōseōn*). Daniel 11:29-31 is even more specific: the king will venture south until the ships of the Kittim (i.e., the Romans) force him to turn back. Then his force will profane the temple and set up "the abomination that makes desolate." Daniel 12:11 adds that the period of this abomination shall be 1,290 days. The distinctive phrase combines religious and political allusions: "abomination" is a term that is often used in the Hebrew writings in reference to idolatry (Deut 29:17; 1 Kgs 11:5, 7; 2 Kgs 23:13; 2 Chr 15:8; Isa 66:3; Jer 4:1; 7:30; Ezek 5:11; Zech 9:7), and "desolation" often occurs in contexts that refer to the ravages of war and utter destruction (Lev 26:34-35; 2 Chr 30:7; 36:21; Jer 4:7; 7:34; 22:5). The events to which Daniel refers are recorded in 1 Maccabees 1:54-59; 6:7, where the term "desolating sacrilege" is also used. In 169 BC the Seleucid King, Antiochus IV Epiphanes, having been blocked by the Romans in Egypt, looted the Jerusalem temple (1 Macc 1:20-24; 2 Macc 5:11-21; Josephus, *J. W.* 1.32). In 167 he abolished the temple cult and erected a pagan altar in the Jewish temple (1 Macc 1:54, 59).[31]

History seemed to be about to fulfill the prophecy of the "desolating sacrilege" in AD 40 when the Roman emperor Caligula ordered his legate to erect his statue in the temple (Philo, *Embassy*; Josephus, *Ant.* 18.261-309; Tacitus, *History* 5.9).[32] After various delays, however, he rescinded the order and was murdered shortly thereafter. Some interpreters postulate that Jesus' words were recalled in this context and that an early version of the discourse on the Mount of Olives emerged at this time.[33]

Scholars are divided on the question of whether or not the reference to the "desolating sacrilege" refers to a specific event during the war of AD 66–70. [Chronology of the Jewish War, AD 66–70] George Beasley-Murray and Martin Hengel both contend that Mark is using traditional prophetic language drawn from the Old Testament, that the writer had only a vague understanding of events in Judea, and that "Mark 13.14-19 . . . does not fit at all into the situation at or after the destruction of the temple and the city or in the time of the siege, from July to September 70."[34] Craig Evans suggests that the reference was related to the Pauline prediction of "the man of lawlessness" in 2 Thessalonians 2:3-4 and the expected appearance of "the antichrist."[35] On the other

---

Chronology of the Jewish War, AD 66–70

April/May 66—Florus, the Roman procurator, took 17 talents from the temple treasury.

Summer 66—Daily sacrifices for the emperor were suspended.

October 66—Cestius Gallus, governor of Syria marched on Jerusalem with more than 30,000 men. After a brief siege, he lost 6,000 men to the Jewish rebels while retreating. The moderate elements in Jerusalem formed a provisional government and prepared for war.

67—Nero appointed Vespasian to subdue the rebels. Roman legions arrived in Galilee; Josephus sought refuge in Jotapata.

June/July 67—The Romans overran Jotapata.

Aug./Sept. 67—Tarichea in Galilee fell to the Romans.

Sept./Oct. 67—The Romans overran Gamla. Refugees fled to Jerusalem.

Winter 67-68—The Zealot party emerged and displaced the moderate leadership in Jerusalem. They appointed Phanni as high priest, although he was not qualified for the office, which provoked public opposition to the Zealots. The Zealots sent for the Idumeans, who joined the Zealots in purging the moderate leadership from Jerusalem. Others (perhaps including the Christians) fled from the city. Some appealed to the Romans to take the city and restore order as soon as possible.

Spring 68—All of Judea, Perea, and Idumea were subdued, except Jerusalem. June 9, 68—Nero died. Vespasian

was forced to await new orders. Galba, Otho, and Vitellius each sought to claim the throne and bring order to the empire.

Jan. 15, 69—Galba was assassinated.

Spring 69—The Romans controlled all of Palestine, except the fortresses at Herodium, Masada, Machaerus, and Jerusalem. John of Gischala and the Zealots held the temple. The Idumeans and the Jerusalem populace laid siege to it. Unable to dislodge the Zealots, the latter called for help from Simon bar Giora. Fighting continued among these factions for more than a year.

July 1, 69—Vespasian was proclaimed emperor in Egypt.

Dec. 20, 69—Vitellius was assassinated, and Vespasian was acknowledged as the emperor.

Spring 70—Vespasian sent Titus, his son, to take Jerusalem.

Summer 70—When the Roman legions took the temple, they set up their standards in the outer court and hailed Titus as Imperatur.

August 30, 70—The temple was destroyed.

71—The table of shewbread and the seven-branched candelabra from the temple were carried in triumph through Rome.

April 74—Masada fell and the remaining Zealots committed suicide there.

L. I. Levine, "Jewish War (66–73 C.E.)," *ABD* 3:839–45; Emil Schürer, *The History of the Jewish People in the Age of Jesus Christ* (rev. and ed. Geza Vermes and Fergus Millar; Edinburgh: T. & T. Clark, 1973), 1:484–513.

hand, William Lane concludes that the early Christians recognized the "farcical investiture of the clown Phanni as high priest" in the winter of 67–68 as "the appalling sacrilege usurping a position which is not his" and fled across the Jordan to Pella.[36] Francis Moloney insists

> the collection of sayings in 13:14-20, which had a complicated prehistory, is to be related to the experience of the Jewish people in and about Jerusalem at the time of the Jewish War. . . . The Markan insistence that the sacrilege will be a male human figure "standing where *he* ought not" determines my acceptance of the suggestion that the "he" is the Roman commander Titus himself, amid the planting of Roman standards, accompanied by his idolatrous acclamation as *imperator* (*autokratora*) within the temple area (Josephus, *J. W.* 6.316).[37]

These various interpretations each have their merits and their weaknesses. While it is clear that Mark is using traditional apocalyptic language in prophesying the destruction of Jerusalem, the intrusive comment, "let the reader understand," and the grammatically odd switch to the masculine participle suggest that he has a particular event in view. The investiture of Phanni as high priest may well have scandalized the believers in Jerusalem and spurred their flight to Pella (see Eusebius, *E.H.* 3.5.3),[38] but Phanni is unlikely to have stirred such feeling outside of Judea or in the church in Rome. The suggestion that Titus fulfilled the prophetic reference fits the evidence well, but by the time Titus appeared in the temple the opportunity to flee to the mountains had passed. It may be best, therefore, to recognize the long history of this verse and allow that it served as a genuine, prophetic warning when the clouds of war gathered over Jerusalem and it became obvious to believers in Rome and elsewhere that the Roman conquest of Jerusalem was imminent and that the Danielic reference to the "desolating sacrilege" would be fulfilled once more by the conquering general.

The command to "flee to the mountains" is puzzling because Jerusalem is in the mountains. On the other hand, it is difficult to accept it as a prophecy after the fact referring to the flight to Pella because Pella was not in the mountains. Nor is it clear that "the mountains" could mean Galilee. In Revelation, when the sixth seal is opened, the kings and generals, the rich and the powerful, the slave and the free, hide in the caves among the rocks of the mountains (Rev 6:15-16). The command may therefore draw on traditional apocalyptic language, however impractical it may have been in the actual circumstances of the Roman control of the area surrounding Jerusalem in AD 70: flee from the city and hide in the mountains surrounding Jerusalem.

Verses 15 and 16 underscore the urgency of readiness. When that time comes, there will be no opportunity to prepare. After killing the king's officer, Mattathias and his five sons "fled to the hills and left all that they had in the town" (1 Macc 2:28). Again, the command does not fit easily into the situation of the protracted siege of Jerusalem from AD 68 to 70, when various groups entered and left the city. Instead, the eschatological urgency is more readily understood in reference to preparation for the coming day of the Lord, as Luke renders these commands in Luke 17:31. In the background is the image of Lot's wife (Gen 19:17): do not even look back. If the warning not to turn back for one's possessions is to be ready for the coming of the Son of Man, then it must be understood figuratively. When the Lord is near, cast aside your garment, like Bartimaeus (10:50).

The typical Palestinian homes had flat roofs that could be used for various purposes (note Mark 2:4). Evans lists the following "rooftop" activities that are attested in the Bible: "prayer or worship (Jer 19:13; Zeph 1:5; Acts 10:9), sleep (1 Sam 9:25), storing or drying fruit (Josh 2:6), proclaiming news (Isa 15:3; 22:1; Matt 10:27), or celebrating festivals (Neh 8:16)."[39] Stairs on the outside of the house allowed easy transit to and from the roof. Come down from the roof and run; do not go back into the house! It is foolish to think about possessions when your life is in danger. If you are working in the field, do not go back to get a cloak. Not only will there not be time to pack up your possessions, there will not even be time to pick up a coat! Run!

Pregnant and nursing women would be incapable of coping with such peril. Jesus' "woe" is not a pronouncement of judgment but a cry of compassion, so "woe" may be better translated "alas for those who are pregnant or nursing" (cf. Luke 23:28-29). If the time came in winter, the cold, rain-swollen wadis and muddy roads would make the travail all the more difficult. Therefore, pray that it may not be in winter. The historical context of the destruction of Jerusalem and the apocalyptic context of the coming of the Son of Man, or the day of the Lord, are mingled in these verses. The one is being interpreted (at least by the false prophets, and no doubt by many others also) as a sign of the other. [Allegorical Interpretations]

Verse 19 is a typical Semitic hyperbole that dramatizes the magnitude of the coming crisis. There has never been anything like it. Verse 19 echoes Daniel 12:1—"There shall be a time of

Allegorical Interpretations

The church fathers ingeniously found moral instruction in these verses through allegorical interpretation:

Origen: "The housetop in this case suggests a lofty and exalted mind. We are commanded not to descend from this housetop. Let one who flees in persecution not fail to go up to this housetop, but also from this housetop let him not come down to scramble for the things down below, in his house." (*Homilies on Jeremiah* 12.13 [18])

Ephrem the Syrian: "Winter is without fruit and sabbath without labor. Do not let it be you who might be led away captive under such circumstances—when you have neither fruit nor work." (*Commentary on Tatian's Diatessaron*).

Thomas C. Oden and Christopher A. Hall, eds., *Ancient Christian Commentary on Scripture: New Testament II, Mark* (Downers Grove IL: InterVarsity Press, 1998), 184–85.

anguish, such as has never occurred since nations first came into existence." Mark's addition, "and there never will be" anything to compare
to it, makes the point that the whole discourse conveys: as terrible as
the destruction of Jerusalem will be, it will not signify the coming of
the Son of Man. The end is not yet. There will be other calamities, but
none as great as the fall of Jerusalem. The hyperbole is typical of
prophecies of destruction. Lane cites Jeremiah 30:7; Joel 2:2; Baruch
2:2; 1 Maccabees 9:27. Deuteronomy 4:32 echoes the same hyperbole,
along with a reference to God's work at creation. The reference is not
gratuitous in Mark 13:19. In this context it not only affirms that God
is the creator; it implies that God, not the Roman armies, still controls
all that happens. God will therefore determine the time of the judgment on Jerusalem. Again the referent of these verses is blurred, and the
description applies also to the great tribulation expected at the end of
time. The destruction of Jerusalem was terrible—and one need only
read Josephus's description of it to be moved by its horror—but the
coming tribulation will be worse. If God had not cut short the time
(i.e., of the coming tribulation), no one would survive it. Nevertheless,
God ordains the times, and God has cut short the time of suffering.
This is good news not only for Jewish Christians in Judea and Gentile
Christians in Rome; it is a reminder of God's provident compassion.
Just as God would not allow the flood to wipe out humanity (Gen
9:11), so God has a purpose for the elect of the covenant community.
Beasley-Murray cautions that while there are parallels to God's cutting
short the time of sinners (*1 En.* 80:2) and hastening the time of the end
(*4 Ezra* 4:26), there are few real parallels to the assertion in 13:20 that
God will cut short the time of suffering for the sake of the faithful.
Beasley-Murray cites *2 Baruch* 20:1, and Evans adds 4Q385=4QpsEzᵃ,
frg 3, lines 3-5, "the days hasten in order that the children of Israel may
inherit. . . . I shall cut short the days and the years."[40]

Verses 21-23 provide a conclusion to this part of the discourse by
returning to a theme that was introduced at its beginning in vv. 5-6: a
warning not to heed false prophets. In the distress of events in Judea
and Rome at that time, false prophets would announce the appearance
of the Messiah, which for the Jews would have meant the coming of the
Messiah and for believers Jesus' return. Jesus warns, "Do not believe
them." Although Mark records secret epiphanies (the raising of Jairus's
daughter, 5:35-43; Jesus' walking on the water, 6:45-52; Jesus' transfiguration, 9:2-8), the coming of the Son of Man will not be a secret to be
spread by prophets. In the terror of the destruction of Jerusalem,
however, prophets arose and Josephus records events that mirror the
prediction in these verses: "Deceivers and impostors, under the pre-
tence of divine inspiration fostering revolutionary changes, they
persuaded the multitude to act like madmen, and led them into the

desert under the belief that God would there give them tokens of deliverance" (*J. W.* 2.259). He also wrote, "Numerous prophets, indeed, were at this period suborned by the tyrants to delude the people, bidding them await help from God" (*J. W.* 6.286). Among the signs adduced by the false prophets were "a star resembling a sword that stood over the city and a comet which continued for a year" (*J. W.* 6. 289), a cow that gave birth to a lamb in the temple (6.292), a gate that opened of its own accord (6.294), the appearance of chariots and armed battalions in the air (6.299). Jesus, son of Ananias, pronounced woes on Jerusalem (6.301-309). Warnings about false prophets who offer "signs and wonders" to confirm their words can be found throughout the Bible.

False Prophets

A sample of the false prophets found in the Bible:

Deut 13:1-2
   False prophets offer signs and wonders but worship other gods.
1 Kgs 22:6, 12
   Court prophets encourage the king to go to war.
Jer 23:9-17, 25-32
   False prophets reassure Israel of God's protection.
Ezek 13:8-10
   False prophets say, "Peace," when there is no peace.
Matt 7:15
   False prophets come in sheep's clothing.
2 Cor 11-13
   Super apostles preaching a different gospel offer signs and wonders.
2 Pet 2:1
   False prophets secretly introduce destructive opinions.
1 John 4:1-2
   False prophets do not confess "Jesus Christ has come in the flesh."
Rev 19:20
   The false prophet will lead people to worship the beast.

Deuteronomy warns the people not to follow "if prophets or those who divine by dreams appear among you and promise you omens and portents" if they follow other gods (Deut 13:1-2) [False Prophets] (see [False Messiahs]). "Signs and wonders" are not always false (Deut 28:46; 29:3; 34:11; Isa 8:18; Acts 2:22; 14:3; 15:12; Rom 15:19; Heb 2:4; 2 Cor 12:12), and Gideon (Judg 6:36-40) and Hezekiah (2 Kgs 20:8-11) were granted signs. Nevertheless, "signs and wonders" were performed by false prophets as well (2 Thess 2:9-10; Rev 13:13; *Didache* 16.4). Perhaps for this reason, Jesus refused to provide signs when he was challenged to do so (8:11-12).

The terms used in the latter part of v. 22 and v. 23 echo terms in 13:5-6, forming a bracket or *inclusion* around the main body of the discourse: "lead astray" (vv. 5, 6, 22), "beware" or "be alert" (*blepete*; vv. 5, 23), and "all things" (vv. 4, 23). The reference to "the elect" at the end of v. 22 suggests that these verses are attached to the previous verses (v. 20) by this "catchword." These brackets relate Jesus' warning about the destruction of Jerusalem to the life setting of the evangelist. The destruction of Jerusalem would bring social anarchy, great terror, terrible suffering, persecution of Jesus' followers, false prophets, and false signs of the end. The church should not be misled by these events. They did not signal the end (13:7-8). Instead, they would offer opportunities to preach the gospel and offer a faithful witness (13:10). If not exactly "all things," therefore, Jesus had told his disciples all they really needed to know about the coming events (cf. John 16:1, 12-13, 33; Gal 5:21; 1 Thess 3:4; 4:6).

Cosmic Signs that Will Precede the Coming of the Son of Man, 13:24-27

Using words and phrases from the Old Testament, these verses describe the coming of the Son of Man as a theophany. Verses 24 and 25 set the time of the appearance of the Son of Man, first in reference to the destruction of Jerusalem (v. 24a), and then in reference to cosmic signs (vv. 24b-25). This section of the discourse opens with a strong adversative, "but" (*alla*). The introductory phrase, "in those days," echoes earlier occurrences in 1:9; 2:20; 8:1 and more immediately in vv. 17 and 19. In the Old Testament this phrase often introduces pronouncements about the end times (e.g., Jer 3:16, 18; 5:18; 31:29; 33:15-16; Joel 3:1; Zech 8:23). The second phrase, "after that suffering [*thlipsis*]," also echoes earlier references: in the interpretation of the parable of the sower in 4:17 and in reference to the suffering at the destruction of Jerusalem in 13:19. The first phrase specifies proximity, "in those days"; the second defines the sequence, "after that suffering," but does not define the interval between the two.

Verses 24b-25 are indented and most of the words are printed in italics in the Nestle (26th ed.) of the Greek New Testament, with marginal notes that indicate that these verses contain quotations of Isaiah 13:10 and 34:4. Beasley-Murray is more precise in observing that this passage "is less a series of citations than a conflation of allusions" to the day of the Lord.[41] The citations are not exact, although the allusions are clear, especially the dependence on Isaiah 13:10. These verses also echo phrases found in Joel 2:10; 3:4, 15-16 [LXX 4:15-16]. Revelation 6:12-13 uses the same traditional language. At the coming of the Lord, the heavens and the earth will shake, the sun and the moon will be darkened, and the stars will fall. Beasley-Murray also notes that the last word in v. 25, "shaken" (*saleuthēsontai*) does not occur in the verses cited above but is common in Old Testament theophanies (Judg 5:5; Job 9:6; Pss 18:7; 114:7; Amos 9:5; Mic 1:4; Nah 1:5; Hab 3:6).[42] The language is entirely metaphorical; it does not mean that the creation will literally be destroyed at the Lord's coming. But if even the powers in the heavens shake at God's coming, earthly powers are certainly not to be compared with God's majesty.

The disciples had asked for the "sign" when "these things" would occur. Jesus told them both the sign of the destruction of Jerusalem (the "desolating sacrilege") and the sign of the coming of the Son of

Man (the darkening and shaking of the heavenly powers). The coming of the Son of Man is described in terms drawn from Daniel 7:13, but there is no reference to the throne of God. The promise "you will see" echoes the reference to Daniel's seeing and Jesus' words to Caiaphas in 14:62. The Son of Man comes in clouds (cf. 9:7; 14:62; 1 Thess 4:17), and since God appeared in a cloud (Exod 34:5), Jesus adds "with great power and glory," which reminds the reader of Jesus' earlier reference to the coming of the Son of Man in 8:38. Again the description suggests comparison with the "power and glory" that attended the arrival of an earthly (Roman) monarch. The glory of the Son of Man will be far, far greater when he comes (see [The Son of Man]).

The Son of Man's coming will be redemptive (but cf. Matt 13:41). He will send the angels to gather "the elect." The angels are mentioned in 8:38, but there their function is not explained. Mark 13:27 completes the description started in the earlier verse. "The elect" is a catchword that links the cutting short of the days (v. 19) with the threat of the false prophets (v. 22) and now the coming of the Son of Man (v. 27), but these are the only verses in Mark in which the term occurs. The gathering of the scattered people of God is part of Israel's hope for the future (Deut 30:3-4; Ps 50:3-5; Isa 43:6; 66:18-20; Jer 32:37; Ezek 34:13; 36:24).[43] The thought of this verse echoes Zechariah 2:6 (LXX) and Deuteronomy 30:3 and combines two descriptions drawn from contemporary cosmology: "from the four winds" and "from the corner of the earth to the corner of heaven." [Adam and the Four Winds] The latter is especially unclear, since one would expect "from one end of heaven to the other" or "from one end of the earth to the other," but it apparently means from the farthest extremities of heaven and earth. Scattering was the result of national defeat; gathering therefore suggested the fulfillment of God's promises to Israel (Isa 11:11; 27:12-13; 43:5-7; Ezek 39:27-28; Zech 10:6-11; cf. John 11:52). Although v. 27 makes no reference to resurrection, Beasley-Murray rightly speculates about its relationship to 1 Thessalonians 4:15-17.[44] Is Jesus alluding to a reunion of the living with the faithful dead? Does he mean an ingathering of the elect from the nations and from Israel (cf. 13:10)? The language is as inclusive as it is ambiguous; when the Son of Man comes, he will gather all of the elect in order to constitute the new community of the faithful.

Adam and the Four Winds

Augustine found an imaginative allusion in the reference to the four winds:

"That he will gather his elect from the four winds means from the whole world. For Adam himself, as I have shown, signifies in Greek the whole world, with the four letters (A, D, A, M). As the Greek think of these matters, the four quarters of the world have these initial letters, *Anatole* (east), *Dysis* (west), *Arktos* (north), and *Mesembria* (south). Adam after the fall has been scattered over the whole world."

Augustine, *On the Psalms* 96.15, in Thomas C. Oden and Christopher A. Hall, eds., *Ancient Christian Commentary on Scripture: New Testament II, Mark* (Downers Grove IL: InterVarsity Press, 1998), 188.

Exhortations to Be Ready, 13:28-37

This section is composed of a compilation of independent sayings: the parable of the fig tree (vv. 28-29), the assurance that Jesus' words will be fulfilled (vv. 30-31), the caveat that even Jesus did not know the exact time of their fulfillment (v. 32), and the parable of the doorkeeper (vv. 33-37).

The parable of the fig tree gives hope that the coming of the Son of Man is imminent. As Beasley-Murray wrote so aptly,

> In the late sixties AD there was nothing the Christians in Rome needed more urgently to know than that God was working his purpose out in the world, in Palestine, and in the church of the empire, not least in view of their having lately come through the most appalling persecution that the church had known to that time or was to know.[45]

The parable of the fig tree, occurring at this point in the Gospel, reminds the reader both of the parables (cf. *parabolē* in v. 28 and in 4:2, 11, 13, 33), especially the parable of the seed growing secretly in 4:26-29, and the cursing of the fig tree in connection with Jesus' judgment on the temple in 11:12-14, 20-21. Although Beasley-Murray rejects the connection, W. R. Telford and recent narrative critics are probably right in observing a suggestive continuity in the role of the fig tree in Mark:

> The fig-tree's *withering* in Chapter 11 was intended in our view to be seen as an eschatological sign prefiguring an imminent *judgement* upon the . . . Temple. In Chapter 13, the disciples, and hence the readers, are invited to look upon the fig tree's blossoming as a sign likewise prefiguring an eschatological event, viz., the coming Age of both *blessing* and *judgement*.[46]

The fig tree is especially suited to this parable because it not only loses its leaves in winter but blossoms late in the spring. Hence, when one sees leaves on a fig tree, one knows that summer is near (Song of Sol 2:11-13). If Jesus spoke this parable on the Mount of Olives (which was known for its fig trees) at the time of Passover, then the fig trees may have been preparing to sprout leaves just then.[47] The parable may have originally been a parable of the coming kingdom of God (cf. *ēngiken* in 1:15 and *engys* in 13:28-29), however, so that its relationship to the present context is secondary. That relationship is made by the introduction, "when you see," which evokes the disciples' question in v. 4 and echoes the beginning of v. 14. The meaning is not that when you see the coming of the Son of Man you will know that the end is near, but rather when you see the destruction of Jerusalem you will know that the coming of the Son of Man is at hand. Do not be misled by the false prophets (vv. 21-22) into thinking that the Son of Man has already come, but do not miss the sign that his coming is imminent. Similarly, the reference to "these things" in v. 29 recalls the reference to "these things" in v. 4 and prepares for "all these things" in v. 30, which again returns to v. 4. The addition of the phrase "at the door" (or gate) in v. 28 looks ahead to the parable of the doorkeeper in vv. 33-37 and may be a play on words (*theros*, "summer," in v. 28; *thyrais*, "doors" in v. 29). Lane notes the famous similar but different play on words in Amos 8:1-2 in Hebrew (*qāits* "summer fruit"; *qēts* "summer").[48] The verb "know" (*ginōskete*) is indicative in v. 28 but imperative in v. 29. The tone of the parable is therefore urgent: "Learn!" (v. 28), "when you see . . . know!"

Coming at the end of the discourse, vv. 30 and 31 claim divine authority for Jesus' words. Verse 30 begins with the solemn formula, "Amen, I say to you," which occurs thirteen times in Mark (e.g., 9:1; 11:23; 12:43; 14:9). See the commentary on 3:28. The two questions on which the interpretation of this verse hinges are the meaning of "this generation" and the meaning of "all these things." Lurking in the background is the concern that Jesus' claims were not fulfilled if (1) "this generation" literally means those alive during Jesus' life, and (2) "all these things" includes the coming of the Son of Man (vv. 24-27). In context there is little reason to search for other meanings. Again, Beasley-Murray is instructive. He notes that elsewhere in the Gospels "this generation" designates Jesus' contemporaries and always carries an implicit criticism (cf. 8:12; 8:38; 9:19).[49] The more difficult question is whether "all these things" includes the signs of the coming of the Son of Man (vv. 24-27) or refers only to the destruction of Jerusalem (vv. 5-23). The phrase wraps the discourse with a natural conclusion since it echoes the disciples' question in 13:4 (cf. "these things" in v. 29). For the first 1,500 years of Christian history, interpreters assumed that the phrase included the coming of the Son of Man, and it was not until Calvin that the alternative became widely accepted.[50] The parallel in Matthew 23:36/Luke 11:51 is not related to the prediction of the coming of the Son of Man. From the context in Mark 13, it is clear Mark understood the events of the war and the imminent (or recent) destruction of Jerusalem as God's judgment, predicted by Jesus. Furthermore, Mark also wished to encourage faithfulness in the persecuted Christian community while cautioning it against the claims of false prophets (vv. 5-6, 21-22). The mission of the church was to preach the gospel to all nations, and this would occur before the end came (13:10). The natural interpretation, therefore, is to assume that Jesus expected the coming of the Son of Man, the Parousia, or "Second Coming," within that generation, just as he foresaw the coming judgment on Jerusalem. Rather than force an artificial interpretation of "this generation" or "all these things," the interpreter can more easily save the accuracy of Jesus' prediction by noting that within the immediate context Jesus said that even he did not know the time of his coming (v. 32).

Apart from these difficult issues, the idiom "this generation will not pass away" is rooted in the Wisdom literature: "My days are past" (Job 17:11), "our life will pass away like the traces of a cloud" (Wis 2:4; cf. Ps 90:6-7), and "the rich will disappear like a flower in the field" (Jas 1:10).[51] In 1 John 2:17 the Elder claims that "the world and its desire are passing away." In contrast to the transience of the created order stands the eternal Creator (Ps 102:25-27). The heavens and the earth may pass away, but God's salvation is forever (Isa 51:6). Moreover, if God is eternal, then God's word will stand forever (Isa 40:6-8). Later Jewish writings apply this claim specifically to the Torah (Bar 4:1; Wis 18:4; *4 Ezra* 9:36-37). Against this background in the Wisdom literature and the Prophets, Jesus makes the same claim for his own words, whether specifically the "Amen" saying in the previous verse, the whole discourse, or all of his words. As we have observed that other parts of Mark 13 echo 8:38 and 9:1, so here the claims for the enduring authority of Jesus' words fill out the passing reference in 8:38, "and my words."

Just as Jesus affirmed the divine authority of the Law in Matthew 5:18/Luke 16:17, so here he makes the same claim for his own words. William Lane's observation is perceptive: "This claim of high authority for Jesus' words implies a christological affirmation: what is said of God in the OT may be equally affirmed of Jesus and his word."[52] The voice from heaven at Jesus' baptism and at the transfiguration affirms that Jesus is the Son of God (1:11; 9:7). Jesus occasionally spoke of God as *abba* (14:36) and obliquely of himself as "Son" (12:6; 14:61). He acts as God's emissary (5:19-20; 11:2-3). As Son of Man, he has authority to forgive sins (2:10) and he is lord of the Sabbath (2:28). The claim that his words, like God's words, will never pass away is therefore a natural extension of Mark's high Christology.

The church father Gregory the Great astutely observed that v. 31 contains a kind of hyperbole. The heavens and the earth are the most enduring, permanent fixtures in human experience. Words, by contrast, are ephemeral. They are scarcely spoken before they are gone. Yet, Jesus' words—because they come from God—are more enduring than the most enduring natural structures.[53]

Nevertheless, there is a clear distinction between Jesus and God, Son and Father. Mark 13:32 affirms that neither the angels nor the Son know "that day or hour," only the Father knows. The intent of this claim is to reinforce the need for vigilance. The disciples had asked for a sign that would tell them when "all these things" would be accomplished (v. 4). The ultimate answer to this question is that no one knows when the coming of the Son of Man will be; therefore, Jesus' disciples must be urgent in their mission and always ready for his coming.

The expression "that day or hour" resonates with prophetic warnings where "that day" means "the Day of the Lord" (Joel 3:18; Amos 3:14; 8:3, 9, 13; 9:11; Obad 8; Mic 4:6; 5:10; 7:11; Zeph 1:9-10; 3:11, 16; Zech 9:16; 12-14 *passim*; see commentary on Mark 13:3).[54] In the era before the invention of clocks with minute hands, an hour was the shortest, most precise measure of time (cf. 13:11; 14:37). It could also designate the coming of a momentous event (14:35). Scholars have debated whether this verse should be interpreted in context or as an independent saying. In context, following v. 30, the sense must be that the end is imminent, within that generation, but even Jesus did not know its exact date. On the other hand, if the saying circulated independent of its present context, it has an even stronger force; the end could come within that generation or at a later time—even Jesus did not know.[55]

The inclusion of "the angels in heaven" is natural in context because of their role in the coming of the Son of Man (8:38; 13:27). First Peter 1:12 says that the angels did not know of the salvation in Christ but longed to look into these things. The assertion that even "the Son" did not know the time of the end maintains the subordination of the Son to the Father (cf. John 14:28; 1 Cor 15:24-28). Nevertheless, the phrase is omitted from Matthew 24:36 in some manuscripts, and Luke does not have it at all. It is unlikely that the early church would have created a saying denying Jesus' knowledge of the time of the end. Still, the absolute reference to "the Son" occurs elsewhere in the synoptics only in Matthew 11:27 (cf. 1 Thess 1:10).

The admonitions to "watch" and the parable of the doorkeeper bring the discourse in Mark 13 to a conclusion. The command to watch, be alert, is the basic theme of the discourse (vv. 5, 9, 23; see [The Structure of Mark 13]). The warning to keep alert serves as a transition to the parable of the doorkeeper that follows and foreshadows Jesus' warning to the sleeping disciples in Gethsemane (14:34, 37, 41). Scribes noted the connection, of course, and some of them added the words "and pray" in v. 33, assimilating the admonition to 14:38, "Keep awake and pray."

The reason for the need for vigilance, of course, is that they do not know when the *kairos* may come. [*Kairos* in Mark] This general term for a significant time or season refers less to the time of the destruction of Jerusalem, for which there was ample warning, than to the coming of the Son of Man. Earlier Jesus had spoken of what they would "see" (vv. 14, 26, 29), but the references to what the disciples "know" and do not know are one of the threads that stitch together the concluding verses of the discourse (*ginōskete*, vv. 28, 29; *oidate* vv. 32, 33, 35). Verse 34 introduces the parable cryptically with a comparative particle, "As . . . ," which evokes an introduction like the one that introduces the parable of the seed growing secretly: "The kingdom of God is as . . ." (4:26). Here the full introduction would have been something like, "Your situation as you await the coming of the Son of Man is as. . . ." The parable is reminiscent of the watching servants in Luke 12:36-38. Indeed the two may be variants of a common original.[56] In Luke the servants await the master's return from a wedding banquet, but a longer absence is suggested by Mark's version, in which the master is away on a journey. He therefore assigns responsibilities to each of his servants. The responsibility of the doorkeeper is to be on watch (*grēgorein*, cf. 13:35, 37; 14:34, 37, 38). Verse 35 admonishes the disciples directly. The instruction given to the doorkeeper in the parable (v. 34) is addressed to them:

Kairos in Mark	*Kairos* is translated variously in the NRSV as "time," "age," and "season."
Mark 1:15	"The time (*kairos*) is fulfilled, and the kingdom of God has come near; repent and believe in the good news."
Mark 10:29-30	"Truly, I tell you, there is no one who has left house or brothers or sisters or mother or father or children or fields, for my sake and for the sake of the good news who will not receive a hundredfold now in this age (*kairos*)—houses, brothers and sisters, mothers and children, and fields with persecutions—and in the age (*aiōn*) to come eternal life."
Mark 11:13	"When he came to it, he found nothing but leaves, for it was not the season (*kairos*) for figs."
Mark 12:2	"When the season (*kairos*) came, he sent a slave to the tenants to collect from them his share of the produce of the vineyard."
Mark 13:33	"Beware, keep alert; for you do not know when the time (*kairos*) will come."

"Watch!" Again the reason is that like the doorkeeper they do not know when the master will return. The parable looks beyond the setting during Jesus' ministry to the time of the waiting church after his death/departure. Beasley-Murray reminds us, however, that the incalculability of the time of the end occurs in Jesus' teachings elsewhere: the parable of the burglar (Matt 24:43-44/Luke 12:39-40), the parable of the wise and foolish maidens (Matt 25:1-13), and the Q apocalypse (Luke 17:24, 26-30).[57] Parenthetically, "the master [*kyrios*] of the house" (13:35) and "the owner [*kyrios*] of the vineyard" (12:9) form an interesting parallel.

As Francis Moloney observes, the sun has set on Jesus' ministry, and night, darkness, an appropriate extension of the disciples' not knowing, pervades most of the rest of the Gospel, where we find preparation for the night, night, and a day marked by darkness.[58] The naming of the four watches of the night, following the Roman system—evening, midnight, cockcrow, and dawn—dramatizes the need for watchfulness throughout the period of the master's absence. The Roman reckoning of four watches, as opposed to the Jewish system of three night watches, is present in Mark 6:48 also, which says literally "about the fourth watch." In context, the naming of the four watches serves also to introduce the coming Passion Narrative that recounts the Passover meal in the evening (*opsias*, 14:17), the prayer vigil in Gethsemane during the night, Peter's denial of Jesus at cockcrow (14:72), and the consultation of the chief priests as soon as it was morning (*prōï*, 15:1; cf. 16:2). The addition of the phrase "or else he may find you asleep when he comes suddenly" (13:36) further connects this passage with the coming account of Jesus finding the disciples sleeping while he prayed in Gethsemane (14:32-42).

Staying awake, being alert, and praying all point to the urgency of being about the tasks of discipleship, cross bearing, bearing a faithful witness when called to trial (13:9, 11), and preaching the gospel to all nations (13:10). Jesus' admonition is not just for the original disciples, however: "what I say to you, I say to all" (13:37).

CONNECTIONS

Mark 13:1-4

The opening verses of this chapter raise two themes that readily connect with human nature in every generation: the disciples marveled at the buildings and sought signs that would foretell coming events. Both expose our human foibles. Marveling at the magnificence of our work, as though it could be lasting or transcend our mortality, marks the long history of human delusion that reaches from the tower of Babel in the period of the Sumerian Ziggurats to the tragic collapse of the twin towers of the World Trade Center on September 11, 2001. It is the essence of humanism to look to the flowering of our God-given potential for creativity and to accept it as the greatest good—the worthy object of our striving. We may easily look to our great cities and take pride in our conquest over the environment. We may look at our technological and medical advances and think that we can now control our destinies. And we may look to our prosperity and material comforts and think that we can provide for our needs. But Jesus confronts the disciples with the cold truth of the transience of all human striving and God's unwavering judgment on all human idolatries: "Not one stone will be left standing on another." The works of the creature are not to be compared with the work of the Creator. All our achievements pale before God's sovereignty. Jesus' prophetic judgment on Jerusalem should not be interpreted as discouraging or disparaging human achievement. Rather, it is a stark reminder that human striving and human achievement endure only when they contribute to God's eternal purposes.

The second place where we may see our own reflection in this text is in the disciples' request to know when "all these things" will be accomplished. Yet, if we cannot secure the future by our work, neither can we know any more of the future than the death and resurrection of Jesus reveal of God's ultimate triumph. As though that were not enough, we attempt to create timetables from Scripture, whether the dispensational charts of the premillennialists of earlier generations, the sensational teachings of Hal Lindsey's *Late Great Planet Earth*, or the contemporary fictions of the "Left Behind" series. Neither tea leaves nor tarot cards, dreams nor visions, shamans nor mediums can lift the veil of our human inability to know the future. As Jesus reminded the disciples, it is not for us to know the future. Our task is to be faithful to the mission to which he has called us.

Mark 13:5-23

Because the prediction of persecution and the destruction of the temple arose out of a particular historical situation, and because Mark was writing for a persecuted church, these verses have a particular historical setting in view that may or may not relate to the time and place of a contemporary reader. The contemporary interpreter should be cautious, therefore, about generalizing or transferring the predictions. We may or may not be handed over by family members, arrested, and put on trial for our beliefs. We may or may not experience the invasion of a foreign army and the destruction of our cities and churches. Nevertheless, Christians in other countries know these experiences all too well. It might be sobering to imagine how we would respond to such devastating crises, and then ask what we should be doing to relieve the distress of persecuted believers today.

A second approach to these verses is to focus on Jesus' exhortations, the imperatives. Jesus' first command is "Beware that no one leads you astray" (v. 5). Regardless of the difference in historical circumstances, the danger of false teachings, religious charlatans, and the cultural captivity of religion is as great today as ever. The presentation of religious messages in the popular media (televisions, books, and films) only heightens the difficulty of distinguishing what is true from what is not. When there were prophets pointing to signs of the end of time, Jesus said "don't be deceived by them" (vv. 5-6, 21-22). When cataclysmic events (wars and famines) threatened, Jesus counseled his disciples, "do not be alarmed" (v. 7); this is the time for faithfulness and renewed effort in preaching the gospel; "the good news must first be proclaimed to all nations" (v. 10). Trials that test our convictions may come in various forms, but they are inevitable. The temptation to compromise and to take the easy way out will always be there: "as for yourselves, beware" (v. 9). In such ordeals the believer should learn to trust the Spirit: "do not worry beforehand what you are to say; but say whatever is given to you at that time" (v. 11). Prepare yourself first. What you will say needs to arise from a readiness to speak the truth honestly and courageously regardless of the circumstances. The next lesson in this survivor's manual to meeting crises with integrity is the importance of endurance: "the one who endures to the end will be saved" (v. 13). James wrote that testing produces endurance (Jas 1:3). By the same token, faith and hope have enabled people of faith to endure ordeals that overcame others who did not have their inner strength or their spiritual resources. Here "endurance" also means "steadfastness," faithfulness in the midst of testing. Endurance can also mean taking measures to assure one's personal safety and the safety of others: "flee to the mountains" (v. 14). Be ready to take decisive action when necessary: do not "go down or enter the house" and do not "turn back" (vv. 15-16). Life is so much more valuable than personal possessions. Be ready to leave everything you have and every *thing* you hold dear. Finally, but not least in importance, disciples should pray when they face crises. Prayer is an important part of taking care of oneself in an ordeal, and it is a measure of whether one is enduring and being steadfast or not. In such circumstances prayer is an act based on the conviction that God is still in control and that God's Spirit will empower those who turn to God for help: "pray that it may not be in winter" (v. 18), "be alert" (v. 23).

Schools have fire drills. Hospitals and "first responders" have disaster drills. Military personnel train for situations that call for taking instinctive action. Just because we are not facing an imminent crisis now is no reason for ignoring Jesus' instructions on how to deal with crises when they arise. Perhaps we should have a spiritual fire drill from time to time and rehearse the things we will need to do to survive a catastrophic ordeal should one ever arise. Pilots and astronauts do not train for what they expect; they train so that they will be ready for whatever might happen.

Mark 13:24-27

These verses combine the Old Testament expectation of the coming of "the day of the Lord" with Jesus' forecast of the coming of the Son of Man in glory. The language is apocalyptic rather than literal—the sun darkened, the stars falling, the Son of Man coming in the clouds. The real issue, however, is not whether one believes that the description of these events is literal or metaphorical. What separates believers from nonbelievers is whether one trusts in a God who is working purposefully to redeem humanity, who is moving history toward this end, who will gather up "the elect" in grace for all eternity beyond time. Believers who share this conviction regarding the future have a context in which to situate their lives that others do not share. It is a context that provides a scale of values by which to determine what is important and what is not. Hope in a secure future regardless of the ordeals we may face provides a "future story" that is just as important for the present as the stories we carry from the past.[59]

The shape of this future adds a further agenda to our present, however, for Jesus said that the Son of Man will gather God's elect "from the four winds, from the ends of the earth to the ends of heaven" (13:27). The extent of God's love reaches beyond our pitiful efforts at diversity and inclusiveness, beyond the range of our experience, and even beyond the limits of our imagination and language. As we grow in the grace and knowledge of God, therefore, we also need to be growing in our ability to find common spiritual ground with those who are outside our culturally defined communities. Because God is love, it is impossible to love God and not love those whom God loves (1 John 4:7-12, 16b-21). Spiritual maturity is defined not just by faith but even more by love (1 Cor 13), and in God's own way and time God's love will encompass us fully. For now, our task is to beware of the ordeals of our time that can tempt us to embrace

The Second Coming

Fra Angelico (Beato Angelico). *The Last Judgement*. Christ in his glory, surrounded by angels and saints. Fresco (around 1436). Museo di S. Marco, Florence, Italy. (Credit: Erich Lessing / Art Resource, NY)

other "future stories," faithfully share the good news we have with "all nations," and live into the future by cultivating the community of the future here and now.

Mark 13:28-37

The theme of the last section of the discourse is the urgency of readiness: "Keep awake, be alert, watch!" This urgency is expressed in temporal terms: "this generation will not pass away until all these things have taken place" (13:30), which leads to a dilemma from which there is no escape because Jesus also declared that even he did not know the time when these things will come to pass. The end will come suddenly, but just as you know that summer is almost here when you see leaves on a fig tree, so when you see the signs of catastrophe (the "desolating sacrilege," 13:14), you know that the end is near. Again, however, the fascinating dilemma should not distract us from the urgency of Jesus' warning to be ready. Mark was writing at a time when the events that led to the destruction of Jerusalem were already unfolding. The warning, therefore, is to be ready. Jesus' predictions for the future—the destruction of Jerusalem and then after that the coming of the Son of Man—were already in process of being fulfilled. The need for readiness is urgent: pray, make the most of opportunities to declare your faith, take care that you are not deceived, be steadfast, and prepare for whatever ordeal you may face. Although we live 2,000 years after this urgent warning, we will do well not to let either the chronological dilemma or the apocalyptic language divert our attention from Jesus' urgent counsel to prepare spiritually for any crisis we may confront. If we are ready for anything today, we will be ready for tomorrow also.

The allusions to what the disciples would experience in the next few days, through the echo of Jesus' exhortation to the disciples at Gethsemane to watch and pray, and the foreshadowing of the events of the Last Supper, Gethsemane, and the arrest and trial of Jesus through the naming of the four watches of the night (see the commentary on 13:35), provides an important hermeneutical bridge for this passage. Mark himself was making a transition from Jesus' warning about readiness for the events of the distant future (the destruction of Jerusalem and the coming of the Son of Man) to the events of the next few days. We may do the same, because the message is the same: "what I say to you I say to all: Keep awake" (13:37).

NOTES

[1] See H. C. Kee, "Testaments of the Twelve Patriarchs," in James H. Charlesworth, ed., *The Old Testament Pseudepigrapha* (Garden City NY: Doubleday, 1983), 1:775-828.

[2] William L. Lane, *The Gospel according to Mark* (NICNT; Grand Rapids: Wm. B. Eerdmans, 1974), 446-47.

[3] Ibid., 450.

[4] George R. Beasley-Murray, *Jesus and the Last Days: The Interpretation of the Olivet Discourse* (Peabody MA: Hendrickson, 1993), 363.

[5] See Martin Hengel, *Studies in the Gospel of Mark* (trans. John Bowden; Philadelphia: Fortress Press, 1985), 16-20, 28, 30; Beasley-Murray, *Jesus and the Last Days*, 363-64; Craig A. Evans, *Mark 8:27–16:20* (WBC 34B; Nashville: Thomas Nelson, 2001), 295.

[6] Cited by Lane, *The Gospel according to Mark*, 451. A cubit was about a foot and a half.

[7] Beasley-Murray, *Jesus and the Last Days*, 379.

[8] See Evans, *Mark 8:27–16:20*, 296, who cites *T. Levi* 16:4; *T. Jud.* 23:3; *Sib. Or.* 3:665 and *Liv. Pro.* 10:10-11; 12:11.

[9] Robert A. Guelich, *The Sermon on the Mount* (Waco: Word Books, 1982), 52.

[10] On the lists of the disciples, see further R. Alan Culpepper, *John the Son of Zebedee: The Life of a Legend* (Columbia: University of South Carolina Press, 1994), 28-36.

[11] Lane, *The Gospel according to Mark*, 454.

[12] Francis J. Moloney, *The Gospel of Mark* (Peabody MA: Hendrickson, 2002), 253.

[13] Beasley-Murray, *Jesus and the Last Days*, 388.

[14] Ibid.

[15] Ibid., 387.

[16] Herbert Braun, "*planaō*," *TDNT* 6:240, 246-47.

[17] Ethelbert Stauffer, "*egō*," *TDNT* 2:353; Lane, *The Gospel according to Mark*, 457; Beasley-Murray, *Jesus and the Last Days*, 391.

[18] Ben Witherington, *The Gospel of Mark: A Socio-Rhetorical Commentary* (Grand Rapids: Wm. B. Eerdmans, 2001), 344.

[19] The experience of POWs offers an interesting parallel. See R. Alan Culpepper, *Eternity as a Sunrise: The Life of Hugo H. Culpepper* (Macon GA: Mercer University Press, 2002), 61, 84-85.

[20] Lloyd Gaston, *No Stone on Another: Studies in the Significance of the Fall of Jerusalem in the Synoptic Gospels* (Leiden: E. J. Brill, 1970), 52, cited by Lane, *The Gospel according to Mark*, 446 n. 4.

[21] See Beasley-Murray, *Jesus and the Last Days*, 398.

[22] Ibid., 148, 371, attributes this insight to F. Busch, *Zum Verständnis der synoptischen Eschatologie: Markus 13 neu Untersucht* (Gütersloh, 1938).

[23] Beasley-Murray, *Jesus and the Last Days*, 401.

[24] Lane, *The Gospel according to Mark*, 462.

[25] Lars Hartman, *Prophecy Interpreted* (Lund: CWK Gleerup, 1966), 169; Lane, *The Gospel according to Mark*, 463; Beasley-Murray, *Jesus and the Last Days*, 405.

[26] Evans, *Mark 8:27–16:20*, 312.

[27] Hengel, *Studies in the Gospel of Mark*, 23.

[28] Ibid., 23-24.

[29] Witherington, *The Gospel of Mark*, 345.

[30] Evans, *Mark 8:27–16:20*, 313.

[31] See Emil Schürer, *The History of the Jewish People in the Age of Jesus Christ* (rev. and ed. Geza Vermes and Fergus Millar; Edinburgh: T. & T. Clark, 1973), 1:151-55.

[32] Ibid., 1:394-96.

[33] Beasley-Murray, *Jesus and the Last Days*, 414-15.

[34] Hengel, *Studies in the Gospel of Mark*, 16, which Beasley-Murray quotes in support of his interpretation of these verses (Beasley-Murray, *Jesus and the Last Days*, 408).

[35] Evans, *Mark 8:27–16:20*, 320.

[36] Lane, *The Gospel according to Mark*, 469.

[37] Moloney, *The Gospel of Mark*, 258-59.

[38] For a recent contribution to the debate over the authenticity of the tradition of the flight to Pella, see Moloney, *The Gospel of Mark*, 260-61. Moloney accepts the Pella tradition as accurate and pre-Markan, making both the reference to the desolating sacrilege and the flight to the mountains *vaticinia ex eventu*. Craig Evans, in contrast, rejects the connection with the Pella tradition and accepts both references as "primitive, probably authentic" to Jesus (Evans, *Mark 8:27–16:20*, 320).

[39] Evans, *Mark 8:27–16:20*, 321.

[40] Beasley-Murray, *Jesus and the Last Days*, 419-20 n. 124; Evans, *Mark 8:27–16:20*, 322. Cf. Florentino, García Martínez, *The Dead Sea Scrolls Translated* (trans. Wilfred G. E. Watson; Leiden: E. J. Brill, 1994), 286.

[41] Beasley-Murray, *Jesus and the Last Days*, 423.

[42] Ibid., 424.

[43] Lane, *The Gospel according to Mark*, 476.

[44] Beasley-Murray, *Jesus and the Last Days*, 433.

[45] Ibid., 442.

[46] W. R. Telford, *The Barren Temple and the Withered Tree* (JSNT Sup 1; Sheffield: JSOT Press, 1980), 216, cited by Beasley-Murray, *Jesus and the Last Days*, 441.

[47] Lane, *The Gospel according to Mark*, 479.

[48] Ibid., 477 n. 97.

[49] Beasley-Murray, *Jesus and the Last Days*, 444.

[50] Ibid., 443.

[51] Ibid., 445.

[52] Lane, *The Gospel according to Mark*, 480.

[53] Gregory the Great, *Homilies* 1, quoted in Thomas C. Oden and Christopher A. Hall, eds., *Ancient Christian Commentary on Scripture: New Testament II, Mark* (Downers Grove IL: InterVarsity Press, 1998), 190.

[54] Lane, *The Gospel according to Mark*, 481.

[55] See Beasley-Murray, *Jesus and the Last Days*, 456-58.

[56] Ibid., 469.

[57] Ibid., 471.

[58] Moloney, *The Gospel of Mark*, 271.

[59] Andrew D. Lester, *Hope in Pastoral Care and Counseling* (Louisville: Westminster John Knox, 1995).

PREPARATIONS FOR JESUS' DEATH

Mark 14:1-72

After the thematic developments of chapter 13, Mark 14 returns to the steady drumbeat of rising conflict leading to Jesus' crucifixion, only now the events begin to move swiftly. As early as Mark 2:1–3:6 the evangelist laid the basis for Jesus' conflict with the authorities, which ends with the Pharisees and Herodians making plans to kill him (3:6). In the next section, Jesus' movement back and forth across the Sea of Galilee, symbolically moving between Jewish and Gentile areas and weaving his ministry with the theme of food, meals, and feasting adds rich overtones to the escalating conflict (Mark 4–7). When Jesus set out for Jerusalem, he tried three times to prepare the disciples for what they would experience there, telling them three times that he would be put to death and rise from the dead (Mark 8–10). Once Jesus arrived in Jerusalem, he challenged the corruption of the temple and then engaged in another series of confrontations with the authorities (Mark 11–12). Mark 13, which in some ways seems to be a digression from the plot of the Gospel, places Jesus' ministry in the larger context of God's judgment on the religious leaders and the temple and looks beyond the death of Jesus to his future coming in glory as the Son of Man. The chapter ends with a warning to the disciples to watch and be ready, evening, midnight, cockcrow, and dawn (13:35). Mark 14 turns to the events of the fateful evening through dawn of the day before Jesus was crucified.

As the chapter opens, the authorities plot to kill Jesus, but not during the Passover festival (14:1-2). When an unnamed woman anoints Jesus at the home of Simon the leper, Jesus interprets her action as an anointing of his body for burial (14:3-9). Returning to the actions of the authorities, Mark reports that Judas agreed to betray Jesus to the religious leaders (14:10-11). The next scene returns again to Jesus' preparations for his death as he shares his last meal with the disciples (14:12-25) and predicts that Peter will deny him three times (14:26-31). At Gethsemane Jesus prepares himself for the coming ordeal, praying while the disciples sleep (14:32-42). When the authorities come to arrest Jesus, Judas betrays him with a kiss, Jesus quells the violence, and a young man following Jesus flees into the night, leaving his linen garment behind (14:43-52). Finally,

Peter's denials of Jesus are intercalated with Jesus' open declarations before the council, and Jesus is led away to be tried before Pilate, the Roman governor (14:54-72).

The Passion Narrative is artfully constructed, alternating between Jesus' actions and those of the disciples and religious leaders. The account of Jesus' last days fills out the center of the early Christian preaching. At Pentecost, Peter announced, "this man, handed over to you according to the definite plan and foreknowledge of God, you crucified and killed by the hands of those outside the law. But God raised him up" (Acts 2:23-24), and Paul said, "but we proclaim Christ crucified, stumbling block to Jews and foolishness to Gentiles" (1 Cor 1:23). The central events were familiar to early Christians, but Mark narrates them within the context of the literary and theological themes he has been developing, thereby casting them in a new light. Jesus' death, not his miracles or his teaching, is foundational for understanding who he was and what it means to be his follower. Jesus' death was the result of his opposition to the corruption of religion, making it a matter of personal or national advantage while excluding others. Through his death, therefore, Jesus identified with the outcast, and God's redemptive love was disclosed in the dark hour of Jesus' complete abandonment and despair.

The familiar rituals of the Christian church draw their meaning from the Gospels' account of the events they recall. Wherever the story is told, a disciple's betrayal and a woman's sincere devotion will be part of that story. The celebration of the Last Supper will always be tempered by the memory that the disciples did not understand what was happening, slept while he prayed, and then denied him and abandoned him. Mark's account of Jesus' death on the cross also prevents it from ever being sentimentalized; the suffering is stark and emotionally devastating. Theologically, Jesus' death is both revelatory and salvific—it reveals Jesus' divinity, ironically, at the moment of his death, and prepares for the salvation of the people of faith precisely while the Jews of Jesus' day were preparing to celebrate the Passover with its commemoration of God's deliverance of the people of Israel from their slavery in Egypt. Readers of the Gospel must therefore pay close attention to all of the ways in which it interprets the meaning of the last day of Jesus' life and the hours leading to his death. Mark's account is far from a simple recounting of events; it is a challenging and provocative interpretation of why and how they are significant for people of every time and era.

COMMENTARY

The Authorities' Preparation for Jesus' Death, 14:1-2

The chapter opens with the narrator's statement introducing the time and characters, and what they were doing. The second verse shifts from third person reporting to direct dialogue, thereby bringing the reader into the scene. This opening scene is the first part of a typical Markan sandwich construction:

A The Authorities' Preparation for Jesus' Death, 14:1-2
  B The Anointing of Jesus, 14:3-9
A' Judas's Agreement with the Authorities, 14:10-11

The time was two days before the Passover, Wednesday of what we call Holy Week. The Passover celebration on the evening of Nisan 14 required the slaughter of a lamb, to commemorate the smearing of lamb's blood on the doorposts of the Israelite homes at the time of the exodus, so that the death angel would "pass over" the homes of the Israelites (Exod 12:1-27; *Jub.* 49). That night and for the next week the Israelites were to eat unleavened bread (Exod 12:17-20). The Passover and the Feast of the Unleavened Bread, which may once have been separate festivals celebrated by different societies, shepherds and farmers, had been combined into one week-long pilgrimage festival by New Testament times. During Passover the population of Jerusalem would swell from around 50,000 to 55,000 to several times that number.[1]

The chief priests and the scribes were plotting how they might seize Jesus and kill him (see [Scribes], [Chief Priests]). These two groups are mentioned together in 11:18, 27 and again in 14:43. The chief priests figure prominently in the events of Mark 14, appearing twelve times in this chapter. Mark characterizes their plan as "by stealth" (NRSV) or "some sly way" (NIV), but the Greek term actually means "deceit," and it is listed among the vices in 7:22. The authorities were concerned because of the crowds that would be present in Jerusalem for the Passover and because of Jesus' popularity. The volatility of the crowds at that particular festival, since it commemorated God's deliverance of Israel from Egyptian oppression, might fuel seditious action against the Roman authorities. The authorities had feared the people earlier (11:32). Now their concern was not that they might violate the religious observance but that there might be a riot (cf. John 11:47-53). Outbreaks and violent incidents during the Passover celebrations were not uncommon during that period. [Riots during Passover]

The Anointing of Jesus, 14:3-9

Mark weaves the irony of the situation. While the people celebrate God's deliverance of their forebears, the religious leaders plot to kill God's deliverer. While they make their preparations, however, an anonymous woman, equally unaware of what she is doing, anoints Jesus' body for burial beforehand. There is also the further irony that when the Messiah comes to Jerusalem, he is not anointed by the chief priests (who plot to kill him) but by an unnamed woman. Finally, the placement of the anointing of Jesus at the beginning of the Passion Narrative forms a bracket with the failure to anoint Jesus for burial at the end of the narrative (cf. 14:8 and 16:1). As noted above, the unnamed woman's anointing of Jesus is the inside of the sandwich formed by the authorities' plot to kill Jesus and Judas's compact with them (14:1-2 and 14:10-11; see [Markan Sandwiches]). John Painter has suggested a further bracketing based on the similarity of this woman's selfless generosity in breaking the flask and pouring the pure nard over Jesus and the widow's giving of her last two coins (12:41-44). These two exemplary acts by devout women bracket Jesus' judgment on the temple in Mark 13.[2]

The parallel traditions of the anointing of Jesus in the four Gospels have challenged interpreters. The account in Matthew 26 is so close to Mark 14 that one must be dependent on the other. In Luke 7 we find a very different account in which a woman of the city weeps on Jesus' feet, wipes them with her hair, and then anoints them almost as an afterthought. In John 12 Mary anoints Jesus' feet, and then wipes off the expensive ointment. The chart in [The Anointing of Jesus in the Four Gospels] highlights other places where the accounts agree and differ. Although interpretations vary, it appears that the accounts report two separate events. Luke reports an incident during Jesus' Galilean ministry in which a woman wept on Jesus' feet and wiped them with her hair. The other Gospels report the anointing of Jesus (probably on his head) at Bethany during the days before Passover. Because of the similarity of the two events, details of each tradition influenced the other.

The story of the anointing of Jesus is similar in some respects to the healing of the paralytic in Mark 2:1-12. Each features a provocative act (healing, anointing), a controversy, and Jesus' response. In each case the function is didactic; the story is used to teach something about Jesus and/or about discipleship. Typically the focus of a pronouncement story is on Jesus' words, but here Jesus' words share the spotlight and indeed point to the woman's exemplary act of devotion.

The narrator first sets the scene. Jesus is in Bethany, presumably with the disciples, but they are not mentioned. Bethany was a village just

---

The Anointing of Jesus in the Four Gospels

	Mark 14:3-9	Matthew 26:6-13	Luke 7:36-50	John 12:1-8
The Place				
	Bethany the house of Simon the leper	Bethany the house of Simon the leper	Galilee the house of Simon the Pharisee	Bethany the house of Lazarus
The Time				
	two days before Passover	two days before Passover	during Jesus' Galilean ministry	six days before Passover
The Woman				
	unnamed	unnamed	a harlot	Mary
The Ointment				
	an alabaster flask of pure nard, very expensive	an alabaster flask of very expensive ointment	an alabaster flask of ointment	a pound of costly ointment, pure nard
The Anointing				
	poured on his head	poured on his head	wet his feet with her tears, wiped her tears with her hair, anointed his feet	anointed his feet wiped them with her hair

The Protest

Some:	The disciples:	The Pharisee:	Judas:
the wasted ointment could have been sold for 300 denarii and given to the poor	the wasted ointment could have been sold for a large sum and given to the poor	If Jesus were a prophet, he would have known what sort of woman this was	the wasted ointment could have been sold for 300 denarii and given to the poor

The Response

(1) Let her alone, why trouble her?	(1) Why trouble her?	(1) the parable of the two debtors	(1) Let her alone.
(2) She has done a beautiful thing.	(2) She has done a beautiful thing.	(2) You gave me no water for my feet.	(2) Let her keep it for the day of my burial.
(3) You always have the poor.	(3) You always have the poor.	(3) Her sins are forgiven.	(3) You always have the poor.
(4) She has anointed my body for burying.	(4) She has done it to prepare my body for burial.	(4) Your faith has saved you. Go in peace.	

over the crest of the Mount of Olives, two or three miles east of Jerusalem, and Jesus stayed there when he was in Jerusalem (cf. 11:1, 11, 12). Jesus was in the home of Simon the leper. Is it coincidence that Luke reports the anointing of Jesus in Galilee in the home of Simon, a Pharisee (Luke 7:36, 40)? Mark reports the name, either to establish the authenticity of the event or because Simon was known to his intended audience (cf. Bartimaeus, 10:46; Alexander and Rufus, 15:21). Painter suggests that Jesus was following the practice he had taught the disciples—to accept hospitality and stay in a home wherever they went (6:10).

Banquets were typically public occasions so that others could watch the grand event and the host could receive public approbation (honor). For that reason, a "woman of the city" could have been present in the home of Simon the Pharisee (Luke 7:37). Similarly, the woman in this scene may or may not have been an invited guest. She is unnamed and described only by her actions. The guests reclined on cushions, making it easy for the woman to approach Jesus' feet. In Mark's account, however, she anoints Jesus' head, which may convey a royal or messianic anointing. Although the woman may have intended nothing more than a spontaneous act of love, Mark may have seen in her act the messianic anointing that should have come from the religious authorities, who were busy plotting to kill him.

Anointing a guest was a common act of hospitality (Pss 23:5; 141:5; Luke 7:46). Breaking a flask of pure nard was incredibly extravagant. Nard was a perfume made from the roots of a plant that grew in India. [Nard] Fine ointments and perfumes were preserved in alabaster flasks,[3] and one broke the slender neck of the flask to pour out the precious perfume. Breaking the flask also meant that none of the ointment would be held back for a later occasion. The value of the fragrance is conveyed by three descriptions, each progressively more specific: "pure" (Gk. *pistikēs*, which can mean "genuine, unadulterated" or may describe a particular kind of nard, *pistakia*, from a pistachio tree),[4] "expensive" (Gk. *polytelous*), and later "worth more than three hundred denarii" (14:5), or about the annual income of a day laborer.

Mark reports that some were "indignant" at the waste of such a precious fragrance. In Luke, the host is scandalized by the woman's reputation and by the sensual demonstration of letting down her hair and wiping Jesus' feet in his house. In Matthew it is the disciples who take issue with her action, and in John it is Judas. Although Mark does not say that it was some of the disciples who were indignant, Jesus' response is more appropriate if it is addressed to the disciples, whom he had previously told that he would be killed (8:31; 9:31; 10:32-34). Mark has also used the term "indignant" on two earlier occasions, once for Jesus being indignant when the disciples refused to let the children come to him (10:14), and once for the response of the ten to James and John (10:41). It was expected that pilgrims for the Passover would give alms for the poor (*m. Pesachim* 9.11; 10.1; John 13:29; [The Poor]; cf. [Beggars]). Those who took offense (cf. 14:4 and 2:6, 24; 3:2) did so because they thought the nard might better have been sold and the money given to the poor, so they rebuked the extravagant woman (Gk. *enebrimōnto*; cf. 1:43).

The rest of the story reports Jesus' response to those who took offense at the woman's selfless act of devotion. Jesus gave three separate responses. First, he defended her and her action by means of a command, a rebuking question, and a defense of what she had done (14:6): "Let her alone; why do you trouble her? She has performed a good service for

---

Nard

"A costly fragrant ointment prepared from the roots and hairy stems of an aromatic Indian herb. . . . In the OT it appears in the Song of Solomon as a perfume giving fragrance to the king's couch (1:12) and as one of several fragrant spices listed symbolically in praise of a bride (4:13–14)."

J. C. Trever, "Nard," *IDB* 3:510.

The Poor

". . . Jerusalem in the time of Jesus was already a centre for mendicancy; it was encouraged because almsgiving was regarded as particularly meritorious when done in the Holy City . . . . Begging in Jerusalem was concentrated around the holy places, i.e. at that time around the Temple."

Joachim Jeremias, *Jerusalem in the Time of Jesus* (trans. F. H. Cave and C. H. Cave; Philadelphia: Fortress Press, 1969), 116–17.

me." The NRSV translation is a bit prosaic here. The command is sharper in Greek, "Leave her!" or "Release her!" and the terms translated "a good service" literally mean "a beautiful work" or "a beautiful thing," and it may have carried the technical meaning of an act of charity.

Second, Jesus explained that she had responded to the opportunity of that moment. They would always have the opportunity to help the poor, but they would not again have the chance to serve him as she had. Jesus' words have often been misunderstood, however. He was not diminishing the importance of relieving the suffering of the poor. In Deuteronomy 15:11, to which Jesus may have been alluding, the observation that "there will never cease to be some in need on the earth" is tied to the command to "open your hand to the poor." The issue is not a forced choice between worship and ministry; there is a time for each, and the poor will always be better served by the spontaneous generosity of the unnamed woman than the calculating plans of those who were critical of the beautiful thing she did for Jesus.

Third, Jesus interpreted the anointing as a proleptic preparation of his body for burial (cf. Mark 16:1; Luke 24:1; John 19:39-40). This third response is powerful because it serves multiple functions. It explains why they will not have Jesus with them much longer, it juxtaposes the woman's action with the maneuvering of the authorities, it sets up a contrast between her and the treachery of Judas, one of the disciples (14:10-11), and it confirms for the reader that the religious authorities will succeed in killing Jesus. With this breathtaking statement, Jesus' sharp response to the indignant critics builds to a climax.

Verse 9 solemnly declares that what she has done will be remembered and told wherever the gospel is preached—"in the whole world." For this declaration Jesus used the weighty formula, "Amen, I say to you" (cf. 3:28; 8:12; 9:1, etc.). Again, the import of what Jesus said is powerful. In spite of—indeed because of—his death, the gospel will be preached (see the commentary on Mark 1:1, 15 and [Gospels]). There will be a period between Jesus' resurrection and the coming of the Son of Man in glory when the gospel will be preached to all nations (13:10). What the woman did in honor of Jesus will be told in memory of her. Her name might not be remembered, but what she did for Jesus will never be forgotten, and Mark ensured that this would be the case by recording it in his Gospel, where it stands as an example for all who would come later. Like other "minor" characters who appear in only one scene in the Gospel, such as the leper (1:40-45), the paralytic's friends (2:1-12), Jairus (5:21-23, 35-43), the Syrophoenician woman (7:24-30), the father of the epileptic boy (9:14-29), Bartimaeus (10:46-52), and the widow with the two mites (12:41-44), the unnamed woman who anointed Jesus models an aspect of true discipleship.

Judas's Agreement with the Authorities, 14:10-11

Sandwiching the anointing of Jesus and completing the report of the authorities' plot to seize Jesus and kill him (14:1-2) is the report of Judas's complicity with the authorities. Mark's brief report of Judas's betrayal takes the form of a negotiation. Verse 10 reports Judas's action in going to the authorities, v. 11a reports their response, and 11b reports what Judas did as a result of their agreement.

Judas Iscariot is identified explicitly as "one of the twelve" (see the commentary on 3:19). He was one of the twelve disciples named by Jesus early in his ministry in Galilee (3:14). Now, forever after he would be remembered as the one who betrayed Jesus (cf. 3:19; John 6:70-71; 12:4). Although elsewhere the chief priests act in collusion with the scribes (11:18, 27; 14:1, 43, 53), Mark reports here that Judas went to the chief priests, whom Evans calls "Jesus' principal and most dangerous opponents."[5] Lane suggests that Judas may have been responding to a public appeal for information leading to Jesus' arrest (cf. John 11:57),[6] but Mark leaves only the assumption that the disciples knew that the authorities were seeking to kill Jesus (cf. 3:6). Likewise, Mark offers no explanation of why Judas betrayed Jesus. If Judas shared with the other disciples the expectation that Jesus would overthrow the Romans and establish his kingdom in Jerusalem (cf. 9:33; 10:37), by now he could see that his hope would not be realized. Jesus condemned the temple authorities rather than the Romans (11:11-19), prophesied the destruction of the Jerusalem and the temple (13:1-23), and spoke again of his death (8:31; 9:31; 10:32-34) and burial (14:8). The clearer Jesus' intentions became, the more alien and disappointing they may have been to Judas.

The authorities needed to find a way to seize Jesus and do away with him without inciting a riot among his followers and the throngs of pilgrims who had come to Jerusalem for the Passover. Judas could serve them well by (1) informing them of a time and place where they could arrest Jesus when others would not be present (14:26, 32, 43), (2) identifying Jesus so they could be sure they got the right man (14:44-46), and perhaps (3) giving them information they could use against Jesus. Citing 14:55-61, Evans contends that Judas "probably also divulged to the ruling priests the essence of Jesus' proclamation and self-understanding."[7] In his defense Jesus pointed to the public nature of his ministry, preaching daily in the temple (14:49; cf. 11:27-12:44), but the accusation that he was the Messiah (14:61) is more explicit than his public proclamations had been.

The authorities were delighted, and indeed Judas's assistance in the matter may have persuaded them to proceed with the arrest before Passover (cf. 14:2). In return, they agreed to pay off the informer, but the money does not seem to have been what induced Judas to go to the chief priests (cf. Matt 26:15; 27:3, where the amount, thirty pieces of silver, is specified). From that moment on Judas was looking for the opportune moment to hand Jesus over to his opponents. Mark uses the verb to seek (*zētein*) for the adulation of the crowd (1:37), his family's misguided effort to protect him (3:32), the Pharisees' desire for a sign (8:11, 12), Jesus' opponents' efforts to do him harm (11:18; 12:12; 14:1, 11, 55), and the women's search for Jesus' body (16:6). Compare the similarly sinister use of "opportune" in 6:21.

Preparations for the Passover Meal, 14:12-16

Another temporal reference introduces this section (cf. 14:1, 3). According to Mark's chronology, the authorities met on Wednesday (two days before Passover), and Jesus was presumably anointed that day at the home of Simon the leper. The next day, which Mark loosely calls "the first day of the Unleavened Bread" and then identifies as the day "when the Passover lamb is sacrificed" (14 Nisan), Jesus makes preparations to eat the Passover meal with his disciples after sunset that evening (14:12, 17; 15 Nisan). After the meal Jesus leads the disciples to Gethsemane, where he is arrested. He is interrogated by the high priest that night, tried before Pilate early the next morning (Friday), and then crucified. Matthew and Luke follow Mark's chronology. [Chronology of the Last Supper and the Crucifixion of Jesus] John, however, reports that the authorities would not enter the Roman praetorium for Jesus' trial because they had not yet eaten the Passover (John 18:28). This means that according to John's chronology, Jesus, "the lamb of God who takes away the sin of the world" (John 1:29, 36), dies on the afternoon when the Passover lambs were slaughtered (14 Nisan) in preparation for the Passover meal, which the Jews would eat after sunset that Friday (cf. John 19:31). All of the Gospel writers record that Jesus was crucified at Passover. The difference is whether the Last Supper occurred at the Passover meal (as in Mark) or Jesus died at the hour the Passover lambs were slain (as in John). Each evangelist could have seen a theological reason for his chronology of these events. While scholars are divided on the resolution of this issue, it is improbable that the authorities would have arrested Jesus, assembled the chief priests, elders, and scribes, and then executed Jesus on the day of Passover (cf. 14:2).

The scene of Jesus sending two disciples to prepare the Passover meal should sound familiar to the reader. At a number of points it reproduces words and phrases from the report that Jesus sent two disciples into the village to bring the colt for his entry into Jerusalem.

Mark 11:1-6	**Mark 14:13-16**
"he sent two of his disciples"	"he sent two of his disciples"
"and said to them"	"saying to them"
"Go into the village"	"Go into the city"
"say"	"say"
"The Lord"	"The Teacher"
"and they went away and found"	"and . . . went . . . and . . . found"
"what Jesus had said"	"as he had told them"

Evidently Mark used the tradition of one of these events as the pattern for his account of the other. In other respects, however, each story is different. While the securing of the colt for the entry into Jerusalem seems to involve Jesus' divine foreknowledge of what would transpire when the disciples untied the colt, the preparation for the Passover meal appears to have been prearranged and then carried out in secrecy.

Following the instruction of Exodus 12:3-11, 21 and Deuteronomy 16:2, a year-old male lamb without blemish was to be slaughtered on the afternoon of the 14th of Nisan. Mark does not say whether Jesus, one of the disciples, or the man in whose home they ate the Passover was the one who slaughtered the lamb. Evans describes the prescribed procedure as follows: "According to Jewish convention, Jesus would have slit the animal's throat, its blood would have been drained into a silver or gold basin held by a priest, and the priest would have taken the basin to the altar where he would have sprinkled the blood at the base of the altar."[8]

The disciples then asked Jesus, perhaps in the temple following the slaughter of the lamb, where they should prepare the Passover meal. At this point, he sent two of them, apparently two who were not among the Twelve, since v. 17 reports that the Twelve accompanied Jesus into the city that evening. Jesus' instructions were that they should go into the city, implying that they were outside the city or perhaps in the temple precinct at the time. A man carrying a jar of water would meet them. They would recognize the man because although men carried wineskins of water, carrying a jar was normally women's work (cf. John 4:28). Such cloak-and-dagger secrecy may have been necessary because Jesus knew the authorities were looking for him. We may infer that Jesus had made these plans in advance with one of his Judean disciples. He would be looking for the two, and the jar of water was the agreed upon signal. Perhaps without even a word being spoken, they would follow him to a house. There they would say, "the Teacher asks, Where is my guest room (*katalyma*) where I may eat the Passover with my disciples?" Without their using Jesus' name, the householder would know who they were, and he would show them "a large room upstairs" furnished, probably with carpets or couches on which Jesus and the

---

Chronology of the Last Supper and the Crucifixion of Jesus

	The Synoptics	John
Preparation for the meal (Thursday afternoon)	"On the first day of Unleavened Bread, when the Passover lamb is sacrificed, his disciples said to him, "Where do you want us to go and make preparations for you to eat the Passover? . . . So the disciples set out and went to the city, and found everything as he had told them; and they prepared the Passover." (Mark 14:12; Nisan 14)	
The meal (Thursday evening)	"When it was evening, he came with the twelve." (Mark 14:17; Nisan 15)	"before the festival of the Passover" (John 13:1; Nisan 14)
The trial (early Friday morning)	"as soon as it was morning" (Mark 15:1; Nisan 15)	"Then they took Jesus from Caiaphas to Pilate's headquarters. It was early in the morning. They themselves did not enter the praetorium, so as to avoid ritual defilement and to be able to eat the Passover." (John 18:28; Nisan 14)
Jesus' death (Friday afternoon)	"At three o'clock" (Mark 15:34; Nisan 15)	"Since it was the day of Preparation, the Jews did not want the bodies left on the cross during the Sabbath, especially because that Sabbath was a day of great solemnity." (John 19:31; Nisan 14)
The burial (late Friday afternoon)	"When evening had come, and since it was the day of Preparation, that is, the day before the Sabbath" (Mark 15:42; Nisan 15)	"And so, because it was the Jewish day of Preparation, and the tomb was nearby, they laid Jesus there." (John 19:38; Nisan 14)

R. Alan Culpepper, *The Gospel and Letters of John* (Nashville: Abingdon Press, 1998), 200–201.

---

disciples could recline for the meal. The word *katalyma* could refer to an inn (Luke 2:7) or a guest room or dining room (1 Sam 1:18; 9:22; Sir 14:25; cf. Luke 22:11).[9] The room would have had to be large if Jesus were accompanied by not only the Twelve but perhaps by other disciples and some women also. It was customary at the Passover meal for a child to ask what made that night special (Exod 12:26). There they would prepare the lamb, bitter herbs, unleavened bread, and wine required for the meal. The plan worked; the disciples followed Jesus' instructions, were met by the man carrying a jar of water, found the upper room, and made the necessary preparations for the meal that would have more significance than they could ever have imagined.

The Passover Meal, Scene 1: The Betrayer, 14:17-21

Following this rather extended account of the preparations for the Passover meal, the meal itself is reported surprisingly briefly, with all attention being focused on Jesus' words, so the meal is merely the setting for what Jesus said. The eating of the Passover lamb is not mentioned at all, and what is reported relates only to parts of the liturgy for the Passover meal as recorded in the *Mishnah*. [Passover Liturgy] Mark's report of the Last Supper falls into three parts: (1) Jesus' announcement that one of the Twelve would betray him (14:17-21), (2) the words of institution (14:22-26), and (3) Jesus' prediction that Peter would deny him (14:27-31).

Following the requirements for the Passover meal, Jesus and the disciples did not come for the meal until evening had fallen, marking the beginning of the 15th of Nisan. If the reference to the Twelve in v. 17 is to be taken literally, then the two who were sent ahead to prepare the meal must have been from the larger circle of disciples. Reclining on couches or mats was required for the Passover meal; it symbolized that the participants were no longer slaves but free people.[10] Reclining for a meal was common, however, when outdoors, or at a party, a feast, or a wedding.

> **Passover Liturgy**
>
> Tractate *Pesahim* in the *Mishnah* is devoted to the Feast of Passover, and gives detailed instructions as to how the meal should be celebrated. The meal should not be eaten until nightfall (10.1). After the first cup of wine, the first benediction was said (10.2). After the food was brought (10.3), there was the breaking of bread and then the second cup. A child then asked, "Why is this night different from other nights," and the father answered with the story of the Exodus, beginning with, "A wandering Aramean was my father . . ." (10.4). The Passover, the unleavened bread, and the bitter herbs were essential parts of the story and the observance. Then, they recited the first part of the Hallel (Psalms 113–118). The benediction over the meal was said after the third cup (10.7), and they chanted the rest of the Hallel. After the fourth cup came the benediction over song, and the meal had to end before midnight (10.9). The celebration gave thanks to God for their deliverance from oppression in Egypt and looked forward to their future redemption.
>
> Herbert Danby, *The Mishnah* (Oxford: Clarendon Press, 1931), 150–51.

The focus of this scene is on Jesus' announcement that one of the disciples will betray him. In contrast to Matthew and John, Mark does not mention Judas. In Matthew the scene is embellished with the addition that Judas also said "Surely not I, Rabbi?" and Jesus responded, "You have said so" (Matt 26:25). In John Jesus dips a morsel and gives it to Judas, Satan enters into Judas, and Judas goes out into the night (John 13:2, 26, 27, 30). Mark reports the scene with greater restraint, brevity, and suspense. Mark's account is therefore open to various interpretations. Reading Mark alone, for example, it is not clear whether Jesus' knowledge of the betrayal is an example of his divine knowledge of the hearts of others (as explicitly in John 2:24-25), or whether one should seek another explanation. Following the latter course, Evans says, "Jesus has evidently heard that the ruling priests have struck a bargain with one of his disciples."[11] It is also not clear from Mark whether Jesus knew that the one who had betrayed him was Judas; he said only that it was someone who was present, eating with him, one of the Twelve. Both of these identifications serve to heighten the treachery of the betrayal. To eat together was an act of intimate fellowship, and the announcement that it was one of the Twelve meant that it was someone in Jesus' inner circle. The reference to one who was eating with him evokes Psalm 41:9, "Even my bosom friend in whom I trusted, who ate of my bread, has lifted his heel against me," and the Gospel of John makes this allusion explicit (John 13:18). Parenthetically, this announcement would make little sense if only the Twelve were present, but it would have a powerful impact if the meal included a larger group of disciples and the Twelve were those reclining closest to Jesus.[12] The reader, however, knows full well that Judas was the betrayer (3:19; 14:10-11).

When they heard this shocking announcement in the middle of what was normally a joyful and optimistic celebration, the disciples were sorrowful. The verb *lypeō* occurs elsewhere in Mark only to describe the response of the would-be disciple who had many possessions (10:22). Their response to Jesus expresses a level of humility and self-awareness that is out of character for the disciples in Mark as they begin to ask him, one by one, "Surely, not I?" The question acknowledges that any one of them was capable of betraying him, but the form of the question expects a negative answer. According to Luke, the disciples began to ask each other who it could be (Luke 22:23), and according to John they looked at one another (John 13:22). Jesus said only that it was one who was dipping bread in the bowl or dish (probably of bitter herbs) with him (14:20). Without identifying the betrayer explicitly, this detail added to the shocking treachery of Judas's betrayal of Jesus.

The fact that Jesus knew that one of the disciples was about to betray him did not lessen that disciple's treachery or guilt. Jesus was remaining faithful to the work God had given him to do, to the very end, even knowing that they were going to kill him. Jesus' death, moreover, would be the means by which God would bring salvation to all who would accept his death as atonement for their sins. Nevertheless, neither Jesus nor Judas was merely playing a predetermined role. Both Jesus' faith and unconditional trust in God and Judas's deceit and treachery were profoundly real. Therefore, Jesus could acknowledge both that his death as the Son of Man was a fulfillment of Scripture and that Judas faced an awful fate. Jesus probably had in mind the suffering servant songs of Isaiah 52–53, and later he alludes to Zechariah 13:7 (14:27), but no Old Testament text speaks of the suffering of the

Son of Man. Jesus' statement therefore implies a connection between the Son of Man and the suffering servant in Isaiah. The "woe" should probably be read as a lament, meaning something like "Alas," or "Oh how terrible it will be." Elsewhere in Mark the term is used only when Jesus laments the suffering of the pregnant and nursing in the last days (13:17), but in the other Gospels Jesus pronounces woes over the towns of Chorazin and Bethsaida (Matt 11:21; Luke 10:13), woes on the hypocritical religious leaders (Matt 23:13-16), and woes on the rich (Luke 6:24-26). The curse formula, "it would have been better for that one not to have been born" (14:21), was a common expression found in Jewish texts of the period (*1 En.* 38.2; *2 En.* 41.2; *m. Hagigah* 2.1).[13] Vincent Taylor captured the spirit of Jesus' lament: "The 'Woe' pronounced over him is not a curse, but a cry of sorrow and of anguish; 'Alas! for that man', and the saying 'It were better, etc.' is not a threat, but a sad recognition of facts."[14]

The Passover Meal, Scene 2: The Institution of the Lord's Supper, 14:22-25

The central point of Mark's account of the Last Supper both structurally and theologically is the institution of the Lord's Supper in the giving of the bread and the wine. Because of the early use of this tradition in the church's worship, it has connections with key passages in the Old Testament, parallel texts elsewhere in the New Testament, meal scenes and pronouncements earlier in Mark, and practices and concepts reflected in a variety of ancient texts. Sacred meals were common in Graeco-Roman paganism as well as in Judaism, and bread and wine, along with fish, were staples of the Mediterranean diet. Not surprisingly, all of these common elements acquired religious significance. The Jewish text *Joseph and Asenath* refers to eating "blessed bread of life" and drinking "a blessed cup of immortality" (8:5, 11; 15:5; 16:16) in contrast to the idolatrous pagan meals that offer "bread of strangulation" and "a cup of insidiousness" (8:5).[15] A Qumran text describes a messianic meal at which the congregation of Israel will eat the first fruit of the bread and drink the new wine (1Q28a[1QSa] II.17-20).[16] The primary background, however, is the liturgy for the Passover meal as derived from Exodus 12 and developed over the centuries (*Jub.* 49; *m. Pesahim*; see [Passover Liturgy]). Significantly, Mark makes no reference to most of the liturgy for the meal and does not mention the lamb or the bitter herbs, only the bread and the wine. Before the meal and after the second cup of wine the paterfamilias pronounced a blessing over the bread. *Mishnah Berakoth* 6.1 prescribes the traditional blessing over bread: "[Blessed art thou] who bringest forth bread from the earth."[17]

Then, the head of the family broke the bread and gave it to each person, who dipped it in the bitter herbs and stewed fruit. Following the meal he blessed the third cup of wine. Again, *Mishnah Berakoth* 6.1 prescribes the traditional blessing over wine: "[Blessed art thou] who createst the fruit of the vine." Following each blessing, Jesus departed from the customary liturgy and infused the meal with new meaning by the words he spoke relating the bread and the cup to himself, his coming death, the new covenant it established, the promise of the coming of the kingdom, and the eschatological banquet they would share when they next ate together.

This Passover meal was but the last of many occasions on which the disciples had eaten with Jesus, privately, as guests in the homes of others, and feeding the crowds who came to Jesus. In these accounts the consistent feature is Jesus' signature act of taking bread, blessing it, breaking it, and giving it (Mark 6:41; 8:6; John 6:11; Luke 24:30; 1 Cor 11:23-24). The early Christian practice of the fellowship meal became known as "the breaking of bread" (Acts 2:42, 46; 20:7; Luke 24:30-31, 35). Mark uses the same verb for blessing (*eulogein*) in v. 22 that he used in 6:41 and 8:7. The parallels in language in the three feeding scenes are striking, with only minor variations in whether the blessing of the bread and fish or bread and cup are reported once or separately, whether *eulogein* or *eucharistein* is used for the blessing, and whether the simple or compound form of the verb "to break" is used. Just as Jesus had given the people bread earlier, so now he gives them himself.

Jesus' pronouncement, "this is my body," would have been startling in the context of the Passover liturgy. It must have meant something like "this represents my body" or "this is a token of my body," but it need not have had the shocking cannibalistic overtones of John 6:53, "unless you eat the flesh of the Son of Man and drink his blood, you have no life in you." Following David Daube, Evans suggests that the bread was the *afikoman*, the piece of bread broken off for the Messiah at the beginning of the meal and then consumed at the end of the meal. By identifying himself as the *afikoman* and offering it to the disciples, Jesus would have been making a messianic claim, and the disciples would have been symbolically acknowledging him as the Messiah by consuming it.[18] Whether this suggestion stands or not, the words of institution of the Lord's Supper confirm that Jesus not only anticipated his imminent death but saw sacrificial significance in it.

Like the suffering servant of Isaiah 53, "he was wounded for our transgressions, crushed for our iniquities" (Isa 53:5), his life was "an offering for sin" (53:10), and "he poured out himself to death" (53:12). Reflection on the deaths of the Maccabean martyrs in the second century BC (see [The Maccabean Martyrs]) had already established a connection between the suffering of the righteous and atonement for the nation. Eleazar, the brother of Judas Maccabaeus, for example, "gave his life to save his people and to win for himself an everlasting name" (1 Macc 6:44). Jesus could therefore have expected the disciples to have grasped the connections between the bread he gave them and the significance of his impending death. [The Eucharist in the Early Church]

The Eucharist in the Early Church

"When the president has given thanks, and the whole congregation has assented, those whom we call deacons give to each of those present a portion of the consecrated bread and wine and water. They then take it to those absent. This food we call Eucharist, of which no one is allowed to partake except one who believes that the things we teach are true, and has received the washing for forgiveness of sins and for rebirth, and who lives according to the way Christ handed down to us."

Justin Martyr, *First Apology* 65-66, in Thomas C. Oden and Christopher A. Hall, eds., *Ancient Christian Commentary on Scripture: New Testament II, Mark* (Downers Grove IL: InterVarsity Press, 1998), 205; *ANF* 1:185.

The giving of the cup symbolized even more graphically the new covenant that would be formed through Jesus' violent death. Here the verb for giving thanks is *eucharistein*. After they all drank of it, Jesus said, "This is my blood of the covenant, which is poured out for many." Blood carried the life force, and in ancient practice covenants were formed through the shedding of blood (Exod 24:3-8; Zech 9:11; Heb 9:18). The people of Israel entered into the covenant by bringing a sacrifice and then by having its blood sprinkled on them by the priests (Exod 24:8; Heb 9:19-22; cf. 1 Pet 1:2). The verb "to pour out" (*ekchynnesthai*) is used in sacrificial contexts. Like the blood of the sacrifice was poured out at the base of the altar (Exod 29:12; Lev 4:7, 18, 25), the life of the suffering servant would be "poured out" (Isa 53:12). Paul referred to his martyrdom, in imitation of Christ, as being poured out on the altar (Phil 2:17), and Luke referred to Stephen's death as pouring out the blood of their martyr (Acts 22:20). Just as the first covenant with Israel had required the shedding of blood, so the new covenant, long anticipated (cf. Jer 31:31-34), would come about through the shedding of Jesus' blood at the Passover. This covenant would atone for the sins of "many" (14:24), another reference with echoes both in Isaiah 53:12, "yet he bore the sin of many," and Mark 10:45, "and to give his life a ransom for many." The meaning of the cup has already been established in Mark as a symbol for suffering and death in Jesus' response to James and John, "Are you able to drink the cup that I drink?" (Mark 10:38). By drinking the cup of wine Jesus offered them in the context of the Passover meal, the disciples not only commemorated God's covenant with Egypt at the exodus but entered into a new covenant that would mark a new deliverance through Jesus' death.

The disciples' last supper with Jesus not only fulfilled the Passover observance that was rooted deep in Israel's history and interpreted the events that were unfolding that very evening, it also looked forward to the fulfillment of all of God's redemptive work in the great eschatological banquet (Isa 25:6; *2 Bar.* 29:5-8; Matt 8:11; Luke 14:15; Rev 19:9). Mark 14 has four of Mark's thirteen solemn "Amen, I say to you" sayings (14:9, 18, 25, 30; see commentary on Mark 3:28). Because the meal ends with the singing of a song, traditionally the latter part of the Hallel (Pss 115–118), with no mention of a further cup—the fourth cup (see [Passover Liturgy]), Lane surmises that Jesus abstained from the fourth cup, making his pronouncement that he would not drink again of "the fruit of the vine" (cf. Num 6:4; Isa 32:12; Hab 3:17) until he drank it new in the kingdom of God (14:25; cf. Luke 22:15-16) even more dramatic.[19] The kingdom of God, the reader will remember, is not an extension of the old, but the inauguration of a radically new reality, the glorious reign of God (cf. Zech 14:9). Old wineskins cannot contain it (2:21-22); it will be new wine.

The Passover Meal, Scene 3: Predicting Peter's Denials, 14:26-31

This scene may be either an extension of the meal, as it is regarded here, or an introduction to the Gethsemane scene that follows. In either case, it presents a series of predictions that will be fulfilled to the letter by the coming events. In this chapter, Jesus has predicted his burial (14:8), the retelling of the woman's anointing of Jesus wherever the gospel is preached (14:9), the disciples' meeting the man carrying a jar of water (14:13), Judas's betrayal (14:18), his own death (14:21), and the coming eschatological banquet (14:25). In this scene Jesus foretells the scattering of the disciples (14:27), his resurrection and reunion with the disciples in Galilee (14:28), and Peter's denial of him later that night (14:30). These prophecies serve both to confirm Jesus' divine authority and foreknowledge and to heighten the reader's sense of suspense as the events unfold. Therefore, when Jesus is mocked and challenged to prophesy (14:65), the reader knows full well that Jesus has prophesied and his prophecies are all coming to pass.

Verse 26 is a transitional verse that can be taken either with the previous scene or with the verses that follow. In keeping with Mark's pattern of carefully setting the scene for Jesus' pronouncements while often moving on abruptly following Jesus' sayings, v. 26 should probably be read as the introduction to the dialogue in vv. 27-31 (as it is in the Nestle text and the NRSV).

Mark does not say what the disciples and Jesus sang. It may have been the latter part of the Hallel (Pss 115–118), or some other psalm. The singing marked the end of the meal. Then they went out to the Mount of Olives, which has already been mentioned prominently

(11:1; 13:3). Joel Marcus suggests that the eschatological expectations related to the Mount of Olives in Zechariah form the background for Jesus' reinterpretation of popular expectations. [Revisioning the Future]

Jesus announces that the disciples "will all become deserters" (literally, they will all be caused to stumble, they will all be "scandalized," *skandalisthēsesthe*). Raymond Brown notes that "while the verb has the general sense of stumbling, falling, and hence sinning, the absolute usage can connote a loss of faith (see Mark 9:42-47; *Didache* 16:5), especially in the face of tribulation or persecution."[20] In the parable of the sower, those who have no root endure only a little while and then fall away "when trouble or persecution arises on account of the word" (4:17). The disciples, then, represent all those who in Mark's time have turned away from the church because of the danger of persecution. Fulfilling Scripture, they will be scattered. Zechariah 13:7 is a declaration of judgment on the people. The Lord calls for the death of their leader: "Awake, O sword, against my shepherd . . . Strike the shepherd, that the sheep may be scattered." The quotation of Zechariah 13:7 departs from the original in two important respects: (1) the imperative, "strike," is changed to the first person, "I will strike," and (2) the scattering of the sheep is the result of striking the shepherd, not the reason for doing so.[21] The Damascus Document, found in the Cairo Geniza and later at Qumran, quotes the same verse and interprets it in relation to the Qumran community (CD 19:7-13). The quotation evokes Jesus' earlier compassion for the people who were like sheep without a shepherd (6:34; see Num 27:17; 1 Kgs 22:17; 2 Chr 18:16; Ezek 34:12) and the expectation that the Messiah would gather the scattered sheep (*Pss. Sol.* 17:16-17, 21, 26). Accordingly, John affirms that Jesus will not die for the nation only but in order "to gather into one the dispersed children of God" (John 11:52). In Mark, which uses the same verb for scattering, the scattering of the sheep (i.e., the disciples) will be their final failure, which will set up their meeting with Jesus, the risen Lord, in Galilee.

Jesus earlier declared that he would rise from the dead (8:31; 9:31; 10:32-34), and the discourse in Mark 13, especially vv. 9-23, provides glimpses of events that would occur following the resurrection. Mark 14:28, however, gives the first indication that Jesus would meet the disciples in Galilee, and the words of the interpreting angel in Mark 16:7

Revisioning the Future

"The allusions to Zechariah 9–14 in Mark 14.22-28, then, may well be read by Mark and his audience in such a way that they provide a contrast to the interpretation of those passages circulating in Jewish revolutionary circles known to them. Instead of seeing the arrival of the kingdom of God in the appearance of a triumphant Messiah figure on the Mount of Olives, a miraculous deliverance of Jerusalem from the Gentile armies that surround it, and a resanctification of the Temple through its cleansing from pagan influence, Mark would see the arrival of the kingdom of God, paradoxically, in the deliverance of Jesus to his Jewish enemies on the Mount of Olives, his humiliating death at the hands of Gentiles in Jerusalem, and the proleptic act of Temple destruction that accompanies that death (see 15.38)."

Joel Marcus, *The Way of the Lord: Christological Exegesis of the Old Testament in the Gospel of Mark* (Louisville: Westminster John Knox, 1992), 161.

return to this point. In Mark, Galilee is the locus of Jesus' declaration of the coming kingdom (see 1:14-15). In contrast to Jerusalem, where Jesus confronts the corruption of the temple authorities and announces God's judgment on the city, Galilee is the place where Jesus crosses the boundaries between Jews and Gentiles, heals the sick, casts out demons, gathers the disciples, and teaches the crowds. The verb *proagein* can mean either to precede (6:45; 11:9) or to lead (10:32), and it often appears in a military context (Thucydides 7.6; 2 Macc 10:1).[22] Jesus therefore announced that he would either lead them in Galilee or go to Galilee ahead of them. Mark 16:7 allows the verb to have both senses. Regardless, Galilee, the place where Jesus announced the coming kingdom, will be the place where the disciples will meet the risen Lord, once again fulfilling the vision of Zechariah: "They will call on my name, and I will answer them. I will say, 'They are my people'; and they will say, 'The LORD is our God'" (Zech 13:9). The third-century "Fayyum Fragment" omits v. 28, but the connection between this verse and 16:7 tilts the argument in favor of the view that the Fayyum Fragment is an abridgement of Mark rather than an earlier version of this tradition. [The Fayyum Fragment]

The Fayyum Fragment

"After> the meal according to custom (?) (he said:) <All ye in this> night will be offended, as> it is written: I will smite the <shepherd, and the> sheep will be scattered. When> Peter <said>: Even if all, <not I, Jesus said:> Before the cock crows twice, <thrice wilt thou> de<ny me today."

Wilhelm Schneemelcher, ed., *New Testament Apocrypha* (trans. R. McL. Wilson; Louisville: Westminster John Knox Press, 1991), 1:102.

As Lane noted, every time Jesus "speaks of his passion, he provokes a crisis for the disciples."[23] Following the first passion prediction, Peter heard only the first thing Jesus said, that he would die, and objected vehemently (8:31-32). Once again, Peter hears only that they will be scattered, and he reacts declaring adamantly that regardless of what the other disciples might do, he would remain faithful to Jesus. Even if the others stumbled (*skandalisthēsontai*), he would not. Jesus' response is even more forceful. It is the last of the thirteen "amen, I say to you" sayings in Mark (see the commentary on 3:28). Three increasingly specific temporal references define the time of Peter's "stumbling"— "today," "this night," and "before the cock crows twice"—and Jesus declares specifically the nature of Peter's failing: "you will deny me three times" (14:30).

Mark is the only Gospel that refers to the cock crowing twice (cf. Matt 26:34; Luke 22:34; John 13:38). The "cockcrow" was the third watch of the night (cf. 13:35), so some interpreters have postulated that Jesus used this common means to refer to the time of Peter's denials. On the other hand, Mark 14:72 returns to Jesus' prediction and specifies that the cock crowed for the second time. In addition, if the Fayyum Fragment is an abridgement of an unknown Gospel, it is interesting that it too refers to the second cockcrow, and there is a parallel in

Juvenal, *Satires* 9.107-08 and in Aristophanes, *Ecclesiazusae* 390-91, which says, "when the rooster calls the second time."[24]

The verb "to deny" (*aparnesthai*) occurred earlier in 8:34, where a disciple is one who denies self and follows Jesus. Peter will now deny Jesus and look out for himself. The simple form of the verb (*arnesthai*) is used elsewhere in the New Testament as the opposite of confessing (*homologein*; John 1:20; 1 John 2:23), or with the technical meaning of denying Jesus Christ (1 John 2:22-23; Acts 3:14; 2 Tim 2:12; 2 Pet 2:1; Jude 4; Rev 3:8) or denying one's faith (1 Tim 5:8; Rev 2:13).

Peter had the last word, but he was wrong. Vehemently, adamantly, but mistakenly, he declared that if necessary he would die with Jesus. This may be more hyperbole than recognition that Jesus was indeed about to die (cf. John 11:16). Like Daniel or the Maccabean martyrs, Peter vowed to be faithful even to the point of death. Either in his defense, or more likely implicating the rest of the disciples in Peter's failure, Mark adds that the other disciples all said the same. Jesus saw exactly what was about to happen, while the disciples once again revealed that they did not grasp the gravity of the situation or their own weakness.

Jesus Prays in Gethsemane, 14:32-42

The Gethsemane scene moves Mark's account of Jesus' passion further into darkness as Jesus leaves the upper room with the disciples and then prays in anguish. This scene stands along with Jesus' baptism, the transfiguration, and "the cry of dereliction" at Jesus' death as crucial moments in the mystery of Jesus' divinity and his relationship to God. Jesus predicts his coming death and moves resolutely toward it. He prays to be spared that death, but the voice from heaven that spoke at Jesus' baptism (1:11) and his transfiguration (9:7) is silent.

In addition to its importance for understanding Jesus' nature and the Trinity, this scene also provides a model for persecuted believers. Jesus prepares himself through prayer, and like later martyrs, he steels himself for the suffering he will endure. He does not seek either death or the glory of martyrdom, but he prepares himself for whatever faithfulness may require of him. By contrast, having failed to understand the transfiguration, the disciples sleep while Jesus prays. Having been charged to watch and stay awake (13:35-37), they sleep in the moment of trial.

Verse 26 indicated that Jesus and the disciples went out to the Mount of Olives. Verse 32 reports that they came to an area called "Gethsemane." As familiar as it is in Christian tradition, it is surprising to note that the New Testament never refers to "the garden of Gethsemane." The Gospel of John says they went across the Kidron

Valley to a garden (18:1), and Mark says they went to a place called Gethsemane, so Christian tradition harmonized the two, calling the place "the garden of Gethsemane." "Gethsemane" is a Semitic name that means "olive press." Tradition has identified the spot as a stone outcropping on the lower slope of the Mount of Olives, just across the Kidron Valley from the temple area.

The group of three disciples, Peter, James, and John, witness three key moments in Jesus' life in the Gospel of Mark: the raising of Jairus's daughter (5:37), the transfiguration (9:2), and Jesus' prayer at Gethsemane. Mark is the only Gospel that names these three disciples at all three of these events. Neither Matthew nor Luke contains the raising of Jairus's daughter, and Luke does not mention the three disciples at Gethsemane. The role of this group of disciples is therefore especially prominent in Mark. Raymond Brown observed that "What is common to the three scenes is not revelation but witness"; the disciples "never understood either Jesus' glory or his anguish."[25]

Having left the other disciples so that he could go and pray, Jesus "took with him" the three. The same verb (*paralambanein*) occurs in Mark 5:40; 9:2; and 10:32 (cf. also 4:36; 7:4). That Jesus sought times of solitude in order to pray is one of the hallmarks of his ministry. He went out by himself to pray after healing the sick in Capernaum (1:35) and after feeding the 5,000 (6:46). The transfiguration occurred while Jesus was on the mountain, presumably at prayer (9:2-8). Shortly thereafter Jesus explained to the disciples that casting out (at least certain) demons required prayer (9:29). In Jerusalem, Jesus reminded the authorities that the temple was to be "a house of prayer for all nations" (11:17; Isa 56:7) and instructed the disciples to have faith (11:24) and forgive others (11:25) when they prayed. He criticized the scribes for making long prayers in pretense (12:40) and admonished the disciples to pray that the fall of Jerusalem might not be in winter (13:18). Prayer was therefore a vital part of both Jesus' life and his teachings.

Mark describes Jesus as being "distressed and agitated" (14:33). The verb translated "distressed" (*ekthambein*) occurs only in Mark in the New Testament. When the crowd saw Jesus following the transfiguration, they were "amazed" or "overcome with awe" (9:15), and the women at the tomb were "alarmed" (16:5, 6), but here the verb has a slightly different nuance. The second verb, "agitated" (*adēmonein*; cf. Phil 2:26), typically means to be anxious, distressed, or troubled.[26] The other Gospels soften Mark's strong language. Matthew reports that Jesus was "grieved and agitated" (26:37). Luke has no immediate parallel but later reports that Jesus was praying "in anguish" (Luke 22:44). Some interpreters find an allusion to the experience recorded in Psalms in these descriptions. In Psalm 116:3, the psalmist laments, "I suffered distress and anguish" (cf. Heb 5:7).[27]

Jesus' instructions to the disciples echo the psalms and his parable of the doorkeeper. The words "I am deeply grieved, even to death" may be a recasting of Psalms 42:6, 11; 43:5 (cf. Jonah 4:9; Sir 37:2; John 12:27). The phrase "even to death" conveys the depth of his grief. The authorities resisted his proclamation of the kingdom and plotted to kill him, his family misunderstood him, his hometown rejected him, his disciples failed him, Judas betrayed him, Peter would deny him, and he knew that his death was imminent—little wonder that Jesus would be "deeply grieved" and identify with the psalms of lament. Earlier Jesus had simply told the disciples to "sit here while I pray" (v. 32; cf. Luke 22:40). In v. 34 his instruction is more specific: "keep awake." It is the same verb that is repeated three times in the parable of the doorkeeper (13:34, 35, 37), which counsels vigilance for the coming of the Son of Man. Now it occurs three times in the Gethsemane scene (14:34, 37, 38). Only Mark has this duplication of the threefold repetition. The final occurrence of the verb makes clear the connection that has been implicit: "keep awake and pray" (14:38). On one level Jesus may have been warning the disciples to stay awake and serve as watchmen to announce the coming of Judas and the authorities. On another level Mark connects the necessity of prayer with faithfulness in the midst of persecution and eschatological urgency. Jesus models faithful watchfulness through prayer in the crisis, while the disciples model the apostasy that threatens those who do not "keep awake and pray."

Jesus' action, leaving first the larger group of disciples and then the three closest to him in order to pray alone, vividly dramatizes the isolation of his passion. The disciples will abandon him, and as he dies Jesus will cry, "My God, my God, why have you abandoned me" (15:34). Similarly, "he threw himself on the ground" gives action to Mark's description that Jesus "began to be distressed and agitated" (14:33) and Jesus' report that he was "deeply grieved, even to death" (14:34). Characteristically, the other evangelists soften this stark image. Matthew echoes biblical language by saying Jesus "fell on his face" (obscured by the NRSV translation; cf. Gen 17:3; Lev 9:24; Num 14:5; 16:4), and Luke says Jesus "knelt down, and prayed" (Luke 22:41).

Jesus' prayer is reported both indirectly and directly with the metaphors of the hour and the cup being used synonymously for Jesus' passion. Both the indirect quotation and the direct quotation refer to what is "possible," a word that resonates with earlier references in Mark. In fact, the verb "to be able" (*dynamai*) occurs thirty-three times in Mark, and the adjective "possible" (*dynatos*) occurs five times. The father of the epileptic boy asked Jesus to help him "if you are able" (9:22), to which Jesus responded, "If you are able!—all things can be done for the one who believes" (9:23). Later, when the disciples asked, "Then who can be saved?" Jesus admonished them, "for God all things are possible" (10:27). In the context of Jesus' prayer, it was not a question of God's power but of the constraints bearing upon the realization of God's redemptive purposes.

As Brown points out, it is not inconsistent that Jesus should have said that his death was "necessary" (8:31) and then prayed that he might not have to die. [Prayer and Providence] The verb "to pass" (*parerchomesthai*) occurs earlier in an eschatological context (13:30-31): "this generation" and "heaven and earth" will pass way, but Jesus' words will not pass away (cf. in a different sense 6:48). Mark and John independently use both "hour" and "cup" as metaphors for Jesus' suffering (cf. John 12:27-28; 18:11), but John develops the theme of Jesus' hour into a distinctively Johannine motif. The "hour" was used earlier in reference to the time of the disciples' trials (13:11), and Jesus' hour is signaled by the arrival of the betrayer (14:41). In the eschatological discourse Jesus said that even the angels do not know the day or the hour of the Son of Man's coming (13:32), and Romans 13:11 may echo the Gethsemane tradition: "You know what time (*kairos*) it is, how it is the moment (i.e., "hour," *hōra*) for you to wake from sleep." The hour of Jesus' death has eschatological significance: it both foreshadows the fulfillment of God's redemptive purposes and moves events toward that end.

Verse 36 reports Jesus' prayer in direct quotation, and Jesus' appeal is more urgent and forceful than the narrator's summary of it in the previous verse. The prayer has four parts: (1) an invocation, (2) a confession of God's sovereign power, (3) a petition for deliverance, and (4) a statement of submission to God's will. Each merits close attention. The confession and the petition essentially repeat the summary of Jesus' prayer in v. 35, while the invocation and the statement of submission are new.

The address "Abba, Father" is the most significant of the Aramaic terms preserved in the Mark (see [Aramaic Words]). Like all the other Aramaic terms except *Hosanna* (11:9), this one is accompanied by a Greek translation, which suggests that some of the early readers would not have known its meaning otherwise. *Abba* also appears twice in Paul's letters (Rom 8:15-16; Gal 4:6). Although neither of the Pauline references link the term directly to Jesus, Joachim Jeremias argued that the Aramaic was preserved because it was characteristic of Jesus' speech, and it was daringly original because although ancient Jews referred to

Prayer and Providence

"In the biblical outlook, it is not irreverent to ask God for a change of mind. Moses intercedes to change the Lord's will about Israel after the incident of the golden calf (Exod 32:10-14); Hezekiah prays to change God's will about his death (II Kings 20:1-6). . . . In such instances, the prayer is not one of rebellion but of confidence in God's love and justice. God will listen and will grant the request if it is reconcilable with overall Providence."

Raymond E. Brown, *The Death of the Messiah* (New York: Doubleday, 1994), 1:166–67.

God as "Father," they did not use the colloquial and familial Aramaic in address to God.[28] Still, there are a few instances of the use of "Father" in invocations in Jewish literature. ["Father" in Invocations] Jeremias probably exaggerated the colloquial familiarity of "Abba," but his contention that Jesus' address to God as "Abba" was so striking that it made a deep impression on his followers still stands.

In contrast to the conditional statement in the indirect discourse of v. 35, Jesus categorically asserts God's sovereign power: "for you all things are possible." Jesus' petition for deliverance from his passion is based on the clear conviction that God is in complete control of his destiny. Jesus turns to God in prayer because he knows God can change the course of events. Whether God does so or not does not raise any question about God's power, God's redemptive purpose, or God's merciful love. Jesus will submit to whatever God determines.

Almost as an extension of Jesus' confession of God's power, he pleads, "remove this cup from me." See the commentary on the cup of suffering in 10:38-39. The metaphor of the cup of suffering or punishment is common in the prophets (Pss 11:6; 75:8; Jer 25:15-28; Lam 4:21; Ezek 23:32-34). Jesus was asking no more than God had done on other occasions, as is evident from Isaiah 55:21, "Thus says your Sovereign, the LORD, . . . See, I have taken from your hand the cup of staggering; you shall drink no more from the bowl of my wrath." The metaphor of the cup is synonymous with the metaphor of the hour in v. 35, but instead of asking that it "pass" from him, Jesus' petition is for God's direct intervention: "remove" this cup! Jesus has already given the cup to his disciples (14:23), however, so his petition stands in tension with his knowledge of what is about to happen.

The statement of submission, the last part of Jesus' prayer, is introduced with a strong adversative, suggesting that it stands in contrast to all that has gone before (the confession and the petition). The contrast is further underscored by the repetition of the adversative: "but not . . . but what. . . ." Jesus' subordination of his will (even when faced with death) to the Father's stands in sharp contrast to the self-seeking attitude of the disciples, expressed especially in James's and John's request that Jesus do "whatever we ask of you" (10:35). Jesus now submits to whatever God will ask of him. Jesus' prayer that God's will be done

"Father" in Invocations

AΩ "Look upon the descendants of Abraham, O Father. . . ." (3 Macc 6:3)

"O Lord, Father and Master of my life, do not abandon me to their designs. . . ." (Sir 23:1)

"O Lord, Father and God of my life, do not give me haughty eyes. . . ." (Sir 23:4)

"Lord, you are my Father, do not forsake me in the days of trouble. . . ." (Sir 51:10)

"It is your providence, O Father, that steers its course. . . ." (Wis 14:3)

"My Father (*abi*) and my God, do not abandon me into the hands of the nations. . . ." (4Q372 1)

Eileen M. Schuller, "The Psalm of 4Q372 1 within the Context of Second Temple Prayer," *CBQ* 54 (1992): 68, 77.

echoes the model prayer (Matt 6:10). Jesus' petition, followed by his acceptance of God's will, whatever it may be, is a significant reflection of Jesus' human nature, his desire to avoid suffering and death, and yet his unwavering commitment to the Father. In John's higher Christology, however, it is inconceivable that Jesus should assert his will in contrast to the Father's in this way, for he and the Father are one (see John 10:30; 11:41-42), so rather than pleading that the Father remove the cup Jesus asks rhetorically, "Am I not to drink the cup that the Father has given me?" (John 18:11). Whether in the Markan or the Johannine form, one senses that the evangelists offer Jesus' faithfulness in crisis at Gethsemane as the model for all those who would later be persecuted for their faith.

Jesus' faithfulness sets the disciples' failure in stark contrast. He charges them to watch and not sleep (13:36-37; 14:34), but after he has prayed for just an hour he comes suddenly, like the master in the parable (13:36), and finds the disciples sleeping. Peter has been the spokesman for the disciples (8:29), but he has also asserted that he will be faithful even if they are not (14:31), so Jesus addresses his rebuke to the disciples directly to Peter. By addressing him as "Simon" Jesus returns to his given name (cf. 1:16, 29, 30, 36; 3:16), which he has not used since Peter's appointment as one of the Twelve (see 5:37; 8:29, 32, 33; 9:2, 5; 10:28; 11:21; 13:3; 14:29, 33). This does not mean that Peter is no longer an apostle, however. Rather, "Simon" is the usual name Jesus uses for Peter in the Gospels (Matt 16:17; 17:25; Luke 22:31; John 1:42; 21:15-17).[29] What Peter is not able to do contrasts sharply both with what he has professed regarding his faithfulness and with God's sovereign power. All things are possible for God; Peter cannot watch for even one hour. Peter thought he would die for Jesus, but he could not even remain watchful and vigilant for an hour. Again, as earlier, watchfulness is not just remaining awake; it connotes spiritual alertness and preparedness. Mark's implied message for his persecuted community is clear. Spiritual preparation is essential when a crisis that will test one's faith is imminent. [Watch and Pray]

Jesus now switches to the second person plural, addressing either the three disciples or the whole group of disciples. The ideal of staying awake and praying through the night hours is attested in the Psalms (42:8; 63:6; 77:2), in the scrolls (1QS 6:7-8), and elsewhere in the New Testament (Luke 2:37; Acts 16:25).[30] The second part of v. 38 explains the reason why watchfulness is imperative and suggests what the disciples should be praying for. Although this is the only occurrence of the term *peirasmos* in Mark, elsewhere in the New Testament it means either "temptation" to sin (1 Tim 6:9) or "trial," in the sense of "testing" (1 Cor 10:13; 1 Pet 1:6; 4:12). The two senses are related,

Watch and Pray

"We do not pray that we will never be tempted at all. For this is impossible. We pray rather that we not be encompassed by temptation." (Origen, *On Prayer* 29.11)

"The Lord has commanded us to watch and pray that we enter not into temptation. Obviously, if we could endow ourselves with this gift merely by willing it, we would not be asking it in prayer. If the will itself sufficed to protect us from temptation, we would not have to pray for it." (Augustine, *Letters*, 218, to Palatinus)

Thomas C. Oden and Christopher A. Hall, eds., *Ancient Christian Commentary on Scripture: New Testament II, Mark* (Downers Grove IL: InterVarsity Press, 1998), 212–13.

however, because a testing by ordeal can lead to sin or apostasy (cf. 2 Pet 4-9; Rev 3:10). Significantly, in view of the earlier echo of the Lord's prayer, "thy will be done" (14:36; Matt 6:10), this phrase echoes the petition, "lead us not into temptation" (NIV) or "do not bring us to the time of trial" (NRSV; Matt 6:13). Jesus' prayer in John 17:15, that God would protect the disciples from the evil one, echoes the themes of the Lord's prayer and the Gethsemane tradition. The latter offers both example and instruction for the tested community.

"The spirit indeed is willing, but the flesh is weak" (14:38) has crossed over into colloquial usage, even by those who are unaware of the origin of this proverbial saying. Although it was once thought to have come from Hellenistic philosophy, the saying is rooted in biblical tradition. The same adjective, "willing" (*prothymon*) describes Paul's eagerness to preach in Rome (Rom 1:15). Psalm 51:12 speaks of "a willing spirit," and the weakness of the flesh of mortals is a common theme in the Wisdom literature (Isa 40:6; Sir 17:31). "Spirit" and "flesh" are common terms in the scrolls (1QS 11:12; 1QH 13:18-19; 18:23), and Paul developed them as metaphors in Romans 7–8 (cf. John 6:63). The spirit here is not the Holy Spirit but the human. The admonition recognizes the disparity between human will and human conduct. Temptation often finds an opening between what we intend and what we do. In the context of Gethsemane, and as instruction for persecuted believers, Jesus explains the need for watchfulness and prayer by reminding the disciples of the fickleness of human resolve.

The alternation between scenes of Jesus with the disciples and Jesus at prayer continues. Without explicitly counting it as a second time, Mark says that Jesus went away again and prayed saying the same words. The repetition is abbreviated because the reader already knows what Jesus prayed. Other repetitions follow the same pattern (cf. for example, the three accounts of Paul's experience on the road to Damascus in Acts 9:1-19; 22:6-16; 26:12-18, or the repetitions in the account of the conversion of Cornelius's household in Acts 10:1–11:18). The phrase "saying the same words" (14:39) is omitted by Codex Bezae and the Old Latin, but Raymond Brown rejects the view that the statement is a gloss because Mark frequently uses "word" (*logos*) to refer to Jesus' sayings (4:33; 8:32, 38; 9:10; 10:24).[31] Matthew says this was the second time and reports Jesus' prayer verbatim: "My Father, if this cannot pass unless I drink it, your will be done" (Matt 26:42). For Mark, however, the focus is not on Jesus' repeated prayer but on the disciples' repeated failure.

Again Jesus comes and finds them sleeping. Jesus instructed them to watch and pray and then he modeled watchfulness by praying again, but still he finds the disciples sleeping. Their failure is inexcusable and stands in sharp contrast to Jesus' faithfulness. The narrator's comment, "for their eyes were heavy" (cf. Gen 48:10), extends Jesus' earlier statement that the flesh is weak, and the explanation repeats the narrator's comment at the transfiguration that Peter "did not know what to say" (9:6). Neither of these comments excuses the disciples. Parenthetically, it is interesting that Luke's account of the transfiguration contains both a reference to being weighed down with sleepiness and the statement that the disciples did not know what to say (Luke 9:32-33). At Gethsemane, however, Luke attempts to ease the disciples' failure by saying that they slept "because of grief" (Luke 22:45).

Without saying that Jesus prayed a third time (cf. Matt 26:44), Mark reports that Jesus came to the disciples the third time. The pattern of threefold prayer, which is clearer in Matthew, is attested in other places (1 Sam 3:2-8; Acts 10:16; 2 Cor 12:8). His words to the disciples pose a series of interpretive difficulties. First, the verb "sleep" can be indicative, imperative, or interrogative. The only way the indicative makes sense, however, is if it is ironic, which makes it virtually the same as the interrogative, which seems to be the best choice (Luke 22:46, followed by both the NRSV and the NIV). Although Jesus uses commands to watch and pray, it is difficult to think that he would command the disciples to sleep and then in the next breath say that the hour has come. The translation "still" (NRSV) is forced; *loipon* generally means "the rest" or "remainder." Hence, "are you sleeping the rest of the time?" One detects both exasperation and resignation in Jesus' question. He recognizes that the disciples have failed him completely and that they are totally unprepared for the coming ordeal. The redundant "and taking your rest" underscores the inappropriateness of their sleep at that moment.

The next word, *apechei*, has been the subject of much debate and a variety of interpretations. Among these, four merit special consideration. (1) Jerome translated it with the meaning "it is enough," a meaning that is attested only in comparatively late sources, but this is the translation favored by most English translations (KJV, RSV, NASB, NIV, NRSV). (2) The verb is often used in commercial texts to indicate that the bill is paid in full. Accordingly, in this context, the verb could mean "the account is closed," or following Brown, "the money is paid."[32] (3) The use of the verb in other contexts to mean "nothing hinders" allows the translation "that is a hindrance"—referring to the disciples' sleep.[33] (4) The verb can also mean "to be distant." Adopting this meaning, Evans connects the statement with what follows, the declaration that the hour has come, and translates it as a question: "Is it far off? The hour has come."[34] Although the data make any decision difficult, the sense of finality conveyed by the first and second options makes the most sense in the context, and the widespread use of the verb for commercial transactions tips the scales in favor of its having been understood in this sense. [Translations of *apexein* in the NRSV] One may still question whether a statement as specific as "the money is paid" (referring to the bribe in 14:11) is warranted instead of a more general rendering: "Are you sleeping the rest of the time and taking your rest? It is done; the account is paid."

Moloney captures the drama of this scene: "There are three fateful forces in play: 'the hour has come,' 'the Son of Man is handed over,' and 'the betrayer is at hand.'"[35] Although Jesus prayed that "the hour" of his travail might pass from him (14:35), he knows that it will not: "The hour has come" (14:41). His predictions have been fulfilled (cf. 8:31; 9:31; 10:32-34; and 13:26; 14:21), and he again refers to himself

---

Translations of *apexein* in the NRSV

Matt 6:2, 5, 16	"Truly I tell you, they *have received* their reward."
Matt 14:24	". . . but by this time the boat, battered by the waves, *was far* from the land. . . ."
Matt 15:8/Mark 7:6	"This people honors me with their lips, but their hearts *are far* from me."
Mark 14:41	"Are you still sleeping and taking your rest? *Enough!* The hour has come; the Son of Man is betrayed into the hands of sinners."
Luke 6:24	"But woe to you who are rich, for you *have received* your consolation."
Luke 7:6	"And Jesus went with them, but when he *was* not *far* from the house, the centurion sent friends to say to him, 'Lord, do not trouble yourself, for I am not worthy to have you come under my roof."
Luke 15:20	"But while he *was* still *far off*, his father saw him and was filled with compassion."
Luke 24:13	"Now on that same day two of them were going to a village called Emmaus, about seven miles *from* Jerusalem."
Acts 15:20	"but we should write to them *to abstain* only from things polluted by idols and from fornication. . . ."
Acts 15:29	"that you *abstain* from what has been sacrificed to idols. . . ."
Phil 4:18	"I *have been paid in full* and have more than enough."
1 Thess 4:3	"For this is the will of God, your sanctification: That you *abstain* from fornication."
1 Thess 5:22	"*Abstain* from every form of evil."
1 Tim 4:3	"The forbid marriage and *demand abstinence* from foods"
Philemon 15	"Perhaps this is the reason he was separated from you for a while, so that you might *have him back* forever."
1 Peter 2:11	"Beloved, I urge you as aliens and exiles *to abstain* from the desires of the flesh that wage war against the soul."

using the term "the Son of Man" (see [The Son of Man]; [The Messianic Son of Man]). The present tense of this statement connotes a declaration that the predicted action is being fulfilled as he speaks. The verb "to give over" (*paradidonai*) was used for handing criminals over for judgment. In the Gospels Judas is the one who hands Jesus over, and hence the verb takes on the connotation of betraying, and Judas is the betrayer. There is also a note of divine agency. The Suffering Servant passage in Isaiah 53:6 (LXX) says, "And the LORD gave him over for our sins," and Romans 8:32 says that God "gave him up for all of us." Because of Jesus' obedience to God's purpose, it is a short step then to the Johannine emphasis that Jesus laid down his own life (10:17-18).[36] Mark leaves the matter ambiguous in 14:41, but in light of Jesus' woe on "that one by whom the Son of Man is betrayed" (i.e., handed over; 14:21) at the Last Supper, an allusion to Judas's role is most likely. Earlier the authorities had castigated Jesus for eating with "sinners" (2:16), and Jesus explained that he had come to save sinners (2:17). Now those he came to save had come for him. Those who were identified in the parallel phrase in 9:31 as "men" and in 10:33 as "chief priests and scribes" are now called "sinners."

Jesus' last words to the disciples in Mark are a command to rise and go with him to meet his betrayer. Presumably they are meant to convey once again Jesus' divine knowledge of the events that were then transpiring, as earlier Jesus had told the disciples about the conversation they would have when they went to bring the colt to him (11:1-6), said that the widow put in everything she had (12:44), foretold the trials of the disciples, the destruction of Jerusalem, and the coming of the Son of Man (13:1-27), predicted that the generosity of the woman who anointed him would be told wherever the gospel was preached (14:9), told the disciples they would meet a man carrying a jar of water (14:13), and predicted Judas's betrayal (14:18) and Peter's denials (14:26-31). It would be no stretch, therefore, for Jesus' announcement that the betrayer was at hand to be another such prediction.

The term "at hand" (or "has come," *ēngiken*) is also used in Jesus' announcement of the coming of the kingdom (1:15), which again lends an eschatological air to the scene. Here as in 1:15 the verb can mean "is near, at hand" rather than "has come" (contra Dodd). Jesus had commanded the disciples to watch and pray with him (14:34, 38); now he commands them to get up and go with him to meet those who have come to kill him (cf. John 14:31).

Jesus Is Arrested, 14:43-52

The transition in v. 43 is typically Markan, with the particle "immediately" (*euthys*), which occurs forty-one times in Mark, and a genitive absolute ("while he was still speaking"). Judas's appearance is dramatic. The reader has been told that Judas was the betrayer (3:19) and that he conspired with the authorities (14:10-11), but the reader was not told that Judas was not with the other disciples at Gethsemane. The unnecessary reminder that Judas was "one of the twelve" may indicate that this was once an independent piece of tradition, or that "this fixed designation vocalized Christian distress that Jesus was betrayed by one of his chosen Twelve" (cf. Matt 26:25; 27:3; John 6:71; 12:4; 18:2, 5).[37]

The "crowd" with Judas was sent by the chief priests, scribes, and elders (cf. [Chief Priests] [Scribes] [Elders]). Jesus named precisely these three groups, though in a different order, in the first passion prediction (8:31), the three groups confronted Jesus in the temple (11:27), and they will constitute the council that will judge Jesus (14:53; 15:1). It was therefore not a mob or a vigilante group.[38] Still, the corrupt first-century chief priests regularly conscripted thugs to do their bidding, as Josephus records:

> But Ananias had servants who were utter rascals and who, combining operations with the most reckless men, would go to the threshing floors and take by force the tithe of the priests; nor did they refrain from beating those who refused to give. (*Ant.* 20.206-207)[39]

A *machaira* was a long knife or sword. Ironically, Jesus' captors come armed with swords, but one of them will be the victim of the slash of a sword (14:47). Other writers say that the sword cannot separate us from the love of Christ (Rom 8:35), civil authority does not "bear the sword in vain" (Rom 13:4), and "if you kill with the sword, with the sword you must be killed" (Rev 13:10; cf. Rev 6:4; Luke 22:36-38, 49). The "sword of the Spirit" is the word of God (Eph 6:17). On occasion, Roman soldiers also used clubs to put down riots (Josephus, *Ant.* 18.62; *J. W.* 2.176).

Today, the Church of All Nations marks the traditional site of Gethsemane. Inside one finds that it is built over a stone outcropping. On either side at the front is a mosaic depicting the arrest of Jesus. One shows Judas kissing Jesus, as in Mark; the other shows the soldiers falling back on the ground before Jesus, as in John. According to Mark, Judas's prearranged sign was a kiss. His role was to lead the authorities to Jesus at a time and place where they could seize him without creating a commotion among the crowds that were gathered in Jerusalem for the Passover (14:2, 10-11). Arresting Jesus at night outside the temple fit this plan, but it introduced the possibility that Jesus might slip away in the night or that they might seize the wrong man, especially if they had not seen Jesus often. A kiss was a normal greeting (Luke 7:45; 1 Esd 4:47). At times it was a sign of reconciliation (Gen 33:4; Luke

15:20), but it also opened the possibility for treachery (2 Sam 20:9; Prov 27:6). The pretended affection of the kiss adds to the depth of Judas's betrayal, and indeed becomes a kind of cipher for it, but the compound verb in Mark, which can mean "to kiss warmly" (*kataphilein*), does not necessarily connote anything out of the ordinary.

The greeting "rabbi," which never occurs in Luke-Acts or Paul's letters, appears earlier in Mark 9:5; 10:51; 11:21. At this time it was still a general term of respect rather than an official title (see [Rabbi]). The agreed upon signal was calculated to appear normal and not to arouse suspicion. Although Jesus has already indicated that he knew one of the Twelve would betray him (14:18-20), in Mark Jesus does not indicate that he knew Judas was the betrayer (contrast John 6:70-71; 13:26). Judas's instructions to his accomplices are to seize Jesus and lead him away securely, safely, or under guard. Judas plays his part flawlessly, approaching Jesus, greeting him, and then kissing him, and then he disappears from Mark without another word (cf. Matt 27:3-5; Acts 1:18).

Judas Betrays Jesus with a Kiss

Christ surrounded by apostles; he is seized by Roman soldiers. Judas' kiss. Saint Peter draws his sword to cut off Malchus' ear.

Mosaic (6th). S. Apollinare Nuovo, Ravenna, Italy. (Credit: Erich Lessing / Art Resource, NY)

The authorities act swiftly, seizing Jesus. The expression "to lay hands on" was used not only in the context of blessing but, as is relevant here, with the meaning to arrest or do harm (Gen 22:12; 2 Sam 18:12; 2 Kgs 11:16). Other events intervene, however, before they lead him away securely (cf. 11:44) in v. 53.

The first of these events is an attack on the slave of the high priest. In spite of the unexpected use of the definite article, Mark is probably not designating a particular official, Judas, or necessarily someone known to the Christian community. Only John identifies the slave as Malchus (John 18:10). Equally uncertain is the designation of the attacker. Mark identifies him simply as a bystander. He does not specify that he was a disciple, and nothing has been said about the disciples having a sword (cf. Luke 22:36-38). If there were others besides the Twelve at the Last Supper with Jesus, it is possible that some of them accompanied Jesus and the Twelve to Gethsemane (see the commentary on 14:20; cf. 14:26). The other Gospels remove the ambiguity in Mark. Matthew and Luke identify the attacker as a disciple (Matt 26:51, "one of those with Jesus"; Luke 22:49-50), and John says that it was Peter (John 18:10).

The attacker struck (*paiein*) the high priest's slave, which might have been understood as an assault on the high priest himself, and cut off his ear. Mark uses the double diminutive *ōtarion* for "ear" (*ous*), as does John 18:10, but diminutives were in common use by this time, so it is better to understand Mark as meaning the ear rather than merely the earlobe. The attack was a serious assault with a sword, apparently in an effort to defend Jesus. If the attacker was Peter, as in John's account, one could surmise that Peter was acting out of the same determination that fueled his protest in vv. 29 and 31, but Mark does not make this connection. Neither does Mark say that it was the right ear (Luke 22:50; John 18:10)

In the other three Gospels Jesus rebukes the attacker, but in Mark he ignores the attack and speaks indignantly to those who have come out to arrest him. First, Jesus reacts to being treated like a bandit or insurrectionist (*lēstēs*; 11:17; 15:27; cf. [Revolutionaries]). Brown describes the *lēstai* as "violent, armed men (not of official police or military status) who were often no better than marauders or thugs."[40] Earlier Jesus had exposed the temple authorities as lawbreakers (11:17); now they falsely arrest Jesus as a lawbreaker.[41] Second, he protests that he has been with them each day in the temple teaching—they did not have to track him down at night, while he was praying, to arrest him. In Mark's chronology, Jesus has been in Jerusalem only a short period of time, and his teaching activities in the temple have been confined to 11:11, 15, 17 and 11:27-13:1 (esp. 12:14, 35). Nevertheless, Jesus' point—that he was doing nothing secretive, he taught in public, and they could have confronted him at any time—was quite true.

Of the Synoptics, Mark gives the least attention to the fulfillment of Scripture, and this is the only occurrence of the formula "that the scriptures might be fulfilled" (*hina plērōthōsin hai graphai*) in Mark (cf. the gloss in 15:28). Still, it is part of the texture of the Gospel tradition (1:2; 7:6; 9:12-13; 11:17; 12:10, 24; 14:21, 27). Allusions and echoes of Scripture throughout the Gospel make it impossible to regard the fulfillment of Scripture as insignificant to Mark (cf. [Isaiah as Subtext] [Isaiah 52:7 and 61:1] [Isaiah 65:3-4] [Walking on Water]). The question of which specific Scripture passages Jesus had in mind is more difficult to resolve. The two most often suggested are Isaiah 53:12, "he was numbered with the transgressors" (cf. the textual variant in 15:28) and Zechariah 13:7 (which he referred to earlier, 14:27). The choice between these two

---

The Secret Gospel of Mark

The Secret Gospel of Mark is a no longer extant document, two fragments of which are quoted in an eighteenth-century manuscript of a letter from Clement of Alexandria to Theodore (c. 180–200). Clement reports that Mark wrote his Gospel (canonical Mark) in Rome while Peter was there. Clement maintains further that Mark later brought it to Alexandria and expanded it into "a more spiritual gospel" (Secret Mark) to guide those seeking perfection. Carpocrates, an early gnostic heretic, used and misinterpreted Secret Mark to advance his own views. In the letter, Clement documents this corruption of the gospel by quoting the following passage, which has connections with the raising of Lazarus in John 11, the young man in Mark 14:51-52, and other passages:

"And they came into Bethany, and a certain woman was there whose brother had died. And, having come, she bowed before Jesus and says to him: 'O Son of David, have mercy on me.' But the disciples rebuked her. And Jesus, angered, went away with her into the garden where the tomb was; and immediately a loud voice was heard from the tomb. And coming forward, Jesus rolled away the stone from the door of the tomb; and immediately going in to where the young man was, he stretched out his hand and raised him up, having taken his hand. Now the young man having looked upon him, loved him and began to beg that he might be with him. And coming out of the tomb, they came into the house of the young man, for he was wealthy. After six days Jesus commanded him; and when it was evening, the young man comes to him clothed with a linen cloth over his nakedness. And he remained with him that night, for Jesus taught him the mystery of the kingdom of God. Then arising, he went from there to the other side of the Jordan." (2:23–3:11)

Raymond E. Brown, *The Death of the Messiah* (New York: Doubleday, 1994), 1:296. For divergent views on the Secret Gospel of Mark, see Morton Smith, *Clement of Alexandria and a Secret Gospel of Mark* (Cambridge MA: Harvard University Press, 1973); Raymond E. Brown, "The Relation of 'The Secret Gospel of Mark' to the Fourth Gospel," *Catholic Biblical Quarterly* 36 (1974): 466–85; John Dominic Crossan, *Four Other Gospels* (Sonoma: Polebridge Press, 1992), 91–121; and Stephen C. Carlson, *The Gospel Hoax: Morton Smith's Invention of Secret Mark* (Waco: Baylor University Press, 2005).

---

hangs on whether one reads Jesus' words in reference to what has just happened (seizing Jesus like a common criminal) or to what is just about to happen (the flight of the disciples). Lane suggests a connection between the latter and Amos 2:16, "and those who are stout of heart among the mighty shall flee away naked in that day."[42] Not to be missed, however, is Brown's observation that these are the last words Jesus speaks to his people, and they "express his summary understanding of all that has happened."[43]

The last time we see the disciples in Mark, they are fleeing into the night, abandoning Jesus. They had been called to "be with Jesus" (3:14), and they had been taught that discipleship required taking up the cross and following him (8:34). They had been warned about the seed that has no root and withers when confronted with persecution (4:17), and they had been told that these events were coming (8:31; 9:31; 10:32-34; 14:18-21, 41). Their repeated failure to understand Jesus' teachings, however, resulted in their inability to follow him when the hour of crisis came. Perhaps it is significant that Mark does not call them disciples at this point; he says merely "All of them deserted him and fled" (14:50). Alternatively, he may mean not only the Twelve but other disciples and bystanders also (cf. 14:47, 51-52). No one remained; Jesus faced his accusers alone. When the disciples were called, they left everything to follow him (1:18, 20; 10:28-30).[44] Now, in their failure, they leave him.

Only Mark includes the flight of a young man (*neaniskos*), clad only in a linen garment, who left the linen garment and fled naked (14:51). Mark gives no other details, but when the women go to the tomb to anoint Jesus at the end of the Gospel, they meet a *neaniskos* there, dressed in a white robe (16:5). As though these tantalizing scenes were not enough to stir the imaginations of Mark's interpreters, a reference to a young man who came to Jesus at night wearing nothing but a linen cloth appears in a mysterious document known as the Secret Gospel of Mark. [The Secret Gospel of Mark]

Mark inserted this third interruption between the time the authorities seize Jesus (v. 46) and the time they lead him away (v. 53) because it fit the theme of the flight of the disciples (v. 50), and both employ the verb "to flee" (*pheugein*, vv. 50, 52). Interpreters have offered various speculations as to the identity of the young man, the most popular being that it was John Mark, whose mother owned a house in Jerusalem (Acts 12:12) and who later wrote the Gospel. While this identification is possible, it is merely speculation. Others have noted the parallel between these verses and the accounts of Joseph's leaving his clothes and fleeing Potiphar's wife (Gen 39:12-13; *T. Joseph* 8:3). Amos 2:16 offers a closer but more obscure parallel. Within the Gospel itself, the description of the young man reverses that of Bartimaeus, who flung aside his garment in order to come to Jesus (10:50). It has also suggested symbolic interpretations related to the *neaniskos* in the white garment at the tomb: that the disciple who follows Jesus in baptism, leaving his garments and dying and rising with Christ, will be with him in glory, symbolized by the empty tomb and the white garment, or that disciples who abandon their faith under persecution can be restored.[45] As suggestive as these interpretations are, a more conservative approach is probably better.

In context, the flight of the young man dramatizes the flight of all the disciples. Linen was expensive (Judg 14:12; Prov 31:24), so a linen garment would only have been worn on special occasions (1 Macc 10:64) or for burial (Mark 15:46). Claiming that this young man was so determined to follow Jesus that he was wearing his burial garment may be too subtle, but when the authorities try to arrest him he flees naked. In doing so he represents the tragic plight of the disciples who left everything to follow Jesus (10:28) and then abandoned him at his arrest. His nakedness reflects their shame.

The Hearing before the Council, 14:53-65

The heading is carefully chosen, for it appears that rather than a formal trial the Jewish authorities held an informal hearing during the night at Caiaphas's house before delivering Jesus to Pilate. This scene relates the assembling of the council (v. 53), Peter's presence in the courtyard (v. 54), the testimony of the false witnesses (vv. 55-59), the chief priest's interrogation of Jesus and his response (vv. 60-62), the condemnation of Jesus (vv. 63-64), and taunting by the authorities (v. 65).

The report that Peter followed Jesus into the courtyard (v. 54) has provoked a great deal of debate because it appears to be another example of a typical Markan sandwich construction (see [Markan Sandwiches]). In this instance, however, unlike the sandwiching of the healing of the woman with a hemorrhage and the raising of Jairus's daughter (5:21-43), or even the cursing of the fig tree and the demonstration in the temple (11:12-21), the account of Peter's denying Jesus is dependent upon the story of the hearing before the Jewish authorities and cannot be told apart from it. As a literary technique, the sandwiching involves introducing Peter in v. 54 rather than waiting until v. 66 to do so. [Does John Have a Markan Sandwich?]

Mark is peculiar in that he does not give the name of the high priest, whereas the other three Gospels all report that Caiaphas was the high priest at the time (Matt 26:3, 57; Luke 3:2; John 11:49; 18:13-14, 24, 28; Acts 4:6). [Caiaphas] The assembling of the council during the night at Passover, even if it was not a formal session, suggests that the authorities had already passed the word that Jesus was being arrested. Later Mark reports that "all the sanhedrin" was seeking testimony against Jesus (v. 55), which would indicate that a council of twenty-three had been assembled. In view of the extraordinary circumstances, it is likely, nevertheless, that the assembly was for something less than a formal capital trial, which was forbidden at night and during the festivals (*m. Sanh.* 4.1; Philo, *Migration* 91).[46] The assembly was composed of the three groups of authorities whose opposition to Jesus has developed throughout the Gospel (see 8:31; 11:27; 14:43; 15:1; cf. [Chief Priests] [Scribes] [Elders]).

Peter alone among the disciples (cf. John 18:15) followed Jesus and his captors into the high priest's court or courtyard (14:54). Mark uses the term for following that is used elsewhere to connote discipleship (*akolouthein*; e.g., 1:18; 8:34), but qualifies it, saying that Peter followed him "at a distance" (cf. 5:6; 8:3; 11:13; 15:40). In this instance the phrase not only fits the circumstances but may suggest the state of Peter's discipleship.[47] The term *aulē* can mean either "court" or "palace" (inside) or "courtyard" (outside). It is clear that Matthew understands the setting as outside (Matt 26:69), and that is probably the meaning in

Does John have a Markan Sandwich?

Because this literary pattern is characteristic of Mark's technique, the similar sandwiching of the hearing before the Jewish authorities in John 18:15-27 within Peter's denials raises the question of whether this pattern was already present in the oral tradition or whether we have here in John an instance of Mark's redactional handling of the tradition—confirming that John was dependent upon Mark. The matter is complicated, however, because Mark merely introduces Peter's presence in the courtyard before the hearing and then relates the three denials following the hearing while John reports the first of the three denials before switching to the scene inside between Jesus and the high priest. If John depended upon Mark, why are they different at this point? It appears that the two independently drew on early tradition of these two closely related scenes and reported them in their own way.

See further John R. Donahue, *Are You the Christ? The Trial Narrative in the Gospel of Mark* (SBLDS 10; Missoula: Scholars, 1973); Kim E. Dewey, "Peter's Curse and Cursed Peter (Mark 14:53–54, 66–72)," in *The Passion in Mark* (ed. Werner Kelber; Philadelphia: Fortress, 1976), 96–114; Robert T. Fortna, "Jesus and Peter at the High Priest's House," *NTS* 24 (1977–1978): 371–83; Raymond E. Brown, *The Death of the Messiah* (New York: Doubleday, 1994), 1:426–28.

Mark also, though Mark describes the separation of the two settings in terms of above and below rather than inside and outside (see 14:66). It is cold in Jerusalem at night in the spring, so Peter sat with the servants who were warming themselves at the fire (cf. 1 Macc 12:28-29).

Inside and upstairs, the council sought testimony they could take to the Roman governor in order to have Jesus put to death. The plot to put Jesus to death has been building since the Pharisees and the Herodians began to conspire against him early in the Gospel (3:6).

Caiaphas

Joseph called Caiaphas, the son-in-law of Annas (high priest from AD 6–15), served as high priest from 18 to 36 or 37. Remarkably little is reported outside the New Testament of the tenure of this longest serving high priest of the 1st century. In 1990, however, two ossuaries inscribed with the name Caiaphas were found in Jerusalem's Peace Forest, about two miles south of the Old City. The inscriptions on one box, which contained the bones of a sixty-year-old man and other members of his family read *Yehosep bar Qayyapa* and *Yehosep bar Qapa*. The spelling of the name has been contested, but it is possible that the ossuary of this most famous of the high priests has been recovered.

Craig A. Evans, *Mark 8:27–16:20* (WBC 34B; Nashville: Thomas Nelson, 2001), 442-43; Raymond E. Brown, *The Death of the Messiah* (New York: Doubleday, 1994), 1:409-11.

Barna da Siena (fl.c.1330–1350). *Christ before Caiaphas*. Collegiata, San Gimignano, Italy. (Credit: Scala / Art Resource, NY)

Raymond Brown noted that the verb "to seek" takes on a sinister tone in Mark's Passion Narrative:

> In 11:18 the chief priests and scribes began "seeking" to destroy Jesus; in 12:12 they *sought* to seize him; in 14:1 they *sought* in stealth to seize and kill him; in 14:11 Judas *sought* how to give him over; now that he is both given over and seized, the authorities *seek* testimony to accomplish what has been the goal from the beginning: to destroy him.[48]

Verse 55 resumes the account introduced by v. 53 after the insertion of the note about Peter. The phrase "the chief priests and the whole council" is Mark's way of emphasizing the role of the highest religious authorities while avoiding a verbatim repetition of the list of the three groups in v. 53 (see [Councils]). The emphasis throughout the first part of Mark's account of this hearing is on the false testimony that is brought against Jesus: the authorities could not find legal evidence (v. 55), the witnesses were false (vv. 56, 57), and their testimony did not agree (v. 56, 59). Pentateuchal law required that there be at least two witnesses and that their testimony agree, especially for a capital offense (Deut 17:6; 19:15; Num 35:30; Josephus, *Ant.* 4.219). The apocryphal story of Susanna turns on the failure of the witnesses against the virtuous Susanna to agree (Sus 52-59). Just as Jesus was condemned by false witnesses, so the Markan community will have to guard against false prophets and false messiahs (13:5-6, 21-22).

Mark has noted Jesus' opposition to the temple in Jesus' demonstration in the temple (11:15-17), his parabolic statement about the destruction of the vineyard and rebuilding on "the stone the builders rejected" (12:10-11), and his prophecy of the destruction of the temple (13:2, where the same verb *katalyein*

Jesus on Trial before the High Priest

Jesus before the Sanhedrin: det. of the Three High Priests. Byzantine fresco, 14th cent. Monastery Church, Ohrid, Macedonia. (Credit: Erich Lessing / Art Resource, NY)

occurs, and 13:14-20), but Jesus has not said that he would destroy the temple. Threats against the temple were punishable by death (Jer 26:1-19),[49] as the later case of Jesus ben Ananias illustrates (Josephus, *J.W.* 6.300-309). Mark introduces the testimony as false testimony, but it is unclear precisely what is false about it. In John 2:19 Jesus actually says something very much like this, and John says that he was speaking metaphorically of his body (i.e., his death and resurrection). If Jesus did say something like this, others may certainly have misunderstood him or turned his words against him. Ironically, the reader knows there is an element of truth to the false testimony.[50] By the time Mark was written, the temple had been destroyed and the church constituted a new, spiritual temple. Mark uses the term *naos* or "sanctuary," the innermost part of the temple, in v. 58, and again when the mockers taunt Jesus at the cross (15:29) and the curtain in the temple is torn in two (15:38). The descriptions "made with hands" (*cheiropoiētos*) and "not made with hands" (*acheiropoiētos*) are unique to Mark and do not occur in the other Gospels. The contrast may have evoked Daniel's interpretation of King Nebuchadnessar's dream:

> And in the days of those kings the God of heaven will set up a kingdom that shall never be destroyed . . . it shall crush all these kingdoms . . . and it shall stand forever; just as you saw that a stone was cut from the mountain not by human hands, and that it crushed the iron, the bronze, the clay, the silver, and the gold. (Dan 2:44-45).

Similarly, Zechariah 6:12, "Here is a man whose name is Branch: for he shall branch out in his place, and he shall build the temple of the LORD," was being interpreted messianically by the first century.[51] Because Jewish polemic against idolatry often charged that idols were gods made by human hands (Ps 135:15; Wis 13:10; 14:8; Ep Jer 51; cf. Isa 44:9-20; Jer 10:1-16; and Bell and the Dragon), the description of the temple as "made with hands" may have been taken as an implicit accusation that it was idolatrous.

The meaning of the "temple not made with hands" (14:58) is more difficult to determine. The phrase "after three days" points to Jesus' predictions of his death and resurrection (8:31; 9:31; 10:34; see ["After Three Days"]). Donald Juel advanced the argument that the temple not made with hands is a reference to the Christian community.[52] Brown discussed the meaning of the new temple in three different time periods and cataloged three major lines of interpretation: the new sanctuary is (1) the Christian community or church, (2) the sanctuary of divine origin that Jewish apocalyptic expected in the last times, and (3) the body of the glorified Christ raised on the third day.[53] Without attempting to respond to these various interpretations, we may note that New Testament imagery for the church embraced each of them, interpreting the church as the expected new temple and as the body of Christ. The quotation of Psalm 118:22 at the conclusion of the parable of the wicked tenants in Mark 12:10-11 prepares the reader to make the connection between the death of Jesus and the building of a new temple. Brown concluded his discussion of the problems surrounding these references by saying,

> What replaces the empty sanctuary of the Jerusalem Temple as the holy place of God is a community of believers such as the centurion, whose true confession of Jesus as the Son of God comes from having comprehended his death on the cross—a community willing to take up the cross and follow Jesus.[54]

Without further explanation, Mark says that the testimony of the witnesses who attributed this claim to Jesus did not agree. As we have seen, although Mark does not report such a saying, John does (John 2:19), and Mark's account of what Jesus said and did related to the temple makes such a statement at least plausible. Moreover, one must assume that those who mock Jesus at the cross had heard the claim either directly or secondhand (15:29). One is left then to assume that (1) their testimony was not consistent as to the circumstances in which Jesus was alleged to have made the claim (similar to the discrepancies Daniel uncovered in the testimony of Susanna's accusers), or (2) while they agreed on the substance of Jesus' claim (v. 58), they differed on exactly what he had said, or (3) the false witnesses misconstrued Jesus' role in the destruction of the temple ("I will destroy"; cf. John 2:19, "[You] destroy"). Pressing the matter further leads only to conjecture. Evidently Jesus' teachings and action related to the temple were raised in the accusations against him by the Jewish authorities (see [E. P. Sanders's Thesis]), but they deemed them inconclusive.

Because their attempt to secure witnesses who could condemn Jesus is unsuccessful, the high priest changes to a more direct approach. Perhaps he could get Jesus to say something incriminating. The modern reader needs to remember that this was probably an informal hearing rather than a formal trial and that in both Jewish and Roman legal process the judge could interrogate the accused. The high priest stands in the midst of the assembly (cf. 3:3) and challenges Jesus to respond to the accusations that have been brought against him (cf. Pss 27:12; 35:11). Jesus' silence even in response to false or inconsistent testimony is frustrating to the authorities. Evans characterizes the tone of the high priest's questions: "The first question is a challenge, even a dare. The second question is a demand."[55] Jesus' persistent silence both expresses contempt for the legal charade of his unjust accusers and fulfills the Scriptures (cf. Isa 53:7 [Acts 8:32]; Pss 38:13-15; 39:7-9; Lam 3:26-30; 1 Pet 2:21, 23).

The high priest therefore changes his approach once again, this time challenging Jesus on a new (but perhaps related) issue, not his threats against the temple but his identity as the Messiah. With the high priest's question the reader senses that Mark has reached a climactic point—the heart of the matter. The reader has been told from the beginning that Jesus was "Christ, the Son of God" (1:1; cf. 1:11; 8:29; 9:7). Nevertheless, Jesus has surrounded his identity with secrecy, making no public claim of his messianic identity and commanding others to say nothing of what they have seen and heard (3:12; 5:43; 7:36; 8:26; 9:9; see [Messianic Secret]).

The high priest's question is composed of an emphatic, and probably derogatory, construction followed by two messianic titles in apposition: "Are *you* the Messiah, the Son of the Blessed One?" (14:61). The construction "You are" (*sy ei*) has been used earlier as a formula of identification (1:11; 3:11; 8:29), but here and in 15:2 it is used interrogatively and seems to convey a note of scorn or incredulity: "Surely *you* are not the Messiah/the King of the Jews?" As we have noted, Mark has used the title "Messiah" or "Christ," the anointed one, for Jesus. The high priest's question echoes the titles for Jesus that appear at key moments in the Gospel: at the beginning (1:1), at Peter's confession at Caesarea Philippi (8:29), and at Jesus' baptism and transfiguration (1:11; 9:7) (see ["Son of God" in Mark]). Since there were various messianic expectations at the time, it may have been necessary for the high priest to qualify the term by means of the appositional "the Son of the Blessed One." The latter is a circumlocution for "the Son of God" (1:1; 3:11; 5:7), and Mark seems to have been saving the title for the centurion's confession in 15:39. Although "the Blessed" does not occur elsewhere as a title for God[56] (cf. its use as a modifier in Rom 1:25; 9:5; 2 Cor 11:31; *m. Berakoth* 7.3), it sounds very Jewish and corresponds to the Jewish practice of using circumlocutions in order to avoid using the word "God." The connection between the Messiah and the Son of God is based on the Davidic covenant in 2 Samuel 7:12, 14 (cf. Ps 2:2; Mark 12:35-37 [Occurrences of "Son" in Early Judaism]). By wording the question in this way, the high priest was asking, probably with some sarcasm, whether Jesus, the abandoned prisoner who stood before him, was really the long-expected royal Messiah (see ["Son of God" in Mark]).

Although Jesus avoided making messianic claims during his ministry, now that the events leading to his death have begun and he is under arrest, he acknowledges his identity directly. The affirmation "I am" (*egō eimi*) is used earlier in Mark as an echo of the divine name disclosed to Moses at the burning bush (Exod 3:14; Mark 6:50), but here it is simply a direct, affirmative response to the high priest's question. Matthew 26:64 has Jesus respond, "You have said so." A few manuscripts harmonize Mark with Matthew at this point, but the shorter reading is stronger.[57]

The quotation from Daniel 7:13 and Psalm 110:1 that follows asserts Jesus' ultimate vindication against his accusers and declares the hope of Mark's persecuted readers. They will *see* these things. Jesus returns to the title he has preferred as a self-designation, "the Son of Man" (see [The Son of Man] [The Messianic Son of Man]); the crucified Son of Man referred to in the passion predictions will become the exalted Son of Man coming in glory. The verses from Daniel and the Psalms focus on key moments of the christological future: the seating of the risen Lord at the right hand of God and the parousia of the Son of Man. The quotation opens with the reference to "the Son of Man" from Daniel 7:13, continues chronologically with "seated at the right hand" from Psalm 110:1 (cf. 12:35-37), and then returns to Daniel 7:13 for "coming with the clouds of heaven" (cf. 8:38; 9:1; 13:26). The phrase Mark adds to these scriptural allusions is "(at the right hand) of the Power," a circumlocution for God that does not occur in contemporaneous Jewish writings but is similar to the high priest's "the Blessed One" and appeals to the power of the Lord to vindicate the righteous servant. Revelation 1:7 uses some of the eschatological language of this passage and combines Daniel 7:13 with Zechariah 12:10—"Look! He is coming with the clouds; every eye will see him, even those who pierced him." Seeing God's vindication of Jesus extends a strand of Jewish eschatology: "Then the glory of the LORD shall be revealed, and all people shall see it together" (Isa 40:5).[58] For Mark this vindication will begin at the cross, with the rending of the veil in the temple, it will continue in the faith of those believers who face the councils and persecutions of the authorities with faith, and it will be fulfilled in the coming of the Lord as the triumphant Son of Man.

Christ Enthroned

Christ Enthroned. 11th-century ivory. Victoria and Albert Museum, London, Great Britain. (Credit: Victoria & Albert Museum, London / Art Resource, NY)

The high priest reacts to Jesus' claims by (1) tearing his garments, (2) declaring by means of a rhetorical question that they no longer need witnesses, (3) charging that Jesus has uttered blasphemy, and (4) asking for a verdict (14:63-64). The council responds by agreeing that Jesus deserves to die (v. 64b). Each of these actions calls for a brief comment.

The act of tearing one's clothes in grief, penitence, or outrage can be traced throughout the biblical period: Reuben tore his clothes when he could not find Joseph (Gen 37:29); David tore his clothes when he heard of the deaths of Saul and Jonathan (2 Sam 1:11-12); Joshua tore his clothes when he was defeated at Ai (Josh 7:6); Tamar put ashes on her head, tore her clothes, and cried aloud after she was violated by Amnon (2 Sam 13:19); Elisha tore his clothes when Elijah was taken up in a whirlwind (2 Kgs 2:12); King Hezekiah and his servants tore their clothes when they heard that God had sent Sennacherib's armies against Judah (2 Kgs 18:37–19:1); Job tore his robe and shaved his head (1:20), and the gesture is mentioned in the Apocrypha also (Ep Jer 31; Jdt 14:19). Later Jewish law prescribed that judges should tear their clothes when they heard blasphemy (*m. Sanh.* 7.5). In all likelihood, the high priest was not wearing his official vestments for this nocturnal assembly of the Sanhedrin [The High Priest's Robes], so the clothes he tore were his "everyday" robes.

The high priest's tactic of questioning Jesus directly had worked. In his judgment Jesus had incriminated himself, and they were all witness to his blasphemy. Further witnesses were unnecessary. Moreover, their judgment against Jesus would now be based not (or at least not merely) on his threat to the temple but on blasphemy.

The scriptural injunctions regarding blasphemy are found in Exodus 22:28 and Leviticus 24. Leviticus 24:16 in particular dictates that "One who blasphemes the name of the LORD shall be put to death." There is ample evidence for injunctions against blasphemy and the judgment that it merited the death penalty in the Qumran scrolls, Philo, and Josephus. Philo, for example, states, "But if anyone, I will not say blasphemes the Lord of gods and men, but even ventures to utter

The High Priest's Robes

Josephus provides us with an elaborate description of the high priest's garments. Like all priests, he put on the *machanases*, "drawers covering the loins, stitched of fine spun linen." Over this he wore a linen robe that reached to the ankles, with long sleeves laced around the arms, and a sash—into which flowers were woven—that was wound to the armpits. The sash trailed to the floor but could be thrown over the left shoulder. On his head he wore a cap without a peak, made of linen that was wound around and around and stitched repeatedly. The high priest added a blue tunic that reached to the feet, held by a brightly colored sash into which gold was woven. Along its lower edge were tassels colored to represent pomegranates and bells of gold, "so that between each pair of bells there hung a pomegranate and between the pome-granates a little bell." Over these he placed a third garment, called an *ephod*, of many colors, with gold embroidery. It left a gap on the breast into which was inserted a piece variegated with gold and the same colors as the ephod, and attached with gold rings to the ephod, with a blue thread passing through the rings to bind them together. The ephod is buckled on to the shoulders by two precious stones which bore the names of the sons of Jacob, six on each stone. Over the priests' cap the high priest wore a second cap with blue embroidery circled by a crown of gold with three tiers from which sprouted a gold calyx, a plant with a fruit with three spikes.

Josephus, *Jewish Antiquities* 3.153–74; cf. Exod 28:31-35.

His Name unseasonably; let him suffer the penalty of death" (*Moses* 2.206; LCL 6:551), and Josephus explains, "Let him who blasphemes God be stoned, then hung for a day, and buried ignominiously and in obscurity" (*Ant.* 4.202). The judgment of blasphemy later became more restricted, being imposed only for uttering God's name (*m. Sanh.* 7.5), but early in the first century any statement that demeaned God or arrogated to oneself divine status or privileges would have been considered blasphemy (see the commentary on 2:7; 3:28-29).[59] Jesus' claim to be "the Messiah, the Son of the Blessed One" and his implicit claim that the Scriptures that spoke of sitting at the right hand of God would be fulfilled by his vindication exceeded his earlier offenses: his claim of the prerogative to forgive sin (2:6-7), his demonstration in the temple (11:15-17), and his parabolic claim to divine sonship (12:1-12) and to being David's son (12:35-37).

By labeling Jesus' response as blasphemy, the high priest moved the proceedings directly to the judgment that Jesus deserved to die (Lev 24:16). The religious authorities were responsible for upholding the law, and in this case the law was clear: blasphemy must be punished by death. The decision of the council is reported in formal language: "All of them condemned him as deserving death" (v. 64; cf. 3:29), which has raised the question of whether the council was holding more than an informal hearing. In any case, the Jewish authorities might judge that Jesus deserved to die, but under Roman law, only the Roman governor could actually impose the death sentence.[60] The effect of their judgment was to send Jesus to Pilate and seek the death penalty from him, thereby fulfilling Jesus' third passion prediction (10:33). Ironically, the religious authorities were also following the pattern of how the wicked deal with the just (Jer 26:11; Wis 2:20).

Later Mark reports that Joseph of Arimathea, "a respected member of the council" (15:43), asked to bury Jesus' body. Mark does not indicate whether Joseph was present when Jesus was condemned, but Luke says that Joseph had not agreed with the council's decision (Luke 23:50-51).

The trial or hearing before the Sanhedrin ends with the members of the Sanhedrin spitting on Jesus, probably spitting in his face since that is commonly attested as a gesture of insult (Num 12:14; Deut 25:9; Job 30:10; Isa 50:6). They also cover Jesus' face, slap him, and challenge him to prophesy. Mark's verb can signify anything from a slap to a beating (1 Cor 4:11; 2 Cor 12:7; 1 Pet 2:20-21). Shocking as Mark's account is in involving the Sanhedrin in this mockery, it clearly plays out the vengeance of the wicked against the just. Matthew clarifies the purpose of this burlesque by reporting that those who slapped Jesus taunted him, saying, "Prophesy to us, you Messiah! Who is it that struck you?" (Matt 26:68). In doing so, Matthew probably simply clarified what Mark assumed. Jesus had been brought to them as a messianic pretender. He had made prophecies about the destruction of the temple (13:14-20; 14:58) and about his vindication (14:62). Now the authorities taunt him. If he can prophesy regarding such weighty matters, surely he could do a simple thing like identify whom it is who has slapped him. Ironically, however, they themselves are in the process of fulfilling Jesus' earlier prophecy about their actions (10:33-34).

The end of v. 65 is translated "the guards also took him over and beat him," but in 15:1 Jesus seems still to be in the custody of the council. Either we are to understand that the guards are simply an extension of the council's authority, or in 15:1 Mark is merely tying together the two main proceedings of the legal action against Jesus. Brown suggests a more colloquial meaning: "The colloquial use of English 'get someone' has the same idea, when they 'got him with slaps.'"[61]

Peter Denies Jesus, 14:66-72

Having introduced Peter's presence in the courtyard in v. 54, Mark returns to Peter for the account of his denials of Jesus. By means of this construction, Mark reports what was happening outside while Jesus was being questioned by the high priest inside. Not only do Peter's denials stand in sharp contrast to Jesus' forthright declaration, "I am" (v. 62), but they ironically fulfill Jesus' prophecy about Peter at the very time that Jesus is being taunted and challenged to prophesy.

The artistry of Mark's storytelling is further evident in the escalating intensity of the three denials. The high priest's house had at least two stories. Peter was "below" and perhaps outside (see the commentary on "courtyard" in v. 54). The first challenge to Peter comes quite unexpectedly, not from one of the guards but from a servant woman. [Peter's Temptation] Had she not seen Peter with Jesus? Her question, however, carries a nuance for Mark's readers because on two occasions Mark has described discipleship as being "with" Jesus. The Twelve were appointed to be "with" him (3:14) and to be sent out, and the Gadarene demoniac, following the exorcism of the evil spirits, asked to be with Jesus (5:18). The servant woman's question may also express contempt for "this Nazarene, Jesus." Mark uses the term *Nazarēnos* three other times (see the commentary on 1:24; 10:47; 16:6). Her contempt may be due to the fact that Jesus was from an

---

Peter's Temptation

"Peter's temptation came in a very unimpressive and incidental way. It was not the appropriate situation for confessing one's faith. The question he was asked did not really concern his faith at all. It was a purely objective question as to whether he was the one whom the servant girl thought she had seen with Jesus on some particular occasion. Furthermore, there was no reason for him to vindicate himself publicly. The one who asked was simply a servant girl who probably had no idea what it really meant to be a 'Nazarene,' so neither a 'yes' nor a 'no' would have indicated anything about faith. Consequently, if Peter had replied in the affirmative, he would have risked his safety without giving any witness to his faith."

Eduard Schweizer, *The Good News according to Mark* (trans. Donald H. Madvig; Atlanta: John Knox Press, 1970), 332.

obscure Galilean town, Nazareth, or more subtly because he was a bound prisoner and hardly a strong Nazirite (like Samson; Judg 13:7 LXX; 16:17).

Peter's response in Mark says nothing directly about his relationship to Jesus: "I do not know or understand what you are talking about" (14:68). In Greek it is awkward, if not ungrammatical, and both Matthew and Luke simplify it, interpreting it differently: "I do not know what you are talking about" (Matt 26:70) or "Woman, I do not know him" (Luke 22:57). William Lane found parallels to Peter's first denial in *m. Shebuoth* 8.3 and 8.6, where it is a formal, legal denial: "'Where is my ox?' He said to him, 'I do not know what you are saying'" (cf. *T. Joseph* 13:1-2).[62] Mark characterizes Peter's response as a denial, which even apart from Jesus' prophecy that Peter would deny him connoted a serious rejection of one's faith: "whoever denies me before others, I also will deny before my Father in heaven" (Matt 10:33; cf. Mark 8:38; 2 Tim 2:12; 2 Pet 2:1; 1 John 2:23; Jude 4; Rev 3:8).[63]

Having put off the servant woman, Peter moves away from the fire, either outside to the courtyard, or if he is already outside, out to the forecourt (*proaulion*). Either way, he is moving further from Jesus and making his escape, if necessary, easier. The statement, "Then the cock crowed" (14:68), is not in some of the early manuscripts and may have been inserted in order to explain the reference to the second cockcrow in 14:72 (cf. 14:30).

Although Peter moved away, the servant woman saw him again and began to tell the bystanders that he was "one of them." The expression implies that Jesus' followers (not necessarily the Twelve) were regarded with suspicion. The situation may also reflect the suspicion under which the Markan community lived—that they might be identified as "one of them." By announcing Peter's identity to the bystanders, the woman may have expected them to take some action against Peter. The situation had become much more serious. Again Peter denied. Mark does not quote his words but changes from the aorist tense to the imperfect, which may mean that Peter was denying repeatedly or continuously.

His own words may have raised further suspicion. One of the bystanders took up the questioning, saying, "Certainly you are one of them; for you are a Galilean" (14:70). Matthew 26:73 explains what is implicit in Mark, adding, "for your accent betrays you" (cf. Acts 2:7; 4:13; [Galilean Accent]). Peter responds by cursing and swearing, but Mark

Galilean Accent

AΩ Craig Evans cites the following text from the Talmud that shows that Judeans thought Galileans pronounced 'aleph as 'ayin and 'ayin as 'aleph:

"A certain Galilean went around saying to people, 'Who has amar? Who has amar? They said to him, 'You Galilean fool, do you mean an ass (hămār) for riding, or wine (hămar) for drinking, wool ('ămar) for clothing, or a lamb ('îmmar) for slaughtering?'" (b. 'Erub. 53b)

Craig A. Evans, *Mark 8:27–16:20* (WBC 34B; Nashville: Thomas Nelson, 2001), 466.

does not say whether Peter was cursing himself, his accusers, or Jesus. Peter may have cursed his accusers, but in context he was attempting to be accepted by them, not antagonize them. Reflexive oaths were common, and may be implied here: "May God punish me if what I am saying is false" (cf. Acts 23:12, 14, 21). Brown, however, concludes that Mark's account of Peter's failure ends with his cursing Jesus.[64] Peter swears that he does not know "this man," thereby implicating himself in Jesus' judgment on "those who are ashamed of me and of my words in this adulterous and sinful generation" (8:38). As Witherington observes, "It is an awful thing to swear to God that one does not know God's Son."[65]

"Immediately" the cock crowed a second time. Mark does not report the first cockcrow, and Matthew and Luke both omit the reference to the "second" crowing of the rooster (cf. the commentary on Mark 14:30). Mark's reference to the second cockcrow is difficult to reconcile with the theory that the cockcrow was the sound of a horn at the beginning of the fourth watch of the night (cf. 13:35). The point is that Jesus' words were being fulfilled to the letter while he was being challenged to prophesy (14:65).

Earlier, Peter remembered Jesus' cursing of the fig tree (11:21). This time his memory is bitter and crushing. Mark's report of Peter's reaction is notoriously ambiguous. The common translation is that he "broke down and wept" (NRSV, NIV), but the verb commonly means to "put on" or "throw over." Brown considers nine alternatives before concluding that it means "having thrown" (himself out; i.e., rushing outside),[66] but Danker is probably right in judging that Mark "intends the reader to understand a wild gesture connected with lamentation."[67] Peter's despair at what he had done would have served as a clear warning to Mark's readers who may have faced similar situations in which they were exposed to ridicule or persecution because they were "one of them"—a "Christian."

Even in complete failure, however, Peter's tears confirm his grief at having failed Jesus and therefore his continuing role as a disciple. Schweizer astutely contrasts Peter's response with Judas's effort to remedy his failure (Matt 27:3).[68] No disciple's story is complete before the resurrection (cf. 16:7).

CONNECTIONS

Mark 14:1-11

The opening of the Passion Narrative presents the reader with contrasting character studies: (1) the scheming religious authorities motivated by responsibility to protect the religious establishment, the uneasy truce with the imperial authority, and apparently a measure of resentment and malice as well; (2) Judas, the betrayer, who for reasons we can no longer recover agreed to hand Jesus over to the authorities; and (3) the unnamed woman whose extravagant gesture lives on in the Gospel. As preparation for entering into the mystery of Jesus' redemptive death, the Gospel leads the reader first to consider these three characters.

Mark traces the development of the opposition to Jesus throughout the Gospel, from the mixed responses to Jesus' exorcisms to the shock of the scribes and Pharisees that Jesus should claim to be able to forgive sin and defend his disciples by appeal to the actions of King David. Later, Jesus created a disturbance in the temple, bested the authorities in debate, characterized the religious leaders as wicked tenants, and castigated the scribes for their pretense. From their point of view, they had reason to feel that they had a responsibility to stop Jesus. He was a loose cannon, a troublemaker, a radical whose erratic behavior threatened the Jews' fragile peace with Rome (John 11:48). There were stories that some of the Galileans even wanted to make him a king (John 6:15; Mark 11:8-10). Did this mix of animosity and responsibility to protect the state and the religious status quo prevent the authorities from seeing who Jesus was?

Judas is the most troubling figure in the Gospel story, not because he betrayed Jesus but because he leads each of us to ask, as the disciples did (14:19), whether we could betray Jesus, indeed whether we are not actually betraying him. Efforts to understand Judas begin with the etymology of his name. Was he a *sicarius*, a dagger man, a zealot, a terrorist? Or was he a man from Kerioth, a town in the Negeb, a southerner, and hence a misfit among the Galileans? The revisionist efforts to rehabilitate Judas by having him conspire with the authorities to arrest Jesus in order to prevent him from throwing in with the Zealots after his demonstration in the temple, or by having Judas seek to force the waffling Jesus to show his hand and move to establish his kingdom, fail to convince. Judas's remorse can be explained in other ways. Nor does greed seem to have been his primary motive. The money seems to be an afterthought in Mark 14:11. The tradition that Judas betrayed Jesus must be respected. For whatever reason, Judas came to believe that

Jesus was not delivering on his promises. Perhaps Judas expected Jesus to establish an earthly kingdom (cf. 10:37), make them rich (10:28-30), or give them supernatural powers (4:41; 9:38). No one should claim to understand Jesus fully, so all are susceptible to holding Jesus to false standards. Judas represents the result of acting on resentment that Jesus did not do for him what he expected.

At the same time, Judas represents Jesus' failure.[69] Jesus was not a poor judge of character. He did not call Judas simply so that Judas would betray him. No, Jesus loved Judas, and Judas presumably had as much potential to become a pillar of the church as Peter or John. Jesus calls him a devil (John 6:70-71), but he also calls Peter Satan (Mark 8:33). The Gospels portray Judas as the betrayer after the fact. It is in that light that he is called "the son of perdition" (John 17:12). John records that Judas was the treasurer for the group (John 12:6) and that he was one of those closest to Jesus at the Last Supper (John 13:26; Mark 14:20). Giving the choice morsel to Judas (John 13:26) may have been Jesus' last appeal for Judas to reconsider what he was about to do—"Love's Last Appeal"—and hence the tragedy that not only did Judas fail Jesus but Jesus failed in his effort to redeem Judas. Even Jesus' immediate presence failed to break through Judas's hostility and malice. Jesus' work, therefore, remains unfinished, and Judas represents all who remain unredeemed and all that remains unredeemed within each of us. The cross creates wholeness and health where sin has sickened and broken, but we live among those who are broken, sick, and alienated. And Jesus has yet to drink the fruit of the vine new in the kingdom of God (14:25).

The woman who anointed Jesus with pure nard, lavishly showering Jesus with her treasure, offers a blinding contrast to the darkness of Judas and the religious authorities. They scheme and calculate, but there is no calculation in her spontaneous splash of spice. Such purity of heart gives her act a surplus of meaning. She may have simply responded to the impulse to give Jesus the most precious thing she had. Anointing Jesus with pure nard was a shockingly extravagant gesture. Jesus saw something further in the anointing—a preparation of his body for burial. How many have wished they had done something for a loved one while they were still alive instead of after they had passed away? The early tradition may have seen still another meaning in what she did: the ironic anointment of the royal Messiah who had entered the Holy City on a colt, not by the high priest but by an anonymous woman. Just as the reader asks with the disciples, "Is it I" (14:19), so the beautiful thing the woman did for Jesus may be the standard by which we measure our own spiritual health. Are we givers, or are we more likely to accuse and find fault?

Mark 14:12-16

Imagine being one of the two disciples sent into the city, looking for a man carrying a jar of water. In the midst of the momentous events that would change the course of human history, this is surely a comic footnote. Yet Mark includes it along with the other events of that fateful week, just before the account of the words of institution at the Last Supper. This vignette, however, reminds us that worship events require careful preparation. The upper room had to be secured and made ready, the furnishing had to be arranged, and the bread, herbs, Passover lamb, and vine had to be prepared, as did the necessary dishes and cups. The others would come later, and the mood for the evening would be set by having everything ready so the meal could proceed, the servers would be ready, and Jesus and the disciples would not be distracted from the Passover observance and the things Jesus needed to say to the disciples.

Supper at the House of Simon

Tintoretto, Jacopo Robusti (1518–1594). *Supper at the House of Simon.* Musei Civici, Padua, Italy. (Credit: Mauro Magliani, 1998. Alinari / Art Resource, NY)

Cleaning, arranging, setting out flowers, cooking, testing sound equipment, or any of the other myriad of preparations may not seem to be holy work, but remember the man carrying the jar of water and the disciples who looked for him. The sanctity of work is defined by why we do it rather than by the task itself, so whether your task be great or small, let it be for you the worship of God.

Mark 14:17-21

Why did Jesus tell the other disciples that one of them would betray him? Was he searching to determine which one of them was the betrayer, or did he already know it was Judas? Was he warning the disciples or appealing to the betrayer to reconsider? Verse 21 calls for further reflection. Much depends on whether the "woe" and the statement "it would have been better for that one not to have been born" carry the force of a threat or the distress of a lament. Was Jesus threatening, warning, stating a stark fact, lamenting, or issuing a final appeal? If we allow the "woe" to express a lament, as it does elsewhere, Jesus was moved by his failure to reach Judas and the terrible thing Judas was about to do. Jesus probably knew that Judas would never be able to forgive himself for his act of betrayal. Matthew records that he took the money back and sought to undo what he had done and that he hanged himself (Matt 27:3-5).

The giving of the bread and the wine at the Last Supper, therefore, is prefaced by Jesus' heartfelt grief over what Judas was about to do. Judas represents every person for whom Jesus died, for he loved all as he loved each one. The giving of the bread and the cup were connected to Judas's moral treachery in the same way that Jesus' death on the cross was connected to human sinfulness. Jesus responded to Judas's terrible failing with completely selfless grace. Similarly, sin led to the cross, but Jesus' death was God's gracious response to human sin. Alas for those who cannot hear this good news.

Mark 14:22-25

The institution of the Lord's Supper was an act so powerful that its liturgical reenactment continues to be the central act in most Christian worship. Countless meditations, homilies, and sermons have mined the significance of the supper, and still it continues to nurture Christian faith and practice. Part of the power of the supper lies in its simplicity. Jesus took the common elements of life and filled them with transcendent meaning. With the specter of his coming death weighing heavily upon him, Jesus sought to reassure the disciples that his death would not mark the end of his presence with them.

Through the mystery of word and faith, the Lord himself is present with the community in every observance of the supper. The elements of the bread and the cup nourish the believer physically while the presence of Christ nourishes and sustains the believer spiritually. The supper is also sheer gift. Mark emphasizes the failure of the disciples, but the giving of the bread and the cup was not a reward for faithfulness; it was a demonstration of unconditional grace. The observance of the supper also ties the worshiping community to the ministry of Jesus, just as it reminded the disciples of all the other times when they had eaten with Jesus. To receive the bread and the cup, therefore, is to receive the love of God revealed in the death of Jesus, affirm the Lordship of the one who ate with outcasts, recognize the deep fellowship of the "temple not made with hands," and look expectantly to the future when we shall drink the cup new in the kingdom of God. The observance of the Lord's Supper is therefore an act of worship in three tenses: a remembrance of the past, worshiping in memory; a recognition of the presence of Christ with the community in the present, worshiping in celebration; and a reminder of the promise of the future consummation of the fellowship with Christ in God's kingdom, worshiping in hope and anticipation. It is the basis for our relationship with God through the new covenant solemnized by the blood of Christ. Ultimately, the meaning of the Lord's Supper eludes analysis and verbalization and touches the deep stirrings of our spirits, bringing about forgiveness, reconciliation, renewal, assurance, community, guidance, celebration, and hope. While the observance of the bread and the cup continues to stir our imaginations, thoughts, and emotions, it continues to effect within us what the ministry, death, and resurrection of Jesus accomplished within human history and experience. It is a declaration of the love and presence of God and a call to live in response to that reality.

Mark 14:26-31

Jesus' divinity allowed him to know what the future held and to be able to prophesy coming events, like Peter's denials before the cock crowed for the second time. There are times when all of us wish we could see into the future. Will I marry? If so, whom? Is this a good business venture? What will my children or grandchildren grow up to be? The argument between Peter and Jesus concerned the future, but it also concerned issues that determined the future. Who was Peter? How would he respond to a life-threatening situation? What was his attitude toward the future?

Peter's future would be determined by his own character. He was apparently headstrong and impulsive, insightful but overly sure of himself. His flaw was that he did not recognize his own weaknesses. Jesus prepared for the trials he knew were coming by spending the night praying in Gethsemane, while Peter was oblivious both to the coming trials and to his own need to prepare himself for them. Peter's responses to Jesus' warning about what was coming are filled with confident declarations about his own strength: "I will not" (14:29) and "even though I must die with you, I will not deny you" (14:31). Blindly, Peter saw no need to look beyond his own abilities, while Jesus recognized his need for prayer. Peter betrayed not just overconfidence but a prideful denial of the possibility that he could fail. Jesus, on the other hand, who was both stronger than Peter and more self-aware, displayed a moving humility both by praying about his future and by recognizing that God might not bend the future to accommodate what Jesus wanted.

Sometimes it is best that we not know the future, and not knowing the future should mean that we treasure the present while being courageously open to whatever the future may hold, relying not on our own strength but on the grace of God for resources to meet the future's trials.

Mark 14:32-42

The Gethsemane scene offers a study in two contrasting role models. Jesus is the suffering Son of Man seeking the Father's direction, strength, and consolation as he faces his coming trial. The disciples, especially the three closest to Jesus, sleep, demonstrating that they cannot be watchful, even for one hour. As Eduard Schweizer observed, the disciples' failure is "the greatest cause of his suffering."[70] Jesus knew that the end of his life was near. Although we cannot know what he thought during those night hours in Gethsemane, Mark shows us that everyone around Jesus failed, abandoned, or opposed Jesus: his hometown, his family, the religious authorities, the crowds, and even his disciples. Still, that did not deter Jesus from remaining faithful to his mission, and he turned to the One who alone could sway the future, or failing that give him the strength he needed to face whatever it might bring. Jesus would not let the failure of others, indeed the apparent failure of his own ministry, crush him.

The sleeping disciples, on the other hand, while they provide no positive role model in this scene, can serve as a reminder that God can work with even the most flawed human vessels to accomplish divine purposes. Mark is unrelenting in his account of the disciples' failure, but at the end of the Gospel he signals that their failure is not the end of the story. The power of the resurrection would touch their lives also, changing them from failed disciples into courageous witnesses (16:7; 13:9-11). And, if God can use such disciples, then surely God can use us too!

Christ's Agony in the Garden

El Greco (1541–1614). *Christ's Agony in the Garden*. S. Maria, Andujar, Spain. (Credit: Scala / Art Resource, NY)

Mark 14:43-52

The arrest scene casts Jesus in the role of a victim of institutional and state-sponsored violence. He had done nothing illegal, but his activities had aroused suspicion, opposition, and then led to a plot to kill him. In a time of heightened resentment of illegal aliens and fear of anti-American terrorists, it is sobering that Jesus was arrested and then executed by the religious and civil authorities for activities they considered to be a threat to their established order.

Jesus was doing nothing wrong. He was praying quietly while his disciples slept when the authorities, led by Judas, came to arrest him. In the pandemonium that followed, someone drew a sword and one of the official's servants was injured before the authorities secured Jesus and his disciples fled into the night. Imagine how modern newspapers might report the scene, molding popular opinion against Jesus: "Messianic Pretender Arrested near the Temple; High Priest's Servant Slashed with a Sword."

Glib answers and knee-jerk reactions often displace reasoned discussion, wise solutions, and advocacy for the outsider. Yet, the scandal of the Gospel, that Jesus was arrested as a troublemaker and executed as a criminal, cannot be escaped. Invariably it reminds us that part of being a follower of Jesus requires that we who are part of the privileged majority have a responsibility to protect the rights of the outsiders in our midst who all too often become the targets of our fears, prejudices, and anxieties.

Mark 14:53-65

The concept of "a temple not made with hands" is suggestive of Mark's vision for the church, even though it enters the Gospel as the words of the false witnesses at Jesus' trial. God denied to David the privilege of building the first temple in Jerusalem, granting that privilege instead to David's son (Solomon). The faithful Jews who returned to Judea from exile in Babylon rebuilt the temple. The temple became the center of Jewish life, and two centuries before Jesus it was the focus of the zeal of the Maccabean heroes who recovered the temple from the Antiochus Epiphanes and rededicated it—the events still celebrated at Hanukkah. During the time of Jesus' life the temple had been undergoing yet another extensive rebuilding, which was started by Herod the Great and continued by his successors. In the parallel to the temple saying in the Gospel of John, the disbelieving Jews respond in amazement at Jesus' claim that he would rebuild the temple in three days, reminding him that it had been under construction for forty-six years (John 2:20).

In Mark the "temple not made with hands" is a metaphor for the church, the community of believers like the failing disciples, the blind Bartimaeus, the generous widow, and the centurion who was able to receive God's revelation. It was a metaphor for the struggling, persecuted church of Mark's time. Although they might have been small in number, insignificant in political power, and living on the margins of Roman society, they were the new temple. They were the new center of God's presence on earth.

At the moment when the religious authorities were in the process of condemning Jesus, the Gospel reminds us that Jesus was not defeated. God would use these events to raise up a new temple, a new place where all people of every land, color, and language can meet God. Unlike every other temple, this one would not be made by human hands; it would be God's work. Paul built on this notion through the metaphor of the church as the body of Christ (see Rom 12:5; 1 Cor 12:27; Eph 2:16; 3:6; 4:12; Col 1:18). The church remains the vital center of God's redemptive work on earth, therefore, and to be faithful it must always be focused on its divine mission.

Saint Peter in Tears

Rutilio Manetti (1571–1639). *Saint Peter in Tears*. Coll. Monte dei Paschi, Siena, Italy. (Credit: Scala / Art Resource, NY)

Mark 14:66-72

Social pressure and fear are powerful forces to which few of us are immune. The fear that we might be singled out as "one of them" is not limited to school children and teenagers. At Gethsemane Peter could not watch with Jesus; in the courtyard he would not dare to be identified with Jesus. In an oppressive and potentially dangerous situation, Peter denied that he even knew Jesus. It would be easy to think that we would have been more courageous, but few of us have ever faced such an overt threat of persecution for our faith in Christ. The tests we face are usually more subtle. When someone speaks scornfully of faith or of all Christians because of the actions of one group or another, the temptation is to remain silent. When someone tells a racist story or puts down a particular group of people, the temptation is to let it pass rather than confront them or speak up for the victimized. When someone makes derogatory comments about the church or about values we hold dear, the temptation is to leave quietly, as Peter did. We live in a highly contentious society, where religious values have become the targets of scorn and the watch words for culture wars. Neither timid silence nor belligerent campaigns to impose our values on others represents the spirit of Jesus, however. When Jesus was silent (14:61; 15:5), it was a silence motivated by integrity and realism, but Peter's silence was a silence born of fear and failure. When Jesus protested the corruption of the temple (11:15-17), it was a measured protest that echoed the Scriptures, and he returned the next day to answer those who questioned him. When the bystander at the arrest of Jesus lashed out with the sword, it was a defensive response that escalated the violence of the situation. Faithfulness always demands a rare and difficult blend of courage, integrity, and prudence if we are ever to be known as truly "one of them."

NOTES

[1] Joachim Jeremias, *Jerusalem in the Time of Jesus* (trans. F. H. and C. H. Cave; Philadelphia: Fortress Press, 1969), 77-84.

[2] John Painter, *Mark's Gospel* (London and New York: Routledge, 1997), 181.

[3] William L. Lane, *The Gospel according to Mark* (NICNT; Grand Rapids: Wm. B. Eerdmans, 1974), 492, cites Pliny the Elder, *Natural History* 13.3.19: "the best ointment is preserved in alabaster."

[4] BAGD, 818.

[5] Craig A. Evans, *Mark 8:27–16:20* (WBC 34B; Nashville: Thomas Nelson, 2001), 365.

[6] Lane, *The Gospel according to Mark*, 496.

[7] Evans, *Mark 8:27–16:20*, 365.

[8] Ibid., 373.

[9] BAGD, 521.

[10] Joachim Jeremias, *The Eucharistic Words of Jesus* (trans. Norman Perrin; Philadelphia: Fortress Press, 1966), 49.

[11] Evans, *Mark 8:27–16:20*, 375.

[12] Ibid., 377.

[13] Ibid., 378.

[14] Vincent Taylor, *The Gospel according to St. Mark* (London: Macmillan, 1952), 542.

[15] James H. Charlesworth, ed., *OTP* (Garden City: Doubleday, 1985), 2:212, 213, 226, 229.

[16] Florentino García Martínez, *The Dead Sea Scrolls Translated* (Leiden: E. J. Brill, 1994), 127.

[17] *The Mishnah* (trans. Herbert Danby; Oxford: Oxford University Press, 1933), 6.

[18] Evans, *Mark 8:27–16:20*, 390-91.

[19] Lane, *The Gospel according to Mark*, 508.

[20] Raymond E. Brown, *The Death of the Messiah* (New York: Doubleday, 1994), 1:127.

[21] Francis J. Moloney, *The Gospel of Mark* (Peabody MA: Hendrickson, 2002), 288.

[22] Evans, *Mark 8:27–16:20*, 402.

[23] Lane, *The Gospel according to Mark*, 511.

[24] Ibid., 512 n. 69.

[25] Brown, *The Death of the Messiah*, 1:152.

[26] BAGD, 19.

[27] Lane, *The Gospel according to Mark*, 516 n. 78.

[28] Joachim Jeremias, *The Prayers of Jesus* (Philadelphia: Fortress, 1967), 11-65; idem, *New Testament Theology: The Proclamation of Jesus* (trans. John Bowden; New York: Charles Scribner's Sons, 1971), 63-68.

[29] Brown, *The Death of the Messiah*, 1:195.

[30] Ibid., 1:196.

[31] Ibid., 1:204.

[32] Ibid., 1:208-09, and Appendix III A, 2:1379-83.

[33] BDAG, 102.

[34] Evans, *Mark 8:27–16:20*, 416-17.

[35] Moloney, *The Gospel of Mark*, 296 n. 104.

[36] See Brown, *The Death of the Messiah*, 1:211-13.

[37] Ibid., 1:246.

[38] Ibid., 1:247.

[39] Evans, *Mark 8:27–16:20*, 422-23.

[40] Brown, *The Death of the Messiah*, 1:283.

[41] Moloney, *The Gospel of Mark*, 298 n. 115, citing Morna D. Hooker, *The Gospel according to St. Mark* (London: A. & C. Black, 1991), 352.

[42] Lane, *The Gospel according to Mark*, 527.

[43] Brown, *The Death of the Messiah*, 1:286.

[44] Ibid., 1:287.

[45] For these and other interpretations, see ibid., 1:299-302.

[46] See ibid., 1:357-63, for a full discussion of these issues.

[47] Moloney, *The Gospel of Mark*, 300 n. 123.

[48] Brown, *The Death of the Messiah*, 1:433.

[49] Lane, *The Gospel according to Mark*, 534.

[50] Moloney, *The Gospel of Mark*, 303 n. 139.

[51] Donald Juel, *Messiah and Temple* (SBLDS 31; Missoula: Scholars Press, 1977), 189; Mary L. Coloe, *God Dwells with Us: Temple Symbolism in the Fourth Gospel* (Collegeville: Liturgical Press, 2001), 171.

[52] Juel, *Messiah and Temple*, 143-57; cf. Eta Linnemann, *Studien zur Passionsgeschichte* (Göttingen: Vandenhoeck und Ruprecht, 1970), 118-24.

[53] Brown, *The Death of the Messiah*, 1:440-43.

[54] Ibid., 1:453.

[55] Evans, *Mark 8:27–16:20*, 448.

[56] Brown, *The Death of the Messiah*, 1:469.

[57] See ibid., 1:489; Evans, *Mark 8:27–16:20*, 450.

[58] Brown, *The Death of the Messiah*, 1:499.

[59] For full discussion of the evidence and issues, see Evans, *Mark 8:27–16:20*, 453-57; Brown, *The Death of the Messiah*, 1:520-27, 1:530-47.

[60] For discussion of the Roman legal authority in Judea, see Brown, *The Death of the Messiah*, 1:331-38.

[61] Ibid., 1:577.

[62] Lane, *The Gospel according to Mark*, 542.

[63] Evans, *Mark 8:27–16:20*, 405.

[64] Brown, *The Death of the Messiah*, 1:605.

[65] Ben Witherington III, *The Gospel of Mark: A Socio-Rhetorical Commentary* (Grand Rapids: Wm. B. Eerdmans, 2001), 387.

[66] Brown, *The Death of the Messiah*, 1:609-10.

[67] BDAG, 368.

[68] Eduard Schweizer, *The Good News according to Mark* (trans. Donald H. Madvig; Atlanta: John Knox Press, 1970), 332.

[69] John A. T. Robinson, *The Roots of a Radical* (London: SCM, 1980), 139-43.

[70] Schweizer, *The Good News according to Mark*, 315.

THE CRUCIFIXION OF JESUS

Mark 15:1-47

By this point Jesus is caught in a vortex of forces. Arrested, abandoned by his disciples, he has been interrogated by the high priest before the Jewish council, where he was condemned not by the testimony of false witnesses but for the truth from his own lips. The authorities determined that he should be executed, something they did not have the legal authority to do, and they may have wanted the Roman soldiers to be the ones to carry out the execution. Mark 15 opens with the trial before Pilate and moves swiftly to the crucifixion, death, and burial of Jesus.

Crucifixion was a familiar form of execution in Palestine. Following the siege of Tyre, Alexander the Great lined the shore with 2,000 crosses (Quintus Curtius, *History of Alexander* 4.4.17), and Alexander Jannaeus (103–76 BC) crucified 800 Pharisees (Josephus, *Ant.* 13.380; *J.W.* 1.97). The challenge Mark faced, therefore, was how to communicate the significance of Jesus' death. What made it different from all the other crucifixions? Since he was not writing an essay or a letter, Mark could not simply explain the meaning of Jesus' death. Instead, he had to use various literary, or narrative, techniques to comment indirectly on the meaning of the events he was recording. The structure of the account is important; Mark follows the reports of the trial, crucifixion, and death of Jesus with reports of the responses to Jesus:

I. The trial before Pilate (15:1-15)
   The soldiers mock Jesus (15:16-20)
II. The crucifixion of Jesus (15:21-27)
   The bystanders mock Jesus (15:29-32)
III. The death of Jesus (15:33-38)
   The centurion confesses Jesus (15:39)

The action in Mark 15, therefore, unfolds in three parts, with the burial of Jesus as a kind of epilogue. Following each of the three parts there is a response. In the first two instances it is mockery, and in the third it is the climactic confession toward which the Gospel has been building from the beginning.

Looking closer, we also see that ironically everything that is said to or about Jesus in mockery is true: he was the king of the Jews

(15:18), he would destroy the temple and build it (metaphorically) in three days (15:29), and he had saved others, yet (for that reason) he could not save himself (15:31). The words that Jesus spoke from the cross are revealing also. Mark records the haunting and ultimately impenetrable cry of abandonment (or "cry of dereliction"), "My God, my God, why have you forsaken me?" (15:34).

In addition, the things that happened while Jesus was on the cross were all significant: the charge against him (15:26), the darkness at midday (15:33), the misunderstanding of his cry (15:35), the sour wine (15:36), and the rending of the veil in the temple (15:38). All of these merit close attention, and many of these elements of the story show that the Scriptures were being fulfilled—another technique for commenting on the meaning of Jesus' death. Jesus' death is theologically the heart of the matter for Mark. It is carefully written, and therefore it calls for close reading.

COMMENTARY

The Trial before Pilate, 15:1-15

This extended scene, nearly one third of the chapter, begins with the conclusion of the hearing before the Sanhedrin and binding Jesus over to Pilate (15:1). Although the scene is a unity, two major parts can be distinguished: Pilate's futile effort to interrogate Jesus (15:2-5) and Pilate's futile effort to placate the chief priests and the crowd (15:6-15). Pilate's efforts fail in both parts, first because of Jesus' silence and second because of the crowd's boisterous demand for the release of Barabbas and the death of Jesus. Mark's theological interests are evident in this brief account of the trial before Pilate: in the phrasing of the charge against Jesus, in Jesus' silence, in Jesus' fulfillment of the model of the suffering servant, and in his example for Mark's persecuted readers.

Mark 15:1 has been read as reporting a second meeting of the Sanhedrin (e.g., NRSV), but more recent scholarship favors interpreting the verse as recapitulating Mark's account of the hearing before Sanhedrin in 14:55-65. The phrase translated "held a consultation" (*symboulion poiēsantes*) can also be translated "having reached a decision" (cf. 3:6).[1] The reason for the urgency in bringing Jesus before Pilate early was that the Roman aristocracy did their business early in the morning so that they could spend the hot part of the day in leisure activities.[2] If they did not present their accusations early that morning, they would not be able to do so until after the Sabbath had passed.

Mark reintroduces the groups that were involved in the arrest and trial of Jesus: the chief priests, the elders, the scribes, and the Sanhedrin. The first three groups are mentioned together in 8:31; 11:27; 14:43, 53, but there is no consistency in the sequence in which they are named (cf. [Chief Priests] [Elders] [Scribes] [Councils]). By renaming the groups, Mark closes the section that began at 14:53. Mark uses four verbs to report their actions: they held counsel, or reached a decision; they bound Jesus, since by this time they had passed judgment on him; they led him to Pilate; and they "handed him over" to Pilate. The latter is an echo of Judas's treachery (cf. 3:19; 14:10, 11, 18, 21, 41, 42, 44), but it also recalls Jesus' passion predictions, especially the third one, in which there are two references to his being handed over (10:33), and his prophecy that his followers would be "handed over" to councils and brought before governors and kings (13:9, 11). The followers of Jesus in the Markan community, therefore, read the account of Jesus' actions when he was brought before the governor knowing that they too might face the same situation.

The change of setting and the introduction of a new character, Pontius Pilate, open the next section. Pilate was a prefect, the governor of Judea. [Pontius Pilate] The location of the trial before Pilate has been debated, however. Since the twelfth century, pilgrims to Jerusalem have been told that the trial took place in the Fortress of Antonia, located at the northwest corner of the temple. The "Way of the Cross," with its various stations, leads from this site to the Church of the Holy Sepulchre, the traditional, and most probable, site of the crucifixion. In addition, since 1870 an impressive paved area, with graffiti that has been identified as the soldiers' "king game," has been identified as the *Lithostrōtos* referred to in John 19:13. Impressive as the case for this site is, it does not hold. More recent archaeologists believe the paved area was part of an entry to the city built on the site in the second century, that the Fortress of Antonia housed Roman troops, but that Pilate probably stayed at Herod's palace when he visited Jerusalem. A *praetorium* was the governor's residence and administrative headquarters. Herod's palace [Herod's Palace] [Map of Jerusalem] was located on the west side of the city, near the three prominent towers Herod named for friends and family members (Hippicus, Phasael, and Mariamme; Josephus, *J. W.* 5.161-75). Josephus describes its extravagance (*J. W.* 1.402; 5.176-79; *Ant.* 15.318) in terms that make it unlikely that Pilate would have stayed at the smaller and less luxurious Fortress of Antonia when he was in Jerusalem. [Josephus's Description of Herod's Palace]

Mark seems to understand that Pilate was not involved in the plan to arrest and try Jesus. Pilate's opening words to Jesus imply that he had received an accusation against Jesus from the Jewish authorities.[3] Pilate's question may be intensive, and if so, scornful, "Are *you* the King

Pontius Pilate

The inscription, which probably commemorates the rebuilding of the harbor at Caesarea, is damaged and various proposals have been advanced for reconstructing its text. The most widely accepted reading is

[CAESARIEN]STIBERIEVM
  [Caesarean]s' Tiberieum
[PON]TIVSPILATVS
  [Pon]tius Pilate,
[PRAEF]ECTVSIVDA[EA]E
[Pref]ect of Jud[ea]
[D]I[DIT]
  [d]e[dicates]

The "Tiberieum" was a building dedicated to Emperor Tiberius, perhaps the lighthouse. The inscription was later reused in the construction of the theater and found there when the theater was excavated. It is now in the archaeological museum in Jerusalem, and a replica stands outside the theater in Caesarea.

Ancient writers offer widely varying accounts of Pilate. Tertullian says he was a Christian at heart (*Apology* 21, *ANF* 3:35); according to Philo, Agrippa charged Pilate with briberies, outrages, and "ceaseless and supremely grievous cruelty" (*Ad Gaium* 28.302; LCL 10:153). Raymond E. Brown discusses six incidents that provide evidence of Pilate's administration. (1) When Pilate attempted to place soldiers with icons of Caesar on their standards in the temple, Jews protested in Caesarea. Pilate surrounded them with troops, but when they showed they were ready to die he relented rather than slaughter the protesters. (2) Pilate minted coins with pagan cultic symbols on them in Jerusalem from AD 29–31. (3) When Pilate appropriated funds from the temple that were *qorban* [Qorban], the Jews again protested. This time Pilate sent soldiers with clubs into the crowd. The violence may have gone beyond anything Pilate intended, but

Pontius Pilate was governor of Judea AD 26–36, under the direct authority of the Roman emperor. "Pontius" was the name of his tribe, and "Pilatus" the name of his family. Legend has it that his personal name was "Lucius," but this is not certain. As a man of equestrian rank, he had probably served in the army before being appointed "prefect," the title given to the Roman governors of Judea prior to the reign of Agrippa I (AD 41–44). This title was confirmed by the discovery of an inscription at Caesarea in 1961.

(Credit: R. Alan Culpepper)

many protesters and bystanders died in the riot that followed. (4) Luke 13:1-2 refers to an incident in which Pilate mingled the blood of Galileans with their sacrifices in Jerusalem. (5) Another incident arose when Pilate dedicated shields coated with gold in Jerusalem. Philo is our only source for this incident. Herodian princes led a protest and appealed to Emperor Tiberius, who ordered Pilate to take the shields to Caesarea. (6) In AD 36 Pilate ordered troops to block an expedition by Samaritans who were preparing to follow a false-prophet who promised to lead them to Moses' sacred vessels. Following this incident the Syrian legate Vitellius, acting no doubt on the emperor's directions, removed Pilate from office. Shortly later, Caiaphas, who may have been involved also, was likewise removed from office.

The portrait that emerges from this record is one of a governor who was at times naïve about the religious sensitivities of the Jews and at times failed to control the brutality of his own soldiers. When pressed, on more than one occasion, he relented rather than order a slaughter of the people. Brown concludes, therefore, "Jesus had not met either the best or the worst of the Roman judges" (1:722).

Raymond E. Brown, *The Death of the Messiah* (New York: Doubleday, 1994), 1:693-705; Craig A. Evans, *Mark 8:27–16:20* (WBC 34B; Nashville: Thomas Nelson, 2001), 476-78; A. N. Sherwin-White, *Roman Society and Roman Law in the New Testament* (Oxford: Oxford University Press, 1963), 6, 24-47.

Herod's Palace

Surrounded by groves of trees, canals, and ponds, King Herod's fortified Palace provided protection to the Upper City. The two main buildings, their banquet halls and baths, could accommodate hundreds of guests. The Palace, like the Temple, was built on a platform approximately 1000 feet (north-south) by 180 feet (east-west).

(Credit: Jim Pitts)

of the Jews?" but it need not carry this force in Mark.[4] This is the first time the title "King" is applied to Jesus in Mark (cf. 15:9, 12, 18, 26, 32). The title "the King of the Jews" was used among the Romans, but it could also have messianic overtones. Mark, however, assumes that the readers will understand the connection between "the Messiah," or God's Anointed One (cf. 1:1; 8:29; 12:35; 14:61), and "the King of the Jews." Jesus' response, "you say so," is carefully noncommittal. If he had openly accepted the title (cf. his response to the high priest, 14:61-62), Pilate would have pronounced him guilty. On the other hand, because of the title's messianic overtones, Jesus could not simply deny it.

Perhaps sensing that their case hung in the balance, the chief priests persisted, either accusing Jesus "vigorously," or accusing him of "many things." The word *polla* is probably the object here (as in 4:2), favoring the latter interpretation, but Mark also uses it adverbially (1:45; 3:12; 5:10, 23; 6:20, 23, etc.). When Pilate interrogates Jesus again, he refers to the many charges brought against him (v. 4), but Jesus is silent, making no further response and thereby fulfilling the characterization of the suffering servant in Isaiah 53:7, "He was oppressed, and he was afflicted, yet he did not open his mouth."

Josephus's Description of Herod's Palace

"Adjoining and on the inner side of these three towers, which lay to the north of it, was the king's palace, baffling all description: indeed, in extravagance and equipment no building surpassed it. It was completely enclosed within a wall thirty cubits high, broken at equal distances by ornamental towers, and contained immense banqueting-halls and bedchambers for a hundred guests. The interior fittings are indescribable—the variety of the stones (for species rare in every country were here collected in abundance), ceilings wonderful both for the length of the beams and the splendour of their surface decoration, the host of apartments with their infinite varieties of design, all amply furnished, while most of the objects in each of them were of silver or gold."

Josephus, *J.W.* 5.176–79; LCL 3:253.

Pilate was amazed at Jesus' silence, another possible echo of the suffering servant songs (Isa 52:15 LXX).[5] In the Roman court, there was no trial by jury, and Jesus had no rights because he was not a Roman citizen. The judge would hear the accusations, discern the facts of the case, interrogate the accused, and pass judgment in the matter. By refusing to respond, Jesus was giving up the only legal defense he had.

Mark explains that Pilate would release a prisoner at the festival. While this practice is credible in light of the available evidence, it is not attested outside the Gospels. John refers to the custom, and Matthew follows Mark, but Luke omits this verse. A reference in the Mishnah allows slaughtering a Passover lamb "for one whom they have promised to bring out of prison" (*m. Pesahim* 8.6).[6] A papyrus text records the governor of Egypt saying to a prisoner named Phibion, "You were worthy of scourging . . . but I give you to the crowds."[7] Josephus also records instances of procurators releasing prisoners and crowds demanding the release of a prisoner on various occasions (*Ant.* 17.204; 20.215). Mark's reference to this custom is credible, therefore. It would have been the kind of gesture of goodwill that the prefect might have made during the Passover celebration as a way of maintaining good relations with the chief priests and the pilgrims who had gathered in Jerusalem.

Mark adds (v. 8) that the crowd gathered explicitly in order to call for the release of a prisoner, and the implication is that they had come to call for the release of Barabbas. Barabbas is introduced in v. 7, but he never actually appears or speaks, and the introduction might have come later since the chief priests do not stir up the crowds to call for his release until v. 11. Nothing is known of Barabbas outside of what the Gospels say about him. There were so many bandits and rebels in first-century Judea that Josephus makes no mention of him, and we cannot even say what incident he may have been involved in. Mark says only that he was in prison with the insurrectionists or rioters who had committed murder. It is doubtful that Barabbas could have been released if he himself were accused of murder (cf. Josephus, *Ant.* 20.215). The name Barabbas can mean "son of a teacher" (*rabban*), "son of [a man named] Abba," or "son of the father."[8] Mark's readers no doubt caught the irony that the crowd called for the "son of the Father" rather than Jesus of Nazareth, and in some manuscripts of Matthew 27:16 and 17 he is called "Jesus Barabbas." Origen insisted that it was not proper for a sinner to be called Jesus,[9] but his insistence supports the argument that it is more likely that scribes omitted the name for this reason than that they added it to draw a closer parallel between Jesus and Barabbas. Either way, the irony remains that the authorities brought Jesus to Pilate on a trumped up political charge and then called for the release of Barabbas, who was guilty of insurrection while Jesus was innocent.

Pilate's action at this point in the trial is important because it characterizes for Mark's readers not only the role of Roman authority in Jesus' death but the sort of Roman justice they themselves might face. In v. 9 Pilate again uses the title "the King of the Jews" (cf. 15:2). The question is whether Pilate is speaking sarcastically, mocking the crowd, or offering them not a rebel but a king. Apparently the Jewish authorities brought Jesus to him with the charge that he was a threat because he claimed to be the King of the Jews, a charge they understood to have messianic overtones but knew would have political ramifications for Pilate. Pilate was at least skeptical and perhaps scornful: "Are you the king of the Jews?" (15:2). Now Mark reports that Pilate knew that the Jewish authorities had handed Jesus over to him out of envy or zeal (Greek *phthonos*). Raymond Brown shows that this term occurs in various accounts of the persecution of the righteous: Daniel (Josephus, *Ant.* 10.250-57; 3 Macc 6:7), Paul (Phil 1:15), and Peter and Paul (*1 Clem.* 5:2).[10] Pilate knew, therefore, that the charge was false. His concern, however, was not justice but defusing the situation that had developed, so he chose to let the crowd decide which prisoner he should release. If he thought they might choose Jesus, he misread the situation. The authorities wanted the Romans to execute Jesus, and the crowd had apparently come to call for the release of Barabbas. The chief priests may have feared that the crowd also included some of Jesus' followers, that they would call for the release of Jesus, and that Pilate would choose to release Jesus, who had done nothing violent, rather than Barabbas. They therefore stirred up the crowd to call for the release of Barabbas. The question that remains, of course, is what should become of Jesus? Pilate puts the question to the crowd, and again uses the title "King of the Jews." The response of the crowd is vehement and violent. They cry out (cf. the cry "Hosanna" in 11:9), "Crucify him!" [Crucifixion]

In Luke and John, Pilate pronounces Jesus innocent three times. In Mark, however, Pilate never pronounces Jesus innocent. He is amazed at Jesus' silence (15:2), he knows that the chief priests handed Jesus over to him out of jealousy (15:10), and he demands to know what Jesus had done that merited the death penalty (15:14), but he never pronounces Jesus

Crucifixion

"I see crosses there, not just of one kind but fashioned in many different ways: Some have their victims with head down toward the ground; some impale their private parts; others stretch out their arms on the crossbeam."

Seneca the Younger, *Ad Marciam de consolatione* 20.3; Raymond E. Brown, *The Death of the Messiah* [New York: Doubleday, 1994], 2:948.

"When caught, they [the fugitives] were driven to resist, and after a conflict it seemed too late to sue for mercy. They were accordingly scourged and subjected to torture of every description, before being killed, and then crucified opposite the walls [of Jerusalem]. Titus indeed commiserated their fate, five hundred or sometimes more being captured daily; on the other hand, he recognized the risk of dismissing prisoners of war, and that the custody of such numbers would amount to the imprisonment of their custodians; but his main reason for not stopping the crucifixions was the hope that the spectacle might perhaps induce the Jews to surrender, for fear that continued resistance would involve them in a similar fate. The soldiers out of rage and hatred amused themselves by nailing their prisoners in different postures; and so great was their number, that space could not be found for the crosses nor crosses for the bodies."

Josephus, *J.W.* 5.449–51; LCL 3:341.

innocent. Instead, he questions the crowd three times (vv. 9, 12, 14). The repetitions build the drama, suspense, and significance of the moment.

The common term for "bad," or "evil" (*kakos*), must carry a legal nuance here: What crime or illegal act has he committed? What legal justification might there be for crucifying him? The crowd does not answer the question. Instead, they cry out all the more vehemently. Mark's account of the trial makes it clear, therefore, that Pilate did not initiate the execution of Jesus. At most, he acquiesced to the demands of the chief priests and the crowd. Although Jesus was crucified by Roman authority on the apparently political charge of claiming to be "King of the Jews," in reality he was a non-political Messiah, the chief priests acted out of jealousy and zeal, and it was the chief priests and the people who were primarily responsible for this miscarriage of justice. Pilate merely acted out of the political expediency that characterized most of the Roman officials of that era.

Pilate's verdict is swift, and Mark reports it with a brevity that underscores its finality. In place of specifying the crime for which Jesus was found guilty, Mark reports the basis for Pilate's judgment: he wished to satisfy the crowd. The idiom here is a Latinism, an unusual Greek construction (*to hikanon poiēsai*) that approximates the Latin *satisfacere*.[11] The term for flogging in the latter half of the verse is also a Latinism, *phragelloun*, which suggests to Brown that Mark is deliberately imitating the Latin style "to supply atmosphere for the Roman governor's legal decision."[12] Scholars have speculated that Jesus was delivered to Pilate and then condemned for violating the *lex Iulia de maiestate*, a revision of an earlier law under Augustus that prescribed exile or execution for anyone who claimed to be a king or in other ways slandered the emperor.[13] In the provinces, however, the particular dictates of the law were often secondary to the governor's desire to maintain order. By his silence on the matter while attributing the verdict to Pilate's desire to satisfy the crowd, Mark conveys that there was no legal basis for the verdict; it was a matter of sheer political expediency. Pilate satisfied the crowd on both counts: he released Barabbas and condemned Jesus.

By reporting that Pilate "handed over" Jesus to be crucified, Mark places him in the line of those responsible for Jesus' death: Judas handed Jesus over to the chief priests (3:19; 14:10-11, 18, 21, 41, 42, 44), who handed Jesus over to Pilate (15:1, 10), who handed Jesus over to be crucified (15:15). The verb echoes Isaiah 53:6, 12 (LXX), so the repetition serves also to underscore the fulfillment of Scripture through this chain of events.

The flogging of Jesus is reported in no more than one verse in any of the Gospels, though they differ regarding whether Jesus was flogged in mid-trial (John 19:1) or at the end as part of the death sentence (Mark

15:15; Matt 27:26). Luke does not report the flogging at all. The Gospels use various terms for flogging or whipping (*paideuein, phragelloun, mastigoun*). The latter is used in the third passion prediction (10:34), but Mark uses *phragelloun* to report the flogging in 15:16. Some Roman sources distinguish levels of severity for various sentences, but even they are not consistent in their terminology.[14] Freedmen and military personnel were beaten with rods or sticks, but others were scourged with leather whips tipped with spikes. The victim was stripped, tied to a post, and sometimes beaten until his bones or entrails were exposed and his flesh hung in strips.

[Flogging] Floggings could be administered either as the prescribed sentence or as preparation for crucifixion.

The Soldiers Mock Jesus, 15:16-20

Following the trial before Pilate there is a scene of mockery, just as there was following the Jewish trial (in 14:65). The trial before the Sanhedrin focused on Jesus' claim to be the Messiah, and in the earlier mockery some of those who were present challenged Jesus to prophesy. The Roman trial concerned the claim that Jesus was the King of the Jews, and this time the soldiers make sport of Jesus, hailing him as a king.

Details of the setting are sparse in Mark. Pilate has addressed the crowd, presumably outside the praetorium. Now Jesus is taken into the courtyard of the praetorium, which was probably Herod's palace (see the commentary on 15:1). If Pilate was concerned not to provoke the Jewish crowd, it is possible that the beating of Jesus took place in the courtyard, away from the crowd, with only the Roman soldiers present. Like the terms noted in v. 15, "praetorium" is a Latinism, a Latin loanword. Earlier, Mark reported that "the whole council" was looking for testimony against Jesus and then bound Jesus over to Pilate (14:55; 15:1); now he reports that they called together "the whole cohort [of soldiers]" to mock Jesus (15:16). A "cohort" (*speira*) was technically 600 soldiers and their equipment, a tenth of a Roman legion, but the term could be used loosely to refer to a somewhat smaller force. The term also appears in John 18:3, 12, where according to John the Roman soldiers were present at the arrest of Jesus.

Flogging

Josephus provides these accounts of the flogging of Jews by the Romans. "Many of the peaceable citizens were arrested and brought before Florus, who had them first scourged and then crucified. The total number of that day's victims, including women and children, for even infancy received no quarter, amounted to about three thousand six hundred. The calamity was aggravated by the unprecedented character of the Romans' cruelty. For Florus ventured that day to do what none had ever done before, namely, to scourge before his tribunal and nail to the cross men of equestrian rank, men who, if Jews by birth, were at least invested with that Roman dignity." (Josephus, *J.W.* 2.306–308; LCL 2:443).

"Thereupon, the magistrates, supposing, as was indeed the case, that the man was under some supernatural impulse, brought him before the Roman governor; there, although flayed to the bone with scourges, he neither sued for mercy nor shed a tear, but, merely introducing the most mournful of variations into his ejaculation, responded to each stroke with 'Woe to Jerusalem!'" (Josephus, *J.W.* 6.304; LCL 3:465).

The Mockery of Karabas

When Agrippa I visited Alexandria in AD 38, an anti-Jewish mob seized Karabas, who was mentally challenged and mocked the Jewish king by making sport of him:

"[The people] drove the poor fellow into the gymnasium and set him up on high to be seen of all and put on his head a sheet of byblus [papyrus] spread out wide for a diadem, clothed the rest of his body with a rug for a royal robe, while someone who had noticed a piece of the native papyrus thrown away in the road gave it to him for his sceptre. And when as in some theatrical farce he had received the insignia of kingship and had been tricked out as a king, young men carrying rods on their shoulders as spearmen stood on either side of him in imitation of a body guard. Then others approached him, some pretending to salute him, others to sue for justice, others to consult him on state affairs. Then from the multitudes standing round him there rang out a tremendous shout hailing him as *Marin* ["My lord"], which is said to be the name for 'lord' in Syria."

Philo, *Flaccus* 6.36–39; LCL 9:323

Various events have been adduced as parallels for the soldiers' mockery of Jesus, especially the mockery of Karabas [The Mockery of Karabas] and the mockery of Herod Agrippa I at his death (AD 44). These parallels show that the mockery of Jesus would have been entirely credible. Tourists and pilgrims to Jerusalem are often told that the inscription of a circle with a "B" (for *basileus*, "king") on the stones of the paved area in the Fortress of Antonia was the place where the soldiers mocked Jesus. Striking as the discovery of this site seems, it is now thought to have been part of a forum constructed in the second century.[15]

First, the soldiers clothed Jesus in a purple cloak, perhaps a faded soldier's cloak (see Matt 27:28) or an old rug. Purple signified royalty, and custom dictated how much purple persons of rank were entitled to wear (1 Macc 10:20, 62; 11:58; 14:43; Josephus, *Ant.* 11.256; 17.197). The crown of thorns was not part of the torture but part of the costume for the mockery. Crowns of the Macedonian and Hellenistic kings were made of delicate, gold leaves. Matthew 27:29 adds that they put a reed in Jesus' hand as a scepter. Having dressed the bloody prisoner as a king, the soldiers began to hail him, imitating the Latin imperial greeting, *Ave, Caesar, victor, imperator*, "Hail, Caesar, victor, emperor."[16] The title "King of the Jews" echoes the treasonous charge brought against Jesus (15:2, 9, 12). For Mark the irony is significant. Everything that is said to or about Jesus in mockery in the Passion Narrative is ironically true.

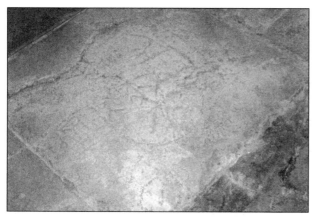

The Game of the King
(Credit: R. Alan Culpepper)

In the second part of the scene the insult and mockery becomes more violent. They strike him about the head with a reed, spit on him, kneel before him, and "worship" (cf. 5:6) him. The spitting, mentioned also in the Jewish mockery (14:65), fulfills the third passion prediction (10:34). The soldiers genuflect before Jesus in a cruel burlesque, but Paul, in what may have been an early Christian confession, looked forward to the time when "every knee should bow, in heaven and on earth and under the earth, and every tongue should confess that Jesus Christ is Lord, to the glory of God the Father" (Phil 2:10-11).

Mark characterizes the scene as "mocking him," a verb (*empaizein*) that literally means to trick, deceive, or "play like a child" (*pais*).[17] Before taking Jesus out to crucify him, the soldiers strip Jesus of the purple robe and put his own clothes on

Macedonian Crown

The gold wreath of myrtle leaves and flowers from the antechamber of the tomb of Philip II in Vergina, Greece. Thessalonike Archaeological Museum.

Gold Wreath, from Vergina. Late 4th BCE. Inside diameter: 18.5 cm. Archaeological Museum, Thessaloniki, Greece. (Credit: Art Resource, NY)

him. Nothing is said about the crown of thorns. Raymond Brown notes that various ancient accounts of crucifixions report that the criminal was forced to walk naked, carrying the crossbeam to the place of crucifixion, and suggests that allowing Jesus to wear his clothes along the way to Golgotha and removing his clothes only when they crucified him (15:24; cf. Josephus, *Ant.* 19.269-70) may have been a concession to the Jewish sensitivity regarding public nudity.[18] With the mockery concluded, the soldiers turned to the grim business at hand.

The Crucifixion of Jesus, 15:21-27

The crucifixion of Jesus is described in a series of third person plural historical present tense verbs (e.g., "Then they lead him out") that lend immediacy to the account. No dialogue is reported in this section. One watches in silence while the soldiers carry out their task without uttering a word.

Mark's account of the crucifixion is dramatically brief. Without explaining why it was necessary, Mark reports that "they" (the Roman soldiers) compelled Simon of Cyrene to carry Jesus' cross. The verb is a Persian loanword that means to "force" or "press into service" (cf. Matt 5:41).[19] Normally the condemned man carried the crossbeam of his own cross to the place of execution. Plutarch reports that "every wrongdoer who goes to execution carries out his own cross" (*Moralia* 554A-B; LCL 7:215). Presumably Jesus was so weakened by the flogging he had received that he could not carry the cross piece. In this sparse account, Simon of Cyrene is introduced in a curious manner. The tag "of

Cyrene" (cf. Acts 6:9; 11:20; 13:1) identifies him as an African from the area of Cyrenaica (now Libya) and distinguishes him from others who had the common Hellenistic name, "Simon." Ptolemy Soter I (300 BC) had settled Jews in Cyrenaic. Interpreters have speculated that Simon was a Jew who had come to Jerusalem for the Passover, but then the detail "coming in from a farm" (CEV) is better translated "who was coming in from the country" (NRSV). In the scene Simon is a random passerby, but he was apparently later known to Mark and to his audience as "the father of Alexander and Rufus." Like "Simon" these are Hellenistic or Roman names. The name Rufus appears in Romans 16:13, where the one being greeted is called "chosen in the Lord," and there is a reference to his mother but not his father. It has been suggested that this might be the same Rufus, a member of a Roman house church and the son of Simon of Cyrene, and hence known to Mark's church in Roman, but the absence of any reference to Rufus's father in this greeting, when it might have been expected if he were not just "chosen in the Lord" but "the son of Simon who bore the Lord's cross," makes this suggestion at least inconclusive if not improbable. William Lane notes that a burial cave from the first part of the first century belonging to a family of Cyrenian Jews was discovered in 1941 in the Kidron Valley. An ossuary recovered from the cave is inscribed in Greek, "Alexander, son of Simon," raising the possibility that this was the ossuary of the son of Simon of Cyrene, but again the combination of common names may simply be coincidence.[20] Within Mark there is a significant echo between Simon's "carrying his cross" in 15:21 and Jesus' earlier command that if anyone would be his disciple that one must "carry his cross" (8:34). Because the disciples have betrayed, abandoned, and denied Jesus, Simon of Cyrene stands in as their surrogate.

The place of crucifixion is called Golgotha, an Aramaic name that is translated "the place of the/a skull," and the traditional interpretation has been that it was a hill outside of Jerusalem that bore some resemblance to a skull. Other explanations are possible, however. According to Jewish legend, Adam's skull was buried there, and others have speculated that skulls lay on the ground at the place used for executions.[21] Stonings and crucifixions were always done outside the city (Lev 24:14; Num 15:35-36; 1 Kgs 21:13; John 19:20; Acts 7:58). From at least the fourth century the traditional site has been near the Church of the Holy Sepulchre. [The Church of the Holy Sepulchre] Most tourists prefer the site of the "Garden Tomb" or "Gordon's Calvary," but as attractive as it is this site has no historical support. Gordon, a British general, proposed this site in the late nineteenth century, but the tomb there probably dates from the second century.

The significance of the wine mingled with myrrh is debated. [Myrrh] Matthew 27:34 says it was "wine mingled with gall," and that Jesus

The Church of the Holy Sepulchre

The Church of the Holy Sepulchre marks the traditional site of Golgotha and the tomb of Jesus. Excavations have confirmed that it was located 100 to 150 yards outside the second north wall of the city (built by Herod the Great). The site was a hill that dropped off to a quarry on its east side. In the time of Jesus the area was used for burials and gardens. The tomb of Jesus was a cave cut in the quarry wall with a rock-cut bench that would accommodate a single body. In AD 135 Emperor Hadrian filled the quarry and built a platform over it on which was constructed a temple to Aphrodite. According to Jerome, Golgotha still protruded above the platform. In 325 Constantine demolished the pagan temple and excavated the cave tomb. The builders cut away the antechamber and most of the surrounding stone, turning it into a shrine, which became the rotunda of the "Anastasis" (Resurrection). The other 4th-century structure, the "Martyrium," was a large five-aisled basilica that was dedicated in September 335. Various pilgrims have left descriptions of the site. These buildings were burned but not totally destroyed by the Persians in 614. In 1009, however, the Fatimid Caliph of Cairo, Kakim, ordered that the church be destroyed, and the tomb itself was virtually leveled. A replica of the tomb was rebuilt forty years later, and the Anastasis rotunda was partially restored. Between 1099 and 1149 the crusaders built an elaborate church over both the Martyrium and the Anastasis. Golgotha was squared off and capped by a marble casing. Earthquakes and restorations continued to alter the Church of the Holy Sepulchre, but the restorations between 1960 and 1980 have revealed the history of the site. Although many tourists prefer the natural beauty of "Gordon's Calvary" and the "Garden Tomb" outside the third north wall (erected in AD 41–44), the historical record suggests that beneath the marble covering of the buildings erected over the centuries known as the Church of the Holy Sepulchre lies the site where Joseph of Arimathea laid to rest the body of Jesus.

Raymond E. Brown, *The Death of the Messiah* (New York: Doubleday, 1994), 2:1279–83; Oliver Nicholson, "Holy Sepulchre, Church of the," *ABD* 3:258–60.

tasted it but would not drink it. Luke 23:36 says the soldiers mocked him and offered him sour wine or vinegar. John only reports that just before Jesus died the soldiers offered him sour wine (cf. Mark 15:36). These later accounts may be allusions to Psalm 69:21, "and for my thirst they gave me vinegar to drink." Did Jewish women offer Jesus wine mingled with myrrh as a humane effort to dull the pain, perhaps following the instruction of Proverbs 31:6, "Give strong drink to one who is perishing, and wine to those in bitter distress"? Mark does not indicate any change in the subject of the verbs, so the presumption must be that the soldiers offered Jesus the mingled drink. The practice of offering the condemned a narcotic drink is attested in Jewish sources (*b. Sanhedrin* 43a), and a first-century army doctor, Dioscorides Pedanius, experimented with 600 plants and 1,000 drugs and found that myrrh had a narcotic effect.[22] On the other hand, Pliny observed that "The finest wines in early days were those spiced with scent of myrrh" (*Natural History* 14.92; 14.107; LCL 4:249). Brown suggested that the dulling effect was from the wine rather than from the myrrh,[23] and Evans abandons the interpretation that the offering of the wine was an act of mercy: it had no narcotic effect; there is no reference to Jewish women at this point, and the soldiers were not acting compassionately. Instead, Evans proposes that the offer of fine wine was a further act of mockery.[24] If that is the case, Jesus' refusal to drink the wine has nothing to do with refusing to diminish his suffering. Rather, it is his refusal to participate in their charade. Earlier, Jesus had referred to drinking the cup (of suffering) in 10:38-39 and vowed that he would

Myrrh

Myrrh was the fragrant gum or resin of various shrubs and trees. It is mentioned as an item of trade in some of our earliest sources, the Ras Shamra documents, Genesis (37:25; 43:11), and the Egyptians apparently used it in embalming (Herodotus 2.86). It was available in liquid (Exod 30:23; Song 5:5, 13; Esth 2:12) as well as solid forms, and was used for sacred anointing oil, perfumes, and as a burial spice (John 19:39).

J. C. Trever, "Myrrh," *IDB* 3:478–79.

not drink again of the fruit of the vine until he drank it new in the kingdom (14:25). Regardless of who offered him the wine mingled with myrrh or their intent, Jesus' refusal of the wine fulfills his vow in 14:25.

The discovery of the remains of a crucified man at Giv'at ha-Mivtar near Jerusalem in 1968 with the leg bones still nailed at the heels to a piece of wood provided new evidence regarding the details of crucifixion.[25] John 20:25 refers to the mark of the nails in Jesus' hands (cf. Ignatius *Smyrnaeans* 1.2, "truly nailed to a tree"), although when nails were used (cf. *m. Shabbath* 6.10) they were probably driven above the wrist to support the weight more effectively. The reference is sometimes seen as an echo of Psalm 22:16, but the meaning of the Hebrew text is uncertain.

The soldiers normally stripped the victim before nailing him to the cross, and since they divided Jesus' garments among themselves we may assume they stripped Jesus also. Whether they left a loin cloth out of deference to Jewish sensitivities (*Jub.* 3:31; 7:20; *m. Sanh.* 6.3), we do not know. The description of casting lots for the garments echoes Psalm 22:18 (cf. John 19:24), the first of a series of allusions to Psalms in Mark's account of Jesus' death. [Psalms in Mark's Account of Jesus' Death] "Casting lots" may have involved stones or some other game of chance.

Verse 25 is problematic because it repeats the report that they crucified Jesus (cf. v. 24), the time of the crucifixion is given here rather than in the first report as one might have expected, and the time, "the third hour" (9:00 a.m., using the Jewish system of counting from daybreak), cannot be harmonized with

Rembrandt's *Raising of the Cross*

Rembrandt Harmensz van Rijn (1606–1669). *Raising of the Cross*. 1634. Alte Pinakothek, Munich, Germany. (Credit: Foto Marburg / Art Resource, NY)

John's report that they crucified Jesus at "about the sixth
hour" (John 19:14), regardless
of whether John uses the
Jewish or the Roman system
for reckoning the hours.[26] A
strong case can be made for
preferring John's account that
the crucifixion occurred on
the day of preparation for the
Passover rather than Mark's
chronology, which places the

Psalms in Mark's Account of Jesus' Death		
Mark	**Topic**	**Psalms**
15:24	division of garments	22:18
15:29	mockery, head shaking	22:7
15:30-31	Save yourself!	22:8
15:32	reviling	22:6
15:34	cry of dereliction	22:1
15:36	gave him vinegar to drink	69:21
15:40	looking on at a distance	38:11

Joel Marcus, *The Way of the Lord: Christological Exegesis of the Old Testament in the Gospel of Mark* (Louisville: Westminster John Knox, 1992), 175.

arrest, trial, and crucifixion following the Passover meal (see [Chronology of the Last Supper and the Crucifixion of Jesus]). On the other hand, if Jesus appeared before Pilate early, "as soon as it was morning" (NRSV; Mark 15:1; John 18:28), Mark's "the third hour" is reasonable, and John's report of an early afternoon crucifixion may reflect his interest in having Jesus' death coincide with the time of the slaughter of the Passover lambs. The reference to the third hour in 15:25 sets up Mark's chronology of the crucifixion at the third hour, darkness at the sixth hour, and Jesus' death at the ninth hour. Nevertheless, none of the other Gospels (Matthew, Luke, or the apocryphal *Gospel of Peter*) picks up Mark's reference to the third hour.

A designation of the condemned man's crime was inscribed on a slab of wood and nailed to the cross. Matthew 27:37 reports that it was placed above Jesus' head, providing evidence that Jesus was crucified upright on a cross that had an extension above the crossbeam—the traditional image of the cross. See [Crucifixion] for reports of crucifixions involving different kinds of crosses; see also *Epistle of Barnabas* 9:8; Justin, *Dialogue* 91.2. The charge "King of the Jews" is a Roman title that echoes the title given to Herod the Great (Josephus, *Ant.* 15.409; *J.W.* 1.282).[27] Josephus reports that Varus, the Roman governor of Syria, crucified self-appointed kings and their followers following the death of Herod (Josephus, *Ant.* 17.285, 295). The title also echoes Roman derision and scorn for their provincial subjects, but the wording of the titulus varies in each Gospel:

Matt 27:37   "This is Jesus, the King of the Jews"
Mark 15:26   "The King of the Jews"
Luke 23:38   "This is the King of the Jews"
John 19:19   "Jesus of Nazareth, the King of the Jews"
(in Hebrew, Latin, and Greek, and lit., "Jesus the Nazorean")

Eusebius reports that when a Christian was martyred, "he was led around the amphitheatre and a placard was carried before him on which was written in Latin, "This is Attalus, the Christian" (*E.H.* 5.1.44).[28]

With Jesus they crucified two others whom Mark calls *lēstai* (cf. 11:17; 14:48), which probably means they were rebels or insurrectionists. Nothing is said about whether they had been condemned that morning or earlier, but given the little information we have it is possible that they were connected with the insurrection referred to in 15:7. The report that they were crucified on Jesus' right and left establishes the traditional picture of three crosses and Jesus on the middle one. The reference to the two criminals was later seen as a fulfillment of Isaiah 53:12, that Jesus was "numbered with the transgressors," and this connection is made explicit in the gloss added in v. 28. Just as the charge against Jesus introduced in v. 26 returns in the mockery in verse 32a, so the other two crucified with Jesus join mocking him in v. 32b.[29] The reference to Jesus' right and left also subtly echoes James and John's earlier request for the places of honor in Jesus' kingdom (10:37, 40) even though a different word for "left" is used here.[30] Ironically, those who are on Jesus' right and left when he is presented as "the King of the Jews" will indeed "drink the cup" that he drinks (see the commentary on 10:35-40).

Verse 28, which is placed in a marginal reference in most modern translations, is a later gloss based on Isaiah 53:12 and Luke 22:37. Metzger notes that this verse entered the text only in later manuscripts and that Mark seldom quotes the Old Testament.[31]

The Bystanders Mock Jesus, 15:29-32

Mark's report of the mocking that followed the crucifixion continues the mocking in vv. 16-20. In vv. 29-32 there are three groups of mockers, the passersby (v. 29), the chief priests (v. 31), and those crucified with Jesus (v. 32). Different words are used to characterize each group: the passersby "blasphemed" (*eblasphēmoun*), the chief priests "mocked" (*empaizontes*), and the criminals taunted (*ōneidizon*). The mockery ironically gathers up many of the Markan themes of Jesus' ministry, his identity, and the Jewish and Roman trials that precede the crucifixion. The unifying motif of the three mockings is the challenge that Jesus come down from the cross, which for Mark is profoundly related to the opposing reality that Jesus is only clearly revealed on the cross.

Mark probably meant for us to understand the "passersby" as Jews who happened upon these events rather than as individuals who were present at the Jewish trial where the false charge that Jesus would destroy the temple was introduced (14:58). Moreover, the chief priests will be introduced in v. 31 as a separate group. The detail that they were "shaking their heads" is an echo of Psalm 22:7, "All who see me mock me; they make mouths at me, they shake their heads" (cf. Ps 109:25; Lam 2:15). The reference to "shaking their heads" in Psalm 22 is followed in the next verse by the taunt that the sufferer should commit his cause to the Lord and let the Lord deliver him (Ps 22:8), so it is likely that Psalm 22 has influenced Mark's account of the mockery of Jesus on the cross.[32]

Mark's anti-temple theme occurs twice in this Gospel's succinct account of Jesus' death. The charge that Jesus would destroy the temple and build another in three days is recalled in mockery by the bystanders (15:29), and when Jesus dies the veil in the temple is rent in two from top to bottom (15:38). The bystanders' taunt in Mark 15:29 lacks the description "not made with hands" that is part of the false witnesses' testimony in 14:58, but the repetition of the charge that Jesus would destroy the temple and build another in three days reminds the reader of the earlier version of the charge (see the commentary on 14:58 and see ["After Three Days"]).[33] Jesus' death is therefore the central event in the building of the new temple, the new locus of God's redemptive activity, the community of those who confess Jesus and take up the cross to follow him.

An early Jewish proverb says, "Before a man puts his trust in flesh and blood (i.e., another man) and asks him to save him, let him (i.e., the other) save himself from death first."[34] To this bit of wisdom one may juxtapose Jesus' challenge to his disciples, "For those who want to save their life will lose it, and those who lose their life for my sake, and for the sake of the gospel will save it" (8:35). Jesus challenges his followers to take up the cross; his opponents challenge him to come down from the cross. One maxim defines the cautious wisdom of the experience, the other the radical reorientation of kingdom of God (see the commentary on 8:35). The first challenge for Jesus to save himself comes from the passersby (v. 30). The second comes from the chief priests and scribes, who played a prominent role in both the Jewish and the Roman trials (14:53-66 and 15:1-11; see [Chief Priests] [Scribes]). It is their final appearance in the Gospel. They extend the challenge by noting the irony that Jesus had saved others but he could not save himself. There is a second level to this irony, however, because the reader knows that by not saving himself Jesus was actually in the act of saving countless others. Jesus is never called "the Savior" in Mark (cf. Luke 2:11; John 4:42), but throughout the Gospel Jesus serves and saves (10:45).[35] The characterization of Jesus as one who saves begins in

Mark 3:4 with the question, "Is it lawful to do good or to do harm on the Sabbath, to save life or to kill?" When the term appears in healing stories, it means to "make well" and hence save from death, but may also carry the suggestion of the theological sense of salvation. Jairus pleads, "My little daughter is at the point of death. Come and lay your hands on her, so that she may be made well (i.e., "saved") and live" (5:23). The woman with the hemorrhage reasons, "If I but touch his clothes, I will be made well" (i.e., "saved"; 5:28), and Jesus later assures her, "Daughter, your faith has made you well" (i.e., "saved you"; 5:34; cf. 10:52). All who touched the fringe of his cloak were healed (i.e., "saved"; 6:56). The term is also used for being saved from persecution and the eschatological travails (13:13, 20) and for the more metaphorical or theological sense of saving one's life (8:35; 10:26).

The chief priests and scribes scornfully refer to Jesus as "the Christ, the king of Israel" (15:32). The title "the Christ" was introduced in the first verse of the Gospel (1:1) and in Peter's confession at Caesarea Philippi (8:29). At the high point of the Jewish trial the high priest asks Jesus, "Are you the Christ?" (14:61). The matter of Jesus' kingship becomes central in the Roman trial (15:2, 9, 12, 18), but this is the only reference to Jesus as "the King of Israel" (cf. Matt 27:42; John 1:49; 12:13), and the term "Israel" appears only one other time in Mark, in the great commandment (12:29). Nevertheless, the title picks up the title inscribed above Jesus on the cross (15:26), while subtly changing it, on the lips of the chief priests, from the idiom of the Romans to a reference to the Jews as the people of God.

The third time the challenge is issued for Jesus to save himself, it is supplemented with the mocking use of the language of discipleship, "so that we may see and believe" (15:32). Throughout the Gospel, Mark uses sight and blindness as metaphors for discipleship to Jesus and opposition to God. Isaiah's prophecy has been fulfilled; Jesus' opponents "may indeed look, but not perceive" (4:12; Isa 6:9-10; cf. Mark 8:17-18). The healing of the blind man in 8:22-26 is a metaphor for the disciples' failure to see clearly who Jesus was, and the corresponding story of the healing of Bartimaeus at the end of that section of the Gospel (10:46-52) portrays Jesus' power to give sight. The chief priests in effect demand a sign (8:11-12),[36] but in reality the cross was the sign for that generation and for all generations.

The scene of mocking ends with a reference to the two crucified with Jesus (15:32b; cf. 15:27). Their mocking completes the sequence of three: first the passersby, then the chief priests and scribes, and now those crucified with Jesus. In contrast to Luke's account, Mark says nothing of the "penitent thief" taking up for Jesus (Luke 23:39-43). Jesus is totally alone, setting the stage for the "cry of abandonment" in v. 34.

The Death of Jesus, 15:33-38

It was not easy to preach a crucified savior to people who had witnessed crucifixions.[37] Death on a cross was an ignominy usually reserved for slaves and traitors.[38] For Jews, crucifixion defiled the land and was evidence of God's curse on the crucified (Deut 21:23); for Gentiles, the idea that a divine man or an immortal could be crucified was foolishness (1 Cor 1:19); and for Mark and his church, proclamation of the crucified Messiah would have been exceedingly difficult during or just after the war of AD 66–70, especially if they were in Rome. If we are to interpret the Second Gospel faithfully, therefore, we will need to answer the question: What did the death and resurrection of Jesus mean to Mark?

The Crucifixion of Christ

Mathais Gruenewald (1455–1528). Detail of Christ's head from the *Crucifixion*, Isenheim Altarpiece. Musee d'Unterlinden, Colmar, France. (Credit: Bridgeman-Giraudon / Art Resource, NY)

Close examination of the Gospel of Mark shows that the shadow of the cross falls across the entire Gospel so that every pericope points ahead to the cross and must be understood in its light.[39] Conversely, the Passion Narrative can and must be understood in the light of the themes developed in the rest of the Gospel that reach their climax in it. The approach followed below is to examine each of the interpretive devices Mark used in narrating the death and resurrection of Jesus: (1) the structure of Mark's account of these events, (2) the phenomena that accompany Jesus' death, (3) the themes that reach a climax or resolution in this section, and (4) Mark's use of the Old Testament in these verses.

Mark is fond of groups of three. He gives three passion predictions (8:31; 9:31; 10:32-34), measures Jesus' time on the cross with references to the third hour (15:25), the sixth hour (15:33), and the ninth hour (15:34); and presents three groups of mockers in 15:29-32: the passersby, the chief priests and scribes, and the two crucified with Jesus. The structure of three events and three responses is further supported by the use of "mock" (*empaizō*) in 15:20 and 15:31 to describe the action of those scenes. The only other occurrence of this word in Mark is in the passion prediction in Mark 10:32-34. The centurion's confession in the third act provides a dramatic contrast to the two scenes of mocking that precede it. The structure of the passion in

Mark, therefore, points emphatically to the third and final act, i.e., the phenomena that accompany and interpret Jesus' death: the darkness (15:33), the cry of dereliction (15:34-37), the rending of the veil (15:38), and the centurion's confession (15:39). These events hold the key to Mark's understanding of the death of Jesus.

The use of accompanying phenomena to interpret the crucifixion is confirmed by the increasing use of this device in the later canonical and apocryphal Gospels (e.g., *Gospel of Peter* 15-27; *Gospel of the Nazareans*, frags. 21 and 36; cf. Matt 27:51b-53).[40] In Mark, however, the four phenomena do not simply heighten the miraculous nature of the event, as they do in the apocryphal Gospels; they interpret its meaning.

Mark states that from the sixth hour (noon) until the ninth (3:00 p.m.) darkness came upon the whole earth. Some interpreters speculate that the darkness was caused by a black sirocco, or dust storm. Others maintain that the parallel in Luke 23:45 implies that the darkness was the result of an eclipse. The cause of the darkness is irrelevant for understanding Mark, however. The better question is What significance did the darkness have for Mark? The Gospel gives us few clues. The word *skotos* does not appear anywhere else in Mark, and the verb form appears only in the quotation in Mark 13:24. In the Old Testament the darkening of the sun was a sign of judgment. As such, it could express God's displeasure toward other peoples (Exod 10:15, 21-23; Ezek 30:18-19; 32:7-8). God's judgment upon Israel in the day of the Lord would also be expressed by darkness upon the land (*ge = eretz*) (Amos 5:18, 20; Joel 2:2, 10, 31; 3:15; Jer 15:6, 9; Isa 13:9-10; 50:2-3; Lam 3:1-2; Zeph 1:15; cf. Wis 17:20-18:4). In the Wisdom of Solomon, the mockers confess, "So it was we who strayed from the way of truth, and the light of righteousness did not shine on us, and the sun did not rise upon us" (5:6).[41] In particular, darkness will come upon the false prophets and rulers of Israel (Mic 3:6). The closest parallel to Mark 15:33 is Amos 8:9:

"On that day," says the Lord GOD,
"I will make the sun go down at noon,
and darken the earth in broad daylight."

The darkness in Mark, therefore, is probably a cosmic, eschatological

Darkness over the Land

sign of God's judgment upon Israel and perhaps on her rulers in particular.[42]

Gentile readers would also understand the darkness as a cosmic sign that often accompanied the death of great men and kings:

> . . . the Sun will give you signs. Who dare say the Sun is false? Nay, he oft warns us that dark uprisings threaten, that treachery and hidden wars are upswelling. Nay, he had pity for Rome when, after Caesar sank from sight, he veiled his shining face in dusky gloom, and a godless age feared everlasting night. (Virgil, *Georgics* 1.463f.)

Similarly, Philo wrote that ". . . eclipses announce the death of kings and the destruction of cities" (*De Providentia* 2.50; cf. Plutarch *Pelopidas* 31.2-3; Diogenes Laertius 4.64). The following interpretations all have some merit: a sign of God's judgment upon Israel (especially its leaders), an indication that the death of Jesus was linked with the day of the Lord and the coming of the Son of Man (cf. Mark 13:24), evidence of the cosmic significance of Jesus' death (especially if "all the earth" is taken to mean more than the land of Israel[43]), and divine confirmation of Jesus' kingship (cf. the references from Virgil and Philo quoted above and Mark 15:2, 9, 12, 18, 26, 32). From all these associations the reader understands that God was at work in the event and that God's purposes would not be thwarted: the sun would shine again on Easter morning (Mark 16:1). Brown notes the irony that by challenging Jesus to come down from the cross the mockers were demanding a sign, but God gave them a sign of the coming judgment on the world.[44]

The cry of abandonment, certainly the most enigmatic word from the cross in all the Gospels, is the only thing Jesus says from the cross in Mark, and it is the last thing he says in this Gospel. It is a quotation of Psalm 22:1 and hence the last of a series of quotations or allusions to this psalm in Mark's Passion Narrative (cf. 14:17; 15:24, 29, 30-31). Discussion of this saying has generally revolved around its authenticity, the wording of Jesus' cry, whether it evokes the rest of Psalm 22, and its theological significance. The verb "to cry" (*boaō*) appears only once earlier in Mark, in the quotation from Isaiah 40:3 in Mark 1:3 that characterizes John the Baptist as "a voice crying in the wilderness." As a result, the Gospel begins with John "crying out" and reaches its climax with Jesus "crying out."

The quotation has been understood both as a "cry of dereliction"[45] and as a prayer that even in the darkness of rejection and suffering began "My God. . ." and evoked the triumphal ending of Psalm 22 as well as its beginning.[46] Interpreters have often attempted to soften the scandal of Jesus' last cry by pointing to the triumphal later verses of

Psalm 22. Jesus may have recited Psalm 22:1 as the "title," which should evoke the remainder of the Psalm,[47] but the reaction of the bystanders (15:35-36) militates against the possibility that Mark wished his readers to understand that Jesus recited the entire psalm in his last moments.[48] As Brown contends, it is better to allow this difficult saying to retain its literal meaning:

> . . . the issue is whether the struggle with evil will lead to victory; and Jesus is portrayed as profoundly discouraged at the end of his long battle because God, to whose will Jesus committed himself at the beginning of the passion (Mark 14:36; Matt 26:39, 42), has not intervened in the struggle and seemingly has left Jesus unsupported.[49]

The interpretation of Jesus' death, which is more evident in Paul (e.g., 2 Cor 5:21) than in Mark, that Jesus in some undefined way became sin or absorbed the sin of the world into himself and therefore had to be abandoned by God, has been popular in evangelical preaching.[50] Mark, however, gives little support for such an interpretation of the death of Jesus. Mark 10:45, which has been used to support a theology of substitutionary atonement, provides no evidence that Jesus thought he would assume the sin of the world; the saying deals with the importance of service and affirms the redemptive power of self-denial.[51] This understanding of Mark 10:45 is given strong support by its position at the end of the section beginning with 8:31, since this section of the Gospel emphasizes the necessity of Jesus' suffering and offers it as a model for the status-seeking disciples.[52] Sin, in fact, is mentioned in only two passages in Mark (1:4-5; 2:5-10). Neither passage is directly related to the death of Jesus, and neither supports the contention that Jesus' death was the necessary prerequisite for the forgiveness of sins. On the contrary, Mark affirms that the forgiveness of sins through the grace of God was proclaimed by John (1:4-5) and mediated by Jesus prior to his death (2:5-10).

In keeping with our pursuit of the meaning of Jesus' death for Mark, our interpretation of Mark 15:34 must be based on two Markan themes that culminate in it: (1) the abandonment of Jesus, the righteous sufferer, and (2) the assurance of God's presence with the persecuted community.

In Mark, Jesus is gradually abandoned by all his supporters. The religious and political leaders, who never supported him, plot his death early on (3:6). His family apparently does not understand his ministry (3:31-35). His hometown rejects him (6:1-6), and even his disciples do not understand him (4:40; 6:52; 8:17, 21, 29-33; 9:32). They seek glory while he is on his way to suffering (9:33-37; 10:28, 35-45), and they fail him when he needs them (14:32-42). Ultimately, Judas betrays him (14:43ff.), the disciples all flee (14:50), and even Peter denies him (14:66-72). The crowd comes after him with swords and clubs (14:43), and Pilate, desiring to please the crowd, hands Jesus over to be crucified (15:15). The soldiers mock him (15:16-20), the spectators blaspheme him (15:29-30), and the two thieves revile him (15:32b). Even the women who stood by the cross and watched the burial fail to carry out the angelic commission in the end (16:8). Jesus' abandonment by his Father, therefore, fits the pattern of progressive betrayal and abandonment that pervades the Gospel of Mark. This abandonment heightens Mark's emphasis on the significance of suffering, but the abandonment by God proves not to be the last word.

Mark is especially interested in affirming that the struggling church should expect to suffer and should accept suffering as an opportunity for expressing its commitment to Christ and his kingdom. John the Baptist suffered and died (1:14; 6:14-29); Jesus suffered and died (cf. 8:31; 9:31; 10:32-34; 12:6-8): the disciples should therefore expect to suffer as well (4:17; 8:34-38; 10:29-30; 13:9, 11-13). They should not interpret their suffering as abandonment by God, however. The Lord will come to the believers in the midst of their turmoil, as he came to the disciples in the midst of the storm (6:45-51). Persecution and distress are necessary, but the Son of Man will come quickly to deliver the oppressed believers (13:14-27). The suffering of Mark's community may have been heightened by the feeling that they had been abandoned by their Lord, but Mark reminds them that Jesus felt abandoned in his suffering as well, and God, just as he was not acting to prevent their suffering, had not acted to prevent Jesus' death. The suffering would not be the end. Beyond the suffering of the obedient Jesus there was the vindicating action of God. Beyond death there was resurrection. If the community could identify with the suffering of its Lord, it could also draw assurance from his resurrection. The Lord had not abandoned the persecuted community; just as the Father had not abandoned His Son, even though he had felt abandoned.

God would accomplish through the suffering of Jesus and the distress of the Christian community what God could achieve in no other way: the disclosure of the divine nature as *suffering love* and the redemption of humankind that could come only through the power of that disclosure. The "cry of abandonment," therefore, reveals the depth of suffering in both the Son and the Father. For Mark it was the moment of the supreme disclosure of God's nature.

The bystanders hear Jesus' cry but misunderstand it. Mark typically translates Hebrew and Aramaic terms (5:41; 7:11; 15:22). It is uncertain, therefore, whether the evangelist knew Aramaic.[53] Hearing *Eloi*, they thought Jesus was calling out to *Ēlias* (Elijah). Mark does not say whether the one who ran to fill a sponge with sour wine was a soldier (as in Luke 23:36) or one of the bystanders. It is doubtful that a soldier would have known the folklore that Elijah was the helper of those who were beyond help.[54] On the other hand, the soldiers would have controlled the movements of the bystanders around the crosses and their access to the condemned men. The sour wine (*oxos*), which was distinct from the wine mixed with myrrh earlier (15:23), was a cheap red wine drunk by peasants to slake thirst (Num 6:3; Ruth 2:14). It may have been the soldiers' wine, but again Mark does not say. More significantly, the action probably signals an allusion to Psalm 69:21, "for my thirst they gave me vinegar to drink."

Mark referred to the expectation of the coming of Elijah earlier in the narrative (9:9-13), and Jesus explained that the expectation of the coming of Elijah (Mal 4:5-6) was fulfilled by John the Baptist. [Elijah's Role in Jewish Expectation] The readers of the Gospel know therefore that Jesus cannot expect help from Elijah (see [Elijah] [Elijah's coming]). On the other hand, the reference to Elijah correctly lends apocalyptic significance to the scene of Jesus' death, as do the darkness over the land and the rending of the veil in the temple. In Mark the one who rushes to offer the sour wine to Jesus explains his actions by saying, "Wait, let us see whether Elijah will come to take him down" (15:36). The term translated "wait" in the NRSV actually means "permit" or "allow" (*me*), as in 1:34; 5:19, 37; 7:12, etc., which may mean that Mark understands that a bystander leaps into action while appealing to the soldiers for permission to offer Jesus the sour wine. In Matthew 27:49 this appeal is voiced by the other bystanders as a reason *not* to give Jesus the sour wine.[55]

The misunderstanding of what Jesus said may also be a final act of mockery that extends the earlier taunt for Jesus to come down from the cross. Perhaps the bystanders thought Jesus was responding to their mockery and calling for Elijah to take him down. Like the other challenges offered in mockery, this one also points to a deeper truth. Jesus will be vindicated, not by Elijah but by God, who will vindicate not by rescuing Jesus from death but by raising him from death.

Jesus' death is reported with great brevity. According to Mark he released a loud but apparently wordless cry and expired. The loud cry

---

Elijah's Role in Jewish Expectation

"Precisely at the beginning of the second-temple period, 'Malachi' announced that God would send a messenger before his own final advent (Mal. 3:1); and a later hand, in all probability, identified this messenger, understandably enough, with the translated Elijah who was therefore expected to come (3:1) in order to restore the hearts of fathers to their children, and the hearts of children to their fathers (3:23f.), thus mitigating God's wrath. To this portrait Ben Sira (48:10) added an element drawn from the 'Servant of Yahweh' traditions (Is. 49:6), thus viewing the coming Elijah as the one who will restore the tribes of Israel. And beyond Ben Sira numerous traditions developed, the major motif being that in preparation for God's eschatological advent—and hence as the 'messianic' figure himself—Elijah would come to accomplish, often miraculously, the *restitutio in integrum* of God's people."

J. Louis Martyn, *The Gospel of John in Christian History* (New York: Paulist Press, 1978), 18.

can be interpreted in various ways (a cry of agony, of defeat, of defiance, of victory, or even of a vanquished spirit as in the accounts of exorcisms[56]). The best clue to the meaning of Jesus' last cry, at least for Mark, may be found in the centurion's response. Mark apparently intended for his readers to understand that the way in which Jesus bore his suffering, the darkness over the land at noon, his appeal to God in the cry of abandonment, and the nature of his final cry led the centurion to the Gospel's climactic confession.

Immediately following Jesus' death, Mark notes, "the curtain of the temple was torn in two from top to bottom" (15:38). Both the use of the passive voice and the direction of the tear, i.e., from the top down, imply that this was God's action. The combination of "in two" and "from top to bottom" is a typical Markan doubling. God has vindicated Jesus' judgment on the temple. From chapter 11 on, Jesus' opposition to the temple is a major concern in Mark.[57] When Jesus entered the Holy City and the temple, its evening had come (11:11). Jesus' opposition to the temple is rooted in both its failure to be a house of prayer and its exclusion of the Gentiles. Mark was intensely interested in the inclusion of the Gentiles in the Christian community. While the temple cult effectively excluded Gentiles from the worship of God by allowing commerce in "their" court, the church would be "a house of prayer for all nations."[58] Jesus also charged that the temple had become a "den of robbers." The thieving money-changers and merchants would find no asylum in the sanctuary.[59] The parable of the wicked husbandmen is related to the temple motif in that the "tenants" are the religious leaders, who know that Jesus told the parable about them (12:12). Because they killed his "beloved son" (12:6), the Lord of the vineyard will take it away from the "tenants" and will give it to others (12:9). Thereafter, Jesus agrees with the scribes' judgment on the lesser value of the sacrifices in relation to love for one's neighbor (12:33-34) and prophesies the destruction of the temple (13:2; cf. 13:14). At the Jewish trial false witnesses testify, "We heard him say, 'I will destroy this temple that is made with hands, and in three days I will build another, not made with hands.' Yet not even so did their testimony agree" (14:57-59). Up to this point Mark has consistently used the term *hieron* (11:11, 15, 16, 27; 12:35; 13:1, 3; 14:49). Here and in the two succeeding references (15:29, 38) he uses *naos*; he does not use *hieron* again. The pattern of Mark's usage suggests that he used the two terms distinctly.[60] Jesus' declarations and prophetic actions had concerned the *hieron*, not the *naos*—he would not destroy the *naos*, the sanctuary of God's presence; his death would open it to the Gentiles. On the other hand, the *hieron*, the temple structure and cult, was condemned and would soon be destroyed; at the cross it became obsolete. The temple made with hands would be replaced by one not made with hands, i.e., the church.[61]

Mark takes up the temple theme at the trial (14:58), the second mocking (15:29), and the death of Jesus (15:38). The rending of the veil indicates that God confirmed Jesus' judgment on the temple. Its destruction was sealed; it would be replaced by the church, the temple not made with hands (cf. John 2:19-21).

Interpreters are rather evenly divided on the question of whether the veil in question was the inner veil concealing the holy of holies or the veil between the forecourt and the sanctuary.[62] Generally, those who choose the former find the symbolism to indicate that now the way to the presence of God through Jesus is open for all (which is developed in Heb 6:19-20; 9:2-3; 10:19-20, the only places outside the Gospels where Mark's term for the veil [*katapetasma*] occurs in the New Testament). Those who think it was the outer veil find a sign of the destruction of the temple. Mark does not make it clear which curtain is meant, nor does he give any indication that the meaning of the sign is related to understanding which curtain was affected. The pattern of references to the temple in Mark strongly suggests that the rending of the veil signifies the destruction of the temple. It has ceased to be a holy place, and its eventual destruction (about the time when Mark was written) is assured. Josephus reports various signs in the temple in the decade of the sixties that were omens of its destruction (*J. W.* 6.288-309), and Jerome illustrates how the rending of the veil was replaced by the tradition that the temple lintel was thrown over and shattered.[63]

The temple in Jerusalem will be replaced by a spiritual temple, one not made with hands, open to all people, Gentile as well as Jew, female as well as male, and lay as well as clergy. Just as the Gospel of Mark begins with the heavens being ripped in two at Jesus' baptism and the voice from heaven announcing "you are my beloved son" (1:11), so it ends with the veil in the temple, which depicted the panorama of the heavens [The Veil in the Temple],[64] ripped in two and the Roman centurion confessing, "Truly this man was God's Son" (15:39).

The vineyard had been given to others (12:9) and the temple had become a house of prayer for all nations (11:17); it was appropriate for the christological high point of the Gospel to follow immediately and to come from a Gentile: "Truly this man was the Son of God" (15:39). Like the breaking down of the "dividing wall of hostility"

The Veil in the Temple

"Before these [golden doors] hung a veil of equal length [fifty cubits high and sixteen broad], of Babylonian tapestry, with embroidery of blue and fine linen, of scarlet also and purple, wrought with marvelous skill. Nor was this mixture of materials without its mystic meaning: it typified the universe. For the scarlet seemed emblematical of fire, the fine linen of the earth, the blue of the air, and the purple of the sea; the comparison in two cases being suggested by their colour, and in that of the fine linen and purple by their origin, as the one is produced by the earth and the other by the sea. On this tapestry was portrayed a panorama of the heavens, the signs of the Zodiac excepted."

Josephus, *Jewish War* 5.213–14; LCL 3:265.

(Eph 2:14-15), the rending of the veil opened the way for the inclusion of Gentiles in the community of believers.[65]

The Centurion's Confession, 15:39

The centurion's confession, "truly this man was the Son of God,"[66] is the last interpretive element in Mark that defines the significance of Jesus' death. Verse 39 connects with v. 37, and v. 38 disrupts the flow of the narrative. The reader also knows of the rending of the veil in the temple, whether or not Mark assumes that the centurion could see that the veil was torn.[67] It was the manner of Jesus' death, and specifically his last cry that prompted the centurion's confession. Mark is precise about the position of the centurion relative to the cross (lit., "he stands by over against Jesus"[68]). The reader is well aware that this is the climax of Mark's revelation of Jesus' identity.

As we have noted, the crucifixion in Mark unfolds in three acts, each of which presents both an event and the response to it. The response to both Jesus' sentencing and his crucifixion was mockery (15:16-20a and 15:29-32). What the mockers say is important because Mark intends for the reader to understand that the vindication of Jesus by the phenomena that accompany his death and resurrection shows that he in fact was that which the unbelieving accomplices in his death refused to believe about him. He was the king of the Jews (15:18), the one worthy of worship (15:19), the one who would build a new temple and destroy the old (15:29), the one who was able to save others (15:31), and the Christ, the King of Israel (15:32).[69] Just as the denial by Peter (predicted by Jesus in 14:30) confirmed at the trial that Jesus was in fact a prophet in spite of the mockery (14:65), so here the manner of Jesus' death and his ensuing resurrection confirm that as the centurion said, "He was the Son of God." Mark underscores this point by bringing the christological titles into the narrative at both the trial and the mockings, just as he inserted the temple theme in both passages.[70] The chief priest asked, "Are you the Christ, the Son of the Blessed [a circumlocution for "Son of God"]?" (14:61), and the chief priests mocked him by calling him "the Christ, the King of Israel" (15:32). Finally, the Gentile centurion sees what the chief priests, the religious leaders of Israel, were unable to see: "Truly," he was the Son of God! This is the "messianic secret" Mark has been disclosing from the start. It was announced by Mark in the opening verse of the Gospel (see the commentary on 1:1), partially revealed by Peter at Caesarea Philippi after Jesus' teaching on the kingdom and his miracles,[71] revealed by Jesus before the high priest (14:61-62), recognized by the centurion (15:39), confirmed by the demons (3:11; 5:7), and declared by God at the baptism of Jesus (1:10) and at the transfiguration (9:7). It is clear, therefore, that the centurion's confession of Jesus as the Son of God is the christological high point of the Gospel (see ["Son of God" in Mark]).

The meaning of the confession can be defined by tracing its association with the "Son of Man" in Mark, the Gentile theme, and the emphasis on suffering. Throughout the Gospel of Mark, the "Son of God" title seems to be waiting in the wings for its moment on center stage.[72] That moment arrives with the confession of the centurion, but it arrives only after the reader has been carefully prepared to understand the significance of the title (see ["Son of God" in Mark]). Up to this point, the title has appeared only obliquely: in the superscription, in utterances of demons who are immediately silenced, and in epiphanic moments that point ahead to the full disclosure of Jesus' identity. Jesus himself avoided the title, consistently preferring "Son of Man."[73] Even when asked directly if he were the "Son of the Blessed" (14:61), Jesus answered in terms of his role as the Son of Man (14:62). It was only in the light of his death on the cross that his identity as the Son of God could be revealed without being misunderstood. Mark, therefore, kept the title waiting in the wings until the reader understood the significance of Jesus' suffering and the way in which his power was disclosed in weakness (a Pauline theme: 2 Cor 12:9). There could now be no possibility that the Gospel could be used to foster a Christology of glory that allowed its adherents to avoid suffering.[74]

The centurion uttered the confession that would have been reserved for the Roman emperor in the emperor cult: a divine being—"God's Son."[75] The specific implications of Mark's message regarding what it meant to follow the Messiah who had been executed by the Jewish and Roman authorities would have been clear to Mark's church when it read his Gospel during or just after the war of AD 66–70.

One other aspect of Mark 15:39 must be given due attention: It is not by accident that the first person to confess that Jesus is the Son of God is a Gentile. The text does not state that the centurion (a Latin loanword) was a Gentile, but we may safely assume that he was and that Mark's audience would have understood him as such. He was a representative of the "Gentiles" to whom Jesus was delivered (10:33), but he was also a representative of the Gentiles to whom the gospel must be preached before the Parousia (13:10) and who would have a place in the new temple not made with hands (cf. 11:17). Just as the shadow of the cross falls back across the entire Gospel, so the echoes of the centurion's confession can be heard throughout it. The associations with the Son of God title and the teachings on suffering have been traced. Associations with Jesus' acceptance of Gentiles into his new community can also be seen.[76]

The references to Gentiles in Mark indicate that the evangelist understood that Jesus by his example had himself launched the Gentile mission of the early church. In an extensive Markan summary section (3:7-12), we find that Jesus drew followers "from Idumea, and across the Jordan, and around Tyre and Sidon" (3:8). After exorcising the demon legion from the Gerasene demoniac, Jesus broke his pattern of commanding the ones he healed or exorcised to "tell no one" (1:24-25, 34, 44; 3:12; 5:43; but also 7:36 [in the Decapolis]) and commanded the man to go to his house and his people and to tell them what the Lord had done for him. Thereafter, the man preached in the Decapolis, a primarily Gentile area (5:20). According to Mark, when Jesus sent the Twelve out on mission, he did not send them only to Israel (6:6b-13); Mark's silence at this point may be significant in view of Matthew 10:5-6, which states that the disciples were not to go to the Gentiles or Samaritans but to Israel only. Then, just following his account of Jesus' rejection of the traditions of the elders in 7:1-23, Mark tells how in Tyre the Syrophoenician woman, a Gentile, persisted in her faith in Jesus and received healing for her daughter (7:24-30). This pericope in turn introduces a period of ministry in Sidon and the area of the Decapolis (7:31). Following the transitional story of the healing of the deaf mute (7:31-37), which Mark may have intended to be illustrative of the way in which Jesus was able to awaken faith in Gentiles, Mark adds the account of the feeding of the 4,000 (8:1-10). This feeding took place in a Gentile area (cf. 7:31), and various references suggest that it was primarily a feeding of Gentiles.[77] Again, Mark probably understood the "others" to whom the vineyard would be given (12:9) to include Gentile Christians. Finally, the reference to the Gentile mission is explicit in 13:10. This command is reminiscent of the words from the risen Lord elsewhere (Matt 28:19-20; Luke 24:47; Acts 1:8; and in the second-century, longer ending of Mark—16:15). These references indicate clearly the importance to Mark of the inclusion of Gentiles in the fellowship of the church. He took pains to be sure the readers of his Gospel would see that their inclusion was ordained by Jesus himself. Hence, the first person to perceive the true identity of Jesus was the Gentile centurion. [Legends about the Centurion]

The centurion's confession stands as the climax of Mark's Gospel, because it is the culmination of his revelation of the hidden identity of Jesus as the Son of God. That revelation takes place only at his death,

Legends about the Centurion

The soldier who thrust the spear into Jesus' side was identified as Longinus by the 4th century (*Acts of Pilate* 16.7). He was said to have been cured of blindness by a drop of Jesus' blood. Still later this soldier was confused with the centurion who confessed that Jesus was the Son of God. The centurion was named as a saint (honored on March 15), and his relics are preserved in Mantua.

Bruce M. Metzger, "Names for the Nameless in the New Testament," in *Kyriakon* (Festschrift for Johannes Quasten; ed. Patrick Granfield and Josef A. Jungmann; 2 vols.; Münster: Aschendorff, 1970), 1:95.

"Longinus," *A Dictionary of Biblical Tradition in English Literature* (ed. David Lyle Jeffrey; Grand Rapids: Wm. B. Eerdmans, 1992), 461.

in the context of his suffering, and it is a Gentile who first understands who Jesus was and is therefore in a position to begin true discipleship to him.

Our survey of the structure, accompanying phenomena, Markan themes, and use of the Old Testament in the third act of Mark 15 has revealed the rich significance Jesus' death had for Mark. Above all, the death of Jesus revealed his identity as the Son of God and the nature of God as suffering love. Only in his abandonment and agony was his divine nature clearly revealed. Hence, the primary significance of the cross for Mark was revelatory. This revelation carried with it several important consequences: It demonstrated that Israel had been judged; the temple was condemned; and the "way" was open for the gathering of a new community, a new temple "not made with hands," i.e., the church. This community would be defined by its faith in Jesus as the Son of God, its appropriation of the way of suffering love in response to God's suffering love, and its inclusion of Gentiles—all peoples. The death of Jesus was a moment of cosmic significance, for it revealed the nature of God and charted the path for the future of those who were able to grasp its significance. The Son of God would be with the community of believers that would gather in Jesus' name and vindicate them in the end in spite of their present sufferings.

The Women at the Cross, 15:40-41

Almost as an addendum to the scene at the cross, Mark adds that there were also some women there who had followed Jesus from Galilee. In contrast to the centurion, who stood facing Jesus (15:39), the women were "looking on from a distance," a phrase used earlier in 5:6; 8:3; 11:13, and most recently in 14:54 to describe Peter's following Jesus into the courtyard at the Jewish trial. Mark has earlier noted that Jesus had many followers beyond the Twelve (2:15; 3:7-8, 13; 8:34), but this is the first time he has named women among Jesus' disciples. It is the first of three lists of women in the closing scenes of the Gospel, and the situation is perplexing because there are variations in

The Lists of Women in Mark

📖

Mark 15:40	Mark 15:47	Mark 16:1
Mary Magdalene	Mary Magdalene	Mary Magdalene
Mary the mother of James the Younger and of Joses	Mary the mother of Joses	Mary the mother of James
Salome	Salome	Salome

the three lists [The Lists of Women in Mark] and differences from the lists in the other Gospels [The Lists of Women at the Cross]. Mary Magdalene, whose name indicates that she was from Magdala, a town on the western shore of the Sea of Galilee that is identified in the Talmud (*b. Pes.* 46a) as *Migdalnunaiya*, which means "Fish Tower,"[78] is named first. Luke

The Lists of Women at the Cross

Mark 15:40	Matt 27:56	Luke 23:49	John 19:25
Mary Magdalene	Mary Magdalene	The women who had fol-	His mother
Mary the mother of James	Mary the mother of James	lowed him in Galilee (cf.	His mother's sister
the Younger and of Joses	and of Joseph	Luke 8:1-3)	Mary the wife of Clopas
Salome	The mother of the sons of		Mary Magdalene
	Zebedee		

8:2 reports that "seven demons had gone out" from her. John 20 records Jesus' appearance to Mary Magdalene in the garden, in which she addresses Jesus as *rabbouni*, "my teacher," and she has become a figure of great interest in Christian hagiography. [Mary Magdalene]

Two identifications have often been suggested based on the lists in the other Gospels. Mary the mother of James the Younger and of Joses may be the wife of Clopas named in John 19:25, and Salome may be the wife of Zebedee named in Matthew 27:56.[79] Mark uses two significant verbs in the identification of these women: they "followed" (*ēkolouthoun*) Jesus in Galilee and they "served" (*diēkonoun*) him. The first term is frequently used of Jesus' disciples (1:18; 2:14-15; 6:1; 10:28, 32; 14:54), but also for the crowds (3:7; 5:24) and the unauthorized exorcist (9:38) and in Jesus' calls to discipleship (2:14; 8:34; 10:21). The second term describes the actions of the angels in the wilderness (1:13), Peter's mother-in-law (1:31), and Jesus' own role (10:45; cf. 9:35; 10:43).

Debate has therefore focused on whether Mark means the women were disciples or whether they merely attended to the food and provisions for Jesus and the disciples (cf. Luke 8:1-3; 10:38-42). Regardless, with the failure and flight of the disciples (14:50), the women now stand in as their surrogates in the Gospel narrative, witnessing Jesus' death and burial and caring for his body (cf. the role of John's disciples in 6:29). Recapping the Gospel story, Mark adds

Mary Magdalene

In recent years the literature on Mary Magdalene has mushroomed. The following list is a sample of recent publications:

Brock, Ann Graham. *Mary Magdalene, the First Apostle: The Struggle for Authority*. Cambridge MA: Harvard Divinity School, 2003.

Coletti, Theresa. *Mary Magdalene and the Drama of Saints: Theater, Gender, and Religion in Late Medieval England*. Philadelphia: University of Pennsylvania, 2004.

De Boer, Esther A. *The Gospel of Mary: Beyond a Gnostic and a Biblical Mary Magdalene*. London: T. & T. Clark International, 2004.

Good, Deidre, editor. *Mariam, the Magdalen, and the Mother*. Bloomington: Indiana University Press, 2005.

Haskins, Susan. *Mary Magdalen: Myth and Metaphor*. New York: Harcourt, Brace & Co., 1993.

Hearon, Holly E. *The Mary Magdalene Tradition: Witness and Counter-Witness in Early Christian Communities*. Collegeville: Liturgical Press, 2004.

Meyer, Marvin W., and Esther A. de Boer. *The Gospels of Mary: The Secret Tradition of Mary Magdalene, the Companion of Jesus*. San Francisco: HarperSanFrancisco, 2004.

Schaberg, Jane. *The Resurrection of Mary Magdalene: Legends, Apocrypha, and the Christian Testament*. New York: Continuum, 2002.

Witherington, Ben, III. *The Gospel Code: Novel Claims about Jesus, Mary Magdalene, and Da Vinci*. Downers Grove IL: InterVarsity Press, 2004.

references to both Galilee and Jerusalem in v. 41, adding that not only these three but many other women had "gone up" to Jerusalem with him (one always "went up" when going to Jerusalem; cf. esp. Acts 13:31).

The Burial of Jesus, 15:42-47

Mark gives a sparse account of the burial of Jesus because it is crucial as background for the discovery of the empty tomb. Mosaic Law required that the bodies of those who were executed by hanging on a tree must not be allowed to remain on the tree overnight (Deut 21:22-23; *m. Sanh.* 6.5). Early Christian tradition confirms that Jesus was buried (1 Cor 15:3-5; Rom 6:4; Col 2:12), and in one of the speeches in Acts Paul recalls that Jesus was buried by those who had crucified him (Acts 13:29). Mark and John agree, independently according to many scholars, that Jesus was buried by Joseph of Arimathea. Still, the details are sparse, and the account suggests an interesting scenario.

Those executed by the Romans, especially if they were accused of treason, were generally not buried but left for birds of prey or thrown on the garbage pits for dogs,[80] and Tacitus records that "people sentenced to death forfeited their property and were forbidden burial" (*Annals* 6.29).[81] Still, the Roman governor could grant permission for an executed criminal to be buried, and Pilate may have been moved to do so if he was suspicious of the motives of the chief priests who had brought Jesus before him (15:10) or if he was acting to appease Jewish sensitivities during the Passover festival. For the Jews burial of the dead was a solemn duty for the pious (2 Sam 21:12-14; Tob 1:17-19; 2:3-7; 12:12-13; Sir 7:33; 38:16), and Philo (*Flaccus* 83) and Josephus affirmed that the Jews considered it a duty "to bury even enemies" (*J. W.* 3.377, LCL 2:683).[82]
[Burial of the Dead]

Burial of the Dead

"They actually went so far in their impiety as to cast out the corpses without burial, although the Jews are so careful about funeral rites that even malefactors who have been sentenced to crucifixion are taken down and buried before sunset."

Josephus, *J. W.* 4.316–17; LCL 3:93.

Normally the request to bury the condemned would have come from family members. Only John (19:26-27) records that Jesus' mother was in Jerusalem at the time, and Jesus' disciples had abandoned him in fear (14:50). Joseph of Arimathea, whom Mark describes as a respected member of the council and one who was "waiting expectantly for the kingdom of God" (15:43), took courage and requested permission from Pilate to bury Jesus. Nothing is said of burying the other two—or even whether they had died yet.

Mark notes the time with two references: evening had come (cf. 1:32; 4:35; 6:47; 14:17), and it was the "day of Preparation," the day before the Sabbath. Since Jesus' death occurred about 3:00 p.m., the time for burying Jesus before the beginning of the Sabbath at sunset was short. Brown lists the things that had to be done in these short hours: "going before Pilate who would call in the centurion, buying a linen cloth, taking the body down, tying it up, and putting it in a burial place."[83] Lane therefore speculates that we should read Joseph's actions as causative and assume that he had servants whom he directed in these actions.[84]

Joseph, who does not appear elsewhere in Mark, is identified by three references: (1) his home, "Arimathea," (2) his status, "a respected member of the council," and (3) his piety, "who was also himself waiting expectantly for the kingdom of God." Various locations have been proposed for Arimathea. [Arimathea] Each town had a council, and Mark identifies Joseph as a member of the council rather than as a member of the Sanhedrin

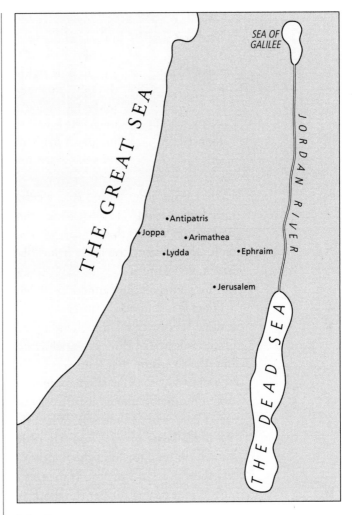

Arimathea

Eusebius and Jerome identify Arimathea with the birthplace of Samuel. 1 Sam 1:1 names Ramah or Ramathaim, in the hill country of Ephraim, as the home of Samuel's father. It is located about twenty miles east of Jaffa, and a monastery named for Joseph of Arimathea is located there. Others identify Arimathea with modern Rentis (fifteen miles east of Jaffa), er-Ram (three miles north of Jerusalem), and el-birah-Ramallah (eight miles north of Jerusalem).

John R. Drayer, "Arimathea," *MDOB*, 61–62; Jerry A. Pattengale, "Arimathea," *ABD* 1:378.

(14:55; 15:1), but because he has not referred to a separate council it is likely that Joseph is to be understood as a member of the Sanhedrin that had condemned Jesus. If that is the case, it may explain why Pilate agreed to release Jesus' body to him and why Mark does not say that the women assisted Joseph in Jesus' burial. The latter point is related to the third descriptive detail. The other Gospels show a tendency toward elevating Joseph to the position of a disciple of Jesus, but if that were the case the women would have assisted in burying Jesus, and Pilate (had he known it) would not have released Jesus' body to him:[85]

Matthew 27:57	"a rich man from Arimathea, named Joseph, who was also a disciple of Jesus"
Luke 23:50	"a good and righteous man named Joseph, who, though a member of the council, had not agreed to their plan and action. He came from the Jewish town of Arimathea. . . ."
John 19:38	"Joseph of Arimathea, who was a disciple of Jesus, though a secret one because of his fear of the Jews"

Earlier Jesus commented that a certain scribe was "not far from the kingdom of God" (12:34), which shows that Mark could have used a description such as this for one who was pious but not one of Jesus' disciples. Requesting the body from Pilate took courage because it could have raised suspicion that Joseph was a sympathizer or follower of Jesus, but his status on the Sanhedrin evidently protected him.

Pilate was "amazed" (the same verb that appears in 15:5 when Jesus refused to answer Pilate) when he heard that Jesus had already died. It often took two or three days before one who was crucified succumbed. In order to ensure that Jesus was in fact dead (a matter that would later be important for Christian apologetics), Pilate summoned the centurion, presumably the same officer who had seen how Jesus died (15:39, see [Legends about the Centurion]). When the centurion confirmed that Jesus was dead, Pilate gave his body (lit., "dead body" or "corpse," *ptōma*, the same term used for John the Baptist's body in 6:29) to Joseph. Neither Matthew nor Luke mentions the role of the centurion at this point.

Without noting further the shortness of the time Joseph had to complete the burial before sundown, Mark reports that Joseph bought a linen cloth (cf. 14:51). John says that he bound the body in cloth strips (19:40). Matthew 27:59-60 takes pains to convey that the burial was a proper one, adding that the cloth was clean and the tomb was new. By contrast, Mark reports only the minimal rites. Joseph apparently secured a tomb in the area of the executions, perhaps near the tombs of others who had been executed (contrast Matt 27:60, which less probably reports that it was Joseph's own tomb), and merely wraps the body in the linen cloth before placing it in the tomb. Nothing is said of washing the body or anointing it. The only anointing the body of Jesus receives in Mark is the anointing at Bethany (14:8-9), and the omission of these steps in the preparation of the body serves as the motivation for the women's return to the tomb on Sunday morning (16:2). The minimal preparations that Mark reports are understandable if Joseph of Arimathea was simply a pious member of the Sanhedrin, who took the initiative to see that the body of Jesus was given a decent burial. John gives a different account of the burial, reporting that Joseph anointed the body with a hundred pounds of spices and laid it in a new tomb that had never been used before (John 19:39-41).

If the tomb was a horizontal one, cut in the quarry wall, as the evidence suggests, the door would have been no more than three feet high (cf. the references to stooping over in Luke 24:12; John 20:5, 11). A stone was then rolled against the opening to seal it. More elaborate tombs had a trough along which to roll the stone. Mark 16:4 reports that the stone was large (cf. Matt 27:60). Joseph may have had help (see the reference to "they" in 16:6), but v. 46 reports all of these actions as though he acted alone. [Joseph of Arimathea in Later Legends]

The report that Mary Magdalene and Mary the mother of Joses [The Lists of Women in Mark] saw where Joseph buried Jesus serves as a transition to the discovery of the empty tomb in the next paragraph. Their presence at Jesus' burial is important because it ensures that the women did not mistakenly go to the wrong tomb. Moreover, the fact that Mark does not say that the women assisted Joseph in the burial, as they presumably would have if he had been a disciple, supports the conclusion that they did not know him and that he was a member of the Sanhedrin fulfilling the duty to bury the dead.[86]

Joseph of Arimathea in Later Legends

In the 4th-c. *Acts of Pilate* the Jewish authorities hold Joseph under house arrest because he provided Jesus' body a proper burial. Jesus himself appeared to Joseph, and Joseph reported Jesus' descent into hell and raising of the dead to Annas and Caiaphas. He then led them to Arimathea to see Simeon and his sons, who had been raised from the dead.

In the medieval histories of Glastonbury in England, Joseph traveled to England from Gaul, where he had worked with Philip the Apostle. He was given the island of Glastonbury (or Avalon in the King Arthur legends). There he built a church in honor of Mary. Still later legend reported that Joseph brought the Holy Grail to England. Joseph therefore figures in the Arthurian legends, in Galahad's vision of the Holy Grail. Finally, the Joseph legend added that Joseph was Jesus' uncle, a merchant, and that he took the boy Jesus with him on a journey to England.

Wilhelm Schneemelcher, ed., *New Testament Apocrypha* (trans. R. McL. Wilson; Louisville: Westminster John Knox, 1991), 1:513–21; Raymond E. Brown, *The Death of the Messiah* (New York: Doubleday, 1994), 2:1232–34; Marie Michelle Walsh, "Joseph of Arimathea," *A Dictionary of Biblical Tradition in English Literature* (ed. David Lyle Jeffrey; Grand Rapids: Wm. B. Eerdmans, 1992), 412.

CONNECTIONS

Mark 15:1-15

The vividness of Mark's description of Jesus' trial before Pilate and the irony of the release of Barabbas and the condemnation of Jesus have imprinted this scene on the memories and imaginations of Christians through the centuries. Mel Gibson's film *The Passion of the Christ* characterizes the chief priests as stern and inflexible while Pilate is much more human. In doing so, the film follows the tendency to blame the Jewish leaders for Jesus' death while exonerating Roman authority that can be traced back to the time of the writing of the Gospels. The Jewish religious leaders probably were more concerned about Jesus' activities than Pilate was, but Christian tradition has all too often seized upon the negative characterization of the chief priests and Pharisees and turned it into a justification for anti-Semitism. Mark is not anti-Jewish or anti-Semitic. The failure of the religious authorities to recognize Jesus as the Messiah is part of Mark's theme that everyone failed Jesus—his hometown, his family, his disciples, and finally even the women at the cross. None was faithful, yet Jesus died for all: "For the Son of Man came not to be served but to serve, and to give his life a ransom for many" (10:45).

The overwhelming emphasis of Gibson's film is on the brutality of the beating and the suffering of Christ. Mark's account places more emphasis on Jesus' suffering than any of the other Gospels with its account of the flogging and mockery of Jesus and by reporting only the cry of abandonment and Jesus' final cry from the cross. By contrast, Jesus speaks coherently from the cross in the other Gospels, prays in Luke, and speaks with his mother and beloved disciple in John before he dies in John. Nevertheless, Mark reports the beating of Jesus in only one verse. If one had not read the Gospels and was led only by the film, he or she would probably think that the Gospel devoted pages to a gruesome account of the flogging. That is not the case. Everyone knew that crucifixion was a brutal, inhuman punishment, but the saving significance of Jesus' death is not based on how much he suffered. The "penal substitution" view of the atonement, that Jesus suffered our punishment, easily leads to the pious tendency to exaggerate Jesus' suffering out of the conviction that as sinners we deserve such suffering and the view that the more Jesus suffered the more grace or merit his death generated. Mark's account of the flogging is reported with no details at all, and his account of Jesus' suffering is actually remarkably restrained. It is not Jesus' suffering that gives his death its saving significance, it is Jesus' identity as the Son of God, confessed by the centurion at the cross (15:39), and his faithfulness to God even in the face of such a terrible death.

The moral failure of "handing over" responsibility is also apparent in Mark. Judas Iscariot agrees to betray (lit., "hand over") Jesus to the Jewish authorities, who try him and then hand him over to Pilate, who gives in to the pressure of the crowd and "hands over" Jesus to be crucified. No one is solely responsible. Each can point to someone else, yet all have a part in the crucifixion of Jesus. Our world is even more complex today. Individuals, groups, organizations, industries, and governments all have a hand in the problems of poverty, exploitation of the environment, racism, and other injustices, so we can always point to the need for others to make changes to address the problems. Mark's clear chain of responsibility and its emphasis on the failure of everyone around Jesus should be a constant reminder that as John Claypool often said, "we are way past innocence," and each of us needs to take responsibility to break the chain of passing blame and do what we can to address the injustices and needs that are all around us.

Mark 15:16-20

Irony and pathos require that the reader or observer know more than the characters or participants. Mark's account of the mockery of Jesus has a profound effect because we know that Jesus really was "the King of the Jews," and not just an earthly king but the divine Son of God. What might have passed as typical soldiers' sport, therefore, becomes a parable of the failure of humanity to recognize God's grace, even when it has come in human form among us. The mockery of Jesus, which adds insult to the brutality of the beating and crucifixion, is a mirror reflecting the blindness and degradation of human sinfulness. Yet, Jesus endures it without uttering a single recorded word.

The Mocked Christ

Annibale Carracci (1560–1609). *The Mocked Christ*. Pinacoteca Nazionale, Bologna, Italy. (Credit: George Tatge, 1999, Alinari / Art Resource, NY)

Could the soldiers not see that he was no ordinary criminal? What caused their blindness, insensitivity, and appetite for cruelty? What are we not seeing? Perhaps the pathos of the mockery should call each of us to examine all the ways we relate insensitively to others, and ask where we are as blind as the soldiers to the work of God around us.

Mark 15:21-27

The crucifixion of Jesus removes any hope that he will be able to escape. The later offer of wine to keep him alive and see if Elijah would come to rescue him (15:36) merely underscores the futility of any hope at this point. Mark reports the events with notable restraint and detachment, with no comment or embellishment. The events speak for themselves, and the pathos of the previous scene gives way to a kind of paradox. Where is God in these unspeakably brutal events? Has God's redemptive love been defeated by the death of Jesus? Contrary to any scenario we might imagine, God is present in the injustice and inhumanity of Jesus' death, not on the side of the institutional power but in the suffering of the abused. The fact that God would choose this scandalous means of responding to sin, violence, and evil through suffering love, grace, and forgiveness reveals both God's love and the futility of engaging in the cycle of violence. God is always on the side of the oppressed and the suffering. Meanwhile, the powerful are blinded by their privileged status. The cross is God's decisive answer to human sin, in part because it unmasks the common abuses of power while calling those who have eyes to see it and ears to hear the cries of the marginalized to confess God's presence with the oppressed and live accordingly.

Mark 15:29-32

The mockery at the cross is the final test in Mark's long string of challenges to the faithfulness of Jesus as God's Son. He resisted the temptation in the wilderness; the temptation of the crowds simply to heal the sick, feed them, and advance their nationalistic aspirations; the cross-examination of the scribes and Pharisees; the attacks of the unclean spirits; the defections and betrayals of those around him; and the authorities' plot to seize him and the interrogations and challenges with which they confronted him in the Jewish and Roman trials. The last temptation is to reveal his true identity by an act of power rather than weakness, by triumph rather than defeat: "Come down from the cross now, so that we may see and believe" (15:32). It was a temptation to achieve his purpose and God's direction in a different way, an easier, self-serving way—the way of the tempter rather than God's way.

Soldiers Casting Lots for Jesus' Clothes

Soldiers dividing Christ's coat, Detail of Byzantine fresco. Monastery Church, Ohrid, Macedonia. (Credit: Erich Lessing / Art Resource, NY)

We may also surmise that at least on the level of the Gospel if not the level of the actual historical events, it is Jesus' faithfulness in this last test that leads the centurion to confess that he is indeed the Son of God. He has passed every test, been faithful in every way, and rejected the taunt of the mockers to prove that he was the Son of God by betraying the faithfulness to which

God had called him. The final test is always a test of character that exposes one's ultimate values.

Mark 15:33-38

Jurgen Moltmann accepts Mark 15:34 as the church's interpretation of the dying cry of Jesus, but asserts that it "seems to be as near as possible to the historical reality of the death of Jesus."[87] Jesus' mission was so linked with his person and the proclamation of the nearness and grace of God that Jesus' death marked also the death of his cause. Therefore, the cry, interpreted by the opening words of Psalm 22, inquires not only "Why hast thou forsaken me?" but also "Why hast thou forsaken thyself?"[88] It is the cry of the Son to his Father, so the abandonment reflects an enmity between God and God that "requires a 'revolution in the concept of God.'"[89] The theology of the cross that Moltmann develops asserts not only the suffering of the Son, who laid down his life in obedience, but also the suffering of the Father, who allowed his Son to die, and the suffering of the Spirit of love and self-surrender. The nature of God, the Trinity, is therefore revealed in the cross: "The unity of this account of Father, Son, and Spirit on the cross can then a posteriori be termed 'God.' The word 'God' means an event, precisely this event."[90]

Mark 15:39

What does it mean to confess that Jesus is the Son of God? The title has become such a part of the church's vocabulary that it has lost most of its metaphorical significance and all of the "edge" it would have carried in Mark. The widely published New Testament scholar John Dominic Crossan once shared with me his response to a reporter who kept trying to elicit a newsworthy confession or denial from him as to whether he believed that Jesus was the Son of God. Crossan knew that neither a simple "yes" nor "no" would clearly express his understanding of the title, so he finally said, "Yes, I believe that Jesus is the 'Son of God,' 'the Word of God,' and 'the lamb of God.'" His point was that all three titles are metaphors that evoke an aspect of who Jesus was, but they are live metaphors, not dead metaphors that can be taken as literal descriptions.

Moreover, in the first century the title "Son of God" was one that was used in the emperor cult. To confess that Jesus rather than the Roman emperor was the Son of God would have been a dramatic challenge to the authority of the state, somewhat akin to saying, "Jesus is my president, so I cannot give to the president the same authority that other

Americans give him." In the era of the Jewish revolt (AD 66–70), such a confession would have been all the more dangerous. Mark's report that the Roman centurion uttered these words is nothing short of shocking. It challenges his readers to be as forthright about their faith, even if doing so would expose them to personal danger. The confession allows no dodging or hiding. It is a public declaration that one places all other authorities under the authority of Jesus, with no compromise. To claim Jesus as the Son of God, therefore, is tantamount to taking up the cross to follow him.

Now, what does it mean to confess that Jesus is the Son of God?

Mark 15:40-41

The group of women at the cross plays an important role as witnesses to his death, burial, and resurrection. The eyewitness testimony for these events came not from the disciples, but from women, even though they were not qualified to serves as witnesses in a court of law. In the Gospel narrative, they stand in where the disciples should have been and perform the tasks the disciples should have done. They are therefore faithful (to a point—see 16:8) in spite of the fact that they were marginalized by society. Their cameo roles in the Gospel stand as a reminder that women have played this role for centuries, looking on "from a distance" (15:40), then quietly stepping in when the men left important or menial tasks unattended. Appropriately, the resurrection brings the women out of the shadows. For the rest of human history the report of the discovery of the empty tomb on Easter Sunday morning will rest on their testimony so that the church cannot discount their role as witnesses to the gospel. Surely women are not to be marginalized and excluded in the "temple not made with hands," as they were in the temple in Jerusalem. Record their names and their words. Women have a place and a voice!

The Pieta

Michelangelo Buonarroti (1475–1564). *The Pieta*. St. Peter's Basilica, Vatican State. (Credit: Alinari / Art Resource, NY)

15:42-47

Joseph of Arimathea is the central figure in the Gospel accounts of the burial of

Jesus, yet he has remained an obscure and overlooked figure for most Christians. From the commentary above he emerges as a pious member of the Sanhedrin who, although he was not a disciple or follower of Jesus, still took the initiative to see that Jesus' body was given a decent burial. In doing so, he represents those who are sincere, devout in their own traditions, but not Christians. Jesus said that such persons are "not far from the kingdom of God" (12:34).

The church has not known what to do with those who are "not far from the kingdom." Obviously, believers will share their faith and invite anyone who has not responded to Jesus' call to discipleship, but what about those, like Joseph, who have not been called or who have not responded yet still give evidence of love, piety, and the knowledge of God by the way they live? In Mark, Jesus takes an accepting posture toward such persons when he chastises the disciples for their response to the one who was casting out demons in Jesus' name even though he was not a disciple, saying, "Whoever is not against us is for us" (9:40) and "whoever gives you a cup of water to drink because you bear the name of Christ will by no means lose the reward" (9:41). Perhaps the best way to relate to the Joseph of Arimatheas and unauthorized exorcists of our time is to work together with them in the commitments we share in common. What might have happened if, instead of watching from a distance, the women had helped Joseph of Arimathea bury Jesus—and the other two who died with him also?

NOTES

[1] BDAG, 957. Cf. William L. Lane, *The Gospel according to Mark* (NICNT; Grand Rapids: Wm. B. Eerdmans, 1974), 545 n. 1; Raymond E. Brown, *The Death of the Messiah* (New York: Doubleday, 1994), 1:632; Craig A. Evans, *Mark 8:27–16:20* (WBC 34B; Nashville: Thomas Nelson, 2001), 475.

[2] A. N. Sherwin-White, *Roman Society and Roman Law in the New Testament* (Oxford: Oxford University Press, 1963), 44-45.

[3] C. E. B. Cranfield, *The Gospel according to St. Mark* (CGTC; Cambridge: Cambridge University Press, 1959), 449.

[4] Brown, *The Death of the Messiah*, 1:733.

[5] Evans, *Mark 8:27–16:20*, 479.

[6] Herbert Danby, trans., *The Mishnah* (Oxford: Oxford University Press, 1933), 147.

[7] Translation adapted from Adolf Deissmann, *Light from the Ancient East* (trans. Lionel R. M. Strachan; New York: George H. Doran Co., 1927), 269.

[8] Cf. Brown, *The Death of the Messiah,* 1:799-800.

[9] Ibid., 1:798, citing Origen, *In Matthew* 27:16-18, #121.

[10] Ibid., 1:802-03.

[11] BDAG, 472.

[12] Brown, *The Death of the Messiah*, 1:850.

[13] Ibid., 1:717-19.

[14] Sherwin-White, *Roman Society and Roman Law*, 27; Brown, *The Death of the Messiah*, 1:851.

[15] Brown, T*he Death of the Messiah*, 1:710, 875.

[16] Evans, *Mark 8:27–16:20*, 490, who cites Suetonius, *Claudius* 21.6.

[17] A. T. Robertson, *Word Pictures in the New Testament* (New York: Richard R. Smith, 1930), 2:201.

[18] Brown, *The Death of the Messiah*, 1:870.

[19] BDAG, 7.

[20] Lane, *The Gospel according to Mark*, 563; cf. N. Avigad, "A Depository of Inscribed Ossuaries in the Kidron Valley," *IEJ* 12 (1962): 1-12.

[21] Origen, *In Matthew* 27:33, #126, cited by Brown, *The Death of the Messiah*, 937 n. 9; Louis Ginzberg, *The Legends of the Jews* (7 vols.; Philadelphia: The Jewish Publication Society of America, 1925), 5:125-27 n. 137.

[22] *Materia Medica* I.lxiv.3, cited by Lane, *The Gospel according to Mark*, 564.

[23] Brown, *The Death of the Messiah*, 2:941.

[24] Evans, *Mark 8:27–16:20*, 501.

[25] V. Tzaferis, "Jewish Tombs at and near Giv'at ha-Mivtar, Jerusalem," *IEJ* 20 (1970): 18-32; N. Haas, "Anthropological Observations on the Skeletal Remains from Giv'at ha-Mivtar," *IEJ* 20 (1970): 49-59.

[26] See R. Alan Culpepper, *Anatomy of the Fourth Gospel* (Philadelphia: Fortress Press, 1983),

[27] Evans, *Mark 8:27–16:20*, 503.

[28] Cited by Evans, *Mark 8:27–16:20*, 504.

[29] Brown, *The Death of the Messiah*, 2:969-70.

[30] See Francis J. Moloney, *The Gospel of Mark* (Peabody MA: Hendrickson, 2002), 322; John Painter, *Mark's Gospel* (London: Routledge, 1997), 204.

[31] See Bruce M. Metzger, *Textual Commentary on the Greek New Testament* (New York: United Bible Societies, 1971), 119.

[32] Brown, *The Death of the Messiah*, 2:989, 994-95.

[33] Cf. R. Alan Culpepper, "Designs for the Church in the Gospel Accounts of Jesus' Death," *NTS* 51 (2005): 380.

[34] Cited by Morton Smith, *Tannaitic Parallels to the Gospels* (Philadelphia: Society of Biblical Literature, 1951), 138.

[35] On this point see Moloney, *The Gospel of Mark*, 323.

[36] Ibid., 324.

[37] Much of this section was first published in R. Alan Culpepper, "The Passion and Resurrection in Mark," *RevExp* 75 (1978): 583-600.

[38] Martin Hengel, *Crucifixion* (Philadelphia: Fortress Press, 1977), gathers references from primary sources, which demonstrate the brutality of crucifixion and illuminate what it would have meant to preach a crucified savior in the first century.

[39] Cf. J. R. Donahue, *Are You the Christ?* (SBLDS 10; Missoula: Scholars Press, 173), 190-91.

[40] See Wilhelm Schneemelcher, ed., *New Testament Apocrypha* (trans. R. McL. Wilson; Louisville: Westminster John Knox Press, 1991), 1:162, 164, 223-24.

[41] Cited by Brown, *The Death of the Messiah*, 2:1035.

[42] Mark repeatedly points an accusing finger at the powerful, especially the leaders of Israel (3:6; 8:15, 31; 10:23-25, 33; 11:18; 12:13; 14:43, 53; 15:1, 31) and affirms the powerless (a leper, 1:40-44; a paralytic, 2:5-10; tax collectors and sinners, 2:15-17; little ones, 9:42; a widow, 12:42-44; a woman, 14:6-9).

[43] Cf. Gospel of Peter 15: "Now it was midday and a darkness covered all Judaea."

[44] Brown, *The Death of the Messiah*, 2:1035.

[45] Ernest Best, *The Temptation and the Passion: The Markan Soteriology* (SNTSMS 2; Cambridge: Cambridge University Press, 1965), 100; Hugh Anderson, *The Gospel of Mark*, (NCB; London: Oliphants, 1976), 346; Cranfield, *The Gospel according to St. Mark*, 458; Lane, *The Gospel according to Mark*, 573.

[46] The quotation affirms Jesus' faith in his vindication: D. E. Nineham, *The Gospel of Saint Mark* (Baltimore: Penguin Books, 1963), 427, 428; Schreiber, *Theologie des Vertrauens*, 163. Rudolf Pesch, *Das Markusevangelium* (HTKNT; Freiburg: Herder, 1977), 2:494-95, emphasizes that the cry is a prayer that expresses Jesus' faith even in his most extreme need.

[47] J. Blinzler, *Der Prozess Jesu* (4 Aufl.; Regensburg: F. Pustet, 1969), 373 n. 64; Nineham, *The Gospel of Saint Mark*, 428.

[48] Cf. J. Jeremias, *New Testament Theology* (New York: Charles Scribner's Sons, 1971), 189.

[49] Brown, *The Death of the Messiah*, 2:1049.

[50] H. C. Read, "The Cry of Dereliction," *Expository Times* 68 (1975): 260-62; Cranfield, *The Gospel according to St. Mark*, 458. Vincent Taylor, *The Gospel According to Saint Mark* (London: Macmillan, 1952), 594, responds that Jesus was not actually abandoned but merely felt abandoned: ". . . Jesus felt the horror of sin so deeply that for a time the closeness of His communion with the Father was obscured."

[51] For various interpretations of this verse see C. K. Barrett, "The Background of Mark 10:45," *New Testament Essays: Studies in Memory of T. W. Manson* (ed. A. J. B. Higgins; Manchester: Manchester University Press, 1959), 1, 18; Anderson, *The Gospel of Mark*, 256-58; Cranfield, *The Gospel according to St. Mark*, 342-44; Nineham, *The Gospel of Saint Mark*, 280, 281.

[52] Cf. Robert C. Tannehill, "The Disciples in Mark: The Function of a Narrative Role," *Journal of Religion* 57 (1977): 400-401.

[53] Brown, *The Death of the Messiah*, 2:1062.

[54] Joachim Jeremias, *"Elias," TDNT* 2:930, 935-36.

[55] Ibid., 2:1065.

[56] Frederick W. Danker, "The Demonic Secret in Mark: A Reexamination of the Cry of Dereliction (15.34)," *ZNW* 61 (1970): 67-68.

[57] For discussion of the anti-temple theme in Mark, see Werner Kelber, ed., *The Passion in Mark* (Philadelphia: Fortress Press, 1976), 121, 129, 168-72.

[58] Mark emphasizes Jesus' teachings on prayer (9:29; 11:24-25; 12:40; 13:33; 14:38) and presents Jesus as an example for the disciples, i.e., Mark's church (1:35; 6:46; 14:32, 35, 39). Cf. D. Juel, *Messiah and Temple: The Trial of Jesus in the Gospel of Mark* (SBLDS 31; Missoula: Scholars Press, 1977), 135.

[59] Paul J. Achtemeier, *Mark* (Proclamation Commentaries; Philadelphia: Fortress Press, 1975), 24: "The brunt of the accusation thus concerns the use to which the temple is put: people think so long as the temple services are continued, they may retreat there, no matter how they have acted outside its walls, and still find forgiveness and fellowship with God."

[60] Cf. Juel, *Messiah and Temple*, 128; against O. Michel, *"naos,"* *TDNT* 4:882.

[61] Cf. Juel, *Messiah and Temple*, 138-39, 143-57; Best, *The Temptation and the Passion*, 99.

[62] Inner veil: Anderson, *The Gospel of Mark*, 347; T. A. Burkill, "St. Mark's Philosophy of the Passion," *NovT* 2 (1957–1958): 268 n. 1; Cranfield, *The Gospel according to St. Mark*, 459-60; C. Schneider, *"katapetasma,"* *TDNT* 3:629-30; Taylor, *The Gospel according to Saint Mark*, 596; H. Strack and P. Billerbeck, *Kommentar zum Neuen Testament aus Talmud und Midrasch* (Munich: Beck, 1922), 1:1045. Outer veil: Donahue, *Are You the Christ?* 202-03; Juel, *Messiah and Temple*, 140-42; Lane, *The Gospel according to Mark*, 574-75. Cf. T. Levi 10:3-4; T. Benjamin 9:4.

[63] See Brown, *The Death of the Messiah*, 2:1113-18.

[64] David Ulansey, "The Heavenly Veil Torn: Mark's Cosmic *Inclusio,*" *JBL* 105 (1991): 123-25.

[65] See Nineham, *The Gospel of Saint Mark*, 430; Best, *The Temptation and the Passion*, 99.

[66] The translation "a son of God" in the Jerusalem Bible and the New English Bible is unfortunate. The absence of the definite article does not necessarily mean that the construction is indefinite. See E. C. Colwell, "A Definite Rule for the Use of the Article in the Greek New Testament," *JBL* 52 (1933): 12-21.

[67] Brown, *The Death of the Messiah*, 2:1145, argues that Mark assumes that the centurion saw the rending of the veil also.

[68] Taylor, *The Gospel according to St. Mark*, 597.

[69] Cf. Best, *The Temptation and the Passion*, 96-97.

[70] Juel, *Messiah and Temple*, 72.

[71] Mark's use of "Christ" in Mark 1:1 indicates that Peter's confession, while inadequate, was not entirely wrong. See the commentary on 8:29.

[72] For studies of the title and its use in Mark, see M. Hengel, *The Son of God* (Philadelphia: Fortress Press, 1976); Juel, *Messiah and Temple*, 77-83, 108-14; H. C. Kee, *Community of the New Age: Studies in Mark's Gospel* (Philadelphia: Westminster Press, 1977), 121-24.

[73] See Norman Perrin, "The Creative Use of the Son of Man Traditions by Mark," *Union Seminary Quarterly Review* 23 (1968): 357-65; Juel, *Messiah and Temple*, 85-95; Kee, *Community of the New Age*, 129-39.

[74] See T. J. Weeden, "The Cross as Power in Weakness," in *The Passion in Mark*, 116-21, and his earlier monograph, *Mark-Traditions in Conflict* (Philadelphia: Fortress Press, 1971).

[75] Evans, *Mark 8:27–16:20*, 510.

[76] See Kee, *Community of the New Age*, 92-97; and Werner Kelber, *The Kingdom in Mark: A New Place and a New Time* (Philadelphia: Fortress Press, 1974), 57-65, for discussions of the Gentiles in Mark. Mark's interest in the Gentile mission is all the more interesting if in fact the evangelist is John Mark and if John Mark withdrew from Paul's first missionary journey because of the conversion of Gentiles, as I have argued elsewhere ["Paul's Mission to the Gentile World: Acts 13-19," *RevExp* 71 (Fall 1974): 488].

[77] Cf. Lane, *The Gospel according to Mark*, 274-75.

[78] R. Alan Culpepper, *John the Son of Zebedee: The Life of a Legend* (Columbia: University of South Carolina Press, 1994), 10.

[79] See ibid., 8-9.

[80] Carl Schneider, *"kathaireō,"* *TDNT* 3:411-12.

[81] Cited by Lane, *The Gospel according to Mark*, 578.

[82] Ibid.

[83] Brown, *The Death of the Messiah*, 2:1211-12.

[84] Lane, *The Gospel according to Mark*, 580.

[85] See Brown, *The Death of the Messiah*, 2:1218.

[86] Ibid.

[87] Jurgen Moltmann, *The Crucified God: The Cross of Christ as the Foundation and Criticism of Christian Theology* (New York: Harper & Row, 1974), 147; cf. p. 149.

[88] Ibid., 151.

[89] Ibid., 152.

[90] Jurgen Moltmann, "The 'Crucified God': A Trinitarian Theology of the Cross," *Int* 26 (1972): 295.

THE RESURRECTION OF JESUS

Mark 16:1-8

The resurrection of Jesus is attested in the New Testament in three forms of material: accounts of the discovery of the empty tomb, reports of appearances of Jesus, and accounts of appearances of Jesus. The earliest confessions affirm the resurrection (1 Cor 15:3-5; Phil 2:6-11; Col 1:15-20; 1 Tim 3:16). All four Gospels report that one or more women went to the tomb early on the first day of the week and found it empty. One or two angels interpret the empty tomb for the women by reciting the core of the early preaching: Jesus of Nazareth, who was crucified and buried, was raised and will appear to his disciples (Mark 16:6-7). The earliest reports of appearances of Jesus appear in Paul's letters (1 Cor 15:3-8), in the apostolic preaching in Acts (2:32; 3:15; 4:33; 10:41; 13:31; cf. 1:3, 22), and embedded in the Gospel accounts of the empty tomb (Mark 16:7; Matt 28:7) and accounts of appearances (Luke 24:34). The reports of appearances (Matt 28:16-20; Luke 24:13-53; John 20:11-29; 21:1-23; Acts 9:1-9; 22:6-11; 26:12-18) fill out the tradition. Generally, the tradition of the empty tomb, which of course is set in Jerusalem, involves women, while the appearances, which occur in Jerusalem, Emmaus, and Galilee, involve male apostles. There are exceptions, however, that may be the result of tying together the early strands of the tradition: the risen Lord appears to women (Matt 28:9-10; John 20:11-18), and disciples go to the empty tomb to check out the report of the women (Luke 24:12, 24; John 20:3-10). Still later in the development of the tradition one finds imaginative descriptions of the resurrection itself. [Descriptions of the Resurrection of Jesus]

In Mark the resurrection is God's answer to Jesus' cry of abandonment (15:34). The Gospel ends not with darkness over the land but with God's decisive act vindicating Jesus and vanquishing evil and death. Mark contains only the account of the discovery of the empty tomb with the embedded promise of an appearance to Peter and the other disciples. Whether the Gospel ended at v. 8, originally contained an account of the appearance to the disciples in Galilee, or was left unfinished is debated. What we can say is that the Gospel circulated in the mid-second century without an account of an appearance and that scribes who knew the tradition of the appearances added a shorter ending and a longer ending (16:9-20). See the notes on these endings below.

Descriptions of the Resurrection of Jesus

📖 "Suddenly, at the third hour of the day, there was darkness over the whole earth, and angels descended from heaven, and rising in the splendor of the living God they ascended together with him, and immediately it was light." (Codex Bobiensis [k] at the end of Mark 16:3)

"Now in the night in which the Lord's day dawned, when the soldiers, two by two in every watch, were keeping guard, there rang out a loud voice in heaven, and they saw the heavens opened and two men come down from there in a great brightness and draw nigh to the sepulchre. That stone which had laid against the entrance to the sepulchre started of itself to roll away to the side, and the sepulchre was opened, and both the young men entered in. When now those soldiers saw this, they awakened the centurion and the elders—for they also were there to assist at the watch. And whilst they were relating what they had seen, they saw again three men come out from the sepulchre, and two of them sustaining the other, and a cross following them, and the heads of the two reaching to heaven, but that of him who was led of them by the hand over-passing the heavens. And they heard a voice out of the heavens crying, 'Hast thou preached to them that sleep?' and from the cross there was heard the answer, 'Yea.'" (*Gospel of Peter* 35-42)

William L. Lane, *The Gospel according to Mark* (NICNT; Grand Rapids: Wm. B. Eerdmans, 1974), 582 n. 3; Wilhelm Schneemelcher, ed., *New Testament Apocrypha* (trans. and ed. R. McL Wilson; Louisville: Westminster John Knox, 1991), 1:224–25.

COMMENTARY

The Empty Tomb, 16:1-8

The activities of the women in 15:47 and 16:1 link the discovery of the empty tomb to the preceding account of the burial of Jesus, but the list of the women is redundant. Emphasis is placed on the witnesses to the event by naming them, and Mark may have drawn on a tradition that had circulated independently. There are subtle differences in the lists of the women (see The Lists of Women in Mark]) that probably indicate that they originated separately. Mary Magdalene appears in all three (15:40, 47; 16:1), Salome appears at the cross and the empty tomb [The Garden Tomb], and the third woman is listed as "Mary the mother of Joses" at the burial, "Mary the mother of James" at the empty tomb, and "Mary the Mother of James the younger and of Joses" at the cross .

When the Sabbath ended at sunset on Saturday, the women bought spices so that they could return to the tomb to anoint the body. The Passion Narrative in Mark begins with the anointing of Jesus before his death by a woman (14:8) and ends with the women's frustrated attempt to anoint his body after his burial. Their plan to anoint the body confirms that Joseph of Arimathea, probably acting out of religious duty, had supplied only the bare minimum required to fulfill the obligation to bury the dead. Myrrh was often used in burials. The purpose of the anointing was not to preserve the body but to reduce the odor of the decomposing body.

Verse 2 sets the time of the women's visit to the tomb by means of two references that stand in some tension to each other: "very early" and "when the sun had risen." Evans surmises that the text is corrupt and hence offers the translation "before the sun had risen."[1] Others suggest that Mark means that the women set out for the tomb while it was still dark but that the sun had risen by the time they arrived,[2] or that the difficulty was created by the insertion of the report that the sun had risen (the same construction occurs in 4:6) because it suggested a metaphorical reference to the resurrection of Jesus in light of Malachi 4:2 (Mal 3:20 LXX).[3] Mark often uses double references, however, and sometimes awkwardly (see 4:1).

The narrator's report of the women's trip to the tomb continues, but from a closer vantage point as he reports their conversation while they walked. They were asking who would roll the stone away from the tomb for them. The narrator offers no explanation for why they had not considered this question earlier. The explana-

The Garden Tomb

The Garden Tomb was proposed as the place of Jesus' burial by General Charles Gordon in 1883 because it was a quiet, reverential place north of the city, near both a garden and a hillside on which one can see the features of a skull in the rock formation. Ever since, pilgrims have found it a worshipful place. Archaeologists, however, have rejected Gordon's identification of the tomb because it is located in the middle of a burial ground that can be dated to Iron Age II (8th to 7th c. BC), and it conforms to the style of tombs of this period. None of the tombs in the area come from the second-temple period. See: John McRay, *Archaeology and the New Testament* (Grand Rapids: Baker, 1991), 206–17.

(Credit: Image courtesy of www.holylandphotos.org)

tion "for it was very large" is out of place at the end of v. 4 and would have produced a smoother reading at the end of v. 3. Both the wording of the question ("Who?") and the placement of the comment about the size of the stone are calculated to draw attention to the wonder of God's action. Who? God—even before the women worried about the stone—and the wonder of the event is telegraphed first by the narrator's comment on its size. A great wonder has occurred. The reference to rolling away the stone corresponds to the description of rolling the stone against the door of the tomb in 15:46, and both suggest a horizontal tomb cut in the wall of the quarry (see above the comment on 15:46). The verb *theōrein* is used in Mark for beholding spectacles and significant events (3:11; 5:15, 38; 12:41), and it is used in each of the three scenes where the women appear (at the cross, 15:40; at the burial, 15:47; and at the empty tomb, 16:4).

Verse 5 introduces the interpreting angel inside the tomb. The entrance to a tomb was usually fairly small. The other Gospels say that those who entered or looked into the tomb had to stoop to do so (Luke 24:12; John 20:5). Inside they saw a figure that Mark describes in three

The Angel at the Tomb

Carracci Annibale (1560–1609). *The Three Marys at the Tomb*. Hermitage, St. Petersburg, Russia. (Credit: Scala / Art Resource, NY)

ways: (1) by referring to him as a "young man" (*neaniskos*), (2) by his position, "sitting on the right side," and (3) by his dress, "a white robe." The description of the young man is sufficiently ambiguous that two questions arise: Is he an angel or a human being? And is there any relationship between this young man and the mysterious young man in the garden who fled leaving his linen garment behind (14:51)? The note that he was on the right side (presumably the right side of where the body had lain) recalls Jesus' promise to the high priest that he would see "the Son of Man seated on the right hand of the Power" (14:62; Ps 110:1), and may suggest that Jesus' prophecy would indeed be fulfilled. This reading may be too subtle, however, and the position may simply be the place of honor or authority (see also 10:40).[4] Mark's comment that the young man was wearing a white robe is remarkably restrained. Earlier Mark described the appearance of the transfigured Jesus' clothing as "dazzling white, such as no one (lit., no fuller) on earth could bleach them" (9:3), and Matthew, who often embellishes the miraculous, says, "His appearance was like lightning, and his clothing white as snow" (Matt 28:3). Angels are described as young men elsewhere (2 Macc 3:26; Josephus, *Ant.* 5.277), and white was often the color associated with heavenly figures (Rev 7:9, 13; cf. 10:1). These three descriptions, taken with the revelatory speech that follows, signal that the mysterious figure is an angel. Luke says there were two men in dazzling clothes (Luke 24:4), Matthew says he was an angel (Matt 28:2), and John says there were two angels (John 20:12).

The question of the relationship between the angel at the tomb and the young man in the garden (14:51) is more difficult. Francis Moloney offers a balanced perspective, judging that "The verbal links are too many, and the passages follow one another too closely within the story to be irrelevant."[5] Aside from the possible links between the young man in the garden and the figure inside the tomb, the appearance of the young man in the garden is mysterious in itself (see the comment on 14:51). He had on only a linen garment (*sindona*), which could have been a burial garment, while the angel at the tomb wore a white robe (*stolēn leukēn*). The two descriptions do not correspond, but the references to what each was wearing invites comparison of the two. There is no basis for finding baptismal symbolism here, but because the young man in the garden apparently symbolizes the failure of the disciples, the description of the angel at the tomb as a "young man" may signal that there is a future for the failed disciples because of the resurrection of Jesus. The symbolism is nevertheless secondary to the primary role of the angel as the heavenly interpreter of the empty tomb.[6] Without the angel's interpretation, the empty tomb would have remained merely a mystery open to the allegation that the disciples had stolen the body (Matt 28:11-15).

The women were "alarmed" (*exethambēthēsan*), which can also mean "amazed" or "distressed" (9:15; 14:33). The compound verb is intensive, and Moloney suggests it literally means "amazed out of themselves."[7] The response is the typical response of human beings at the appearance of angels (Judg 6:22-23; 13:22; Luke 1:12, 29-39).

The words of the angel in the tomb are a summary of the early Christian preaching. Peter's Pentecost sermon contains the following references to the tomb and Jesus' resurrection: "this man . . . you crucified and killed by the hands of those outside the law. But God raised him up" (Acts 2:23-24); "I may say to you confidently of our ancestor David that he both died and was buried, and his tomb is with us to this day [the implication is that although David's body lay in the tomb, as they all knew, Jesus' body did not]" (Acts 2:29); and "This Jesus God raised up, and of that all of us are witnesses" (Acts 2:32). Similarly, the early tradition that Paul recites in 1 Corinthians 15:3-5 summarizes the kerygma, the content of the Christian gospel, in four balanced clauses:

a. "that Christ died for our sins in accordance with the scriptures,"
b. "that he was buried,"
c. "that he was raised on the third day in accordance with the scriptures, and"
d. "that he appeared to Cephas, then to the twelve."

The parallel to the words of the angel is striking:

a. "you are looking for Jesus of Nazareth, who was crucified."
c. "He has been raised; he is not here."
b. "Look, there is the place they laid him."
d. "But go, tell his disciples and Peter that he is going ahead of you to Galilee; there you will see him."

Mark therefore caps his account of "the beginning of the gospel of Jesus Christ, Son of God" (1:1) by linking the preaching of the gospel to the historical datum of the empty tomb and the revelatory words of the interpreting angel.

The angel declares knowingly that the women were "seeking" Jesus. In Mark this verb (*zēteō*) typically carries a derogatory sense (1:37; 3:32; 8:11-12; 11:18; 12:12; 14:1, 11, 55).[8] They seek Jesus' body, not knowing that he has already been raised. Jesus is identified specifically as "the Nazarene" (see the commentary on 1:24; 10:47; 14:67). The Nazarene was the descendant of David who would build the temple. Hence, the reference here may imply fulfillment of the promise of "the temple not made with hands."[9] The reference to the crucifixion, "who was crucified," is superfluous, but it performs the important function of recalling the Passion Narrative and the saving significance of Jesus' death. The NRSV rightly translates the climactic announcement of the resurrection in the passive—not "he is risen," but "he has been raised." The resurrection is God's action, God's decisive victory over the power of evil that tested Jesus, and God's response to Jesus' cry of abandonment, "My God, My God, why have you forsaken me?" (15:34). The comment "he is not here" should not be exaggerated into a statement of the absence of God; it merely emphasizes the significance of the empty tomb. The women themselves could examine the place where they had seen Joseph lay the body of Jesus and verify that indeed he was not there. It has been suggested that these words were later recalled in ceremonial visits to the tomb where Jesus had been buried.

The gospel story does not end at the empty tomb, however. The proclamation of the resurrection does not rest on the physical evidence of the tomb or even the revelatory words of the angel but on personal encounters with the risen Lord. The strong adversative conjunction ("but," *alla*) is important. The women cannot remain at the tomb. Even though the testimony of women was not legally admissible (*m. Rosh Ha-Shanah* 1.8; *m. Shebuoth* 4.1; Josephus, *Ant.* 4.219), the women were charged to carry the news of the resurrection to the disciples. Peter is singled out because of his denials of Jesus in the courtyard. As Jesus had told the disciples earlier, he would go ahead of them to Galilee (see the commentary on 14:28), and they would see him there. Galilee was the place of Jesus' announcement of the kingdom, the place where the disciples had witnessed his teaching, the sea crossings, the demon exorcisms, and the meals with Jews and Gentiles alike. It is not insignificant therefore that (in Mark) this would be the place where the disciples would meet the risen Lord.

The earliest manuscripts of the Gospel end with v. 8. The question naturally arises as to whether the evangelist could have actually ended the Gospel at this point, whether he intended to write more but did not, or whether the original ending (and perhaps the beginning, see the commentary on 1:1) of the Gospel is lost.

The report of the angel's words ends with v. 7, and the narrator reports the failure of the women to carry out their commission. The verb "to flee" (*pheugō*) is used elsewhere in Mark in relation to Jesus' miracles (5:14), eschatological urgency (13:14), and the failure of the disciples (14:50, 52), and all three contexts are relevant here. The women flee from the tomb in fear because of what they had witnessed there, but their flight and subsequent silence convey that they no less than Jesus' disciples have moved from fear to failure. The verse is a couplet, each part of which contains a statement and an explanation:

1. a. "So they went out and fled from the tomb,
   b. "for terror and amazement had seized them;"
2. a. "and they said nothing to anyone,
   b. "for they were afraid."

Both explanatory statements attribute the women's actions to fear. Their fear is described first with two words that have not been used earlier in this scene: "terror" (*tromos*) and "amazement" (*ekstasis*, see 5:42; Ps 55:4-5), and in the final statement with the verb "they were afraid" (*phobeomai*). The latter is used throughout Mark to describe the failure of the disciples and others to grasp the significance of Jesus' mighty acts (4:41; 5:15, 33, 36; 6:50; 9:32; 10:32; 11:18). Like the disciples, therefore, the women fail in their commission. The theme of human failure is therefore complete. The religious authorities, Jesus' hometown, the disciples, the crowds, the Roman authorities, and even the women who accompanied Jesus to Jerusalem failed him. On the other hand, God's promises have been fulfilled. The fulfillment of the Scriptures and the words of Jesus, the voice from heaven, the phenomena that accompanied Jesus' death, and finally God's resurrection of Jesus are all signs of God's unfailing trustworthiness. There is no doubt that the promised meeting in Galilee will take place, although it is uncertain whether the tradition Mark knew contained a mountaintop appearance as in Matthew 28:16-20 or a lakeside appearance as in John 21.

Much has been made of the grammatical construction of the last words in v. 8. The word "for" (*gar*) is postpositive, meaning that it never comes first in a clause, so the word order in Greek is "they were afraid, for," which has led to continuing debate as to whether it is plausible that Mark could have intended this to be the end of the Gospel. Beyond the grammatical issue stand the more substantive questions of the meaning of this ending and possible clues that Mark actually composed a further ending. William Lane contends that ending the Gospel with v. 8 dramatically underscores that "'the gospel of Jesus the Messiah' (Ch. 1:1) is an event beyond human comprehension and therefore awesome and frightening."[10] Francis Moloney observes that "there is something profoundly Pauline in what

Mark is trying to do as he takes away all initiative from human beings and places it with God."[11] Paul Danove, more trenchantly, argues that v. 8 is the intended ending and that it demands a literal interpretation (the message of the empty tomb was not delivered), which establishes a paradox that can only be resolved in the life of the reader.[12] On the other hand, Craig Evans and Ben Witherington are persuaded by Robert Gundry's arguments that Mark actually wrote more than our earliest manuscripts contain: (1) Mark consistently reports the fulfillment of Jesus' predictions; (2) if v. 8 reports disobedience of the angel's command, Mark would have used an adversative conjunction ("but") rather than "and"; (3) the parallel accounts in Matthew and Luke report the actions of the women after they left the tomb, which suggests that Mark's account did too; (4) parallels in the appearance accounts in Matthew and Luke suggest that they drew from a common source—Mark; (5) elsewhere Mark begins rather than ends scenes with a reference to fear; (6) only six out of sixty-six of Mark's "for" clauses conclude pericopae; and (7) the centrality of the resurrection in the early Christian preaching makes it probable that Mark included a resurrection appearance.[13]

Apart from the discovery of a very early manuscript of Mark that contains a previously unknown ending, the ending of Mark will remain one of the great mysteries of the New Testament. Internal clues give the reader a general idea of what Mark would have written, if indeed he wrote (or intended to write) more. Matthew may have drawn on Mark for the report that as the women fled from the tomb Jesus met them and said, "Do not be afraid; go and tell my brothers to go to Galilee; there they will see me" (Matt 28:10). The women found the disciples, hiding in fear, told them what they had seen, and instructed them to go to Galilee. There the risen Lord appeared to Peter and the others, either on a mountain (Matt 28:16-20) or at the Sea of Galilee (John 21). Since the angel's command mentioned Peter specifically, Mark may have included an account of a pastoral charge to Peter (similar to John 21:15-17) and a command to all the disciples to preach the good news to all nations (13:10) and be faithful in the midst of the trials they would experience (13:9-13). Whether Mark wrote such an ending, we may never know.[14] Nevertheless, there are enough clues in the Gospel to allow us to reconstruct this much of its future story. The rest is not a matter of history but of the reader's response, either in fear or in faith.

The Later Endings of Mark

So startling is the ending of Mark at v. 8 that early scribes added both a "shorter ending" and a "longer ending" to bring the Gospel to a more satisfactory conclusion. Only four manuscripts conclude with v. 8:

Codex Sinaiticus (א), Codex Vaticanus (B), and minuscules 304 and 2386. The paucity of manuscripts that end at 16:8, therefore, serves as further testimony to the prevalence of the feeling that the Gospel could not end at that point. Once the longer and shorter endings were available, later scribes felt obliged to include one or both of them. Nevertheless, Eusebius (writing in the fourth century) reports that "accurate" copies of Mark ended at v. 8, and both Eusebius and Jerome comment that the longer ending of the Gospel is missing from "almost all manuscripts."[15]

A Note on the Shorter Ending

The shorter ending was probably composed in the second century specifically to serve as the conclusion for the Gospel, though it is not attested until the fourth century. The placement of the shorter ending before the longer ending in manuscripts up to the thirteenth century also argues for an early date for it. The only manuscript that has only the shorter ending following v. 8 is Codex Bobbiensis (*k*), which was copied in the fourth or fifth century from a much earlier text. Codex Bobbiensis also omits v. 8b, thereby removing the problem of the women's silence. In addition to its weak manuscript support, its vocabulary and rhetorical tone ("the sacred and imperishable proclamation of eternal salvation") confirm that it was not written by the evangelist. The scribe, moreover, apparently had no knowledge of the longer ending.

Portrait of Mark the Evangelist

The purple *Codex Rossanensis*, a 6th c. manuscript on purple parchment, contains the Gospel of Matthew and almost the entire Gospel of Mark. Portrait of evangelist Mark, shown writing in the posture of a scribe. The figure of Sophia, wisdom, stands in front of Mark. Origin perhaps Aleppo, Syria. Biblioteca Arcivescovile, Rossano, Italy. (Credit: Erich Lessing / Art Resource, NY)

A Note on the Longer Ending, vv. 9-20

The longer ending is a compilation of traditions related to the appearances of the risen Lord drawn from the other Gospels and Acts. Unlike the shorter ending, it does not seem to have been written to serve as the ending of Mark. Verse 9 provides the composition with an introduction that makes no reference to the women, the discovery of the empty tomb, the charge to tell Peter and the other disciples, or the women's silence. Instead, Mary Magdalene is introduced as the one from whom Jesus had cast out seven demons (Luke 8:2). It seems clear, therefore, that the longer ending served other functions before it was added to Mark, and it has been suggested that it was a catechetical summary of the grounds for belief in Jesus' resurrection[16] or encouragement for early missionaries.[17]

The theme of the composition is the overcoming of doubt. The disciples did not believe Mary Magdalene's report that she had seen the risen Lord (16:11). Neither did they believe the two who met the Lord while walking in the country (an allusion to the appearance to the two on the road to Emmaus, Luke 25:13-35). Therefore, when the Lord appeared to the Eleven while they were at table (perhaps an echo of Luke 24:36-43), he rebuked them for their lack of faith (16:14). A commissioning follows, along with the command to baptize (a summary of Matt 28:16-20). Signs will certify the faith of those who believe: casting out demons, speaking in tongues, picking up snakes, drinking poison without being hurt, and healing the sick (16:17-18). A reference to the ascension and the later work of the apostles concludes the longer ending. [Outline of the Longer Ending]

In addition to the evidence that the longer ending is a later summary of material contained elsewhere in the Gospels and Acts, its language and style are not those of the evangelist. Most commentators assign the composition of the longer ending to the middle of the second century.[18] The earliest attestation for the longer ending comes from Irenaeus (*Against Heresies* 3.10.6) and Tatian (based on the Arabic version of his *Diatessaron*).[19] In 1546 the Council of Trent declared that the longer ending was part of the Catholic canon of sacred Scriptures.

A Note on the Freer Logion

The discovery of a fifth-century manuscript of the Gospels in Egypt in 1906 (Codex W) added a further gloss to the Gospel of Mark. [The Freer Logion] A local tradition of the disciples' response to Jesus' rebuke of their unbelief in follows v. 14 of the longer ending. It is named the "Freer Logion" for the first owner of the manuscript, which is preserved in the Freer Museum in Washington. Part of the Freer Logion was already known from a Latin citation in the writings of Jerome (*Dialogue against the Pelagians* 2.15). The saying, while clearly a later gloss, pre-

---

Outline of the Longer Ending

V. 11 Lack of belief (cf. Luke 24:11)
V. 12 Two on the road (cf. Luke 24:13-35)
V. 14 Reproach for unbelief (cf. John 20:19, 26)
V. 15 Great Commission (cf. Matt 28:19)
V. 16 Salvation/judgment (cf. John 3:18, 36)
V. 17 Speaking in tongues (cf. Acts 2:4; 10:46)
V. 18 Serpents and poison (cf. Acts 28:3-5)
V. 19 Ascension (cf. Luke 24:51; Acts 1:2, 9)
V. 20 General summary of Acts

Craig A. Evans, *Mark 8:27–16:20* (WBC 34B; Nashville: Thomas Nelson, 2001), 546.

The Freer Logion

[Inserted between 16:14 and 16:15]
"And they excused themselves with the words, 'This aeon (age) of lawlessness and unbelief is under Satan, who through the unclean spirits does not allow the true power of God to be comprehended. Therefore,' they said to Christ, 'reveal your righteousness now.' And Christ replied to them, 'The measure of the years of Satan's power is filled up. But other fearful things draw near, also (for those) for whom I, because they have sinned, was delivered to death, that they might turn back to the truth and sin no more in order to inherit the spiritual and imperishable glory of righteousness (preserved) in heaven."

Wilhelm Schneemelcher, ed., *New Testament Apocrypha* (trans. R. McL. Wilson; Louisville: Westminster John Knox, 1991), 1:248–49.

serves elements of an early eschatology that emphasized the requirement of repentance as a condition for the blessings of the age of the Messiah and established a periodization of history that foresaw "other terrible things" before the arrival of the "days of the Messiah." William Lane called attention to the parallels in thought between the Freer Logion and Acts 3:19-21.[20]

CONNECTIONS

"Eternity as a Sunrise"

Is it reasonable to hope for life beyond death? This question fascinated my father, Hugo H. Culpepper, and engaged his reflection and study through much of his adult life. He was drawn to the writings of the Spanish philosopher Miguel de Unamuno for this reason, and wrote his dissertation on Unamuno. The following is an excerpt from one of my father's sermons, "Eternity as a Sunrise," that gathers up much of his reflection on death and the hope of eternal life:

Job knew what it was to feel the weight of this fear of death. In the fourteenth chapter of the book of Job, he was speaking for all mankind. He depicted man's mortality. One of the tragic dimensions of life is its brevity. Even the longest life is all too brief. The religious rites and beliefs in the ancient Near East cultivated the hope of a resurrection after the grave. But Job spoke bluntly against these attractive illusions, as he saw them. "Man lies down and rises not again," he said. Emil Brunner listed, as one of the axioms of modern man, the statement, "If you are dead, then you *are* dead." Men today have an idea that they know what kind of world they are living in. Death seems to them on the face of it to be fairly conclusive.

But Job was speaking out of the context of the Hebrew religion. The popular Hebrew notion of the so-called "life" after death was that it goes on as being, but it amounts to no more than a dreary sort of not-being. It has been said that the pessimism of the author of Job is more profound than that of any other of the writers of Israel, profounder even than that of Ecclesiastes; for in Job life seems "incurably evil, unbearably sad, atrociously tragic."

The determination with which Job rejects the hope of life after death betrays the fascination that such beliefs exercise on his mind. He rejects them, but he cannot help dwelling upon them a little longer. He gropes toward some assurance of an afterlife, then he rises from the level of meditation to that of warm and intimate dialogue. "O that thou . . . wouldst . . . remember me!" This call from person to person enables him to restate his wildly imaginative hope in the form of a question, "If a man die, shall he live again?" This is the cry of anguish from the heart of man, "If a man die, shall he live again?" With all the stored-up yearning of his soul, he reaches out his hands for what his mind has forbidden him. Is the wish father to the thought, or is God father to the wish?

We are reminded of the life-long struggle of Miguel de Unamuno, president of the University of Salamanca at the early age of thirty-seven. The purpose of his major work, *The Tragic Sense of Life*, was to draw his reader's attention to "*the* problem." At the very close of the book, he states this purpose in an indirect manner, which at the same time strikingly suggests that usually people try to evade it, when he says, "I took up my pen to distract you for a while from your distractions." In other words, most of what we do in life, he thought, was to distract us from remembering our mortality. One does not read long in *The Tragic Sense of Life* before the centrality of the problem becomes emphatic. He says, "I mean the only real vital problem, the problem that strikes at the very root of our being, is the problem of our individual and personal destiny, of the immortality of the soul." As the only "real" problem, it caused Unamuno anguish in his deepest being. He wrote, "The problem of the duration of my soul, of my own soul, tortures me." Death and the uncertainty of any life beyond were ever present with him. Again he said, "This thought that I must die and the enigma of what will come after death is the very palpitation of my consciousness." It was a deep conviction with him that if his soul was not immortal, and the souls of all the rest of men and even everything, then nothing is worthwhile or worth the effort. Life's value is utterly dependent on immortality, he believed. Again he wrote, "If consciousness is, as some inhuman thinker has said, nothing more than a flash of light between two extremities of darkness, then there is nothing more execrable than existence."

Unamuno learned eighteen languages to read philosophy and the religious literature of the world in the original languages as he quested for some sure answer to his problem. The more he read, the more he became convinced that it is not reasonable to expect to live on beyond death. But the more his mind became convinced of this, the more his heart cried out that there must be life beyond death, because he so deeply longed for it to be so. There resulted a tension between mind and heart which he called the tragic sense of life. By this tension he came to live, as though it were his sustaining faith. At least it kept him from despair, he believed. His courage to face up fully to what he called the only real question in our existence was admirable. He challenged us to have the courage to look life and death squarely in the face! He believed in the value of the agony of soul struggle it caused him. His final legacy to us would be, "May God deny you peace, but give you glory!"

The tragedy of his life is that he seems never to have found the answer to his only real problem—and Job's: "If a man die, shall he live again?"

It was the privilege of a humble woman, who lived with her sister and brother in a village near Jerusalem, to hear the answer to this ultimate question from the lips of the Lord of life and death. Jesus said to Martha, "I am the resurrection and the life. The one believing in me, even if he should die, shall live; and everyone living and believing in me shall never die."

. . . Sometimes we give our most honest answers to this question in attitudes expressed when we are caught off-guard. On one occasion I was a guest in the home of an uncle. We were seated at the table. Someone mentioned having read of the death of a well-known pastor whom I had known as a truly spiritual minded man. I made the comment, "Death for him must have been a glorious experience. I imagine it was like walking through that door into the immediate presence of the Lord whom he knew so well and loved so much." My uncle was somewhat startled. "Do you really believe that?" he asked. His reaction was a surprise to me. All his life he had been an active church member, a Sunday School teacher, and a deacon. I thought to myself then, "How strange that what he professes to believe seems not to make a real difference." Since then I have lived longer and can empathize more fully with my uncle. But I still have a conviction that death was a glorious experience for my friend.

It was not the intention of Jesus that Martha should come to have a morbid preoccupation with death. Neither is this his desire for us. He came that we might have *life* and have it abundantly! The point of his conversation with Martha was *not* to emphasize death, but rather to emphasize eternal life and the consequent insignificance of death for those believing in him. As close as Martha and her brother and sister had been to Jesus in their friendship, only now did she seem to move *from* assent to the teaching of the Pharisees *to* a personal trust as the basis of an eternal quality of life in the present. And even yet, she relied upon the concepts of her Jewish religion to express this trust. Her answer to Jesus was, "Yes, Lord; I have believed and keep on believing that *you* are the Christ (the Messiah), the Son of God, the one coming into the world." But she was well on her way. She was growing in grace and the knowledge of God.

So it is with us. We do not begin the Christian pilgrimage as fully mature disciples. We are learners. We must go to school in God's school of life. We catch visions of inspired hope, but then at times we are lost in the darkness for a while. As Robert Browning wrote in "Bishop Blougram's Apology":

Just when we are safest, there's a sunset touch,
A fancy from a flower-bell, someone's death,
A chorus-ending from Euripides,—
And that's enough for fifty hopes and fears
As old and new at once as nature's self,
To rap and knock and enter in our soul.

And so we must turn our eyes once again to the Lord and look steadfastly enough to see life in the context of eternity. But we *can* grow in grace and knowledge of God to the point that we can have a steady assurance, a clarity of vision, an expectant hope. Life can become an exciting experience of living each day fully free, captive neither to the past nor the future. Then God can use us more fully in serving others and in bringing them to know him. We awake to welcome each day as a bright new challenge for creative living. We live on the tiptoes of expectancy![21]

[Grünewald's *Resurrection*]

"Go to Galilee; There You Will See Him"

A person cannot live in the cemetery, the place of the dead. The figure who does so in Mark is the Gerasene demoniac (5:3-5). It is natural that we want to visit the final resting place of our loved ones, but as the angel at the tomb said, they are not there. Their memory and influence continues on most powerfully in the work they gave their lives to and in the homes where they lived. That is where we meet them and see the fruit of their lives. It is appropriate, therefore, that the angel at the tomb sent the women to tell the disciples to "go to Galilee; there you will see him" (16:7). Galilee was the place of Jesus' ministry, where he taught the crowds, cast out demons, prayed alone, healed the sick,

---

Grünewald's *Resurrection*

Mathis Grünewald's (c. 1470/80–1528) masterpiece was his depiction of the crucifixion and resurrection of Jesus for the Isenheim Altarpiece, which he painted for the hospital church of the Anthonite Abbey at Isenheim during one of the plagues (about 1515). The *Crucifixion* shows Jesus' wrenching agony, his body mangled, as he died on the cross, reminding the plague victims that Jesus too had suffered terribly before he conquered death. In the *Resurrection* Grünewald allows the risen Lord to display the nail and spear wounds, but the lacerations that cover his body in the *Crucifixion* are gone, declaring to those who suffered there that the marks of disease and sin would be removed from them also. The *Resurrection* makes use of dramatic color, movement, and expressive distortion. Ironically, Grünewald's career declined toward the end of his life, and he was dismissed from his court position because of his Protestant sympathies during the Peasant's War. Ultimately he fled to Halle, where he died of the plague.

Ian Chilvers, ed., *The Concise Oxford Dictionary of Art and Artists* (Oxford: Oxford University Press, 1990), 201–02.

Mathias Gruenewald (1455–1528). *Resurrection*, from the Isenheim Altarpiece, ca. 1515. Musee d'Unterlinden, Colmar, France. (Credit: Erich Lessing / Art Resource, NY)

called disciples, and fed multitudes. Galilee was the place where Jesus crossed the boundaries between "clean" and "unclean," and the symbolic boundaries between Jew and Gentile and male and female. Galilee was the place where, through all these activities, Jesus announced the coming of the kingdom of God (1:15). The angelic commission therefore continues, at least figuratively, to be an invitation for every reader of the Gospel: Go to Galilee, continue the work of the kingdom that Jesus left unfinished, and there you will see him. He is not in the tomb. You will find him still among the suffering, needy, oppressed, and estranged in Galilee, with all who share their bread, give a cup of water, receive children, protect women, care for widows, and extend grace and hope for all. "Go to Galilee; there you will see him."

A Future Beyond Faith

The theme of the failure of the disciples is resolved by the angel's charge to the women at the tomb: "Go, tell his disciples and Peter . . ." (16:7). Throughout the commentary we have traced the depressing theme of the disciples' failure that is epitomized by Peter, who denied Jesus three times. Regardless of how often or how miserably the disciples failed, however, Jesus always called them back to discipleship. There was always a future for them, and Jesus always moved to open their eyes and set them again on the journey with him.[22] That is the hope to which the gospel calls us all, regardless of how often we have failed in the past.

Fear or Faith?

The reader is shocked. How could the women, who had witnessed the death of Jesus and who had seen the empty tomb and heard the words of the angel, go and not tell anyone? Mark was a skillful writer. Perhaps shock and surprise were the reactions he intended for the church to have, for now it knew everything the women knew. So the question comes home to haunt those who hear Mark's Gospel. How could they, how can we, hear these words, go, and tell no one?

NOTES

[1] Craig A. Evans, *Mark 8:27–16:20* (WBC 34B; Nashville: Thomas Nelson, 2001), 529, 534.

[2] John Painter, *Mark's Gospel* (London: Routledge, 1997), 210.

[3] Hugh Anderson, *The Gospel of Mark* (NCB; London: Oliphants, 1976), 354.

[4] Evans, *Mark 8:27–16:20*, 536.

[5] Francis J. Moloney, *The Gospel of Mark* (Peabody MA: Hendrickson, 2002), 345.

[6] Raymond E. Brown, *The Death of the Messiah* (New York: Doubleday, 1994), 1:299-304.

[7] Ibid., 344.

[8] William L. Lane, *The Gospel according to Mark* (NICNT; Grand Rapids: Wm. B. Eerdmans, 1974), 588 n. 16; Moloney, *The Gospel of Mark*, 346 n. 29.

[9] See the commentary on 14:58; Mary L. Coloe, *God Dwells with Us: Temple Symbolism in the Fourth Gospel* (Collegeville: Liturgical Press, 2001), 171; see also Edwin K. Broadhead, *Naming Jesus: Titular Christology in the Gospel of Mark* (JSNTSup 175; Sheffield: Sheffield Academic Press, 1999), 31-42.

[10] Lane, *The Gospel according to Mark*, 592.

[11] Moloney, *The Gospel of Mark*, 351.

[12] Paul L. Danove, *The End of Mark's Story: A Methodological Study* (BIS 3; Leiden: E. J. Brill, 1993), 1.

[13] Robert H. Gundry, *Mark: A Commentary on His Apology for the Cross* (Grand Rapids: Wm. B. Eerdmans, 1993), 1009-12; Evans, *Mark 8:27–16:20*, 539; Ben Witherington III, *The Gospel of Mark: A Socio-Rhetorical Commentary* (Grand Rapids: Wm. B. Eerdmans, 2001), 416-18.

[14] Evan Powell, *The Unfinished Gospel* (Westlake Village CA: Symposium Books, 1994), 121-25, actually argues that John 21 is the lost ending of Mark.

[15] Lane, *The Gospel of Mark*, 601, citing Eusebius, *Quaestiones ad Marinum* 1 [MPG XXII, 937] and Jerome, Epistle CXX.3, *ad Hedibiam* [MPL XXII, 987].

[16] Oxford Annotated NRSV marginal notes.

[17] J. A. Kelhoffer, *Miracle and Mission: The Authentication of Missionaries and Their Message in the Longer Ending of Mark* (WUNT 2, Reihe 112; Tübingen: J. C. B. Mohr, 2000).

[18] William R. Farmer, *The Last Twelve Verses of Mark* (SNTSMS 25; Cambridge: Cambridge University Press, 1974), argues that it is authentically Markan. This thesis supports his view of the priority of Matthew and Mark's status as a compiler of material from Matthew and Luke.

[19] Lane, *The Gospel of Mark*, 604-605.

[20] Ibid., 610-11.

[21] R. Alan Culpepper, *Eternity as a Sunrise: The Life of Hugo H. Culpepper* (Macon GA: Mercer University Press, 2002), 294-95, 298-99.

[22] Eduard Schweizer, *The Good News according to Mark* (trans. Donald H. Madvig; Atlanta: John Knox Press, 1970), 373.

BIBLIOGRAPHY

Selected Commentaries on Mark

Anderson, Hugh. *The Gospel of Mark*. New Century Bible. Greenwood SC: Attic Press, 1976.

Broadhead, Edwin K. *Mark*. Sheffield: Sheffield Academic Press, 2001.

Cranfield, C. E. B. *The Gospel according to Saint Mark*. The Cambridge Greek Testament Commentary. Cambridge: Cambridge University Press, 1959.

Danove, Paul L. *The End of Mark's Story: A Methodological Study*. Biblical Interpretation Series, vol. 3. Leiden: E. J. Brill, 1993.

Donahue, John R., and Daniel J. Harrington. *The Gospel of Mark*. Sacra Pagina. Collegeville MN: The Liturgical Press, 2002.

Dowd, Sharyn. *Reading Mark: A Literary and Theological Commentary on the Second Gospel*. Macon GA: Smyth & Helwys, 2000.

Edwards, James R. *The Gospel according to Mark*. The Pillar New Testament Commentary. Grand Rapids: Wm. B. Eerdmans, 2002.

Evans, Craig A. *Mark 8:27–16:20*. Word Biblical Commentary 34B. Nashville: Thomas Nelson, 2001.

France, R. T. *The Gospel of Mark: A Commentary on the Greek Text*. The New International Greek Testament Commentary. Grand Rapids: Wm. B. Eerdmans, 2002.

Guelich, Robert A. *Mark 1–8:26*. Word Biblical Commentary 34A. Dallas: Word, 1989.

Gundry, Robert H. *Mark: A Commentary on His Apology for the Cross*. Grand Rapids: Wm. B. Eerdmans, 1993.

Hooker, Morna D. *The Gospel according to St. Mark*. London: A. & C. Black, 1991.

Howcroft, Kenneth G. *The Gospel of Mark*. Epworth Commentaries. London: SCM Press, 2003.

Juel, Donald H. *The Gospel of Mark*. Nashville: Abingdon Press, 1999.

Lane, William L. *The Gospel according to Mark*. The New International Commentary on the New Testament. Grand Rapids: Wm. B. Eerdmans, 1974.

LaVerdiere, Eugene. *The Beginning of the Gospel: Introducing the Gospel according to Mark*. 2 volumes. Collegeville: Liturgical Press, 1999.

Malina, Bruce J., and Richard L. Rohrbaugh. *Social-Science Commentary on the Synoptic Gospels*. Minneapolis: Fortress, 1992.

Marcus, Joel. *Mark 1–8*. Anchor Bible 27. New York: Doubleday, 2000.

Moloney, Francis J. *The Gospel of Mark*. Peabody MA: Hendrickson, 2002.

Nineham, D. E. *The Gospel of Saint Mark*. Baltimore: Penguin Books, 1963.

Painter, John. *Mark's Gospel: Worlds in Conflict*. New Testament Readings. London and New York: Routledge, 1997.

Perkins, Pheme. "The Gospel of Mark." In *The New Interpreter's Bible*. Volume 8. Nashville: Abingdon, 1995.

Schweizer, Eduard. *The Good News according to Mark*. Translated by Donald H. Madvig. Atlanta: John Knox Press, 1970.

Taylor, Vincent. *The Gospel according to St. Mark*. London: Macmillan, 1952.

Van Iersel, Bas M. F. *Mark: A Reader-Response Commentary*. Translated by W. H. Bisscheroux. Journal for the Study of the New Testament: Supplement Series 164. Sheffield: Sheffield Academic Press, 1998.

Williamson, Lamar, Jr. *Mark*. Interpretation. Atlanta: John Knox, 1983.

Witherington, Ben, III. *The Gospel of Mark: A Socio-Rhetorical Commentary*. Grand Rapids, Wm. B. Eerdmans, 2001.

Monographs and Other Resources

Anderson, Janice Capel, and Stephen D. Moore, editors. *Mark & Method: New Approaches in Biblical Studies*. Minneapolis: Fortress Press, 1992.

Black, C. Clifton. *Mark: Images of an Apostolic Interpreter*. Columbia: University of South Carolina Press, 1994.

Blount, Brian K., and Gary W. Charles. *Preaching Mark in Two Voices*. Louisville: Westminster John Knox, 2002.

Bolt, Peter G. *Jesus' Defeat of Death: Persuading Mark's Early Readers*. Society for New Testament Studies Monograph Series 125. Cambridge: Cambridge University Press, 2004.

Crossley, James G. *The Date of Mark's Gospel*. Journal for the Study of the New Testament: Supplement Series 266. London: T. & T. Clark International, 2004.

Croy, N. Clayton. *The Mutilation of Mark's Gospel*. Nashville: Abingdon, 2003.

Danove, Paul L. *The Rhetoric of Characterization of God, Jesus, and Jesus' Disciples in the Gospel of Mark*. Journal for the Study of the New Testament: Supplement Series 290. London: T. & T. Clark, 2005.

Gaventa, Beverly Roberts, and Patrick D. Miller. *The Ending of Mark and the Ends of God: Essays in Memory of Donald Harrisville Juel*. Louisville: Westminster John Knox Press, 2005.

Harrington, Daniel J. *What Are They Saying about Mark?* New York: Paulist Press, 2004.

Hatina, Thomas R. *In Search of a Context: The Function of Scripture in Mark's Narrative*. Journal for the Study of the New Testament: Supplement Series 232. London: Sheffield Academic Press, 2002.

Horsley, Richard A. *Hearing the Whole Story: The Politics of Plot in Mark's Gospel*. Louisville: Westminster John Knox Press, 2001.

Incigneri, Brian J. *The Gospel to the Romans: The Setting and Rhetoric of Mark's Gospel*. Leiden: E. J. Brill, 2003.

Iverson, Kelly R. *Gentiles in the Gospel of Mark*. Library of New Testament Studies, 339. London: T. & T. Clark, 2007.

Kaminouchi, Alberto de Mingo. *But It Is Not So among You: Echoes of Power in Mark 10:32-45*. Journal for the Study of the New Testament: Supplement Series 249. London: T. & T. Clark, 2003.

Levine, Amy-Jill, with Marianne Blickenstaff, editors. *A Feminist Companion to Mark*. Sheffield: Sheffield Academic Press, 2001.

MacDonald, Dennis R. *The Homeric Epics and the Gospel of Mark*. New Haven: Yale University Press, 2000.

Maloney, Elliott C. *Jesus' Urgent Message for Today: The Kingdom of God in Mark's Gospel*. New York: Continuum, 2004.

Miller, Susan. *Women in Mark's Gospel*. Journal for the Study of the New Testament: Supplement Series 259. London: T. & T. Clark International, 2004.

Minor, Mitzi L. *The Power of Mark's Story*. St. Louis: Chalice Press, 2001.

———. *The Spirituality of Mark: Responding to God*. Louisville: Westminster John Knox, 1996.

Moeser, Marion C. *The Anecdote in Mark, the Classical World and the Rabbis*. Journal for the Study of the New Testament: Supplement Series 227. London: T. & T. Clark International, 2004.

Neirynck, Franz. *The Gospel of Mark: A Cumulative Bibliography, 1950–1990*. Bibliotheca ephemeridum theologicarum lovaniensium 102. Louvain: Louvain University Press, 1992.

Oden, Thomas C., and Christopher A. Hall, editors. *Ancient Christian Commentary on*

Scripture, New Testament, II: Mark. Downers Grove IL: InterVarsity, 1998.

Orton, David E., editor. *The Composition of Mark's Gospel.* Leiden: E. J. Brill, 1999.

Peterson, Dwight N. *The Origins of Mark: The Markan Community in Current Debate.* Biblical Interpretation Series 48. Leiden: E. J. Brill, 2000.

Rhoads, David. *Reading Mark, Engaging the Gospel.* Minneapolis: Fortress, 2004.

Rhoads, David M., Joanna Dewey, and Donald Michie. *Mark as Story: An Introduction to the Narrative of a Gospel.* Revised edition. Minneapolis: Fortress Press, 1999.

Roskam, H. N. *The Purpose of the Gospel of Mark in Its Historical and Social Setting.* Supplements to Novum Testamentum 114. Leiden: E. J. Brill, 2004.

Sabin, Marie Noonan. *Reopening the Word: Reading Mark as Theology in the Context of Early Judaism.* New York: Oxford University Press, 2002.

Samuel, Simon. *A Postcolonial Reading of Mark's Story of Jesus.* Library of New Testament Studies, 340. London: T. & T. Clark, 2007.

Santos, Narry F. *Slave of All: The Paradox of Authority and Servanthood in the Gospel of Mark.* Journal for the Study of the New Testament: Supplement Series 237. London: Sheffield Academic Press, 2003.

Shiner, Whitney. *Proclaiming the Gospel: First-Century Performance of Mark.* Harrisburg: Trinity Press International, 2003.

Thurston, Bonnie Bowman. *Preaching Mark.* Minneapolis: Fortress, 2002.

Tolbert, Mary Ann. *Sowing the Gospel: Mark's World in Literary Historical Perspective.* Minneapolis: Fortress Press, 1989.

Trainor, Michael F. *The Quest for Home: The Household in Mark's Community.* Collegeville MN: Liturgical Press, 2001.

Upton, Bridget Gilfillan. *Hearing Mark's Endings: Listening to Ancient Popular Texts through Speech Act Theory.* Biblical Interpretation Series 79. Leiden: E. J. Brill, 2006.

Vines, Michael E. *The Problem of Markan Genre: The Gospel of Mark and the Jewish Novel.* Atlanta: Society of Biblical Literature, 2002.

INDEX OF AUTHORS

INDEX OF SCRIPTURES

INDEX OF SIDEBARS

INDEX OF TOPICS